THE
COLLECTED
POEMS
of
SIR
CHARLES
G. D. ROBERTS

Charles G. D. Roberts

THE
COLLECTED
POEMS

of

SIR
CHARLES
G. D. ROBERTS

A Critical Edition

Edited by

DESMOND PACEY

Assistant Editor

GRAHAM ADAMS

THE WOMBAT PRESS

Design by GDA, Steven Slipp

Frontispiece: Portrait of Roberts by John Wentworth
Russell; oil on canvas, 40" x 32," painted in Toronto,
1934; signed by both artist and poet; used by kind
permission of the artist's widow, Anna Russell.

Canadian Cataloguing in Publication Data

Roberts, Charles G.D., 1860-1943
    The Collected Poems of Sir Charles G.D. Roberts

Includes index.
Bibliography: p.
ISBN 0-9690828-3-5.

I. Pacey, Desmond, 1917-1975. II. Adams, Graham.
Clevearn, 1937-   . III. Title.

PS8485.023A17 1985   C811'.4   C85-098338-X
PR9199.2.R62A17 1985

This book is

dedicated to the memory of

SIR CHARLES G. D. ROBERTS

ACKNOWLEDGEMENTS

This book has been published with the help of a grant from the Canadian Federation for the Humanities, using funds provided by the Social Sciences and Humanities Research Council of Canada.

The Publisher acknowledges as well the generous aid of the Nova Scotia Department of Culture, Recreation and Fitness, whose Assistance to Established Publishers program provided a grant for this book.

Financial assistance toward publication was also received with gratitude from the Office of the President, Acadia University.

The Publisher wishes to thank the following for their co-operation and support:

> Acadia University
> Nelson Ball
> Historical Society of Pennsylvania
> Professor William J. Keith, University College, Toronto
> Library of Congress
> Rachel M. Mansfield, McGraw-Hill Ryerson Ltd.
> McGill University
> Queens University
> St. John's Seminary, Camarillo, California
> Tulane University
> University of British Columbia
> University of New Brunswick

* * * * * * * * * * *

The following worked as research assistants on this project; support for the last three workers was provided by the Canada Council/Social Sciences and Humanities Research Council of Canada:

> Michael Pacey
> David Yarrow
> J.C. Mahanti
> Graham Adams

CONTENTS

ACKNOWLEDGEMENTS   vii

INTRODUCTION   xix

POEMS

Sonnet / On the Dying Year   1
Spring   1
Amoris Vincula   2
The Maple   3
To Winter   3
Memnon   5
Ode to Drowsihood   9
Ariadne   10
To the Spirit of Song   15
Epistle to Bliss Carman   15
Orion   18
Iterumne   29
Rondeau.—"Hesper Appears."   29
The Shannon and the Chesapeake   30
A Farewell   32
Ballade of the Poet's Thought   32
At Pozzuoli   33
Ballad of a Bride   33
A Ballad of Three Mistresses   34
Ballad to a Kingfisher   35
A Blue Blossom   36
Dedication of "Orion and Other Poems"   36
The Flight   37
Launcelot and the Four Queens   38
Love-Days   46
Miriam.—I. / Sapphics   47
Miriam.—II. / Choriambics   47
Ode to Night   48
One Night   49
Rondeau to A.W. Straton   51
Rondeau.—"Without One Kiss."   51
Sappho   52
A Song of Morning   55
Off Pelorus   55

A Ballade of Philomela 57
To Fredericton in May-Time 57
The Slave Woman 58
Lotos 58
Out of Pompeii 59
To the Memory of Sidney Lanier 61
A Ballade of Calypso 62
Rondeau / To Louis Honore Fréchette 62
A Song of Regret 63
Soliloquy in a Monastery 64
On the Eve of Departure 66
Actæon 66
Canoe Song 71
Before the Breath of Storm 72
In September 73
A Breathing Time 73
In the Afternoon 73
Sonnet on Spring 76
The Pipes of Pan 76
Tantramar Revisited 78
La Belle Tromboniste 80
The Poet is Bidden to Manhattan Island 81
The Sower 82
The Footpath 83
In Notre Dame 84
Canada 85
Mist 87
To My Friend, / Edmund Collins 87
To Bliss Carman / With a Copy of Lang's "Helen of Troy" 88
On Reading the Poems of Sidney Lanier 88
Tides 88
Promise 89
Collect for Dominion Day 89
An Ode for the Canadian Confederacy 90
The Potato Harvest 91
Dark 91
Afloat 92
Birch and Paddle 94
A Birthday Ballade 96
A Blue Violet 97
A Break 97
Consolation 98
The Departing of Gluskâp 98
Impulse 99
The Isles—An Ode 100
Khartoum 101

Liberty 101
The Marvellous Work 102
On the Creek 104
On the Lagoon 106
The Quelling of the Moose 106
Rain 108
Reckoning 108
Salt 109
A Serenade 109
A Song of Dependence 110
To a Lady, / After Hearing Her Read Keats' "Nightingale" 110
To S——— M——— 111
Tout ou Rien 111
Winter Geraniums 112
Mother of Nations 112
A Song of Cheer 113
How the Mohawks Set Out for Medoctec 114
Burnt Lands 116
Frogs 117
The Keepers of the Pass 117
Canadians Are We 119
Severance 119
The Waking Earth 120
The Night Sky 120
When Milking-Time is Done 121
The Summer Pool 121
The Valley of the Winding Water 122
Autochthon 122
A Christmas-Eve Courtin' 123
The Fortress 126
The Fir Woods 126
Life 127
Triumph 127
The Winter Fields 128
Blomidon 128
The Deserted City 129
The Flight of the Geese 129
The Furrow 130
The Night-Hawk 130
A Song of Growth 131
The Mowing 132
A Vesper Sonnet 132
Lines for the Times 133
In the Wide Awe and Wisdom of the Night 133
Quebec, 1757 133
The Autumn Thistles 134

New Year's Eve 134
Moonlight 136
The Salt Flats 136
For a Bust of Lanier 137
The Clearing 137
Grey Rocks and Greyer Sea 137
The Pea-Fields 138
The Hawkbit 138
My Trees 139
The Silver Thaw 139
The Bird's Song, the Sun, and the Wind 141
The Lily of the Valley 141
The Wild-Rose Thicket 141
The Canada Lily 142
O Solitary of the Austere Sky 142
To G.B.R. 142
The Hermit-Thrush 143
The Cricket 144
Ave! (An Ode for the Shelley Centenary, 1892) 144
Epitaph for a Sailor Buried Ashore 153
Bringing Home the Cows 154
The Cicada in the Firs 155
Whitewaters 155
Buckwheat 159
Canadian Streams 159
The Chopping Bee 161
The Cow Pasture 163
The Herring Weir 163
In an Old Barn 164
Indian Summer 164
Marsyas 165
Midwinter Thaw 166
The Oat-Threshing 166
Oh, Purple Hang the Pods! 167
Prologue 167
The Pumpkins in the Corn 167
The Succour of Gluskâp 168
The Tide on Tantramar 170
The Stillness of the Frost 174
Resurrection 175
The Quest of the Arbutus 175
Renewal 176
Sleepy Man 176
The Trout Brook 177
The Unsleeping 178
Admittance 179

A Homing Song 179
The Piper and the Chiming Peas 180
The Ballad of Crossing the Brook 180
Kinship 181
Golden-Rod 183
Up and Away in the Morning 183
Home, Home in the Evening 184
The Vengeance of Gluskâp 185
Immanence 186
Origins 187
The Brook in February 187
Ebb 188
The Frosted Pane 188
Ice 188
An April Adoration 189
The Comedy 189
The Forest Fire 191
Twilight on Sixth Avenue at Ninth Street 192
Her Glove Box 192
A Modern Dialogue 193
Three Good Things 193
An Epitaph for a Husbandman 194
The Train Among the Hills 195
Earth's Complines 196
Her Fan 196
The Wrestler 197
An August Wood Road 198
The Weaver 198
The Muse and the Wheel 200
Oliver Wendell Holmes 200
Recessional 201
Recompense 202
Phillida's Birthday 203
The Witches' Flight 204
A Child's Prayer at Evening 204
Bohemia 205
The Deserted Wharf 206
The Elephant and the Pansy-Blossom 207
Nativity 207
A Spring Colloquy 208
The Stirrup Cup 208
The Laughing Sally 210
The Little Field of Peace 211
The Flocks of Spring 212
The Jonquil 212
An Oblation 212

With All Her Faults 213
Inspiration 214
The Jar 215
Two Spheres 215
O Clearest Pool 216
Ye Poet and His Ideal 217
The Stack Behind the Barn 218
In the Orchard 219
Dew 220
The Farmer's Winter Morning 220
Afoot 221
Apple Song 222
Beside the Winter Sea 223
Butterflies 224
The Heal-All 224
July 225
Love's Translator 226
Mothers 226
Trysting Song 227
A Wake-Up Song 228
Where the Cattle Come to Drink 228
Aylesford Lake 228
The Solitary Woodsman 229
Life and Art 231
To a Mirror 231
Phillida's Lent 231
The Tower Beyond the Tops of Time 232
When the Clover Blooms Again 234
The Hermit 235
Marjory 236
Ascription 237
Tears 238
Night in a Down-Town Street 238
A Nocturne of Consecration 239
My Garden 241
A Street Vigil 242
At the Railway Station 242
In a City Room 243
In the Solitude of the City 243
A Nocturne of Exile 244
A Nocturne of Trysting 245
Presence 245
Life and the Artist 245
Thaw 246
A Nocturne of Spiritual Love 246
In the Crowd 247

xiv

On the Elevated Railway at 110th Street 247
At Thy Voice My Heart 247
A Ballad of Manila Bay 248
The Atlantic Cable 250
At Tide Water 250
Dream-Fellows 251
An Evening Communion 253
The Falling Leaves 254
A Foreword to *Northland Lyrics* 254
The Ideal 254
In Darkness 255
Nocturnes of the Honeysuckle 255
O Thou Who Bidd'st 256
The Street Lamps 256
At the Drinking Fountain 257
Jonathan and John 257
Kinsmen Strong 258
A Remorse 259
A Song for April 259
Brooklyn Bridge 260
A Street Song at Night 260
The White Frost 261
Child of the Infinite 261
The Aim 263
Attar 263
The Stranded Ship 264
O Little Rose, O Dark Rose 265
The Rose of My Desire 266
Away, Sad Voices 267
The Fear of Love 267
The Covert 268
How Little I Knew 268
New Dead 269
In Apia Bay 270
The Rose's Avatar 272
The Pipers of the Pools 272
The Rose of Life 273
The Native 274
Invocation 275
The Wisdom of Love 276
In the Barn-Yard's Southerly Corner 277
The Logs 278
New Life 279
The Skater 279
The Great and the Little Weavers 280
Heat in the City 282

At the Wayside Shrine 282
Shepherdess Fair 283
The Unknown City 284
When in the Rowan Tree 285
When the Cloud Comes Down the Mountain 286
Coal 286
The Conspirators 286
The First Ploughing 287
Lines for an Omar Punch-Bowl 288
My Heart is a House 289
On the Upper Deck 290
When Mary the Mother Kissed the Child 293
All Night the Lone Cicada 294
Beppo's Song 295
Philander's Song 295
Monition 295
From the High Window of Your Room 296
The Hour of Most Desire 296
Wayfarer of Earth 297
The Good Earth 298
O Earth, Sufficing All Our Needs 299
Under the Pillars of the Sky 299
Eastward Bound 300
The Banquet 300
Hill Top Songs: I 300
Hill Top Songs: II 301
The Place of His Rest 301
In the Valley of Luchon 303
On the Road 303
Going Over 304
Cambrai and Marne 305
To Shakespeare, In 1916 306
The Stream 306
The Summons 307
Epitaph for a Certain Architect 308
The Sweet o' the Year 308
The Flower 309
With April Here 309
Sister to the Wild Rose 310
Asterope 310
To-Day 311
Hath Hope Kept Vigil 311
Spring Breaks in Foam 312
The Vagrant of Time 312
In the Night Watches 314
These Three Score Years 315

Be Quiet, Wind 317
Pan and the Rose 318
Unsaid 319
Bat, Bat, Come Under My Hat 319
Spirit of Beauty 320
The Iceberg. 321
To a Certain Mystic 327
Taormina 328
Presences 329
Re-Birth 330
The Squatter 331
Westcock Hill 333
Twilight Over Shaugamauk 334
Those Perish, These Endure 335
As Down the Woodland Ways 335
Two Rivers 336
Peace With Dishonour 339
In Time of Earth's Misuse 339
Forget Not, Thou 340
Canada to France 340
The Ravaged Lands 341
Canada Speaks of Britain 342
Epitaph for a Young Airman 342
Song for Victory Delayed 343
Resurgant 344
Phillida's Blue Ribbon 344
May-Night 345
Colour Toasts 346

CHRONOLOGY   349

A NOTE ON BIBLIOGRAPHICAL PROCEDURES   357

NOTES   363

INDEX OF FIRST LINES   637

INDEX OF TITLES   654

SOURCES OF THE POEMS   663

BIBLIOGRAPHY   669

INTRODUCTION

This book is the brain-child of the late Desmond Pacey, who conceived it as an entity, obtained a grant from the Canada Council for its compilation, and brought it toward its final form when death intervened and took it from him. When I was called in, at the request of the University of New Brunswick, to supervise the final year of research and to write the introduction, I debated whether or not to allow Desmond Pacey to speak for himself from his previous writings on Roberts or to attempt an introduction of my own. I chose the latter course because Desmond Pacey's writings on Roberts are already well known and readily available.

Upon reading the *corpus* of Roberts' poems arranged here chronologically and in its entirety for the first time, I decided to abandon my original idea of writing a comprehensive essay upon the whole in favour of the more modest— and I feel at this stage of our knowledge of Roberts more useful—task of classifying the poetry according to genre and commenting upon each genre in general, formally and/or thematically, as that genre deserves. These comments represent my own individual impressions formed not only by my own knowledge of poetry and history and my reading of Roberts but also by my own experience as poet, editor, publisher, teacher, and human being. They are designed both to inform and clarify and to raise questions in the readers' minds. At the same time, it is hoped that some general impression of Roberts as a poet may emerge out of these fragments.

Roberts began to write poetry early and remained constant in attitude and technique to the paths on which he set out in his early poems. Although he was forced by the need to earn a living for two households—his own and that of his wife and children—to write almost exclusively prose for a quarter of a century in mid-career, the poetry of his second phase marks no break with that of his first. As a poet, Roberts was shaped by his New Brunswick background, by his classical and literary upbringing, and by an innate mystical acceptance and belief in life which he early adopted and which was always to be part of his nature. His rise to early fame owes much to the merit of his poetry. It owes much, too, to the fact that influences akin to those which shaped his work were abroad in society and reinforced one another. The current relative lack of esteem in which his poetry is held is a testimony to how far we have departed from the beliefs, interests, and values of our ancestors.

In New Brunswick, Roberts grew up in a society which had substituted ritual behaviour for intelligence based upon thought: religion, sex, commerce, speech habits, politics, work—all were subject to implicit tacit procedures that tended to absorb or eliminate any attempts at personal expression which might be at odds with ways of thinking and acting evolved by hard-working people through generations of living together on an isolated frontier that seemed to demand standardization for survival. In such a society, one did not need to think; one had only to accept and conform.

Roberts' mind was kept alive by his reading, fostered by education, inclination, and the personal influence of his father and his teachers. Given his colonial frontier background, it would have been very odd indeed had he studied and read with any attitude other than acceptance. After acceptance came imitation of the poets of his time then writing in England and America. By the age of seventeen, he had also accepted an Anglo-American blend of transcendentalism whose hall-mark was an intuitive faith in the ultimate value of life. It would have been indeed strange had he done otherwise. Compared to his fellows, he was well endowed and of a healthy constitution. The family circumstances were happy. The society and nation to which he belonged was homogeneous, developing in material prosperity, and holding meaningful goals in eternity.

Later events were not to shake Roberts' initial beliefs nor to cause him to become iconoclastic. He belonged to a generation whose individuals tended to blame their own shortcomings rather than the system for their personal misfortunes, and his mysticism, fortified throughout his life by various uncanny experiences, explained away as temporal or illusory the vicissitudes that affected mankind. Moreover, the acclaim which his poems received throughout most of his career was bound to discourage technical innovation. In short, Roberts was ideally fitted to become what Canada in the late nineteenth century required, a poet who could embody the spirit of his age in verse that was recognizably Canadian, recognizably part of the verse tradition of his time, and recognizably good.

It was second nature for a young man receiving a sound classical education and with his head full of the works of the great Romantic and Victorian poets to turn classical legends into verse. Roberts wrote twelve poems on overtly classical themes, and of the twelve, nine belong to the period of his poetic apprenticeship, 1873-1883.

As might be expected, the stylistic devices—and in many cases the phrases—of Roberts' classical poems echo the poems on similar themes by Keats and Shelley. There was not, however, on the young man living comfortably in colonial Fredericton the ideological and social pressure that had led Keats and Shelley to re-write in terms of their own time the Greek myths, and thereby revitalize them. He also lacked the psychological acuteness, the social *savoir faire,* and the speech rhythms that in the hands of a Shakespeare or a Browning made legendary characters seem as real as contemporaries. The classical poems which Roberts produced between his seventeenth and twenty-second years were more akin to the "Oenone" and the "Ulysses" of Tennyson than they were to anything else. They are basically monologues in which the narrator combines emotion with the unfolding of poignant event against a background of picturesque detail expressed in dignified, rhythmic language. For this purpose, Roberts' remarkable command of grammar and his grasp of involved sentence structure—particularly learned from translations into and from the classical languages—stood him in excellent stead.

The problem of bringing a landscape remote in space and time to life in these poems hardly presented itself at all. Classical landscape as rendered in literature was very much a generalized one which a host of poets and translators had domesticated to words and phrases that were at the same time euphonious and rich in associations. In fact, by the late nineteenth century it had become difficult to deal with such landscapes other than in clichés. Although in a "Ballad to a Kingfisher" Roberts shows that he is aware of the incongruity between the bird of legend and the kingfisher of his native New Brunswick rivers, he is throughout his classical poems as content with clichés as were his contemporaries, Tennyson, Swinburne, and Matthew Arnold.

In "Orion," Roberts suppressed the rape of Merope in order to make his protagonist more attractive, and in "Actæon" the narrator is most un-Greek in her condemnation of the Olympians. In the main, however, Roberts took and embroidered his classical material as he found it. His narrator, within each myth or legend, is well chosen for effect, and where, as in "Out of Pompeii," he has to invent, he writes with conviction and spirit.

Roberts' last three classical poems, scattered in time of composition between 1893 and 1928, are shorter, sharper, and owe their interest to the themes they embody rather than to the mere word-painting of a legend. "Marsyas," perhaps the best of all Roberts' classical poems although its conclusion owes something to that of Emerson's "Days," is really about aesthetics— the gap between human and divine harmonies. The only thing classical about "Asterope" is its title, and "Pan and the Rose" is essentially a lament for a moment of illumination gone beyond recall.

Roberts, then, brought to the poem in English based on classical myth what that genre demanded and no more. He soon tired of its lack of challenge and abandoned it for other forms. It did, however, give him his first spectacular success in an established vogue, ready publication, favourable critical attention, and invaluable practice in the selection and arrangement of landscape material.

Supplemental to the poems on classical themes and more important in their consequences were "Miriam I. Sapphics," "Miriam II. Choriambics" (1880), and "A Breathing Time" (1882). These poems demonstrate that Roberts, like most nineteenth century poets before him, experimented with the feasibility of adapting standard classical metres to the rhythms of the English language. They also lead up to, and account largely for, the form of Roberts' earliest masterpiece, "Tantramar Revisited" (1883).

What matters about these metrical experiments is not their fidelity to ancient quantities, which is illusory and can only be achieved arbitrarily, by distorting the sound as one reads; it is rather the ways in which they may force a poet out of the iambic grooves into which so much English poetry has fallen and make him aware of subtler nuances of sound that can be conveyed by other alternatives. By forcing English verse into an alien pattern, a poet may unwittingly come upon patterns that are essentially "sprung rhythm."

When, therefore, Roberts chose to write "Tantramar Revisited" in elegiacs— probably because he felt he could use some phrases from a recent similar poem "A Breathing Time" in it—he was able to work in a music that was essentially his own and not borrowed. When, using the techniques of classical description, he chose to describe the landscape in exact physical phrases rather than in the clichés of classical poetry, here again Roberts was his own man. "Tantramar Revisited" is, paradoxically, the culmination of Roberts' classicism and a magnificent, if short-lived, declaration of independence from the bondage of traditional English metre.

Linked by origin and association with classicism and hallowed by past achievement was the ode. Roberts wrote four odes in the manner of Keats and Shelley. In these works, the use of invocation, personification with compound epithets, classical and literary allusion, the hypothetical negative, and the shape and movement of the stanzas are reminiscent of early nineteenth century verse. Two odes, however, the first, "Ode to Drowsihood" (1877), and the last, "Ave (An Ode for the Shelley Centenary, 1892)," are noteworthy for their deliberate blending of European literary and classical material with realistic descriptions of the New Brunswick landscape.

In "Ode to Drowsihood," a remarkable composition for a youth of seventeen, Drowsihood is invoked and its effects described *à la* Keats. Drowsihood is a state between sleep and waking in which associations derived from reading blend with those derived from sensory perception:

> The mistletoe dissolves to Indian willow,
> Glassing its red stems in the stream that flows
> Through the broad interval. A lazy billow
> Flung from my oar lifts the long grass that grows
> To be the Naiad's pillow.

But such blending is beyond the power of the conscious will, and the poet concludes:

> I have thy favours but I fear thy treason.
> Fain would I hold thee by the dusk wing-tips
> Against a grievous season.

"Ave," an ambitious poem of thirty-one ten-lined stanzas, calls forth all the technical skill of the then mature Roberts in an attempt, using Shelley as its theme, to emulate "Adonais," Shelley's great poem on the death of Keats. In pace and fervour, the diction is consciously Shelleyan, and the topical allusions pertaining to Shelley's life and work are handled masterfully throughout. The texture of the verse is unflawed, and the nobility of the language keeps pace with the nobility of thought and feeling displayed. If there is an incongruity in the poem, it is in Roberts' attempt to link himself with the dead Shelley and to link the associations brought to him by an obscure New Brunswick river, the Tantramar, with the associations that tradition has heaped upon the storied cities of Europe. Roberts was conscious of this possible incongruity and did his best—successful, in my opinion—to dispel it. The first

xxii

nine stanzas of the poem are devoted to describing the relationship which exists between Roberts and the Tantramar. The river has shaped his soul, has made him into a man and a poet who is responsive to its every changing mood. At the close of stanza nine, Roberts perceives that the Tantramar's literary counterpart in nature is, for him, the poet Shelley. Stanza ten describes the similarity, and in stanza eleven Roberts is able to devote his poem to tracing the life and work of his hero, returning in stanza thirty to the Tantramar for one closing stanza which, although adequate in itself, is an anticlimax when compared to the close of "Adonais." Despite the ending, "Ave" is one of the few poems produced in North America that can compete on their own ground with Matthew Arnold's "Thyrsis" and "The Scholar Gypsy."

One of the oldest established, most widely practised forms of the lyric in English was the sonnet. It is not therefore surprising that Roberts' first poem, composed at the age of fourteen, was a sonnet, "On the Dying Year." What is surprising, at a time when sonnet sequences by George Meredith and Dante Gabriel Rossetti were still popular, is that Roberts attempted no sonnet sequence and normally wrote no more than one sonnet a year if any at all. (The period between 1886 and 1891 during which Roberts wrote twenty-eight sonnets and the year 1893 in which he composed nine are exceptions.)

Roberts' sonnets occasionally begin with the alternative rhyming quatrains of a Shakespearean sonnet, but the sestet almost invariably becomes Petrarchan. He seems to have realized very early on that the "turn" of wit introduced by a concluding couplet was not for him. In most instances, the divisions in thought and form between octave and sestet are distinctly marked in a Roberts sonnet. His sonnets can be divided into three categories.

The most important group of Roberts sonnets, by the standards of contemporary taste, are the "objective" sonnets—sonnets in which Roberts in both octave and sestet is content to delineate an aspect of landscape through a careful selection of concrete detail and an equally careful modulation of tone and pace. ("The Herring Weir" is a good example.) Although these poems are usually as empty of thought as the Parnassian sonnets of Heredia, they are important in the history of Canadian poetry, for they represent the first completely unmixed "domestication" of the Canadian landscape into English verse through a technique which found ready imitators in Archibald Lampman, William Wilfred Campbell, and Duncan Campbell Scott.

In all likelihood, Roberts regarded his "objective" sonnets less highly than he did those of a second group in which he used the sestet to draw conclusions from the "objective" data contained in the octave ("The Cow Pasture" is typical of the eleven sonnets in this category), for he belonged to an age in which poets prided themselves on having specific messages to communicate to mankind.

In Roberts' remaining sonnets, he is either literary ("Iterumne"), imitative of sonnets by other writers ("At Pozzuoli"), or personal on themes of love, mysticism, and war to such a degree that objective details throughout both octave and sestet are obscured by the thought and/or feeling which pervade them. Although less highly regarded than those of Roberts' other groups, some of these personal sonnets ("Iterumne," "Mist," "Dark," "Rain," and "Twilight over Shaugamauk") are among his best.

Apart from the "domestication" of the Canadian landscape, Roberts added nothing new to the sonnet, and he was never quite the painstaking craftsman which that medium deserved in its formal aspects. Almost every sonnet— however fine it may be in conception and general execution—is flawed by an inversion to fit a rhyme, an archaism, a cliché, or a descriptive word or phrase that is out of keeping. Nevertheless, even a casual reader can recognize that, despite these flaws, Roberts possessed in his command of grammar and in his habits of thought great natural ability as a sonnet writer. In my opinion, his work is equal to and more varied in range than that achieved in this form by his Canadian contemporaries, J.F. Herbin and Archibald Lampman. Roberts has the additional distinction of showing both men the way to go in the sonnet.

In other traditional set verse forms, Roberts experimented early with the rondeau and the ballade, which he usually mis-spelled as "ballad." His four rondeaux and five ballades need not detain us. Each represents the successful metrical completion of a formal exercise, and each—with the possible exception of the refrain of "Ballade of the Poet's Thought"—is utterly banal.

Although Roberts wrote thirty-one epigrams, none has received critical attention. Some were buried in the pages of the *University Monthly;* others appeared in *Lippincott's Magazine,* and apart from this volume, few have appeared in any book whatever. They range from autograph verse and clever but slight extended metaphors to a kind of distilled wisdom ("Immanence," "The Comedy," "Tears," "The Falling Leaves," "The Banquet") that is rare in the work of Canadian poets. A few of them ("Golden-Rod," "Ice," "Inspiration," "The Stirrup-Cup," "Life and Art," "Life and the Artist," "The Street Lamps," "At the Drinking Fountain") express more clearly and vividly Roberts' essential attitudes to life, art, and love than do many of his longer, more ambitious poems.

Roberts wrote seven true ballads and two ballad-like poems. Of the ballads, one celebrates Adam Daulac's heroic defence of the Long Sault in seventeenth century Quebec and four deal with sea battles. "The Shannon and the Chesapeake" celebrates a rare British triumph during the War of 1812; "The Laughing Sally," based upon an incident in the Spanish Main, demonstrates that even with pirates the call of blood is stronger than the love of life:

> "There's English rope that bides for our necks,
> But we all be English men!"

"A Ballad of Manila Bay" and "In Apia Bay" were written in New York and pay tribute to U.S. achievement in the Spanish-American War. All are stirring, well-executed verse, but they depend for their interest upon a society of readers to whom the courage displayed by the military in wartime is the paramount chauvinistic fact of history. Later generations have learned to revalue war, and with that revaluation has gone the kinetic response its celebration in verse can call forth.

"The Forest Fire" and "Whitewaters" are more truly representative ballads in that they are rooted in frontier experience and are faithful to that experience by the simplicity with which they develop tension between fear and relief. An eighth poem, "The Tide on Tantramar," probably the germ of Roberts' later novel, *The Heart That Knows,* has the ingredients of a ballad. Although not so slavishly imitative as the Tennysonian "Launcelot and the Four Queens" and the Browningesque "Soliloquy in a Monastery," its simple pathos is too heavily overlaid by pre-Raphaelite decoration to be effective. "How the Mohawks Set Out for Medoctec" employs and extends the technique of Shelley's "The Waters are Flashing" rather than that of the ballad proper, but, unlike Shelley's poem, it is too long for the effect it achieves.

More satisfying than any ballad Roberts wrote are the four poems based on myths surrounding Gluskâp or Clote Scarp, the tribal god of the Algonquin Indians of Eastern Canada. In these poems, Roberts discovered a mine of material that was essentially poetic, original, and of the universality of fable. It seems to me to be a pity that he did not work it more often and produce more poems of the calibre of "The Departing of Gluskâp."

Although Roberts translated Philip Aubert de Gaspé's novel, *Les Anciens Canadiens* and was interested in the history and tradition of French Canada, he translated only four poems from the French: two are by Louis Honore Fréchette, one is by de Gaspé, and the original of the fourth has not been traced. Even here, Roberts is something of a pioneer. Archibald Lampman, Bliss Carman, William Wilfred Campbell, and Duncan Campbell Scott did not seem to realize that any poetry other than that in the English language was being produced in Canada during their hey-day; if they did, they certainly did not succumb to the urge to translate it.

Although Roberts was raised as an Anglican and was primarily a religious poet, there was little in the myths and history of orthodox Christianity that inspired his verse. What little there was, however, that led to the writing of the five short poems that can be classified as "Christian" was surprisingly free from being stereotyped. "A Child's Prayer at Evening" fits, as we shall see below, into the second category of his mystical poems. In "Mothers" and "Nativity," Roberts extends the special prerogative of the Virgin Mary to every mother of every child. In "When Mary the Mother Kissed the Child" (1903), he finds true divinity in the human bond between a mother and her son, and in "At the Wayside Shrine" (1903) he identifies Saint Anne with the trivial sins of petty sinners and infers that for great human beings at odds with the world something more is needed than she can offer.

At only two phases of history can a poet write patriotic poetry and expect a strong response. One is during a period when a people are coalescing as a nation; the other is during a time of crisis. Under both circumstances, a poet can easily become a catalyst. To polarize emotion in other minds and hearts, he has but to evoke those emotions in familiar language. Roberts was a patriotic poet of both phases. He gave voice to the growing Canadian nationalism of the 1880's and 1890's, and he expressed what people felt during World War I and during the early years of World War II. Roberts' patriotic verse is manly, sincere, and admirably constructed for its purpose. In its own time, it received an appropriate response. But like so many works of art constructed for a particular occasion—Noel Coward's film, *In Which We Serve* is a similar instance—the symbols lose their magic once the occasion has passed and the work must depend for continued interest on qualities of imagination which at the time of its composition it did not require. Poems like Roberts' "Canada," "An Ode for the Canadian Confederacy," "Jonathan and John," "To Shakespeare, In 1916," "Cambrai and Marne," "These Three Score Years," and "Canada Speaks of Britain" are dated and have no appeal to a generation that in self defence has tuned out public utterances and their rhetoric, however well-intentioned. Of all Roberts' patriotic poems, modern readers are more apt to prefer the divided humanity of "Going Over" (1918). They must admire, too, the indomitable spirit of the octogenarian who produced no less than eight competent poems within a twelve-month span during 1941 and 1942.

It was customary for nineteenth century poets to write elegiacs on dead relatives and distinguished men and to compose dedicatory and occasional poems. Roberts followed the custom. The best of these poems are "In the Afternoon" (1882) and "Westcock Hill" (1934), poems in which the poignancy of personal grief presses against but does not break the symmetry of the form. "An Epitaph for a Husbandman," expressive of the desire to merge with the universe which—as will be shown below—was so characteristic of Roberts, is his finest achievement in this genre. No other poems in this category deserve special mention.

So far, I have dealt with Roberts' work in forms where—either through tradition or the demands of verse patterns—nineteenth century poets have usually chosen to be most public and subject to conventions. Like most of his contemporaries, Roberts put what was essentially personal in his views of love, nature, and life into the lyric.

Roberts grew up in a genteel, respectable household in a homogeneous respectable society in New Brunswick and became imbued so strongly with certain then universally-held ideas of morality and love that they remained a part of him, whatever he may have seen and done during the bohemian wanderings of his last fifty years. In Victorian England—and to an equal degree in nineteenth century North America—convention decreed that women fell into two categories, ladies and the other kind. A moral man behaved nobly to ladies; he could, however, behave otherwise to a woman who was not a lady and still be considered a gentleman. *She,* after all, had first forfeited her right to consideration. A third situation occurred when a gentleman became involved with a lady in a relationship unsanctioned by wedlock. In such a case, both gentleman and lady turned usually to literature to find reinforcement for their feelings—and an excuse if not a justification for their behaviour—in the cult of romantic love. There sexual attraction based on beauty is united with a union of mind and spirit that transcends sex. Roberts was to write poems in all categories.

His poems celebrating a gentleman's attitude towards a lady include the religious poems referred to earlier, the Lowellesque "A Christmas-Eve Courtin'," the boyish "Amoris Vincula" and "Love-Days," and such blameless lyrics as "A Homing Song," "Home, Home in the Evening," and "Up and Away in the Morning." A small group of poems ("A Modern Dialogue," "Phillida's Birthday," "Three Good Things," "Phillida's Lent," "With All Her Faults," "Beppo's Song," and "Colour Toasts") range from witty attempts at a masculine hedonism in the classical manner to smoking-room crudity. The remainder of Roberts' love poems are tributes, in varying degrees of depth and sincerity, to romantic love.

Roberts' first, and most important, burst of poetic passion toward a woman reached its apotheosis in 1886 and found its ending in 1896. It produced at least twenty-two love poems and, as Roberts documents in "The Elephant and the Pansy-Blossom," was in response to a love whose continued and complete fruition was doomed:

> For he thought, you see, of his wife and child,
>   And she of her aged mother;
> They thought till they felt quite weird and wild;
>   Then—said "Good-by" to each other.

These poems celebrate the joy of a love that, through the persistence of mnemonic associations, cannot die while consciousness lasts—a persistence that is sometimes sweet ("A Break," "On the Creek," "Trysting Song," "Love's Translator"), sometimes bitter ("The Footpath"), and sometimes bitter-sweet ("In Notre Dame"). They vacillate between faith that love is all ("A Serenade," "At the Drinking Fountain") and knowledge that it is not ("Tout ou Rien," "Severance"). Two poems from this period ("Afloat," "Beside the Winter Sea") rank among the most interesting love poems written during the latter half of the nineteenth century.

"Afloat" is akin in fervor and intellectual daring to Shelley's "Epipsychidion" but is more rigid in its logic and less compromising in its conclusion. In it, the poet realizes that the intense experience of love he seeks is impossible in space and time for

>   . . . the love of the flesh . . .
>   Is yet finite, attains not the height
>   Of the spirit enfranchised, and must
>   With the body slip back into dust.
>   Our soul-passion is deathless, divine.

Therefore:

>   It is only a plunge, a quick roll
>   Of our skiff—I will gather and fold
>   You close, for the waters are cold,—
>   A few sobs, and we rise one soul,
>   Undisservered for ever and ever.

By comparison, "Beside the Winter Sea" is a valedictory to love; it is quiet, subdued, but infused with a blend of tenderness and unconscious pride of mastery that is chauvinistic without being offensively so.

A second group of love poems begins with "A Nocturne of Consecration" (1897) and ends with "The Hour of Most Desire" (1906). The setting is New York, but the beloved is more elusive. Sometimes she seems a mere personification of the power of woman to heal, comfort, and inspire ("The Ideal," "At Thy Voice My Heart," "An Evening Communion," "The Wisdom of Love," "A Nocturne of Exile"). Sometimes she is felt as a woman of flesh and blood: one who can be late at a station ("At the Railway Station"); one who can blot out emptiness by her presence ("In a City Room," "A Street Song at Night," "The Covert") or cause it by her absence ("In the Solitude of the City"); one who the poet can doubt ("A Street Vigil") or betray ("A Remorse"). Too many of these poems, however, seem shrill and over-decorated ("My Garden," "A Nocturne of Spiritual Love," "A Nocturne of Trysting," "Nocturne of the Honeysuckle," "The Rose of My Desire," "Invocation," "The Rose's Avatar"), and their usual blend of the transcendent glory of creation with some portion of the beloved's anatomy is almost always anticlimactic and off-putting. Roberts' most ambitious poem of this group, "A Nocturne of Consecration," well-written though it is, seems contrived by comparison with the earlier "Afloat." Nevertheless, three poems which link fear with love ("The Conspirators," "The Fear of Love," "On the Upper Deck") testify to the reality of Roberts' experience and his skill in presenting it during his New York years. These—along with the best of the group of poems in which the beloved is flesh and blood—do much to redeem Roberts as a poet who could write genuine love poems when his feelings were sufficiently engaged.

Of Roberts' final love poems, two ("The Flower," "With April Here") are sharp evocations of the feelings of a man who, at fifty-nine, had won the heart of a young girl. More poignant are the imaginative and tender "In the Night Watches" (1926) and the much-anthologized "Taormina" (1932), Roberts' poetic farewell to love.

The fact of the matter was that, however much human love meant to Roberts, it was but a facet of a greater love, the love of life, which is best expressed in his transcendental poems.

To give expression to the inexpressible through expressible objects is almost, if not entirely, an insurmountable task. In "A Blue Blossom," (1880) Roberts enunciated the problem with which his mystical poems were, in one way or another, consistently to grapple. In this poem, he states that Nature utters an eternal language addressed to the soul. Man's work and speech are a mere temporal phase addressed to the mind and senses. The flower, for example, has a temporal message, "Forget me not," but it also speaks another message to the spirit. Unfortunately

> Forgotten is our ancient tongue;
> Too dull our ears, our eyes too blind,

Even quite to catch its notes, or find
Its symbols written bright among
All shapes of beauty. But 't is hard
When one *can* hear, to be debarred
From knowledge of the meaning sung.

Ralph Waldo Emerson had maintained that Nature was a metaphor for Spirit and that therefore natural objects were symbols for spiritual truths. Accepting this belief, Roberts attempts to convey the correspondence between natural objects and spiritual truths that his intuitive wisdom perceived. The poem "Impulse" (1885) is typical of his method in this regard. Here a plant frustrated by an obstacle persists and ultimately flowers. Roberts finds in this fact a message for his soul:

The good
The blossom craved was near, tho' hid.
Fret not that thou must doubt, but rid
Thy sky-path of obstruction strewed
By winds of folly. Then, do thou
The Godward impulse room allow
To reach its perfect air and food!

The difficulty with this kind of argument is that it speaks only to the believing; others are apt to find the parallel a simplistic and not necessarily logical correspondence. Be that as it may, Roberts made use of Nature in this way for spiritual instruction in a good many poems of no more than average quality ("My Trees," "In the Orchard," "The Hermit-Thrush," "Prologue," "Aylesford Lake," "All Night the Lone Cicada," "Eastward Bound," "On the Road," "Hath Hope Kept Vigil") and in four very good ones ("Resurgant," "At Tide Water," "The Skater," "Hill Top Songs: II").

An important facet of the transcendentalism that treats time and space as illusory is paradox, and in his mystical poems Roberts gives free reign to this facet of existence. At the heart of action is calm ("A Song of Growth"); the infinitesimal in space and time is equivalent to the gigantic ("Two Spheres," "The Great and the Little Weavers"); animate life is equated with inanimate ("The Native"); life is at once trivial and wonderful ("Under the Pillars of the Sky"); however, the greatest paradox of all is the triviality-magnificence of the living process which Roberts celebrates in some of his finest poems.

Life is trivial from the point of view of the self that judges merely by space and time. It is wonderful in terms of the divinity that informs the whole—a divinity which Roberts sometimes subsumes under the name of God and which expands and contracts space and time according to its own inscrutable purpose which Roberts sometimes calls "God's face" and sometimes "the dream of God." This purpose cannot be accomplished without change, of which life, death, growth, and decay are necessary facets. In two of his most eloquent poems, "Autochthon" and "The Unsleeping," Roberts becomes the cosmic "I" at the heart of this process and gives voice to the unconscious joy of all things which stems from it and which to him is the dynamic of the universe. In poems only a little less compelling, the pulse of the life-process is expressed by the alteration of its external manifestations ("Afoot," "Recessional," "Kinship," "An Oblation," "Ascription," "The Hermit," "The Solitary Woodsman," "Child of the Infinite," "To a Certain Mystic," "O Earth, Sufficing All Our Needs"). Roberts' own immediate experience of this illumination is rendered in "Earth's Complines," "The Tower Beyond the Tops of Time," "Hill Top Songs: I," "The Vagrant of Time," "Spirit of Beauty," "Presences," "Be Quiet, Wind," "As Down the Woodland Ways," and, on the level of personal experience rendered through dream, in one of his finest, most original poems, "Dream Fellows."

It is difficult for any man, however much a mystic, to keep at all times the totality of his transcendental vision. In two poems, "The Marvellous Work" (1886) and "To-Day" (1926), Roberts departs from it sufficiently to make two temporal ideas—the evolution of man and the progress of man—more central than a true mystic has the right to assume. The former poem is noteworthy for lines which must have evoked an answering chord in the mind of E.J. Pratt when he read them, for they typify so much that is characteristic of Pratt's own verse:

> How the Eternal's unconcern of time,—
> Omnipotence that hath not dreamed of haste,—
> Is graven in granite-moulding aeons' gloom;
> Is told in stony record of the roar
> Of long Silurian storms, and tempests huge
> Scourging the circuit of Devonian seas;
> Is whispered in the noiseless mists, the gray
> Soft drip of clouds about rank fern-forests,
> Through dateless terms that stored the layered coal;
> Is uttered hoarse in strange Triassic forms
> Of monstrous life; or stamped in ice-blue gleams
> Athwart the death-still years of glacial sleep!

More sharp, however, in a few poems is the wrestle of Roberts' ego to maintain its vision of timelessness. As a man, he was conscious of age and death. In one gruesomely fantastic poem, "The Wrestler," he allows the concept of death to triumph throughout the universe; more often, however, he assumes that death, pain, and the dullness of temporality are necessary parts of the life-process ("The Wild-Rose Thicket," "Recompense," "The Rose of Life") and are to be blessed and responded to ("The Aim," "Wayfarer of Earth," "The Summons," "Re-Birth"). The discomfort which this ego-pressure gives is probably the factor which impels Roberts' desire to merge with and lose his individual being in the universe at times when his consciousness is at odds with the cosmic process. In "Afloat," as we have seen, he had imagined the possibility of death as an ideal consummation of love. In "The Solitary

Woodsman," "The Stranded Ship," and "The Squatter," acceptance of impending death is equated with oneness with the universe.

Roberts united in "The Iceberg" an ideal symbol with a form of cadenced verse that suited him. The result is his greatest single long poem. As he envisioned it, the iceberg is an ideal vehicle for what Roberts imagined the mystical voyage of life to be. It has no ego-centre, no will of its own; it floats wherever the currents may move its unconscious undersea bulk; yet it is a force to be reckoned with and feels the beauty and wonder of its strange journey, most consciously of all, perhaps, at the final moment of its merger:

> And then my fragile, scintillating frame
> Dissolved in ecstasy
> Of many coloured light,
> And I breathed my soul into the air
> And merged forever in the all-solvent sea.

While in New York, Roberts wrote a few poems which are modern in the sense that in general they reflect the alienation, loneliness, and separation from Nature that is inevitably one aspect of urban life. "Twilight on Sixth Avenue at Ninth Street," "Night in a Down-Town Street," "Heat in the City" are stark nineteenth century evocations of a landscape that was to loom large in twentieth century verse. Yet even here, Roberts did not break with conventional forms or wax politically indignant as Lampman did. He is able to escape the city pressures in "On the Elevated Railway at 110th Street" and "Brooklyn Bridge" and to demonstrate in his beautiful poem "Monition" that New York could be like Francis Thompson's London, "no strange land" to the spirit.

Roberts' approach to art ("To the Spirit of Song," "Ye Poet and His Ideal," "Bohemia," and "The Unknown City") reinforces his mysticism. Poetry is independent of the will in its origin and can only be received through the poet's having patience until the epiphany comes of its own accord. Its result, if it is well-made, transcends time. In "Two Rivers," Roberts attempts to explain the apparent contradictions of his personality by his mystical union during childhood with each of two contradictory streams, the Tantramar and the Saint John.

In my opinion, Roberts' mystical poems have never received sufficient credit. For the sake of their fullest appreciation it was unfortunate that he wrote them for an age that superficially accepted them without being aware of the depth and consistency of the philosophy that underlay them and that they have since been undervalued by an age antithetical to almost all the things for which they stand.

Roberts' poetry expresses the deepest, most cherished concepts of his being; hence its key-note is its insistence upon an overriding unity which transcends time and space; in his prose work, Roberts was more receptive to discords, to the values of time and space, and to the Darwinism which was also a facet of the age in which he lived. But even here, it can be argued, he was not

SONNET
ON THE DYING YEAR

1   The winds are whispering low their dirges drear,
Sobbing and sighing in a sad lament,
And all the clouds of heaven seem hither sent
To watch around the deathbed of the year.

All Nature softens as his end draws near,
The winds cling round him thick and heavy now,—
O'er burdened with the death-damps of his brow;
The drooping elms let fall the chilly tear.

The clouds draw closer round, and stoop to hear
10 His dying moans; their bosoms swell with rain,
As swells my troubled heart with tears and pain,
At the near loss of one to me so dear:
For, from the New Year, hastening here to reign,
I have thought much to hope yet more to fear.

1874; 1878

SPRING

1   When snows the dead earth cumber
And weary Winter reigns
When streams in frozen slumber
Lie torpid in the plains;
Though all seems dead forever,
We know that nought can sever
Cold earth and rigid river
From Spring's awakening.

When trees are bare, and shining
10 With Winter's frozen breath,
The buds in their warm lining
Know 'tis but seeming death;
Know that not all his keenness,
Nor North Wind's hungry leanness
Can freeze their sleeping greenness
From waking in the spring.

When winter winds of sorrow
Warp brightness from his brow,
Would that man might borrow
20 Fresh leaves, from Hope's green bough;

1

But, crouched o'er Joy's dead embers,
Full seldom he remembers
That these drear, dark Decembers
Foretell the coming Spring.

1875; 1878

AMORIS VINCULA

1   Subtler than all sorceries
This tender breath upon mine eyes;
Surer than steel, though soft as air,
These fetters of caressing hair;
Yet they gall not me, nor smart,
Heart-fast to a girlish heart.

Wakes upon the quiet night
Clamor of strife of might and right,
And bears unto a girlish ear
10   Vague messages of pain and fear,
And girlish arms more close enlace
To shield me in their weak embrace.

Ah, I too had girded me
And stood among the strong and free,—
Had struck, and shrunk not, for the right,
Amid the red death of the fight,—
Had fought and won, or fallen with them
That wear the hero's diadem.

I even now were smiting strong
20   In the front ranks, to smite the wrong,
But a girlish voice saith nay,—
Bids me stay, and I must stay:
Let Freedom rise, or faint, or fall,
Here is my faith, my fame, my all.

1876-77; 1880

2

THE MAPLE

1   Oh, tenderly deepen the woodland glooms,
       And merrily sway the beeches;
Breathe delicately the willow blooms,
       And the pines rehearse new speeches;
The elms toss high till they reach the sky,
       Pale catkins the yellow birch launches,
But the tree I love all the greenwood above
       Is the maple of sunny branches.

Let who will sing of the hawthorn in spring,
10   Or the late-leaved linden in summer;
There's a word may be for the locust-tree,
       That delicate strange new-comer;
But the maple it glows with the tint of the rose
       When pale are the spring-time regions,
And its towers of flame from afar proclaim
       The advance of Winter's legions.

And a greener shade there never was made
       Than its summer canopy sifted,
And many a day as beneath it I lay
20   Has my memory backward drifted
To a pleasant lane I may walk not again,
       Leading over a fresh, green hill,
Where a maple stood just clear of the wood—
       And oh! to be near it still!

1876-77; 1880

TO WINTER

1   Ruling with an iron hand
O'er the intermediate land
Twixt the plains of rich completeness,
And the realms of budding sweetness,
Winter! from thy crystal throne,
With a keenness all thy own
Dartest thou, through gleaming air,
O'er the glorious barren glare
Of thy sunlit wildernesses,
10 Thine undazzled level glances,
Where thy minions' silver tresses
Stream among their icy lances;
While thy universal breathing,

Frozen to a radiant swathing
For the trees, their bareness hides,
And upon their sunward sides
Shines and flushes rosily
To the chill pink morning sky.
Skilful artists thou employest,
20   And in chastest beauty joyest,—
Forms most delicate, pure, and clear,
Frost-caught starbeams fallen sheer
In the night, and woven here
In jewel-fretted tapestries.
But what magic melodies,
As in the bord'ring realms are throbbing,
Hast thou, Winter?—Liquid sobbing
Brooks, and brawling waterfalls,
Whose responsive-voicéd calls
30   Clothe with harmony the hills,
Gurgling meadow-threading rills,
Lakelets' lisping wavelets lapping
Round a flock of wild ducks napping,
And the rapturous-noted wooings,
And the molten-throated cooings,
Of the amorous multitudes
Flashing through the dusky woods,
When a veering wind hath blown
A glare of sudden daylight down?—
40   Naught of these!—And fewer notes
Hath the wind alone that floats
Over naked trees and snows;
Half its minstrelsy it owes
To its orchestra of leaves.
Ay! weak the meshes music weaves
For thy snaréd soul's delight,
'Less, when thou dost lie at night
'Neath the star-sown heavens bright,
To thy sin-unchokéd ears
50   Some dim harmonies may pierce
From the high-consulting spheres:
'Less the silent sunrise sing
Like a vibrant silver string
When its prison'd splendors first
O'er the crusted snow-fields burst.
But thy days the silence keep,
Save for grosbeaks' feeble cheep,
Or for snow-birds' busy twitter
When thy breath is very bitter.

60 So my spirit often acheth
    For the melodies it lacketh
    'Neath thy sway, or cannot hear
    For its mortal-chokéd ear.
    And full thirstily it longeth
    For the beauty that belongeth
    To the Autumn's ripe fulfilling;—
    Heapéd orchard-baskets spilling
    'Neath the laughter-shaken trees;
    Fields of buckwheat full of bees,
70 Girt with ancient groves of fir
    Shod with berried juniper;
    Beech-nuts mid their russet leaves;
    Heavy-headed nodding sheaves;
    Clumps of luscious blackberries;
    Purple-cluster'd traceries
    Of the cottage climbing-vines;
    Scarlet-fruited eglantines;
    Maple forests all aflame
    When thy sharp-tongued legates came.

80 Ruler with an iron hand
    O'er an intermediate land!
    Glad am I thy realm is border'd
    By the plains more richly order'd,—
    Stock'd with sweeter-glowing forms,—
    Where the prison'd brightness warms
    In lush crimsons thro' the leaves,
    And a gorgeous legend weaves.

1876-77; 1880

MEMNON

I

1 Weary, forsaken by fair, fickle sleep,
       A traveller rose, and stood outside his tent,
   That shrouded was in dusky shadows deep,
       By palm-trees cast, that o'er it kindly leant.
       A low moon lingered o'er a wide extent
   Of lifeless, shifting sands; her pallid rays
       Had kissed the scorchéd waste to sweet content;
   And now her farewells whispering, still she stays,
   As loth to leave the land to Phoebus' fiery blaze.

II

10 Slowly she sinks; and faint streaks quietly creep
　　Up from the East into the dusky sky;
Aurora's yellow hair, that up the steep
　　Streams to the rear of night full breezily,
　　Shaken from her flushed fingers that now dye
The under-heavens crimson; now she springs
　　Full-blown before the Day, and hastens by
With silver-footed speed and yearning wings,
　　To kiss a form of stone that at her coming sings.

III

Thrilled at the voice, the traveller starts aside,
20　　And sees the image, prostrate, half enwound
With red, unstable sand-wreaths, and its wide
　　Forehead, and lips that moved not with their sound
　　Celestial, lined with many a furrowed wound,
Deep-graven by the gnawing desert blast:
　　Half-buried sphinxes strewed the waste around,
And human-headed bulls, now mouldering fast,—
Their impious shapes half gone, their greatness wholly past.

IV

Out of this desolation vast and dead,
　　Now glorified and clothed in red and gold,—
30 Brightness befitting Egypt's hero's bed,—
　　A matin to his goddess mother rolled
　　From dawn-kissed lips, that also kissed the mould
Of their decaying substance. The sweet psalm
　　Thrilled in the listener's ears, with manifold
Cool music mingled of the murmuring palm;
And accents large and sad deepened the lifeless calm.

V

"Sweet mother, stay; thy son requireth thee!
　　All day the sun, with massive, maddening glare,
Beats on my weary brow and tortures me.
40　　All day the pitiless sand-blasts gnaw and wear
　　Deep furrows in my lidless eyes and bare.
All day the palms stand up and mock at me,
　　And drop cool shade over the dead bones there,
And voiceless stones, that crave no canopy:
O beautiful mother, stay; 'tis thy son prayeth thee.

"O mother, stay; thy son's heart needeth thee!
    The night is kind and fans me with her sighs,
But knoweth not nor feeleth sad for me.
    Hyenas come and laugh into my eyes,
50   The weak bats fret me with their small shrill cries,
And toads and lizards crawl in slimy glee.
    Thou comest—and my torturers dost surprise,
And fondlest me with fresh hands tearfully.
O dewy-lipped mother, stay; thy son desireth thee.

"O mother, why so quickly wouldst thou flee?
    Let Echo leave her mountain rocks and twine
My words with triple strength to cling to thee
    And clog thy limbs from flight as with strong wine;
    Let them recall sweet memories of thine,
60 Of how the long-shadowed towers of wind-swept Troy
    Were dear to thee and near, whilst thou didst pine
For the god-faced Tithonus, and the joy
Thou drank'st when thou hadst gained the willing, kingly boy.

VIII

"O mother, how Scamander chided thee,
    And swelled his tawny floods with grief for him,
And drowned his oozy rushes by the sea!
    For often have I heard such tales from him,
    Thou listening, whilst the purple night did swim
Reluctant past, and young Æmathion hung
70   Upon thy wealthy bosom; music, dim
In ears not all divine, the nigh stars sung,
Of thine high origin Hyperion's courts among.

"O mother, what forebodings visited thee
    From the Laconian's ravish'd bridal bed;
What mists of future tears half blinded thee
    When Ilion's god-built gates, wide-openéd,
    Let in the fatal Spartan woman wed
To Troy in flames, dogs gorged with Trojan slain,
    And tears of thine, mother, for thy son dead.
80 Dead; would my soul were with the body slain,
Nor stony-fetter'd here upon this Theban plain!

"O mother, what glooms darkened down on thee,
   And tearful fears made thy scared eyelids red,
When me thou sawest by some god's enmity
   Madly to meet Pelides' fury led,
   Sparing the aged Nestor's childless head
By me made childless. On the Phrygian plain
   Between the bright-eyed Greeks and Trojans bred
Warriors, I met the Phthian ash in vain,
90   Which bade my breast's bright wine the trampled stubble stain.

XI

"Then, mother, weeping, thou to Jove didst flee,
   And wring thy fingers, and, a suppliant,
Didst kneel before him, grasping his great knee
   And awful beard, and clinging like a plant
   Of ivy to an oak, till he should grant
Peculiar honours, not vouchsafed before,
   To thy son's obsequies; nor didst thou pant
And pray in vain, and kiss his beard all hoar,
And large ambrosial locks that veiled the sapphire floor.

XII

100   "For, mother, when the ruddy-bosomed sea
   Had drunk its fill of fire, and, climbing high,
Smoke of my funeral pyre, with savoury
   Odours of oil and honey, 'riched the sky,
   Out of the seething flames a cloud did fly
Of shrill-voiced birds,—like swarms of swarthy bees
   That move their household gods in young July,—
And, screaming, fought and perished, to appease
My manes and fulfil impelling Jove's decrees.

XIII

"O mother, hath my song no charm for thee,
110   To hamper thee from flight? Thou then didst wait
Scarce till the lustral drops were dry for me,
   And embers parch'd with dark wine satiate;
   But wast away through the Hesperean gate
To mourn o'er waters Atlantean. Now
   Thy loose locks trailéd are in golden state
Down the far side of yon keen peaks of snow;
The brazen sun hath come, and beareth on my brow.

"Soon will for me the many-spangled night
   Rise, and reel round, and tremble toward the verge.
120 Soon will the sacred Ibis her weird flight
   Wing from the fens where shore and river merge,
   With long-drawn sobbings of the reed-choked surge.
The scant-voiced ghosts, in wavering revelry,
   For Thebes' dead glory gibber a fitful dirge.
Would thou wert here, mother, to bid them flee!
O beautiful mother, hear; thy chained son calleth thee."

1877; 1879

ODE TO DROWSIHOOD

1 Breather of honeyed breath upon my face!
   Teller of balmy tales! Weaver of dreams!
   Sweet conjurer of palpitating gleams
And peopled shadows trooping into place
    In purple streams
Between the drooped lid and the drowsy eye!
   Moth-winged seducer, dusky-soft and brown,
Of bubble gifts and bodiless minstrelsy
   Lavish enough! Of rest the restful crown!
10 At whose behest are closed the lips that sigh,
   And weary heads lie down.

Thee, Nodding Spirit! Magic Comforter!
   Thee, with faint mouth half speechless, I invoke,
   And straight uplooms through the dead centuries' smoke
The aged Druid in his robe of fur,
    Beneath the oak
Where hang uncut the paly mistletoes.
   The mistletoe dissolves to Indian willow,
Glassing its red stems in the stream that flows
20   Through the broad interval. A lazy billow
Flung from my oar lifts the long grass that grows
   To be the Naiad's pillow.

The startled meadow-hen floats off, to sink
   Into remoter shades and ferny glooms;
   The great bees drone about the thick pea-blooms;
The linkéd bubblings of the bobolink,
    With warm perfumes
From the broad-flowered wild parsnip, drown my brain;
   The grackles bicker in the alder-boughs;

9

30   The grasshoppers pipe out their thin refrain
        That with intenser heat the noon endows.
    Then thy weft weakens, and I wake again
        Out of my dreamful drowse.

    Ah! fetch thy poppy-baths, juices exprest
        In fervid sunshine, where the Javan palm
        Stirs, scarce awakened from its odorous calm
    By the enervate wind, that sinks to rest
        Amid the balm
    And sultry silence, murmuring, half asleep,
40   Cool fragments of the ocean's foamy roar,
    And of the surge's mighty throbs that keep
        Forever yearning up the golden shore,
    Mingled with song of Nereids that leap
        Where the curled crests downpour.

    Who sips thy wine may float in Baiæ's skies,
        Or flushed Maggiore's ripples, mindless made
        Of storming troubles hard to be allayed.
    Who eats thy berries, for his ears and eyes
        May vineyard shade
50   Melt with soft Tuscan, glow with arms and lips
        Cream-white and crimson, making mock at reason.
    Thy balm on brows by care uneaten drips;
        I have thy favors but I fear thy treason.
    Fain would I hold thee by the dusk wing-tips
        Against a grievous season.

1877; 1879

ARIADNE

I

1   Hung like a rich pomegranate o'er the sea
        The ripened moon; along the tranced sand
    The feather-shadowed ferns drooped dreamfully;
    The solitude's evading harmony
        Mingled remotely over sea and land;
    A light wind woke and whispered warily,
        And myriad ripples tinkled on the strand.

II

    She lay face downward on the sighing shore,
        Her head upon her bended arm; her hair

10   Loose-spreading fell, a heart-entangling store;
Her shoulder swelling through it glimmered more
    Divinely white than snows in morning air;
One tress, more wide astray, the ripples bore
Where her hand clenched the ooze in mute despair.

III

A wandering wind laughed over her, then slunk
    Shamefast away, laden with her deep woe,
Smit with the consciousness that she had drunk
Grief's numbing chalice to the dregs, and sunk,
    As deep as ever mortal soul could go,
20   To sleep's dim caves: while, like a wave-borne trunk,
    Did her still body no life-promise show.

IV

Then stronger stirred her pulses; and a sound
    Of her deep-drawn and slowly-measured breath,
Now shattered by a gasping sob, or drowned
By sudden rustlings of the leaves around,
    Told of her spirit driven back from Death,
Whom it had sought with forehead duly bound
    With fillets, where the hemlock wavereth.

V

A many-throated din came echoing
30   Over the startled trees confusedly,
From the inmost mountain folds hurled clamouring
Along the level shore to droop its wing;
    She blindly rose, and o'er the moon-tracked sea
Towards Athens stretched her hands,—"With shouts
      they bring
    Their conquering chieftain home. Ah me! ah me!"

VI

But clearer came the music, zephyr-borne,
    And turned her yearnings from the over-seas,
Hurtled unmasked o'er glade and belted bourne,—
Of dinning cymbal, covert-rousing horn,
40   Soft waxen pipe, shrill-shouted EVOES.
Then sat she down unheeding and forlorn,
Half dreaming of old Cretan melodies.

VII

Like thought quick-frozen in the vivid brain
    At need of sudden, vast emergency,
She sat there dazed and motionless; the main
Sobbed round and caught her longest tress again,
    And clasped her shell-like foot, nor heeded she;
And nearer, and nearer, like thick gusts of rain,
    The clamour swelled and burst upon the sea.

VIII

50 The thickets rocked; the ferns were trampled down;
    The shells and pebbles splashed into the waves;
The white sands reeked with purple stains and brown,
With crushed grape-clusters and fig-bunches strown;
    Hoof'd sylvans, fauns, satyrs from mossy caves,
Fur-clad Bacchantes, lept around to drown
    God Bacchus' voice, whose lip the crimson laves.

IX

His thyrsus, wreathed with many-veined vine
    That magically blossomed and bare fruit,
He waved above the crowd with grace divine,
60 And straightway by the silver waste of brine
    They laid them gently down with gesture mute;
The while he twinéd his persuasions fine
    And meshed her grief-clipt spirit with his lute.

X

These sweet entanglements he closely wove,—
    "A god hath heard thy plainings piteous;
A god's deep heart thy shrill shriek shuddering clove;
A god hath left his incense-teeming grove,
    And sought thee by the chill sea's barrenness;
A god's strong spirit night-long vainly strove,
70   And fell before thy mortal loveliness.

XI

"Forget the subtle-tongued Ionian's love,
    His speech that flowed like honey, and his vows;
Forget the deaf, black ship that fleetly drove,
Leaving thee hopeless in this moaning cove;

Forget the past's dumb misery, and rouse
Thy heart and lift thy spirit clear above
    Dead griefs, as fitteth godhead's promised spouse.

XII

"And hearken, maiden! I will love thee well.
Then rise and follow, rise and follow, rise
And give a god thine hand, and come and dwell
With gods, and drink the purpling œnomel,
    And slake desire with aught that lures thine eyes,
From flowerful hermitage in some green dell
    To sphere-realms in the star-entangled skies.

XIII

"Rich largess of all crystalline delights,
    With converse of the well-persuading lyre,
Shall satisfy thee of sweet sounds and sights,
And each compelling beauty that excites
    A yearning shall fulfil its own desire;
And vintagers shall worship thee with rites
    Of wine outpoured and vervain-nourished fire.

XIV

"And all these pleasures shall be sure for thee;
    And woven through them like a golden thread
The certainty of one fixt love for thee,
And that a god's, shall bind them fast for thee,—
    So fast that by no finely-stinging dread,
Lest they should prove some dream-wrought mockery,
    Shall thy heart's joyance e'er be visited."

XV

And so with silver-linkéd melodies
    He wooed her till the moon lay pale and low;
And first she lifted up her dreaming eyes
And dreamed him her old love in fairer guise;
    And then her soul drew outwards, and a glow
Woke in her blood of pleasure and surprise,
    To think it was a god that loved her so.

And last she rose up happily, and gave
    Her hand to him, by sudden love made bold,—
The while the sun got up refreshed and drave
Square-shouldered through the lucent mists, that clave
110   To the clear-echoed inland hills, and rolled
Along their peaks in many a pallid wave,
    Or floated coldly o'er the molten gold,—

XVII

And went with him where honey-dew distils
    Through swimming air in odorous mists and showers,
Where music the attentive stillness fills;
And every scent and colour drips and spills
    From myriad quivering wings of orchid flowers;
And there they dwelt deep in the folded hills,
    Blissfully hunting down the fleet-shod hours.

XVIII

120   And who shall say her love was incomplete?
    For love fares hardly on ingratitude,
And love dies quickly nurtured on deceit,
And love turns hatred, captured by a cheat;
    And love had died while in despair immewed;
And this god's love was surely very sweet,
    For she was a forsaken maid he wooed.

1877; 1880

TO THE SPIRIT OF SONG

1　White as fleeces blown across the hollow heaven
　　　Fold on fold thy garment wraps thy shining limbs;
　Deep thy gaze as morning's flamed thro' vapours riven,
　　　Bright thine hair as day's that up the ether swims.
　Surely I have seen the majesty and wonder,
　　　Beauty, might and splendour of the soul of song;
　Surely I have felt the spell that lifts asunder
　　　Soul from body, when lips faint and thought is strong;
　　　　　Surely I have heard
10　　　　　The ample silence stirred
　By intensest music from no throat of bird:—
　　　　Smitten down before thy feet
　　　　From the paths of heaven sweet,
　Lowly I await the song upon my lips conferred.

1877; 1880

EPISTLE TO BLISS CARMAN
September, 1878

1　　An azure splendour floats upon the world.
　　Around my feet the blades of grass, impearled
　　And diamonded, are changing radiantly.
　　At every step new wonders do I see
　　Of fleeting sapphire, gold and amethyst,—
　　Enchanting magic of the dew sun-kissed.
　　The felon jay mid golden-russet beeches
　　Ruffles his crest, and flies with startled screeches.
　　Ever before me the shy cricket whistles
10　　From underneath the dry, brown, path-side thistles.
　　His gay note leads me, and I quickly follow
　　Where dips the path down through a little hollow
　　Of young fir-seedlings. Then I cross the brook
　　On two grey logs, whose well-worn barkless look
　　Tells of the many black-gown-shadowed feet
　　Which tread them daily, save when high June's heat
　　Scatters us wide, to roll in cool, salt billows
　　Of Fundy's make, or under hanging willows
　　Slide the light birch, and dream, and watch the grasses
20　　Wave on the intervale as the light wind passes,
　　Puffing a gentle cloud of smoke to scare
　　The sand-flies, which are ravening everywhere.

Such our enjoyment, Bliss, few weeks ago;
And the remembrance warms me with a glow
Of pleasure, as I cross the track and climb
The rocky lane I've clambered many a time.
On either side, where birch and maples grow,
The young firs stand with eager hands below,
And catch the yellow dropping leaves, and hold
30   Them fast, as if they thought them dropping gold;
But fairy gold they'll find them on the morrow,
When their possessing joy shall turn to sorrow.
    Now thro' the mottled trunks, beneath the boughs,
I see the terrace, and the lower rows
Of windows drinking in the waking air;
While future Freshmen stand around and stare.

. . . .

    Last week the bell cut short my happy strain.
Now half in pleasure, half in a vague pain,
For you I undertake my rhyme again.
40   Last week in its first youth saw you begin
Your happy three-years' course with us, and win
The highest honours, half of which are due
To your own strength of brain, and half accrue
To that wise master from whose hands you came
Equipped to win, and win yourself a name.
But I,—I have but one quick-slipping year
To spend amid these rooms and faces dear,
And then must quit this fostering roof, these walls
Where from each door some bright-faced memory calls,
50   And halt outside in sore uncertainty,
Not knowing which way lies the path for me
Through the unlighted, difficult, misty world.
Ah, whither must I go? Thick smoke is curled
Close round my feet, but lifts a little space
Further ahead, and shows to me the face—
Distorted, dim, and glamourous—of Life;
With many ways, all cheerless ways, and rife
With bristling toils crowned with no fitting fruit,—
All songless ways, whose goals are bare and mute.
60   But *one* path leads out from my very feet,—
The only one which lures me, which is sweet.
Ah! might I follow it, methinketh then
My childhood's brightest dreams would come again.
Indeed, I know they dwell there, and I'd find
Them meeting me, or hastening up behind.

16

See where it windeth, always bright and clear,
Though over stony places here and there;
Up steep ascents, thro' bitter obstacles,
But interspersed with glorious secret dells;
70 And vocal with rich promise of delight,
And ever brightening with an inward light
That soothes and blesses all the ways that lie
In reach of its soft light and harmony.
And were this path made for my following,
Then would I work and sing, and work and sing;
And though the songs were cryings now and then
Of me thus singing in the midst of men,—
Where some are weary, some are **weeping**, some
Are hungering for joys that never come;
80 And some drive on before a bitter fate
That bends not to their prayers importunate;
Where some say God is deaf and hears not now,
And speaks not now, some that He *is* not now,
Nor ever was, and these in fancied power
See not the mighty workings of each hour,
Or, seeing, read them wrong. Though now and then
My songs were wailings from the midst of men,
Yet would I deem that it were ever best
To sing them **out** of weariness to rest;
90 Yet would I cheer them, sharing in their ills,
Weaving them dreams of waves, and skies, and hills;
Yet would I sing of Peace, and Hope, and Truth,
Till softly o'er my song should beam the youth,—
The morning of the world. Ah, yes, there hath
The goal **been** planted all along that path;
And as the swallow were my heart as free,
Might I but hope that path belonged to me.

I've prated so, I scarce know what I've said.
But you'll not think me to have lost the thread,
100 Seeing I had none. Do not say I've kept
My promises too amply, and o'erleapt
A letter's bounds; not harshly criticise;
But miss the spots and blots with lenient eyes.
Scan not its outer, but its inner part;
'T was not the head composed it, but the heart.

1878; 1880

ORION

1   Two mighty arms of thunder-cloven rock
Stretched ever westward toward the setting sun,
And took into their ancient, scarred embrace
A laughing valley and a crooning bay.
The gods had stilled them in their primal throes,
And broken down their writhed extremities
Sheer to the open sea. And now pine-belts
And strayed fir-copses lined their shaggy sides;
And inland toward the island's quiet heart

10   White torrents cleft the screens and answered each
To other from the high cliffs closer drawn;
Kept ever brimming from eternal caves
In azure deeps of snow, and feeding full
A strong, swift river. And the river flowed
With tumult, till it caught the mighty speech
Rolled upward from the ocean, when it paused,
And hushed its rapid song in reverence,
And wound slow-footed through the summer vale,
And met its sovereign with majestic calm.

20   The sunset with its red and purple banners
Hung softly o'er the bay, whose rippled breast
Flushed crimson; and the froth-streaks round the beach
Were glowing pink. The sands burned ruddy gold,
And foot-marks crossing them lay sharp and black.
A flood of purple glory swept the shores,
And spread upon the vineyards, and the groves
Of olives round the river-banks, and clothed
The further matted jungles; whence it climbed
The ragged scaurs and jagg'd ravines, until

30   It lay a splendour on the endless snow.

Where the slow swirls were swallowed in the tide,
Some stone-throws from the stream's mouth, there the sward
Stretched thick and starry from the ridge's foot
Down to the waves' wet limits, scattering off
Across the red sand-level stunted tufts
Of yellow beach-grass, whose brown panicles
Wore garlands of blown foam. Amidst the slope
Three sacred laurels drooped their dark-green boughs
About a high-piled altar. There the king,

40   Œnopion, to whose sceptre bowed with awe
The people dwellers in the steep-shored Chios,
Stood praying westward; in his outstretched hand
The griding knife, well whetted, clothed with dread.

The royal priest's dark tresses, made aware
Of coming winter by some autumn snows,
Hung down his blue-dyed mantle, which he girt
Up seemly for the sacrifice; a beard,
Short, black, and silken, clothed his lips and chin;
Beneath deep brows his keen eyes lurked half hid,
50 And never rested. Now they drank the stream
Poured from the fiery sunset's sunken springs.
A supplication moved his silent lips,
Swift-winged to seek Apollo and beseech
Regard unto the rites e'en now begun.
Anon he dropped his arm; and straight the youths,
Chosen of Chios' fairest race, upbore
The victim to the pile,—a tawny wolf,
Blood-stained, fast bound in pliant withes, fed fat
On many a bleating spoil of careless folds,
60 His red tongue lolling from his fanged jaws,
His eyes, inflamed, shrinking with terror and hate,
His writhen sinews strained convulsively.

Meanwhile from out a neighbour gorge, which spake
Rough torrent-thunders through its cloak of pines,
Along the shore came one who seemed to wear
The grandeur of the mountains for a robe,
The torrent's strength for girdle, and for crown
The sea's calm, for dread fury capable,—
A Hunter laden with the spotted pride
70 Of kingly beasts before not dared of men,—
And stood without the laurel's sacred shade,
Which his large presence deepened. When the knife
Let blood well-pleasing to Apollo forth
The victim's gasping throat,—who yet cried not,
But glared still hate upon his murderers
And died uncraven,—then the Hunter bent
His godlike head with awe unto the gods,
And so kept bowed, the while the King drew forth
Wine from a full skin-bottle nigh, and poured
80 A beaded, dark libation. Then he raised
His head again,—like a tall pine that bends
Unto a sudden blast, and so keeps bent
Some moments, till the tempest passes by,—
And cast his burden down before the King,
And said,—
       "With skins of lions, leopards, bears,
Lynxes and wolves, I come, O King, fulfilling
My pledge, and seeking the delayed fulfilling

Of some long hopes. For now the mountain lairs
90   Are empty, and the valley folds secure.
The inland jungles shall be vexed no more
With muffled roarings through the clouded night,
And heavy splashings in the misty pools.
The echo-peopled crags shall howl no more
With hungry yelpings 'mid the hoary firs.
The breeding ewe in the thicket shall not wake
With wolves' teeth at her throat, nor drinking bull
Bellow in vain beneath the leopard's paw.
Your maidens shall not fear to quit by night
100   Their cottages to meet their shepherd lads;
And these shall leave safe flocks, and have no need
Of blazing faggots. Nor without some toils
Are these things so. For mighty beasts did yield
Their ornament up most reluctantly;
And some did grievous battle. But the pledge
And surety of a blissful harbourage,
Whither through buffets rude I needs must fare,
Made heavy labours light. And if, hard pressed,
My knees perchance waxed faint, or mine eyes dim,
110   The strong earth stayed me, and the unbowed hills,
The wide air and the ever-joyous sun,
The free sea leaping up beneath the sun,—
All were to me for kindly ministrants,
And lent glad service to their last-born, man,
Whom, reverent, the gods, too, favoured well.
And if to me, sleepless, alone, by night
Came phantoms from polluted spots, and shades
Unfettered, wavering round my cliff-edged couch,
Fain to aghast me; them I heeded not,
120   As not worth heed. For there the deep-eyed Night
Looked down on me; unflagging voices called
From unpent waters falling; tireless wings
Of long winds bare me tongueless messages
From star-consulting, silent pinnacles;
And breadth, and depth, and stillness fathered me.
But now, O King, seeing I have at cost
Of no slight labour done thy rugged hest,
And seeing hard strife should win sweet favours, grant
The good long wrought for, that amid the groves
130   And sunny vineyards I may drink deep draughts
Of love's skilled mixing, and of sweet mouth's gift
Of maiden-lipped, snow-breasted Merope."

So sped the winged words. And thus the King,
Œnopion, to whose sceptre bowed with awe

The people, dwellers in the steep-shored Chios:
"Great honour hast thou won and shalt possess,
And I will pay thee to the uttermost.
Thy couch this night be softer, and more blest
Thy visions,"—but in subtlety he spake,
140   And went apart a little from the place,
And filled with sullen wine two cups, well wrought.
But one he tinctured with a Colchian drug
And gave his guest to drink, with honeyed words,
But crooked, serpent-smooth,—"Drink this, in pledge
Of those deep draughts for which thou art athirst.
And now I go to bid the maid be glad
And make all ready. Rest thee here with these,
And I will come and fetch thee." And he went
Up from the shore and in among the vines,
150   Until his mantle gleamed athwart the lanes
Of sunset through the far, grey olive-groves.
The Hunter turned and heeded not the men,
But went apart close by the sleepless sea
And sat him down, because his eyes were dim,
And his head heavy, and his sinews faint.

And now it was about the set of sun,
And the west sea-line with its quivering rim
Had hid the sun-god's curls. A sanguine mist
Crept up, and to the Hunter's heavy eyes
160   Became as if his eyes were filled with blood.
He guessed the traitorous cup, and his great heart
Was hot, his throat was hot; but heavier grew
His head, and he sank back upon the sand,
Nor saw the light go out across the sea,
Nor heard the eagle scream among the crags,
Nor stealthy laughter echo up the shore,
Nor the slow ripple break about his feet.

The deep-eyed Night drew down to comfort him,
And lifted her great lids and mourned for him,
170   Foreknowing all his woe, and herself weak
To bend for him the indomitable fates;
And heavier dews wet all the trees and fields;
And sighs cool-drawn from infinite wells of space
Breathed round him; and from forth the unbowed hills
Came strength, and from the ocean essences
And influences to commune with him,
But found his spirit blind, and dumb, and deaf,
Not eager and expectant, as of old,
At every portal of the sleepless mind.

180   But hark! what feet are these that stir the vines
        Beneath the big, sweet-smelling grape-clusters?
        What feet are these that leave the muffling grass
        And crush the shingle sharply up the beach?
        Out of the foamless sea a heavy fog
        Steamed up, rolled in on all the island shores,
        But heavier, denser, like a cloak, where lay
        The Hunter; and the darkness gathered thick,
        More thick the fog and darkness where he lay,—
        Like as a mother folds more close her child
190   At night when sudden street-brawl jars her dreams.
        But now the folding vapours veiled him not,
        The ineffectual darkness hid him not,
        For one came with the King and bare a torch,
        And stood beside the Hunter where he lay;
        And all the darkness shuddered and fled back
        Sullenly into the grim-visaged crags,
        Beneath their battered foreheads; and the fog
        Crept up a chilly horror round the King,
        Made huge the writhed and frowning mountain-brows,
200   Till cliff, and cloud, and chaos of thick night
        Toppled about the place, and each small sound
        Of footstep or of stealthy whisper rang
        Tortured and shrill within the cavernous hollows.
        Before the King, before the torch-bearer,
        Stood one beside the Hunter's head,—a slave
        Beside the god-begotten,—and he bare
        Back with one arm his cloak, and in his hand
        He bare a cup—with suchlike juice in it
        As slew Alcmena's son—above the face,
210   The strong, white godlike face, more deathly white
        Even than death. Then into each close lid
        He dropped the poison with a loathing hand,
        While he whose light made manifest the deed
        Winced in his eyes and saw not, would not see,
        Those eyes that knew not of their light gone out.
        And heavy drops stood forth on all the rocks,
        And ocean moaned unseen beneath the fog.
        But the King laughed—not loud—and drew his cloak
        Closer about him and went up the beach,
220   And they two with him.
                        Now the fog rolled back
        And a low moon came out across the sea,
        And o'er the sea flocked out the pasturing stars,
        And still he lay upon the trodden sand,
        And still the ripple brake about his feet.

So moved the burdened hours toward the dawn;
But suddenly their burden was forgot,
For music welled from out the throbbing waves,
And melody filled all the silver air.
230   And silver shoulders under wondrous gold
Of dripping tresses brake the shining waste
Whence came the maids beloved of Doris, fair
As stars and lovely for the stars to see,
And stood and mourned about the Hunter there,—
And cursed were his eyes that could not see.
And had he seen, as grievous were his case,
Blinded with love and stricken with delight.
So came they weeping, and their yellow hair
Fell round them, while they smote their lyres and sang:

240   "O god-begotten
        And dear to all the gods!
            For thee quick-dropping tears
                Make heavy our eyes and hot.
      Be he of gods forgotten
            That smote thee, their gifts as rods
                To scourge him all his years,
                    Sparing him not.

        "For thee the long-heaving
        Ocean, fruitful of foam,
250   Groaned in his depths and was sore
                Troubled, grieving for thee.
    Grew Clotho sick of her weaving,
        And the fury of storms that come
            Out of the wilderness hoar
                Went pitying thee.

        "For thee the all-bearing
        Mother, the bountiful Earth,
            Who hath borne no fairer son
                In her kindly bosom and broad,
260   Will not be comforted, wearing
        Thy pain like her labour of birth,
            And hath veiled her in vapours as one
                Stricken down, overawed.

        "For thee the all-covering
        Night, the comforting mother,
            Wept round thee pitifully,
                Nor withheld her compassionate hands;

And sleep from her wings low-hovering
Fell kindly and sweet to no other
270
Between the unharvested sky
And the harvested lands.

"We are all made heavy of heart, we weep with thee, sore
with thy sorrow,—
The Sea to its uttermost part, the Night from the dusk to the
morrow,
The unplumbed spaces of Air, the unharnessed might of the
Wind,
The Sun that outshaketh his hair before his incoming, behind
His outgoing, and laughs, seeing all that is, or hath been, or
shall be,
The unflagging waters that fall from their well-heads soon to
the sea,
The high Rocks barren at even, at morning clothed with the
rime,
The strong hills propping up heaven, made fast in their place
for all time.
280
Withal the abiding Earth, the fruitful mother and kindly,
Who apportions plenty and dearth, nor withholds from the
least thing blindly,
With suchlike pity would hide they reverent eyes indeed
Wherewith the twin Aloides fain she would hide at their need.
But they withstood not Apollo, they brake through to Hades,
o'erthrown;
But thee the high gods follow with favour, kind to their own;
For of thee they have not lacked vows, nor yellow honey, nor
oil,
Nor the first fruit red on the boughs, nor white meal sifted
with toil,
Nor gladdening wine, nor savour of thighs with the fat burned
pure,—
Therefore now of their favour this ill thing shall not endure.
290
It endures but a little, seeing the gods make ready their
mercy,
Giving for thy well-being a skillfuller goddess than Circe,
For the putting away of thy trouble, the setting far off of
thy pain,
And she shall repay thee double, making thy loss thy gain.
But come, for the night fulfils, the grey in the sky gives
warning;-
Then get thee up to the hills and thou shalt behold the
MORNING."

The Hunter stirred, and all the long grey shore
Lay empty, and the ripple whispered not,
Awed by the wide-spread silence. Then he rose,
Groping, and strove to put aside the night
300 That clung beneath his eyelids,—till he knew,
And his whole heart sank, knowing. Then his voice
Brake thus from out his utter misery
(The while a sound went,—"Get thee up to the hills;
Thou shalt behold the morning"; but he heard not):
"Oh, black night, black forever! No light forever!
Oh, long, long night, just fallen to hang forever,
Never to break or lighten! Whose the heart
That dared it? Whose the hateful thought? What hand
Wrought me this curse, dealt me this ruin, this woe
310 Unutterable, pitiless, unmeasured,—
Put out my light, portioned me night forever?
Oh, ye that die not, ye that suffer not,
Gods that are mindful, seeing good and evil!
If ever unto you have risen a savour
Acceptable, of honey, and oil, and wine,
Me offering; and if a frequent smoke
Have circled up to heaven from me to you
Acceptable, of spotless hecatombs;
And if from vows fulfilled and reverence
320 Be favour in your sight,—then hear my prayer,
And soon be it accomplished: let the hand
Wither that wrought me this, the brain that planned
Rave and henceforth be mocked and plagued of devil.
Let every good be turned for him to gall,
And those his heart most cherishes become
A horror, till he flee from them as fiends.
But is this pain forever, this my night
Eternal? Thou that mad'st the day and night,
Make thou a day for me! O Earth, my mother,
330 All bountiful, all pitiful, take heed
Into what evil on thy breast hath fallen
Thy son! O sleepless sea, behold my woe!
O air all-folding, sky immovable,
With everlasting contemplation wise,
Know ye no remedy? Forest and fields,
Tempests untiring, streams, and steadfast hills,
Flame-riven caverns, hear me, for ye know me!
Tell me; I hearken." And his bended head
Besought the rocks.
340   "Thou shalt behold the morning,"
Brake clearly on the ample-bosomed silence,

And straight begot as many widening waves
As doth a pebble on a resting lake.
The echoes hurtled inland, startling all
The olive-groves and vineyards, rippling up
The green foot-hills, and lapping faint and low
About the low fir-copses; then they reached
The upper gorges, dying in that region,–
Region of sounding pines and cataracts
350 Impregnable to silence. Then, again,
Even in the lifting of his head, and making
Thanksgiving with mute lips, clear, far, and fine,
Out of the vaporous raiment round their tops
Came comfort from the hills:
       "Up to the hills!
Thou shalt behold the morning!"
         Then he bowed
With godlike reverence, reverencing the gods
And ancient powers that watched him, and made quick
360 His sense to their communion.
          Now a sound
Of hammers rose behind a jagged cape
Not many paces hence, with windy roar
Of new-awakened fire. With pain and toil,
Groping and staggering, hands, and knees, and feet
Bruised with the crags, and faint, he came where men
Wrought arms and forged the glowing bronze for war.
There one came forth to meet him; him he took
Upon his kingly shoulder, and him bade
370 Of courtesy to be to him for eyes,
To guide his feet that quickly he might fare
To the hill-crests, or ere the fiery flower
Of dawn bloomed fully.
      So they two went thus
Up from the sombre, bitter-breathing sea,
Beside the river, o'er the slumbrous sward
Gossamer-spread, dew-drenched, and in among
The vineyards and the olives. The fresh earth
Heavy about his feet, the bursting wealth
380 Of big grape-bunches, and the cool, green coils
Of dripping vines breathed richly. Swift they moved
'Mid gnarled trunks and still, grey stretch of leaves,
Without a sound save of wet twigs snapped dully
Or flit of startled bird. And now their way
They kept with toil, fallen on toilsome ways,–
Up shattered slopes half-clothed with juniper,
Through ragged-floored ravines, whose blasted scars

Held mighty pines root-fast in their black depths,
Still climbing, till a keen wind met them full
390 From eastward breathed, free-scented from the brine.
His labouring feet stood still, and while his lips
Drank the clear wind, his guide, descending home,
Left him alone, facing the gates of dawn.
The cliffs are rent, and through the eternal chasm
A far-heard moan of many cataracts,
With nearer, ceaseless murmur of the pines,
Came with the east wind, whilst the herald gold
From cloven pinnacles on either hand
On gradual wings sank to that airy glen;
400 And many-echoed dash of many waves
Rose dimly from the cliff-base where they brake,
Far down, unseen; and the wide sea spread wan
In the pale dawn-tide, limitless, unportioned—
Aye sentinelled by these vast rocky brows
Defaced and stern with unforgotten fires.

But he, intent, leaned toward the gates of dawn
With suppliant face, unseeing, and the wind
Blew back from either brow his hair, and cooled
His eyes that burned with that so foul dishonour
410 Late wrought upon them, **whispering** many things
Into his inmost soul. Sudden the day
Brake full. The healing of its radiance fell
Upon his eyes, and straight his sightless eyes
Were opened. All the morning's majesty
And mystery of loveliness lay bare
Before him; all the limitless blue sea
Brightening with laughter many a league around,
Wind-wrinkled, keel-uncloven, far below;
And far above the bright sky-neighbouring peaks;
420 And all around the broken precipices,
Cleft-rooted pines swung over falling foam,
And silver vapours flushed with the wide flood
Of crimson slanted from the opening east
Well ranked, the vanguard of the day,—all these
Invited him, but these he heeded not.
For there beside him, veiled in a mist
Wherethrough the enfolded splendour issued forth,—
As delicate music unto one asleep
Through mist of dreams flows softly,—all her hair
430 A mist of gold flung down about her feet,
Her dewy, cool, pink fingers parting it
Till glowing lips, and half-seen snowy curves

Like Parian stone, unnerved him, waited SHE,—
Than Circe skillfuller to put away
His pain, to set his sorrow afar off,—
Eos, with warm heart warm for *him*. His toils
Endured in vain, his great deeds wrought in vain,
His bitter pain, Œnopion's house accurst,
And even his sweet revenge, he recked not of;
440   But gave his heart up straightway unto love.

Now Delos lay a great way off, and thither
They two rejoicing went across the sea.
And under their swift feet, which the wave kissed
But wet not,—for Poseidon willed it so,
Honouring his son,—and all along their way
Was spread a perfect calm. And every being
Of beauty or of mirth left his abode
Under the populous flood and journeyed with them.
Out of their deep green caves the Nereids came
450   Again to do him honour; shining limbs
And shining bosoms, cleaving, waked the main
All into sapphire ripples, eachwhere crowned
With yellow tresses streaming. Triton came
And all his goodly company, with shells
Pink-whorled and purple, many-formed, and made
Tumultuous music. Ocean's tawny floor
They all left vacant, empty every bower,
And solitary the remotest courts.
Following in the midst of the array
460   Their mistress, her white horses paced along
Over the unaccustomed element,
Submissive, with the wonted chariot
Pillowed in vapours silver, pink and gold,
Itself of pearl and fire. And so they reached
Delos, and went together hand in hand
Up from the water and their company,
And the green wood received them out of sight.

1878; 1880

ITERUMNE

1   Ah me! No wind from golden Thessaly
     Blows in on me as in the olden days;
     No morning music from its dew-sweet ways,
   No pipings, such as came so clear to me
   Out of green meadows by the sparkling sea;
     No goddess any more, no Dryad strays,
     And glorifies with song the laurel maze;
   Or else I hear not and I cannot see.

   For out of weary hands is fallen the lyre,
10   And sobs in falling; all the purple glow
     From weary eyes is faded, which before
   Saw bright Apollo and the blissful choir
     In every mountain grove. Nor can I know
     If I shall surely see them any more.

1879: 1880

RONDEAU.—"HESPER APPEARS."

1   Hesper appears when flowing gales
   Have filled the sunset's fervid sails,
     When down the low dim orient hills
     The purple gloaming soft distils
   To nestle in the crooning vales.

   To fretted hearts whom want assails,
   Whom Youth, nor Hope, nor Love avails
     To loose their wearying load of ills,
       Hesper appears,

10   Lifting the sordid dusty veils
   That wrap us till our courage fails:
     Ah, vexéd hearts! The hour fulfils
     Your yearnings with its peace, and stills
   Awhile man's myriad fretful wails,—
       Hesper appears.

1879

29

THE SHANNON AND THE CHESAPEAKE

1   Oh, shout for the good ship Shannon,
      And cheer for the gallant Brooke,
For hot was the fight she fought
      And staunch the ship he took.

When the might of the land was astonished,
      And wreck on wreck had gone down,
The old flag fast at the peak,
      But the old flag's fame o'erthrown,

Then Brooke in the good ship Shannon
10   Set it forth in face of the world
That "hearts of oak" still flourished
      To keep the old flag unfurled.

'Twas the fair-starred first of June,
      A day of glorious days,
When York and Penn drove the Dutch,
      And Howe put the French to amaze;

And out from Boston Harbor
      The frigate Chesapeake steered;
Not a sound save the wash on her bows,
20   Till her crew broke silence and cheered.

In curt return from the Shannon
      Came a round shot over the rail,
And sullenly, one by one,
      Fell the first of the deadly hail.

Then full in its blind, white thunder
      Burst the wrath of that iron rain,
Sweeping the broad decks bare
      Till their timbers staggered again.

And the men crouch down for their lives,
30   And the heavy pall of the smoke
Is rent by the fierce, red flashes
      And the splinter's hurtling stroke.

Hot work at the belching cannon,
      In the sweat, and powder, and grime,
Till the Chesapeake's steersman falls,
      And firing slacks for a time;

For she drops afoul of our quarter,
    And her gallant captain dies.
Grapple now, for her mightiest bulwark
40   Is fallen where Lawrence lies.

We swarm in over the taffrail,
    With hot strokes taken and given,
And Brooke at our head, till the foe
    To the hold or the chains are driven.

We haul down the "Stars and Stripes";
    But, oh, the grief and the woe!—
A matter of twisted halliards,
    And the storm-worn flag *below*.

But it costs us dear, that blunder,
50   For our gunner misunderstands,
And Watt and five brave seamen
    Take death at their comrades' hands.

But, hark you, there is the summons!
    And sullenly they comply.
Brave men; they fought till hope perished,
    But better surrender than die.

Now cheer for the good ship Shannon,
    And the good fight fought that morn,
For the old flag's vindication,
60   And its ancient honor upborne!

But woe must be in such warfare,
    Though lost be the battle or won,
For brother's slaughter of brother
    And father smitten of son.

Pray God that England no more
    Stand wroth from her daughter apart!
Pray God one blood and one tongue
    Be one in hand and in heart!

But let a great wrong cry to heaven;
70   Let a giant necessity come;
And now, as of old, she can strike,
    She will strike, and strike home.

1879

A FAREWELL

My feet are set for other ways,
    And I go forth alone,
Crushing aside the heartsickness
    With careless look and tone.
I dash my hand across my eyes
    With a laugh that's half a moan:—
Good-bye! Good-bye! God rest with thee,
    My City—Fredericton.

Jan., 1880; 1881

BALLADE OF THE POET'S THOUGHT

1   A poet was vexed with the fume of the street,
    With tumult wearied, with din distraught;
And very few of the passing feet
    Would stay to listen the truths he taught.
    And he said,—"My labour is all for naught;
I will go, and at Nature's lips drink deep."
    For he knew not the wealth of the poet's thought,
Though sweet to win, was bitter to keep.

So he left the hurry, and dust, and heat
10   For the free, green forest where man was not;
And found in the wilderness' deep retreat
    That favour with Nature which he sought.
    She spake with him, nor denied him aught,
In waking vision or visioned sleep,
    But little he guessed the wealth she brought,
Though sweet to win, was bitter to keep.

But now when his bosom, grown replete,
    Would lighten itself in song of what
It had gathered in silence, he could meet
20   No answering thrill from his passion caught.
    Then grieving he fled from that quiet spot
To where men work, and are weary, and weep;
    For he said,—"The wealth for which I wrought
Is sweet to win, but bitter to keep."

ENVOI

Oh, poets, bewailing your hapless lot,
    That ye may not in Nature your whole hearts steep,

Know that the wealth of the poet's thought
Is sweet to win, but bitter to keep.

1880

AT POZZUOLI

1   At Pozzuoli on the Italian coast
      A ruined temple stands. The thin waves flow
      Upon its marble pavements; and in row
   Three columns, last of a majestic host
   Which once had heard the haughty Roman's boast,
      Rise in the mellow air. Long years ago
      The unstable floor sank down. Now from below
   The shining flood of sapphire,—like the ghost

   Of youth's bright aspirations and high hopes,
10   More real than castles in the air, and laid
   On some foundation, though of sand that slopes
      Seaward to lift again,—it comes arrayed
   In olive sea-weeds; but a raven mopes
      Upon its topmost stone, and casts a shade.

1880

BALLAD OF A BRIDE

1   Bring orange-blossoms fairly twined,
      Fair-plaited wreaths to wreathe her hair,
   Sweet-smelling garlands meet to bind
      Her brows, and be out-glistened there;
      Bring radiant blooms and jewels rare
   Against the happy bridal day;—
      A sound of parting thrills the air:—
   Hearken a little to my lay.

   Now, blossoms shine, but ye shall find
10   Beside her brow ye are not fair;
   Breathe sweetly an' ye have a mind,
      But with her breath can ye compare?
      Bright garlands, ye less lovely are,
   Nathless adorn her while ye may,—
      Even now her thoughts are otherwhere:—
   Hearken a little to my lay.

Now hasten, maids; the flowérs wind
   Amidst her hair with loving care;
Wind roses, for their red consigned
20   Beside her blushes to despair,
   Such happy beauty doth she wear;
But haste,—her glad feet scarce will stay,
   Nor us she heeds, for *he* is near:—
Hearken a little to my lay.

ENVOI

He comes, they go, a blissful pair;
   Full willingly she speeds away;
Full lightly heeds she this my prayer,—
   Hearken a little to my lay.

1880

A BALLAD OF THREE MISTRESSES

1   Fill high to its quivering brim
     The crimson chalice, and see
The warmth and whiteness of limb
     Light-draped luxuriously;
     Hark the voice love-shaken for thee,
My heart,—and thou liest ere long
     In the close captivity
Of wine, and woman, and song.

Though sweetly the dark wine swim,
10   More sweet, more tyrannous she
Who, till the moon wax dim,
     Rules man from east sea to west sea.
     And strong tho' the red wine be,
Ne'ertheless is woman more strong,
     Most fair of the Jove-given three,—
Of wine, and woman, and song.

But the rhyme of thy **Rhine-sung** hymn
     Is more sweet than thyself, Lorelie!
As over the night's blue rim
20   Thou chantest voluptuously;
     So stronger is song for me
To bind with a subtiler thong,—
     Her only may I not flee
Of wine, and woman, and song.

34

Then her must I serve without plea
    Who doeth her servants much wrong,
Queen Song of the Jove-given three,—
    Of wine, and woman, and song.

1880

BALLAD TO A KINGFISHER

1   Kingfisher, whence cometh it
    That you perch here, collected and fine,
On a dead willow alit
    Instead of a sea-watching pine?
    Are you content to resign
The windy, tall cliffs, and the fret
    Of the rocks in the free-smelling brine?
O, Kingfisher, do you forget?

Here do you chatter and flit
10   Where bowering branches entwine,
Of Ceyx not mindful a whit,
    And that terrible anguish of thine?
    Can it be that you never repine?
Aren't you Alcyone yet?
    Eager only on minnows to dine,
O Kingfisher, how you forget!

To yon hole in the bank is it fit
    That your bone-woven nest you consign,
And the ship-wrecking tempests permit
20   For lack of your presence benign?
    With your name for a pledge and a sign
Of seas calmed and storms assuaged set
    By John Milton, the vast, the divine,
O Kingfisher, still you forget.

ENVOI

But here's a reminder of mine,
    And perhaps the last you will get;
So, what's due your illustrious line
    Now, Kingfisher, *do* not forget.

1880

A BLUE BLOSSOM

1   A small blue flower with yellow eye
      Hath mightier spell to move my soul
      Than even the mightiest notes which roll
    From man's most perfect minstrelsy.
      A flash, a momentary gleam,
      A glimpse of some celestial dream,
    And tears alone are left to me.

    Filled with a longing vague and dim,
      I hold the flower in every light;
10   To purge my soul's redarkened sight
    I grope till all my senses swim.
      In vain; I feel the ecstacy
      Only when suddenly I see
    This pale star with the sapphire rim.

    Nor hath the blossom such strange power
      Because it saith "Forget me not"
      For some heart-holden, distant spot,
    Or silent tongue, or buried hour.
      Methinks immortal memories
20   Of some past scene of Paradise
    Speak to my spirit through the flower.

    Forgotten is our ancient tongue;
      Too dull our ears, our eyes too blind,
      Even quite to catch its notes, or find
    Its symbols written bright among
      All shapes of beauty. But 't is hard
      When one *can* hear, to be debarred
    From knowledge of the meaning sung.

              1880

DEDICATION OF "ORION AND OTHER POEMS"
To G. Goodridge Roberts

1   These first-fruits, gathered by distant ways,
    In brief, sweet moments of toilsome days,
      When the weary brain was a thought less weary
    And the heart found strength for delight and praise,—

I bring them and proffer them to thee,
All blown and beaten by winds of the sea,
   Ripened beside the tide-vexed river,—
The broad, ship-laden Miramichi.

Even though on my lips no Theban bees
10 Alighted,—though harsh and ill-formed these,
   Of alien matters in distant regions
Wrought in the youth of the centuries,—

Yet of some worth in thine eyes be they,
For bare mine innermost heart they lay;
   And the old, firm love that I bring thee with them
Distance shall quench not, nor time betray.

1880

THE FLIGHT

1   She rose in the night and fled;
    Such a night there was never another.
And her small hands shewed they red?
    What need! It is cleanly to smother.
In warm arms sleeps the young wife,
And he fondles her,—"Love! my life!"—
Ha! ha! but the child lies dead—
    Sweet dreams to you, father and mother!

Her hair streams out on the wind,
10   The tree-tops wail and mutter,
The dry leaves patter behind,
    And before the gray bats flutter;
Three crows are hastening after,—
But whence is that flying laughter?
She knows not, following blind,
    Nor heeds what the voices utter.

Down the long, moon-lighted glades
    Where the pale ghosts moan and shiver,
Through writhen, poisonous shades
20   Where the night-shades heavily quiver;
Where the reeking hollows are mute
She treads down the toad and the newt,
And thro' hemlock, sweet when love fades,
    She hastens, and rests not ever.

Shun yon thicket of grass!—
   A body lies there forgotten.
Strange it should come to pass
   Before the body is rotten.
They have crushed his head with a stone—
30   "Ha! ha! I am not alone."
And she flies; while up the morass
   Roll the night-mists swamp-begotten.

Her light feet scale the crags
   Where the **wild-goat scarce** could follow,
And never her swift flight flags
   Till she reaches a yawn-mouthed hollow
Where a goodly company feast—
Of man, and devil, and beast,
And by torch-light revel the hags,
40   And the beasts they grovel and wallow.

She comes among them by night,
   Her long hair over her falling,
Her white feet torn in her flight,
   And they gather around her brawling.
They shriek, they applaud, they groan,—
"Lady, we welcome our own.
Come and feast, thou hast won the right,—
   To wake him will need much calling."

1880

LAUNCELOT AND THE FOUR QUEENS

PART I.

1   Launcelot sleepeth under an apple-tree.

Where a little-trodden byway
Intersects the beaten highway
      Running downward to the river,
Stands an ancient apple-tree
In whose blossoms drowsily
      The bees are droning ever.

Back along the river's edge
Twists a tangled hawthorn hedge,
10   In whose thickets lurks the thrush;

Broods the skylark in the meads,
Floats the teal among the reeds,
    The warm wild-roses flush;

The sundews clasp their glistening beads,
The sun in mid-sky reins his steeds,
    And languid noon enwraps the earth;
Scarce a living creature stirs,
Save some gadding grasshoppers
    That heedless prate their mirth.

20 'Neath the fruit-tree's latticed shade
An errant knight at length is laid,
    In opiate noon's deep slumber sunk;
His helm, well proved in conflicts stern,
Lies in a tuft of tender fern
    Against the mossy trunk.

A robin on a branch above,
Nodding by his dreaming love
    Whose four blue eggs are hatched not yet,
Winks, and watches unconcerned
30 A spider o'er the helm upturned
    Weaving his careful net.

The sleeper's hair falls curling fair
From off his forehead broad and bare,
    Entangling violets faint and pale;
Beside his cheek a primrose gleams,
And breathes her sweetness through his dreams,
    Till grown too sweet they fail.

PART II.

And as he sleeps four queens come by
    And spy him 'neath the apple-tree.
40 Of his fair show enamored sore
    They 'prison him by sorcery.

Hark, the voices blithe and gay!
Four queens of great estate are they,
And riding come they up this way,—
    Come they up from out the river;
On four white horses do they ride,
And four fair knights do ride beside,
    As is their custom ever.

On upright spear each knight doth bear
50 One corner of an awning rare
Of silk, all green, and bordered fair
      With mystic-symbolled broidery;
And o'er the ladies' milky-white,
Soft shoulders falls the tinted light,
      And nestles tremblingly.

Now come they where they well may see
The blossom-veiléd apple-tree.
Quoth Eastland's queen,—"It grieveth me
      That on the branch but blossoms are!
60 If it were only autumn now,
And apples crowned the stooping bough,
      I'd deem it fairer far:

"Drooping so ripe and melting mellow,
Rind-streaked red and flecked with yellow,
Each one fairer than its fellow,
      Oh, methinks I see them now!"
Thus quoth she; but Morgane le Fay
Hath cast her eyne another way,
      And peereth 'neath the bough.

70 "Now swear I on my life," quoth she,
"Fairer fruit is 'neath the tree
Than e'er will be upon the tree.
      See ye yon knight in armor black?
Can looks so brave and limbs so strong
To any lowlier knight belong
      Than Launcelot du Lac?

"Faith! we the fairest knight have found
That ever lady's arms enwound,
Or ever lady's kisses crowned;
80   Myself can wish no royaller lover." . . .
"Nay! Think you then to choose for him,"
Quoth Eastland's queen, "while shadows dim
      His sheeny eyelids cover?

"Certes, 'twere discourtesie!
But put a spell of secrecy
Upon his drowsy eyne, till we
      May bring him to our magic towers;
Then let him choose which one of us
Shall deck for him the amorous,
90   Deep, blossom-scented bowers."

They weave a spell of witchery
Above his drowsy eyne, till he
Is breathing slow and heavily;
  Then bear him homeward on his shield.
His war-horse neighs behind the hedge,
The duck drops back into the sedge,
  The lark into the field.

PART III.

 He waketh in a chamber high,
  With tapestries adornéd fair;
100 Unto a window climbeth up,
   And chanteth unto Guinevere.

 In place of green o'ershadowing
  Launcelot sees above his head—
And, smiling, turns his magic ring—
A dragon fixt with brooding wing,
  And dismal claws outspread.

 He gives the ring a prayerful turn,
  Which aye was wont to put to flight
All lying visions; but the stern,
110 Black dragon's eyeballs seem to burn
  With smouldering, inward light.

 Now doth he slowly come aware
  No glamour 'tis, nor painted dream,
But oak, all carved with cunning care,
And for its eyes a sullen pair
  Of mighty jewels gleam.

 From samite soft he lifts his head,
  Instead of earthy-scented moss;
Four walls he sees all fair bespread
120 With yellow satins, garnishéd
  With legends wrought across.

 Half-hidden by a storied fold
  An archéd door he sees, shut close;
The sun, far-sunken o'er the wold,
Through archéd windows sluicing gold
  In sloping, moted rows,

 Gleameth upon the topmost tier
  Of armor on the farther walls;

Shimmers in gules and argent clear;
130 Bathes the carven rafters bare;
Then seeks adown the ocean sheer
    His sleepless azure halls.

Now paleth silver on the floor
    In place of gold upon the roof;
From a young moon the still gleams pour,
That from the sun, her paramour,
    Yet walketh not aloof.

Where bars the window-niche emboss,
    Launcelot, climbing, chanteth clear;
140 His song it floateth soft across
The dreaming trees that fringe the foss,
    And seeketh Guinevere:

    "Hearken, Guinevere!
        Hear me, oh, my love!
    Waketh thy soul wistfully?
        Hither let it rove;
    Hither tripping swift
        O'er the silvered meadows,
    With whispers for my prisoned ears
150   Fill the vacant shadows,
                Guinevere.

    "Hearken, Guinevere!
        Warm about my neck
    Might I feel thy claspéd arms,
        Little would I reck
    Prisonment or chains;
        Bitterer bonds hast thou
    Link'd of rippled locks upon me,
        And I kiss them now,
160   Guinevere.

    "Hearken, Guinevere!
        Spake thine eyes in silence,
    As a stream that fareth softly
        Thorough summer islands;
    Uttered suddenly
        What I never guess'd,—
    How could I betray my king
        At his queen's behest,
                Guinevere.

42

170   "Hearken, Guinevere!
      Magic potenter
Than hath brought me to this plight
     Hath thy bosom's stir;
Subtler witchery
     Hath thy whispering,
To make me foul before my God
     And false unto my king,
          Guinevere.

PART IV.

    The queens essay to have his love;
180   Denies he them **disdainfully.**
   A damsel comes and pledges her
     For service due to set him free.

A dewy breeze laughs through the bars,
   With meadow scents and early light;
And soon appear the ladies fair
   In silken vestures richly dight:
"The noblest knight of Arthur's court
   We know thee for, Sir Launcelot!
Who, save for Lady Guinevere,
190   For lady carest not.

"And now thou art our prisoner,
   And shalt lose her, and she lose thee;
So it behoveth thee to choose
   One of us four for **thy** ladye.
And choose thou not, here shalt thou die.
   So choose: I am Morgane le Fay,
Here Eastland's queen, there she of the Isles,
   North Wales accepts *her* sway."

Saith he: "This is a grievous case,
200   That either I must quit sweet life
Or keep it bitter with one of ye;
   Yet liefer will I death to wife
With worship, than a sorceress,
   As ye are each, I'll lay me by.
What boots it that one's body live
   An' his dear honor die!"

"Is this your answer?" question they.
   "Yea, is it," laughs he carelessly.

Then go they sorely sorrowing,
210   Leaving his spirit only free.
And training that to lonely flight,
     He seats him on his couch's side,
Till scent and song are heavy-winged
     About the hot noontide.

A breeze slips in refreshingly,
     As slowly swings the oaken door,—
Swings slow and lets a damsel in
     Bearing a most enticing store
Of fare to cheer his sinking heart,
220   And set his slackened strings in tune,—
Collops of meat that taste of the woods,
     And mead that smells of June.

"Ill fareth it with thee, Sir Knight!"
     "Ne'er spakest thou a truer word,
Fair damsel," saith he, heavily,
     While up the walls the arras stirred.
Saith she: "This magic-bred mischance
     Shall vaunt not to have mastered thee;
I'll see thee clearly quits with it
230   And thou'lt be ruled by me."

"What service wouldst thou?" asketh he.
     "To help my father Tuesday next,
Who hath agreed a tournament
     Him and North Wales's king betwixt;
For Tuesday last we lost the field."
     "Fair maid, who may thy father be?
Needs is it that thou tell me this,
     Then will I answer thee."

"King Bagdemagus is his name."
240   Saith he: "A knightly knight, and true,
And gentle; by my body's faith
     I will thee willing service do."
She turns, and lifts the trencher up,
     And seeks the door with paces steady:
"When dripping Phosphor flickers gray
     Be ready."

PART V.

When western folds are flocked with stars,
    And larks are quivering up the blue,
    Four clampéd doors, eleven locks,
250   And seven gates, she leads him through.

The blue has killed the gray;
White fleeces swiftly stray
From the shepherd feet of day
    Over their azure pasture;
To their morning baths addrest,
The gusts with wrinkling zest
Over the river's breast
    Are following fast and faster.

The door swings open wide,
260 And quickly side by side
Adown the steps they glide
    To an iron-bolted gateway;
What Magic makes Truth mars;
And through her fortunate stars
These hell-forged bolts and bars
    Open before her straightway.

She brings him to his steed,
Hidden with mindful heed
Where mossy foot-paths lead
270   From a broken pier on the river;
He draws his saddle-girth
And tries his lance's worth,
Then canters with lightsome mirth
    Out from the thickets that quiver.

* * * * * * * * * * * * *

In primal sympathy
All nature laughed with glee,
Shouted to feel him free,
    Drank of his breath and kissed him;
Nothing of sound and scent,
280 Color and coolness blent,
Nothing the morning meant
    In its myriad speeches missed him.

Over a knoll or two,
Grassy, and drenched with dew,
His blossomed pathway drew
    Till a screen between had risen;
Then in his iron shoes
He rose and waved his "adieus:"
"Methinketh neither I'll choose,
290   Nor die in your witches' prison."

1880

LOVE-DAYS

1   The sweet-mouthed shore hath wed the singing sea,
    And winds are joyous with their kissing chime.
    The voice-beseeching rapture of the time
An utterance hath found in every tree,
    In bursts of happy rhyme.

All nature loves, and loves are all fulfilled.
    Me only hope deferred and waitings long
    Keep silent; me these rich completions wrong:
Ah! when shall I have leave my lips to gild
10   With a sweet marriage-song?

From scenes of glad love crownéd, long gone down
    The droning-billowed reaches of the years,
    The lotus-flutes are shrilling in mine ears,
And torches flash into mine eyes, and drown
    Their sight in envious tears.

All lovers surely now are satisfied,
    Save only we, whom yet no threshold waits,
    For whom not yet the inner temple's gates
Have lifted: how much longer must we bide,
20   Pressing reluctant fates?

Oh, too long tarryings make a weary way!
    Then kiss me, Love, and kiss me; for the wings
    Of time are ever dropping divers things;
And who may from the promise of to-day
    Guess what the morrow brings!

1880

MIRIAM.—I.

SAPPHICS.

1   Miriam, loved one, were thy goings weary?
  Journeyed not with thee one to brighten thy way?
  Lighted with love-light how could it be dreary?
        Was it not my way?

  Why wert thou weary? All the golden glories
  Streaming from love's lamp thy enraptured sight won;
  Sweetly we whispered old self-heroed stories,
        Miriam, bright one!

  Crimson lipp'd love-flowers sprang about us going,
10   Clustering closely, rosy shadows weaving;
  Straight from our footsteps glowing ways were flowing,
        Vistas far-cleaving.

  Silvery lute-notes thrilled athrough the **noonlight**,
  Flutings of bird-throats light as flight of swallow;
  Scents rose around us thick as in the moonlight
        Leaves fall and follow.

  How could I dream that thou wert growing weary?
  Never I guessed it till I saw thee fading;
  Saw thee slip from me,—and my way fell dreary.
20   Cease thine upbraiding!

  Cease thine upbraiding, ah, my widowed spirit!
  Trace on thy path by rays from backward sight won.
  More than I gave thee the bliss thou dost inherit,
        Miriam, bright one!

1880

MIRIAM.—II.

CHORIAMBICS.

1   Ah, Love, what would **I give** just for a little light!
    Cryings born of the wind wake on its undertones.
  Vainly praying the shore wearily all the night
    Round me the ocean moans.

Ebb-tides laden with woe flee with a wailful song
       Far down out of the dark, calling my trembling soul.
Ah, Love, where is the light? Why is the way so long? . . .
       Hearken how sad their roll!

Ay, sad surely, but sweet! Why do they always call,—
10   All night through the thick dark calling me out to thee?
Lured by surf-whispers soft, feebly my footsteps fall
       Toward the enfolding sea.

Nay! I cover my ears; 'tis not the way to thee.
       Why doth it play me false now that my paths are blind?
When they lay in the light born of thy love to me,
       Never it seemed unkind.

Sweet it sang in the light, scarce could it dream a dirge;
       Fringed with ripples of blue tinkled the strand like bells;
When, thy hand in my hand, crushed we along its verge
20   Pebbles and pink-lipp'd shells.

Ah! but full were the hours, full to the heart's desire;
       Flowing over with love, golden to their flying feet.
Deep and sweet was the air, shining and clear like fire,
       Vital with balmy heat.

Warm,—but now it is cold; bright,—it is wild and dark;
       Dimly over the sea lieth the gleamless pall;
Dimly out of the sea murmur the voices. Hark!
       Do not they sweetly call?

Stay me, Miriam, Love; chill is the drifting foam.
30   Come, Love, meet me with strength; fierce is the moaning sea.
Peace! peace! vainly I call; thou wilt not quit thy home;
       Wait; I will come to thee.

1880

ODE TO NIGHT

I.

1   The noon has dried thy dewdrops from my wings,
       My spirit's wings, so they no longer soar;
              And, drooping more and more,
I pant, O Night, for thy soft whisperings
       Of bounteous blessings which thou hast in store
              For me, and all who serve thee with due rites;

48

Not with a riotous loose merriment,
      That thy soft wrath excites;
But with sweet yielding to thy lavishment
10   Of warm syringa-scented breathings, blent
        With trancéd draughts of subtle-souled delights.

II.

Low-sighing zephyr, pulsing from the west,
      Before thee sheds earth-purifying dew,
        As priests were wont to do
With lustral waters, ere the victims, dressed
For sacrifice, felt the keen-searching knife.
Then, thy light-fingered forager, and rife
      With thefts from all lush odors and sweet sounds,
        He drowses on thy skirt;
20   Whilst thou, breast-full of new, sweet milk of life,
      Loosest the robe thy bounteous bosom bounds,
        With heart's-ease blooms and marigolds begirt.

III.

Dear goddess, come. Thy feather-sandalled feet
      Tread out the dying crimsons of the day,
        Whose warm, red-spirted spray
I'll find soft-changed to flushes rosy sweet,
Dowered by thee to my love's lips and cheeks:
My love, with whom is covert from the freaks
      Of Folly, so heart-vexing through the light,
30   With whom a safe retreat,
In whose dusk bower sour Envy never speaks,
      Nor poison drips from venomed fangs of Spite;
        Thither, dear Night, we'll haste on happy feet.

1880

ONE NIGHT

1   The wood is cold, and dank, and green;
      The trunks stand close in sullen row;
A crookéd moon through a creeping screen
      Of night-fog rots in the roots below.

The pool is thick, and dead, and green;
      Its bubbles gleam the roots below;
To feed the slimy growths between
      The slimy roots the ooze drips slow.

My feet can find no standing-place,
10   The monstrous trunk my arms grasp not;
Across the roots upon my face
       I fall, and pray my soul can not.

And one came by, and bare a load—
       An unstrange form—to where I lay;
Into the pool he cast his load:
       "Look to it," he said, and went away.

The thick scum closed; the body slid
       Beneath the roots to where I lay,
And rose face up: I fain had hid
20   My eyes; their lids forgot the way.

And fain my hands had hid my face,
       But could not quit their slimy hold;
Close to my face its loathly face
       Uprose, and back its swathings rolled.

Its dead eyes woke and with mine met
       Familiarly; at that I wept.
My tears fell big and fast, and set
       More foulness forth the scum had kept.

And more I wept more foul it grew;
30   All else grew black, and my heart dropped down.
I had lain there for an age, I knew,
       And must lie there till the body sank down.

Then One came by to where I lay;
       He had heard my tears and come to me.
He had heard my tears (for I could not pray),
       And pitied me, and had come to me.

He touched the body, and it sank down
       Beyond my sight, though the pool was clear;
And the space above was a sapphire crown
40   Upon their heads, for the trees to wear.

He stood me up upon my feet,
       And the trunks were dry and my hands were clean;
The breath of laughing leaves was sweet:
       And he left me in this pleasant scene.

1880

RONDEAU TO A.W. STRATON
(Written in his autograph album.)

1   To fledge the hours with mirth and ease
And wing their feet with pleasantries,
    Till heedlessly they hasten by
    As cloudlets down the summer sky,
Or bats mid twilight shadowed trees,

Or petals on the noontide breeze,
Full oft our laboring minds should please.
    So now to you I come to try
    To fledge the hours.

10   And oft when they shall seem to lie
    Wingless and footless, we may buy
Wings for them from such names as these,
And happy-colored feathers seize
From their upspringing memories
    To fledge the hours.

1880

RONDEAU.—"WITHOUT ONE KISS."

1   Without one kiss she's gone away,
And stol'n the brightness out of day;
    With scornful lips and haughty brow
    She's left me melancholy now,
In spite of all that I could say.

And so, to guess as best I may
What angered her, awhile I stay
    Beneath this blown acacia bough,
    Without one kiss;

10   Yet all my wildered brain can pay
My questioning, is but to pray
    Persuasion may my speech endow,
    And Love may never more allow
My injured sweet to sail away
    Without one kiss.

1880

51

SAPPHO

1   Her hair it floated fair and free
In the blushful evening sky;
    The purple sea
    Sobbed wearily,
To the curlew's mournful cry;
    Her white feet mock'd
    The barren rock,
With their warmth and beauty and life;
    Her white hands prest
10   All close her breast,
To stifle its bursting strife.
    The musical sea
    Sobbed musically,
The warm wind whispered her,—"Flee:
    Counsel I thee
    That thou warily flee
The fair-seeming snare of the sea."
    But deeper she drank,
    As the gold sun sank,
20   The mist of the sea's purple breath;
    While the sun's last embrace
    Lit flame in her face,
And her eyes searched the shadows of Death.

    But the shadows are driven,
    Like night-clouds riven,
From her eyes by a heaven of song,
    That trembles and floats,
    In silver-lipped notes,
From a light skiff drifting along:
30   All the singers save one
    Full-faced to the sun,
But the one to the rim of the moon;
    And it seeméd the tune
    Was the voice of the moon,
Or the moon the embodied tune.

    O'er the tingling pink
    Of her eager ear's brink
The golden melody swells,
    As a ripple's song slips
40   In the dawn-kissed lips
Of listening, mimicking shells;

And chases away—
So enchanting the lay—
Her purpose and pain, forsooth,
Till she sees the face,
In the thin moon's embrace,
Of the Mitylenian youth;
And the shadows return,
And her drooped lids burn,
50   And she calls to him under her breath;
Then leaps to meet,
At the cliff's chilled feet,
The hungry embraces of Death.

And the slumbrous sea
Wakes tremulously,
And thrills to his furthest streams;
And a sudden glow
Through the depths below
Gives the Nereids blissful dreams;
60   And the deepest sea-graves
In Leucadian caves
Are lighted with golden gleams,
As though the sunk sun
Had thitherward run
To pry with his fronting beams.
And the musical sea
Sings more musically
Than he ever has sung before,
And the whole night long
70   His syrenal song
Beguiles the soul of the shore.
And at peep of morrow
In red-eyed sorrow
The Lesbian maids come by;
And search the sand
Of the rippled strand,
And the shallows remote and nigh;
But they see the maiden
All tenderly laid in
80   A coral bed deep from harms;
And for all their endeavor
The sea will not give her
From his encircling arms.

Nor ever could they
Have won her away,

For all their Ionian cunning,
    Had not the sea-maids,
    In their emerald braids,
Who were wont to sit a-sunning
90   In the sea-monarch's smile,
    In their envy and guile
Upborn her again to the shore,
Which shall gleam with the blaze of her funeral-pile,
    But throb with her song no more.

Chorus of Lesbian youth, singing around the funeral-pyre.

SEMI-CHORUS I.

Scatter roses from full hands;
    Wreathe bright garlands; bring white heifers.
Call sweet savors from far lands,
100   Borne on wings of morning zephyrs.

SEMI-CHORUS II.

Burn, with olives' outpressed fatness,
    Riches of the swarthy bees.
Bring to slake the thirsty embers
    Wine new-purgéd from the leas.

SEMI-CHORUS I.

Twine the voices; wreathe **the song;**
    Weave a dirge of mythic numbers.

SEMI-CHORUS II.

110   Breathe it high and sweet and strong,
    For ye will not pierce her slumbers.

CHORUS

Jove-bestowed, thy passioned singing
    O'er the Grecian nations came;
Was in Grecian ears a heaven,
    And in Grecian blood a flame.

Now thy songful lips are silent;
    But thy deathless song shall dwell
In men's bosoms, and its echoes
120   Down far-distant ages swell.

And forever thy sweet singing
    Rich to hearts of men shall come,
In its meaning and its music
    A full goblet crowned with foam.

Now the sea lies gray and chilly
    Under the wet streaks of dawn;
Now the dull red embers darken,
    And their glow is almost gone:

Quench them; pour the last libation;
130   Slake them with red Lesbian wine;
In wrought brass enclose her ashes;
    Once more are the Muses nine.

                                    1880

A SONG OF MORNING

1   Weird Night has withdrawn
        Her gleaming black tresses,
            And, sighing for sorrow,
    Has fled from the dawn,
Sinking her sleep-woven wings in the west,
        To breathe there her kisses
            On tired hearts that borrow
    Her balm of sweet lethe and rest.

    And Morning, upspringing
10   From out the gray ocean
            With rosy-lipped laughter,
    Her yellow locks flinging
O'er forest and fountain, field, fallow, and sky,
        With breezy, bright motion,
            Is hastening after,
    While vapor-veiled glamours sail by.

                                    1880

OFF PELORUS

1   Crimson swims the sunset over far Pelorus;
        Burning crimson tops its frowning crest of pine.
    Purple sleeps the shore and floats the wave before us,
        Eachwhere from the oar-stroke eddying warm like wine.

Soundless foams the creamy violet wake behind us;
　　We but *see* the creaking of the labored oar;
We have stopped our ears,—mad were we not to blind us,
　　Lest our eyes behold our Ithaca no more.

See the purple splendor o'er the island streaming,
10　　O'er the prostrate sails and equal-sided ship!
Windless hangs the vine, and warm the sands lie gleaming;
　　Droop the great grape-clusters melting for the lip.

Sweet the golden calm, the glowing light elysian.
　　Sweet were red-mouthed plenty mindless grown of pain.
Sweeter yet behold—a sore-bewildering vision!
　　Idly took we thought, and stopped our ears in vain.

Idly took we thought, for still our eyes betray us.
　　Lo, the white-limbed maids, with love-soft eyes aglow,
Gleaming bosoms bare, loosed hair, sweet hands to slay us,
20　　Warm lips wild with song, and softer throats than snow!

See the King! he hearkens,—hears their song,—strains forward,—
　　As some mountain snake attends the shepherd's reed.
Now with urgent hand he bids us turn us shoreward,—
　　Bend the groaning oar now; give the King no heed!

Mark the luring music by his eyes' wild yearning,
　　Eager lips, and mighty straining at the cords!
Well we guess the song, the subtle words and burning,
　　Sung to him, the subtle king of burning words.

"Much-enduring Wanderer, wondrous-tongued, come nigher!
30　　Sage of princes, bane of Ilion's lofty walls!
　　Whatsoe'er in all the populous earth befalls
We will teach thee, to thine uttermost desire."

So, we rise up twain, and make his bonds securer.
　　Seethes the startled sea now from the surging blade.
Leaps the dark ship forth, as we, with hearts grown surer,
　　Eyes averse, and war-worn faces made afraid,

O'er the waste warm reaches drive our prow, sea-cleaving,
　　Past the luring death, into the folding night.
Home shall hold us yet, and cease our wives from grieving,—
40　　Safe from storm, and toil, and flame, and clanging fight.

Feb., 1881; 1881

A BALLADE OF PHILOMELA

1   From gab of jay and chatter of crake
       The dusk wood covered me utterly.
And here the tongue of the thrush was awake.
       Flame-floods out of the low bright sky
       Lighted the gloom with gold-brown dye,
Before dark; and a manifold chorussing
       Arose of thrushes remote and nigh,—
For the tongue of the singer needs must sing.

Midmost a close green covert of brake
10   A brown bird listening silently
Sat; and I thought—"She grieves for the sake
       Of Itylus,—for the stains that lie
       In her heritage of sad memory."
But the thrushes were hushed at evening.
       Then I waited to hear the brown bird try,—
For the tongue of the singer needs must sing.

And I said—"The thought of the thrushes will shake
       With rapture remembered her heart; and her shy
Tongue of the dear times dead will take
20   To make her a living song, when sigh
       The soft night winds disburthened by.
Hark now!"—for the upraised quivering wing,
       The throat exultant, I could descry,—
And the tongue of the singer needs must sing!

L'ENVOI

But the bird dropped dead with only a cry.
       I found its tongue was withered, poor thing!
Then I no whit wondered, for well knew I
       That the heart of the singer will break or sing.

April, 1881; 1882

TO FREDERICTON IN MAY-TIME

1   This morning, full of breezes and perfume,
       Brimful of promise of midsummer weather,
       When bees and birds and I are glad together,
Breathes of the full-leaved season, when soft gloom
Chequers thy streets, and thy close elms assume
       Round roof and spire the semblance of green billows;

Yet now thy glory is the yellow willows,
The yellow willows, full of bees and bloom.

Under their dusty blossoms blackbirds meet,
10   And robins pipe amid the cedars nigher;
Thro' the still elms I hear the ferry's beat;
    The swallows chirp about the towering spire;
The whole air pulses with its weight of sweet;
    Yet not quite satisfied is my desire!

May 24, 1881; 1881

THE SLAVE WOMAN

1 Shedding cool drops upon the sun-baked clay,
    The dripping jar, brimful, she rests a space
    On the well's dry white brink, and leans her face,
Heavy with tears and many a heartsick day,
Down to the water's lip, whence slips away
    A rivulet thro' the hot, bright square apace,
    And lo! her brow casts off each servile trace—
The wave's cool breath hath won her thoughts astray.

Ah desolate heart! Thy fate thou hast forgot
10   One moment; the dull pain hath left those eyes
    Whose yearning pierces time, and space, and tears.
Thou seest what was once, but now is not,—
    By Niger thy bright home, thy Paradise,
    Unscathed of flame, and foe, and hostile spears.

June, 1881; 1881

LOTOS

1   Wherefore awake so long,
    Wide-eyed, laden with care?
    Not all battle is life,
    But a little respite and peace
    May fold us round as a fleece
    Soft-woven for all men's wear.
    Sleep, then, mindless of strife;
    Slumber, dreamless of wrong;—
    Hearken my slumber-song,
10   Falling asleep.

Drowsily all noon long
The warm winds rustle the grass
Hush'dly, lulling thy brain,—
Burthened with murmur of bees
And numberless whispers, and ease.
Dream-clouds gather and pass
Of painless remembrance of pain.
Havened from rumor of wrong,
Dreams are thy slumber-song,
20   Fallen asleep.

August, 1881; 1882

OUT OF POMPEII

1   Save what the night-wind woke of sweet
      And solemn sound, I heard alone
The sleepless ocean's ceaseless beat,
      The surge's monotone.

Low down the south a dreary gleam
      Of white light smote the sullen swells,
Evasive as a blissful dream,
      Or wind-borne notes of bells.

The water's lapping whispers stole
10   Into my brain, and there effaced
All human memories from my soul,—
      An atom in a shifting waste.

Weird fingers, groping, strove to raise
      Some numbing horror from my mind;
And ever, as it met my gaze,
      The sharp truth struck me blind.

The keen-edged breath of the salt sea
      Stung; but a faint, swift, sulphurous smell
Blew past, and I reeled dizzily
20   As from the brink of hell,

One moment; then the swan-necked prow
      Sustained me, and once more I scanned
The unfenced flood, against my brow
      Arching my lifted hand.

O'er all the unstable vague expanse
    I towered the lord supreme, and smiled;
And marked the hard, white sparkles glance,
    The dark vault wide and wild.

Again that faint wind swept my face—
30   With hideous menace swept my eyes.
I cowered back in my straitened place
    And groped with dim surmise,

Not knowing yet. Not knowing why,
    I turned, as one asleep might turn,
And noted with half curious eye
    The figure crouched astern.

On heaped-up leopard skins she crouched,
    Asleep, and soft skins covered her,
And scarlet stuffs where she was couched,
40   Sodden with sea-water,

Burned lurid with black stains, and smote
    My thought with waking pangs; I saw
The white arm drooping from the boat,
    Round-moulded, pure from flaw;

The yellow sandals even-thonged;
    The fair face, wan with haunting pain,—
Then sudden, crowding memories thronged
    Like unpent sudden rain.

Clear-stamped, as by white lightning when
50   The swift flame rends the night, wide-eyed
I saw dim streets, and fleeing men,
    And walls from side to side

Reeling, and great rocks fallen; a pall
    Above us, an encumbering shroud
About our feet, and over all
    The awful Form that bowed

Our hearts, the fiery scourge that smote
    The city,—the red Mount. Clear, clear
I saw it,—and this lonely boat,
60   And us two drifting here!

With one sharp cry I sprang and hid
　　My face among the skins beside
Her feet, and held her safe, and chid
　　The tumult till it died.

And crouched thus at her rescued feet,
　　Save her low breath, I heard alone
The sleepless ocean's ceaseless beat,
　　The surge's monotone.

1876 and Oct., 1881; 1881

TO THE MEMORY OF SIDNEY LANIER

1　Sullenly falls the rain,
　　Still hangs the dripping leaf,
And ah, the pain!—
　　The slow, dull ache of my grief,
That throbs—"In vain, in vain,—
　　You have garnered your sheaf!"

You have **garnered** your sheaf, with the tares
　　Therein, and unripe wheat,—
All that Death spares,
10　　Who has come with too swift feet,
Not turning for any prayers
　　Nor all who entreat.

They entreated with tears. But I—
　　Ah me, all I can say
Is only a cry!
　　I had loved you many a day,
Yet never had fate drawn nigh
　　My way to your way.

My spirit made swift with love
20　　Went forth to you in your place
Far off and above.
　　Tho' we met not face to face,
My Elder Brother, yet love
　　Had pierced through space!

Oct., 1881; 1881

A BALLADE OF CALYPSO

1   The loud black flight of the storm diverges
       Over a spot in the loud-mouthed main,
Where, crowned with summer and sun, emerges
       An isle unbeaten of wind or rain.
       And here, of its sweet queen grown full fain,—
By whose kisses the whole broad earth seems poor,—
       Tarries the wave-worn prince, Troy's bane,
In the green Ogygian Isle secure.

To her voice our sweetest songs are dirges.
10   She gives him all things, counting it gain.
Ringed with the rocks and ancient surges,
       How could Fate dissever these twain?
       But him no loves nor delights retain;
New knowledge, new lands, new loves allure;
       Forgotten the perils, and toils, and pain,
In the green Ogygian Isle secure.

So he spurns her kisses and gifts, and urges
       His weak skiff over the wind-vext plain,
Till the gray of the sky in the gray sea merges,
20   And nights reel round, and waver, and wane.
       He sits once more in his own domain.
No more the remote sea-walls immure.—
       But ah, for the love he shall clasp not again
In the green Ogygian Isle secure!

L'ENVOI

Princes, and ye whose delights remain,
       To the one good gift of the gods hold sure,
Lest ye too mourn, in vain, in vain,
       Your green Ogygian Isle secure!

Nov., 1881; 1881

RONDEAU
To Louis Honore Fréchette

1   Laurels for song! And nobler bays,
In old Olympian golden days
       Of clamor thro' the clear-eyed morn,
       No bowed triumphant head hath borne,
Victorious in all Hellas' gaze!

They watched his glowing axles graze
The goal, and rent the heavens with praise;—
   Yet the supremer heads have worn
      Laurels for song.

10 So thee, from no palaestra-plays
A conqueror, to the gods we raise,
   Whose brows of all our singers born
   The sacred fillets chief adorn,—
Who first of all our choir displays
      Laurels for song.

Nov., 1881; 1881

A SONG OF REGRET

1 In the southward sky
The late swallows fly,
   The low red willows
      In the river quiver;
From the beeches nigh
Russet leaves sail by,
   The tawny billows
      In the chill wind shiver;
The beech-burrs burst,
10   And the nuts down-patter;
   The red squirrels chatter
O'er the wealth disperst.

Yon carmine glare
Would the west outdare;—
   'Tis the Fall attire
      Of the maples flaming.
In the keen late air
Is an impulse rare,
   A sting like fire,
20   A desire past naming.
But the crisp mists rise
   And my heart falls a-sighing,—
   Sighing, sighing
That the sweet time dies!

1881

SOLILOQUY IN A MONASTERY

1   Cuthbert, open! Let me in!
      Cease your praying for a minute!
    Here the darkness seems to grin,
      Holds a thousand horrors in it.
    Down the stony corridor
    Footsteps pace the stony floor.

    Here they foot it, pacing slow,
      Monk-like, one behind another!—
    Don't you hear me? Don't you know
10   I'm a little nervous, Brother?
    Won't you speak? Then, by your leave,
    Here's a guest for Christmas Eve!

    Shrive me, but I got a fright!
      Monks of centuries ago
    Wander back to see to-night
      How the old place looks—Hello!
    This the kind of watch you keep!
    Come to pray—and go to sleep!

    Ah, this mortal flesh is weak!
20   Who is saintly there's no saying.
    Here are tears upon his cheek,
      And he sleeps that should be praying;—
    Sleeps, and dreams, and murmurs. Nay,
    I'll not wake you.—Sleep away!

    Holy saints, the night is keen!
      How the nipping wind does drive
    Through yon tree-tops, bare and lean,
      Till their shadow seems alive,—
    Patters through the bars, and falls,
30   Shivering, on the floor and walls!

    How yon patch of freezing sky
      Echoes back their bell-ringings!
    Down in the grey city, nigh
      Severn, every steeple swings.
    All the busy streets are bright.
    Many folk are out to-night.

    —What's that, Brother? Did you speak?—
      Christ save them that talk in sleep!

Smile they howsoever meek,
40   Somewhat in their hearts they keep.
We, good souls, what shifts we make
To keep talking whilst awake!

Christ be praised, that fetched me in
    Early, yet a youngling, while
All unlearned in life and sin,
    Love and travail, grief and guile!
For your world of two-score years,
Cuthbert, all you have is tears.

Dreaming, still he hears the bells
50   As he heard them years ago,
Ere he sought our quiet cells
    Iron-mouthed and wrenched with woe,
Out of what dread storms who knows—
Faithfulest of friends and foes!

Faithful was he aye, I ween,
    Pitiful, and kind, and wise;
But in mindful moods I've seen
    Flame enough in those sunk eyes!
Praised be Christ, whose timely hand
60   Plucked from out the fire this brand!

Now in dreams he's many miles
    Hence, he's back in Ireland.
Ah, how tenderly he smiles,
    Stretching a caressing hand!
Backward now his memory glides
To old, happy Christmastides.

Now once more a loving wife
    Holds him; now he sees his boys,
Smiles at all their playful strife,
70   All their childish mirth and noise;
Softly now she strokes his hair.—
Ah, their world is very fair!

—Waking, all your loss shall be
    Unforgotten evermore!
Sleep alone holds these for thee.
    Sleep then, Brother!—To restore
All your heaven that has died
Heaven and Hell may be too wide!

Sleep, and dream, and be awhile
80   Happy, Cuthbert, once again!
Soon you'll wake, and cease to smile,
     And your heart will sink with pain.
You will hear the merry town,—
And a weight will press you down.

Hungry-hearted you will see
     Only the thin shadows fall
From yon bleak-topped poplar-tree,—
     Icy fingers on the wall.
You will watch them come and go,
90   Telling o'er your count of woe.

—Nay, now, hear me, how I prate!
     I, a foolish monk, and old,
Maundering o'er a life and fate
     To me unknown, by you untold!
Yet I know you're like to weep
Soon, so, Brother, this night sleep.

Dec. 17, 1881; 1881

ON THE EVE OF DEPARTURE

S.M.B.

To you, dear girl, and other friends like you,
No many, but well proved and loved, my pen,
To steal a little from the sting of parting,
Writes not "Farewell" but "Till we meet again."

January 29, 1882

ACTÆON
A Woman of Platæa Speaks

1   I have lived long, and watched out many days,
And seen the showers fall and the light shine down
Equally on the vile and righteous head.
I have lived long, and served the gods, and drawn
Small joy and liberal sorrow,—scorned the gods,
And drawn no less my little meed of good,
Suffered my ill in no more grievous measure.
I have been glad—alas, my foolish people,
I have been glad with you! And ye are glad,

66

10   Seeing the gods in all things, praising them
In yon their lucid heaven, this green world,
The moving inexorable sea, and wide
Delight of noonday,—till in ignorance
Ye err, your feet transgress, and the bolt falls!
Ay, have I sung, and dreamed that they would hear;
And worshiped, and made offerings,—it may be
They heard, and did perceive, and were well pleased,—
A little music in their ears, perchance,
A grain more savour to their nostrils, sweet
20   Tho' scarce accounted of. But when for me
The mists of Acheron have striven up,
And horror was shed round me; when my knees
Relaxed, my tongue clave speechless, they forgot.
And when my sharp cry cut the moveless night,
And days and nights my wailings clamoured up
And beat about their golden homes, perchance
They shut their ears. No happy music this,
Eddying through their nectar cups and calm!
Then I cried out against them,—and died not;
30   And rose, and set me to my daily tasks.
So all day long, with bare, uplift right arm,
I drew out the strong thread from the carded wool,
Or wrought strange figures, lotus-buds, and serpents,
In purple on the himation's saffron fold;
Nor uttered praise with the slim-wristed girls
To any god, nor uttered any prayer,
Nor poured out bowls of wine and smooth bright oil,
Nor brake and gave small cakes of beaten meal
And honey, as this time, or such a god
40   Required; nor offered apples summer-flushed,
Scarlet pomegranates, poppy-bells, or doves.
All this with scorn, and waiting all day long,
And night long with dim fear, afraid of sleep,—
Seeing I took no hurt of all these things,
And seeing mine eyes were driéd of their tears
So that once more the light grew sweet for me,
Once more grew fair the fields and valley streams,
I thought with how small profit men take heed
To worship with bowed heads and suppliant hands
50   And sacrifice the everlasting gods,
Who take small thought of them to curse or bless,
Girt with their purples of perpetual peace!
Thus blindly deemed I of them,—yet—and yet—
Have late well learned their hate is swift as fire,
Be one so wretched as to encounter it;

Ay, have I seen a multitude of good deeds
Fly up in the pan like husks, like husks blown dry.
Hereafter let none question the high gods!
I questioned; but these watching eyes have seen
60 Actæon, thewed and sinewed like a god,
Godlike for sweet speech and great deeds, hurled down
To hideous death,—scarce suffered space to breathe
Ere the wild heart in his changed, quivering side
Burst with mad terror, and the stag's wide eyes
Stared one sick moment 'mid the dogs' hot jaws.

*   *   *   *   *   *   *

Cithæron, mother mount, set steadfastly
Deep in Bœotia, past the utmost roar
Of seas, beyond Corinthian waves withdrawn,
Girt with green vales awake with brooks or still,
70 Towers up mid lesser-browed Bœotian hills—
These couched like herds secure beneath its ken—
And watches earth's green corners. At mid-noon
We of Platæa mark the sun make pause
Right over it, and top its crest with pride.
Men of Eleusis look toward north at dawn
To see the long white fleeces upward roll
Smitten aslant with saffron, fade like smoke,
And leave the grey-green dripping glens all bare,
The drenched slopes open sunward; slopes wherein
80 What gods, what godlike men to match with gods,
Have roamed, and grown up mighty, and waxed wise
Under the law of him whom gods and men
Reverence, and call Cheiron! He, made wise
With knowledge of all wisdom, had made wise
Actæon, till there moved none cunninger
To drive with might the javelin forth, or bend
The corded ebony, save Leto's son.

But him the Centaur shall behold no more
With long stride making down the beechy glade,
90 Clear-eyed, with firm lips laughing,—at his heels
The clamour of his fifty deep-tongued hounds.
Him the wise Centaur shall behold no more.

I have lived long, and watched out many days,
And am well sick of watching. Three days since,
I had gone out upon the slopes for herbs,
Snake-root, and subtle gums; and when the light

Fell slantwise through the upper glens, and missed
The sunk ravines, I came where all the hills
Circle the valley of Gargaphian streams.
100   Reach beyond reach all down the valley gleamed,—
Thick branches ringed them. Scarce a bowshot past
My platan, thro' the woven leaves low-hung,
Trembling in meshes of the woven sun,
A yellow-sanded pool, shallow and clear,
Lay sparkling, brown about the further bank
From scarlet-berried ash-trees hanging over.
But suddenly the shallows brake awake
With laughter and light voices, and I saw
Where Artemis, white goddess incorrupt,
110   Bane of swift beasts, and deadly for straight shaft
Unswerving, from a coppice not far off
Came to the pool from the hither bank to bathe.
Amid her maiden company she moved,
Their cross-thonged yellow buskins scattered off,
Unloosed their knotted hair; and thus the pool
Received them stepping, shrinking, down to it.

        Here they flocked white, and splashed the waterdrops
On rounded breast and shoulder snowier
Than the washed clouds athwart the morning's blue,—
120   Fresher than river grasses which the herds
Pluck from the river in the burning noons.
Their tresses on the summer wind they flung.
And some a shining yellow fleece let fall
For the sun's envy; others with white hands
Lifted a glooming wealth of locks more dark
Than deepest wells, but purple in the sun.
And She, their mistress, of the heart unstormed,
Stood taller than they all, supreme, and still,
Perfectly fair like day, and crowned with hair
130   The colour of nipt beech-leaves: Ay, such hair
Was mine in years when I was such as these.
I let it fall to cover me, or coiled
Its soft, thick coils about my throat and arms;
Its colour like nipt beech-leaves, tawny brown,
But in the sun a fountain of live gold.

        Even as thus they played, and some lithe maids
Upreached white arms to grasp the berried ash,
And, plucking the bright bunches, shed them wide
By red ripe handfuls, not far off I saw
140   With long stride making down the beechy glade,

Clear-eyed, with firm lips laughing,—at his heels
The clamour of his fifty deep-tongued hounds,
Actæon. I beheld him not far off,
But unto bath and bathers hid from view,
Being beyond that mighty rock whereon
His wont was to lie stretched at dip of eve,
When frogs are loud amid the tall-plumed sedge
In marshy spots about Asopus' bank,—
Deeming his life was very sweet, his day
150 A pleasant one, the peopled breadths of earth
Most fair, and fair the shining tracts of sea;
Green solitudes, and broad low-lying plains
Made brown with frequent labours of men's hands,
And salt, blue, fruitless waters. But this mount,
Cithæron, bosomed deep in soundless hills,
Its fountained vales, its nights of starry calm,
Its high chill dawns, its long-drawn golden days,—
Was dearest to him. Here he dreamed high dreams,
And felt within his sinews strength to strive
160 Where strife was sorest, and to overcome;
And in his heart the thought to do great deeds,
With power in all ways to accomplish them.
For had not he done well to men, and done
Well to the gods? Therefore he stood secure.

But him,—for him—Ah that these eyes should see!—
Approached a sudden stumbling in his ways!
Not yet, not yet he knew a god's fierce wrath,
Nor wist of that swift vengeance lying in wait.

And now he came upon a slope of sward
170 Against the pool. With startled cry the maids
Shrank clamouring round their mistress, or made flight
To covert in the hazel thickets. She
Stirred not; but pitiless anger paled her eyes,
Intent with deadly purpose. He, amazed,
Stood with his head thrust forward, while his curls,
Sun-lit, lay glorious on his mighty neck,—
Let fall his bow and clanging spear, and gazed
Dilate with ecstacy; nor marked the dogs
Hush their deep tongues, draw close, and ring him round,
180 And fix upon him strange, red, hungry eyes,
And crouch to spring. This for a moment. Then
It seemed his strong knees faltered, and he sank.
Then I cried out,—for straight a shuddering stag
Sprang one wild leap over the dogs; but they

Fastened upon his flanks with a long yell,
And reached his throat; and that proud head went down
Beneath their wet, red fangs and reeking jaws.

I have lived long and watched out many days,
Yet have not seen that aught is sweet save life,
190 Nor learned that life hath other end than death.
This horror like a cloud had veiled my sight,
That for a space I saw not, and my ears
Were shut from hearing; but when sense grew clear
Once more, I only saw the vacant pool
Unrippled,—only saw the dreadful sward,
Where dogs lay gorged, or moved in fretful search,
Questing uneasily; and some far up
The slope, and some at the low water's edge,
With snouts set high in air and straining throats
200 Uttered keen howls that smote the echoing hills.
They missed their master's form, nor understood
Where was the voice they loved, the hand that reared,—
And some lay watching by the spear and bow
Flung down.

And now upon the homeless pack
And paling stream arose a stealthy wind
Out of the hollow west awhile, and stirred
The branches down the valley; then blew off
To eastward toward the long grey straits, and died
210 Into the dark, beyond the utmost verge.

March, 1882; 1882

CANOE SONG

1 Sing, Boys, sing!
Down the tent and baggage bring.
See her seams are rozened tight,
For we'll start at morning's light,
And we'll sing: —

Oh, here's to the paddle!
To the dogs with the saddle!
And to tug on the oar
Is a bore!

10 Sing, Boys, Sing!
Off the laughing ripples fling

71

From the paddle, flashing bright
In the breezy morning light—
So we sing:—

> Oh, here's to the paddle!
> To the dogs with the saddle!
> And to tug on the oar
> Is a bore!

Sing, Boys, Sing!
20   Swift we fly with fin or wing
As we paddle or we sail.
So in silver calm or gale
Will we sing:—

> Oh, here's to the paddle!
> To the dogs with the saddle!
> And to tug on the oar
> Is a bore!

1882

BEFORE THE BREATH OF STORM

1   Before the breath of storm,
While yet the long, bright afternoons are warm,
Under this stainless arch of azure sky
    The air is filled with gathering wings for flight;
    Yet with the shrill mirth and the loud delight
Comes the foreboding sorrow of this cry—
"Till the storm scatter and the gloom dispel,
    Farewell! Farewell!
    Farewell!"

10   Why will ye go so soon,
In these soft hours, this sweeter month than June?
The liquid air floats over field and tree
    A veil of dreams;—where do ye find the sting?
A gold enchantment sleeps upon the sea
    And purple hills;—why have ye taken wing?
But faint, far-heard, the answers fall and swell—
    "Farewell! Farewell!
    Farewell!"

Sept., 1882; 1882

72

IN SEPTEMBER

1   This windy, bright September afternoon
     My heart is wide awake, yet full of dreams.
     The air, alive with hushed confusion, teems
  With scent of grain-fields, and a mystic rune,
  Foreboding of the fall of Summer soon,
     Keeps swelling and subsiding; till there seems
     O'er all the world of valleys, hills, and streams,
  Only the wind's inexplicable tune.

  My heart is full of dreams, yet wide awake.
10   I lie and watch the topmost tossing boughs
  Of tall elms, pale against the vaulted blue;
  But even now some yellowing branches shake,
     Some hue of death the living green endows:—
     If beauty flies, fain would I vanish too.

Sept., 1882; 1882

A BREATHING TIME

1   Here is a breathing time, and rest for a little season.
  Here have I drained deep draughts out of the springs of life.
  Here, as of old, while still unacquainted with toil and faintness,
  Stretched are my veins with strength, fearless my heart and at peace.
  I have come back from the crowd, the blinding strife and the tumult,
  Pain, and the shadow of pain, sorrow in silence endured;
  Fighting, at last I have fallen, and sought the breast of the Mother,—
  Quite cast down I have crept close to the broad sweet earth.
  Lo, out of failure triumph! Renewed the wavering courage,
10   Tense the unstrung nerves, steadfast the faltering knees!
  Weary no more, nor faint, nor grieved at heart, nor despairing,
  Hushed in the earth's green lap, lulled to slumber and dreams!

1882

IN THE AFTERNOON

1   Wind of the summer afternoon,
     Hush, for my heart is out of tune!

  Hush, for thou movest restlessly
     The too light sleeper, memory!

Whate'er thou hast to tell me, yet
'T were something sweeter to forget,—

Sweeter than all thy breath of balm
An hour of unremembering calm.

Blowing over the roofs, and down
10   The bright streets of this inland town,

These busy crowds, these rocking trees—
What strange note hast thou caught from these?

A note of waves and rushing tides,
Where past the dykes the red flood glides,

To brim the shining channels far
Up the green plains of Tantramar.

Once more I sniff the salt, I stand
On the long dykes of Westmoreland;

I watch the narrowing flats, the strip
20   Of red clay at the water's lip;

Far off the net-reels, brown and high,
And boat-masts slim against the sky;

Along the ridges of the dykes
Wind-beaten scant sea-grass, and spikes

Of last year's mullein; down the slopes
To landward, in the sun, thick ropes

Of blue vetch and convolvulus
And matted roses glorious.

The liberal blooms o'erbrim my hands;
30   I walk the level, wide marsh-lands;

Waist-deep in dusty-blossomed grass
I watch the swooping breezes pass

In sudden, long, pale lines, that flee
Up the deep breast of this green sea.

I listen to the bird that stirs
The purple tops, and grasshoppers

Whose summer din, before my feet
Subsiding, wakes on my retreat.

Again the droning bees hum by;
40 Still-winged, the grey hawk wheels on high;

I drink again the wild perfumes,
And roll, and crush the grassy blooms

Blown back to olden days, I fain
Would quaff the olden joys again;

But all the olden sweetness not
The old unmindful peace hath brought.

Wind of this summer afternoon,
Thou hast recalled my childhood's June.

My heart—still is it satisfied
50 By all the golden summer-tide?

Hast thou one eager yearning filled,
Or any restless throbbing stilled,

Or hast thou any power to bear
Even a little of my care?—

Ever so little of this weight
Of weariness canst thou abate?

Ah, poor thy gift indeed, unless
Thou bring the old child-heartedness,—

And such a gift to bring is given,
60 Alas, to no wind under heaven!

Wind of the summer afternoon,
Be still; my heart is not in tune.

Sweet is thy voice; but yet, but yet—
Of all 't were sweetest to forget!

1882; 1882

SONNET ON SPRING

1 Through cold and dreary winter Nature sleeps,
    And hushed in peaceful rest seems lying dead,
  With heavy snows heaped on her frosty head.
    Fond Spring stoops o'er the lovely form and weeps

Great, bitter tears of agony. She steeps
    The flowers buried in their earthy bed
  With woe-sprung showers of agony and dread
    At this, their death. Up lovely Nature leaps

And smiles, won back to life by tearful Spring.
10   Spring's night of sorrow changed to morn of joy
  Aloud o'er hill and dale, she'll blithely sing

With gentle, soothing voice so sweet and coy
    That scarce the soft responsive echoes ring
  Lest they her smoothly-flowing notes destroy.

1883

THE PIPES OF PAN

1 Ringed with the flocking of hills, within shepherding
    watch of Olympus,
Tempe, vale of the gods, lies in green quiet withdrawn,—
Tempe, vale of the gods, deep-couched amid woodland
    and woodland,
Threaded with amber of brooks, mirrored in azure of
    pools,
All day drowsed with the sun, charm-drunken with
    moonlight at midnight,
Walled from the world forever under a vapour of
    dreams,
Hid by the shadows of dreams, not found by the
    curious footstep,
Sacred and secret forever, Tempe, vale of the gods.

How, through the cleft of its bosom, goes sweetly the
    water Penëus!
10 How by Penëus the sward breaks into saffron and blue!
How the long slope-floored beech-glades mount to the
    wind-wakened uplands,
Where, through flame-berried ash, troop the hoofed
    Centaurs at morn!

Nowhere greens a copse but the eye-beams of Artemis
    pierce it.
Breathes no laurel her balm but Phœbus' fingers caress.
Springs no bed of wild blossom but limbs of dryad have
    pressed it.
Sparkle the nymphs, and the books chime with shy
    laughter and calls.

Here is a nook. Two rivulets fall to mix with Penëus,
Loiter a space, and sleep, checked and choked by the
    reeds.
Long grass waves in the windless water, strown with the
    lote-leaf.
20 Twist thro' dripping soil great alder roots; and the air
Glooms with the dripping tangle of leaf-thick branches,
    and stillness
Keeps in the strange-coiled stems, ferns, and wet-
    loving weeds.
Hither comes Pan, to this pregnant earthy spot, when his
    piping
Flags; and his pipes outworn breaking and casting away,
Fits new reeds to his mouth with the weird earth-
    melody in them,
Piercing, alive with a life able to mix with the god's.
Then, as he blows, and the searching sequence delights
    him, the goat-feet
Furtive withdraw; and a bird stirs and flutes in the
    gloom,
Answering. Float with the stream the outworn pipes,
    with a whisper,—
30 "What the god breathes on, the god never can wholly
    evade!"
God-breath lurks in each fragment forever. Dispersed by
    Penëus
Wandering, caught in the ripples, wind-blown hither
    and yon,
Over the whole green earth and globe of sea they are
    scattered,
Coming to secret spots, where in a visible form
Comes not the god, though he come declared in his
    workings. And mortals,
Straying at cool of morn, or bodeful hasting at eve,
Or in the depths of noonday plunged to shadiest
    coverts,
Spy them, and set to their lips; blow, and fling them
    away!

Ay, they fling them away,—but never wholly! Thereafter
40   Creeps strange fire in their veins, murmur strange tongues
         in their brain,
Sweetly evasive; a secret madness takes them,—a charm-
         struck
Passion for woods and the wild, the solitude of the hills.
Therefore they fly the heedless throngs and traffic of
         cities,
Haunt mossed **caverns**, and wells bubbling ice-cool;
         and their souls
Gather a magical gleam of the secret of life, and the god's
         voice
Calls to them, not from afar, teaching them wonderful
         things.

1883; 1886

TANTRAMAR REVISITED

1   Summers and summers have come, and gone with the flight of the
         swallow;
Sunshine and **thunder** have been, storm, and winter, and frost;
Many and many a sorrow has all but died from remembrance,
Many a dream of joy fall'n in the shadow of pain.
Hands of chance and change have marred, or moulded, or broken,
Busy with spirit or flesh, all I most have adored;
Even the bosom of Earth is strewn with heavier shadows,—
Only in these green hills, aslant to the sea, no change!
Here where the road that has climbed from the inland valleys and
         woodlands,
10   Dips from the hill-tops down, straight to the **base** of the hills,—
Here, from my vantage-ground, I can see the scattering houses,
Stained with time, set warm in orchards, meadows, and wheat,
Dotting the broad bright slopes outspread to southward and
         eastward,
Wind-swept all day long, blown by the south-east wind.

Skirting the sunbright uplands stretches a riband of meadow,
Shorn of the labouring grass, bulwarked well from the sea,
Fenced on its seaward border with long clay dykes from the turbid
Surge and flow of the tides vexing the Westmoreland shores.
Yonder, toward the left, lie broad the Westmoreland marshes,—
20   Miles on miles they extend, level, and grassy, and dim,
Clear from the long red sweep of flats to the sky in the distance,
Save for the outlying heights, green-rampired Cumberland Point;
Miles on miles outrolled, and the river-channels divide them,—
Miles on miles of green, barred by the hurtling gusts.

Miles on miles beyond the tawny bay is Minudie.
There are the low blue hills; villages gleam at their feet.
Nearer a white sail shines across the water, and nearer
Still are the slim, grey masts of fishing boats dry on the flats.
Ah, how well I remember those wide red flats, above tide-mark
30   Pale with scurf of the salt, seamed and baked in the sun!
Well I remember the piles of blocks and ropes, and the net-reels
Wound with the beaded nets, dripping and dark from the sea!
Now at this season the nets are unwound; they hang from the rafters
Over the fresh-stowed hay in upland barns, and the wind
Blows all day through the chinks, with the streaks of sunlight,
          and sways them
Softly at will; or they lie heaped in the gloom of a loft.

Now at this season the reels are empty and idle; I see them
Over the lines of the dykes, over the gossiping grass,

Now at this season they swing in the long strong wind, thro'
          the lonesome
40   Golden afternoon, shunned by the foraging gulls.
Near about sunset the crane will journey homeward above them;
Round them, under the moon, all the calm night long,
Winnowing soft grey wings of marsh-owls wander and wander,
Now to the broad, lit marsh, now to the dusk of the dike.
Soon, thro' their dew-wet frames, in the live keen freshness of morning,
Out of the teeth of the dawn blows back the awakening wind.
Then, as the blue day mounts, and the low-shot shafts of the sunlight
Glance from the tide to the shore, gossamers jewelled with dew
Sparkle and wave, where late sea-spoiling fathoms of drift-net
50   Myriad-meshed, uploomed sombrely over the land.

Well I remember it all. The salt, raw scent of the margin;
Surging in ponderous lengths, uprose and coiled in its station;
Then each man to his home,—well I remember it all!

Yet, as I sit and watch, this present peace of the landscape,—
Stranded boats, these reels empty and idle, the hush,
One grey hawk slow-wheeling above yon cluster of haystacks,—
More than the old-time stir this stillness welcomes me home.
Ah, the old-time stir, how once it stung me with rapture,—
60   Old-time sweetness, the winds freighted with honey and salt!
Yet will I stay my steps and not go down to the marshland,—
Muse and recall far off, rather remember than see,—
Lest on too close sight I miss the darling illusion,
Spy at their task even here the hands of chance and change.

                                        1883; 1883

LA BELLE TROMBONISTE

1   How grave she sits and toots
       In the glare!
  From her dainty bits of boots
       To her hair
  Not the sign remotest shows
  If she either cares or knows
  How the **beer-imbibing** beaux
       Sit and stare.

  They're most prodigal with sighs,
10   Or they laugh;
  Or they cast adoring eyes
       As they quaff.
  They exert their every wile
  Her attention to **beguile**.
  Do they ever win a smile?
       Not by half!

  She leans upon her chin
       (Not a toot!),
  While the leading violin
20   And the flute
  Wail and plead in low duet
  Till, it may be, eyes are **wet**.
  She her trombone doth forget—
       She is mute.

  The music louder grows;
       She's awake!
  She applies her lips and blows—
       Goodness sake! . . . . .
  To think that such a peal
30   From such throat and frame ideal,
  From such tender lips could steal—
       Takes the cake!

  To the dinning cymbals shrill
       Kiss and clash.
  Drum and kettle-drum at will
       Roll and crash.
  But that trombone over all
  Toots unto my heart a call;—
  Maid petite, and trombone tall—
40   *It's a mash!*

Yet, I hesitate—for lo,
    What a pout!
She's poetic; and I know
    I am stout.
In her little room would she
On her trombone, tenderly,
Sit and toot as thus to me?—
    Ah, I doubt!

1884; 1885

THE POET IS BIDDEN TO MANHATTAN ISLAND

1   Dear Poet, quit your shady lanes
    And come where more than lanes are shady.
Leave Phyllis to the rustic swains
    And sing some Knickerbocker lady.
O hither haste, and here devise
    Divine *ballades* before unuttered.
Your poet's eyes *must* recognize
    The side on which your bread is buttered!

Dream not I tempt you to forswear
10   One pastoral joy, or rural frolic.
I call you to a city where
    The most urbane are most bucolic.
'Twill charm your poet's eyes to find
    Good husbandmen in brokers burly;—
Their stock is ever on their mind;
    To water it they rise up early.

Things you have sung, but ah, not seen—
    Things proper to the age of Saturn—
Shall greet you here; for we have been
20   Wrought quaintly, on the Arcadian pattern.
Your poet's lips will break in song
    For joy, to see at last appearing
The bulls and bears, a peaceful throng,
    While a lamb leads them—to the shearing!

And metamorphoses, of course,
    You'll mark in plenty, *à la* Proteus:
A bear become a little horse—
    Presumably from too much throat-use!
A thousandfold must go untold;
30   But, should you miss your farm-yard sunny,

And miss your ducks and drakes, behold
    We'll make you ducks and drakes—of money!

Greengrocers here are fairly read.
    And should you set your heart upon them,
We lack not beets—but some are dead,
    While others have policemen on them.
And be the dewfall dear to you,
    Possess your poet's soul in patience!
Your *notes* shall soon be falling dew,—
40   Most mystical of transformations!

Your heart, dear Poet, surely yields;
    And soon you'll leave your uplands flowery,
Forsaking fresh and bowery fields,
    For "pastures new"—upon the Bowery!
You've piped at home, where none could pay,
    Till now, I trust, your wits are riper.
Make no delay, but come this way,
    And pipe for them that pay the piper!

1884; 1886

THE SOWER

1 A brown, sad-coloured hillside, where the soil
    Fresh from the frequent harrow, deep and fine,
    Lies bare; no break in the remote sky-line,
Save where a flock of pigeons streams aloft,
Startled from feed in some low-lying croft,
    Or far-off spires with yellow of sunset shine;
    And here the Sower, unwittingly divine,
Exerts the silent forethought of his toil.

Alone he treads the glebe, his measured stride
10   Dumb in the yielding soil; and though small joy
    Dwell in his heavy face, as spreads the blind
Pale grain from his dispensing palm aside,
    This plodding churl grows great in his employ;—
    God-like, he makes provision for mankind.

1884

THE FOOTPATH

1   Path by which her feet have gone,
    Still you climb the windy hill,
Still the hillside fronts the dawn,
    Fronts the clustering village still.

On the bare hill-summit waves
    Still the lonely poplar-tree.
Where the blue lake-water raves,
    Still the plover pipe and flee.

Still you climb from windy pier,
10   Where the white gull drops and screams,
Through the village grown so dear,
    Till you reach my heaven of dreams.

Ah, the place we used to meet,
    I and she,—where sharp you turn,
Shun the curious village street,
    Lurk thro' hollows, hide in fern!

Then, the old house, ample-eaved,
    Night-long quiet beneath the stars,—
How the maples, many-leaved,
20   Screened us at the orchard bars!

Path by which her feet have gone,
    Still you climb the windy hill;
Still the hillside fronts the dawn,
    Fronts the clustering village still;

But no longer she, my own,
    Treads you, save as dreams allow.
And these eyes in dreams alone
    Dare to look upon you now.

1884?; 1886

IN NOTRE DAME

1   When first did I perceive you, when take heed
     Of what is now so deep in heart and brain
That tears shall not efface it, nor the greed
     Of time or fate destroy, nor scorn, nor pain?

Long summers back I trembled to the vision
     Of your keen **beauty**,—a delirious sense
That he you loved might hold in like derision
     Or Hell or Heaven, or sin or innocence.

This in my heart of hearts, while outwardly
10   Nor speech nor guarded glance my dream betrayed;
Till one day, so past thought you maddened me,
     My dream escaped my lips, glad and afraid.

Afraid, where no fear was. For lo, the gift
     (Worlds could not purchase it) was mine, was mine!
And oh, my Sweet, how swift we went adrift
     On wild sweet waters, warmer-hued than wine!

My very eyes are dizzy with delight
     At your recalled caresses. Peace, my heart!
She whom you beat so wild for lies to-night
20   From you too many bitter leagues apart.

Be calm, and I will talk to you of her;
     And you shall listen, **passionately** still;
And as the pauses in my verse recur,
     Think, heart, all this does fealty to your will!

All this,—a lithe and perfect-moulded form,
     Instinct with subtle gesture, soft, intense.
Head small and queenlike, dainty feet that warm
     Even the dull world's ways into rapturous sense.

Clear, broad, white forehead, crowned low down
         with hair
30   Darker than night, more soft than sleep or tears.
Nose neither small nor great, but straight, and fair.
     Like naught but smooth sea-shells her delicate ears.

But how to tell about her mouth and eyes!
     Her strange, sweet, maddening eyes, her subtle mouth!
Mouth in whose closure all love's sweetness lives,—
     Eyes with the warm gleam of the lustrous south!

Fathomless dusk by night, the day lets in
    Glimmer of emerald,—thus those eyes of hers!
Above the firm sweep of the moulded chin
40   The lips, than whose least kiss Heaven's gifts
       were worse.

Her bosom,—ah that now my head were laid
    Warm in that resting-place! But, heart, be still!
I will refrain, and break my dreams, afraid
    To stir the yearning I can not fulfil.

Love, in the northern night of Brittany
    Hear you no voice divide the night like flame?
In these gray walls the inmost soul of me
    Is swooning with the music of your name.

                        1884

CANADA

1   O Child of Nations, giant-limbed,
    Who stand'st among the nations now
Unheeded, unadored, unhymned,
    With unanointed brow,—

How long the ignoble sloth, how long
    The trust in greatness not thine own?
Surely the lion's brood is strong
    To front the world alone!

How long the indolence, ere thou dare
10   Achieve thy destiny, seize thy fame,—
Ere our proud eyes behold thee bear
    A nation's franchise, nation's name?

The Saxon force, the Celtic fire,
    These are thy manhood's heritage!
Why rest with babes and slaves? Seek higher
    The place of race and age.

I see to every wind unfurled
    The flag that bears the Maple Wreath;
Thy swift keels furrow round the world
20   Its blood-red folds beneath;

Thy swift keels cleave the furthest seas;
    Thy white sails swell with alien gales;
To stream on each remotest breeze
    The black smoke of thy pipes exhales.

O Falterer, let thy past convince
    Thy future,—all the growth, the gain,
The fame since Cartier knew thee, since
    Thy shores beheld Champlain!

Montcalm and Wolfe! Wolfe and Montcalm!
30   Quebec, thy storied citadel
Attest in burning song and psalm
    How here thy heroes fell!

O Thou that bor'st the battle's brunt
    At Queenston and at Lundy's Lane,—
On whose scant ranks but iron front
    The battle broke in vain!—

Whose was the danger, whose the day,
    From whose triumphant throats the cheers,
At Chrysler's Farm, at Chateauguay,
40   Storming like clarion-bursts our ears?

On soft Pacific slopes,—beside
    Strange floods that northward rave and fall,—
Where chafes Acadia's chainless tide—
    Thy sons await thy call.

They wait; but some in exile, some
    With strangers housed, in stranger lands,—
And some Canadian lips are dumb
    Beneath Egyptian sands.

O mystic Nile! Thy secret yields
50   Before us; thy most ancient dreams
Are mixed with far Canadian fields
    And murmur of Canadian streams.

But thou, my country, dream not thou!
    Wake, and behold how night is done,—
How on thy breast, and o'er thy brow,
    Bursts the uprising sun!

January, 1885; 1885

MIST

1   Its hand compassionate guards our restless sight
     Against how many a harshness, many an ill!
     Tender as sleep, its shadowy palms distil
Strange vapours that ensnare our eyes with light.
Rash eyes, kept ignorant in their own despite,
     It lets not see the unsightliness they will,
     But paints each scanty fairness fairer still,
And still deludes us to our own delight.

It fades, regathers, never quite dissolves.
10   And ah that life, ah that the heart and brain
     Might keep their mist and glamour, not to know
So soon the disenchantment and the pain!
     But one by one our dear illusions go,
     Stript and cast forth as time's slow wheel revolves.

1885; 1886

TO MY FRIEND,
EDMUND COLLINS

1   In divers tones I sing,
     And pray you, Friend, give ear!
My medley of song I bring
     You, who can rightly hear.

Themes gathered far and near,
     Thoughts from my heart that spring,
     In divers tones I sing,
And pray you, Friend, give ear!

Here's many a serious thing—
10   You'll know if it's sincere.
Where the light laughters ring
     You may detect a tear.
In divers tones I sing,
     And pray *you*, Friend, give ear!

1885

TO BLISS CARMAN
WITH A COPY OF LANG'S "HELEN OF TROY"

This antique song, new sung in fashion new,
From me, half silent fallen, with love to you,
O singer of unvexed scenes and virgin themes
In strait, quaint, ancient metres, thronged with dreams!

April 22, 1885; 1885

ON READING THE POEMS OF SIDNEY LANIER

Poet and Flute-player, that flute of thine
To me must ever seem thy perfect sign!
   Tho' strenuously with breath divine inspired,
To thy strait law is due thy deathless line.

April 22, 1885; 1885

TIDES

1 Through the still dusk how sighs the ebb-tide out,
    Reluctant for the reed-beds! Down the sands
    It washes. Hark! Beyond the wan grey strand's
Low limits how the winding channels grieve,
Aware the evasive waters soon will leave
    Them void amid the waste of desolate lands,
    Where shadowless to the sky the marsh expands,
And the noon-heats must scar them, and the drought.

Yet soon for them the solacing tide returns
10   To quench their thirst of longing. Ah, not so
    Works the stern law our tides of life obey!
Ebbing in the night-watches swift away,
    Scarce known ere fled forever is the flow;
    And in parched channel still the shrunk stream mourns.

1885

PROMISE

1 Ere the spring comes near
    Over the smoking hills,
    Stirring a million rills
  To laughter low and clear
  That the winds hush to hear,—

  Ere the eaves at noon
    Thaw and drip, there flies
    A Presence through the skies
  With promise of the boon
10 Of birds and blossoms soon.

  Elusive though it be,
    Yet can I trust that word.—
    Even such my soul hath heard,
  Athwart life's wintry lea,
  Of Immortality.

1885

COLLECT FOR DOMINION DAY

1 Father of nations! Help of the feeble hand!
    Strength of the strong! to whom the nations kneel!
  Stay and destroyer, at whose just command
    Earth's kingdoms tremble and her empires reel!
  Who dost the low uplift, the small make great,
    And dost abase the ignorantly proud,
  Of our scant people mould a mighty state,
    To the strong, stern,—to Thee in meekness bowed!
  Father of unity, make this people one!
10   Weld, interfuse them in the patriot's flame,—
  Whose forging on thine anvil was begun
    In blood late shed to purge the common shame;
  That so our hearts, the fever of faction done,
    Banish old feud in our young nation's name.

1885; 1886

AN ODE FOR THE CANADIAN CONFEDERACY

1   Awake, my country, the hour is great with change!
      Under this gloom **which** yet obscures the land,
From ice-blue strait and stern Laurentian range
      To where giant peaks our western bounds command,
A deep voice stirs, vibrating in men's ears
      As if their own hearts throbbed that thunder forth,
A sound wherein who hearkens wisely hears
      The voice of the desire of this strong North,—
         This North whose heart of fire
10   Yet knows not its desire
Clearly, but dreams, and murmurs in the dream.
The hour of dreams is done. Lo, on the hills the gleam!

Awake, my country, the hour of dreams is done!
      Doubt not, nor dread the greatness of thy fate.
Tho' faint souls fear the keen confronting sun,
      And fain would bid the morn of splendour wait;
Tho' dreamers, rapt in starry visions, cry
      "Lo, yon thy future, yon thy faith, thy fame!"
And stretch vain hands to stars, thy fame is nigh,
20   Here in Canadian hearth, and home, and name,—
         This name which yet shall grow
         Till all the nations know
Us for a patriot people, heart and hand
Loyal to our native earth, our own Canadian land!

O strong hearts, guarding the birthright of our glory,
      Worth your best blood this heritage that ye guard!
These mighty streams resplendent with our story,
      These iron coasts by rage of seas unjarred,—
What fields of peace these bulwarks well secure!
30   What vales of plenty those calm floods supply!
Shall not our love this rough, sweet land make sure,
      Her bounds preserve inviolate, though we die?
         O strong hearts of the North,
         Let flame your loyalty forth,
And put the craven and base to an open shame,
Till earth shall know the Child of Nations by her name!

1885; 1886

THE POTATO HARVEST

1   A high bare field, brown from the plough, and borne
      Aslant from sunset; amber wastes of sky
      Washing the ridge; a clamour of crows that fly
    In from the wide flats where the spent tides mourn
    To yon their rocking roosts in pines wind-torn;
      A line of grey snake-fence that zigzags by
      A pond and cattle; from the homestead nigh
    The long deep summonings of the supper horn.

    Black on the ridge, against that lonely flush,
10   A cart, and stoop-necked oxen; ranged beside
      Some barrels; and the day-worn harvest-folk,
    Here emptying their baskets, jar the hush
      With hollow thunders. Down the dusk hillside
      Lumbers the wain; and day fades out like smoke.

1886; 1886

DARK

1   Now, for the night is hushed and blind with rain,
      My soul desires communion, Dear, with thee.
      But hour by hour my spirit gets not free,—
    Hour by still hour my longing strives in vain.
    The thick dark hems me, ev'n to the restless brain.
      The wind's confusion vague encumbers me.
      Ev'n passionate memory, grown too faint to see
    Thy features, stirs not in her straitening chain.

    And thou, dost thou too feel this strange divorce
10   Of will from power? The spell of night and wind,
      Baffling desire and dream, dost thou too find?
    Not distance parts us, Dear; but this dim force,
      Intangible, holds us helpless, hushed with pain,
      Dumb with the dark, blind with the gusts of rain!

1886; 1886

AFLOAT

1   Afloat!—
Ah Love, on the mirror of waters
All the world seems with us afloat,—
All the wide, bright world of the night;
But the mad world of men is remote,
And the prating of tongues is afar.
We have fled from the crowd in our flight,
And beyond the gray rim of the waters
All the turmoil has sunk from our sight.

10 Turn your head, Love, a little, and note
Low down in the south a pale star.
The mists of the horizon-line drench it,
The beams of the moon all but quench it,
Yet it shines thro' this flood-tide of light.
Love, under that star is the world
Of the day, of our life, and our sorrow,
Where defamers and envious are.
Here, here is our peace, our delight,—
To our closest love-converse no bar.

20 Yet, as even in the moonbeam's despite
Still is seen the pale beam of the star,
So the light of our rapture this hour
Cannot quench the remembrance of morrow.
Though the wings of all winds are upfurled
And a limitless silence hath power,
Still the envious strife we forget not;
For the future is skilful to mar,
And the past we have banished not quite.

But this hour—Ah Love, if it might
30 With this splendor, this shining moon, set not!
If only forever as now
In this silence of silver adrift,
In this reeling, slow, luminous sphere,
This hollow great round of the night,
We might drift with the tide-flow, and lift
With the infinite pulse of the waters,
See each but the other, and hear
Our own language alone, I and thou,
I here at the stern, at the prow
40 The one woman, God's costliest gift!
So only to see you, to hear you,
To speak with you, Love, to be near you,—
I should reckon this life, well content.

But this dream is in vain, is in vain;
I will dream you one other. Suppose
This one hour some nepenthe were lent,
So pain, nor remembrance of pain,
Nor remembrance nor knowledge of care,
Nor distrust, nor fear, nor despair,—
50   For these, and more also, God knows
We have known and endured them, full share,—
Should have power to approach us! Suppose
To us drifting and dreaming afloat
On this shadowless shining of waters,
This mirror of tide without stain,
It were possible just for one hour
To forebode, or remember, or fear,
Nothing; of one thing aware
And one only, that we two are here,
60   And together, unhindered: then, Dear,
This one hour were our life,—all the past
But the ignorant sleep before birth,
All the future a trance, that should last
Till we turn us again to our earth!
And this dream, hadst thou courage to hear
Me interpret, were dreamed not in vain.
For this hour, O Love, was not meant,
With its rapture of peace, to endure,
Intense, calm, passionate, pure,—
70   My spirit with thy spirit blent
As the odor of flower and flower,
Of hyacinth blossom and rose.
Heart, spirit, and body, and brain,
Thou art utterly mine, as I thine;
But the love of the flesh, tho' at first
When I saw you and loved you it burst
With the love of the spirit one flame,
Neither greater nor less, but the same,
Is yet finite, attains not the height
80   Of the spirit enfranchised, and must
With the body slip back into dust.
Our soul-passion is deathless, divine.

So, we strike now the perfectest note
That man's heart is attuned to, attain
The white light of the zenith supreme,
Pierce the seventh and innermost sphere;
We are gods! Let us cast us adrift
From the world of the flesh and its power!

It is only a plunge, a quick roll
90   Of our skiff—I will gather and fold
You close, for the waters are cold,—
A few sobs, and we rise one soul,
Undissevered for ever and ever.

1886

BIRCH AND PADDLE
To Bliss Carman

1   Friend, those delights of ours
Under the sun and showers,—

Athrough the noonday blue
Sliding our light canoe,

Or floating, hushed, at eve,
Where the dim pine-tops grieve!

What tonic days were they
Where shy streams dart and play,—

Where rivers brown and strong
10   As caribou bound along,

Break into angry parle
Where wildcat rapids snarl,

Subside, and like a snake
Wind to the quiet lake!

We've paddled furtively,
Where giant boughs hide the sky,—

Have stolen, and held our breath,
Thro' coverts still as death,—

Have left with wing unstirred
20   The brooding phœbe-bird,

And hardly caused a care
In the water-spider's lair.

For love of his clear pipe
We've flushed the zigzag snipe,—

94

Have chased in wilful mood
The wood-duck's flapping brood,—

Have spied the antlered moose
Cropping the young green spruce,

And watched him till betrayed
30   By the kingfisher's sharp tirade.

Quitting the bodeful shades
We've run thro' sunnier glades,

And dropping craft and heed
Have bid our paddles speed.

Where the mad rapids chafe
We've shouted, steering safe,—

With sinew tense, nerve keen,
Shot thro' the roar, and seen,

With spirit wild as theirs,
40   The white waves leap like hares.

And then, with souls grown clear
In that sweet atmosphere,

With influences serene
Our blood and brain washed clean,

We've idled down the breast
Of broadening tides at rest,

And marked the winds, the birds,
The bees, the far-off herds,

Into a drowsy tune
50   Transmute the afternoon.

So, Friend, with ears and eyes
Which shy divinities

Have opened with their kiss,
We need no balm but this,—

A little space for dreams
On care-unsullied streams,—

'Mid task and toil, a space
To dream on Nature's face!

1886

A BIRTHDAY BALLADE

1   All deserted to wind and to sun
    You have left the dear, dusky canoe.
The amber cool currents still run,
    But our paddle forgets to pursue.
    Our river wears still the rare blue,
But its sparkle seems somehow less gay;
    It confides me this greeting for you—
Many Happy Returns of the Day!

Where's the mirth that with morn was begun,
10   Nor dreaded the dark and the dew?
Some sweet thieves have made off with our fun!
    Would our paddles were free to pursue!
    Ah, could we but catch them anew,
Clip their wings, forbid them to stray,
    Then more blithely we'd sing than we do—
Many Happy Returns of the Day!

Dear remembrances die, one by one,
    So cunning Time's craft to undo!
But ours must be never undone.
20   Oft again must the paddle pursue,
    Oft the treasured impression renew!
Then, return our Acadian way,
    For our days of delight were too few—
Many Happy Returns of the Day!

L'ENVOI

Now an easy enigma or two
    This ballade is devised to convey.
Unto you, and us lonely ones too,
    Many Happy Returns of the Day!

1886

A BLUE VIOLET

1   Blossom that spread'st, ere spring brings in
        Her sudden flights of swallows,
    Thy nets of blue, cool-meshed and thin,
        In rain-wet pasture hollows,

    Thronging the dim grass everywhere
        Amid thy heart-leaves tender,
    Thy temperate fairness seems more fair
        Even than August's splendour!

    Yet do I hear complaints of thee,
10   Men doubting of thy fragrance!
    Ah, Dear, thou hast revealed to *me*
        That shyest of perfume vagrants!

    Do ever so, my Flower discreet,
        And all the world be fair to,
    While men but guess that rarest sweet
        Which one alone can swear to.

                                        1886

A BREAK

1   Oh, the scent of the hyacinth blossom!
        The joy of that night,
        But the grievous awaking!
        The speed of my flight
        Thro' the dawn redly breaking!
        Gray lay the still sea;
        Naked hillside and lea;
        And gray with night frost
        The wide garden I crossed!
10   But the hyacinth beds were a-bloom.
        I stooped and plucked one—
        In an instant 'twas done,—
        And I heard, not far off, a gun boom!
        In my bosom
        I thrust the crushed blossom;
        And turned, and looked back
        Where She stood at her pane
        Waving sadly farewell once again;

Then down the dim track
20   Fled amain,
With the flower in my bosom.
Oh, the scent of the hyacinth blossom!

1886

CONSOLATION

1   Dear Heart, between us can be no farewell.
We have so long to live, so much to endure,
What ills despair might work us who can tell,
Had we not help in that one trust secure!

Time cannot sever, nor space keep long apart,
Those whom Love's sleepless yearning would
draw near.
Fate bends unto the indomitable heart
And firm-fixt will.—What room have we for fear!

1886

THE DEPARTING OF GLUSKÂP

1   It is so long ago; and men well-nigh
Forget what gladness was, and how the earth
Gave corn in plenty, and the rivers fish,
And the woods meat, before he went away.
His going was on this wise.

All the works
And words and ways of men and beasts became
Evil, and all their thoughts continually
Were but of evil. Then he made a feast.
10   Upon the shore that is beside the sea
That takes the setting sun, he ordered it,
And called the beasts thereto. Only the men
He called not, seeing them evil utterly.
He fed the panther's crafty brood, and filled
The lean wolf's hunger; from the hollow tree
His honey stayed the bear's terrific jaws;
And the brown rabbit couched at peace, within
The circling shadow of the eagle's wings.
And when the feast was done he told them all
20   That now, because their ways were evil grown,
On that same day he must depart from them,

And they should look upon his face no more.
Then all the beasts were very sorrowful.

It was near sunset, and the wind was still,
And down the yellow shore a thin wave washed
Slowly; and Gluskâp launched his birch canoe,
And spread his yellow sail, and moved from shore,
Though no wind followed, streaming in the sail,
Or roughening the clear waters after him.
30   And all the beasts stood by the shore, and watched.
Then to the west appeared a long red trail
Over the wave; and Gluskâp sailed and sang
Till the canoe grew little, like a bird,
And black, and vanished in the shining trail.
And when the beasts could see his form no more,
They still could hear him, singing as he sailed,
And still they listened, hanging down their heads
In long row, where the thin wave washed and fled.
But when the sound of singing died, and when
40   They lifted up their voices in their grief,
Lo! on the mouth of every beast a strange
New tongue! Then rose they all and fled apart,
Nor met again in council from that day.

1886

IMPULSE

1   A hollow on the verge of May,
        Thick strewn with drift of leaves. Beneath
        The densest drift a thrusting sheath
Of sharp green striving toward the day!
        I mused—"So dull Obstruction sets
        A bar to even violets,
When these would go their nobler way!"

My feet again, some days gone by,
        The self-same spot sought idly. There,
10   Obstruction foiled, the adoring air
Caressed a blossom woven of sky
        And dew, whose misty petals blue,
        With bliss of being thrilled athrough,
Dilated like a timorous eye.

Reck well this rede, my soul! The good
        The blossom craved was near, tho' hid.

Fret not that thou must doubt, but rid
Thy sky-path of obstruction strewed
By winds of folly. Then, do thou
20   The Godward impulse room allow
To reach its perfect air and food!

                      1886

THE ISLES—AN ODE

I

1 Faithful reports of them have reached me oft!
    Many their embassage to mortal court,
    By golden pomp, and breathless-heard consort
        Of music soft,—
By fragrances accredited, and dreams.
    Many their speeding herald, whose light feet
Make pause at wayside brooks, and fords of streams
    Leaving transfigured by an effluence fleet
        Those wayfarers they meet.

II

10 No wind from out the solemn wells of night
    But hath its burden of strange messages,
    Tormenting for interpreter; nor less
        The wizard light
That steals from noon-stilled waters, woven in shade,
    Beckons somewhither, with cool fingers slim.
No dawn but hath some subtle word conveyed
    In rose ineffable at sunrise rim,
        Or charactery dim.

III

One moment throbs the hearing, yearns the sight.
20   But tho' not far, yet strangely hid—the way,
    And our sense slow; nor long for us delay
        The guides their flight!
The breath goes by; the word, the light, elude;
    And we stay wondering. But there comes an hour
Of fitness perfect and unfettered mood,
    When splits her husk the finer sense with power,
        And—yon their palm-trees tower!

Here Homer came, and Milton came, tho' blind.
    Omar's deep doubts still found them nigh and nigher,
30   And learned them fashioned to the heart's desire.
          The supreme mind
Of Shakspere took their sovereignty, and smiled.
    Those passionate Israelitish lips that poured
The Song of Songs attained them; and the wild
    Child-heart of Shelley, here from strife restored,
          Remembers not life's sword.

1886

KHARTOUM

1   Set in the fierce red desert for a sword,
    Drawn and deep-driven implacably! The tide
    Of scorching sand that chafes thy landward side
Storming thy palms; and past thy front outpoured
The Nile's vast dread and wonder! Late there roared
    (While far off paused the long war, long defied)
    Mad tumult thro' thy streets; and Gordon died,
Slaughtered amid the yelling rebel horde!

Yet, spite of shame and wrathful tears, Khartoum,
10   We owe thee certain thanks, for thou has shown
    How still the one a thousand crowds outweighs,—
Still one man's moods sways millions,—one man's doom
    Smites nations;—and our burning spirits own
    Not sordid these nor unheroic days!

1886

LIBERTY
(From the French of Louis Honore Frèchette.)

1   A child, I set the thirsting of my mouth
    To the gold chalices of loves that craze.
Surely, alas, I have found therein but drouth,
    Surely has sorrow darkened o'er my days.
While worldlings chase each other **madly** round
    Their giddy track of frivolous gayety,
Dreamer, my dream earth's utmost longings bound:
    One love alone is mine, my love is Liberty.

I have sung them all;—youth's lightsomeness that fleets,
10   Pure friendship, my most fondly cherished dreams,
Wild blossoms and the winds that steal their sweets,
    Wood odors, and the star that whitely gleams.
But our hearts change; the spirit dulls its edge
    In the chill contact with reality;
These vanished like the foam-bells on the sedge:
    I sing one burden now, my song is Liberty.

I drench my spirit in ecstacy, consoled,
    And my gaze trembles toward the azure arc,
When in the wide world-records I behold
20   Flame like a meteor God's finger thro' the dark [.]
But if, at times, bowed over the abyss
    Wherein man crawls toward immortality,—
Beholding here how sore his suffering is,
    I make my prayer with tears, it is for Liberty.

1883; 1886

THE MARVELLOUS WORK

"Rise after rise bow the phantoms behind me."—Whitman.

1   Not yet, for all their quest of it, have men
Cast wholly by the ignoble dread of truth!
Each of God's laws, if but so late discerned
Their faiths upgrew unsuckled in it, fills
Their hearts with angry fears, perchance lest God
Be dwarfed behind his own decrees, or made
Superfluous through his perfectness of deed!
But large increase of knowledge in these days
Is come about us, fraught with ill for them
10   Whose creeds are cut too straight to hold new growth,
Whose faiths are clamped against access of wisdom;
Fraught with some sadness, too, for those just souls
Who, clothed in rigid teachings found too scant,
Are fain to piece the dear accustomed garb,
Till here a liberal, there a literal fragment,
Here new, there old, here bright, there dark, disclose
Their vesture a strange discordant motley.
But O rare motley,—starred with thirst of truth,
Patched with desire of wisdom, zoned about
20   With passion for fresh knowledge, and the quest
Of right! Such motley may be made at last,
Through grave sincerity, a dawn-clear garment!

102

But, for the enfranchised spirit, this expanse
Immeasurable of broad-horizoned view,—
What rapt, considerate awe it summons forth,
What adoration of the Eternal Cause!
His days unmeasured ages, His designs
Unfold through age-long silences, through surge
Of world upheaval, coming to their aim
30   As swerveless in fit time as tho' His finger
But yesterday ordained, and wrought to-day.
How the Eternal's unconcern of time,—
Omnipotence that hath not dreamed of haste,—
Is graven in granite-moulding æons' gloom;
Is told in stony record of the roar
Of long Silurian storms, and tempests huge
Scourging the circuit of Devonian seas;
Is whispered in the noiseless mists, the gray
Soft drip of clouds about rank fern-forests,
40   Through dateless terms that stored the layered coal;
Is uttered hoarse in strange Triassic forms
Of monstrous life; or stamped in ice-blue gleams
Athwart the death-still years of glacial sleep!

Down the stupendous sequence, age on age,
Thro' storm and peace, thro' shine and gloom, thro'
        warm
And pregnant periods of teeming birth,
And seething realms of thunderous overthrow,—
In the obscure and formless dawn of life,
In gradual march from simple to complex,
50   From lower to higher forms, and last to Man
Through faint prophetic fashions,—stands declared
The God of order and unchanging purpose.
Creation, which He covers, Him contains,
Even to the least up-groping atom. His
The impulse and the quickening germ, whereby
All things strive upward, reach toward greater good;
Till craving brute, informed with soul, grows Man,
And Man turns homeward, yearning back to God.

1886

ON THE CREEK

1   Dear Heart, the noisy strife
      And bitter carpings cease.
Here is the lap of life,
      Here are the lips of peace.

Afar from stir of streets,
      The city's dust and din,
What healing silence meets
      And greets us gliding in!

Our light birch silent floats;
10   Soundless the paddle dips.
Yon sunbeam thick with motes
      Athro' the leafage slips,

To light the iris wings
      Of dragon-flies alit
On lily-leaves, and things
      Of gauze that float and flit.

Above the water's brink
      Hush'd winds make summer riot;
Our thirsty spirits drink
20   Deep, deep, the summer quiet.

We slip the world's grey husk,
      Emerge, and spread new plumes;
In sunbeam-fretted dusk,
      Thro' populous golden glooms,

Like thistledown we slide,
      Two disembodied dreams,—
With spirits alert, wide-eyed,
      Explore the perfume-streams.

For scents of various grass
30   Stream down the veering breeze;
Warm puffs of honey pass
      From flowering linden-trees;

And fragrant gusts of gum,
      Breath of the balm-tree buds,
With fern-brake odours, come
      From intricate solitudes.

The elm-tops are astir
   With flirt of idle wings.
Hark to the grackles' *chirr*
40   Whene'er an elm-bough swings!

From off yon ash-limb sere
   Out-thrust amid green branches,
Keen like an azure spear
   A kingfisher down launches.

Far up the creek his calls
   And lessening laugh retreat.
Again the silence falls,
   And soft the green hours fleet.

They fleet with drowsy hum
50   Of insects on the wing.
We sigh—the end must come!
   We taste our pleasure's sting.

No more, then, need we try
   The rapture to regain.
We feel our day slip by,
   And cling to it in vain.

But, Dear, keep thou in mind
   These moments swift and sweet!
Their memory thou shalt find
60   Illume the common street;

And thro' the dust and din,
   Smiling, thy heart shall hear
Quiet waters lapsing thin,
   And locusts shrilling clear.

1886

ON THE LAGOON

1   Soothe, soothe
      The day-fall, soothe,
  Till wrinkling winds and seas are smooth,
      Till yon low band
      Of purpling strand
Breathe seaward dreams from the inner land,
Till lapped in mild half-lights our dream-blown boat
      Is felt to float,
      To fall, to float.

10   The sundown rose
      Delays and glows
O'er yon spired peak's remoter snows.
      Uprolling soon
      The red-ripe moon
Lolls in the pines in drowsed half swoon;
Till thin moon shades entangle us, and shift
      Our visions as we drift
      And drift.

      From musk-rose blooms
20   In the coppice glooms
Glide argosies of spice perfumes.
      The slow-pulsed seas,
      The shadowy trees,
The night spell holds us one with these,
Till, Dear, we scarce know life from sleep, but seem
      Dissolved together
      In sweet half dream.

           1886

THE QUELLING OF THE MOOSE
A Melicite Legend

1 When tent was pitched, and supper done,
  And forgotten were paddle, and rod, and gun,
  And the low, bright planets, one by one,

  Lit in the pine-tops their lamps of gold,
  To us by the fire, in our blankets rolled,
  This was the story Sacóbi told:—

"In those days came the Moose from the east,
A monster out of the white north-east,
And as leaves before him were man and beast.

10   "The dark rock-hills of Saguenay
Are strong,—they were but straws in his way.
He leapt the St. Lawrence as in play.

"His **breath** was a storm and a flame; his feet
In the mountains thundered, fierce and fleet,
Till men's hearts were as milk, and ceased to beat.

"But in those days dwelt Clote Scarp with men.
It is long to wait till he comes again,—
But a friend was near, and could hear us, then!

"In his wigwam, built by the Oolastook,
20   Where the ash-trees over the water look,
A voice of trouble the stillness shook.

"He rose, and took his bow from the wall,
And listened; he heard his people's call
Pierce up from the villages one and all.

"From village to village he passed with cheer,
And the people followed; but when drew near
The stride of the Moose, they fled in fear.

"Like smoke in a wind they fled at the last.
But he in a pass of the hills stood fast,
30   And down at his feet his bow he cast.

"That terrible forehead, maned with flame,
He smote with his open hand,—and tame
As a dog the raging beast became.

"He smote with his open hand; and lo!
As shrinks in the rains of spring the snow,
So shrank the monster beneath that blow,

"Till scarce the bulk of a bull he stood,
And Clote Scarp led him down to the wood,
And gave him the tender shoots for food."

40   He ceased. And a voice said, "Understand
How huge a peril will shrink like sand,
When stayed by a prompt and steady hand."

1886

RAIN

1   Sharp drives the rain, sharp drives the endless rain.
The rain-winds wake and wander, lift and blow.
The slow smoke-wreaths of vapour to and fro
Wave, and unweave, and gather and build again.
Over the far grey reaches of the plain,—
Grey miles on miles my passionate thought must go,—
I strain my sight, grown dim with gazing so,
Pressing my face against the streaming pane.

How the rain beats! Ah God, if love had power
10   To voice its utmost yearning, even tho'
Thro' time and bitter distance, not in vain,
Surely Her heart would hear me at this hour,
Look thro' the years, and see! But would She know
The white face pressed against the streaming pane?

1886

RECKONING

1   What matter that the sad gray city sleeps,
Sodden with dull dreams, ill at ease, and snow
Still falling chokes the swollen drains! I know
That even with sun and summer not less creeps
My spirit thro' gloom, nor ever gains the steeps
Where Peace sits, inaccessible, yearned for so.
Well have I learned that from my breast my woe
Starts,—that as my own hand hath sown, it reaps.

I have had my measure of achievement, won
10   Most I have striven for; and at last remains
This one thing certain only, that who gains
Success hath gained it at too sore a cost,
If in his triumph hour his heart have lost
Youth, and have found its sorrow of age begun.

1886

SALT

1   O breath of wind and sea,
     Bitter and clear,
  Now my faint soul springs free,
     Blown clean from fear!

  O hard sweet strife, O sting
     Of buffeting salt!
  Doubt and despair take wing,
     Failure, and fault.

  I dread not wrath or wrong,—
10   Smile, and am free;
  Strong while the winds are strong,
     The rocks, the sea.

  Heart of my heart, tho' life
     Front us with storm,
  Love will outlast the strife,
     More pure, more warm.

1886

A SERENADE

1   Love hath given the day for longing,
     And for joy the night.
  Dearest, to thy distant chamber
     Wings my soul its flight.

  Though unfathomed seas divide us,
     And the lingering year,
  'T is the hour when absence parts not,—
     Memory hath no tear.

  O'er the charmed and silent river
10   Drifts my lonely boat;
  From the haunted shores and islands
     Tender murmurs float,

  Tender breaths of glade and forest,
     Breezes of perfume;—
  Surely, surely thou canst hear me
     In thy quiet room!

Unto shore, and sky, and silence,
　　Low I pour my song.
All the spell, the summer sweetness,—
20　　These to thee belong.

Thou art love, the trance and rapture
　　Of the midnight clear!
Sweet, tho' world on world withhold thee,
　　I can clasp thee here.

1886

A SONG OF DEPENDENCE

1　Love, what were fame,
　　And thou not in it,
That I should hold it worth
　　Much toil to win it?

What were success
　　Didst thou not share it?
As Spring can spare the snows
　　I well could spare it!

Love, what were love
10　　But of thy giving
That it should much prevail
　　To sweeten living?

Nay, what were life,
　　Save thou inspire it,
That I should bid my soul
　　Greatly desire it?

1886

TO A LADY,

AFTER HEARING HER READ KEATS' "NIGHTINGALE"

1　This supreme song of him who dreamed
　　All beauty, and whose heart foreknew
The anguish of vain longing, seemed
　　To breathe new mystery, breathed by you.

As if the rapture of the night,
    Moon-tranced, and passion-still, were stirred
To some undreamed divine delight
    By sudden singing of a bird!

1886

TO S——— M———

The disciple of Master Herrick returneth thanks for the gift
of a band of pansies for his hat.

I

1
        Never poet
    From Musæus down,
Crowned with rose, or myrtle-wreath, or laurel,
    Had of daintier hand
        Dearer trophy!
      Therefore (I know it,
Castaly! and, Daphne's lover, quarrel!)
      I for crown
Flout the bay and wear thy pansy-band,
10
      Mistress Sophie.

II

    As these petals
      Die not,
So the thought that settles
Softly in the purple petals
      Fly not!
Half a memory, which a world of men
      Can buy not,—
Half a prayer, that till we meet again
      Thou sigh not!

1886

TOUT OU RIEN

1 Love, if you love me, love with heart and soul!
    I am not liberal as some lovers are,
Accepting small return, and scanty dole,
    Gratefully glad to worship from afar.

Ah, love me passionately, or not at all!
    For love that counts the cost I have small need.
My fingers would with laughing scorn let fall
    That poor half-love so many lovers heed.

Then be mine wholly,—body, soul, and brain!
10   Your memory shall outlive kings. For Time
Forgets his cunning and assails in vain
    Her whose name rings along the poet's rhyme.

1886

WINTER GERANIUMS

O what avails the storm,
When o'er my sense this Magian flower enweaves
    His charm of slumbrous summer, green and warm,
And laps me in his luxury of leaves!

O where the frost that chills,
Whilst these rich blooms burn red about my face,
    Luring me out across the irised hills
Where Autumn broods o'er purple deeps of space!

1886

MOTHER OF NATIONS

1   To Her whose fame, these fifty years
    Of triumph and of tears,
    Beneath the searching radiance shed
    On every loftiest head.

Hath stood with skirts unstained, and shown
How, even on a throne,
The grace may thrive and wifely good
Of tender womanhood;

To Her whose gaze thro' storm and peace
10   Hath marked her power increase,
Her people keep their steadfast way
Beneath her temperate sway.

Who wears in her Imperial place
The splendor of the race,
This reverent greeting speed we forth
From out our sanguine north;

Saying, that not for these alone
Our praise surrounds her throne,
Graces which other crowns have worn,
20   By other rulers borne

—For justice, power, and counsel sage
Are hers by heritage,
And she would scorn a faith less pure
Than common hearths keep sure—

But rather than beneath her care
Hath ripened brave and fair
This Canada of north and storm,
Whose blood yet beats so warm—

This nation that hath weighed the worth
30   Of its heroic birth,
And now in manhood shall not shame
The loins from whence it came.

1886; 1887

Á SONG OF CHEER

1   The winds are up with wakening day
     And tumult in the tree;
Across the cool and open sky
     White clouds are streaming free;
The new light breaks o'er flood and field
     Clear like an echoing horn,
While in loud flight the crows are blown
     Athwart the sapphire morn.

What tho' the maple's scarlet flame
10   Declares the summer done,
Tho' finch and starling voyage south
     To win a softer sun;
What tho' the withered leaf whirls by
     To strew the purpling stream,—
Stretched are the world's glad veins with strength,
     Despair is grown a dream!

The acres of the goldenrod
     Are glorious on the hills.
Tho' storm and loss approach, the year's
20   High heart upleaps and thrills.

Dearest, the cheer, the brave delight,
   Are given to shame regret,
That when the long frost falls, our hearts
   Be glad, and not forget!

1888

HOW THE MOHAWKS SET OUT FOR MEDOCTEC

(*When the invading Mohawks captured the outlying Melicite village of Madawaska, they spared two squaws to guide them downstream to the main Melicite town of Medoctec, below Grand Falls. The squaws steered themselves and their captors over the Falls.*)

I

1   Grows the great deed, though none
   Shout to behold it done!
   To the brave deed done by night
   Heaven testifies in the light.

   Stealthy and swift as a dream,
   Crowding the breast of the stream,
   In their paint and plumes of war
   And their war-canoes four score,

   They are threading the Oolastook,
10 Where his cradling hills o'erlook.
   The branchy thickets hide them;
   The unstartled waters guide them.

II

   Comes night to the quiet hills
   Where the Madawaska spills,—
   To his slumbering huts no warning,
   Nor mirth of another morning!

   No more shall the children wake
   As the dawns through the hut-door break;
   But the dogs, a trembling pack,
20 With wistful eyes steal back.

   And, to pilot the noiseless foe
   Through the perilous passes, go
   Two women who could not die—
   Whom the knife in the dark passed by.

III

Where the shoaling waters froth,
Churned thick like devils' broth,—
Where the rocky shark-jaw waits,
Never a bark that grates.

And the tearless captives' skill
30   Contents them. Onward still!
And the low-voiced captives tell
The tidings that cheer them well;

How a clear stream leads them down
Well-nigh to Medoctec town,
Ere to the great Falls' thunder
The long wall yawns asunder.

IV

The clear stream glimmers before them;
The faint night falters o'er them;
Lashed lightly bark to bark,
40   They glide the windless dark.

Late grows the night. No fear
While the skillful captives steer!
Sleeps the tired warrior, sleeps
The chief; and the river creeps.

V

In the town of the Melicite
The unjarred peace is sweet,
Green grows the corn and great,
And the hunt is fortunate.

This many a heedless year
50   The Mohawks come not near.
The lodge-gate stands unbarred;
Scarce even a dog keeps guard.

No mother shrieks from a dream
Of blood on the threshold stream,—
But the thought of those mute guides
Is where the sleeper bides!

VI

Gets forth those caverned walls
No roar from the giant Falls,
Whose mountainous foam treads under
60   The abyss of awful thunder.

But the river's sudden speed!
How the ghost-grey shores recede!
And the tearless pilots hear
A muttering voice creep near.

A tremor! The blanched waves leap.
The warriors start from sleep.
Faints in the sudden blare
The cry of their swift despair,

And the captives' death-chant shrills.
70   But afar, remote from ills,
Quiet under the quiet skies
The Melicite village lies.

1888

BURNT LANDS

1   On other fields and other scenes the morn
     Laughs from her blue,—but not such fields are these,
     Where comes no cheer of summer leaves and bees,
And no shade mitigates the day's white scorn.
These serious acres vast no groves adorn;
     But giant trunks, bleak shapes that once were trees,
     Tower naked, unassuaged of rain or breeze,
Their stern grey isolation grimly borne.

The months roll over them, and mark no change.
10   But when spring stirs, or autumn stills, the year,
     Perchance some phantom leafage rustles faint
Through their parched dreams,—some old-time notes
      ring strange,
     When in his slender treble, far and clear,
     Reiterates the rain-bird his complaint.

1888

FROGS

1   Here in the red heart of the sunset lying,
      My rest an islet of brown weeds blown dry,
      I watch the wide bright heavens, hovering nigh,
    My plain and pools in lucent splendour dyeing.
    My view dreams over the rosy wastes, descrying
      The reed-tops fret the solitary sky;
      And all the air is tremulous to the cry
    Of myriad frogs on mellow pipes replying.

    For the unrest of passion here is peace,
10   And eve's cool drench for midday soil and taint.
    To tired ears how sweetly brings release
      This limpid babble from life's unstilled complaint;
      While under tired eyelids lapse and faint
    The noon's derisive visions—fade and cease.

                         1888

THE KEEPERS OF THE PASS

(When the Iroquois were moving in overwhelming force to obliterate the infant town of Montreal, Adam Daulac and a small band of comrades, binding themselves by oath not to return alive, went forth to meet the enemy in a distant pass between the Ottawa River and the hills. There they died to a man, but not till they had slain so many of the savages that the invading force was shattered and compelled to withdraw.)

1   Now heap the branchy barriers up.
      No more for us shall burn
    The pine-logs on the happy hearth,
      For we shall not return.

    We've come to our last camping-ground.
      Set axe to fir and tamarack.
    The foe is here, the end is near,
      And we shall not turn back.

    In vain for us the town shall wait,
10   The home-dear faces yearn,
    The watchers in the steeple watch,—
      For we shall not return.

For them we're come to these hard straits,
    To save from flame and wrack
The little city built far off;
    And we shall not turn back.

Now beat the yelling butchers down.
    Let musket **blaze**, and axe-edge burn.
Set hand to hand, lay brand to brand,
20   But we shall not return.

For every man of us that falls
    Their hordes a score shall lack.
Close in about the Lily Flag!
    No man of us goes back.

For us no morrow's dawn shall break.
    Our sons and wives shall learn
Some day from lips of flying scout
    Why **we** might not return.

A dream of children's laughter comes
30   Across the battle's slack,
A vision of familiar streets,—
    But we shall not go back.

Up roars the painted **storm** once more.
    Long rest we soon shall earn.
Henceforth the city safe may sleep,
    But we shall not return.

And when our last has fallen in blood
    Between these waters black,
Their tribe shall no more lust for war,—
40   For we shall not turn back.

In vain for us the town shall wait,
    The **home-dear** faces yearn,
The watchers in the steeple watch,
    For we shall not return.

1888

CANADIANS ARE WE

(A TOAST FOR DOMINION DAY)

1   Here's to the glory of the land that we name
        The dear Land of Canada the Free,
    Where our hope is, and our home, and our faith, and
          our fame,—
      For Canadians—Canadians are we!

    Dominion is to us from Columbia's shores of balm
        To the shouting tides of glad Acadie,
    From the laughing waves of Erie to the Arctic fields of
          calm,—
      For Canadians—Canadians are we!

    Here the lily and the thistle, the shamrock and the rose,
10   Are at one beneath our goodly maple tree,
    From our union confusion shall come down about our foes,—
      For Canadians—Canadians are we!

    Then here's to our Land! Lundy's Lane—Chateauguay—
        Would they win by bribe or battle? They shall see
    Our Maple Flag forever proclaim our nation's sway,—
      For Canadians—Canadians are we!

1889

SEVERANCE

1   The tide falls, and the night falls,
        And the wind blows in from the sea,
    And the bell on the bar it calls and calls,
        And the wild hawk cries from his tree.

    The late crane calls to his fellows gone
        In long flight over the sea,
    And my heart with the crane flies on and on,
        Seeking its rest and thee.

    O Love, the tide returns to the strand,
10   And the crane flies back oversea,
    But he brings not my heart from his far-off land
        For he brings not thee to me.

1889

THE WAKING EARTH

1   With shy bright clamour the live brooks sparkle and
        run.
      Freed flocks confer about the farmstead ways.
      The air's a wine of dreams and shining haze,
Beaded with bird-notes thin,—for Spring's begun!
The sap flies upward. Death is over and done.
      The glad earth wakes; the glad light breaks; the
        days
      Grow round, grow radiant. Praise for the new life!
        Praise
For bliss of breath and blood beneath the sun!

What potent wizardry the wise earth wields,
10   To conjure with a perfume! From bare fields
      The sense drinks in a breath of furrow and sod.
And lo, the bound of days and distance yields;
      And fetterless the soul is flown abroad,
      Lord of desire and beauty, like a god!

                            1889

THE NIGHT SKY

1   O deep of Heaven, 't is thou alone art boundless,
      'T is thou alone our balance shall not weigh,
      'T is thou alone our fathom-line finds soundless,—
      Whose infinite our finite must obey!
Through thy blue realms and down thy starry reaches
      Thought voyages forth beyond the furthest fire,
And, homing from no sighted shoreline, teaches
      Thee measureless as is the soul's desire.
O deep of Heaven, no beam of Pleiad ranging
10   Eternity may bridge thy gulf of spheres!
The ceaseless hum that fills thy sleep unchanging
      Is rain of the innumerable years.
Our worlds, our suns, our ages, these but stream
Through thine abiding like a dateless dream.

                         1889; 1890

WHEN MILKING-TIME IS DONE

1 When milking-time is done, and over all
     This quiet Canadian inland forest home
     And wide rough pasture-lots the shadows come,
  And dews, with peace and twilight voices, fall,
  From moss-cooled watering-trough to foddered stall
     The tired plough-horses turn,—the barnyard loam
     Soft to their feet,—and in the sky's pale dome
  Like resonant chords the swooping night-hawks call.

  The frogs, cool-fluting ministers of dream,
10   Make shrill the slow brook's borders; pasture bars
     Down clatter, and the cattle wander through,—
  Vague shapes amid the thickets; gleam by gleam
     Above the wet grey wilds emerge the stars,
     And through the dusk the farmstead fades from view.

                        1889

THE SUMMER POOL

1 This is a wonder-cup in Summer's hand.
     Sombre, impenetrable, round its rim
     The fir-trees bend and brood. The noons o'erbrim
  The windless hollow of its iris'd strand
  With mote-thick sun and water-breathings bland.
     Under a veil of lilies lurk and swim
     Strange shapes of presage in a twilight dim,
  Unwitting heirs of light and life's command.

  Blind in their bondage, of no change they dream,
10   But the trees watch in grave expectancy.
     The spell fulfils,—and swarms of radiant flame,
  Live jewels, above the crystal dart and gleam,
     Nor guess the sheen beneath their wings to be
     The dark and narrow regions whence they came.

                      1889; 1891

THE VALLEY OF THE WINDING WATER

1   The valley of the winding water
      Wears the same light it wore of old.
   Still o'er the purple peaks the portals
      Of distance and desire unfold.

   Still break the fields of opening June
      To emerald in their ancient way.
   The sapphire of the summer heaven
      Is infinite, as yesterday.

   My eyes are on the greening earth,
10   The exultant bobolinks wild [a-wing.]
   And yet, of all this kindly gladness,
      My heart beholds not anything.

   For in a still room far away,
      With mourners round her silent head,
   Blind to the quenchless tears, the anguish—
      I see, to-day, a woman dead.

           1889

AUTOCHTHON

I

1   I am the spirit astir
         To swell the grain
      When fruitful suns confer
         With labouring rain;
      I am the life that thrills
         In branch and bloom;
    I am the patience of abiding hills,
         The promise masked in doom.

II

      When the sombre lands are wrung
10   And storms are out,
     And giant woods give tongue,
       I am the shout;
     And when the earth would sleep,
       Wrapped in her snows,
  I am the infinite gleam of eyes that keep
       The post of her repose.

I am the hush of calm,
　　I am the speed,
The flood-tide's triumphing psalm,
20　　　The marsh-pool's heed;
I work in the rocking roar
　　Where cataracts fall;
I flash in the prismy fire that dances o'er
　　The dew's ephemeral ball.

IV

I am the voice of wind
　　And wave and tree,
Of stern desires and blind,
　　Of strength to be;
I am the cry by night
30　　　At point of dawn,
The summoning bugle from the unseen height,
　　In cloud and doubt withdrawn.

V

I am the strife that shapes
　　The stature of man,
The pang no hero escapes,
　　The blessing, the ban;
I am the hammer that moulds
　　The iron of our race,
The omen of God in our blood that a people beholds,
40　　　The foreknowledge veiled in our face.

1889

A CHRISTMAS-EVE COURTIN'

1　The snow'd laid deep that winter from the middle of November;
The goin', as I remember, was the purtiest kind of goin';
An' as the time drawed nigh fur turkeys an' mince pie
The woods, all white an' frosted, was a sight worth showin'.

The snow hung down the woodpiles all scalloped-like an' curled.
You'd swear in all the world ther' warn't no fences any more.
The cows kep' under cover, an' the chickens scratched twice over
The yaller ruck of straw a-layin' round the stable door.

'Twas Christmas Eve, in the afternoon, an' the store was jest a-hummin'
10   When we seen the parson comin' in his pung along the road;
An' as he passed the store he called in through the door,
"Church to-night at the Crossroads! Come, boys, and bring a load!"

'Twas a new idee in them parts, an' Bill Simmons made 'n oration
About "High Church innovation," an' "a-driftin' back to Rome,"
But I backed the parson's rights to have Church o' moonlight nights;
An' I thought of Nance's cute red lips, an' pinted straight fur home.

I wasn't long a-gittin' the chores done up, you bet,
An' the supper that I eat wouldn't more'n a' fed a fly!
Then I hitched the mare in the pung an' soon was bowlin' along
20   Down by the crick to Nance's while the moon was white an' high.

She didn't keep me waitin', fur church was at half-pas' seven;
An' my idee of Heaven, as I tucked her into the furs,
Was a-riding' with Nance at night when the moon was high an' white,
An' the deep sky all a-sparkle like them laughin' eyes of hers.

I had a heap to say, but I couldn't jest find my tongue;
But my heart it sung an' sung, like canaries was into it.
So I chirruped to the mare with a kind of easy air,
An' Nance had to do the talkin',—as was jest the one could do it!

An' I could feel her shoulder, kind of comfortin' an' warm,
30   Nestlin' agin my arm,—sech a sweet an' cunnin' shoulder.
My heart was all afire, but I kep' gittin' shyer an' shyer,
An' wished that I'd been born a leetle sassier an' bolder.

We come to them there Crossroads 'fore I'd time to say a word;
An' I reckon as how I heard mighty little of the sarvice.
But 'twas grand to hear Nance sing "Glory to the newborn King,"
Tho' the way the choir folks stared at us, it made me kind of narvous.

I wished the parson'd stop an' give me another chance
Out there in the night with Nance, under the stars an' moon;
An' I vowed I'd have my say in the tidiest kind of way,
40   An' she shouldn't have no more call to think me a blame gossoon.

At last the preachin' come to an end, an' the folks all crowded out.
'Fore I knowed what I was about we was on the road fur home.
But the sky was overcast an' a thick snow droppin' fast,
An' a big wind down from the mountins got a-rantin' an' moanin' some.

124

We hadn't rode two mile when it blowed like all possessed,
An' at that I kind of guessed we was in fur a ticklish night.
We couldn't go more'n a walk, an' Nance she forgot to talk;
Then I jest slipped my arm around her, an' she never kicked a mite.

Well, now, if the hull blame roof'd blowed off I wouldn't 'a keered,
50 But I seen as how Nance was skeered, so I sez, "By gracious, Nance,
I guess if we don't turn, an' cut back for the Crossroads, durn
The shelter we'll git to-night by any kind of a chance!"

Then the mare stopped short an' whinnied, an' Nance jest said, "Oh, Si!"
An' then commenced to cry, till I felt like cryin' too;
I forgot about the storm, an' jest hugged her close an' warm,
An' kissed her, an' kissed her, an' swore as how I'd be true.

Then Nance she quit her cryin' an' said she wastn't skeered
So long's she knowed I keered jest a leetle mite fur her;
But she guessed we'd better try an' git home, an' "by-an'-by
60 The storm'll stop, an' anyways, it ain't so very fur!"

My heart was that chock full I couldn't find a word to say,
But she understood the way that I looked into her eyes!
In buffaler robe an' rug I wrapped her warm an' snug,
An' got out an' broke the mare a road all the way to Barnes's Rise.

'Twas a tallish tramp, I tell you, a-leadin' that flounderin' mare
Thro' snow drifts anywheres from four to six foot deep.
An' a "painter" now an' then howled out from his mountin den;
But Nance, she never heered it, fur she must 'a fell to sleep.

It wasn't fur from mornin' when we come to Barnes's Rise,—
70 An' I found to my surprise I'd tramped nine mile an' wasn't tired.
I was in sech a happy dream it didn't hardly seem
As the ride had been any tougher'n jest what I'd desired.

It was easier goin' now, an' Nance woke up all rosy.
She was sweeter'n any posy as I kissed her at the gate.
The dawn was jest a-growin' so I wished her a Merry Christmas,
An' remarked I must be goin' as it might be gittin' late!

We was married at the Crossroads jest six weeks from Christmas Eve;
An' Nance an' me believe in our parson's innovations;
We ain't much skeered o' Rome, an' we reckon he can preach some,
80 An' we call that evenin' sarvice a Providential Dispensation.

1889

THE FORTRESS

1   While raves the midnight storm,
    And roars the rain upon the windy roof,
    Heart held to heart and all the world aloof,
    We laugh secure and warm.

    This chamber of our bliss
    Might seem a fortress by a haunted main,
    Which shouting hosts embattled charge in vain,
    Powerless to mar our kiss.

    O life, O storm of years,
10   Our walls are built against your shattering siege;
    Our dwelling is with Love, our sovereign liege,
    And fenced from change and tears.

                     1889

THE FIR WOODS

1   The wash of endless waves is in their tops,
    Endlessly swaying, and the long winds stream
    Athwart them from the far-off shores of dream.
    Through the stirred branches filtering, faintly drops
    Mystic dream-dust of isle, and palm, and cave,
    Coral and sapphire, realms of rose, that seem
    More radiant than ever earthly gleam
    Revealed of fairy mead or haunted wave.

    A cloud of gold, a cleft of blue profound,—
10   These are my gates of wonder, surged about
    By tumult of tossed bough and rocking crest.
    The vision lures. The spirit spurns her bound,
    Spreads her unprisoned wing, and drifts from out
    This green and humming gloom that wraps my rest.

                     1889

LIFE

(After the French)

O Life, how slight!
  A little sweet,
A brief delight,
  And then—we meet!

O Life, how vain!
  A little spite,
A little pain,
  And then—good-night!

1889; 1891

TRIUMPH

1   For a little while,
A heartsick **season**,
Blind fate's unreason
Withheld thy face,—
For a sunless space
Thy voice, thy smile.

But now on the hills
There is health and laughter.
No more hereafter
10   The voiceless pain.
There's mirth in the rain,
There's May in the rills.

Now earth's far corners
No more withhold thee;
No more enfold thee
The fetters of change;
And thou art stranger
To the tears of mourners.

For me and thee
20   No more—no longer—
The hopeless hunger,
The hearts of fire;—
The unquenched desire
No more for me!

For now the gleam
Of the dew thy glance is.
My heart's deep trance is
Forever on thee.
Yea, I have won thee
30   From death and dream!

Circa *1889*

THE WINTER FIELDS

1   Winds here, and sleet, and frost that bites like steel.
The low bleak hill rounds under the low sky.
Naked of flock and fold the fallows lie,
Thin streaked with meagre drift. The gusts reveal
By fits the dim grey snakes of fence, that steal
    Through the white dusk. The hill-foot poplars sigh,
    While storm and death with winter trample by,
And the iron fields ring sharp, and blind lights reel.
Yet in the lonely ridges, wrenched with pain,
10   Harsh solitary hillocks, bound and dumb,
Grave glebes close-lipped beneath the scourge and chain,
    Lurks hid the germ of ecstasy—the sum
Of life that waits on summer, till the rain
    Whisper in April and the crocus come.

1890

BLOMIDON

1   This is that black rock bastion, based in surge,
    Pregnant with agate and with amethyst,
Whose foot the tides of storied Minas scourge,
    Whose top austere withdraws into its mist.
This is that ancient cape of tears and storm,
    Whose towering front inviolable frowns
O'er vales Evangeline and love keep warm—
    Whose fame thy song, O tender singer, crowns.
Yonder, across these reeling fields of foam,
10   Came the sad threat of the avenging ships.
What profit now to know if just the doom,
    Though harsh! The streaming eyes, the praying lips,
The shadow of inextinguishable pain,
The poet's deathless music—these remain!

1890

THE DESERTED CITY

1   There lies a little city leagues away.
      Its wharves the green sea washes all day long.
      Its busy, sun-bright wharves with sailors' song
    And clamour of trade ring loud the livelong day.
    Into the happy harbour hastening, gay
      With press of snowy canvas, tall ships throng.
      The peopled streets to blithe-eyed Peace belong,
    Glad housed beneath these crowding roofs of grey.

    'Twas long ago this city prospered so,
10   For yesterday a woman died therein.
    Since when the wharves are idle fallen, I know,
      And in the streets is hushed the pleasant din;
      The thronging ships have been, the songs have been,—
    Since yesterday it is so long ago.

1890

THE FLIGHT OF THE GEESE

1   I hear the low wind wash the softening snow,
      The low tide loiter down the shore. The night,
      Full filled with April forecast, hath no light.
    The salt wave on the sedge-flat pulses slow.
    Through the hid furrows lisp in murmurous flow
      The thaw's shy ministers; and hark! The height
      Of heaven grows weird and loud with unseen flight
    Of strong hosts prophesying as they go!

    High through the drenched and hollow night their wings
10   Beat northward hard on Winter's trail. The sound
    Of their confused and solemn voices, borne
    Athwart the dark to their long Arctic morn,
      Comes with a sanction and an awe profound,
    A boding of unknown, foreshadowed things.

1890

THE FURROW

1   How sombre slope these acres to the sea
     And to the breaking sun! The sun-rise deeps
     Of rose and crocus, whence the far dawn leaps,
   Gild but with scorn their grey monotony.
   The glebe rests patient for its joy to be.
     Past the salt field-foot many a dim wing sweeps;
     And down the field a first slow furrow creeps,
   Pledge of near harvests to the unverdured lea.

   With clank of harness tramps the serious team.
10   With sea air thrills their nostrils. Some wise crows
     Feed confidently behind the ploughman's feet.
   In the early chill the clods fresh cloven steam,
     And down its griding path the keen share goes.
     So, from a scar, best flowers the future's sweet.

                        1890

THE NIGHT-HAWK

1   When frogs make merry the pools of May,
       And sweet, oh, sweet,
       Through the twilight dim
       Is the vesper hymn
   Their myriad mellow pipes repeat
     As the rose-dusk dies away,
     Then hark, the night-hawk!
       (For now is the elfin hour.)
     With melting skies o'er him,
10   All summer before him,
   His wild brown mate to adore him,
       By the spell of his power
       He summons the apples in flower.

   In the high pale heaven he flits and calls;
       Then swift, oh, swift,
       On sounding wing
       That hums like a string,
   To the quiet glades where the gnat-clouds drift
     And the night-moths flicker, he falls.
20   Then hark, the night-hawk!
       (For now is the elfin hour.)

With melting skies o'er him,
All summer before him,
His wild brown mate to adore him,
　　By the spell of his power
　　He summons the apples in flower.

1890

A SONG OF GROWTH

1　In the heart of a man
　　　Is a thought upfurled.
　Reached its full span
　　　It shakes the world,
　And to one high thought
　Is a whole race wrought.

　Not with vain noise
　　　The great work grows,
　Nor with foolish voice,
10　　　But in repose,—
　Not in the rush
　But in the hush.

　From the cogent lash
　　　Of the cloud-herd wind
　The low clouds dash,
　　　Blown headlong, blind;
　But beyond, the great blue
　Looks moveless through.

　O'er the loud world sweep
20　　　The scourge and the rod;
　But in deep beyond deep
　　　Is the stillness of God,—
　At the Fountains of Life
　No cry, no strife.

1890

THE MOWING

1   This is the voice of high midsummer's heat.
        The rasping vibrant clamour soars and shrills
        O'er all the meadowy range of shadeless hills,
    As if a host of giant cicadae beat
    The cymbals of their wings with tireless feet,
        Or brazen grasshoppers with triumphing note
        From the long swath proclaimed the fate that smote
    The clover and timothy-tops and meadowsweet.

    The crying knives glide on; the green swath lies.
10   And all noon long the sun, with chemic ray,
        Seals up each cordial essence in its cell,
    That in the dusky stalls, some winter's day,
        The spirit of June, here prisoned by his spell,
    May cheer the herds with pasture memories.

                        1890

A VESPER SONNET

1   This violet eve is like a waveless stream
        Celestial, from the rapt horizon's brink,
        Assuaging day with the diviner drink
    Of temperate ecstasy, and dews, and dream.
    The wine-warm dusks, that brim the valley, gleam
        With here and there a lonely casement. Cease
        The impetuous purples from the sky of peace,
    Like God's mood in tranquillity supreme.

    The encircling uplands east and west lie clear
10   In thin aërial amber, threaded fine,—
    Where bush-fires gnaw the bramble-thickets sere,—
        With furtive scarlet. Through the hush benign
    One white-throat voices, till the stars appear,
        The benediction of the Thought Divine.

                        1890

LINES FOR THE TIMES

1   Now that Canadian barley can't go in,
     We fancy Uncle Sam may think it queer
That he with meaner stuff must fill his skin,
     While Brother Bull enjoys the better beer!

The Bird of Freedom stretched his mighty legs,
And eyed the duty on Canadian eggs.
"Children," he shrieked in ire, "it makes me ill!
What addled egg has hatched this monstrous Bill?"

Dear to the pampered tooth of Uncle Sam
10 Were savory baked-meats of Canadian lamb,
Till one McKinley, thinking to make clearer
The old man's duty, made his mutton dearer.

1890

IN THE WIDE AWE AND WISDOM OF THE NIGHT

1   In the wide awe and wisdom of the night
     I saw the round world rolling on its way,
Beyond significance of depth or height,
     Beyond the interchange of dark and day.
I marked the march to which is set no pause,
     And that stupendous orbit round whose rim
The great sphere sweeps, obedient unto laws
     That utter the eternal thought of Him.
I compassed time, outstripped the starry speed,
10   And in my still Soul apprehended space,
Till, weighing laws which these but blindly heed,
     At last I came before Him face to face,—
And knew the universe of no such span
As the august infinitude of man.

1890

QUEBEC, 1757

(From the French of Philippe Aubert de Gaspé)

1   An eagle city on her heights austere,
     Taker of tribute from the chainless flood,
She watches wave above her in the clear
     The whiteness of her banner purged with blood.

Near her grim citadel the blinding sheen
    Of her cathedral spire triumphant soars,
Rocked by the Angelus, whose peal serene
    Beats over Beaupré and the Lévis shores.

Tossed in his light craft on the dancing wave,
10   A stranger where he once victorious trod,
The passing Iroquois, fierce-eyed and grave,
    Frowns on the flag of France, the cross of God.

1890

THE AUTUMN THISTLES

1 The morning sky is white with mist, the earth
    White with the inspiration of the dew.
    The harvest light is on the hills anew,
And cheer in the grave acres' fruitful girth.
Only in this high pasture is there dearth,
    Where the grey thistles crowd in ranks austere,
    As if the sod, close-cropt for many a year,
Brought only bane and bitterness to birth.

But in the crisp air's amethystine wave
10   How the harsh stalks are washed with radiance now,
    How gleams the harsh turf where the crickets lie
Dew-freshened in their burnished armour brave!
    Since earth could not endure nor heaven allow
    Aught of unlovely in the morn's clear eye.

1891

NEW YEAR'S EVE

(After the French of Fréchette)

1 Ye night winds, shaking the weighted boughs
    Of snow-blanched hemlock and frosted fir,
While crackles sharply the thin crust under
    The passing feet of the wayfarer;

Ye night cries, pulsing in long-drawn waves
    Where beats the bitter tide to its flood,—
A tumult of pain, a rumour of sorrow,
    Troubling the starred night's tranquil mood;

Ye shudderings where, like a great beast bound,
10   The forest strains to its depths remote;
Be still and hark! From the high gray tower
    The great bell sobs in its brazen throat.

A strange voice out of the pallid heaven,
    Twelve sobs it utters and stops. Midnight!
'Tis the ominous *Hail!* and the stern *Farewell!*
    Of Past and Present in passing flight.

This moment, herald of hope and doom,
    That cries in our ears and then is gone,
Has marked for us in the awful volume
20   One step toward the infinite dark—or dawn!

A year is gone, and a year begins.
    Ye wise ones, knowing in Nature's scheme,
Oh tell us whither they go, the years
    That drop in the gulfs of time and dream!

They go to the goal of all things mortal,
    Where fade our destinies, scarce perceived,
To the dim abyss wherein time confounds them—
    The hours we laughed and the days we grieved.

They go where the bubbles of rainbow break—
30   We breathed in our youth of love and fame,
Where great and small are as one together
    And oak and windflower counted the same.

They go where follow our smiles and tears,
    The gold of youth and the gray of age,
Where falls the storm and falls the stillness,
    The laughter of spring and winter's rage.

What hand shall gauge the depth of time
    Or a little measure eternity?
God only, as they unroll before Him,
40   Conceives and orders the mystery.

1891

MOONLIGHT

1   The fifers of these amethystine fields,
     Whose far fine sound the night makes musical,
     Now while thou wak'st and longing would'st recall
   Joys that no rapture of remembrance yields,
   Voice to thy soul, lone-sitting deep within
     The still recesses of thine ecstasy,
     My love and my desire, that fain would fly
   With this far-silvering moon and fold thee in.

   But not for us the touch, the clasp, the kiss,
10   And for our restlessness no rest. In vain
     These aching lips, these hungering hearts that strain
   Toward the denied fruition of our bliss,
     Had love not learned of longing to devise
     Out of desire and dream our paradise.

                           1891

THE SALT FLATS

1   Here clove the keels of centuries ago
     Where now unvisited the flats lie bare.
     Here seethed the sweep of journeying waters, where
   No more the tumbling floods of Fundy flow,
   And only in the samphire pipes creep slow
     The salty currents of the sap. The air
     Hums desolately with wings that seaward fare,
   Over the lonely reaches beating low.

   The wastes of hard and meagre weeds are thronged
10 With murmurs of a past that time has wronged;
     And ghosts of many an ancient memory
   Dwell by the brackish pools and ditches blind,
   In these low-lying pastures of the wind,
     These marshes pale and meadows by the sea.

                           1891

FOR A BUST OF LANIER

To him the vision and the peace belong,
Who was high priest of music and of song.
Ministering where lesser lips forbear,
His soul an offering and his song a prayer.

1891

THE CLEARING

1   Stumps, and harsh rocks, and prostrate trunks all charred,
     And gnarled roots naked to the sun and rain,—
     They seem in their grim stillness to complain,
And by their plaint the evening peace is jarred.
These ragged acres fire and the axe have scarred,
     And many summers not assuaged their pain.
     In vain the pink and saffron light, in vain
The pale dew on the hillocks stripped and marred!

But here and there the waste is touched with cheer
10   Where spreads the fire-weed like a crimson flood
And venturous plumes of goldenrod appear;
     And round the blackened fence the great boughs lean
With comfort; and across the solitude
     The hermit's holy transport peals serene.

1891

GREY ROCKS AND GREYER SEA

1   Grey rocks, and greyer sea,
     And surf along the shore—
     And in my heart a name
     My lips shall speak no more.

The high and lonely hills
     Endure the darkening year—
     And in my heart endure
     A memory and a tear.

Across the tide a sail
10   That tosses, and is gone—
     And in my heart the kiss
     That longing dreams upon.

137

Grey rocks, and greyer sea,
   And surf along the shore—
And in my heart the face
   That I shall see no more.

1891

THE PEA-FIELDS

1   These are the fields of light, and laughing air,
   And yellow butterflies, and foraging bees,
   And whitish, wayward blossoms winged as these,
And pale green tangles like a seamaid's hair.
Pale, pale the blue, but pure beyond compare,
   And pale the sparkle of the far-off seas
   A-shimmer like these fluttering slopes of peas,
And pale the open landscape everywhere.

From fence to fence a perfumed **breath exhales**
10   O'er the bright pallor of the well-loved fields,—
My fields of Tantramar in summer-time;
   And, scorning the poor feed their pasture yields,
Up from the bushy lots the cattle climb
   To gaze with longing through the grey, mossed rails.

1891

THE HAWKBIT

1   How sweetly on the autumn scene,
When haws are red amid the green,
The hawkbit shines with face of cheer,
The favourite of the faltering year!

When days grow short and nights grow cold
How fairly gleams its eye of gold,
On pastured field and grassy hill,
Along the roadside and the rill!

It seems the spirit of a flower,
10   This offspring of the autumn hour,
Wandering back to earth to bring
Some kindly afterthought of spring.

A dandelion's ghost might so
Amid Elysian meadows blow,
Become more fragile and more fine
Breathing the atmosphere divine.

1891

MY TREES

1   At evening, when the winds are still,
     And wide the yellowing landscape glows,
My firwoods on the lonely hill
     Are crowned with sun and loud with crows.
Their flocks throng down the open sky
     From far salt flats and sedgy seas;
Then dusk and dewfall quench the cry,—
     So calm a home is in my trees.

At morning, when the young wind swings
10   The green slim tops and branches high,
Out puffs a noisy whirl of wings,
     Dispersing up the empty sky.
In this dear refuge no roof stops
     The skyward pinion winnowing through.
My trees shut out the world;—their tops
     Are open to the infinite blue.

1891

THE SILVER THAW

1   There came a day of showers
     Upon the shrinking snow.
The south wind sighed of flowers,
     The softening skies hung low.
Midwinter for a space
Foreshadowing April's face,
The white world caught the fancy,
     And would not let it go.

In reawakened courses
10   The brooks rejoiced the land.
We dreamed the Spring's shy forces
     Were gathering close at hand.

The dripping buds were stirred,
As if the sap had heard
The long-desired persuasion
    Of April's soft command.

But antic Time had cheated
    With hope's elusive gleam.
The phantom Spring, defeated,
20   Fled down the ways of dream.
And in the night the reign
Of Winter came again,
With frost upon the forest
    And stillness on the stream.

When morn in rose and crocus
    Came up the bitter sky,
Celestial beams awoke us
    To wondering ecstasy.
The wizard Winter's spell
30   Had wrought so passing well,
That earth was bathed in glory,
    As if God's smile were nigh.

The silvered saplings, bending,
    Flashed in a rain of gems.
The statelier trees, attending,
    Blazed in their diadems.
White fire and amethyst
All common things had kissed,
And chrysolites and sapphires
40   Adorned the bramble-stems.

In crystalline confusion
    All beauty came to birth.
It was a kind illusion
    To comfort waiting earth—
To bid the buds forget
The Spring so distant yet,
And hearts no more remember
    The iron season's dearth.

1892

THE BIRD'S SONG, THE SUN, AND THE WIND

The bird's song, the sun, and the wind—
   The wind that rushes, the sun that is still,
The song of the bird that sings alone,
   And wide light washing the lonely hill!

The spring's coming, the buds and the brooks—
   The brooks that clamour, the buds in the rain,
The coming of spring that comes unprayed for,
   And eyes that welcome it not for pain!

1892; 1892

THE LILY OF THE VALLEY

Did Winter, letting fall in vain regret
   A tear among the tender leaves of May,
Embalm the tribute, lest she might forget,
   In this elect, imperishable way?

Or did the virgin Spring sweet vigil keep
   In the white radiance of the midnight hour,
And whisper to the unwondering ear of sleep
   Some shy desire that turned into a flower?

1892

THE WILD-ROSE THICKET

1   Where humming flies frequent, and where
   Pink petals open to the air,

   The wild-rose thicket seems to be
   The summer in epitome.

   Amid its gold-green coverts meet
   The late dew and the noonday heat;

   Around it, to the sea-rim harsh,
   The patient levels of the marsh;

   And o'er it the pale heavens bent,
10   Half sufferance and half content.

1892

THE CANADA LILY

The northern summer, bright like flame,
Grew troubled at the tranquil core,
And from the sudden passion came
This blossom, blazoned as for war;
And as the tropic bloom unfurled,
Strange heats assailed our temperate world,
And o'er the burning petals drew
The heavens with a sultrier blue.

1892

O SOLITARY OF THE AUSTERE SKY

1 O Solitary of the austere sky,
    Pale presence of the unextinguished star,
That from thy station where the spheres wheel by,
    And quietudes of infinite patience are,
Watchest this wet, grey-visaged world emerge,—
    Cold pinnacle on pinnacle, and deep
On deep of ancient wood and wandering surge,—
    Out of the silence and the mists of sleep;
How small am I in thine august regard!
10   Invisible,—and yet I know my worth!
When comes the hour to break this prisoning shard,
    And reunite with Him that breathed me forth,
Then shall this atom of the Eternal Soul
Encompass thee in its benign control!

August 17, 1892; 1893

TO G. B. R.

1 How merry sings the aftermath,
    With crickets fifing in the dew!
The home-sweet sounds, the scene, the hour,
    I consecrate to you.

All this you knew and loved with me;
    All this in our delight had part;
And now—though us earth sees no more
    As comrades, heart to heart—

This kindly strength of open fields,
10   This faith of eve, this calm of air,
They lift my spirit close to you
    In memory and prayer.

August 19, 1892; 1893

THE HERMIT-THRUSH

1   Over the tops of the trees,
        And over the shallow stream,
    The shepherd of sunset frees
        The amber phantoms of dream[.]
    The time is the time of vision;
        The hour is the hour of calm;
    Hark! On the stillness Elysian
        Breaks how divine a psalm!
            Oh, clear in the sphere of the air,
10   *Clear, clear, tender and far,*
            Our aspiration of prayer
            Unto eve's clear star!

    O singer serene, secure!
        From thy throat of silver and dew
    What transport lonely and pure,
        Unchanging, endlessly new,—
    An unremembrance of mirth,
        And a contemplation of tears,
    As if the musing of earth
20   Communed with the dreams of the years!
            Oh, clear in the sphere of the air,
            Clear, clear, tender and far,
            Our aspiration of prayer
            Unto eve's clear star!

    O cloistral ecstatic! thy cell
        In the cool green aisles of the leaves
    Is the shrine of a power by whose spell
        Whoso hears aspires and believes!
    O hermit of evening! thine hour
30   Is the sacrament of desire,
    When love hath a heavenlier flower,
        And passion a holier fire!

Oh, clear in the sphere of the air,
Clear, clear, tender and far,
Our aspiration of prayer
Unto eve's clear star!

August 23, 1892; 1893

THE CRICKET

1   Oh, to be a cricket,
     That's the thing!
To scurry in the grass
     And to have one's fling!
And it's oh, to be a cricket
In the warm thistle-thicket,
     Where the sun-winds pass,
     Winds a-wing,
And the bumble-bees hang humming,
10   Hum and swing,
And the honey-drops are coming!

It's to be a summer rover,
     That can see a sweet, and pick it
     With the sting!
     Never mind the sting!

And it's oh, to be a cricket
     In the clover!
     A gay summer rover
In the warm thistle-thicket,
20   Where the honey-drops are coming,
Where the bumble-bees hang humming—
     That's the thing!

1892; 1896

AVE!

(An Ode for the Shelley Centenary, 1892)

I

1   O tranquil meadows, grassy Tantramar,
     Wide marshes ever washed in clearest air,
Whether beneath the sole and spectral star
     The dear severity of dawn you wear,

144

Or whether in the joy of ample day
    And speechless ecstasy of growing June
You lie and dream the long blue hours away
      Till nightfall comes too soon,
Or whether, naked to the unstarred night,
10 You strike with wondering awe my inward sight,—

II

You know how I have loved you, how my dreams
    Go forth to you with longing, though the years
That turn not back like your returning streams
    And fain would mist the memory with tears,
Though the inexorable years deny
    My feet the fellowship of your deep grass,
O'er which, as o'er another, tenderer sky,
      Cloud phantoms drift and pass,—
You know my confident love, since first, a child,
20 Amid your wastes of green I wandered wild.

III

Inconstant, eager, curious, I roamed;
    And ever your long reaches lured me on;
And ever o'er my feet your grasses foamed,
    And in my eyes your far horizons shone.
But sometimes would you (as a stillness fell
    And on my pulse you laid a soothing palm)
Instruct my ears in your most secret spell;
      And sometimes in the calm
Initiate my young and wondering eyes
30 Until my spirit grew more still and wise.

IV

Purged with high thoughts and infinite desire
    I entered fearless the most holy place,
Received between my lips the secret fire,
    The breath of inspiration on my face.
But not for long these rare illumined hours,
    The deep surprise and rapture not for long.
Again I saw the common, kindly flowers,
      Again I heard the song
Of the glad bobolink, whose lyric throat
40 Pealed like a tangle of small bells afloat.

The pounce of mottled marsh-hawk on his prey;
    The flicker of sand-pipers in from sea
In gusty flocks that puffed and fled; the play
    Of field-mice in the vetches,—these to me
Were memorable events. But most availed
    Your strange unquiet waters to engage
My kindred heart's companionship; nor failed
      To grant this heritage,—
That in my veins forever must abide
50   The urge and fluctuation of the tide.

VI

The mystic river whence you take your name,
    River of hubbub, raucous Tantramar,
Untamable and changeable as flame,
    It called me and compelled me from afar,
Shaping my soul with its impetuous stress.
    When in its gaping channel deep withdrawn
Its waves ran crying of the wilderness
      And winds and stars and dawn,
How I companioned them in speed sublime,
60   Led out a vagrant on the hills of Time!

VII

And when the orange flood came roaring in
    From Fundy's tumbling troughs and tide-worn caves,
While red Minudie's flats were drowned with din
    And rough Chignecto's front oppugned the waves,
How blithely with the refluent foam I raced
    Inland along the radiant chasm, exploring
The green solemnity with boisterous haste;
      My pulse of joy outpouring
To visit all the creeks that twist and shine
70   From Beauséjour to utmost Tormentine.

VIII

And after, when the tide was full, and stilled
    A little while the seething and the hiss,
And every tributary channel filled
    To the brim with rosy streams that swelled to kiss
The grass-roots all awash and goose-tongue wild

And salt-sap rosemary,—then how well content
I was to rest me like a breathless child
     With play-time rapture spent,—
To lapse and loiter till the change should come
80   And the great floods turn seaward, roaring home.

                    IX

And now, O tranquill marshes, in your vast
     Serenity of vision and of dream,
Wherethrough by every intricate vein have passed
     With joy impetuous and pain supreme
The sharp, fierce tides that chafe the shores of earth
     In endless and controlless ebb and flow,
Strangely akin you seem to him whose birth
          One hundred years ago
With fiery succour to the ranks of song
90   Defied the ancient gates of wrath and wrong.

                    X

Like yours, O marshes, his compassionate breast,
     Wherein abode all dreams of love and peace,
Was tortured with perpetual unrest.
     Now loud with flood, now languid with release,
Now poignant with the lonely ebb, the strife
     Of tides from the salt sea of human pain
That hiss along the perilous coasts of life
          Beat in his eager brain;
But all about the tumult of his heart
100 Stretched the great calm of his celestial art.

                    XI

Therefore with no far flight, from Tantramar
     And my still world of ecstasy, to thee,
Shelley, to thee I turn, the avatar
     Of Song, Love, Dream, Desire, and Liberty;
To thee I turn with reverent hands of prayer
     And lips that fain would ease my heart of praise,
Whom chief of all whose brows prophetic wear
          The pure and sacred bays
I worship, and have worshipped since the hour
110 When first I felt thy bright and chainless power.

XII

About thy sheltered cradle in the green
    Untroubled groves of Sussex, brooded forms
That to the mother's eye remained unseen,—
    Terrors and ardours, passionate hopes, and storms
Of fierce retributive fury, such as jarred
    Ancient and sceptred creeds, and cast down kings,
And oft the holy cause of Freedom marred
        With lust of meaner things,
With guiltless blood, and many a frenzied crime
120   Dared in the face of unforgetful Time.

XIII

The star that burns on revolution smote
    Wild heats and change on thine ascendant sphere,
Whose influence thereafter seemed to float
    Through many a strange eclipse of wrath and fear,
Dimming awhile the radiance of thy love.
    But still supreme in thy nativity,
All dark, invidious aspects far above,
        Beamed one clear orb for thee,—
The star whose ministrations just and strong
130   Controlled the tireless flight of Dante's song.

XIV

With how august contrition, and what tears
    Of penitential, unavailing shame,
Thy venerable foster-mother hears
    The sons of song impeach her ancient name,
Because in one rash hour of anger blind
    She thrust thee forth in exile, and thy feet
Too soon to earth's wild outer ways consigned,—
        Far from her well-loved seat,
Far from her studious halls and storied towers
140   And weedy Isis winding through his flowers.

XV

And thou, thenceforth the breathless child of change,
    Thine own Alastor, on an endless quest
Of unimagined loveliness didst range,
    Urged ever by the soul's divine unrest.

Of that high quest and that unrest divine
  Thy first immortal music thou didst make,
Inwrought with fairy Alp, and Reuss, and Rhine,
  And phantom seas that break
In soundless foam along the shores of Time,
150 Prisoned in thine imperishable rhyme.

XVI

Thyself the lark melodious in mid-heaven;
  Thyself the Protean shape of chainless cloud,
Pregnant with elemental fire, and driven
  Through deeps of quivering light, and darkness loud
With tempest, yet beneficent as prayer;
  Thyself the wild west wind, relentless strewing
The withered leaves of custom on the air,
  And through the wreck pursuing
O'er lovelier Arnos, more imperial Romes,
160 Thy radiant visions to their viewless homes.

XVII

And when thy mightiest creation thou
  Wert fain to body forth,—the dauntless form,
The all-enduring, all-forgiving brow
  Of the great Titan, flinchless in the storm
Of pangs unspeakable and nameless hates,
  Yet rent by all the wrongs and woes of men,
And triumphing in his pain, that so their fates
  Might be assuaged,—oh then
Out of that vast compassionate heart of thine
170 Thou wert constrained to shape the dream benign.

XVIII

—O Baths of Caracalla, arches clad
  In such transcendent rhapsodies of green
That one might guess the sprites of spring were glad
  For your majestic ruin, yours the scene,
The illuminating air of sense and thought;
  And yours the enchanted light, O skies of Rome,
Where the giant vision into form was wrought;
  Beneath your blazing dome
The intensest song our language ever knew
180 Beat up exhaustless to the blinding blue!—

149

XIX

The domes of Pisa and her towers superb,
   The myrtles and the ilexes that sigh
O'er San Giuliano, where no jars disturb
   The lonely aziola's evening cry,
The Serchio's sun-kissed waters,—these conspired
   With Plato's theme occult, with Dante's calm
Rapture of mystic love, and so inspired
      Thy soul's espousal psalm,
A strain of such elect and pure intent
190   It breathes of a diviner element.

XX

Thou on whose lips the word of Love became
   A rapt evangel to assuage all wrong,
Not Love alone, but the austerer name
   Of Death engaged the splendours of thy song.
The luminous grief, the spacious consolation
   Of thy supreme lament, that mourned for him
Too early haled to that still habitation
      Beneath the grass-roots dim,—
Where his faint limbs and pain-o'erwearied heart
200   Of all earth's loveliness became a part,

XXI

But where, thou sayest, himself would not abide,—
   Thy solemn incommunicable joy
Announcing Adonais has not died,
   Attesting death to free but not destroy,
All this was as thy swan-song mystical.
   Even while the note serene was on thy tongue
Thin grew the veil of the Invisible,
      The white sword nearer swung,—
And in the sudden wisdom of thy rest
210   Thou knewest all thou hadst but dimly guessed.

XXII

Lament, Lerici, mourn for the world's loss!
   Mourn that pure light of song extinct at noon!
Ye waves of Spezzia that shine and toss
   Repent that sacred flame you quenched too soon!

Mourn, Mediterranean waters, mourn
    In affluent purple down your golden shore!
Such strains as his, whose voice you stilled in scorn,
    Our ears may greet no more,
Unless at last to that far sphere we climb
220   Where he completes the wonder of his rhyme!

                    XXIII

How like a cloud she fled, thy fateful bark,
    From eyes that watched to hearts that waited, till
Up from the ocean roared the tempest dark—
    And the wild heart Love waited for was still!
Hither and thither in the slow, soft tide,
    Rolled seaward, shoreward, sands and wandering shells
And shifting weeds thy fellows, thou didst hide
        Remote from all farewells,
Nor felt the sun, nor heard the fleeting rain,
230   Nor heeded Casa Magni's quenchless pain.

                    XXIV

Thou heedest not? Nay, for it was not thou,
    That blind, mute clay relinquished by the waves
Reluctantly at last, and slumbering now
    In one of kind earth's most compassionate graves!
Not thou, not thou,—for thou wert in the light
    Of the Unspeakable, where time is not.
Thou sawest those tears; but in thy perfect sight
        And thy eternal thought
Were they not even now all wiped away
240   In the reunion of the infinite day!

                    XXV

There face to face thou sawest the living God
    And worshippedst, beholding Him the same
Adored on earth as Love, the same whose rod
    Thou hadst endured as Life, whose secret name
Thou now didst learn, the healing name of Death.
    In that unroutable profound of peace,
Beyond experience of pulse and breath,
        Beyond the last release
Of longing, rose to greet thee all the lords
250   Of Thought, with consummation in their words:

XXVI

He of the seven cities claimed, whose eyes,
    Though blind, saw gods and heroes, and the fall
Of Ilium, and many alien skies,
    And Circe's Isle; and he whom mortals call
The Thunderous, who sang the Titan bound
    As thou the Titan victor; the benign
Spirit of Plato; Job; and Judah's crowned
        Singer and seer divine;
Omar; the Tuscan; Milton, vast and strong;
260   And Shakespeare, captain of the host of Song.

XXVII

Back from the underworld of whelming change
    To the wide-glittering beach thy body came;
And thou didst contemplate with wonder strange
    And curious regard thy kindred flame,
Fed sweet with frankincense and wine and salt,
    With fierce purgation search thee, soon resolving
Thee to the elements of the airy vault
        And the far spheres revolving,
The common waters, the familiar woods,
270   And the great hills' inviolate solitudes.

XXVIII

Thy close companions there officiated
    With solemn mourning and with mindful tears,—
The pained, imperious wanderer unmated
    Who voiced the wrath of those rebellious years;
Trelawney, lion-limbed and high of heart;
    And he, that gentlest sage and friend most true,
Whom Adonais loved. With these bore part
        One grieving ghost, that flew
Hither and thither through the smoke unstirred
280   In wailing semblance of a wild white bird.

XXIX

O heart of fire, that fire might not consume,
    Forever glad the world because of thee;
Because of thee forever eyes illume
    A more enchanted earth, a lovelier sea!

O poignant voice of the desire of life,
   Piercing our lethargy, because thy call
Aroused our spirits to a nobler strife
   Where base and sordid fall,
Forever past the conflict and the pain
290   More clearly beams the goal we shall attain!

XXX

And now once more, O marshes, back to you
   From whatsoever wanderings, near or far,
To you I turn with joy forever new,
   To you, O sovereign vasts of Tantramar!
Your tides are at the full. Your wizard flood,
   With every tribute stream and brimming creek,
Ponders, possessor of the utmost good,
   With no more left to seek,—
But the hour wanes and passes; and once more
300   Resounds the ebb with destiny in its roar.

XXXI

So might some lord of men, whom force and fate
   And his great heart's unvanquishable power
Have thrust with storm to his supreme estate,
   Ascend by night his solitary tower
High o'er the city's lights and cries uplift.
   Silent he ponders the scrolled heaven to read
And the keen stars' conflicting message sift,
   Till the slow signs recede,
And ominously scarlet dawns afar
310   The day he leads his legions forth to war.

October 29, 1892; 1892

EPITAPH FOR A SAILOR BURIED ASHORE

1   He who but yesterday would roam
     Careless as clouds and currents range,
   In homeless wandering most at home,
     Inhabiter of change;

   Who wooed the west to win the east,
     And named the stars of North and South,
   And felt the zest of Freedom's feast
     Familiar in his mouth;

153

Who found a faith in stranger speech,
10   And fellowship in foreign hands,
And had within his eager reach
    The relish of all lands—

How circumscribed a plot of earth
    Keeps now his restless footsteps still,
Whose wish was wide as ocean's girth,
    Whose will the water's will!

1892

BRINGING HOME THE COWS

1   When potatoes were in blossom,
    When the new hay filled the mows,
Sweet the paths we trod together,
    Bringing home the cows.

What a purple kissed the pasture,
    Kissed and blessed the alder-boughs,
As we wandered slow at sundown,
    Bringing home the cows!

How the far-off hills were gilded
10   With the light that dream allows,
As we built our hopes beyond them,
    Bringing home the cows!

How our eyes were bright with visions,
    What a meaning wreathed our brows,
As we watched the cranes, and lingered,
    Bringing home the cows!

Past the years, and through the distance,
    Throbs the memory of our vows.
Oh, that we again were children,
20   Bringing home the cows!

1893

THE CICADA IN THE FIRS

1   Charm of the vibrant, white September sun—
      How tower the firs to take it, tranced and still!
      Their scant ranks crown the pale, round pasture-hill,
And watch, far down, the austere waters run
Their circuit thro' the serious marshes dun.
      No bird-call stirs the blue; but strangely thrill
      The blunt-faced, brown cicada's wing-notes shrill,
A web of silver o'er the silence spun.

      O zithern-winged musician, whence it came
10   I wonder, this insistent song of thine!
      Did once the highest string of Summer's lyre,
Snapt on some tense chord slender as a flame,
      Take form again in these vibrations fine
      That o'er the tranquill spheres of noon aspire?

                          1893

WHITEWATERS

1   Beside the wharf at Whitewaters
    The loitering ebb with noon confers;
    And o'er the amber flats there seems
    A sleep to brood of sun and dreams.

    The white and clustering cottages,
    Thick shadowed by their windless trees,
    Inhabit such a calm, that change
    Goes by and lets her face grow strange.

    And not far off, on tiptoe seen,
10   The brown dyke and the sky between,
    A shifting field that heaves and slides,—
    The blue breast of the Minas tides.

    A-through the little harbour go
    The currents of the scant Pereau,
    Drawn slowly, drawn from springs unseen
    Amid the marsh's vasts of green.

    Up from the wharf at Whitewaters,
    Where scarce a slim sandpiper stirs,
    A yellow roadway climbs, that feels
20   Few footsteps and infrequent wheels.

It climbs to meet the westering sun
Upon the heights of Blomidon,—
Bulwark of peace, whose bastioned form
Out-bars the serried hosts of storm.

. . . .

Down to the wharf at Whitewaters,
The children of the villagers
One drowsy, windless hour of noon
Deep in the green mid-heart of June,

Like swallows to a sunset pool
30   Came chattering, just let loose from school;
And with them one small lad of four,
Picked up as they flocked past his door.

His sea-blue, merry eyes, his hair
Curling and like the corn-silk fair,
His red, sweet mouth, made Hally Clive
Comely as any lad alive.

His father, master of *The Foam,*
Drave his tight craft afar from home.
His mother—peaceful life was hers
40   With Hally, safe in Whitewaters.

And in his sun-brown arms the boy
Carried his last, most cherished toy;
A small white kitten, free from fleck,
With a blue ribbon round its neck.

In the old timbers lapping cool,
About the wharf the tide hung full;
And at the wharf-side, just afloat,
Swung lazily an old grey boat.

About the froth-white water's edge,
50   The weedy planks, the washing sedge,
And in and out the rocking craft,
The children clambered, splashed, and laughed,

Till presently, grown tired of play,
Up the bright road they raced away;
But in the boat, a drowsy heap,
Curled boy and kitten, sound asleep.

Warm in the sunny boat they slept.
Soon to its ebb the slow tide crept.
By stealthy fingers, soft as dream,
60   The boat was lured into the stream.

Out from the wharf it slipped and swung—
On the old rope one moment hung—
Then snapped its tether and away
For the storm-beaten outer bay.

In Whitewaters, in Whitewaters,
No watcher heeds, no rescuer stirs.
Out from the port the currents sweep
With Hally, smiling in his sleep.

An hour they drifted, till the boat
70   From the low shore one scarce might note.
The kitten climbed the prow, and mewed
Against the watery solitude.

Then Hally woke, and stared with eyes
Grown round and dark with grieved surprise.
Where were the children gone? And where
The grey old wharf, the weedy stair?

Bewildered, and but half awake,
He sobbed as if his heart would break;
Then, as his lonely terror grew,
80   Down in the boat himself he threw,

And passionately for comfort pressed
The kind white kitten to his breast.
Through the thin plank his hand could feel
The little eddies clutch the keel.

Lost and alone, lost and alone,
He heard the long wave hiss and moan,
He heard the wild ebb seethe and mourn
Along the outer shoals forlorn.

And now a wind that chafed the flood
90   Blew down from Noel's haunted wood;
And now in the dread tides that run
Past the grim front of Blomidon,

Over the rolling troughs, between
The purple gulfs, the slopes of green,
With sickening glide and sullen rest
The old boat climbed from crest to crest.

.   .   .   .

That day in his good ship, *The Foam,*
Shipmaster Clive was speeding home;
His heart was light, his eyes elate;
100 His voyage had been fortunate.

"If the wind holds," said he, "to-night
We'll anchor under Kingsport Light;—
I'll change the fogs of Fundy wild
For Whitewaters and wife and child."

He marked the drifting boat, and laughed,
"What clumsy lubber's lost his craft?"
"What's that that walks the gunwale?" cried
A sailor leaning o'er the side.

The captain raised his glass. Said he:
110 "A kitten! Some one's pet, maybe!
We'll give it passage in *The Foam*"—
Soft is the heart that's bound for home!

"Stop for a kitten?" growled the mate:
"Look to the sun; we're getting late!
If we lose this tack we'll lie to-night
A long ways off o' Kingsport Light."

The captain paused irresolute
"To leave the helpless little brute
To the wrecked seaman's death accurst,
120 The slow, fierce hunger, the mad thirst.—

"I wish not my worst enemy
Such death as that! Lay to!" said he.
The ship came up into the wind;
The slackening canvas flapped and dinned;

And the ship's boat with scant delay
Was swung and lowered and away,—
The captain at the helm, and four
Stout men of Avon at the oar.

They neared the drifting craft; and when
130 They bumped against her gunwale, then
Hally upraised his tumbled head!
"My God! My boy!" the captain said.

. . . .

And now with bellying sails *The Foam*
Up the tossed flood went straining home;
The wind blew fair; she lay that night
At anchor under Kingsport Light.

And late that night in gladness deep,
Sank father, mother, child, to sleep,—
Where no storm breaks, nor terror stirs
140 The peace of God in Whitewaters.

by November, 1893; 1896

BUCKWHEAT

1 This smell of home and honey on the breeze,
    This shimmer of sunshine woven in white and pink
    That comes a dream from memory's visioned brink,
Sweet, sweet and strange across the ancient trees,—
It is the buckwheat, boon of the later bees,
    Its breadths of heavy-headed bloom appearing
    Amid the blackened stumps of this high clearing,
Freighted with cheer of comforting auguries.

But when the blunt, brown grain and red-ripe sheaves,
10 Brimming the low log barn beyond the eaves,
    Crisped by the first frost, feel the thresher's flail,
Then flock the blue wild-pigeons in shy haste
    All silently down Autumn's amber trail,
To glean at dawn the chill and whitening waste.

1893

CANADIAN STREAMS

1 O rivers rolling to the sea
From lands that bear the maple-tree,
    How swell your voices with the strain
Of loyalty and liberty!

A holy music, heard in vain
By coward heart and sordid brain,
   To whom this strenuous being seems
Naught but a greedy race for gain.

O unsung streams—not splendid themes
10   Ye lack to fire your patriot dreams!
   Annals of glory gild your waves,
Hope freights your tides, Canadian streams!

St. Lawrence, whose wide water laves
The shores that ne'er have nourished slaves!
   Swift Richelieu of lilied fame!
Niagara of glorious graves!

Thy rapids, Ottawa, proclaim
Where Daulac and his heroes came!
   Thy tides, St. John, declare La Tour,
20   And, later, many a loyal name!

Thou inland stream, whose vales, secure
From storm, Tecumseh's death made poor!
   And thou small water, red with war,
'Twixt Beaubassin and Beauséjour!

Dread Saguenay, where eagles soar,
What voice shall from the bastioned shore
   The tale of Roberval reveal,
Or his mysterious fate deplore?

Annapolis, do thy floods yet feel
30   Faint memories of Champlain's keel,
   Thy pulses yet the deeds repeat
Of Poutrincourt and D'Iberville?

And thou far tide, whose plains now beat
With march of myriad westering feet,
   Saskatchewan, whose virgin sod
So late Canadian blood made sweet?

Your bulwark hills, your valleys broad,
Streams where De Salaberry trod,
   Where Wolfe achieved, where Brock was slain,—
40   Your voices are the voice of God!

160

O sacred waters! not in vain,
Across Canadian height and plain,
Ye sound us in triumphant tone
The summons of your high refrain.

1893

THE CHOPPING BEE

1   The morning star was bitter bright, the morning sky was grey;
  And we hitched our teams and started for the woods at break of day.
    Oh, the frost is on the forest, and the snow piles high!

Along the white and winding road the sled-bells jangled keen
Between the buried fences, the billowy drifts between.
    Oh, merry swing the axes, and the bright chips fly!

So crisp sang the runners, and so swift the horses sped,
That the woods were all about us ere the sky grew red.
    Oh, the frost is on the forest, and the snow piles high!

10   The bark hung ragged on the birch, the lichen on the fir,
  The lungwort fringed the maple, and grey moss the juniper.
    Oh, merry swing the axes, and the bright chips fly!

So still the air and chill the air the branches seemed asleep,
But we broke their ancient visions as the axe bit deep.
    Oh, the frost is on the forest, and the snow piles high!

With the shouts of the choppers and the barking of their blades
How rang the startled valleys and the rabbit-haunted glades!
    Oh, merry swing the axes, and the bright chips fly!

The hard wood and the soft wood, we felled them for our use;
20   And chiefly, for its scented gum, we loved the scaly spruce;
    Oh, the frost is on the forest, and the snow piles high!

And here and there, with solemn roar, some hoary tree came down,
And we heard the rolling of the years in the thunder of its crown.
    Oh, merry swing the axes, and the bright chips fly!

So, many a sled was loaded up above the stake-tops soon;
And many a load was at the farm before the horn of noon;
    Oh, the frost is on the forest, and the snow piles high!

And ere we saw the sundown all yellow through the trees,
The farmyard stood as thick with wood as a buckwheat patch with bees;
30   *Oh, merry swing the axes, and the bright chips fly!*

And with the last-returning teams, and axes burnished bright,
We left the woods to slumber in the frosty shadowed night.
    Oh, the frost is on the forest, and the snow piles high!

And then the wide, warm kitchen, with beams across the ceiling,
Thick hung with red-skinned onions, and homely herbs of healing.
    Oh, merry swing the axes, and the bright chips fly!

The dishes on the dresser-shelves were shining blue and white,
And o'er the loaded table the lamps beamed bright.
    Oh, the frost is on the forest, and the snow piles high!

40 Then, how the ham and turkey and the apple-sauce did fly,
The heights of boiled potatoes and the flats of pumpkinpie!
    Oh, merry swing the axes, and the bright chips fly!

With bread-and-cheese and doughnuts fit to feed a farm a year!
And we washed them down with tides of tea and oceans of spruce beer.
    Oh, the frost is on the forest, and the snow piles high!

At last the pipes were lighted and the chairs pushed back,
And Bill struck up a sea-song on a rather risky tack;
    Oh, merry swing the axes, and the bright chips fly!

And the girls all thought it funny—but they never knew 't was worse,
50 For we gagged him with a doughnut at the famous second verse.
    Oh, the frost is on the forest, and the snow piles high!

Then someone fetched a fiddle, and we shoved away the table,
And 't was jig and reel and polka just as long as we were able,
    Oh, merry swing the axes, and the bright chips fly!

Till at last the girls grew sleepy, and we got our coats to go.
We started off with racing-teams and moonlight on the snow;
    Oh, the frost is on the forest, and the snow piles high!

And soon again the winter world was voiceless as of old,
Alone with all the wheeling stars, and the great white cold.
60   *Oh, the frost is on the forest, and the snow piles high!*

1893

THE COW PASTURE

1   I see the harsh, wind-ridden, eastward hill,
      By the red cattle pastured, blanched with dew;
      The small, mossed hillocks where the clay gets through;
  The grey webs woven on milkweed tops at will.
  The sparse, pale grasses flicker, and are still.
      The empty flats yearn seaward. All the view
      Is naked to the horizon's utmost blue;
  And the bleak spaces stir me with strange thrill.

  Not in perfection dwells the subtler power
10   To pierce our mean content, but rather works
      Through incompletion, and the need that irks,—
  Not in the flower, but effort toward the flower.
      When the want stirs, when the soul's cravings urge,
      The strong earth strengthens, and the clean heavens purge.

1893

THE HERRING WEIR

1   Back to the green deeps of the outer bay
      The red and amber currents glide and cringe,
      Diminishing behind a luminous fringe
  Of cream-white surf and wandering wraiths of spray.
  Stealthily, in the old reluctant way,
      The red flats are uncovered, mile on mile,
      To glitter in the sun a golden while.
  Far down the flats, a phantom sharply grey,

  The herring weir emerges, quick with spoil.
10   Slowly the tide forsakes it. Then **draws** near,
      Descending from the farm-house on the height,
  A cart, with gaping tubs. The oxen toil
      Sombrely o'er the level to the weir,
      And drag a long black trail across the light.

1893

IN AN OLD BARN

1   Tons upon tons the brown-green fragrant hay
      O'erbrims the mows beyond the time-warped eaves,
      Up to the rafters where the spider weaves,
Though few flies wander his secluded way.
Through a high chink one lonely golden ray,
      Wherein the dust is dancing, slants unstirred.
      In the dry hush some rustlings light are heard,
Of winter-hidden mice at furtive play.

Far down, the cattle in their shadowed stalls,
10   Nose-deep in clover fodder's meadowy scent,
      Forget the snows that whelm their pasture streams,
The frost that bites the world beyond their walls.
      Warm housed, they dream of summer, well content
      In day-long contemplation of their dreams.

1893

INDIAN SUMMER

1   What touch hath set the breathing hills afire
      With amethyst, to quench them with a tear
      Of ecstasy? These common fields appear
The consecrated home of hopes past number.
So many visions, so entranced a slumber,
      Such dreams possess the noonday's luminous sphere,
      That earth, content with knowing heaven so near,
Hath done with aspiration and desire.

In these unlooked-for hours of Truth's clear reign
10   Unjarring fitness hath surprised our strife.
This radiance, that might seem to cheat the view
      With loveliness too perfect to be true,
      But shows this vexed and self-delusive life
Ideals whereto our Real must attain.

1893

MARSYAS

1   A little grey hill-glade, close-turfed, withdrawn
Beyond resort or heed of trafficking feet,
Ringed round with slim trunks of the mountain ash.
Through the slim trunks and scarlet bunches flash—
Beneath the clear chill glitterings of the dawn—
Far off, the crests, where down the rosy shore
The Pontic surges beat.
The plains lie dim below. The thin airs wash
The circuit of the autumn-coloured hills,
10 And this high glade, whereon
The satyr pipes, who soon shall pipe no more.
He sits against the beech-tree's mighty bole,—
He leans, and with persuasive breathing fills
The happy shadows of the slant-set lawn.
The goat-feet fold beneath a gnarléd root;
And sweet, and sweet the note that steals and thrills
From slender stops of that shy flute.
Then to the goat-feet comes the wide-eyed fawn
Hearkening; the rabbits fringe the glade, and lay
20 Their long ears to the sound;
In the pale boughs the partridge gather round,
And quaint hern from the sea-green river reeds;
The wild ram halts upon a rocky horn
O'erhanging; and, unmindful of his prey,
The leopard steals with narrowed lids to lay
His spotted length along the ground.
The thin airs wash, the thin clouds wander by,
And those hushed listeners move not. All the morn
He pipes, soft-swaying, and with half-shut eye,
30 In rapt content of utterance,—
                              nor heeds
The young god standing in his branchy place,
The languor on his lips, and in his face,
Divinely inaccessible, the scorn.

1893

MIDWINTER THAW

1   How shrink the snows upon this upland field,
      Under the dove-grey dome of brooding noon!
      They shrink with soft reluctant shocks, and soon
In sad brown ranks the furrows lie revealed.
From radiant cisterns of the frost unsealed
      Now wakes through all the air a watery rune—
      The babble of a million brooks atune,
In fairy conduits of blue ice concealed.

     Noisy with crows, the wind-break on the hill
10   Counts o'er its buds for summer. In the air
Some shy foreteller prophesies with skill—
      Some voyaging ghost of bird, some effluence rare;
And the stall-wearied cattle dream their fill
      Of deep June pastures where the pools are fair.

                       1893

THE OAT-THRESHING

1   A little brown old homestead, bowered in trees
      That o'er the autumn landscape shine afar,
      Burning with amber and with cinnabar.
A yellow hillside washed in airy seas
Of azure, where the swallow drops and flees.
      Midway the slope, clear in the beaming day,
      A barn by many seasons beaten grey,
Big with the gain of prospering husbandries.

     In billows round the wide red welcoming doors
10   High piles the golden straw; while from within,
      Where plods the team amid the chaffy din,
The loud pulsation of the thresher soars,
      Persistent as if earth could not let cease
      This happy proclamation of her peace.

                       1893

OH, PURPLE HANG THE PODS!

1   Oh, purple hang the pods
      On the green locust-tree,
And yellow turn the sods
      On a grave that's dear to me!

And blue, softly blue,
      The hollow autumn sky,
With its birds flying through
      To where the sun-lands lie!

In the sun-lands they'll bide
10   While winter's on the tree;—
And oh, that I might hide
      The grave that's dear to me!

1893

PROLOGUE

1   Across the fog the moon lies fair.
      Transfused with ghostly amethyst,
O white Night, charm to wonderment
      The cattle in the mist!

Thy touch, O grave Mysteriarch,
      Makes dull, familiar things divine.
O grant of thy revealing gift
      Be some small portion mine!

Make thou my vision sane and clear,
10   That I may see what beauty clings
In common forms, and find the soul
      Of unregarded things!

1893

THE PUMPKINS IN THE CORN

1   Amber and blue, the smoke behind the hill,
      Where in the glow fades out the morning star,
      Curtains the autumn cornfield, sloped afar,
And strikes an acrid savour on the chill.

The hilltop fence shines saffron o'er the still
  Unbending ranks of bunched and bleaching corn,
    And every pallid stalk is crisp with morn,
Crisp with the silver autumn morns distil.

Purple the narrowing alleys stretched between
10   The spectral shooks, a purple harsh and cold,
      But spotted, where the gadding pumpkins run,
With bursts of blaze that startle the serene
    Like sudden voices,—globes of orange bold,
      Elate to mimic the unrisen sun.

1893

THE SUCCOUR OF GLUSKÂP

(*A Melicite Legend*)

1   The happy valley laughed with sun,
      The corn grew firm in stalk,
    The lodges clustered safe where run
      The streams of Peniawk.

    The washing-pools and shallows rang
      With shout of lads at play;
    At corn-hoeing the women sang;
      The warriors were away.

    The splashed white pebbles on the beach,
10   The idling paddles, gleamed;
    Before the lodge doors, spare of speech,
      The old men basked and dreamed.

    And when the windless noon grew hot,
      And the white sun beat like steel,
    In shade about the simmering pot
      They gathered to their meal.

    Then from the hills, on flying feet,
      A desperate runner came,
    With cry that smote the peaceful street,
20   And slew the peace with shame.

    "Trapped in the night, and snared in sleep,
      Our warriors wake no more!
    Up from Wahloos the Mohawks creep—
      Their feet are at the door!"

The grey old sachems rose and mocked
　　The ruin that drew near;
And down the beach the children flocked,
　　And women wild with fear.

Launched were the red canoes; when, lo!
30　　Beside them Gluskâp stood,
Appearing with his giant bow
　　From out his mystic wood.

With quiet voice he called them back,
　　And comforted their fears;
He swore the lodges should not lack,
　　He dried the children's tears;

Till sorrowing mothers almost deemed
　　The desperate runner lied,
And the tired children slept, and dreamed
40　　Their fathers had not died.

That night behind the mystic wood
　　The Mohawk warriors crept;
A spell went through the solitude
　　And stilled them, and they slept.

And when the round moon, rising late,
　　The Hills of Kawlm had crossed,
She saw the camp of Mohawk hate
　　Swathed in a great white frost.

At morn, behind the mystic wood
50　　Came Gluskâp, bow in hand,
And marked the ice-bound solitude,
　　And that unwaking band.

But as he gazed his lips grew mild,
　　For, safe among the dead,
There played a ruddy, laughing child
　　By a captive mother's head;

And child and mother, nestling warm,
　　Scarce knew their foes had died,
As past their sleep the noiseless storm
60　　Of strange death turned aside.

1893?

THE TIDE ON TANTRAMAR

1 Tantramar! Tantramar!
    I see thy cool green plains afar.
    Thy dykes where grey sea-grasses are,
        Mine eyes behold them yet.

But not the gladness breathed of old
Thy bordering, blue hill-hollows hold;
Thy wind-blown leagues of green unrolled,
    Thy flats the red floods fret,

Thy steady-streaming winds—no more
10 These work the rapture wrought of yore,
When all thy wide bright strength outbore
    My soul from fleshly bar.

A darkness as of drifted rain
Is over tide, and dyke, and plain.
The shadow-pall of human pain
    Is fallen on Tantramar.

II

A little garden gay with phlox,
Blue corn-flowers, yellow hollyhocks,
Red poppies, pink and purple stocks,
20   Looks over Tantramar.

Pale yellow drops the road before
The hospitable cottage-door,—
A yellow, upland road, and o'er
The green marsh seeks the low red shore
    And winding dykes afar.

Beyond the marsh, and miles away,
The great tides of the tumbling bay
Swing glittering in the golden day,
    Swing foaming to and fro;

30 And nearer, in a nest of green,
A little turbid port is seen,
Where pitch-black fishing-boats careen,
    Left when the tide runs low.

The little port is safe and fit.
About its wharf the plover flit,
The grey net-reels loom over it,
    With grass about their feet.

In wave and storm it hath no part,
This harbour in the marshes' heart;
Behind its dykes, at peace, apart
    It hears the surges beat.

40

The garden hollyhocks are tall;
They tower above the garden wall,
And see, far down, the port, and all
    The creeks, and marshes wide;

But Margery, Margery,
'T is something further thou wouldst see!
Bid all thy blooms keep watch with thee
    Across the outmost tide.

Bid them keep wide their starry eyes
To warn thee should a white sail rise,
Slow climbing up, from alien skies,
    The azure round of sea.

50

He sails beneath a stormy star;
The waves are wild, the Isles afar;
Summer is ripe on Tantramar,
    And yet returns not he.

Long, long thine eyes have watched in vain,
Waited in fear, and wept again.
Is it no more than lovers' pain
    That makes thy heart so wild?

60

At dreams within the cottage door
The old man's eyes are lingering o'er
The little port,—the far-off shore,—
    His dear and only child.

And at her spinning-wheel within
The mother's hands forget to spin.
With loving voice she calls thee in,—
    Her dear and only child.

70 To leave the home-dear hearts to ache
Was not for thee, though thine should break.
For their dear sake, for their dear sake,
    Thou wouldst not go with him.

But always wise, and strong, and free,
Is given to which of us to be?
A gathering shadow, Margery,
    Makes all thy daylight dim!

Yet surely soon will break the day
For which thine anxious waitings pray,—
80 His sails, athwart the yellow bay,
    Shall cleave the sky's blue rim.

III

To-night the wind roars in from sea;
The crow clings in the straining tree;
Curlew and crane and bittern flee
    The dykes of Tantramar.

To-night athwart an inky sky
A narrowing sun dropped angrily,
Scoring the gloom with dreadful dye,
    A bitter and flaming scar.

90 But ere night falls, across the tide
A close-reefed barque has been descried,
And word goes round the country-side—
    "The *Belle* is in the bay!"

And ere the loud night closes down
Upon that light's terrific frown,
Along the dyke, with blowing gown,
    She takes her eager way.

Just where his boat will haste to land,
On the open wharf she takes her stand.
100 Her pale hair blows from out its band.
    She does not heed the storm.

Her blinding joy of heart they know
Who so have fared, and waited so.
She heeds not what the winds that blow.
    She does not feel the storm.

But fiercer roars the gale. The night
With cloud grows black, with foam gleams white.
The creek boils to its utmost height.
    The port is seething full.

110   The gale shouts in the outer waves
Amid a world of gaping graves;
Against the dyke each great surge raves,
    Blind battering like a bull.

The dyke! The dyke! The brute sea shakes
The sheltering wall. It breaks,—it breaks!
The sharp salt whips her face, and wakes
    The dreamer from her dream.

The great flood lifts. It thunders in.
The broad marsh foams, and sinks. The din
120   Of waves is where her world has been;—
    Is this—is this the dream?

One moment in that surging hell
The old wharf shook, then cringed and fell.
Then came a lonely hulk, the *Belle,*
    And drove athwart the waste.

. . . .

They know no light, nor any star,
Those ruined plains of Tantramar.
And where the maid and lover are
    They know nor fear nor haste.

IV

130   After the flood on Tantramar
The fisher-folk flocked in from far.
They stopped the breach; they healed the scar.
    Once more the marsh grew green.

But at the marsh's inmost edge,
Where a tall fringe of flag and sedge
Catches a climbing hawthorn hedge,
    A lonely hulk is seen.

It lies forgotten of all tides.
The grass grows round its bleaching sides.
140 An endless inland peace abides
About its mouldering age.

But in the cot-door on the height
An old man sits with fading sight,
And memories of one cruel night
Are all his heritage.

And at her spinning-wheel within
The mother's hands forget to spin,—
So weary all her days have been
Since Margery went away.

150 Tantramar! Tantramar!
Until that sorrow fades afar,
Thy plains where birds and blossoms are
Laugh not their ancient way!

1893

THE STILLNESS OF THE FROST

1 Out of the frost-white wood comes winnowing through
No wing; no homely call or cry is heard.
Even the hope of life seems far deferred.
The hard hills ache beneath their spectral hue.
A dove-grey cloud, tender as tears or dew,
From one lone hearth exhaling, hangs unstirred,
Like the poised ghost of some unnamed great bird
In the ineffable pallor of the blue.

Such, I must think, even at the dawn of Time,
10 Was thy white hush, O world, when thou lay'st cold,
Unwaked to love, new from the Maker's word,
And the spheres, watching, stilled their high accord,
To marvel at perfection in thy mould,
The grace of thine austerity sublime!

1894

RESURRECTION

1   Daffodil, lily, and crocus,
     They stir, they break from the sod,
    They are glad of the sun, and they open
     Their golden hearts to God.

    They, and the wilding families,—
     Windflower, violet, may,—
    They rise from the long, long dark
     To the ecstasy of day.

    We, scattering troops and kindreds,
10   From out of the stars wind-blown
    To this wayside corner of space,
     This world that we call our own,—

    We, of the hedgerows of Time,
     We, too, shall divide the sod,
    Emerge to the light, and blossom,
     With our hearts held up to God.

                1894

THE QUEST OF THE ARBUTUS

1   For days the drench of noiseless rains,
    Then sunshine on the vacant plains,
    And April with her blind desire
    A vagrant in my veins!

    Because the tardy gods grew kind,
    Unrest and care were cast behind;
    I took a day, and found the world
    Was fashioned to my mind.

    The **swelling** sap that thrilled the wood
10   Was cousin to my eager blood;
    I caught the stir of waking roots,
    And knew that life was good.

    But something in the odors fleet,
    And in the sap's suggestion sweet,
    Was lacking,—one thing everywhere
    To make the spring complete.

At length within a leafy nest,
Where spring's persuasions pleaded best,
I found a pale, reluctant flower,
20   The purpose of my quest.

And then the world's expectancy
Grew clear: I knew its need to be
Not this dear flower, but one dear hand
To pluck the flower with me.

                                    1894

RENEWAL

1   Comrade of the whirling planets,
        Mother of the leaves and rain,
     Make me joyous as thy birds are,
        Let me be thy child again.

     Show me all the troops of heaven
        Tethered in a sphere of dew,—
     All the dear familiar marvels
        Old, child-hearted singers knew.

     Let me laugh with children's laughter,
10   Breathe with herb and blade and tree,
     Learn again forgotten lessons
        Of thy grave simplicity.

     Take me back to dream and vision
        From the prison-house of pain,
     Back to fellowship with wonder—
        Mother, take me home again!

                                    1894

SLEEPY MAN

1   When the Sleepy Man comes with the dust on his eyes
        (Oh, weary, my Dearie, so weary!)
     He shuts up the earth, and he opens the skies.
        (So hush-a-by, weary my Dearie!)

     He smiles through his fingers, and shuts up the sun;
        (Oh, weary, my Dearie, so weary!)
     The stars that he loves he lets out one by one.
        (So hush-a-by, weary my Dearie!)

176

He comes from the castles of Drowsy-boy Town;
10   (Oh, weary, my Dearie, so weary!)
At the touch of his hand the tired eyelids fall down.
        (So hush-a-by, weary my Dearie!)

He comes with a murmur of dream in his wings
        (Oh, weary, my Dearie, so weary!)
And whispers of mermaids and wonderful things.
        (So hush-a-by, weary my Dearie!)

Then the top is a burden, the bugle a bane
        (Oh, weary, my Dearie, so weary!)
When one would be faring down Dream-a-way Lane,
20   (So hush-a-by, weary my Dearie!)

When one would be wending in Lullaby Wherry
        (Oh, weary, my Dearie, so weary!)
To Sleepy Man's Castle by Comforting Ferry.
        (So hush-a-by, weary my Dearie!)

1894

THE TROUT BROOK

1   The airs that blew from the brink of day
Were fresh and wet with the breath of May.
I heard the babble of brown brooks falling
And golden-wings in the woodside calling.

Big drops hung from the sparkling eaves;
And through the screen of the thin young leaves
A glint of ripples, a whirl of foam,
Lured and beckoned me out from home.

My feet grew eager, my eyes grew wide,
10   And I was off by the brown brook's side.
Down in the swamp-bottom, cool and dim,
I cut me an alder sapling slim.

With nimble fingers I tied my line,
Clear as a sunbeam, strong and fine.
My fly was a tiny glittering thing,
With tinsel body and partridge wing.

With noiseless steps I threaded the wood,
Glad of the sun-pierced solitude.
Chattered the kingfisher, fierce and shy,
20 As like a shadow I drifted by.

Lurked in their watery lairs the trout,
But, silver and scarlet, I lured them out.
Wary were they, but warier still
My cunning wrist and my cast of skill.

I whipped the red pools under the beeches;
I whipped the yellow and dancing reaches.
The purple eddy, smooth like oil, ,
And the tail of the rapid yielded spoil.

So all day long, till the day was done,
30 I followed the stream, I followed the sun.
Then homeward over the ridge I went,
The wandering heart of me well content.

1894

THE UNSLEEPING

1 I soothe to unimagined sleep
The sunless bases of the deep.
And then I stir the aching tide
That gropes in its reluctant side.

I heave aloft the smoking hill;
To silent peace its throes I still.
But ever at its heart of fire
I lurk, an unassuaged desire.

I wrap me in the sightless germ
10 An instant or an endless term;
And still its atoms are my care,
Dispersed in ashes or in air.

I hush the comets one by one
To sleep for ages in the sun;
The sun resumes before my face
His circuit of the shores of space.

178

The mount, the star, the germ, the deep,
They all shall wake, they all shall sleep.
Time, like a flurry of wild rain,
20   Shall drift across the darkened pane.

Space, in the dim predestined hour,
Shall crumble like a ruined tower.
I only, with unfaltering eye,
Shall watch the dreams of God go by.

1894

ADMITTANCE

I might not, coming to the realms of bliss,
   Of her white presence be at once aware;
But on my lips the light of her last kiss
   Would win me welcome there.

1894

A HOMING SONG

Oh, fierce is the heat,
And weary is the street,
   And all day long
It is work, work, work!
But farewell work
   For love and a song,
When twilight's come
And the heart turns home.
   Oh, the nest for the bird,
10   And the hive for the bee,
And home, home, home
    For my dearies and me!

Oh, care flies far
From the twilight star;
   And the long, kind night
It is love, love, love!
And warm breathes love,
   Breathes low, breathes light,
O'er the small, kissed faces
20   In their pillowed places.

Oh, the nest for the bird [,]
  And the hive for the bee,
  And home, home, home
  For my dearies and me!

1894

THE PIPER AND THE CHIMING PEAS

1   There was a little piper man
  As merry as you please,
  Who heard one day the sweet-pea blossoms
  Chiming in the breeze.

  He murmured with a courtly grace
  That set them quite at ease,—
  "I never knew that you had such
  Accomplishments as these!

  "If I should pipe until you're ripe
10   I think that by degrees
  You might become as wise as I
  And chime in Wagnerese!"

  "Oh, no, kind Sir! That could not be!"
  Replied the modest peas.
  "We only play such simple airs
  As suit the bumble-bees."

1894

THE BALLAD OF CROSSING THE BROOK

Oh, it was a dainty maid that went a-Maying in the morn,
  A dainty, dainty maiden of degree.
The ways she took **were** merry and the ways she missed forlorn,
  And the laughing water tinkled to the sea.

The little leaves above her loved the dainty, dainty maid;
  The little winds they kissed her, every one.
At the nearing of her little feet the flowers were not afraid;
  And the water lay a-whimpling in the sun.

Oh, the dainty, dainty maid to the borders of the brook
10   Lingered down as lightly as the breeze;
And the shy **water-spiders** quit their scurrying to look;
  And the happy water whispered to the trees.

She was fain to cross the brook, was the dainty, dainty maid;
    But first she lifted up her elfin eyes
To see if there were cavalier or clown a-near to aid,—
    And the water-bubbles blinked in surprise.

The brook bared its pebbles to persuade her dainty feet,
    But the dainty, dainty maid was not content.
She had spied a simple country lad (for dainty maid unmeet),
20   And the sly water twinkled as it went.

As the simple lad drew nigh, then this dainty, dainty maid,
    (O maidens, well you know how it was done!)
Stood a-gazing at her feet until he saw she was afraid
    Of the water there a-whimpling in the sun.

Now that simple lad had in him all the makings of a man;
    And he stammered, "I had better lift you over!"
Said the dainty, dainty maid—"Do you really think you can?"
    And the water hid its laughter in the clover.

So he carried her across, with his eyes cast down,
30   And his foolish heart a-quaking with delight.
And the maid she looked him over with her elfin eyes of brown;
    And the impish water giggled at his plight.

He reached the other side, he set down the dainty maid;
    But he trembled so he couldn't speak a word.
Then the dainty, dainty maid—"Thank you, Sir! Good-day!" she said.
    And the water bubbles chuckled as they heard.

Oh, she tripped away so lightly, a-Maying in the morn,
    That dainty, dainty maiden of degree.
She left the simple country lad a-sighing and forlorn
40   Where the mocking water twinkled to the sea.

1894

KINSHIP

1   Back to the bewildering vision
        And the borderland of birth;
    Back into the looming wonder,
        The companionship of earth;

Back unto the simple kindred—
    Childlike fingers, childlike eyes,
Working, waiting, comprehending,
    Now in patience, now surprise;

Back unto the faithful healing
10   And the candour of the sod—
Scent of mould and moisture stirring
    At the secret touch of God;

Back into the ancient stillness
    Where the wise enchanter weaves,
To the twine of questing tree-root,
    The expectancy of leaves;

Back to hear the hushed consulting
    Over bud and blade and germ,
As the Mother's mood apportions
20   Each its pattern, each its term;

Back into the grave beginnings
    Where all wonder-tales are true,
Strong enchantments, strange successions,
    Mysteries of old and new;

Back to knowledge and renewal,
    Faith to fashion and reveal,
Take me, Mother,—in compassion
    All thy hurt ones fain to heal.

Back to wisdom take me, Mother;
30   Comfort me with kindred hands;
Tell me tales the world's forgetting,
    Till my spirit understands.

Tell me how some sightless impulse,
    Working out a hidden plan,
God for kin and clay for fellow,
    Wakes to find itself a man.

Tell me how the life of mortal,
    Wavering from breath to breath,
Like a web of scarlet pattern
40   Hurtles from the loom of death.

How the caged bright bird, desire,
　　Which the hands of God deliver,
Beats aloft to drop unheeded
　　At the confines of forever;

Faints unheeded for a season,
　　Then outwings the farthest star,
To the wisdom and the stillness
　　Where thy consummations are.

1894

GOLDEN-ROD

Ripe grew the year. Then suddenly there came,
　　With the significance of a smile of God,
O'er all the edges of the world a flame,—
　　The mild apocalypse of the golden-rod.

1894

UP AND AWAY IN THE MORNING

1　Tide's at full; the waves break white.
　　(Oh, up and away in the morning!)
Blue is the blown grass, red is the height;
Washed with the sun the sail shines white.
　　(Oh, up and away in the morning!)

Wide is the world in the laughing sun.
　　(Oh, up and away in the morning!)
Work's to be done and wealth's to be won
Ere a man turn home with the homing sun.
10　　(Oh, up and away in the morning!)

Long is the heart's hope, long as the day.
　　(Oh, up and away in the morning!)
Heart has its will and hand has its way
Till the world rolls over and ends the day.
　　(Oh, up and away in the morning!)

It's home that we toil for all day long.
    (Oh, up and away in the morning!)
Hand on the line and heart in the song,
The labour of love will not seem long.
20   (Oh, up and away in the morning!)

1894

HOME, HOME IN THE EVENING

1   When the crows fly in from sea
    (Oh, home, home in the evening!)
My love in his boat comes back to me,
Over the tumbling leagues of sea.
    (Oh, home, home in the evening!)

And when the sun drops over the hill
    (Oh, home, home in the evening!)
My happy eyes they take their fill
Of watching my love as he climbs the hill.
10   (Oh, home, home in the evening!)

And when the dew falls over the land
    (Oh, home, home in the evening!)
I hold in my hand his dearest hand,
The happiest woman in all the land.
    (Oh, home, home in the evening!)

*   *   *   *   *

All day she sang by the cottage door.
    (Oh, home, home in the evening!)
At sundown came his boat to the shore—
But he to the hearthside comes no more
20   Home, home in the evening.

1894

THE VENGEANCE OF GLUSKÂP

(*A Melicite Legend*)

1   Gluskâp, the friend and father of his race,
With help in need went journeying three days' space.

His village slept, and took no thought of harm,
Secure beneath the shadow of his arm.

But wandering wizards watched his outward path,
And marked his fenceless dwelling for their wrath.

They came upon the tempest's midnight wings,
With shock of thunder and the lightning's slings,
And flame, and hail, and all disastrous things.

10 When home at length the hero turned again,
His huts were ashes and his servants slain;
And o'er the ruin wept a slow, great rain.

He wept not; but he cried a mighty word
Across the wandering sea, and the sea heard.

Then came great whales, obedient to his hand,
And bare him to the demon-haunted land,

Where, in malign morass and ghostly wood
And grim cliff-cavern, lurked the evil brood.

And scarce the avenger's foot had touched their coast
20 Ere horror seized on all the wizard host,
And in their hiding-places hushed the boast.

He grew and gloomed before them like a cloud,
And his eye drew them till they cried aloud,

And withering like spent flame before his frown
They ran forth in a madness and fell down.

Rank upon rank they lay without a moan,—
His finger touched them, and their hearts grew stone.

All round the coasts he heaped their stiffened clay;
And the sea-mews wail o'er them to this day.

1894

IMMANENCE

Not only in the cataract and the thunder,
    Or in the deeps of man's uncharted soul,
But in the dew-star dwells alike the wonder,
    And in the whirling dust-mote the control.

1894

ORIGINS

1   Out of the dreams that heap
    The hollow hand of sleep,—
    Out of the dark sublime,
    The echoing deeps of time,—
    From the averted Face
    Beyond the bournes of space,
    Into the sudden sun
    We journey, one by one.
    Out of the hidden shade
10   Wherein desire is made,—
    Out of the pregnant stir
    Where death and life confer,—
    The dark and mystic heat
    Where soul and matter meet,—
    The enigmatic Will,—
    We start, and then are still.

       Inexorably decreed
    By the ancestral deed,
    The puppets of our sires,
20   We work out blind desires,
    And for our sons ordain
    The blessing or the bane.
    In ignorance we stand
    With fate on either hand,
    And question stars and earth
    Of life, and death, and birth.
    With wonder in our eyes
    We scan the kindred skies,
    While through the common grass
30   Our atoms mix and pass.
    We feel the sap go free
    When spring comes to the tree;
    And in our blood is stirred
    What warms the brooding bird.
    The vital fire we breathe
    That bud and blade bequeath,
    And strength of native clay
    In our full veins hath sway.

       But in the urge intense
40   And fellowship of sense,
    Suddenly comes a word
    In other ages heard.

On a great wind our souls
Are borne to unknown goals,
And past the bournes of space
To the unaverted Face.

1895

THE BROOK IN FEBRUARY

A snowy path for squirrel and fox,
　It winds between the wintry firs.
Snow-muffled are its iron rocks,
　And o'er its stillness nothing stirs.

But low, bend low a listening ear!
　Beneath the mask of moveless white
A babbling whisper you shall hear—
　Of birds and blossoms, leaves and light.

1895

EBB

1　The tide goes out, the tide goes out; once more
The empty day goes down the empty shore.

The tide goes out; the wharves deserted lie
Under the empty solitude of sky.

The tide goes out; the dwindling channels ache
With the old hunger, with the old heartbreak.

The tide goes out; the lonely wastes of sand
Implore the benediction of thy hand.

The tide goes out, goes out; the stranded ships
10　Desire the sea,—and I desire thy lips.

The tide goes out, the tide goes out; the sun
Relumes the hills of longing one by one.

The tide goes out, goes out; and goes my heart
On the long quest that ends but where thou art.

1895

THE FROSTED PANE

One night came Winter noiselessly, and leaned
    Against my window-pane.
In the deep stillness of his heart convened
    The ghosts of all his slain.

Leaves, and ephemera, and stars of earth,
    And fugitives of grass,—
White spirits loosed from bonds of mortal birth,
    He drew them on the glass.

1895

ICE

When Winter scourged the meadow and the hill
And in the withered leafage worked his will,
The water shrank, and shuddered, and stood still,—
Then built himself a magic house of glass,
Irised with memories of flowers and grass,
Wherein to sit and watch the fury pass.

1895

AN APRIL ADORATION

1   Sang the sunrise on an amber morn—
    "Earth, be glad! An April day is born.

"Winter's done, and April's in the skies
Earth, look up with laughter in your eyes!"

Putting off her dumb dismay of snow,
Earth bade all her unseen children grow.

Then the sound of growing in the air
Rose to God a liturgy of prayer;

And the thronged succession of the days
10   Uttered up to God a psalm of praise.

Laughed the running sap in every vein,
Laughed the running flurries of warm rain,

Laughed the life in every wandering root,
Laughed the tingling cells of bud and shoot.

God in all the concord of their mirth
Heard the adoration-song of Earth.

1895

THE COMEDY

Penning his comedy called "Man," the Master
   Who shapes his word in symbol and in trope
Made love a gay enigma of disaster,
   And life an epigram on the tomb of hope.

1895

THE FOREST FIRE

1   The night was grim and still with dread;
    No star shone down from heaven's dome;
   The ancient forest closed around
    The settler's lonely home.

There came a glare that lit the north;
   There came a wind that roused the night;
But child and father slumbered on,
   Nor felt the growing light.

There came a noise of flying feet,
10   With many a strange and dreadful cry;
  And sharp flames crept and leapt along
   The red verge of the sky.

There came a deep and gathering roar.
   The father raised his anxious head;
He saw the light, like a dawn of blood,
   That streamed across his bed.

It lit the old clock on the wall,
   It lit the room with splendour wild,
It lit the fair and tumbled hair
20   Of the still sleeping child;

And zigzag fence, and rude log barn,
    And chip-strewn yard, and cabin grey,
Glowed crimson in the shuddering glare
    Of that untimely day.

The boy was hurried from his sleep;
    The horse was hurried from his stall;
Up from the pasture clearing came
    The cattle's frightened call.

The boy was snatched to the saddle-bow.
30   Wildly, wildly, the father rode.
Behind them swooped the hordes of flame
    And harried their abode.

The scorching heat was at their heels;
    The huge roar hounded them in their flight;
Red smoke and many a flying brand
    Flew o'er them through the night.

And past them fled the wildwood forms—
    Far-striding moose, and leaping deer,
And bounding panther, and coursing wolf,
40   Terrible-eyed with fear.

And closer drew the fiery death;
    Madly, madly, the father rode;
The horse began to heave and fail
    Beneath the double load.

The father's mouth was white and stern,
    But his eyes grew tender with long farewell.
He said: "Hold fast to your seat, Sweetheart,
    And ride Old Jerry well!

"I must go back. Ride on to the river.
50   Over the ford and the long marsh ride,
Straight on to the town. And I'll meet you, Sweetheart,
    Somewhere on the other side."

He slipped from the saddle. The boy rode on.
    His hand clung fast in the horse's mane;
His hair blew over the horse's neck;
    His small throat sobbed with pain.

"Father! Father!" he cried aloud.
　　The howl of the fire-wind answered him
With the hiss of soaring flames, and crash
60　　Of shattering limb on limb.

But still the good horse galloped on,
　　With sinew braced and strength renewed.
The boy came safe to the river ford,
　　And out of the deadly wood.

　　　　. . . . .

And now with his kinsfolk, fenced from fear,
　　At play in the heart of the city's hum,
He stops in his play to wonder why
　　His father does not come!

1895

TWILIGHT ON SIXTH AVENUE AT NINTH STREET

1　Over the tops of the houses
　　Twilight and sunset meet.
The green, diaphanous dusk
　　Sinks to the eager street.

Astray in the tangle of roofs
　　Wanders a wind of June.
The dial shines in the clock-tower
　　Like the face of a strange-scrawled moon.

The narrowing lines of the houses
10　　Palely begin to gleam,
And the hurrying crowds fade softly
　　Like an army in a dream.

Above the vanishing faces
　　A phantom train flares on
With a voice that shakes the shadows,—
　　Diminishes, and is gone.

And I walk with the journeying throng
　　In such a solitude
As where a lonely ocean
20　　Washes a lonely wood.

1895

HER GLOVE BOX

What bold
Adventurers I hold
In my enameled walls of gold!
Gallants who have dared, I guess,
Her hands' white loveliness
With close caress
To press.

1895

A MODERN DIALOGUE

1 She—

> If I should take my pen in hand
>> To write whole reams on Woman's Wrongs,
> To libel men, like Sarah Grand,
>> Or scribble naughty songs:
> If I should don my brother's coat,
>> And skirts not much below the knee;
> If I should claim the right to vote,
>> *Would* you be true to me?

He—   I swear—

10 She—   *Dear* Jack!

He—

> I swear my heart
> Would love that girl—perhaps an hour!

She (*rising*)—

> You—*Thank* you, sir! We two will part!
> Your ring!—Consider our
> Engagement—

He—

> Solid as the sun!
> You shake your head? I'll tell you how.
> My constant heart can love but one,
> *The girl that you are now!*

1895

THREE GOOD THINGS

Bona in terrâ tria inveni,
Ludum, venerem, vinum.

1   *Three good things I've thanked the Gods for,—*
      Play, and love, and wine!
   So by Tiber sang my poet;—
      Would the song were mine!

   Yet methinks, I would not turn it
      Just the Roman way,
   But for *ludum* say read *libros,—*
      Books are more than play!

   Through the togaed Latin trembles
10   Laughter half divine;
   Flash the dice beside the column;
      Rosy flagons shine.

   I, for gleams of yellow Tiber,
      Down my garden way
   See a water blue and beaming
      In the northern day.

   Ovid, Meleager, Omar,
      In the orchard shade,
   With a jug that gurgles gently,
20   And a white-armed maid.

   Three good things I thank the Gods for,—
      Books, and love, and wine:
   So, my poet, singing later,
      Would have run your line!

                  1895

AN EPITAPH FOR A HUSBANDMAN

1   He who would start and rise
      Before the crowing cocks,—
   No more he lifts his eyes,
      Whoever knocks.

He who before the stars
　　Would call the cattle home,—
They wait about the bars
　　For him to come.

Him at whose hearty calls
10　　The farmstead woke again
The horses in their stalls
　　Expect in vain.

Busy and blithe and bold
　　He laboured for the morrow,—
The plough his hands would hold
　　Rusts in the furrow.

His fields he had to leave,
　　His orchards cool and dim;
The clods he used to cleave
20　　Now cover him.

But the green, growing things
　　Lean kindly to his sleep,—
White roots and wandering strings,
　　Closer they creep.

Because he loved them long
　　And with them bore his part,
Tenderly now they throng
　　About his heart.

1895

THE TRAIN AMONG THE HILLS

1　Vast, unrevealed, in silence and the night
　　Brooding, the ancient hills commune with sleep.
　　Inviolate the solemn valleys keep
Their contemplation. Soon from height to height
Steals a red finger of mysterious light,
　　And lion-footed through the forests creep
　　Strange mutterings; till suddenly, with sweep
And shattering thunder of resistless flight
And crash of routed echoes, roars to view,
10　　Down the long mountain gorge the Night Express
Freighted with fears and tears and happiness.

194

The dread form passes; silence falls anew.
   And lo! I have beheld the thronged, blind world
   To goals unseen from God's hand onward hurled.

1895

EARTH'S COMPLINES

1   Before the feet of the dew
   There came a call I knew,
      Luring me into the garden
   Where the tall white lilies grew.

   I stood in the dusk between
   The companies of green,
      O'er whose ethereal ranks
   The lilies rose serene.

   And the breathing air was stirred
10   By an unremembered word,
      Soft, incommunicable—
   And wings not of a bird.

   I heard the spent blooms sighing,
   The expectant buds replying;
      I felt the life of the leaves,
   Ephemeral, yet undying.

   The spirits of earth were there,
   Thronging the shadowed air,
      Serving among the lilies,
20   In an ecstasy of prayer.

   Their speech I could not tell;
   But the sap in each green cell,
      And the pure initiate petals,
   They knew that language well.

   I felt the soul of the trees—
   Of the white, eternal seas—
      Of the flickering bats and night-moths
   And my own soul kin to these.

And a spell came out of space
30   From the light of its starry place,
    And I saw in the deep of my heart
The image of God's face.

1895

HER FAN

Its breath, which cools her breast to snow,
Fans many a lover's heart to fire.
How came this silken toy to know
Such subtle lordships of desire?

1895

THE WRESTLER

1   When God sends out His company to travel through the stars,
    There is every kind of wonder in the show;
There is every kind of animal behind its prison bars;
    With riders in a many-coloured row.
The master showman, Time, has a strange trick of rhyme,
    And the clown's most ribald jest is a tear;
But the best drawing card is the Wrestler huge and hard,
    Who can fill the tent at any time of year.

His eye is on the crowd and he beckons with his hand,
10   With authoritative finger, and they come.
The rules of the game they do not understand,
    But they go as in a dream, and are dumb.
They would fain say him nay, and they look the other way,
    Till at last to the ropes they cling.
But he throws them one by one till the show for them is done,
    In the blood-red dust of the ring.

There's none to shun his challenge—they must meet him soon or late,
    And he knows a cunning trick for all heels.
The king's haughty crown drops in jeers from his pate
20   As the hold closes on him, and he reels.
The burly and the proud, the braggarts of the crowd,
    Every one of them he topples down in thunder.
His grip grows mild for the dotard and the child,
    But alike they must all go under.

Oh, many a mighty foeman would try a fall with him;—
    Persepolis, and Babylon, and Rome,
Assyria and Sardis, they see their fame grow dim
    As he tumbles in the dust every dome.
At last will come an hour when the stars shall feel his power,
30   And he shall have his will upon the sun.
Ere we know what he's about the lights will be put out,
    And the wonder of the show will be undone.

1895

AN AUGUST WOOD ROAD

1   When the partridge coveys fly
   In the birch-tops cool and high;

When the dry cicadas twang
Where the purpling fir-cones hang;

When the bunch-berries emboss—
Scarlet beads—the roadside moss;

Brown with shadows, bright with sun,
All day long till day is done

Sleeps in murmuring solitude
10   The worn old road that threads the wood.

In its deep cup—grassy, cool—
Sleeps the little roadside pool;

Sleeps the butterfly on the weed,
Sleeps the drifted thistle-seed.

Like a great and blazing gem,
Basks the beetle on the stem.

Up and down the shining rays
Dancing midges weave their maze.

High among the moveless boughs,
20   Drunk with day, the night-hawks drowse.

Far up, unfathomably blue,
August's heaven vibrates through.

The old road leads to all things good;
The year's at full, and time's at flood.

1895

THE WEAVER

In an enchanted gloom
Behind the shadowy curtains of the Past,
He sits and weaves, with shuttle flying fast,—
Strange colors of the sun, and threads our sires have spun,—
The figures of our joy and of our doom,
While creeps the web from the low-murmuring loom.

1895

THE MUSE AND THE WHEEL

1 The poet took his wheel one day
   A-wandering to go,
  But soon fell out beside the way,
   The leaves allured him so.

  He leaned his wheel against a tree
   And in the shade lay down;
  And more to him were bloom and bee
   Than all the busy town.

  He listened to the Phoebe-bird
10   And learned a thing worth knowing.
  He lay so still he almost heard
   The merry grasses growing.

  He lay so still he dropped asleep;
   And then the Muse came by.
  The stars were in her garment's sweep
   But laughter in her eye.

  "Poor boy!" she said, "how tired he seems!
20   His vagrant feet must follow
  So many loves, so many dreams—
   (To find them mostly hollow!)

198

"Can you be Pegasus," she mused,
    "To modern mood translated,
But poorly housed, and meanly used,
30   And grown attenuated?

"Ah, no, you're quite another breed
    From him who once would follow
Across the clear Olympian mead
    The calling of Apollo!

"No Hippocrene would leap to light
    If you should stamp your hoof.
You never knew the pastures bright
    Wherein we lie aloof.

"You never drank of Helicon,
40   Or strayed in Tempe's vale.
You never soared against the sun
    Till earth grew faint and pale.

"You bear my poor deluded boy
    Each latest love to see!
But Pegasus would mount with joy
    And bring him straight to me!"

He woke. The olden spell was strong
    Within his eager bosom,
And so he wrote a mystic song
50   Upon the nearest blossom.

He wrote, until a sudden whim
    Set all his bosom trembling;
Then sped to woo a maiden slim
    His latest love resembling.

1895; 1896

OLIVER WENDELL HOLMES

1   He that so often bade us smile—
     What later whim hath bid us weep?
Or was it some new jest, that while
     He jested, he should fall asleep?

His mirth, we now remember, stood
     Next neighbour always to regret.
Responding to his merriest mood
     We sometimes found our lashes wet.

With courtly quip, and kindly scoff,
10   And laughter never long or loud,
His fun was not the common stuff,
     His fancy fooled not for the crowd;

But, Humour's wild aristocrat,
     He wandered through these busy days,
Half wondering what the world was at,
     And shrewdly smoothing it with praise.

And now he lives but in his page,
     Where wit and wisdom are comprised,—
The gentlest breeding of the age
20   Most graciously epitomized.

                        1895

RECESSIONAL

1   Now along the solemn heights
Fade the Autumn's altar-lights;
     Down the great earth's glimmering chancel
Glide the days and nights.

Little kindred of the grass,
Like a shadow in a glass
     Falls the dark and falls the stillness;
We must rise and pass.

We must rise and follow, wending
10   Where the nights and days have ending,—
     Pass in order pale and slow
Unto sleep extending.

Little brothers of the clod,
Soul of fire and seed of sod,
    We must fare into the silence
At the knees of God.

Little comrades of the sky
Wing to wing we wander by,
    Going, going, going, going,
20 Softly as a sigh.

Hark, the moving shapes confer,
Globe of dew and gossamer,
    Fading and ephemeral spirits
In the dusk astir.

Moth and blossom, blade and bee,
Worlds must go as well as we,
    In the long procession joining
Mount, and star, and sea.

Toward the shadowy brink we climb
30 Where the round year rolls sublime,
    Rolls, and drops, and falls forever
In the vast of time.

                                    1895

RECOMPENSE

1   To Beauty and to Truth I heaped
        My sacrificial fires.
    I fed them hot with selfish thoughts
        And many proud desires.

    I stripped my days of dear delights
        To cast them in the flame,
    Till life seemed naked as a rock,
        And pleasure but a name.

    And still I sorrowed patiently,
10   And waited day and night,
    Expecting Truth from very far
        And **Beauty** from her height.

Then laughter ran among the stars;
And this I heard them tell:
"Beside his threshold is the shrine
Where Truth and Beauty dwell!"

1895; 1896

PHILLIDA'S BIRTHDAY

1   Although you might surmise
She descended from the skies
    Yesterday,
My Phillida would scorn
To deny that she was born
    Quite the ordinary way.

But should you ask her "when?"
She will smile upon you then,
    With an air
10   That would seem to indicate
She was just as old as fate,
    With the ages in her hair.

The month, the day, perchance,
She'll confess with merry glance;
    For she knows
A birthday-box may come,—
Something that may tell, though dumb,
    More than words would dare disclose.

But never will you gain
20   What is locked within her brain,—
    Videlicet:
What year, most happy one,
First awakened to the sun
    Those deep eyes of violet.

And yet she is, in truth,
Such a paragon of youth,
    You'll agree
The subject of her years
Could not be a source of fears,
30   To a maid so young as she.

But Phillida is sage!
If to-day she told her age
   Frank and fair,
Five and twenty years from now
Some one might the truth avow,
   When she does begin to care.

1895

THE WITCHES' FLIGHT

1   Come, Red Mouse,
      And come, Black Cat!
   Oh, see what the goat
      And the toad are at!
   Oh, see them where
   They rise in the air,
   And wheel and dance
      With the whirling bat!

   We rise, we rise
10   On the smoking air;
   And the withered breast
      Grows young and fair;
   And the eyes grow bright
   With alluring light,
   And the fierce mouth softens
      With love's soft prayer.

   Come, White Sisters,
      Naked of limb!
   The horned moon reddens;
20   The stars grow dim;
   The crags in the gloom
   Of our caldron's fume
   Shudder and topple
      And reel and swim.

   We mount, we mount
      Till the moon seems nigh.
   Our rout possesses
      The middle sky.
   With strange embraces,
30   And maddened faces,
   And streaming tresses,
      We twist and fly.

Come, White Sisters,
   And four-foot kin,
For the horned moon sinks
   And the reek grows thin,
And brief is the night
Of our delight,
And brief the span
40   Of our secret sin.

1895

A CHILD'S PRAYER AT EVENING

(Domine, cui sunt Pleiades curae)

Father, who keepest
   The stars in Thy care,
Me, too, Thy little one,
   Childish in prayer,
Keep, as Thou keepest
The soft night through,
Thy long, white lilies
   Asleep in Thy dew.

1895

BOHEMIA

1   Oh the coast of green Bohemia,
Where the shining sea
Laughs to shame the learned fables
Of geography!

Whither from inclement seasons
Flee uncaptained ships
Freighted with forbidden raptures
Ripe for lovers' lips!

Shining paths of green Bohemia!
10 Sweetly there holds sway
One who smiles on all our homage
In her gracious way.

Tall and stately, white and shapely,
From her slender hands
Falls the spell of foreign longing
Flower of far-off lands [.]

Love and laughter, tears and kisses,
Joy of passéd pain,
Purposes that missed completion,
20   Battles gained in vain!

Oh the ways where things are fairer
Even than they seem,
And our Lady lures us always,
Almoner of dream!

1896

THE DESERTED WHARF

1   The long tides sweep
      Around its sleep,
The long red tides of Tantramar.
      Around its dream
      They hiss and stream,
Sad for the ships that have sailed afar.

How many lips
    Have lost their bloom,
How many ships
10   *Gone down to gloom,*
Since keel and sail
    Have fled out from me
Over the thunder and strain of the sea!

Its kale-dark sides
Throb in the tides;
The long winds over it spin and hum;
    Its timbers ache
    For memory's sake,
And the throngs that never again will come.

20   *How many lips*
    Have lost their bloom,
How many ships
    Gone down to gloom,
Since keel and sail
    Have fled out from me
Over the thunder and strain of the sea!

1896

205

THE ELEPHANT AND THE PANSY-BLOSSOM

1   An elegant Elephant walked one day
        Beside the wondering sea,
    And a Pansy-Blossom he met by the way,
        A Puritan saint was she.

    She bowed with an indescribable air,
        And murmured, "What repose!
    I love you for your wonderful hair
        And Aubrey Beardsley clo'es!"

    Now, delicate breeding had made him shy,
10   As you well may understand;
    So the startled eye-glass fell from his eye,
        As he clasped her by the hand.

    He blushed to the tips of his diffident ears,
        But never a word said he,
    And the Pansy-Blossom saw, through her tears,
        That it certainly could not be.

    "But why?" she whispered, and wailed, "But why?"
        —And he heard as in a dream—
    "I know of a beautiful spot, near by,
20   Where the crocodile keeps ice-cream.

    "I know of a wilderness just divine,
        Where I could love you so!"
    He only said—"The idea is fine,
        But I really could not go!"

    For he thought, you see, of his wife and child,
        And she of her aged mother;
    They thought till they felt quite weird and wild;
        Then—said "Good-by" to each other.

                                    1896

NATIVITY

Not only far away and long ago,
With wondering joy and prescience of woe,
   Came God to man on that transfiguring morn,
But now, but now, with wordless ecstasy,
Yet trembling for a grief that is to be,
   In every mother's bosom Christ is born.

1896

A SPRING COLLOQUY

1   Violet, Violet, where did you capture
      Your pure, unspeakable blue?
    "Her eyes in the springtime I copied, with pencil
      Of magic, and heaven, and dew."

    Apple-bloom, Apple-bloom, why are your petals
      So blended of roses and snow?
    "All my long bud-time I dreamed of her blushes,
      And like them elected to grow."

    Buttercup, Buttercup, why are you golden?
10   "I looked on the light of her hair,
    And loved it, till God, who is kind to his flowers,
      Made me, too, shining and fair."

    Maple-bud, Maple-bud, how comes your scarlet
      As warm as the heart of the South?
    "She tasted my sap once, and every faint leaflet
      Took fire at the touch of her mouth."

    Mayflower, Mayflower, why is your sweetness
      So subtle, and cool, and divine?
    "I think it's because she once wore in her bosom
20   One fortunate blossom of mine."

1896

THE STIRRUP CUP

Life at my stirrup lifted wistful eyes,
    And as she gave the parting cup to me,—
    Death's pale companion for the silent sea,—
"I know," she said, "that land and where it lies.
    A pledge between us now before you go,
    That when you meet me there your soul may know!"

1896

THE LAUGHING SALLY

1   A wind blew up from Pernambuco.
      (Yeo heave ho! the *Laughing Sally!*
        Hi yeo, heave away!)
    A wind blew out of the east-sou'-east
      And boomed at the break of day.

The *Laughing Sally* sped for her life,
    And a speedy craft was she.
The black flag flew at her top to tell
    How she took toll of the sea.

The wind blew up from Pernambuco;
10   And in the breast of the blast
Came the King's black ship like a hound let slip
    On the trail of the *Sally* at last.

For a day and a night, a night and a day,
    Over the blue, blue round,
Went on the chase of the pirate quarry,
    The hunt of the tireless hound.

"Land on the port bow!" came the cry;
    And the *Sally* raced for shore,
20   Till she reached the bar at the river-mouth
    Where the shallow breakers roar.

She passed the bar by a secret channel
    With clear tide under her keel,—
For he knew the shoals like an open book,
    The captain at the wheel.

She passed the bar, she sped like a ghost,
    Till her sails were hid from view
By the tall, liana'd, unsunned boughs
    O'erbrooding the dark bayou.

30 At moonrise up to the river-mouth
        Came the King's black ship of war.
    The red cross flapped in wrath at her peak,
        But she could not cross the bar.

And while she lay in the run of the seas,
    By the grimmest whim of chance
Out of the bay to the north came forth
    Two battle-ships of France.

On the English ship the twain bore down
    Like wolves that range by night;
40 And the breakers' roar was heard no more
        In the thunder of the fight.

The crash of the broadsides rolled and stormed
    To the *Sally,* hid from view
Under the tall, liana'd boughs
    Of the moonless, dark bayou.

A boat ran out for news of the fight,
    And this was the word she brought—
"The King's ship fights the ships of France
    As the King's ships all have fought!"

50 Then muttered the mate, "I'm a man of Devon!"
        And the captain thundered then—
    "There's English rope that bides for our necks,
        But we all be English men!"

The *Sally* glided out of the gloom
    And down the moon-white river.
She stole like a grey shark over the bar
    Where the long surf seethes forever.

She hove to under a high French hull,
    And the red cross rose to her peak.
60 The French were looking for fight that night,
        And they had not far to seek.

Blood and fire on the streaming decks,
    And fire and blood below;
The heat of hell, and the reek of hell,
    And the dead men laid a-row!

And when the stars paled out of heaven
    And the red dawn-rays uprushed,
The oaths of battle, the crash of timbers,
    The roar of the guns were hushed.

70   With one foe beaten under his bow,
    The other afar in flight,
The English captain turned to look
    For his fellow in the fight.

The English **captain** turned, and stared;—
    For where the *Sally* had been
Was a single spar upthrust from the sea
    With the red-cross flag serene!

*   *   *   *   *

A wind blew up from Pernambuco,—
    (Yeo heave ho! the *Laughing Sally!*
80   Hi yeo, heave away!)
And boomed for the doom of the *Laughing Sally,*
    Gone down at the break of day.

1896

THE LITTLE FIELD OF PEACE

1   By the long wash of his ancestral sea
He sleeps how quietly!
How quiet the unlifting eyelids lie
Under this tranquil sky!
The little busy hands and restless feet
Here find that rest is sweet;
For sweetly, from the hands grown tired of play,
The child-world slips away,
With its confusion of forgotten toys
10   And kind, familiar noise.

Not lonely does he lie in his last bed,
For love o'erbroods his head.
Kindly to him the comrade grasses lean
Their fellowship of green.
The wilding meadow companies give heed,—
Brave tansy, and the weed
That on the dyke-top lifts its dauntless stalk,—
Around his couch they talk.
The shadows of his oak-tree flit and play
20 Above his dreams all day.
The wind, that was his playmate on the hills,
His sleep with music fills.

Here in this tender acre by the tide
His vanished kin abide.
Ah! what compassionate care for him they keep,
Too soon returned to sleep!
They watch him in this little field of peace
Where they have found release.
Not as a stranger or alone he went
30 Unto his long content;
But kissed to sleep and comforted lies he
By his ancestral sea.

1896

THE FLOCKS OF SPRING

1 When winter is done, and April's dawning
    Shatters the dark of the year,
And the rain-fed rivulet under the bridge
    Again runs clear,

And the shepherd sun comes over the hill
    To let out the flocks of Spring,
With laughter and light in the pastures of air
    The flocks take wing.

They scatter on every lingering wind,—
10   The perfume, and the bee,
And the whispers of the jostling grass,
    Glad to be free,

The minstrelsy of the shining pools,
   The dancing troops of the hours;
And over the sod in a sudden rapture
   Flame the flowers.

1896

THE JONQUIL

1 Through its brown and withered bulb
   How the white germ felt the sun
In the dark mould gently stirring
   His spring children one by one!

Thrilled with heat, it split the husk,
   Shot a green blade up to light,
And unfurled its orange petals
   In the old enchanter's sight.

One step more and it had floated
10   On the palpitating noon
Winged and free, a butterfly
   Soaring from the rent cocoon.

But it could not leave its earth,
   And the May-dew's tender tears,—
So it wavers there forever
   'Twixt the green and azure spheres.

1896

AN OBLATION

1 Behind the fateful gleams
Of Life's foretelling streams
   Sat the Artificer
Of souls and deeds and dreams.

Before him April came;
And on her mouth his name
   Breathed like a flower
And lightened like a flame.

She offered him a world
10 With showers of joy empearled;
   And a spring wind
With iris wings unfurled.

She offered him a flight
Of birds that fare by night,
  Voyaging northward
By the ancestral sight.

She offered him a star
From the blue fields afar,
  Where unforgotten
20 The ghosts of gladness are.

And every root and seed
Blind stirring in the mead
  Her hand held up,—
And still he gave no heed.

Then from a secret nook
Beside a pasture brook,—
  A place of leaves,—
A pink-lipped bloom she took.

Softly before his feet,
30 Oblation small and sweet,
  She laid the arbutus,
And found the offering meet.

Over the shadowy tide,
Where **Birth** and **Death** abide,
  He stretched his palm,
And strewed the petals wide;

And o'er the ebbing years,
Dark with the drift of tears,
  A sunbeam broke,
40 And summer filled the spheres.

1896

WITH ALL HER FAULTS

1 When I was but a lad,
  Long ago,
This simple lore I had,
  Don't you know,
That every maiden fair
Was an angel unaware,—
And I wondered when and where
  The wings would grow.

But wiser now am I,
10   A good deal,
Tho' I've sometimes seen them fly,
        Yet I feel
They are something just between
Man and angel in their mien,
Since my Phillida I've seen
        On her wheel.

She does not show a sign
        Of a wing;
But her figure is divine
20   And the fling
Of her abbreviated gown,
As she flickers through the town,
Might buy the throne and crown
        Of a king!

No halo of a saint
        Does she wear,
Such as Lippo loved to paint;
        But her hair—
As when all heaven streams
30 Thro' the landscape of my dreams—
In such glory floats and gleams
        On the air!

But not all for heaven she,—
        Not *too* good!
Yet she's good enough for me
        In any mood.
And if her dashing wheel
Took her even to the de'il,
Thither, too, I'd gently steal,—
40   Yes, I would!

1896

INSPIRATION

He builds not anxiously by rule and line
Who, as he toils at the august design,
    Hears in his heart the summons from the height,
Sees in his soul the truth of beauty shine.

1896

THE JAR

Time is a deep-mouthed jar, pictured and dim,
Wherein Life's potent purple juices swim,
With Mirth the vanishing bubble at the brim.

1896

TWO SPHERES

1   While eager angels watched in awe,
     God fashioned with his hands
Two shining spheres to work his law,
     And carry his commands.

With patient art he shaped them true,
     With calm, untiring care;
And none of those bright watchers knew
     Which one to call most fair.

He dropped one lightly down to earth
10   Amid the morning's blue—
And on a gossamer had birth
     A bead of blinding dew.

It flamed across the hollow field,
     On tiptoe to depart,
Outvied Arcturus, and revealed
     All heaven in its heart.

He tossed the other into space
     (As children toss a ball)
To swing forever in its place
20   With equal rise and fall;

To flame through the ethereal dark,
     Among its brother spheres,
An orbit too immense to mark
     The little tide of years.

1896

O CLEAREST POOL

1 Clearest pool, my wondering joy
When a fancy-haunted boy,
From the troubled world of men
I've come back to thee again.

Loosed by my imperious star
I've come back from very far,
Dusty from the clash of years,
Worn with life and love and tears.

When I came to thee of old
10 Treasures rare my hands would hold,—
Wondrous blooms, or glass of dye
To transfigure earth and sky.

Now the best that I can bring
Seems a very little thing.
Let me cast it all away
To win back one boyhood's day.

O'er thy globe of crystal space,
Clearest pool, I lean my face.
What's the happy mask I see
20 Wisely smiling back on me?

Surely those glad eyes were mine
When the earth looked all divine!—
Knowing less, remembering more,
How enchanted was their lore!

Surely mine, this weary while
Agone, was that unshadowed smile!
Clearest pool, thou showest me
All my boyhood used to be.

Keep thy waters, clearest pool,
30 Always tranquil, pure and cool.
I, alas, must turn again
To the troubled world of men!

1896

YE POET AND HIS IDEAL

1 A wistful poet long and slim,
  Went down the greenwood way;
 The shy spring blossoms leaned to him,
  He seemed as shy as they.

 Plucking a flower here and there,
  And here and there a leaf,
 He moralized—"That things so fair
  Should be, alack, so brief!"

 With heedful finger at his lip
10 He strayed, until he came
 Where sat a slender young she-slip
  With eyes of dancing flame.

 She laughed, like sunlight on the stream,
  And he forgot the leaves;
 No more of blossoms he could dream
  Than Izrafel of beeves.

 She laughed; he knew not what to say,
  But gasped, he knew not why;
 She laughed; and he,—it was his way,—
20 Forgot that he was shy!

 "What fount, of wave pellucid, lends
  Thee to the air?" said he,
 "Or round thy dim abode extends
  The sap-rind of what tree?

 "Or art thou Helen, for whose kiss,
  The ten-years-anguished fray
 And woes that crimsoned Simois
  Were not too much to pay?

 "Or art thou Lilith, whose deep eyes
30 Made our great father glad,
 Ere Eve came into Paradise
  And drove him to the bad?

 "Or"—But her lips now grew so red,
  His trembled and were dumb.
 "Oh, yes, I'm all of these!" she said;
  "And more I may become!

"The Muse of late begins to feel
    The plight that you are in,
She sees the quest of your ideal
40   Has made you really thin.

"So, I am she whose face and form
    You've always hoped to find
In every love that took by storm
    Your much beleaguered mind.

"Now, you may rest. You'll need to chase
    No more from clime to clime
Each **haunting** form, each witching face!
    I'll be here all the time!"

Deep in his heart the poet mused:
50   "I like the good old way,
The methods I have always used,—
    I like those maids of clay!

"I dread her threatened constancy!
    But oh, her lips are real!
And, if I should grow wearied, why,
    I'll make a new ideal!"

1896

THE STACK BEHIND THE BARN

1   September is here, with the ripened seeds,
And the homely smell of the autumn weeds.
My heart goes back to a vanished day,
And I am again a boy at play
    In the stack behind the barn.

Dear memory of the old home-farm,—
The hedge-rows fencing the crops from harm,
The cows, too heavy with milk for haste,
The barn-yard, yellow with harvest waste,
10   And the stack behind the barn.

Dear, dear, dear the old garden-smell,
Sweet William and phlox that I loved so well,
And the seeding mint, and the sage turned grey,
But dearer the smell of the tumbled hay
    In the stack behind the barn.

218

In the side of the stack we made our nest,
And there was the play-house we loved the best.
A thicket of goldenrod, bending and bright,
Filled us with glory and hid us from sight
20   In the stack behind the barn.

Then, when the stack, with the year, ran low,
And our frosty, morning cheeks were aglow,
When time had forgotten the dropping leaves,
What joy to drop from the barn's wide eaves
     To the stack behind the barn!

O childhood years! Your heedless feet
Have slipped away with how much that's sweet!
But dreams and memory master you,
Till the make-believe of Life is through
30   I still may play as the children do
     In the stack behind the barn.

1896

IN THE ORCHARD

1   O apple leaves, so cool and green
     Against the summer sky,
You stir, although the wind is still
     And not a bird goes by.
      You start,
     And softly move apart
      In hushed expectancy.
Who is the gracious visitor
     Whose form I cannot see?

10   O apple leaves, the mystic light
     All down your dim arcade!
Why do your shadows tremble so,
     Half glad and half afraid?
      The air
     Is an unspoken prayer.
      Your eyes look all one way.
Who is the secret visitor
     Your tremors would betray?

1896

DEW

At evening, when the noise of life is done,
   And Earth lets fall her labors with the sun,
And calls her children, weary with their play,
   In from the busy tumult one by one,
How tenderly the heat and hurts of day
She washes in her infinite baths away!

1896

THE FARMER'S WINTER MORNING

1   The wide, white world is bitter still,
    (Oh, the snow lies deep in the barn-yard.)
And the dawn bites hard on the naked hill;
And the kitchen smoke from the chimney curls
Unblown, and hangs with a hue of pearls.
    (Oh, the snow lies deep in the barn-yard.)

The polished well-iron burns like a brand.
    (Oh, the frost is white on the latch.)
The horses neigh for their master's hand;
10   In the dusky stable they paw the floor
As his steps come crunching up to the door.
    (Oh, the frost is white on the latch.)

In the high, dim barn the smell of the hay
    (Oh, the snow lies deep in the barn-yard.)
Breathes him the breath of a summer's day.
The cows in their stanchions heavily rise
And watch him with slow, expectant eyes [.]
    (Oh, the snow lies deep in the barn-yard.)

Into the mangers, into the stalls,
20   (Oh, the frost is white on the latch.)
The fodder, cheerily rustling, falls.
And the sound of the feeding fills the air
As the sun looks in at the window-square.
    (Oh, the frost is white on the latch.)

With a rhythmic din in the echoing tins
    (Oh, the snow lies deep in the barn-yard.)
The noise of the milking soon begins.
With deepening murmur up to the brims
The foamy whiteness gathers and swims.
30   (Oh, the snow lies deep in the barn-yard.)

When the ice is chopped at the great trough's brink,
    (Oh, the frost is white on the latch.)
The cattle come lazily out to drink;
And the fowls come out on the sun-lit straw,—
For the sun's got high, and the south eaves thaw,
    (And the frost is gone from the latch.)

1896

AFOOT

1   Comes the lure of green things growing,
Comes the call of waters flowing,—
    And the wayfarer Desire
Moves and wakes and would be going.

Hark the migrant hosts of June
Marching nearer noon by noon!
    Hark the gossip of the grasses
Bivouacked beneath the moon!

Hark the leaves their mirth averring;
10   Hark the buds to blossom stirring;
    Hark the hushed, exultant haste
Of the wind and world conferring!

Hark the sharp, insistent cry
Where the hawk patrols the sky!
    Hark the flapping, as of banners,
Where the heron triumphs by!

Empire in the coasts of bloom
Humming cohorts now resume,—
    And desire is forth to follow
20   Many a vagabond perfume.

Long the quest and far the ending
Where my wayfarer is wending,—
    When Desire is once afoot,
Doom behind and Dream attending!

Shuttle-cock of indecision,
Sport of chance's blind derision,
    Yet he may not fail nor tire
Till his eyes shall win the Vision[.]

221

In his ears the phantom chime
30 Of incommunicable rhyme,
    He shall chase the fleeting camp-fires
Of the Bedouins of Time.

Farer by uncharted ways,
Dumb as Death to plaint or praise,
    Unreturning he shall journey,
Fellow to the nights and days;

Till upon the outer bar
Stilled the moaning currents are,
    Till the flame achieves the zenith,
40 Till the moth attains the star,

Till, through laughter and through tears,
Fair the final peace appears,
    And about the watered pastures
Sink to sleep the nomad years!

1896

APPLE SONG

1 O the sun has kissed the apples,
        Kissed the apples;
    And the apples, hanging mellow,
        Red and yellow,
    All down the orchard seen
    Make a glory in the green.

The sun has kissed the apples,
        Kissed the apples;
    And the hollow barrels wait
10   By the gate.
    The cider-presses drip
    With nectar for the lip.

The sun has kissed the apples,
        Kissed the apples;
    And the yellow miles of grain
        Forget the rain.
    The happy gardens yet
    The winter's blight forget.

222

The sun has kissed the apples,
20   Kissed the apples;
O'er the marsh the cattle spread,
      White and red.
The sky is all as blue
As a gentian in the dew.

The sun has kissed the apples,
      Kissed the apples;
And the maples are ablaze
      Through the haze.
The crickets in their mirth
30   Fife the fruiting song of earth.

The sun has kissed the apples,
      Kissed the apples;
Now with flocking call and stir
      Birds confer,
As if their hearts were crost
By fear of coming frost.

O the sun has kissed the apples,
      Kissed the apples;
And the harvest air is sweet
40   On the wheat.
Delight is not for long,—
Give us laughter, give us song!

                              1896

BESIDE THE WINTER SEA

1   As one who sleeps, and hears across his dream
    The cry of battles ended long ago,
    Inland I hear the calling of the sea.
    I hear its hollow voices, though between
    My wind-worn dwelling and thy wave-worn strand
    How many miles, how many mountains are!
    And thou beside the winter sea alone
    Art walking, with thy cloak about thy face.
    Bleak, bleak the tide, and evening coming on;
10   And grey the pale, pale light that wans thy face.
    Solemnly breaks the long wave at thy feet;
    And sullenly in patches clings the snow
    Upon the low, red rocks worn round with years.
    I see thine eyes, I see their grave desire,

223

Unsatisfied and lonely as the sea's;—
Yet how unlike the wintry sea's despair!
For could my feet but follow thine, my hands
But reach for thy warm hands beneath thy cloak,
What summer joy would lighten in thy face,
20   What sunshine warm thine eyes, and thy sad mouth
Break to a dewy rose and laugh on mine!

1896

BUTTERFLIES

Once in a garden, when the thrush's song,
   Pealing at morn, made holy all the air,
Till earth was healed of many an ancient wrong,
   And life appeared another name for prayer,

Rose suddenly a swarm of butterflies,
   On wings of white and gold and azure fire;
And one said, "These are flowers that seek the skies,
   Loosed by the spell of their supreme desire."

1896

THE HEAL-ALL

1   Dear blossom of the wayside kin,
     Whose homely, wholesome name
Tells of a potency within
     To win thee country fame!

The sterile hillocks are thy home,
     Beside the windy path;
The sky, a pale and lonely dome,
     Is all thy vision hath.

Thy unobtrusive purple face
10   Amid the meagre grass
Greets me with long-remembered grace,
     And cheers me as I pass.

And I, outworn by petty care,
     And vexed with trivial wrong,
I heed thy brave and joyous air
     Until my heart grows strong.

A lesson from the Power I crave
That moves in me and thee,
That makes thee modest, calm, and brave,—
20   Me restless as the sea.

Thy simple wisdom I would gain,—
To heal the hurt Life brings,
With kindly cheer, and faith in pain,
And joy of common things.

1896

JULY

1 I am for the open meadows,
Open meadows full of sun,
Where the hot bee hugs the clover,
The hot breezes drop and run.

I am for the uncut hayfields
Open to the cloudless blue,—
For the wide unshadowed acres
Where the summer's pomps renew;

Where the grass-tops gather purple,
10   Where the oxeye daisies thrive,
And the mendicants of summer
Laugh to feel themselves alive;

Where the hot scent steams and quivers,
Where the hot saps thrill and stir,
Where in leaf-cells' green pavilions
Quaint artificers confer;

Where the bobolinks are merry,
Where the beetles bask and gleam,
Where above the **powdered** blossoms
20   Powdered moth-wings poise and dream;

Where the bead-eyed mice adventure
In the grass-roots green and dun.
Life is good and love is eager
In the playground of the sun!

1896

LOVE'S TRANSLATOR

1   When the white moon divides the mist,
     My longing eyes believe
  'T is the white arm my lips have kissed
     Flashing from thy sleeve.

  And when the tall white lily sways
     Upon her queenly stalk,
  Thy white form fills my dreaming gaze
     Down the garden walk.

  When, rich with rose, a wandering air
10   Breathes up the leafy place,
  It seems to me thy perfumed hair
     Blown across my face.

  And when the thrush's golden note
     Across the gloom is heard,
  I think 't is thy impassioned throat
     Uttering one sweet word.

  And when the scarlet poppy-bud
     Breaks, breathing of the south,
  A sudden warmth awakes my blood
20   Thinking of thy mouth.

  And when that dove's wing dips in flight
     Above the dreaming land,
  I see some dear, remembered, white
     Gesture of thy hand.

  Wonder and love upon me wait
     In service fair, when I
  Into thy sweetness thus translate
     Earth and air and sky.

1896

MOTHERS

1   Mary, when the childing pain
     Made thy patient eyes grow dim,
  Of that anguish wert thou fain,
     Wert thou glad because of Him?
  How thou smiledst in thy woe
  Every mother's heart doth know.

Mary, when the helpless Child
    Nursed and slumbered at thy breast,
In the rosy form and mild
10   Didst thou see the Heavenly Guest?
Such a guest from Paradise
Gladdens every mother's eyes.

1896

TRYSTING SONG

1   Dear! Dear!
As the night draws nigh draw near.
    The world's forgotten;
      Work is done;
    The hour for loving
      Is begun.

    Sweet! Sweet!
It is love-time when we meet.
    The hush of desire
10   Falls with the dew,
    And all the evening
      Turns to you.

    Child! Child!
With the warm heart wise and wild.
    My spirit trembles
      Under your hand;
    You look in my eyes
      And understand.

    Mine! Mine!
20 Mistress of mood divine.
    What lore of the ages
      Bids you know
    The heart of a man
      Can love you so?

1896

A WAKE-UP SONG

1   Sun's up; wind's up! Wake up, dearies!
      Leave your coverlets white and downy.
    June's come into the world this morning.
      Wake up, Golden Head! Wake up, Brownie!

    Dew on the meadow-grass, waves on the water,
      Robins in the rowan-tree wondering about you!
    Don't keep the buttercups so long waiting.
      Don't keep the bobolinks singing without you.

    Wake up, Golden Head! Wake up, Brownie!
10   Cat-bird wants you in the garden soon.
    You and I, butterflies, bobolinks, and clover,
      We've a lot to do on the first of June.

1896

WHERE THE CATTLE COME TO DRINK

1   At evening, where the cattle come to drink,
      Cool are the long marsh-grasses, dewy cool
      The alder thickets, and the shallow pool,
    And the brown clay about the trodden brink.
    The pensive afterthoughts of sundown sink
      Over the patient acres given to peace;
      The homely cries and farmstead noises cease,
    And the worn day relaxes, link by link.

    A lesson that the open heart may read
10   Breathes in this mild benignity of air,
      These dear, familiar savours of the soil,—
    A lesson of the calm of humble creed,
      The simple dignity of common toil,
      And the plain wisdom of unspoken prayer.

1896

AYLESFORD LAKE

1   All night long the light is lying
    Silvery on the birches sighing,
    All night long the loons are crying
    Sweetly over Aylesford Lake.

Berry-copse and brake encumber
Granite islands out of number;
All night long the islands slumber,
   But my heart is wide awake.

Listening where the water teaches
10   Magic to the shining beaches,—
Watching where the waveless reaches
   Hold communion with the sky,—

Soon my spirit grows serener,
Hearing saner, vision keener.
In the night's benign demeanour
   Peace and Wisdom venture nigh.

                                   1897

THE SOLITARY WOODSMAN

1   When the grey lake-water rushes
Past the dripping alder-bushes,
   And the bodeful autumn wind
In the fir-tree weeps and hushes,—

When the air is sharply damp
Round the solitary camp,
   And the moose-bush in the thicket
Glimmers like a scarlet lamp,—

When the birches twinkle yellow,
10   And the cornel bunches mellow,
   And the owl across the twilight
Trumpets to his downy fellow,—

When the nut-fed chipmunks romp
Through the maples' crimson pomp,
   And the slim viburnum flushes
In the darkness of the swamp,—

When the blueberries are dead,
When the rowan clusters red,
   And the shy bear, summer-sleekened,
20   In the bracken makes his bed,—

On a day there comes once more
To the latched and lonely door,
　　Down the wood-road striding silent,
One who has been here before.

Green spruce branches for his head,
Here he makes his simple bed,
　　Couching with the sun, and rising
When the dawn is frosty red.

All day long he wanders wide
30　With the grey moss for his guide,
　　And his lonely axe-stroke startles
The expectant forest-side.

Toward the quiet close of day
Back to camp he takes his way,
　　And about his sober footsteps
Unafraid the squirrels play.

On his roof the red leaf falls,
At his door the bluejay calls,
　　And he hears the wood-mice hurry
40　Up and down his rough log walls;

Hears the laughter of the loon
Thrill the dying afternoon;
　　Hears the calling of the moose
Echo to the early moon.

And he hears the partridge drumming,
The belated hornet humming,—
　　All the faint, prophetic sounds
That foretell the winter's coming.

And the wind about his eaves
50　Through the chilly night-wet grieves,
　　And the earth's dumb patience fills him,
Fellow to the falling leaves.

1897

230

LIFE AND ART

Said Life to Art—"I love thee best
    Not when I find in thee
My very face and form, expressed
    With dull fidelity,

"But when in thee my craving eyes
    Behold continually
The mystery of my memories
    And all I long to be."

1897

TO A MIRROR

Haughty glass, be not so vain,
    So superb in thy disdain,
Deeming that she doth adore thee
    Over all the world of men!
If the splendid sun were not,
Who would give the moon a thought?
    And without her face before thee,
    Where would be thy beauty then?

1897

PHILLIDA'S LENT

1   In smart attire my Phillida
    Was gayest of the gay,
The giddy world was all to her;
    But that was yesterday!
For, strange to tell, she seems content
With serious things—because it's Lent!

She goes to matins every day
    And bows her knee demurely,
A nun of moonlight-colored mood
10   You would esteem her surely.
Some young Madonna she might be,
Made pale with prayer and ecstasy.

You'll swear 'tis fasting makes her cheek
　　Seem just a trifle thinner,
As plaintively she calls herself
　　A miserable sinner,
And finds in that convenient sentence
The fervor of profound repentance.

And yet **be sure** her utmost warmth
20　　Of picturesque devotion
Will not be suffered to provoke
　　A too severe emotion.
With timely tears her eyes may swim—
But not enough to make them dim.

To play the part of penitent
　　To her is most becoming,
Or else I fear that round her feet
　　The world would still be humming.
Less for her soul than her complexion
30　Is Lent a much desired protection.

Just watch her eyes and you will see
　　The naughty imp still in them;
And if you tempt her witcheries
　　She'll very soon begin them;
For when she's deepest in her prayers
The spell may take you unawares.

1897

THE TOWER BEYOND THE TOPS OF TIME

1　How long it was I did not know,
　　That I had waited, watched, and feared.
It seemed a thousand years ago
　　The last pale lights had disappeared.
I knew the place was a narrow room
Up, up beyond the reach of doom.

Then came a light more red than flame;—
　　No sun-dawn, but the soul laid bare
Of earth and sky and sea became
10　　A presence burning everywhere;
And I was glad my narrow room
Was high above the reach of doom.

Windows there were in either wall,
     Deep cleft, and set with radiant glass,
Wherethrough I watched the mountains fall,
     The ages wither up and pass.
I knew their doom could never climb
My tower beyond the tops of Time.

A sea of faces then I saw,
20   Of men who had been, men long dead.
Figured with dreams of joy and awe,
     The heavens unrolled in lambent red;
While far below the faces cried—
"Give us the dream for which we died!"

Ever the woven shapes rolled by
     Above the faces hungering.
With quiet and incurious eye
     I noted many a wondrous thing,—
Seas of clear glass, and singing streams,
30   In that high pageantry of dreams;

Cities of sard and chrysoprase
     Where choired Hosannas never cease;
Valhallas of celestial frays,
     And lotus-pools of endless peace;
But still the faces gaped and cried—
"Give us the dream for which we died!"

At length my quiet heart was stirred,
     Hearing them cry so long in vain.
But while I listened for a word
40   That should translate them from their pain
I saw that here and there a face
Shone, and was lifted from its place,

And flashed into the moving dome
     An ecstasy of prismed fire.
And then said I, "A soul has come
     To the deep zenith of desire!"
But still I wondered if it knew
The dream for which it died was true.

I wondered—who shall say how long?
50   (One heart-beat?—Thrice ten thousand years?)
Till suddenly there was no throng
    Of faces to arraign the spheres,—
No more white faces there to cry
To those great pageants of the sky.

Then quietly I grew aware
    Of one who came with eyes of bliss
And brow of calm and lips of prayer.
    Said I, "How wonderful is this!
Where are the faces once that cried—
60   'Give us the dream for which we died'?"

The answer fell as soft as sleep,—
    "I am of those who, having cried
So long in that tumultuous deep,
    Have won the dream for which we died."
And then said I, "Which dream was true?
For many were revealed to you!"

He answered, "To the soul made wise
    All true, all beautiful they seem.
But the white peace that fills our eyes
70   Outdoes desire, outreaches dream.
For we are come unto the place
Where always we behold God's face!"

1897

WHEN THE CLOVER BLOOMS AGAIN

1   "When the clover blooms again,
    And the rain-birds in the rain
        Make the sad-heart noon seem sweeter
        And the joy of June completer,
    I shall see his face again!"

Of her lover over sea
So she whispered happily;
    And she prayed, while men were sleeping,
    "Mary, have him in thy keeping
10   As he sails the stormy sea!"

White and silent lay his face
In a still, green-watered place,
    Where the long, grey weed scarce lifted,
    And the sand was lightly sifted
O'er his unremembering face.

1897

THE HERMIT

1   Above the blindness of content,
        The ignorance of ease,
    Inhabiting within his soul
        A shrine of memories,

    Between the silences of sleep
        Attentively he hears
    The endless crawling sob and strain,
        The spending of the years.

    He sees the lapsing stream go by
10   His unperturbéd face,
    Out of a dark, into a dark,
        Across a lighted space.

    He calls it Life, this lighted space
        Upon the moving flood.
    He sees the water white with tears,
        He sees it red with blood.

    And many specks upon the tide
        He sees and marks by name,—
    Motes of a day, and fools of Fate,
20   And challengers of fame;

    With here a people, there a babe,
        A blossom, or a crown,—
    They whirl a little, gleam, and pass,
        Or in the eddies drown.

    He waits. He waits one day to see
        The lapsing of the stream,
    The eddying forms, the darknesses,
        Dissolve into a dream.

1897

MARJORY

1   Spring, summer, autumn, winter,
    Over the wild world rolls the year.
Comes June to the rose-red tamarack buds,
    But Marjory comes not here.

The pastures miss her; the house without her
    Grows forgotten, and grey and old;
The wind, and the lonely light of the sun
    Are heavy with tears untold.

Spring, summer, autumn, winter,
10   Morning, evening, over and o'er!
The swallow returns to the nested rafter,
    But Marjory comes no more.

The grey barn-doors in the long wind rattle
    Hour by hour of the long white day.
The horses fret by the well-filled manger
    Since Marjory went away.

The sheep she fed at the bars await her.
    The milch cows low for her down the lane.
They long for her light, light hand at the milking,—
20   They long for her hand in vain.

Spring, summer, autumn, winter,
    Morning and evening, over and o'er!
The bees come back with the willow catkins,
    But Marjory comes no more.

The voice of the far-off city called to her.
    Was it long years or an hour ago?
She went away, with dear eyes weeping,
    To a world she did not know.

The berried pastures they could not keep her,
30   The brook, nor the buttercup-golden hill,
Nor even the long, long love familiar,—
    The strange voice called her still.

She would not stay for the old home garden;—
    The scarlet poppy, the mignonette,
The fox-glove bell, and the kind-eyed pansy,
    Their hearts will not forget.

Oh, that her feet had not forgotten
　　The woodland country, the homeward way!
Oh, to look out of the sad, bright window
40　　And see her come back, some day!

Spring, summer, autumn, winter,
　　Over the wild world rolls the year.
Comes joy to the bird on the nested rafter;
　　But Marjory comes not here.

　　　　　　　　　　　　1897

ASCRIPTION

1　O Thou who hast beneath Thy hand
　　The dark foundations of the land,—
　　The motion of whose ordered thought
　　An instant universe hath wrought,—

　　Who hast within Thine equal heed
　　The rolling sun, the ripening seed,
　　The azure of the speedwell's eye,
　　The vast solemnities of sky,—

　　Who hear'st no less the feeble note
10　Of one small bird's awakening throat,
　　Than that unnamed, tremendous chord
　　Arcturus sounds before his Lord,—

　　More sweet to Thee than all acclaim
　　Of storm and ocean, stars and flame,
　　In favour more before Thy face
　　Than pageantry of time and space,

　　The worship and the service be
　　Of him Thou madest most like Thee,—
　　Who in his nostrils hath Thy breath,
20　Whose spirit is the lord of death!

　　　　　　　　　　　　1897

237

TEARS

When chars the heart to ashes in its pain,
    Or withers in its vain desire,
Tears are the benediction of the rain
    Falling to quench the fire.

1897

NIGHT IN A DOWN-TOWN STREET

1   Not in the eyed, expectant gloom,
    Where soaring peaks repose
And incommunicable space
    Companions with the snows;

Not in the glimmering dusk that crawls
    Upon the clouded sea,
Where bourneless wave on bourneless wave
    Complains continually;

Not in the palpable dark of woods
10   Where groping hands clutch fear,
Does Night her deeps of solitude
    Reveal unveiled as here.

The street is a grim cañon carved
    In the eternal stone,
That knows no more the rushing stream
    It anciently has known.

The emptying tide of life has drained
    The iron channel dry.
Strange winds from the forgotten day
20   Draw down, and dream, and sigh.

The narrow heaven, the desolate moon
    Made wan with endless years,
Seem less immeasurably remote
    Than laughter, love, or tears.

1897

A NOCTURNE OF CONSECRATION

1   I talked about you, Dear, the other night,
Having myself alone with my delight.
Alone with dreams and memories of you,
All the divine-houred summer stillness through
I talked of life, of love the always new,
Of tears, and joy,—yet only talked of you.

To the sweet air
That breathed upon my face
The spirit of lilies in a leafy place,
10   Your breath's caress, the lingering of your hair,
I said—"In all your wandering through the dusk,
Your waitings on the marriages of flowers
Through the long, intimate hours
When soul and sense, desire and love confer,
You must have known the best that God has made.
What do you know of her?"

Said the sweet air—
"Since I have touched her lips,
Bringing the consecration of her kiss,
20   Half passion and half prayer,
And all for you,
My various lore has suffered an eclipse.
I have forgot all else of sweet I knew."

To the wise earth,
Kind, and companionable, and dewy cool,
Fair beyond words to tell, as you are fair,
And cunning past compare
To leash all heaven in a windless pool,
I said—"The mysteries of death and birth
30   Are in your care.
You love, and sleep; you drain life to the lees;
And wonderful things you know.
Angels have visited you, and at your knees
Learned what I learn forever at her eyes,
The pain that still enhances Paradise.
You in your breast felt her first pulses stir;
And you have thrilled to the light touch of her feet,
Blindingly sweet.
Now make me wise with some new word of her."

40   Said the wise earth—
"She is not all my child.
But the wild spirit that rules her heart-beats wild
Is of diviner birth
And kin to the unknown light beyond my ken.
All I can give to her have I not given?
Strength to be glad, to suffer, and to know;
The sorcery that subdues the souls of men;
The beauty that is as the shadow of heaven;
The hunger of love
50   And unspeakable joy thereof.
And these are dear to her because of you.
You need no word of mine to make you wise
Who worship at her eyes
And find there life and love forever new!"

To the white stars,
Eternal and all-seeing,
In their wide home beyond the wells of being,
I said—"There is a little cloud that mars
The mystical perfection of her kiss.
60   Mine, mine, she is,
As far as lip to lip, and heart to heart,
And spirit to spirit when lips and hands must part,
Can make her mine. But there is more than this,—
More, more of her to know.
For still her soul escapes me unaware,
To dwell in secret where I may not go.
Take, and uplift me. Make me wholly hers."

Said the white stars, the heavenly ministers,—
"This life is brief, but it is only one.
70   Before to-morrow's sun
For one or both of you it may be done.
This love of yours is only just begun.
Will all the ecstacy that may be won
Before this life its little course has run
At all suffice
The love that agonizes in your eyes?
Therefore be wise.
Content you with the wonder of love that lies
Between her lips and underneath her eyes.
80   If more you should surprise,
What would be left to hope from Paradise?["]

So, Dear, I talked the long, divine night through,
And felt you in the chrismal balms of dew.

240

The thing then learned
Has ever since within my bosom burned —
One life is not enough for love of you.

1897

MY GARDEN

1   I have a garden in the city's grime
Where secretly my heart keeps summer-time;

Where blow such airs of rapture on my eyes
As those blest dreamers know in Paradise,

Who after lives of longing come at last
Where anguish of vain love is overpast.

When the broad noon lies shadeless on the street,
And traffic roars, and toilers faint with heat,

Where men forget that ever woods were green,
10   The wonders of my garden are not seen.

Only at night the magic doors disclose
Its labyrinths of lavender and rose;

And honeysuckle, white beneath its moon,
Whispers me softly thou art coming soon;

And led by Love's white hand upon my wrist
Beside its glimmering fountains I keep tryst.

O Love, this moving fragrance on my hair, —
Is it thy breath, or some enchanted air

From far, uncharted realms of mystery
20   Which I have dreamed of but shall never see?

O Love, this low, wild music in my ears,
Is it the heart-beat of thy hopes and fears,

Or the faint cadence of some fairy song
On winds of boyhood memory blown along?

O Love, what poignant ecstasy is this
Upon my lips and eyes? Thy touch, — thy kiss.

1898

A STREET VIGIL

1 Here is the street
Made holy by the passing of her feet,—
    The little, tender feet, more sweet than myrrh,
    Which I have washed with tears for love of her.

Here she has gone
Until the very stones have taken on
    A glory from her passing, and the place
    Is tremulous with memory of her face.

Here is the room
10 That holds the light to lighten my life's gloom.
    Beyond that blank white window she is sleeping
    Who hath my hope, my health, my fame in keeping.

A little peace
Here for a little, ere my vigil cease
    And I turn homeward, shaken with the strife
    Of hope that struggles hopeless, sick for life.

Surely the power
That lifted me from darkness that one hour
    To a dear heaven whereof no word can tell
20   Not wantonly will thrust me back to hell.

1898

AT THE RAILWAY STATION

1   Here the night is fierce with light,
      Here the great wheels come and go,
    Here are partings, waitings, meetings,
      Mysteries of joy and woe.

Here is endless haste and change,
      Here the ache of streaming eyes,
    Radiance of expectant faces,
      Breathless askings, brief replies.

Here the jarred, tumultuous air
10   Throbs and pauses like a bell,
    Gladdens with delight of greeting,
      Sighs and sorrows with farewell.

Here, ah, here with hungry eyes
    I explore the passing throng.
Restless I await your coming
    Whose least absence is so long.

Faces, faces pass me by,
    Meaningless, and blank, and dumb,
Till my heart grows faint and sickens
20   Lest at last you should not come.

Then—I see you. And the blood
    Surges back to heart and brain.
Eyes meet mine,—and Heaven opens.
    You are at my side again.

1898

IN A CITY ROOM

1 O city night of noises and alarms,
    Your lights may flare, your cables clang and rush,
But in the sanctuary of my love's arms
    Your blinding tumult dies into a hush.

My doors are surged about with your unrest;
    Your plangent cares assail my realm of peace;
But when I come unto her quiet breast
    How suddenly your jar and clamour cease!

Then even remembrance of your strifes and pains
10   Diminishes to a ghost of sorrows gone,
Remoter than a dream of last year's rains
    Gusty against my window in the dawn.

1898

IN THE SOLITUDE OF THE CITY

1 Night; and the sound of voices in the street.
    Night; and the happy laughter where they meet,
      The glad boy lover and the trysting girl.
    But thou—but thou—I cannot find thee, Sweet!

243

Night; and far off the lighted pavements roar.
Night; and the dark of sorrow keeps my door.
   I reach my hand out trembling in the dark.
Thy hand comes not with comfort any more.

O Silent, Unresponding! If these fears
10 Lie not, nor other wisdom come with years,
   No day shall dawn for me without regret,
No night go uncompanioned by my tears.

1898

A NOCTURNE OF EXILE

1 Out of this night of lonely noise,
   The city's crowded cries,
Home of my heart, to thee, to thee
   I turn my longing eyes.

Years, years, how many years I went
   In exile wearily,
Before I lifted up my face
   And saw my home in thee.

I had come home to thee at last.
10   I saw thy warm lights gleam.
I entered thine abiding joy,—
   Oh, was it but a dream?

Ere I could reckon with my heart
   The sum of our delight,
I was an exile once again
   Here in the hasting night.

Thy doors were shut; thy lights were gone
   From my remembering eyes.
Only the city's endless throng!
20   Only the crowded cries!

1898

A NOCTURNE OF TRYSTING

1 Broods the hid glory in its sheath of gloom
Till strikes the destined hour, and bursts the bloom,
A rapture of white passion and perfume.

So the long day is like a bud
That aches with coming bliss,
Till flowers in light the wondrous night
That brings me to thy kiss.

Then, with a thousand sorrows forgotten in one hour,
In thy pure eyes and at thy feet I find at last my goal;
10 And life and hope and joy seem but a faint prevision
Of the flower that is thy body and the flame that is thy soul.

1898

PRESENCE

1 Dawn like a lily lies upon the land
Since I have known the whiteness of your hand.
Dusk is more soft and more mysterious where
Breathes on my eyes the perfume of your hair.
Waves at your coming break in livelier blue;
And solemn woods are glad because of you.
Brooks of your laughter learn their liquid notes.
Birds to your voice attune their pleading throats.
Fields to your feet grow smoother and more green;
10 And happy blossoms tell where you have been.

1898

LIFE AND THE ARTIST

Life said to the Artist: Tell my dream,
That man may know me loftier than I seem,—
Not only kin and servitor to the clod,
But the veiled oracle of the Thought of God.

1898

THAW

Time in the long, chill Norland silence slept,
While the white warder, snow, his chamber kept.

Dreaming the stars were young, and he a child,
His wise old lips did mutter, and he smiled.

Then went a warm stir through the wintry land,
And waking brooks sang, "Surely spring's at hand!"

1898

A NOCTURNE OF SPIRITUAL LOVE

1   Sleep, sleep, imperious heart! Sleep, fair and undefiled!
      Sleep and be free.
Come in your dreams at last, comrade and queen and child,
      At last to me.

Come, for the honeysuckle calls you out of the night.
      Come, for the air
Calls with a tyrannous remembrance of delight,
      Passion, and prayer.

Sleep, sovereign heart! and now,—for dream and memory
10   Endure no door,—
My spirit undenied goes where my feet, to thee,
      Have gone before.

A moonbeam or a breath, above thine eyes I bow,
      Silent, unseen,—
But not, ah, not unknown! thy spirit knows me now
      Where I have been.

Surely my long desire upon thy soul hath power.
      Surely for this
Thy sleep shall breathe thee forth, soul of the lily flower,
20   Under my kiss.

Sleep, body wonderful. Wake, spirit wise and wild,
      White and divine.
Here is our heaven of dream, O dear and undefiled,
      All thine, all mine.

1898

IN THE CROWD

I walk the city square with thee.
   The night is loud; the pavements roar.
Their eddying mirth and misery
Encircle thee and me.

The street is full of lights and cries.
   The crowd but brings thee close to me.
I only hear thy low replies;
I only see thine eyes.

1898

ON THE ELEVATED RAILWAY AT 110TH STREET

1   Above the hollow deep where lies
   The city's slumbering face,
Out, out across the night we swing,
   A meteor launched in space.

The dark above is sown with stars.
   The humming dark below
With sparkle of ten thousand lamps
   In endless row on row.

Tall shadow towers with glimmering lights
10   Stand sinister and grim
Where upper deep and lower deep
   Come darkly rim to rim.

Our souls have known the midnight awe
   Of mount, and plain, and sea;
But here the city's night enfolds
   A vaster mystery.

1898

AT THY VOICE MY HEART

1   At thy voice my heart
   Wakes as a bird
Wakes in the night
   With sudden rapture stirred.

At thy look my soul
        Soars as a flame
Soars from the dark
        Toward heaven, whence it came.

At thy love my life
10   Lifts from the clod
As a lily lifts
        From its dark sleep toward God.

                                        1898

A BALLAD OF MANILA BAY

1   Your threats how vain, Corregidor;
    Your rampired batteries, feared no more;
    Your frowning guard at Manila gate,—
        When our Captain went before!

    Lights out. Into the unknown gloom
    From the windy, glimmering, wide sea-room.
    Challenging fate in that dark strait
        We dared the hidden doom.

    But the death in the deep awoke not then;
10 Mine and torpedo they spoke not then;
    From the heights that loomed on our passing line
        The thunders broke not then.

    Safe through the perilous dark we sped,
    Quiet each ship as the quiet dead,
    Till the guns of El Fraile roared—too late,
        And the steel prows forged ahead.

    Mute each ship as the mute-mouth grave,
    A ghost leviathan cleaving the wave;
    But deep in its heart the great fires throb,
20   The travailing engines rave,

    The ponderous pistons urge like fate,
    The red-throat furnaces roar elate,
    And the sweating stokers stagger and swoon
        In a heat more fierce than hate.

So through the dark we stole our way
Past the grim warders and into the bay,
Past Kalibuyo, and past Salinas,—
    And came at the break of day

Where strong Cavité stood to oppose,—
30 Where, from a sheen of silver and rose,
A thronging of masts, a soaring of towers,
    The beautiful city arose.

How fine and fair! But the shining air
With a thousand shattering thunders there
Flapped and reeled. For the fighting foe—
    We had caught him in his lair.

Surprised, unready, his proud ships lay
Idly at anchor in Bakor Bay;—
Unready, surprised, but proudly bold,
40   Which was ever the Spaniard's way.

Then soon on his pride the dread doom fell,
Red doom,—for the ruin of shot and shell
Lit every vomiting, bursting hulk
    With a crimson reek of hell.

But to the brave though beaten, hail!
All hail to them that dare and fail!
To the dauntless boat that charged our fleet
    And sank in the iron hail!

    . . . .

Manila Bay! Manila Bay!
50 How proud the song on our lips to-day!
A brave old song of the true and strong
    And the will that has its way;

Of the blood that told in the days of Drake
When the fight was good for the fighting's sake!
For the blood that fathered Farragut
    Is the blood that fathered Blake;

And the pride of the blood will not be undone
While war's in the world and a fight to be won.
For the master now, as the master of old,
60   Is "the man behind the gun."

The dominant blood that daunts the foe,
That laughs at odds, and leaps to the blow,—
It is Dewey's glory to-day, as Nelson's
    A hundred years ago!

                   1898

THE ATLANTIC CABLE

1   This giant nerve, at whose command
    The world's great pulses throb or sleep,—
It threads the undiscerned repose
    Of the dark bases of the deep.

Around it settle in the calm
    Fine tissues that a breath might mar,
Nor dream what fiery tidings pass,
    What messages of storm and war.

Far over it, where filtered gleams
10   Faintly illume the mid-sea day,
Strange, pallid forms of fish or weed
    In the obscure tide softly sway.

And higher, where the vagrant waves
    Frequent the white, indifferent sun,
Where ride the smoke-blue hordes of rain
    And the long vapours lift and run,

Passes perhaps some lonely ship
    With exile hearts that homeward ache,—
While far beneath is flashed a word
20   That soon shall bid them bleed or break.

                   1898

AT TIDE WATER

1   The red and yellow of the Autumn salt-grass,
    The grey flats, and the yellow-grey full tide,
The lonely stacks, the grave expanse of marshes,—
    O Land wherein my memories abide,
I have come back that you may make me tranquil,
    Resting a little at your heart of peace,
Remembering much amid your serious leisure,
    Forgetting more amid your large release.

For yours the wisdom of the night and morning,
10   The word of the inevitable years,
The open heaven's unobscured communion,
    And the dim whisper of the wheeling spheres.
The great things and the terrible I bring you,
    To be illumined in your spacious breath,—
Love, and the ashes of desire, and anguish,
    Strange laughter, and the unhealing wound of death.
These in the world, all these, have come upon me,
    Leaving me mute and shaken with surprise.
Oh, turn them in your measureless contemplation,
20   And in their mastery teach me to be wise.

1898

DREAM-FELLOWS

1   Behind the veil that men call sleep
    I came upon a golden land.
A golden light was in the leaves
    And on the amethystine strand.

Amber and gold and emerald
    The unimaginable wood.
And in a joy I could not name
    Beside the emerald stream I stood.

Down from a violet hill came one
10   Running to meet me on the shore.
I clasped his hand. He seemed to be
    One I had long been waiting for.

All the sweet sounds I ever heard
    In his low greeting seemed to blend.
His were the eyes of my true love.
    His was the mouth of my true friend.

We spoke; and the transfigured words
    Meant more than words had ever meant.
Our lips at last forgot to speak,
20   For silence was so eloquent.

We floated in the emerald stream;
    We wandered in the wondrous wood.
His soul to me was clear as light.
    My inmost thought he understood.

Only to be was to be glad.
 Life, like a rainbow, filled our eyes.
In comprehending comradeship
 Each moment seemed a Paradise.

And often, in the after years,
30 I and my dream-fellow were one
For hours together in that land
 Behind the moon, beyond the sun.

At last, in the tumultuous dream
 That men call life, I chanced to be
One day amid the city throng
 Where the great piers oppose the sea.

A giant ship was swinging off
 For other seas and other skies.
Amid the voyaging companies
40 I saw his face, I saw his eyes.

Oh, passionately through the crowd
 I thrust, and then—our glances met!
Across the widening gulf we gazed,
 With white, set lips, and eyes grown wet.

And all day long my heart was faint
 With parting pangs and tears unwept;
Till night brought comfort, for he came
 To meet me, smiling, when I slept.

Beyond the veil that men call sleep
50 We met, within that golden land.
He said—or I—"We grieved to-day.
 But now, more wise, we understand!

"Communing in the common world,
 The flesh, for us, would be a bar.
Strange would be our familiar speech;
 And earth would seem no more a star.

"We'd know no more the golden leaves
 Beside the amethystine deep;
We'd see no more each other's thought
60 Behind the veil that men call sleep!"

1898

AN EVENING COMMUNION

1 The large first stars come out
     Above the open hill,
   And in the west the light
     Is lingering still.

   The wide and tranquil air
     Of evening washes cool
   On open hill, and vale,
     And shining pool.

   The calm of endless time
10   Is in the spacious hour
   Whose mystery unfolds
     To perfect flower.

   The silence and my heart
     Expect a voice I know,—
   A voice we have not heard
     Since long ago.

   Since long ago thy face,
     Thy smile, I may not see,
   True comrade, whom the veil
20   Divides from me.

   But when earth's hidden word
     I almost understand,
   I dream that on my lips
     I feel thy hand.

   Thy presence is the light
     Upon the open hill.
   Thou walkest with me here,
     True comrade still.

   My pain and my unrest
30   Thou tak'st into thy care.
   The world becomes a dream,
     And life a prayer.

                    1898

THE FALLING LEAVES

1   Lightly He blows, and at His breath they fall,
      The perishing kindreds of the leaves; they drift,
    Spent flames of scarlet, gold aërial,
      Across the hollow year, noiseless and swift.
    Lightly He blows, and countless as the falling
      Of snow by night upon a solemn sea,
    The ages circle down beyond recalling
      To strew the hollows of Eternity.
    He sees them drifting through the spaces dim,
10   And leaves and ages are as one to Him.

                        1898

A FOREWORD TO *NORTHLAND LYRICS*

To E.R. MacD., W.C.R., T.G.R.

1   Sisters and brothers, not by blood alone
    Kinship inalienably dear we own,
    Nor hearts close-knit in common joys and tears
    And memories of sweet, familiar years
      That pledge the deep endurance of our love;

    But also by the fellowship of song,—
    One art, one aim, one impulse,—we belong
    Each to the others! Therefore let this word,
    Though poor, amid your Northland notes be heard
10   For craft and kin and the loyal warmth thereof.

                        1898

THE IDEAL

1   To Her, when life was little worth,
      When hope, a tide run low,
    Between dim shores of emptiness
      Almost forgot to flow,—

    Faint with the city's fume and stress
      I came at night to Her.
    Her cool white fingers on my face—
10   How wonderful they were!

More dear they were to fevered lids
    Than lilies cooled in dew.
They touched my lips with tenderness,
    Till life was born anew.

The city's clamour died in calm;
    And once again I heard
The moon-white woodland stillnesses
    Enchanted by a bird;

      The wash of far, remembered waves;
20   The sigh of lapsing streams;
And one old garden's lilac leaves
    Conferring in their dreams.

A breath from childhood daisy fields
    Came back to me again,
Here in the city's weary miles
    Of city-wearied men.

1898

IN DARKNESS

I have faced life with courage,—but not now!
    O Infinite, in this darkness draw thou near.
Wisdom alone I asked of thee, but thou
    Hast crushed me with the awful gift of fear.

1898

NOCTURNES OF THE HONEYSUCKLE

I

1   Forever shed your sweetness on the night,
Dear honeysuckle, flower of our delight!

Forever breathe the mystery of that hour
When her hand touched me, lightlier than a flower,—

And life became forever strange and sweet,
A gift to lay with worship at her feet.

Oh, flower of the honeysuckle,
   Tell me how often the long night through
She turns in her dream to the open window,
10   She turns in her dream to you.

Oh, flower of the honeysuckle,
   Tell me how tenderly out of the dew
You breathe her a dream of that night of wonder
   When life was fashioned anew.

Oh, flower of the honeysuckle,
   Tell me how long ere, the sweet night through,
She will turn not to you but to me in the darkness,
   And dream and desire come true.

                    1898

O THOU WHO BIDD'ST

O Thou who bidd'st a million germs decay
That one white bloom may soar into the day,
Mine eyes unseal to see their souls in death
Borne back to Thee upon the lily's breath.

                    1898

THE STREET LAMPS

   Eyes of the city,
Keeping your sleepless watch from sun to sun,
     Is it for pity
You tremble, seeing innocence undone;
   Or do you laugh, to think men thus should set
   Spies on the folly day would fain forget?

                    1898

AT THE DRINKING FOUNTAIN

He stops beside the crowded curb, and lifts
The chained cup to his lips. And now he hears
The water thinly tinkling thro' the roar
Of wheels and trade. Back, back his memory drifts.
To his tired eyes the pasture spring appears,
And the dear fields that he shall see no more.

1899

JONATHAN AND JOHN

1   Should Jonathan and John fall out
The world would stagger from that bout.
With John and Jonathan at one
The world's great peace will have begun.

With Jonathan and John at war
The hour that havoc hungers for
Will strike, in ruin of blood and tears,—
The world set back a thousand years.

With John and Jonathan sworn to stand
10 Shoulder to shoulder, hand by hand,
Justice and peace shall build their throne
From tropic sea to frozen zone.

When Jonathan and John forget
The scar of an ancient wound to fret
And smile to think of an ancient feud
Which the God of the nations turned to good;

When the bond of a common creed and speech
And kindred binds them each to each,
And each in the other's victories
20 The pride of his own achievement sees,—

How paltry a thing they both will know
That grudge of a hundred years ago,—
How small that blemish of wrath and blame
In the blazonry of their common fame!

1899

KINSMEN STRONG

1   This is the song
Of kinsmen strong
Standing at guard
In the gates of earth:—

"Side by side
Our flags flung wide
Proclaim the pride
Of our kindred birth.

"All ye of the brood
10   Of an alien blood
Take count of our folk
No longer twain.
Not twain, but one,
By the tides that run
With new warmth won
In each kindred vein.

"Take note all ye,
Of the alien knee,
Of the faith that fires
20   Our hearts and thews.
One in our creed
And one in our need,
In daring and deed
We shall win, not lose.

"Be counseled, each
Of the alien speech,
From polar barren,
To isle empearled:
This shout you hear
30   So near and clear
Is the marching cheer
Of the lords of the world.

"Stout heart by heart
We work our part
That light may broaden
And law command.
This is our place
By right of race,
By God's good grace
40   And the strength of our hand.

"The strength of our hand
On every land
Till the master-work
Of the world be done:
For the slave's release,
For the bond of peace,
That wars may cease
From under the sun."

1899

A REMORSE

1   I dreamed last night my love was dead.
The dreadful thing was this!—
Not that my lips would feel no more
The kindness of her kiss;
Not that my feet the weary years
Would go uncomraded;
Not that of all my love for her
So much remained unsaid;—
But, sickening, I remembered how
10 I had been false to her!
"O God!" I cried aloud—"*She knows
I have been false to her!*"

1899

A SONG FOR APRIL

1   List! list! The buds confer.
This noonday they've had news of her;
The south bank has had views of her;
The thorn shall exact his dues of her;
    The willows adream
    By the freshet stream
Shall ask what boon they choose of her.

Up! up! The world's astir;
The would-be green has word of her;
10 Root and germ have heard of her,
    Coming to break
    Their sleep and wake
Their hearts with every bird of her.

See! see! How swift concur
Sun, wind, and rain at the name of her,
A-wondering what became of her;
The fields flower at the flame of her;
    The glad air sings
    With dancing wings
20   And the silvery shrill acclaim of her.

1899

BROOKLYN BRIDGE

1   No lifeless thing of iron and stone,
    But sentient, as her children are,
Nature accepts you for her own,
    Kin to the cataract and the star.

She marks your vast, sufficing plan,
    Cable and girder, bolt and rod,
And takes you, from the hand of man,
    As some new handiwork of God.

You thrill through all your chords of steel
10   Responsive to the living sun,
And quickening in your nerves you feel
    Life with its conscious currents run.

Your anchorage upbears the march
    Of time and the eternal powers.
The sky admits your perfect arch.
    The rock respects your stable towers.

1899

A STREET SONG AT NIGHT

1   Here mid the hasting and eddying faces,
    Here in the whirl of the crowd,
Where the car lights flame and the windows glare
    And the night is white and loud,

Here we two are together, we two
    Unheeded, content, unknown.
Not in the wilderness could we be
    More wonderfully alone.

No face of them all is a face we know.
10   No too familiar eye
Will peer from the throng to vex our joy
     As we two wander by.

Yon towering walls with the lights that soar
     Are gnome-land palaces.
Yon airy train is a dragon rushing
     To carry us overseas.

I press you close to my side, secure
     In the solitude of the throng.
And the laughter of children comes to our lips
20   For we know that love is long.

                                                      1899

THE WHITE FROST

The earth lay black and weeping, till from God
Came a reflection of the Eternal Face;
And every common weed and branch and clod
Knew itself kindred to the spheres of space.

                                                      1900

CHILD OF THE INFINITE

1   Sun, and Moon, and Wind, and Flame,
              Dust, and Dew, and Day and Night,—
              Ye endure. Shall I endure not,
              Though so fleeting in your sight?
              Ye return. Shall I return not,
              Flesh, or in the flesh's despite?
              Ye are mighty. But I hold you
              Compassed in a vaster might.

    Sun.   Sun, before your flaming circuit
10   Smote upon the uncumbered dark,
              I, within the Thought Eternal
              Palpitant, a quenchless spark,
              Watched while God awoke and set you
              For a measure and a mark.

                                                      261

Moon.	Dove of Heaven, ere you brooded
	Whitely o'er the shoreless waste
	And upon the driven waters
	Your austere enchantment placed,
	I was power in God's conception,
20	Without rest and without haste.

Wind. Breath of Time, before your whisper
Wandered o'er the naked world,
Ere your wrath from pole to tropic
Running Alps of ocean hurled,
I, the germ of storm in stillness,
At the heart of God lay furled.

Flame. Journeying Spirit, ere your tongues
Taught the perished to aspire,
Charged the clod, and called the mortal
30   Through the reinitiant fire,
I was of the fiery impulse
Urging the Divine Desire.

Dust. Seed of Earth, when down the void
You were scattered from His hand,
When the spinning clot contracted,
Globed and greened at His command,
I, behind the sifting fingers,
Saw the scheme of beauty planned.

Dew. Phantom of the Many Waters,
40   When no more you fleet and fall,
When no more your round you follow,
Infinite, ephemeral,
At the feet of the Unsleeping
I shall toss you like a ball.

Day and Rolling Masks of Life and Death,
Night. When no more your ancient place
Knows you, when your light and darkness
Swing no longer over space,
My remembrance shall restore you
50   To the favour of His face.

1900

262

THE AIM

1   O Thou who lovest not alone
The swift success, the instant goal,
But hast a lenient eye to mark
The failures of the inconstant soul,

Consider not my little worth,—
The mean achievement, scamped in act,
The high resolve and low result,
The dream that durst not face the fact.

But count the reach of my desire.
10   Let this be something in Thy sight:—
I have not, in the slothful dark,
Forgot the Vision and the Height.

Neither my body nor my soul
To earth's low ease will yield consent.
I praise Thee for my will to strive.
I bless Thy goad of discontent.

                  1900

ATTAR

1   The dark rose of your mouth
Is summer and the south to me;
The attar of desire and dream
Its tendernesses seem to me.

The clear deep of your eyes
A lure of wonder lies to me,
Whereto my longing soul descends
While love comes by and bends to me.

The hushed night of your hair
10   Breathes an enchanted air to me—
Strange heats from many a mystic clime
And far-off, perished time to me.

The pulses of your throat,
What madness they denote to me,—
Passion, and hunger, and despair,
And ecstasy, and prayer to me!

The dusk bloom of your flesh
Is as a magic mesh to me,
Wherein our spirits lie ensnared,
20   Your wild, wild beauty bared to me.

1900

THE STRANDED SHIP

1   Far up the lonely strand the storm had lifted her.
And now along her keel the merry tides make stir
No more. The running waves that sparkled at her prow
Seethe to the chains and sing no more with laughter now.
No more the clean sea-furrow follows her. No more
To the hum of her gallant tackle the hale Nor'-westers roar.
No more her bulwarks journey. For the only boon they crave
Is the guerdon of all good ships and true, the boon of a deep-sea
    grave.

Take me out, sink me deep in the green profound,
10   *To sway with the long weed, swing with the drowned,*
Where the change of the soft tide makes no sound,
Far below the keels of the outward bound.

No more she mounts the circles from Fundy to the Horn,
From Cuba to the Cape runs down the tropic morn,
Explores the Vast Uncharted where great bergs ride in ranks,
Nor shouts a broad "Ahoy" to the dories on the Banks.
No more she races freights to Zanzibar and back,
Nor creeps where the fog lies blind along the liners' track.
No more she dares the cyclone's disastrous core of calm
20   To greet across the dropping wave the amber isles of palm.

Take me out, sink me deep in the green profound,
To sway with the long weed, swing with the drowned,
Where the change of the soft tide makes no sound,
Far below the keels of the outward bound.

Amid her trafficking peers, the wind-wise, journeyed ships,
At the black wharves no more, nor at the weedy slips,
She comes to port with cargo from many a storied clime.
No more to the rough-throat chantey her windlass creaks in time.
No more she loads for London with spices from Ceylon,—
30   With white spruce deals and wheat and apples from St. John.
No more from Pernambuco with coffee-bags,—no more
With hides from Buenos Ayres she clears for Baltimore.

264

Take me out, sink me deep in the green profound,
To sway with the long weed, swing with the drowned,
Where the change of the soft tide makes no sound,
Far below the keels of the outward bound.

Wan with the slow vicissitudes of wind and rain and sun
How grieves her deck for the sailors whose hearty brawls are done!
Only the wandering gull brings word of the open wave,
40   With shrill scream at her taffrail deriding her alien grave.
Around the keel that raced the dolphin and the shark
Only the sand-wren twitters from barren dawn till dark;
And all the long blank noon the blank sand chafes and mars
The prow once swift to follow the lure of the dancing stars.

    Take me out, sink me deep in the green profound,
    To sway with the long weed, swing with the drowned,
    Where the change of the soft tide makes no sound,
    Far below the keels of the outward bound.

And when the winds are low, and when the tides are still,
50   And the round moon rises inland over the naked hill,
And o'er her parching seams the dry cloud-shadows pass,
And dry along the land-rim lie the shadows of thin grass,
Then aches her soul with longing to launch and sink away
Where the fine silts lift and settle, the sea-things drift and stray,
To make the port of Last Desire, and slumber with her peers
In the tide-wash rocking softly through the unnumbered years.

    Take me out, sink me deep in the green profound,
    To sway with the long weed, swing with the drowned,
    Where the change of the soft tide makes no sound,
60   *Far below the keels of the outward bound.*

1900

O LITTLE ROSE, O DARK ROSE

1   O little rose, O dark rose,
    With smouldering petals curled,
    I am the wind that comes for you
    From the other side of the world.

    O little rose, O dark rose,
    With the wild and golden heart,
    I am your bee with burdened wings,
    Too laden to depart.

O little rose, O dark rose,
10 Your soul a seed of fire,
I am the dew that dies in you,
In the flame of your desire.

O little rose, O dark rose,
The madness of your breath!
I am the moth to drain your sweet,
Even though the dregs be death.

O little rose, O dark rose,
When the garden day is done
I am the dusk that broods o'er you
20 Until the morrow's sun.

1900

THE ROSE OF MY DESIRE

1 O wild, dark flower of woman,
Deep rose of my desire,
An eastern wizard made you
Of earth and stars and fire.

When the orange moon swung low
Over the camphor-trees,
By the silver shaft of the fountain
He wrought his mysteries.

The hot, sweet mould of the garden
10 He took from a secret place
To become your glimmering body
And the lure of your strange face.

From the swoon of the tropic heaven
He drew down star on star
And breathed them into your soul
That your soul might wander far—

On earth forever homeless
But intimate of the spheres,
A pang in your mystic laughter,
20 A portent in your tears.

From the night's heat, hushed, electric,
He summoned a shifting flame
And cherished it and blew on it
Till it burned into your name.

And he set the name in my heart
For an unextinguished fire,
O wild, dark flower of woman,
Deep rose of my desire.

1900

AWAY, SAD VOICES

Away, sad voices, telling
Of old, forgotten pain!
My heart, at grief rebelling,
To joy returns again.
My life, at tears protesting,
To long delight returns,
Where, close of all my questing,
Her dear eyes love discerns.

1900

THE FEAR OF LOVE

1 Oh, take me into the still places of your heart,
And hide me under the night of your deep hair;
For the fear of love is upon me;
I am afraid lest God should discover the wonderfulness
    of our love.

Shall I find life but to lose it?
Shall I stretch out my hands at last to joy
And take but the irremediable anguish?
For the cost of heaven is the fear of hell;
The terrible cost of love
10 Is the fear to be cast out therefrom.

Oh, touch me! Oh, look upon me!
Look upon my spirit with your eyes
And touch me with the benediction of your hands!

Breathe upon me, breathe upon me,
And my soul shall live.
Kiss me with your mouth upon my mouth
And I shall be strong.

1900

THE COVERT

Sharp drives the rain for me,
Bitter the long night's pain for me,
Bitter the dawn's disdain for me,
    And breath so vain a prayer!

But open your heart and let me in.
The deep of your soul, oh, set me in!
And sorrow of life shall forget me in
    The hiding of your hair!

1900

HOW LITTLE I KNEW

1 How little I knew, when I first saw you,
    And your eyes for a moment questioned mine,
    It amounted to this,—that the dawn and the dew,
    The midnight's dark, and the midnoon's shine,
    The awe of the silent, soaring peak,
    The harebell's blue, and the cloud in the blue,
    And all the beauty I sing and seek,
    Would come to mean—just you!

    Yet I might have known; for that one deep look
10 Which you gave me from under your hat's low brim
    Months afterward in my memory shook
    And made my pulses swim.
    It will burn in my heart the long years through;
    And when this life of the flesh is done
    I will open my heart and show it to you
    In the world beyond the sun.

1900

NEW DEAD

1   Where are the kind eyes gone
That watched me so?
Was it but now they wept,
Or long ago?

Why did they run with tears
And yearn to me?
What was it in my face
They feared to see?

Ah, world, when did I pass
10   Beyond your smile,—
Forget you, for a long
Or little while?

Descending from the sun
Into this night,—
Impenetrable dark
That chokes my sight,—

Ah, now I know why stirs
No more my breath!
My mouth is stopt with dust,
20   My dream with death.

Where is this seed of self
I clutch to hold?
Will it dissolve with me
Into the mould?

It slips,—ah, let me sleep,
Worn, worn, outworn!
So to be strong when I
Arise, new born!

1900

IN APIA BAY

(*Morituri vos salutamus*)

1   Ruin and death held sway
        That night in Apia Bay,
And smote amid the loud and dreadful gloom.
        But, Hearts, no longer weep
        The salt unresting sleep
Of the great dead, victorious in their doom.

        Vain, vain the strait retreat
        That held the fated fleet,
Trapped in the two-fold threat of sea and shore!
10   Feel reefs on either hand,
        And the devouring strand!
Above, below, the tempest's deafening roar!

        What mortal hand shall write
        The horror of that night,
The desperate struggle in that deadly close,
        The yelling of the blast,
        The wild surf, white, aghast,
The whelming seas, the thunder and the throes!

        How the great cables surged,
20   The giant engines urged,
As the brave ships the unequal strife waged on!
        Not hope, not courage flagged;
        But the vain anchors dragged,
Down on the reef they shattered, and were gone!

        And now were wrought the deeds
        Whereof each soul that reads
Grows manlier, and burns with prouder breath,—
        Heroic brotherhood,
        The loving bonds of blood,
30 Proclaimed from high hearts face to face with death.

        At length, the English ship
        Her cables had let slip,
Crowded all steam, and steered for the open sea,
        Resolved to challenge Fate,
        To pass the perilous strait,
And wrench from jaws of ruin Victory.

With well-tried metals strained,
In the storm's teeth she gained,
Foot by slow foot made head, and crept toward life.
40   Across her dubious way
The good ship *Trenton* lay,
Helpless, but thrilled to watch the splendid strife.

Helmless she lay, her bulk
A blind and wallowing hulk,
By her strained hawsers only held from wreck,
But dauntless each brave heart
Played his immortal part
In strong endurance on the reeling deck.

They fought Fate inch by inch,—
50   Could die, but could not flinch;
And, biding the inevitable doom,
They marked the English ship,
Baffling the tempest's grip,
Forged hardly forth from the expected tomb.

Then, with exultant breath,
These heroes waiting death,
Thundered across the storm a peal of cheers,—
To the triumphant brave
A greeting from the grave,
60 Whose echo shall go ringing down the years.

"To you, who well have won,
From us, whose course is run,
Glad greeting, as we face the undreaded end!"
The memory of those cheers
Shall thrill in English ears
Where'er this English blood and speech extend.

No manlier deed comes down,
Blazoned in broad renown,
From men of old who lived to dare and die!
70   The old fire yet **survives**,
Here in our modern lives,
Of splendid chivalry and valor high!

1900

THE ROSE'S AVATAR

1   There grew a rose more wonderful
      Than ever Saadi sang.
    Its loveliness occult and strange,
      A rapture and a pang.
    Its petals had the pulsing touch
      That shakes the blood with fire.
    Its warm deeps were the avatar
      Of unassuaged desire.
    His scents and hushed seraglio dreams
10   Were in its subtle breath,
    The madness of the Mænad's joy,
      The tenderness of death.
    Its soul was all the mystic East,
      Its heart was all the South,—
    Till love and tears transmuted it
      To the dark rose of thy mouth.

                          1901

THE PIPERS OF THE POOLS

1   Pipers of the chilly pools
    Pipe the April in.
    Summon all the singing hosts,
    All the wilding kin.

    Through the cool and teeming damp
    Of the twilight air
    Call till all the April children
    Answer everywhere.

    From your cold and fluting throats
10   Pipe the world awake,
    Pipe the mould to move again,
    Pipe the sod to break.

    Pipe the mating song of earth
    And the fecund fire,—
    Love and laughter, pang and dream,
    Desire, desire, desire.

    Then a wonder shall appear,
    Miracle of time:
    Up through root and germ and sapwood
20   Life shall climb, and climb.

Then the hiding things shall hear you
And the sleeping stir,
And the far-off troops of exile
Gather to confer;

Then the rain shall kiss the bud
And the sun the bee,
Till they all, the painted children,
Flower and wing get free;

And amid the shining grass
30   Ephemera arise;
And the windflowers in the hollow
Open starry eyes;

And delight comes in to whisper—
"Soon, soon, soon
Earth shall be but one wild blossom
Breathing to the moon!"

1901

THE ROSE OF LIFE

1   The Rose spoke in the garden:
"Why am I sad?
The vast of sky above me
Is blue and glad;
The hushed deep of my heart
Hath the sun's gold;
The dew slumbers till noon
In my petals' hold.
Beauty I have, and wisdom,
10   And love I know,
Yet cannot release my spirit
Of its strange woe."

Then a Wind, older than Time,
Wiser than Sleep,
Answered: "The whole world's sorrow
Is yours to keep.
Its dark descends upon you
At day's high noon;
Its pallor is whitening about you
20   From every moon;
The cries of a thousand lovers,
A thousand slain,

273

The tears of all the forgotten
Who kissed in vain,
And the journeying years that have vanished
Have left on you
The witness, each, of its pain,
Ancient yet new.
So many lives you have lived;
30   So many a star
Hath veered in the Signs to make you
The wonder you are!
And this is the price of your beauty:
Your wild soul is thronged
With the phantoms of joy unfulfilled
That beauty hath wronged;
With the pangs of all secret betrayals,
The ghosts of desire,
The bite of old flame, and the chill
40   Of the ashes of fire."

1901

THE NATIVE

1   Rocks, I am one with you;
Sea, I am yours.
Your rages come and go,
Your strength endures.

Passion may burn and fade;
Pain surge and cease.
My still soul rests unchanged
Through storm and peace.

Fir-tree, beaten by wind,
10   Sombre, austere,
Your sap is in my veins
O kinsman dear.

Your fibres rude and true
My sinews feed—
Sprung of the same bleak earth,
The same rough seed.

The tempest harries us.
It raves and dies;
And wild limbs rest again
20   Under wide skies.

Grass, that the salt hath scourged,
Dauntless and grey,
Though the harsh season chide
Your scant array,

Year by year you return
To conquer fate.
The clean life nourishing you
Makes me, too, great.

O rocks, O fir-tree brave,
30 O grass and sea!
Your strength is mine, and you
Endure with me.

1901

INVOCATION

1   O Voice,
Whose sound is as the falling of the rain
On harp-strings strung in casements by the sea,
Low with all passion, poignant with all pain,
In dreams, out of thy distance, come to me.
I hear no music if I hear not thee.

O Hands,
Whose touch is like the balm of apple-bloom
Brushed by the winds of April from the bough,
10 Amid the passionate memories of this room
Flower out, sweet hands, a presence in the gloom,
And touch my longing mouth and cool my brow.

O Eyes,
Whose least look is a flame within my soul,
(Still burns that first long look, across the years!)
Lure of my life, and my desire's control,
Illume me and my darkness disappears.
Seeing you not, my eyes see naught for tears.

O Lips,
20 The rose's lovelier sisters, you whose breath
Seems the consummate spirit of the rose—
Honey and fire, delirium and repose,
And that long dream of love that laughs at death—
All these, all these your scarlet blooms enclose.

O Hair,
Whose shadows hold the mystery of a shrine
Heavy with vows and worship, where the pale
Priests who pour out their souls in incense pine
For dead loves unforgot—be thou the veil
30 To my heart's altar, secret and divine.

O Voice, O Hands, O Eyes, O Lips, O Hair,
Of your strange beauty God Himself hath care,
So deep the riddle He hath wrought therein—
Whether for love's delight, or love's despair.

1901

THE WISDOM OF LOVE

1 My life she takes between her hands;
My spirit at her feet
Is taught the lore inscrutable [,]
The wisdom bitter sweet.

The world becomes a little thing;
Art, travel, music, men,
And all that these can ever give
Are in her brow's white ken.

I look into her eyes and learn
10 The mystery of tears;
The pang of doubt; the doom that haunts
The fleeting of the years;

And pale foreknowledge, hid from all
But those who fear to know;
And memory's treason, that betrays
Joy to the nameless woe;

Compassion, like the rain of spring;
And truth without a flaw;
And one great gladness, hushed and still
20 With love's initiate awe.

In her deep hair I hide my heart;
And in that scented shade
I sail sleep's immemorial sea,
Expectant, unafraid;

And take the enigmatic word
Of dream upon my breath,
And learn the secrecy of joy,
The long content of death.

Her sad mouth, scarlet, passionate,
30   Shows me the world's desire,
The mirth that is the mask of pain,
And that immortal fire

Drawn by the touch of kiss on kiss
From life's eternal core,
Frail, flickering, mordant, keen, unquenched
When time shall be no more.

Then worship, love's last wisdom, learned,
I bow my spirit there,
And let my soul in silence plead
40   The passion which is prayer.

1901

IN THE BARN-YARD'S SOUTHERLY CORNER

1   When the frost is white on the fodder-stack,
The haws in the thorn-bush withered and black,
When the near fields flash in a diamond mail
And the far hills glimmer opaline pale,
Oh, merrily shines the morning sun
   In the barn-yard's southerly corner.

When the ruts in the cart-road ring like steel
And the birds to the kitchen door come for their meal,
And the snow at the gate is lightly drifted
10 And over the wood-pile thinly sifted,
Oh, merrily shines the morning sun
   In the barn-yard's southerly corner.

When the brimming bucket steams at the well,
And the axe on the beech-knot sings like a bell,
When the pond is loud with the skaters' calls,
And the horses stamp in the littered stalls,
Oh, merrily shines the morning sun
   In the barn-yard's southerly corner.

When the hay lies loose on the wide barn-floor,
20 And a sharp smells puffs from the stable door,
When the pitchfork handle stings in the hand
And the stanchioned cows for the milking stand,
Oh, merrily shines the morning sun
    In the barn-yard's southerly corner.

And the steers, let out for a drink and a run
Seek the warm corner one by one,
And the huddling sheep, in their dusty white,
Nose at the straw in the pleasant light,
When merrily shines the morning sun
30   In the **barn-yard's** southerly corner.

                                              1901

THE LOGS

1 In thronged procession gliding slow
The great logs sullenly seaward go.

A blind and blundering multitude
They jostle on the swollen flood,

Nor guess the inevitable fate
To greet them at the river-gate

When noiseless hours have lured them down
To the wide booms, the busy town,

The mills, the chains, the screeching jaws
10 Of the eviscerating saws.

Here in the murmur of the stream
Slow journeying, perchance they dream,

And hear once more their branches sigh
Far up the solitary sky,

Once more the rain-wind softly moan
Where sways the high green top alone,

Once more the inland eagle call
From the white crag that broods o'er all.

But if, beside some meadowy brink
20 Where flowering willows lean to drink,

Some open beach at the river bend
Where shallows in the sun extend,

They for a little would delay,
The huge tide hurries them away.

1901

NEW LIFE

1 Since I have felt upon my face thy tears
    I have been consecrated, Dear, to thee.
Cleansed from the stain of hot and frivolous years
    By thy white passion, I have bowed the knee,
Worshiping thee as sovereign and as saint,
    While with desire all human thou wert **leaning**
To my long kiss, thy lips and eyes grown faint,
    Thy spirit eloquent with love's new meaning.

Since I have seen within thy heart my heaven,
10   Life has been changed and earth has grown divine.
Hope, health, and wisdom, these thy love hath given,
    And if my song have any worth, 't is thine.
Thy hands are benediction, Dear. Thy feet
    Are flowers upon the altar of my soul,
Whereat my holiest aspirations meet,
    Humble and wondering in thy rapt control.

1901

THE SKATER

1 My glad feet shod with the glittering steel
I was the god of the wingéd heel.

The hills in the far white sky were lost;
The world lay still in the wide white frost;

And the woods hung hushed in their long white dream
By the ghostly, glimmering, ice-blue stream.

Here was a pathway, smooth like glass,
Where I and the wandering wind might pass

To the far-off palaces, drifted deep,
10 Where Winter's retinue rests in sleep.

I followed the lure, I fled like a bird,
Till the startled hollows awoke and heard

A spinning whisper, a sibilant twang,
As the stroke of the steel on the tense ice rang;

And the wandering wind was left behind
As faster, faster I followed my mind;

Till the blood sang high in my eager brain,
And the joy of my flight was almost pain.

Then I stayed the rush of my eager speed
20 And silently went as a drifting seed,—

Slowly, furtively, till my eyes
Grew big with the awe of a dim surmise,

And the hair of my neck began to creep
At hearing the wilderness talk in sleep.

Shapes in the fir-gloom drifted near.
In the deep of my heart I heard my fear.

And I turned and fled, like a soul pursued,
From the white, inviolate solitude.

1901

THE GREAT AND THE LITTLE WEAVERS

1 The great and the little weavers,
They neither rest nor sleep.
They work in the height and the glory,
They toil in the dark and the deep.

The rainbow melts with the shower,
The white-thorn falls in the gust,
The cloud-rose dies into shadow,
The earth-rose dies into dust.

But they have not faded forever,
10 They have not flowered in vain,
For the great and the little weavers
Are weaving under the rain.

Recede the drums of the thunder
When the Titan chorus tires,
And the bird-song piercing the sunset
Faints with the sunset fires,

But the trump of the storm shall fail not,
Not the flute-cry fail of the thrush,
For the great and the little weavers
20 Are weaving under the hush.

The comet flares into darkness,
The flame dissolves into death,
The power of the star and the dew
They grow and are gone like a breath,

But ere the old wonder is done
Is the new-old wonder begun,
For the great and the little weavers
Are weaving under the sun.

The domes of an empire crumble,
30 A child's hope dies in tears;
Time rolls them away forgotten
In the silt of the flooding years;

The creed for which men died smiling
Decays to a beldame's curse;
The love that made lips immortal
Drags by in a tattered hearse.

But not till the search of the moon
Sees the last white face uplift,
And over the bones of the kindreds
40 The bare sands dredge and drift,

Shall Love forget to return
And lift the unused latch,
(In his eyes the look of the traveller,
On his lips the foreign catch),

Nor the mad song leave men cold,
Nor the high dream summon in vain,—
For the great and the little weavers
Are weaving in heart and brain.

1902

HEAT IN THE CITY

1   Over the scorching roofs of iron
The red moon rises slow.
Uncomforted beneath its light
The pale crowds gasping go.

The heart-sick city, spent with day,
Cries out in vain for sleep.
The childless wife beside her dead
Is too outworn to weep.

The children in the upper rooms
10 Lie faint, with half-shut eyes.
In the thick-breathing, lighted ward
The stricken workman dies.

From breathless pit and sweltering loft
Dim shapes creep one by one
To throng the curb and crowd the stoops
And fear to-morrow's sun.

1902

AT THE WAYSIDE SHRINE

(Ste. Anne De Beaupré)

1   So little and so kind a shrine!
So homely and serene a saint!—
No violent sorrow can be thine,
Thou patient pensioner of constraint!

This gentle gloom that wraps thee in
Mistaking for a soul's despair,
Thou griev'st, perchance, for some small sin,
Too trivial for such fervent prayer.

Not sin hath wanned thy weary face,
10 Nor living woe made dark thine eyes,
Nor memory wrought this pleading grace,—
But ignorance, and dumb surmise.

The bleeding feet of shameful pain
Have passed not up this tranquil way,
Nor late **repentance**, haply vain,
By these slim poplars knelt to pray.

Thine is the sadness of the breast
That has not known the human strife—
Weighed down with shelter, worn with rest,
20 Athirst for the free storms of life.

Thine is the ache of lips that ache
For unknown pangs, unknown delight,—
The emptiness of hearts that break
With dreaming through the empty night.

The woe thou canst not understand,
Poor soul and body incomplete!
Thou hungerest for a little hand
And touch of little unknown feet.

But now, because all sorrows cease
30 Assuaged by such sweet faith as thine,
The dear Saint Anne shall give thee peace
Here at her little, kindly shrine.

                                    1902

SHEPHERDESS FAIR

1   O shepherdess fair, the flocks you keep
Are dreams and desires and tears and sleep.

O shepherdess brown, O shepherdess fair,
Where are my flocks you have in care?

My wonderful, white, wide-pasturing sheep
Of dream and desire and tears and sleep?

Many the flocks, but small the care
You give to their keeping, O shepherdess fair!

O shepherdess gay, your flocks have fed
10   By the iris pool, by the saffron bed,

Till now by noon they have wandered far,
And you have forgotten where they are!

O shepherdess fair, O shepherdess wild,
Full wise are your flocks, but you a child!

You shall not be chid if you let them stray.
In your own wild way, in your own child way,
You will call them all back at the close of day.

1902

THE UNKNOWN CITY

1   There lies a city inaccessible,
Where the dead dreamers dwell.

Abrupt and blue, with many a high ravine
And soaring bridge half seen,
With many an iris cloud that comes and goes
Over the ancient snows,
The imminent hills environ it, and hold
Its portals from of old,
That grief invade not, weariness, nor war.
10   Nor anguish evermore.

White-walled and jettied on the peacock tide,
With domes and towers enskied,
Its battlements and balconies one sheen
Of ever-living green,
It hears the happy dreamers turning home
Slow-oared across the foam.

Cool are its streets with waters musical
And fountains' shadowy fall.
With orange and anemone and rose
20   And every flower that blows
Of magic scent or unimagined dye,
Its gardens shine and sigh.
Its chambers, memoried with old romance
And faëry circumstance,—
From any window love may lean some time
For love that dares to climb.

284

This is that city babe and seer divined
With pure, believing mind.
This is the home of unachieved emprise.
30   Here, here the visioned eyes
Of them that dream past any power to do,
Wake to the dream come true.
Here the high failure, not the level fame,
Attests the spirit's aim.
Here is fulfilled each hope that soared and sought
Beyond the bournes of thought.
The obdurate marble yields; the canvas glows;
Perfect the column grows;
The chorded cadence art could ne'er attain
40   Crowns the imperfect strain;
And the great song that seemed to die unsung
Triumphs upon the tongue.

March 14, 1903; 1903

WHEN IN THE ROWAN TREE

1   When in the rowan tree
The coloured light fades slowly,
And the quiet dusk,
All lilied, breathes of you,
Then, Heart's Content,
I feel your hair enfolding me,
And tender comes the dark,
Bringing me—you.

And when across the sea
10   The rose-dawn opens slowly,
And the gold breaks, and the blue,
All glad of you,
Then, Heart's Reward,
Red, red is your mouth for me,
And life to me means love,
And love means—you.

March 15, 1903; 1905

WHEN THE CLOUD COMES DOWN THE MOUNTAIN

When the cloud comes down the mountain,
   And the rain is loud on the leaves,
And the slim flies gather for shelter
   Under my cabin eaves,—

Then my heart goes out to earth,
   With the swollen brook runs free,
Drinks life with the drenched brown roots,
   And climbs with the sap in the tree.

March 15, 1903; 1919

COAL

Deep in the hush of those unfathomed glooms
Whereunder steamed the wet and pregnant earth,
Pulsing thick sap and pungent, hot perfumes,
This providence of unguessed needs had birth.
From drench of the innumerable rain
And drowse of unrecorded noon on noon
It sucked the heat and plucked the light, to gain
For times unborn a boon.

1903

THE CONSPIRATORS

1   Come, Death, sit down with me,
    Thou and Love, we three
    In a sad conspiracy
    Against life, our enemy.

    Thine, Death, the briefer score,
    Though she hate thee evermore.
    Hate of hers is less sore
    Than her treasons honeyed o'er
    With old, sweet lies and false, sweet lore.
10 Whom she hurts thou healest, Death.
    That is what she hates thee for.

Thine, Love, the bitterer plaint,
She has kissed thee, fooled thee, shamed thee,
Clasped thee, and disclaimed thee,
Found thee white, child and saint,
Left thee with the world's taint,
Found thee strong, left thee faint,
Used thee, and defamed thee.

I, who love life, needs must live;
20 But, loving most, can least forgive.

Leave her, Love! Forsake her, Death!
So shall men come to curse their breath!

1903

THE FIRST PLOUGHING

1 Calls the crow from the pine-tree top
When the April air is still.
He calls to the farmer hitching his team
In the farmyard under the hill.
"Come up," he cries, "come out and come up,
For the high field's ripe to till.
Don't wait for word from the dandelion
Or leave from the daffodil."

Cheeps the flycatcher—"Here old earth
10 Warms up in the April sun;
And the first ephemera, wings yet wet,
From the mould creep one by one.
Under the fence where the flies frequent
Is the earliest gossamer spun.
Come up from the damp of the valley lands,
For here the winter's done."

Whistles the high-hole out of the grove
His summoning loud and clear:
"Chilly it may be down your way
20 But the high south field has cheer.
On the sunward side of the chestnut stump
The woodgrubs wake and appear.
Come out to your ploughing, come up to your
ploughing,
The time for ploughing is here."

Then dips the coulter and drives the share,
And the furrows faintly steam.
The crow drifts furtively down from the pine
To follow the clanking team.
The flycatcher tumbles, the high-hole darts
30   In the young noon's yellow gleam;
And wholesome sweet the smell of the sod
Upturned from its winter's dream.

1903

LINES FOR AN OMAR PUNCH-BOWL

To C.B.

1   Omar, dying, left his dust
To the rose and vine in trust.

———————

"Through a thousand springs"—said he,
"Mix your memories with me.

"Fire the sap that fills each bud
With an essence from my blood.

"When the garden glows with June
Use me through the scented noon,

"Till the heat's alchemic art
10   Fashions me in every part.

"You, whose petals strew the grass
Round my lone, inverted glass,

"Each impassioned atom mould
To a red bloom with core of gold.

"You, whose tendrils, soft as tears,
Touch me with remembered years,

"When your globing clusters shine,
Slow distil my dreams to wine,

"Till by many a sweet rebirth
20   Love and joy transmute my earth,

"Changing me, on some far day,
To a more ecstatic clay,

"Whence the Potter's craft sublime
Shall mould a shape to outlast Time."

———————

Omar's body, Omar's soul,
Breathe in beauty from this bowl,

At whose thronged, mysterious rim
Wan desires, enchantments dim,

Tears and laughter, life and death,
30 Fleeing love and fainting breath,

Seem to waver like a flame,
Dissolve,—yet ever rest the same,

Fixed by your art, while art shall be [,]
In passionate immobility.

1903

MY HEART IS A HOUSE

1 My heart is a house, deep-walled and warm,
To cover you from the night of storm.

O little wild feet, too softly white
To roam the world's tempestuous night,
The years like sleet on my windows beat,—
Come in and be cherished, O little wild feet.
  For my heart is a house, deep-walled and warm,
  To cover you from the night of storm.

In the hillside hollow each lonely flower
10 Is closed against the disastrous hour.
The wet crow rocks in the wind-blown tree;
The tern drives in from the lashing sea.
  But my heart is a house, deep-walled and warm,
  To cover you from the night of storm.

Down from the naked heights of cloud
Care and despair cry low, cry loud.
The dark woods mutter with thronging fears;
The rocks are drenched with the rain of tears.
    But my heart is a house, deep-walled and warm,
20   To cover you from the night of storm.

O little dark head, too dear and fair
For the buffeting skies and the bitter air,
Time sweeps the wold with his wings of dread,—
Come in and be comforted, little dark head.
    For my heart is a house, deep-walled and warm,
    To cover you from the night of storm.

1903

ON THE UPPER DECK

1   *As the will of last year's wind,*
As the drift of the morrow's rain,
As the goal of the falling star,
As the treason sinned in vain,
As the bow that shines and is gone,
As the night cry heard no more—
Is the way of the woman's meaning
Beyond man's eldest lore.

HE

This hour to me is like a rose just open,
10   The wonder of its golden heart not yet
Fully revealed. So long I've waited for it,
Prefigured it in dream, and scourged my hope
With fear lest jealous fortune should deny,
That now I hardly dare—Am I awake?
Can it be true I have you here beside me?
Can it be true I have you here alone—
Most wonderfully alone among these strangers
Who seem to me like senseless shapes of air?
The throb of the great engines, the obscure
20   Hiss of the water past our speeding hull
Seem to enfold and press you closer to me.
No, do not move! Alone although we be,
I dare not touch your hand; your gown's dear hem
I will not touch lest I should break my dream
And just an empty deck-chair mock my longing.

290

But (for the beggar may in dreams be king),
Oh, let your eyes but touch me, let my spirit
But drink, but drain, but bathe in their deep light,
And slake its cherished anguish. Look at me!

SHE

30   Look how the water's waiting holds the sky!
I think I never saw the Sound so still.
That wash of beryl green, that melting violet,
That fine rose-amber veiling deeps of glory
Our eyes could not endure—how each is doubled,
Lest we should miss some marvel of strange tone,
And be forever poor. Such beauty seems
To cry like violins. Hush, and you'll hear it.
Don't look at me when God is at his miracles.

HE

He topped all miracle in making you.
40   Your mouth, your throat, your eyes, your hands, your hair—
To look at these is harps within my soul,
The music of the stars at Time's first morning.
How can I see the wide, familiar world
When all my being drowns in your deep eyes?
What is the maddest sunset to your eyes?
Let us not talk of sunsets.

SHE

                Soon this rose
Of incommunicable light will fade,
Its ultimate petals sinking in the sea.
50   Be still, and watch the vaster bloom unfold
Whose pollen is the dust of stars, whose petals
The tissue of strange tears, desire and sleep.

HE

We talk of roses, meaning all things fair
And rare and enigmatic; but the rose
Transcending all, the Rose of Life, is you!

O Rose, blossom of wonder, dark blossom of ancient dream,
Wan tides of the Wandering Sorrow through your deep
        slumber stream;

Warm winds of the Wavering Passion are lost in your
      crimson fold,
And memory and foreboding at the hush of your
      heart lie cold.

60   *O Rose, blossom of mystery, holding within your deeps*
The hurt of a thousand vigils, the heal of a thousand
      sleeps,
There breathes upon your petals a power from the ends
      of earth.
Your beauty is heavy with knowledge of life and
      death and birth.

O Rose, blossom of longing—the faint suspense, and
      the fire,
The wistfulness of time, and the unassuaged desire,
The pity of tears on the pillow, the pang of tears unshed—
With these your spirit is weary, with these your beauty
      is fed.

SHE

Woman or rose, your verses do her credit,
Barring some small confusion in the figure.

HE

70   'Tis fusion, not confusion. So the rose
Be beautiful enough, and strange enough,
Love in his haste may take its sweet for you;
And sun and rain, wise gardeners, seeing you
With face uplift, will know the rose you are.

SHE

Let us not talk of roses. Don't you think
The engines' pulse throbs louder now the light
Has gone? The hiss of water past our hull
Is more mysterious, with a menace in it?
And that pale streak above the unseen land,
80   How ominous! A sword has just such pallor!
(Yes, you may put the scarf around my shoulders.)
Never has life shown me the face of beauty
But near it I have seen the fear of fear.

HE

I knew not fear until I knew your beauty.

SHE

Let us not talk of me. Look down, close in,
There where the night-black water breaks and seethes.
How its heart, torn and shuddering, burns to
     splendour!
What climbing lights! What rapture of white fire!
Clear souls of flame returning to the infinite!

HE

90   If you should ever come to say "I love you,"
I think that even thus my life's dark tide
Would flame to sudden glory, and the gloom
Of long grief lift forever! Dear, your eyes,
Your great eyes, shine upon me, soft as with tears.
Your shoulder touches me. What does it mean?
I hold you to me. Is it love—and life?

SHE

Let us not talk of—love! I know so little
Of love! I only know that life wears not
The face of beauty, but the face of fear.
100   The face of fear is gone. The face of beauty
Comes when you hold me so! Help me to live!
Help me to live, and hold me from the terror!

                         1903

WHEN MARY THE MOTHER KISSED THE CHILD

1   When Mary the Mother kissed the Child
And night on the wintry hills grew mild,
And the strange star swung from the courts of air
To serve at a manger with kings in prayer,
Then did the day of the simple kin
And the unregarded folk begin.

When Mary the Mother forgot the pain,
In the stable of rock began love's reign.

When that new light on their grave eyes broke
10   The oxen were glad and forgot their yoke;
And the huddled sheep in the far hill fold
Stirred in their sleep and felt no cold.

When Mary the Mother gave of her breast
To the poor inn's latest and lowliest guest,—
The God born out of the woman's side,—
The Babe of Heaven by Earth denied,—
Then did the hurt ones cease to moan,
And the long-supplanted came to their own.

When Mary the Mother felt faint hands
20   Beat at her bosom with life's demands,
And naught to her were the kneeling kings,
The serving star and the half-seen wings,
Then was the little of earth made great,
And the man came back to the God's estate.

1903

ALL NIGHT THE LONE CICADA

1   All night the lone cicada
        Kept shrilling through the rain,
    A voice of joy undaunted
        By unforgotten pain.

    Down from the tossing branches
        Rang out the high refrain,
    By tumult undisheartened,
        By storm assailed in vain.

    To looming vasts of mountain,
10   To shadowy deeps of plain
    The ephemeral, brave defiance
        Adventured not in vain,—

    Till to my faltering spirit,
        And to my weary brain,
    From loss and fear and failure
        My joy returned again.

March 20, 1903; December 11, 1904; 1907

BEPPO'S SONG

(From "The Sprightly Pilgrim")

Oh some are for the cities of men,
    And some are for the sea,
And some for a book in a musty nook,—
    But the lips of a maid for me!

And some are for the forest and field,
    For their whim is to be free.
But the lips of a maid in the chestnut shade
    Are freedom enough for me!

1904; 1927

PHILANDER'S SONG

(From "The Sprightly Pilgrim")

I sat and read Anacreon.
    Moved by the gay, delicious measure
I mused that lips were made for love,
    And love to charm a poet's leisure.

And as I mused a maid came by
    With something in her look that caught me.
Forgotten was Anacreon's line,
    But not the lesson he had taught me.

1904; 1927

MONITION

1   A faint wind, blowing from World's End,
    Made strange the city street.
A strange sound mingled in the fall
    Of the familiar feet.

Something unseen whirled with the leaves
    To tap on door and sill.
Something unknown went whispering by
    Even when the wind was still.

295

And men looked up with startled eyes
10   And hurried on their way,
As if they had been called, and told
How brief their day.

October 13, 1904;
December 5, 1905; 1907

FROM THE HIGH WINDOW OF YOUR ROOM

1   From the high window of your room,
Above the roofs, and streets, and cries,
Lying awake and still, I watch
The wonder of the dawn arise.

Slow tips the world's deliberate rim,
Descending to the baths of day:
Up floats the pure, ethereal tide
And floods the outworn dark away.

The city's sprawled, uneasy bulk
10   Illumines slowly in my sight.
The crowded roofs, the common walls,
The grey streets, melt in mystic light.

It passes. Then, with longing sore
For that veiled light of paradise,
I turn my face,—and find it in
The wonder of your waking eyes.

December 23, 24, 1905; 1919

THE HOUR OF MOST DESIRE

1   It is not in the day
That I desire you most,
Turning to seek your smile
For solace or for joy.

Nor is it in the dark,
When I toss restlessly,
Groping to find your face,
Half waking, half in dream.

It is not while I work—
10   When, to endear success,
Or rob defeat of pain,
I weary for your hands.

Nor while from work I rest,—
And rest is all unrest
For lack of your dear voice,
Your laughter, and your lips.

But every hour it is
That I desire you most—
Need you in all my life
20   And every breath I breathe.

January 4, 9, 1906; 1919

WAYFARER OF EARTH

1   Up, heart of mine,
Thou wayfarer of earth!
Of seed divine,
Be mindful of thy birth.
Though the flesh faint
Through long-endured constraint
Of nights and days,
Lift up thy praise
To life, that set thee in such strenuous ways,
10   And left thee not
To drowse and rot
In some thick-perfumed and luxurious plot.

Strong, strong is earth
With vigor for thy feet,
To make thy wayfaring
Tireless and fleet.
And good is earth,—
But earth not all thy good,
O thou with seed of suns
20   And star-fire in thy blood!

And though thou feel
The slow clog of the hours
Leaden upon thy heel,
Put forth thy powers.

Thine the deep sky,
The unpreëmpted blue,
The haste of storm,
The hush of dew.

Thine, thine the free
30   Exalt of star and tree,
The reinless run
Of wind and sun,
The vagrance of the sea.

January 4, 11, 1906; 1906

THE GOOD EARTH

1   The smell of burning weeds
Upon the twilight air;
The piping of the frogs
From meadows wet and bare;

A presence in the wood,
And in my blood a stir;
In all the ardent earth
No failure or demur.

O spring wind, sweet with love
10   And tender with desire,
Pour into veins of mine
Your pure, impassioned fire.

O waters, running free
With full, exultant song,
Give me, for outworn dream,
Life that is clean and strong.

O good Earth, warm with youth,
My childhood heart renew.
Make me elate, sincere,
20   Simple and glad, as you.

O springing things of green,
O waiting things of bloom,
O winging things of air,
Your lordship now resume.

1906

O EARTH, SUFFICING ALL OUR NEEDS

1   O earth, sufficing all our needs, O you
With room for body and for spirit too,
   How patient while your children vex their souls
Devising alien heavens beyond your blue!

Dear dwelling of the immortal and unseen,
How obstinate in my blindness have I been,
   Not comprehending what your tender calls,
Veiled promises and reassurance, mean.

Not far and cold the way that they have gone
10 Who through your sundering darkness have withdrawn;
   Almost within our hand-reach they remain
Who pass beyond the sequence of the dawn.

Not far and strange the Heaven, but very near,
Your children's hearts unknowingly hold dear.
   At times we almost catch the door swung wide.
An unforgotten voice almost we hear.

I am the heir of Heaven—and you are just.
You, you alone I know—and you I trust.
   I have sought God beyond His farthest star—
20 But here I find Him, in your quickening dust.

> lines one and two, *April 16, 1905,*
> lines three and four, *December 26, 1905,*
> stanzas three and four, *January 28, 1906,*
> stanzas two and five, *June 21, 1906;* 1907

UNDER THE PILLARS OF THE SKY

Under the pillars of the sky
I played at life, I knew not why.

The grave recurrence of the day
Was matter of my trivial play.

The solemn stars, the sacred night,
I took for toys of my delight,

Till now, with startled eyes, I see
The portents of Eternity.

> *March 17, 20, 1907;* 1907

EASTWARD BOUND

1   We mount the arc of ocean's round
      To meet the splendours of the sun;
  Then downward rush into the dark
      When the blue, spacious day is done.

  The slow, eternal drift of stars
      Draws over us until the dawn,
  Then the grey steep we mount once more,
      And night is down the void withdrawn.

  Space, and interminable hours,
10   And moons that rise, and sweep, and fall,—
  On-swinging earth, and orbéd sea,—
      And voyaging souls more vast than all!

November 2, 1907; 1910

THE BANQUET

Though o'er the board the constellations shine,
  Austere the feast for Time's retainers spread,—
Laughter the salt of life, and love the wine,
  Sleep the sweet herbs, and toil the gritty bread.

1907

HILL TOP SONGS: I

1   Here on the hill
  At last the soul sees clear,
  Desire being still,
  The High Unseen appear.
  The thin grass bends
  One way, and hushed attends
  Unknown and gracious ends.
  Where the sheep's pasturing feet
  Have cleft the sods
10   The mystic light lies sweet;
  The very clods,
  In purpling hues elate,
  Thrill to their fate;
  The high rock-hollows wait,
  Expecting gods.

April 26, 27, 1909; 1919

HILL TOP SONGS: II

1   When the lights come out in the cottages
     Along the shores at eve,
And across the darkening water
     The last pale shadows leave;

And up from the rock-ridged pasture slopes
     The sheep-bell tinklings steal,
And the folds are shut, and the shepherds
     Turn to their quiet meal;

And even here, on the unfenced height,
10   No journeying wind goes by,
But the earth-sweet smells, and the home-sweet sounds,
     Mount, like prayer, to the sky;

Then from the door of my opened heart
     Old blindness and pride are driven,
Till I know how high is the humble,
     The dear earth how close to heaven.

April 21, 1909; 1910

THE PLACE OF HIS REST

1   The green marsh-mallows
     Are over him.
Along the shallows
     The pale lights swim.

Wide air, washed grasses,
     And waveless stream;
And over him passes
     The drift of dream;—

The pearl-hue down
10   Of the poplar seed;
The elm-flower brown;
     And the sway of the reed;

The blue moth, winged
     With a flake of sky;
The bee, gold ringed;
     And the dragon-fly.

Lightly the rushes
        Lean to his breast;
A bird's wing brushes
20   The place of his rest.

The far-flown swallow,
        The gold-finch flame,—
They come, they follow
        The paths he came.

'Tis the land of No Care
        Where now he lies,
Fulfilled the prayer
        Of his weary eyes,

And while around him
30   The kind grass creeps,
Where peace hath found him
        How sound he sleeps.

Well to his slumber
        Attends the year:
Soft rains without number
        Soft noons, blue clear,

With nights of balm,
        And the dark, sweet hours
Brooding with calm,
40   Pregnant with flowers.

See how she speeds them,
        Each childlike bloom,
And softly leads them
        To tend his tomb!—

The white-thorn nears
        As the cowslip goes;
Then the iris appears;
        And then, the rose.

            May 24, 25, 1909; 1919

IN THE VALLEY OF LUCHON

1   Day long, and night long,
        From the soaring peaks and the snow,
    Down through the valley villages
        The cold white waters flow.

    Quiet are the villages;
        And very quiet the cloud
    At rest on the breast of the mountain;
        But the falling waves are loud

    Through the little, clustering cottages,
10   Through the little, climbing fields,
    Where every sunburnt vineyard
        Its patch of purple yields.

    High hung, a steel-bright scimitar,
        The crooked glacier gleams.
    The white church dreams in the valley
        Where the red oleander dreams.

    And every wonder of beauty
        Comes, as a dream comes, true,
    Where the sun drips rose from the ledges
20   And the moon by the peak swims blue.

                                    1909

ON THE ROAD

1   Ever just over the top of the next brown rise
    I expect some wonderful thing to flatter my eyes.
    "What's yonder?" I ask of the first wayfarer I meet.
    "Nothing!" he answers, and looks at my travel-worn feet.

    "Only more hills and more hills, like the many you've passed,
    With rough country between, and a poor enough inn at the last."
    But already I am a-move, for I see he is blind,
    And I hate that old grumble I've listened to time out of mind.

    I've tramped it too long not to know there is truth in it still,
10 That lure of the turn of the road, of the crest of the hill.
    So I breast me the rise with full hope, well assured I shall see
    Some new prospect of joy, some brave venture a-tiptoe for me.

For I have come far and confronted the calm and the strife.
I have fared wide, and bit deep in the apple of life.
It is sweet at the rind, but oh, sweeter still at the core;
And whatever be gained yet the reach of the morrow is more.

At the crest of the hill I shall hail the new summits to climb.
The demand of my vision shall beggar the largess of time.
For I know that the higher I press, the wider I view,
20 The more's to be ventured and visioned, in worlds that are new.

So when my feet, failing, shall stumble in ultimate dark,
And faint eyes no more the high lift of the pathway shall mark,
There under the dew I'll lie down with my dreams, for I know
What bright hill-tops the morning will show me, all red in the glow.

January 19, 1913; 1913

GOING OVER

[The Somme, 1917]

1 A girl's voice in the night troubled my heart
Across the roar of the guns, the crash of the shells,
Low and soft as a sigh, clearly I heard it.

Where was the broken parapet, crumbling about me?
Where my shadowy comrades, crouching expectant?
A girl's voice in the dark troubled my heart.

A dream was the ooze of the trench, the wet clay slipping.
A dream the sudden out-flare of the wide-flung Verys.
I saw but a garden of lilacs, a-flower in the dusk.

10 What was the sergeant saying?—I passed it along.—
Did *I* pass it along? I was breathing the breath of the lilacs.
For a girl's voice in the night troubled my heart.

Over! How the mud sucks! Vomits red the barrage.
But I am far off in the hush of a garden of lilacs.
For a girl's voice in the night troubled my heart.
Tender and soft as a sigh, clearly I heard it.

October 20, 1918; 1919

CAMBRAI AND MARNE (1914-1918)

1   Before our trenches at Cambrai
We saw their columns cringe away.
We saw their masses melt and reel
Before our line of leaping steel.

A handful to their storming hordes
We scourged them with the scourge of swords,
And still, the more we slew, the more
Came up for every slain a score.

Between the hedges and the town
10   Their cursing squadrons we rode down.
To stay them we outpoured our blood
Between the beetfields and the wood.

In that red hell of shrieking shell
Unfaltering our gunners fell.
They fell, or ere that day was done,
Beside the last unshattered gun.

But still we held them, like a wall
On which the breakers vainly fall—
Till came the word, and we obeyed,
20   Reluctant, bleeding, undismayed.

Our feet, astonished, learned retreat,
Our souls rejected still defeat.
Unbroken still, a lion at bay,
We drew back grimly from Cambrai.

In blood and sweat, with slaughter spent,
They thought us beaten as we went;
Till suddenly we turned and smote
The shout of triumph in their throat.

At last, at last we turned and stood—
30   And Marne's fair water ran with blood.
We stood by trench and steel and gun,
For now the indignant flight was done.

We ploughed their shaken ranks with fire.
We trod their masses into mire.
Our sabres drove through their retreat,
As drives the whirlwind through young wheat.

At last, at last we flung them back
Along their drenched and smoking track.
We hurled them back, in blood and flame,
40   The reeking ways by which they came.

By cumbered road and desperate ford,
How fled their shamed and harassed horde!
Shout, Sons of Freemen, for the day
When Marne so well avenged Cambrai!

1918

TO SHAKESPEARE, IN 1916

1   With what white wrath must turn thy bones,
     What stern amazement flame thy dust,
To feel so near this England's heart
     The outrage of the assassin's thrust!

How must thou burn to have endured
     The acclaim of these whose fame unclean
Reeks from the *Lusitania's* slain,
     Stinks from the orgies of Malines!

But surely, too, thou are consoled
10   (Who knew'st thy stalwart breed so well)
To see us rise from sloth, and go,
     Plain and unbragging, through this hell.

And surely, too, thou art assured.
     Hark how that grim and gathering beat
Draws upwards from the ends of earth,—
     The tramp, tramp, of thy kinsmen's feet.

1918

THE STREAM

1   I know a stream
     Than which no lovelier flows.
     Its banks a-gleam
     With yarrow and wild rose,
     Singing it goes
     And shining through my dream.

Its waters glide
Beneath the basking noon,
A magic tide
10   That keeps perpetual June.

There the light sleeps
Unstirred by any storm;
The wild mouse creeps
Through tall weeds hushed and warm;
And the shy snipe,
Alighting unafraid,
With sudden pipe
Awakes the dreaming shade.

So long ago!
20   Still, still my memory hears
Its silver flow
Across the sundering years—
Its roses glow,
Ah, through what longing tears!

December 26, 29, 1918,
January 1, 1919; 1919

THE SUMMONS

1   Deeps of the wind-torn west,
    Flaming and desolate,
Upsprings my soul from his rest
    With your banners at the gate.

'Neath this o'ermastering sky
    How could the heart lie still,
    Or the sluggish will
Content in the old chains lie,
    When over the lonely hill
10   Your torn wild scarlets cry?

Up, Soul, and out
    Into the deeps alone,
To the long peal and the shout
    Of those trumpets blown and blown!

January 13, 1919; 1919

EPITAPH FOR A CERTAIN ARCHITECT

1 His fame the mock of shallow wits,
His name the jest of fool and child,
Remains the dream he fixed in form,
Remains the stone he hewed and piled.

Untouched by scorn that dogged his way
Ere the great task was well begun,
He drudged to give the vision life
And died content when it was done.

They pass, the mockers, and are dust,
10 While stars conspire to enscroll his name.
When roaring guns are fallen to rust
This granite shall attest his fame.

Eternal as the returning rose,
Impregnable as the perfect rhyme,
Through the long sequence of the suns
His dream in stone shall outwear Time.

November 3, 1918;
January 10 and 16, 1919; 1925

THE SWEET O' THE YEAR

1 The upland hills are green again;
The river runs serene again;
All down the miles
Of orchard aisles
The pink-lip blooms are seen again;
To garden close
And dooryard plot
Come back the rose
And bergamot.

10 The ardent blue leans near again;
The far-flown swallow is here again;
To his thorn-bush
Returns the thrush,
And the painted-wings appear again.
In young surprise
The meadows run
All starry eyes
To meet the sun.

Warm runs young blood in the veins again,
20   And warm loves flood in the rains again.
      Earth, all aflush
      With the fecund rush,
To her Heart's Desire attains again;
      While stars outbeat
         The exultant word—
      "Death's in defeat,
         And Love is Lord."

                    March 25, 1908 and January 6,
                    February 5, 1919; 1920

THE FLOWER

1   I am the man who found a flower,
      A blossom blown upon the wind,
More radiant than the sunrise rose,
      More sweet than lotus-airs of Ind.

I clutched the flower, and on my heart
      I crushed its petals, red and burning.
O ecstasy of life new-born!
      O youth returned, the unreturning!

I am the man who dared the Gods
10   And under their thunderbolts lay blest,
Because I found the flower, and wore it
      One wild hour upon my breast.

                                        1919

WITH APRIL HERE

1   With April here,
      And first thin green on the awakening bough,
What wonderful things and dear,
      My tired heart to cheer,
      At last appear!
Colours of dream afloat on cloud and tree,
      So far, so clear,
      A spell, a mystery;

And joys that thrill and sing,
10 New come on mating wing,
The wistfulness and ardour of the Spring,—
And Thou!

1919

SISTER TO THE WILD ROSE

1 I know a maiden like a flower,
    (Flower-sweet, dainty-sweet!)
Sister to the wild rose
    And the wild marguerite.

Petal-soft are the lips of her,
    (Flower-sweet, dainty-sweet!)
And blue her eyes as the misty blue
    Where the dew and the blue-bells meet.

Light her hands as the cherry blossom,
10   (Flower-sweet, dainty-sweet!)
And never so light the wind on the grass
    As the lightness of her feet.

August 27, 1926; 1927

ASTEROPE

1 Whither down the ways of dream
    Went my starry-eyed,
Tears and laughter at her lips
    And longing by her side?

Went the joy of day with her
    From the shining lands,—
All the wonder of the night
    In her unheeding hands.

Wind of June hath gone with her
10   From the sighing tree,—
Dove-neck marvel from the mists
    Of the morning sea.

Flowers she forgot to take
Smell no longer sweet.
Earth has no more pleasantness
Save where fell her feet.

So I seek that place of dream
Where waits my starry-eyed,
All the happy things of earth
20   A-crowding at her side.

February 16, 1903; 1904
revised
1926; 1927

TO-DAY

1   As once by Hybna's emerald flow
The goatboy saw in dream
The old gods to their hunting go,
And heard their eagles scream,
So I, by Nashwaak's amber stream,
See gods and heroes pass,
While these drab days and deeds but seem
Like shadows in a glass.

But when a thousand years are done
10   My eyes, unsealed, will know
Beauty and glory new begun
As in the long ago;
And then, astonished, I shall know
The splendour of To-Day,
When men outdare the old gods, and grow
In reach more vast than they.

August 28 and September 1, 1926; 1926

HATH HOPE KEPT VIGIL

1   Frail lilies that beneath the dust so long
Have lain in cerements of musk and slumber,
While over you hath fled the viewless throng
Of hours and winds and voices out of number,

Pulseless and dead in that enswathing dark
　　Hath hope kept vigil at your core of being?
Did the germ know what unextinguished spark
　　Held these white blooms within its heart unseeing?

Once more into the dark when I go down,
10　　And deep and deaf the black clay seals my prison,
Will the numbed soul foreknow how light shall crown
　　With strong young ecstasy its life new risen?

　　　　　stanza one, incomplete, *January 16, 1919,*
　　　　　f^ull poem, *September 3, 1926;* 1926

SPRING BREAKS IN FOAM

1　Spring breaks in foam
　　　Along the blackthorn bough.
　　Whitethroat and goldenwing
　　　Are mating now.
　　With green buds in the copse
　　　And gold bloom in the sun
　　Earth is one ecstasy
　　　Of life begun.
　　And in my heart
10　　Spring breaks in glad surprise
　　As the long frosts of the long years melt
　　　At your dear eyes.

　　　　　April 12, 1922;
　　　　　September 4, 1926; 1927

THE VAGRANT OF TIME

1　I voyage north, I journey south,
　　　I taste the life of many lands,
　　With ready wonder in my eyes
　　　And strong adventure in my hands.

　　I join the young-eyed caravans
　　　That storm the portals of the West;
　　And sometimes in their throng I catch
　　　Hints of the secret of my quest.

　　The musks and attars of the East,
10　　Expecting marvels, I explore.
　　I chase them down the dim bazaar,
　　　I guess them through the close-shut door.

312

In the lone cabin, sheathed in snow,
  I bide a season, well content,
Till forth again I needs must fare,
  Called by an unknown continent.

I loiter down remembered shores
  Where restless tide-flows lift and surge,—
In my wild heart their restlessness
20 And in my veins their tireless urge.

In old grey cities oft I dwell,
  Down storied rivers drift and dream.
Sometimes in palaces I lose,
  Sometimes in hovels catch, the gleam.

Great fortune in my wayfaring
  I stumble on, more oft than not,—
Grip comrade hands in hall or camp,
  Greet ardent lips in court or cot.

Down country lanes at noon I stray,
30 Loaf in the homely wayside heat,
And with bright flies and droning bees
  Rifle the buckwheat of its sweet.

In solitudes of peak or plain,
  When vaulted space my sense unbars,
I pitch my tent, and camp the night
  Beyond the unfathomed gulfs of stars.

At times I thirst, at times I faint,
  Sink mired in swamp, stray blind in storm,
See high hopes shattered, faiths betrayed,—
40 But stout heart keeps my courage warm.

And sometimes rock-ridged steeps I climb
  In chill black hours before the dawn.
With battered shins and bleeding feet
  And obstinate fists I blunder on.

And then, when sunrise floods my path,
  I pause to build my dreams anew.
But, take the gipsying all in all,
  I find a-many dreams come true.

So when, one night, I drop my pack
50   Behind the Last Inn's shadowy door,.
To take my rest in that lone room
    Where no guest ever lodged before,

In sleep too deep for dreams I'll lie,—
    Till One shall knock, and bid me rise
To quest new ventures, fare new roads,
    Essay new suns and vaster skies.

Stanza one *April, 1908*
Full Text, *September 5-7, 1926;* 1926

IN THE NIGHT WATCHES

1   When the little spent winds are at rest in the tamarack tree
In the still of the night,
And the moon in her waning is wan and misshapen,
And out on the lake
The loon floats in a glimmer of light,
And the solitude sleeps,—
Then I lie in my bunk wide awake,
And my long thoughts stab me with longing,
Alone in my shack by the marshes of lone Margaree.

10 Far, oh so far in the forests of silence they lie,
The lake and the marshes of lone Margaree,
And no man comes my way.
Of spruce logs my cabin is builded securely;
With slender spruce saplings its bark roof is battened down surely;
In its rafters the mice are at play,
With rustlings furtive and shy,
In the still of the night.

Awake, wide-eyed, I watch my window-square,
Pallid and grey.
20 (O Memory, pierce me not! O Longing, stab me not!
O ache of longing memory, pass me by, and spare,
And let me sleep!)
Once and again the loon cries from the lake.
Though no breath stirs
The ghostly tamaracks and the brooding firs,
Something as light as air leans on my door.

314

Is it an owl's wing brushes at my latch?
Are they of foxes, those light feet that creep
Outside, light as fall'n leaves
30 On the forest floor?
From the still lake I hear
A feeding trout rise to some small night fly.
The splash, how sharply clear!
Almost I see the wide, slow ripple circling to the shore.

The spent winds are at rest, But my heart, spent and faint, is unresting,
Long, long a stranger to peace . . .
O so Dear, O so Far, O so Unforgotten-in-dream,
Somewhere in the world, somewhere beyond reach of my questing.
Beyond seas, beyond years,
40 You will hear my heart in your sleep, and you will stir restlessly;
You will stir at the touch of my hand on your hair;
You will wake with a start,
With my voice in your ears
And an old, old ache at your heart,
(In the still of the night)
And your pillow wet with tears.

September 10 and 22, 1926; 1927

THESE THREE SCORE YEARS

(*An Ode for Canada's Diamond Jubilee*)

I

1 Oh to be back where the oatfields are blowing
In my own Canadian home;
Where the shadows chase the shadows across the water meadows
And the deep grass seethes like foam!

II

So sang the exile, wearying for dead days;
And homeward turned o'er the long-furrowed sea
To find new wonder in the old dear ways,
And drown in dreams fulfilled the ache of memory.

III

Deliberate Time, toiling for age on age
10   To chisel one lean channel down the steep,
Or grave in stone some enigmatic page
     Of aeons lapsed in immemorial sleep,
What impulse urged you to this ecstatic haste,
     Drove you to spurn the dragging centuries,
     To beat blind oafish Ignorance to her knees,
        And, in a space as brief
        To immortal eyes as that twixt bud and leaf,
To fling the marvel of a million hearths
And towered and teaming cities o'er the waste?

IV

20   These three score fateful years!
     So swiftly have they sped, so fleetly wrought,
     Our eyes, confused by dust of toil and strife,
By turmoil of desires and hopes and fears,
     Have scarce perceived the miracles they wrought,
     Or sensed the splendours burgeoning into life;
Till now, on this proud day we celebrate,
     Pausing to count the cost and gain, we stand
With eyes unsealed, with wondering hearts elate,
     To view the task complete as our great Fathers planned.

V

30   Theirs was the vision, theirs the faith far-seeing,
     And theirs the force that forged our unity,
That called a nation into instant being
     And stretched its boundaries from sea to sea.
They snared a savage continent in steel.
     They bowed the eternal icepeaks to their will.
     The clamour of old hates they bade be still.
They tamed old factions to the common weal.
And one, our poet, statesman, seer combined,
Sealed with a martyr's blood the bond his faith had signed.

VI

40   And are we worthy these heroic sires,
     These twain world-mastering peoples whence they sprang?
     Doth still the breed run true,
Still in our veins upflame the ancient fires?

316

Make answer, Fields of Flanders, Fields of France,
    Where late our young battalions marched and sang,
        Our airmen soared the shrapnel-shattered blue!
Bear witness, Ypres and Vimy, with what cheer,
And courage clear,
And high contempt of fear,
50 Embattled at the grim old Lion's side,
Our scarred battalions triumphed, laughed and died!

VII

Dying, they live imperishable, and proclaim
    Our manhood's stature to the world, their blood
A sacrament of glory, and their fame
    The enduring pledge of that new brotherhood
Of equal nations which we "Empire" name,—
That Commonwealth in which we proudly own
Love to our peers, allegiance to our Throne.

VIII

And so I end my random song, returning
60   To that which makes perchance its only worth,—
The patriot warmth within my bosom burning
        Through all my wanderings o'er the curious earth.
Friends have I found in far and alien places,
Beauty and ardour in unfamiliar faces,
But first in my heart this land I call my own!
Canadian am I in blood and bone!

June 3, 1909, June 26, 1927; 1927

BE QUIET, WIND

1   Be quiet, wind, a little while,
        And let me hear my heart.
    You chiming rivulet, still your chant
        And stealthily depart.

    You whisperings in the aspen leaves,
        You far-heard whip-poor-will,
    You slow drop spilling from the rose—
        You, even you, be still.

I must have infinite silence now,
10   Lest I should miss one word
Of all my heart would say to me—
      Now, when its deeps are stirred.

Hardly I dare my breath to draw
      Lest breathing break the spell,—
While we commune, my heart and I,
      In dreams too deep to tell.

August 6, 22, 23, 1928; 1928

PAN AND THE ROSE

1   Came Pan to the garden
On a golden morning,
The dew of the thickets
Adrip on his thighs.
He thrust through the hollyhocks,
Stamped the bright marigolds,
And scanned pale Dianthe
With indifferent eyes.

But aloof in the garden
10 He spied one blossom,
A rose but half open
To the insistent sun,—
Her petals enclosing
The dew of young ecstasy,
The perilous perfume
Of life just begun.

His hot heart pounding
In his shaggy bosom,
The tender red petals
20 To his lips he drew.
With aching rapture
And a wild, wild wonder,
He drained the distillage
Of that honeyed dew.

* * * * * * * * *

318

And ever thereafter
He needs must wander,
Piping his lone plaint
Beside the shadowy stream,—
Nor heeds the enticing
30   Of white nymphs in the copses,—
His heart tormented,
And his parched lips thirsting
For the draught that assuages them
No longer save in dream.

July 31, August 2 and 24, 1928;
1934

UNSAID

1   I thieved a skein of gossamer thread
And wove me a web of moonbeam wings,
That I might hover over your head
And dare to whisper into your dream
The lovely, disastrous, scarce-thought things
That even my eyes had left unsaid.

Under the veil of your slumbering eyes
I caught the heart of your dream by surprise.
I uncovered your dream; and found there hidden,—
10   Sleeping cherished though waking forbidden,—
All the disastrous, scarce-thought things,
The wonderful things I had left unsaid.

December 29, 30, 31, 1928/
January 11, 1929; 1929

BAT, BAT, COME UNDER MY HAT

(A Modernity)

1   Twelve good friends
Passed under her hat,
And devil a one of them
Knew where he was at.

Had they but known,
Then had they known all things,—

The littleness of great things,
The unmeasured immensity of small things.
They had known the *Where* and the *Why,*
10 The *When* and the *Wherefore,*
And how the Eternal
Conceived the Eternal, and therefore
Beginning began the Beginning;
They had apprehended
The ultimate virtue of sinning;
They had caught the whisper
That Vega vibrates to Arcturus,
Piercing the walls
Of heavy flesh that immure us.

20 But if they had known,
Then had there been no mystery;
And Life had been poorer,
And laughter unsurer,
And the shadow of **death** securer,
By lack of this brief history.

June 12, 1929; 1934

SPIRIT OF BEAUTY

1 Spirit of Beauty,
    Never shall you escape me.
Through glad or bitter days
    Hearten and shape me.

Since first these eyes could see
    Still **have** they sought you.
Since first my soul knew dream
    My dreams have wrought you.

Since first my ears were unsealed
10   To the whitethroat's plaining,
Between the gusts of the wind
    And the low sky's raining,

Your voice I hear
    In the laughter of leaves, in the falling
Of waves on an empty shore
    And a far bell calling.

When I clasp a warm, dear hand
  I know you are holding me.
When I lean to the lips of my love
20   Your arms are enfolding me.

And when Night comes
  And the faithless senses forsake me,
Out of my cold, last sleep
  You, you shall awake me.

June 11-13, 1930; 1930

THE ICEBERG

1   I was spawned from the glacier,
A thousand miles due north
Beyond Cape Chidley;
And the spawning,
When my vast, wallowing bulk went under,
Emerged and heaved aloft,
Shaking down cataracts from its rocking sides,
With mountainous surge and thunder
Outraged the silence of the Arctic sea.

10   Before I was thrust forth
A thousand years I crept,
Crawling, crawling, crawling irresistibly,
Hid in the blue womb of the eternal ice,
While under me the tortured rock
Groaned,
And over me the immeasurable desolation slept.

Under the pallid dawning
Of the lidless Arctic day
Forever no life stirred.
20 No wing of bird—
Of ghostly owl low winnowing
Or fleet-winged ptarmigan fleeing the pounce of death,—
No foot of backward-glancing fox
Half glimpsed, and vanishing like a breath,—
No lean and gauntly stalking bear,
Stalking his prey.
Only the white sun, circling the white sky.
Only the wind screaming perpetually.

And then the night—
30 The long night, naked, high over the roof of the world,
Where time seemed frozen in the cold of space,—
Now black, and torn with cry
Of unseen voices where the storm raged by,
Now radiant with spectral light
As the vault of heaven split wide
To let the flaming Polar cohorts through,
And close ranked spears of gold and blue,
Thin scarlet and thin green,
Hurtled and clashed across the sphere
40 And hissed in sibilant whisperings,
And died.
And then the stark moon, swinging low,
Silver, indifferent, serene,
Over the sheeted snow.

But now, an Alp afloat,
In seizure of the surreptitious tide,
Began my long drift south to a remote
And unimagined doom.
Scornful of storm,
50 Unjarred by thunderous buffeting of seas,
Shearing the giant floes aside,
Ploughing the wide-flung ice-fields in a spume
That smoked far up my ponderous flanks,
Onward I fared,
My ice-blue pinnacles rendering back the sun
In darts of sharp radiance;
My bases fathoms deep in the dark profound.

And now around me
Life and the frigid waters all aswarm.
60 The smooth wave creamed
With tiny capelin and the small pale squid,—
So pale the light struck through them.
Gulls and gannets screamed
Over the feast, and gorged themselves, and rose,
A clamour of weaving wings, and hid
Momently my face.
The great bull whales
With cavernous jaws agape,
Scooped in the spoil, and slept,
70 Their humped forms just awash, and rocking softly,—
Or sounded down, down to the deeps, and nosed
Along my ribbed and sunken roots,
And in the green gloom scattered the pasturing cod.

322

And so I voyaged on, down the dim parallels,
Convoyed by fields
Of countless calving seals
Mild-featured, innocent-eyed, and unforeknowing
The doom of the red flenching knives.
I passed the storm-racked gate
80   Of Hudson Strait,
And savage Chidley where the warring tides
In white wrath seethe forever.
Down along the sounding shore
Of iron-fanged, many-watered Labrador
Slow weeks I shaped my course, and saw
Dark Mokkowic and dark Napiskawa,
And came at last off lone Belle Isle, the bane
Of ships and snare of bergs.
Here, by the deep conflicting currents drawn,
90   I hung,
And swung,
The inland voices Gulfward calling me
To ground amid my peers on the alien strand
And roam no more.
But then an off-shore wind,
A great wind fraught with fate,
Caught me and pressed me back,
And I resumed my solitary way.
Slowly I bore
100   South-east by bastioned Bauld,
And passed the sentinel light far-beaming late
Along the liners' track,
And slanted out Atlanticwards, until
Above the treacherous swaths of fog
Faded from the view the loom of Newfoundland.

      Beautiful, ethereal
In the blue sparkle of the gleaming day,
A soaring miracle
Of white immensity,
110   I was the cynosure of passing ships
That wondered and were gone,
Their wreathed smoke trailing them beyond the verge.
And when in the night they passed—
The night of stars and calm,
Forged up and passed, with churning surge
And throb of huge propellers, and long-drawn
Luminous wake behind,
And sharp, small lights in rows,

I lay a ghost of menace chill and still,
120   A shape pearl-pale and monstrous, off to leeward,
Blurring the dim horizon line.

      Day dragged on day,
And then came fog,
By noon, blind-white,
And in the night
Black-thick and smothering the sight.
Folded therein I waited,
Waited I knew not what
And heeded not,
130   Greatly incurious and unconcerned.
I heard the small waves lapping along my base,
Lipping and whispering, lisping with bated breath
A casual expectancy of death.
I heard remote
The deep, far carrying note
Blown from the hoarse and hollow throat
Of some lone tanker groping on her course.
Louder and louder rose the sound
In deepening diapason, then passed on,
140   Diminishing, and dying,—
And silence closed around.
And in the silence came again
Those stealthy voices,
That whispering of death.

      And then I heard
The thud of screws approaching.
Near and more near,
Louder and yet more loud,
Through the thick dark I heard it,—
150   The rush and hiss of waters as she ploughed
Head on, unseen, unseeing,
Toward where I stood across her path, invisible.
And then a startled blare
Of horror close re-echoing,—a glare
Of sudden, stabbing searchlights
That but obscurely pierced the gloom;
And there
I towered, a dim immensity of doom.

      A roar
160   Of tortured waters as the giant screws,
Reversed, thundered full steam astern.

Yet forward still she drew, until,
Slow answering desperate helm,
She swerved, and all her broadside came in view,
Crawling beneath me;
And for a moment I saw faces, blanched,
Stiffly agape, turned upward, and wild eyes
Astare; and one long, quavering cry went up
As a submerged horn gored her through and through,
170   Ripping her beam wide open;
And sullenly she listed, till her funnels
Crashed on my steep,
And men sprang, stumbling, for the boats.
But now, my deep foundations
Mined by those warmer seas, the hour had come
When I must change.
Slowly I leaned above her,
Slowly at first, then faster,
And icy fragments rained upon her decks.
180   Then my enormous mass descended on her,
A falling mountain, all obliterating,—
And the confusion of thin, wailing cries,
The Babel of shouts and prayers
And shriek of steam escaping
Suddenly died.
And I rolled over,
Wallowing,
And once more came to rest,
My long hid bases heaved up high in air.

190   And now, from fogs emerging,
I traversed blander seas,
Forgot the fogs, the scourging
Of sleet-whipped gales, forgot
My austere origin, my tremendous birth,
My journeyings, and that last cataclysm
Of overwhelming ruin.
My squat, pale, alien bulk
Basked in the ambient sheen;
And all about me, league on league outspread,
200   A gulf of indigo and green.
I laughed in the light waves laced with white,—
Nor knew
How swiftly shrank my girth
Under their sly caresses, how the breath
Of that soft wind sucked up my strength, nor how
The sweet, insidious fingers of the sun
Their stealthy depredations wrought upon me.

Slowly now
I drifted, dreaming.
210 I saw the flying-fish
With silver gleaming
Flash from the peacock-bosomed wave
And flicker through an arc of sunlit air
Back to their element, desperate to elude
The jaws of the pursuing albacore.

Day after day
I swung in the unhasting tide.
Sometimes I saw the dolphin folk at play,
Their lithe sides iridescent-dyed,
220 Unheeding in their speed
That long grey wraith,
The shark that followed hungering beneath.
Sometimes I saw a school
Of porpoise rolling by
In ranked array,
Emerging and submerging rhythmically,
Their blunt black bodies heading all one way
Until they faded
In the horizon's dazzling line of light.
230 Night after night
I followed the low, large moon across the sky,
Or counted the large stars on the purple dark,
The while I wasted, wasted and took no thought,
In drowsed entrancement caught;—
Until one noon a wave washed over me,
Breathed low a sobbing sigh,
Foamed indolently, and passed on;
And then I knew my empery was gone;
As I, too, soon must go.
240 Nor was I ill content to have it so.

Another night
Gloomed o'er my sight,
With cloud, and flurries of warm, wild rain.
Another day,
Dawning delectably
With amber and scarlet stain,
Swept on its way,
Glowing and shimmering with heavy heat.
A lazing tuna rose
250 And nosed me curiously,
And shouldered me aside in brusque disdain,

326

So had I fallen from my high estate.
A foraging gull
Stooped over me, touched me with webbed pink feet,
And wheeled and skreeled away,
Indignant at the chill.

Last I became
A little glancing globe of cold
That slid and sparkled on the slow-pulsed swell.
260   And then my fragile, scintillating frame
Dissolved in ecstasy
Of many coloured light,
And I breathed up my soul into the air
And merged forever in the all-solvent sea.

September-October 1928,
March 9, 1931; 1931

TO A CERTAIN MYSTIC

1   Sometimes you saw what others could not see.
       Sometimes you heard what no one else could hear:—
A light beyond the unfathomable dark,
       A voice that sounded only to your ear.

And did you, voyaging the tides of vision
       In your lone shallop, steering by what star,
Catch hints of some Elysian fragrance, wafted
       On winds impalpable, from who knows how far?

And did dawn show you driftage from strange continents
10   Of which we dream but no man surely knows,—
Some shed gold leafage from the Tree Eternal,
       Some petals of the Imperishable Rose?

And did you once, Columbus of the spirit,
       Essay the crossing of that unknown sea,
Really touch land beyond the mists of rumour
       And find new lands where they were dreamed to be?

Ah, why brought you not back the word of power,
       The charted course, the unambiguous sign,
Or even some small seed, whence we might grow
20   A flower unmistakably divine?

But you came empty-handed, and your tongue
    Babbled strange tidings none could wholly trust.
And if we half believed you, it was only
    Because we would, and not because we must.

Fourth stanza, September 18, 1909,
Full text March 20, 22, 23, 1931; 1931

TAORMINA

1 A little tumbled city on the height,
    Basking above the cactus and the sea!
What pale, frail ghosts of memory come to-night
    And call back the forgotten years to me!
      Taormina, Taormina,
      And the month of the almond blossom.

In an old book I find a withered flower,
    And withered dreams awake to their old fire.
How far have danced your feet since that fair hour
10   That brought us to the land of heart's desire!
      Taormina, Taormina,
      Oh, the scent of the almond blossom.

The grey-white monastery-garden wall
    O'erpeers the white crag, and the flung vines upclamber
In the white sun, and cling and seem to fall,—
    Brave bougainvilleas, purple and smoky amber.
      Taormina, Taormina,
      And the month of the almond blossom.

You caught your breath, as hand in hand we stood
20   To watch the luminous peak of Aetna there
Soaring above the cloudy solitude,
    Enmeshed in the opaline Sicilian air.
      Taormina, Taormina,
      Oh, the scent of the almond blossom.

We babbled of Battos and brown Corydon,—
    Of Amaryllis coiling her dark locks,—
Of the sad-hearted satyr grieving on
    The tomb of Helicé among the rocks
      O'erhung with the almond blossom,—

Of how the goat-boy wrenched apart the vines
30   That veiled the slim-limbed Chloe at her bath,
And followed her fleet-foot flight among the pines
     And caught her close, and kissed away her wrath.
          Taormina, Taormina,
          And the month of the almond blossom.

And then—you turned impetuously to me!
     We saw the blue hyacinths at our feet; and came
To the battlements, and looked down upon the sea—
     And the sea was a blue flame!

          * * * * * * * * * * *

40   The blue flame dies. The ghosts come back to me.
          Taormina, Taormina,
          Oh, the scent of the almond blossom.

                              May 3, 5, and 6, 1932; 1932

PRESENCES

1   The shadow of the poplar
      Beside my cabin door
      Has trembled on the floor.
      Tho' no wind walks the forest tops
      Across my window sill
      It trembled and was still.

      The broad noon sunlight basking
      On every flower and tree
      Was still as light can be.
10   What made those withered leaves whirl up,
      And drift a space, and fall—
      As they had heard a call?

      Why are those harebells nodding
      As if an unseen wing
      Had set them all aswing,
      Tho' up and down the forest glade
      No other blade or bough
      Stirs from its slumber now?

The stillness and the brightness
Companion me. I hear
20 A footfall drawing near
Tho' no sound breaks the noonday hush.
A sweet breath stirs my hair,—
But there is nothing there!

What gracious presences
Are these I cannot see
Tho' they come close to me?

* * * * * * * * *

I think I shall have pleasant dreams
In silence charmed and deep
30 When I lie down to sleep.

First stanza, *March 17, 1907,*
Full poem, *May 12, 13, 1932;* 1932

RE-BIRTH

1 I had stumbled up thro' Time from the slime to the heights,
    Then fallen into the stillness of the tomb.
For an age I had lain in the pulseless, senseless dark,
    I had swooned in the darkness of the tomb.

I had slept for an age without a dream or stir
    Till a voice came, troubling the pools of sleep.
From the long-forgotten bones, the immemorial dust,
    I fled up from the smother of my sleep.

A naked soul, I bathed in the light ineffable,
10   I floated in the ecstasy of light.
Yet I ached with desire for a dream I could not grasp,
    And I struggled to pierce beyond the light.

As the light had been a veil I swam through the veil
    And sank through shadows to a blissful gloom.
And the ache of my desire was sweetly assuaged
    As I sheathed me blindly in the gloom.

In my heart, as it seemed, I heard a craving, faint cry.
    I was darkly aware of moving warmth.
I thirsted, and my groping thirst was satisfied;
20   And I slumbered, wrapt and folded in the warmth.

330

Once again was I snared in the kindly flesh of man.
The kind flesh closed away my sight.
But before the mists of temporal forgetting shut me in
I had seen, far off, the Vision and the Height.

September 22, 1932; 1934

THE SQUATTER

1   Round the lone clearing
Clearly the whitethroats call
Across the marge of dusk and the dewfall's coolness.

Far up in the empty
Amber and apple-green sky
A night-hawk swoops, and twangs her silver chord.

No wind's astir,
But the poplar boughs breathe softly
And the smoke of a dying brush-fire stings the air.

10   The spired, dark spruces
Crowd up to the snake fence, breathless,
Expectant till the rising of the moon.

In the wet alders,
Where the cold brook flows murmuring,
The red cow drinks,—the cow-bell sounds *tonk-tonk.*

*   *   *   *   *   *

From his cabin door
The squatter lounges forth,
Sniffs the damp air, and scans the sky for rain.

He has made his meal,—
20   Fat bacon, and buckwheat cakes,
And ruddy-brown molasses from Barbados.

His chores all done,
He seats himself on the door-sill,
And slowly fills his pipe, and smokes, and dreams.

He sees his axe
Leaning against the birch logs.
The fresh white chips are scattered over the yard.

331

He hears his old horse
Nosing the hay, in the log barn
30 Roofed with poles and sheathed with sheets of birchbark.

Beyond the barn
He sees his buckwheat patch,
Its pink-white bloom pale-gleaming through the twilight.

Its honeyed fragrance
Breathes to his nostrils, mingled
With the tang of the brush-fire smoke, thinly ascending.

Deepens the dusk.
The whitethroats are hushed; and the night-hawk
Drops down from the sky and hunts the low-flying night-moths.

* * * * * * *

40 The squatter is dreaming.
Vaguely he plans how, come winter,
He'll chop out another field, just over the brook.

He'll build a new barn
Next year, a barn with a haymow,
No more to leave his good hay outside in the stack.

He rises and stretches,
Goes in and closes the door,
And lights his lamp on the table beside the window.

The light shines forth.
50 It lights up the wide-strewn chips.
For a moment it catches the dog darting after a rabbit.

It lights up the lean face
Of the squatter as he sits reading,
Knitting his brow as he spells out a month-old paper.

* * * * * * *

Slowly the moon,
Humped, crooked, red, remote,
Rises, tangled and scrawled behind the spruce-tops.

Higher she rises,—
Grows rounder, and smaller, and white,
60   And sails up the empty sky high over the spruce-tops.

She washes in silver,
Illusively clear, the log barn,
The lop-sided stack by the barn, and the slumbering cabin.

She floods in the window,—
And the squatter stirs in his bunk,
On his mattress stuffed with green fir-tips, balsamy scented.

*   *   *   *   *   *   *

From the dark of the forest
The horned owl hoots, and is still.
Startled, the silence descends, and broods once more on the clearing.

September 23 and October 2, 1932; 1933

WESTCOCK HILL

1   As I came over Westcock Hill
     My heart was full of tears.
   Under the summer's pomp I heard
     The spending of the years.
   Oh, the sweet years! The swift years!
   The years that lapse away!

   I saw the green slopes bathed in sun,
     The marshlands stretched afar,
   And, hurrying pale between its dikes,
10   My memoried Tantramar.
   Oh, the sweet years! The swift years!
   The years that lapse away!

   The salt tang and the buckwheat scents
     Were on the breathing air;
   And all was glad. But I was sad
     For one who was not there.
   Oh, the sweet years! The swift years!
   The years that lapse away!

I wandered down to Westcock Church,
20   The old grey church in the wood.
Kneeling, I heard my father's voice
    In that hushed solitude.
Oh, the sweet years! The swift years!
    The years that lapse away!

I saw again his surpliced form.
    I heard the hymning choir.
Shadows!—and dreams! Alone remained
    The ache of my desire.
Oh, the sweet years! The swift years!
30   *The years that lapse away!*

He sleeps;—how many a year removed,
    How many a league withdrawn
From these dear woods, these turbid floods,
    These fields that front the dawn.
Oh, the sweet years! The swift years!
    The years have lapsed away!

July 14, 1929; November 27, 1932;
October 13, 14, 1934; 1934

TWILIGHT OVER SHAUGAMAUK

1 Back to you, Shaugamauk, my heart is turning!
    Your shallow rapids call to me through the dusk.
I sniff the acrid sweet of your brush-fires burning.
    I breathe your dew-drenched tamaracks' **poignant** musk.

I see once more your thin young moon appearing
    Through the black branches, pale, remote, apart.
From the lone cabin on the hillside clearing
    A dog's bark echoes faintly through my heart.

I pass. But I commit to your long keeping
10   Some part of me that passes not. I know
My words, my songs, my memories unsleeping
    Will mingle unforgotten in your flow.

Waters of Shaugamauk, when your dusk is falling
My dust will stir, hearing your shallows calling.

August 5, 1905; October 15, 1928; February 18
and 25, October 18 and 20, 1936; 1937

THOSE PERISH, THESE ENDURE

1 On the pale borders of evening
     The hawthorn **breaths** are cool.
The frogs pipe in the sedges
     About the shadowy pool.

The cows, turned out from the milking, through
     The bars go one by one;
And the lusty farm-lad whistles free
     For soon his chores are done.

In war-torn lands afar
10   Red hates flare up and fade.
Temples and towers crumble down
     And children cower dismayed.
The streets are loud with shouting,
     The peoples bleed and riot;
The blood soaks into the reeking sod,—
     Then comes, for a little, **quiet**.

On scenes like these the moon
     Looks down with heedless face.
The sly inexorable years
20   Their horrors shall efface.
But still shall cows to pasture
     Trail leisurely one by one;
And frogs in the pale sedge go on piping
     After the set of sun;
And hawthorn breathe on the air;
And farm-lads homeward fare;
And men come gossiping in from fields—
     The day's work done.

February 14, 16, 17, 1937; 1937

AS DOWN THE WOODLAND WAYS

1   As down the woodland ways I went
      With every wind asleep
    I felt the surge of endless life
      About my footsteps creep.

    I felt the urge of quickening mould
      That had been once a flower
    Mount with the sap to bloom again
      At its appointed hour.

I saw gray stumps go crumbling down
10   In sodden, grim decay,
To soar in pillared green again
    On some remoter day.

I saw crushed beetles, mangled grubs,
    All crawling, perished things,
Whirl up in air, an ecstasy
    Of many-coloured wings.

Through weed and world, through worm and star,
    The sequence ran the same:—
Death but the travail-pang of life,
20   Destruction but a name.

February 5, 1936, March 11, 19??,
March 31, 1937; 1937

TWO RIVERS

[The Tantramar and the St. John]

1   Two rivers are there hold my heart
    And neither would I leave.
When I would stay with one too long
    The other tugs my sleeve.

For both are in my blood and bone
    And will be till I die.
Along my veins their argument
    Goes on incessantly.

The one, inconstant as the wind
10   And fickle as the foam,
Disturbs my soul with strange desires
    And pricks my feet to roam.

The other, a strong and tranquil flood
    With stars upon its breast,
Would win me back from wandering
    And snare desire with rest.

336

II. The Tantramar

To you, my moon-led Tantramar,
    I turn, who taught my feet to range,—
You and the vagrant moon conspiring,
20   Twin arbiters of change,—

To you I turn, my Tantramar.
    A wide-eyed boy I played beside
Your wastes of wind-swept green and chased
    Your ever-changing tide.

I watched your floods come tumbling in
    To fill your inland creeks remote,
Assail your prisoning dykes, and set
    Your long marsh grass afloat.

I watched your venturing floods at full
30   Falter and halt, turn and retreat,
And race with laughter back to sea,
    Mocking their own defeat.

Far up to Midgic's farms you flow
    And there for a brief space rest your fill,
Then back past Sackville's studious halls
    To Westcock on her hill.

Draining your vast red channels bare
    To shine like copper in the sun
You tremble down the gleaming chasm
40   And whimper as you run;

But, soon repenting your dismay,
    With challenging roar you surge again
To brim your dykes and reassume
    Your lordship of the plain.

.   .   .   .

Across the estranging, changing years,
    Blind puppet of my restless star,
In discontent content alone,
    You urge and drive me, Tantramar.

To you I turn again, St. John,
50   Great river, constant tide,—return
With a full heart to you, beside
     Whose green banks I was born.

A babe I left you, and a youth
     Returned to you, ancestral stream,
Where sits my city, Fredericton,
     A jewel in a dream.

Your broad tide sweeps her storied shores
     Where loyalties and song were bred,
And that green hill where sleeps the dust
60   Of my beloved dead.

From many a distant source withdrawn
     You drain your waters,—from the wash
Of Temiscouata's waves, and lone
     Swamps of the Allegash,—

From many a far and nameless lake
     Where rain-birds greet the showery noon
And dark moose pull the lily pads
     Under an alien moon.

Full-fed from many a confluent stream
70   Your fortunate waters dream toward sea,—
And reach the barrier heights that hold
     Your calm estates in fee.

In that strait gate you stand on guard
     While Fundy's floods, without surcease,
In giant wrath assault in vain
     The portals of your peace.

Outside, reared on that iron rock
     Where first the Ships of Freedom came,
Sits the proud city, foam begirt,
80   That bears your name and fame,—

Saint John, rock-bound, rock-ribbed, secure,
  To her stern birthright constant still,
She fronts the huge o'er mastering tides
  And bends them to her will.

.   .   .   .   .

Dear and great River, when my feet
  Have wearied of the endless quest,
Heavy with sleep I will come back
  To your calm shores for rest.

March 20 - May 18, 1937; 1937

PEACE WITH DISHONOUR

1   The red flame of war, the anguish of woman,
The dropped bomb, the gas-choked breath,
The groans of the stricken, or the swift death—
These, alas, are but human!

'Tis not for these my heart sinks—not for these!
Their horrors pass like a sick dream.
Their scars fade in Time's detergent stream.
Oh! not for these!

But oh, for faith betrayed cringes my soul.
10   For long dishonour brief, cowed peace.
For Freedom stripped and cast to the loud pack.
This stain endures. For this cringes my soul.

September 18 and 20, 1938; 1938

IN TIME OF EARTH'S MISUSE

1   Outside the wind sobs in the old spruce.
  One dead branch taps my window pane.
  Drips the slow rain
    And grieves,
Lamenting Earth's misuse—

Lamenting the blood-lust of bestial men
  Who spew their hate over the raped lands
  Where children stretch to heaven red, maimed hands,
And shriek to be avenged.

10   Slow drips the rain. But oh, more slow, alas—
      What if too late?—comes the Avenging Thrust!
    —Profitable is neutrality! Let the sword rust!
  The storm—and shame—may pass!

March 16, 1936;
February 8 and 9, 1940; 1940

FORGET NOT, THOU

1   Forget not, Thou who saidst
  "Vengeance is Mine. I will repay."

  Forget not Thou,
  God of Compassion! Surely now
  The cup of Thy wrath is filled
  To overflowing!
  (Thou God hear our prayer! Oh, hear us now!)

  Is it nothing to Thee, Thou All-Knowing,
  That they perish in flame,
10   Thy children,
  While the obscene Beast reviles Thy name,
  And vaunts the wrong unspeakable,
  Treading them down, mother and babe,
  In the blood and spew of his hate?
  Is it nothing to Thee?

  Thou God who seest all,
  Too long we wait!
  Too long!

May 12, 26, 27, 1940; 1940

CANADA TO FRANCE

1 Not upon thee the shame, not upon thee,
    O France, our France, from whose bright loins are sprung
  The half of all our sons,—not upon thee
    The ignominy of betrayal, vilely wrung
  From dotards who would lick the butchering hand,
    Drooling of "Honour" while they slit her throat!—
  Never for these, cowed traitors, to demand
    The right to speak for thee, while thy foes gloat
  Upon thy glory eclipsed, thy pride brought low,
10   Thy homes a shambles and thy soul enchained.

340

But now, in this thy darkest hour, we know
    There stands a remnant that shall purge thy stained
Banner, and above thy martyred dead
See thee uplift again thy sacred head.

June 26 and 30, 1940; 1940

THE RAVAGED LANDS

[*Poland*]

1   Oh, not this year comes spring
        To the darkened lands,
    Gutted with fire, laid waste
        By ravaging hands.

    Not this year, not here,
        Comes the glad rebirth
    Of mating blooms and wings
        And pregnant earth.

    Not here will fields be sweet
10   With summer's breath:—
    Watered are they with blood,
        Deep-sown with death!

    These fields—no sound they hear
        Save women's weeping
    And children's starving cries
        And anguish unsleeping.

    Oh, bitter the harvest here
        (Far off, but fated,)
    Of hate that will not be assuaged
20   Till vengeance be sated,—

    Till comes at length the hour
        (Too long delayed)
    When the grim score shall be,
        To the last tear, paid.

May 12, 16,
July 21, 22, 28, 29, 1940; 1940

CANADA SPEAKS OF BRITAIN

1   This is that bastioned rock where dwell the Free,
      That citadel against whose front in vain
   Storm up the mad assaults of air and sea
      To shatter down in flaming wreck again.

   This, this is Britain, bulwark of our breed,
      Our one sure shield against the hordes of hate.
   Smite her, and we are smitten; wound her, we bleed.
      Yet firm she stands and fears no thrust of fate.

   Stands she, and shall;—but not by guns alone,
10   And ships and planes and ramparts. Her own soul
   That knows neither to bend nor break,—her own
      Will, hammered to temper,—keeps her whole.

   She calls. And we will answer to our last breath,—
   Make light of sacrifice, and jest with Death.

July 28, August 18 and 19, 1940; 1940

EPITAPH FOR A YOUNG AIRMAN

[Shot down over the Channel]

1   He who would mount on eager wing
      With morning in his eyes
   To climb through cloud and storm, and hurl
      His challenge through the skies,—

   Would scale the heights of air too thin
      For toil of labouring breath,
   Alone to front the foe and fling
      His dare to flaming death,—

   Would plunge through scathing hail of fire
10   And blast of screaming shell
   To scourge with steel the ravening horde
      Back to their hell,—

He sleeps today, how deep a sleep,
    Beneath the Channel wave,
Nor heeds how well his task was done
    For those he died to save.

September 28,
October 13, 17, and 18, 1940;
revised December 4, 1940; 1940

SONG FOR VICTORY DELAYED
("Une heure viendra qui tout paiera.")

1   No easy task is ours.
    Far off is victory yet.
For us the doubtful battle,
    For us the tears and sweat.

For us with will unbowed
    And strength that shall not tire
And clenched teeth to endure
    The test of blood and fire.

For blindness, folly, sloth,
10   Still must we pay the price,—
The heartstrings rent asunder,
    The anguished sacrifice.

On every shore we die.
    In every sea we drown.
Adventuring every sky
    Our sons to death go down.

Yet purged by flame we front
    The fury unafraid,
With faith that flinches not
20   And high hearts undismayed,

Till strikes the destined hour,
    Big with the world's fate,
When we shall scourge to their just doom
    The shattered hordes of hate.

May 27, 1941; July 18 and 19, 1941;
March 16, 1942; 1942

RESURGANT

(A Song for the Nations Submerged)

1   *Oh, clear and high summons the trumpet*
    Before the gates of Dawn [.]

    What tho' their ramparts be fallen,
      Their streets with blood run red,
    And over cradle and altar
      The brute battalions tread;
    Tho' gutted by flame their villages,
      Tho' desolate byre and stead,
    And ever for vengeance cry the bones
10   Of their unburied dead:—

    Yet clear and high summons the trumpet
    Before the gates of Dawn.

    In the black slough of defeat
      Still are their heads unbowed;
    Defiant they front death still,
      In their chains still proud;
    But they all shall rise again:—
      From the long dark shall they rise,
    With the daybreak on their foreheads
20   And the New Dawn flooding their eyes,
    To a new world purged with blood
      As it never before has been,—
    A world for justice, faith, good will
      Made free at last and clean.

    Oh, clear and high summon [s] *the trumpets*
    Before the gates of Dawn.

        August 12, 1934; January 6, 1941;
        March 29, 1942;
        April 4, 7, 8, 9, 1942; 1942

PHILLIDA'S BLUE RIBBON

1   This band of true patrician hue
      I hold in tender thrall:
    But the dear rebel holds me too
      For it remembers all.

It dreams of its proud office, ere
It fell to me from you
When—was it your ethereal hair
It cintured with its blue?

Or was it your white ambrosial throat
10   Its azure thrilled to kiss
While envious lips and eyes might note
The sweet antithesis?

Or your slim waist, adored, desired,
It clasped with joy perchance,
And felt each silken fibre fired
With ardent circumstance?

Nay, happier yet! To play its part
What lover might not barter
His hopes of heaven and pawn his heart?
20   This ribbon was—your garter!

mid 1890's ?

MAY-NIGHT

1   Dear, you have come into my loving heart
In these last fateful days,
Nearer and dearer, and I have learned in part
Your tender, wistful ways.

Thy gentle, loving thoughts have come to me
As one, who waiting, stands
Expectant for some gift of poesy
With eager heart and hands.

And oh! my very dear one, I have given
10   To thee that inner stream
Of tender thoughts linked happily with heaven,
Love's vision and Love's dream.

Such peace, such joy a moment seems to stay
'Ere other cares divide,
But its divine sense cannot fade away
On misty time or tide.

345

Beneath the dusky, wistful, soft, sweet night,
　　　There in the shadowy lane
I gave thee thanks for all the dear delight
20　　　Thou broughtest me again.

And, hand and hand beneath the liquid stars,
　　　Children in love we stood;
No longer prisoners behind the bars
　　　Of sentient solitude;—

But happy that affection and regard
　　　Might flow between us free
Each giving silently, save that one word
　　　I whispered unto thee.

I love thee! and thou knowest it, and yet
30　　　This gift that we exchange
Has neither pain, nor sorrow, nor regret
　　　Within its widening range.

My *very dear one*—take the love I give
　　　Freely,—'tis clear and fair,
It is the very hope by which I live
　　　The one sweet dream I share.

For my heart fills with joy and tenderness
　　　That cannot rest alone,
So take my love, and, if it be to bless,
40　　　Then give me of thine own.

May, 1919

COLOUR TOASTS

1　Here's to the girl who dresses in *white,*
And declares she has never stopped out over night.
But if you're all right, and you take her all right,
I don't say she will,—but I do think she might.

Here's to the girl who dresses in *blue,*
And swears to her lover she'll always be true.
But give her a kiss and a cocktail or two
And the devil knows what she will do.

346

Here's to the girl who dresses in *rose,*
10 What she does with her lover nobody knows.
A kiss and a hug, that's as far as it goes;
At least so *they* say,—but nobody knows.

Here's to the girl who dresses in *gold,*
And tries to pretend she's so timid and cold.
Well, in public perhaps. But at times she's quite bold.
So the rest of the story is best left untold.

Here's to the girl who dresses in *black,*
So demure she is almost secure from attack.
But there's something about her makes others seem slack;
20 So if once you have known her you'll always come back.

Here's to the girl who dresses in *jade,*
And wouldn't get up for a zeppelin raid;
But if to her room that night you had strayed
You might have found out *why* she wasn't afraid.

Here's to the girl who dresses in *plaid,*
And declares she has never been kissed by a lad.
But—look deep in her eyes and you'll swear she has had
A wee taste of *something* that's mad, bad and glad.

Here's to the girl who is dressed in *magenta;*
30 She's cold—on the surface; but warm at the centre.
If she does find a lad who she thinks will content her
She'll have him, begad, and no power can prevent her.

Here's to the girl who dresses in *green,*
Of provocative glance and delectable mien.
But beware of her wiles and don't get too keen,
For those naughty bright glances say more than they mean.

Here's to the girl who dresses in *red,*
And can say with her eyes what her lips leave unsaid.
She'll stir a man up till he looses his head,
40 Then—run away off to her *own* little bed.

Here's to the girl who dresses so neat,
For the sake of the army,—and also the fleet.
And when she kisses, she kisses so sweet
That she makes something stand that hasn't got feet!

CHRONOLOGY

1860   Born January 10, in the Parish of Douglas, near Fredericton. Eldest child of the Reverend George Goodridge Roberts and Emma (Bliss) Roberts. Sisters and brothers: Fanny (b. 1862, died at eleven months), Jane Elizabeth Gostwycke Roberts (i.e., Elizabeth Roberts MacDonald, b. 1864), Goodridge Bliss Roberts (b. 1870), Theodore Roberts (b. 1871), and William Carman Roberts (b. 1874). For Roberts' full genealogy see the "Appendix" in E.M. Pomeroy, *Sir Charles G.D. Roberts* (Toronto: Ryerson, 1943), pp. 357-8.

                August, family moves to Westcock, N.B.

1874   Family moves to Fredericton. Reverend Roberts appointed Rector of St. Ann's Church and Canon of Christ Church Cathedral.

                September, enrols in Fredericton Collegiate School, (Sir) George R. Parkin, Headmaster.

1874-75   "Sonnet: On the Dying Year" and "Spring" composed, first published verses, in *The Canadian Illustrated News,* March 30, 1878.

1876   Summer, graduates from Fredericton Collegiate School with highest honours.

                Fall, enrols in University of New Brunswick.

1879   June, graduates from University with honours in mental and moral philosophy and political economy, scholarships in Latin and Greek, medal in Latin prose composition.

                September, appointed Headmaster, Chatham Grammar and High School, Chatham, N.B.

1880   December, marries Mary Fenety.

                Orion and Other Poems.

1881   M.A. degree, University of New Brunswick.

1881-82   *Later Poems* privately printed.

349

1882 January, resigns from Chatham School.

February, appointed Headmaster, York Street School, Fredericton.

May, Athelstan, eldest child and first son born.

"New Brunswick" in *Picturesque Canada.*

1883 June, delivers Convocation Address on "The Beginnings of Canadian Literature" at University of New Brunswick.

Resigns, York Street School.

November, moves to Toronto; appointed editor of Goldwin Smith's *The Week.*

1884 February, resigns from *The Week.*

Brief free-lance period, first trip to New York, return to Fredericton.

Lloyd Roberts born.

1885 September, takes appointment as Professor of English and French at King's College, Windsor, N.S.

November, address on "The Making of a Nation" at University of New Brunswick.

1886 Edith Roberts born.

1886-87 *In Divers Tones.*

1887 "Echoes of Old Acadia" in *Canadian Leaves.*

1888 Douglas Roberts born.

Poems of Wild Life, edited and with an Introduction by Roberts.

1889 *Autochthon* privately printed.

1890 Roberts' translation of Phillippe Aubert de Gaspé's *Canadians of Old.*

Elected Fellow of Royal Society of Canada.

350

1891   *The Canadian Guide-Book.*

1892   February, Goodridge Bliss Roberts dies.

Ave: An Ode for the Centenary of the Birth of Percy Bysshe Shelley.
"The Poetry of Wordsworth" in *Selections from Wordsworth.*
"Do Seek Their Meat from God", first animal story.

1893   Elected Fellow of the Royal Society of Literature.

Songs of the Common Day and Ave.

1894   *The Raid from Beauséjour and How the Carter Boys Lifted the Mortgage: Two Stories of Acadie,* first volume of fiction.
"Mr. Bliss Carman's Poems" in *The Chap-Book.*

1895   Summer, resigns from King's College.

Return to Fredericton, free-lance period to 1897.

Reube Dare's Shad Boat: A Tale of the Tide Country.
The Land of Evangeline and the Gateways Thither.

1896   *The Book of the Native.*
The Forge in the Forest, first novel.
Earth's Enigmas, first nature stories.
Around the Camp Fire.

1897   February, moves to New York, appointed assistant editor of *The Illustrated American.*

Elected member of the Author's Club of America.

A History of Canada.

1898   Elected charter member of the National Institute of Arts and Letters, the only non-American admitted to membership.

October 16, Athelstan Roberts dies.

Resigns from *The Illustrated American.*

Free lance from this time.

New York Nocturnes and Other Poems.
A Sister to Evangeline.

351

1899	April, leaves New York for London.
	"Introduction" to *Walden: Or Life in the Woods.*
	"Prologue" in *Northland Lyrics.*
1900	Return to New York.
	By the Marshes of Minas.
	The Heart of the Ancient Wood.
1901	*Poems.*
1902	*Barbara Ladd.*
	The Kindred of the Wild.
	Alastor and Adonais, edited and with an introduction by Roberts.
1903	Visit with Francis Sherman in Cuba.
	The Book of the Rose.
1904	Trip to France and Holland.
	The Prisoner of Mademoiselle.
	The Watchers of the Trails.
	"Introduction" in Carman's *Sappho: One Hundred Lyrics.*
1905	October, Reverend Roberts dies.
	Second visit with Sherman in Cuba.
	Cameron of Lochiel, a new edition of *The Canadians of Old.*
	Red Fox.
1906	May, honorary LL.D. conferred by University of New Brunswick.
	The Heart That Knows.
1907	November, leaves for Europe, does not return to Canada for seventeen years, resides in Paris and Pont Levoy until 1910, first visit to Italy.
	Poems, new edition.
	The Haunters of the Silences.
1908	*The House in the Water.*

1909	*The Red Oxen of Boval.*
	The Backwoodsmen.
	Kings in Exile.

1909
: *The Red Oxen of Boval.*
The Backwoodsmen.
Kings in Exile.

1910
: Resides in Munich until 1912.

"Jean Michaud's Little Ship" in *International Short Stories.*

1911
: *More Kindred of the Wild.*
Neighbours Unknown.

1912
: Returns to London.

Babes of the Wild.
The Feet of the Furtive.

1913
: *A Balkan Prince.*
Hoof and Claw.

1914
: September, joins the Legion of Frontiersmen.

December, commissioned as First Lieutenant in the 16th Battalion of the King's (Liverpool) Regiment.

Promoted to Captain.

1916
: Transferred to Canadian Staff in London in the Canadian War Records Office.

Promoted to Major.

December, sent to France as Special Press Correspondent attached to the Canadian Corp.

Remains in France until Spring, 1918.

The Secret Trail.

1918
: *Canada in Flanders,* Vol. III.
The Ledge on Bald Face (Jim: The Story of a Backwoods Police Dog).

1919
: Demobilized from Army.

Resides in London.

New Poems.
In the Morning of Time.

1921   Visits to North Africa, Italy, and Switzerland.

     Some Animal Stories.

1922   November, Elizabeth Roberts MacDonald dies.

     Wisdom of the Wilderness.
     More Animal Stories.

1923   February, Roberts' mother, Emma Roberts, dies.

1924   *Lovers in Acadie* (new edition of *A Sister to Evangeline*).
     They That (Who) Walk in the Wild.

1925   February, returns to Canada, first recital tour, resides in Toronto.

     The Sweet o' the Year and Other Poems.

1926   Second recital tour.

     Elected National President of the Canadian Authors' Association.

     Awarded Lorne Pierce Gold Medal of the Royal Society of Canada.

1927   Winter 1927-8, lecture series on Canadian Literature at University of British Columbia.

     The Vagrant of Time.

1929   June, Bliss Carman dies.

1930   May, Mary (Fenety) Roberts dies.

     "Introduction" in E. J. Pratt's *Verses of the Sea.*

1933   *Eyes of the Wilderness.*

1934   *The Iceberg and Other Poems.*

1935   June, Knighted.

     "Foreword" in Francis Sherman's *The Complete Poems of Francis Sherman.*

354

1936   *Selected Poems.*
            Further Animal Stories.

1937   *Twilight Over Shaugamauk and Three Other Poems.*

1941   *Canada Speaks of Britain.*

1942   May, Doctor of Letters degree conferred by Mount Allison University.

            Flying Colours: An Anthology, edited and with an Introduction by Roberts.

1943   October, marries Joan Montgomery.

            November 25, dies in Toronto, burial in Fredericton.

            Sir Charles G.D. Roberts: A Biography. (E.M. Pomeroy)

A NOTE ON
BIBLIOGRAPHICAL PROCEDURES

The format of this edition presents the following features: (1) the poem itself with marginal line numbers in groups of ten, (2) the date of composition when possible and the date of the first known publication. Provided in a separate section are: (3) a complete record of the known publishing history of each poem and, occasionally, apposite comments on it, and (4) where necessary a complete record of variants and a glossary.

All of the known publications, manuscripts, and typescripts for each poem have been collected and a copy-text, as authoritative as possible, has been selected. The copy-text was chosen on the established principle that the last publication, unless it is demonstrably corrupt, during the author's lifetime should represent his final intention. In the majority of cases, the selection of the copy-text has presented no difficulty. Of the three hundred eighty-four poems in this edition, the copy-texts for three hundred forty-four were taken from books either by Roberts or from books edited by him. The following list shows the distribution of copy-texts taken from these sources.

Orion, and Other Poems	19
Later Poems, 1881	1
In Divers Tones	29
Songs of the Common Day and Ave	3
The Book of the Native	2
Poems, 1901/7	88
The Vagrant of Time	16
The Iceberg	1
Selected Poems	165
Canada Speaks of Britain	13
Poems of Wild Life	1
Flying Colours	2
Sir Charles G.D. Roberts: A Biography	4
(Pomeroy)	

Of the remaining forty poems, none appeared in books by or edited by Roberts. In thirty-two cases the copy-text was taken from the last non-corrupt, and frequently the only, publication in a periodical. One poem was taken from its unique appearance in the 1896 Calendar of the Toronto Art Students' League, and one was taken from *Poems of American History.* Four never previously published poems derive their copy-texts from manuscripts or typescripts, and two others were taken from autographed typescripts demonstrably later than their earlier and unique printing. The distribution from these sources is as follows.

357

The Truth	8
Grip	1
The Independent	2
Lippincott's Magazine	10
The University Monthly	2
King's College Record	2
Dominion Illustrated Magazine	1
Bookman	1
McBride's Magazine	1
The Century Magazine	1
Harper's Weekly	1
Saturday Night	1
1896 Calendar	1
Poems of American History	1
Argosy	1
Unpublished manuscripts or typescripts	4
Typescripts (later than printed texts)	2

Once selected, the copy-text has been scrupulously followed except in rare instances. Any alteration of the copy-text is enclosed in brackets in the text of the poem and an explanatory note appears in the record of variants.

At the end of each poem is a date or set of dates. If only a single date appears, it is that of the first known publication; if more than one date is shown, the last is the publication date. Any italicized dates are the dates of composition, determined by information found in manuscripts, typescripts, letters, or Pomeroy's biography. The poems are arranged chronologically, and within each year they are further ordered by date of composition or by month in the case of periodical publication and finally alphabetically by title when only the year of publication is known.

The history of publication is also arranged chronologically and lists all of the known printings of each poem as well as each manuscript or typescript. Some indication of the popularity of a given poem may be suggested by the number of publications, and some indication of Roberts' changing tastes or interests may be further suggested by the poems he chose to include or omit in succeeding volumes. Critical, biographical, or other commentary is provided for a number of poems.

The conventional distinctions between substantives and accidentals, between variants which affect the meaning of a poem or merely the presentation of a poem, are inapplicable in the case of Roberts. All variants except differences between Canadian, British, and American spellings, whether verbal or non-verbal, have been recorded. Roberts was extraordinarily concerned with the punctuation of his poems, and one suspects that he was trying quite consciously to re-create the sound of the poem on the printed page. Certainly no claim is made that all of the punctuation variants in all of the publications were made by Roberts, but it is undeniable that he deliberately and frequently altered the punctuation in a number of poems in each succeeding publication which he personally saw through the press.

358

The record of variants falls into roughly four categories: (1) those dealing with punctuation, (2) those dealing with verbal variants, (3) those dealing simultaneously with verbal and non-verbal variants, and (4) explanatory notes. A few examples should clarify the method of presentation.

3   deep,]   ~ *Scribner's*

In line 3 of the copy-text *deep* is followed by a comma. The curved line is a symbol for *deep* and in *Scribner's* the word is not followed by a comma or by any other punctuation.

11   sky;]   ~ − *Scribner's*

In line 11 of the copy-text *sky* is followed by a semi-colon; in *Scribner's* it is followed by a dash.

30   citadel]   ~ , *Globe, Univ. Monthly, Century*

In line 30 of the copy-text *citadel* is not followed by any punctuation, but in the listed texts it is followed by a comma. Here, and in all succeeding examples when more than one text appears in a list, they appear in the order of publication.

6   dawn,]   ~ ; *Century*   ~ . *NP*

In line 6 of the copy-text *dawn* is followed by a comma; in *The Century Magazine* it is followed by a semi-colon and in *New Poems* it is followed by a period.

11   smells, . . . sounds,]   **smells . . . sounds**   *NB, McLure's*

In line 11 of the copy-text *smells* and *sounds* are followed by commas; in the listed texts no comma appears after either word but the rest of the line, represented by the ellipsis, is identical in all texts.

1   trenches]   **columns** *Bookman*

In line 1 of the copy-text *trenches* is used; in *The Bookman* the word is *columns.*

24   shall]   **will** *NB, ENB, Harper's*

In line 24 of the copy-text *shall* is used; in each of the texts listed the word is *will.*

240 Nor . . . content]   **And well content I was**   *NB, ENB, TS*(1), *TS*(2), *UTQ, TS*(3), *Iceberg*

In line 240 of the copy-text the phrase is *Nor was I ill content;* in each of the texts listed the phrase is *And well content I was.*

168   Astare;]   **Staring,** *NB*

In line 168 of the copy-text *Astare* is followed by a semi-colon; in Roberts' notebook the word is *Staring* and it is followed by a comma.

18   damp air,]   **cool air**   *NB*

In line 18 of the copy-text the phrase *damp air* is followed by a comma; in Roberts' notebook the phrase is *cool air* and there is no punctuation.

The explanatory notes deal largely with variants between manuscripts and printed texts and describe modifications that Roberts made during the process of composition. Two additional symbols, $< \ldots >$ and $< >$ appear in these notes. If a word or part of a word has been obscured but the number of letters may be counted, the number of periods indicates the number of letters. If a word or phrase has been obliterated, $< >$ represents the mutilated part of the line.

At the end of the record of variants a glossary is provided to explain any unfamiliar references or allusions.

Graham C. Adams

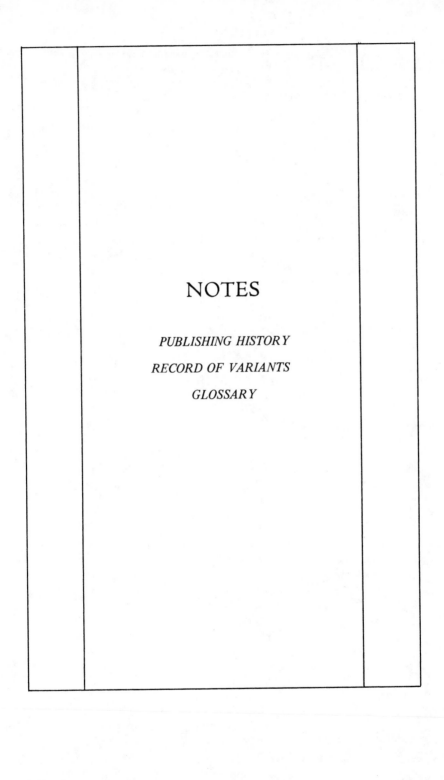

NOTES

PUBLISHING HISTORY

RECORD OF VARIANTS

GLOSSARY

NOTES

p. 1 SONNET ON THE DYING YEAR

The poem was published only in *The Canadian Illustrated News* (March 30, 1878). A typescript also survives in the files of Lloyd Roberts. A marginal note in the typescript says, "Written at 14½ C G D R Childish stuff, of course, but correct in form." Also in Roberts' hand, above the typed signature, is, "signed 'Douglas'." After mentioning the facts of publication, Pomeroy (p. 22) writes of this poem and "Spring," "Only the wish for more 'spending money' prompted the poet to publish them—two poems which were written when he was barely fifteen. (He received five dollars.) They were signed merely *Douglas*, as he had so little faith in them; and he kept no copy. Although he entirely forgot the sonnet it was his recollection of the publication of the Keatsian lyric, which led to a search among old files of illustrated papers, resulting in the discovery of both. The sonnet, although uninspired, was technically perfect; the lyric, derivative enough, yet marked by excellent craftsmanship and charming cadences."

Variants
12   dear:]   ~ ;   *Can. Ill. News*

p. 1 SPRING

The poem was published only in *The Canadian Illustrated News* (March 30, 1878). See the note on "Sonnet on the Dying Year." A typescript of this poem also survives in the files of Lloyd Roberts, and the accompanying marginal note says, "written at 15. obvious imitation of Keats. C. G. D. R." The typescript is signed by Roberts.

Variants
1   cumber]   ~ ,   *Can. Ill. News*
2   reigns]   ~ ,   *Can. Ill. News*
14   leanness]   ~ ,   *Can. Ill. News*
20   leaves, from]   **leaves from**   *Can. Ill. News*
22   Full]   **Too** *Can. Ill. News*   The typescript has *For,* which is
        crossed through, and *Full* is written in the margin in Roberts' hand.
24   Foretell   In both the typescript and *The Canadian Illustrated News,*
        the spelling is *Fortel.*

p. 2　AMORIS VINCULA

The poem first appeared in *Orion, and Other Poems,* 1880; and was later published in *The Magazine of Poetry* (Jan., 1889). Pomeroy (p. 26) notes that

> It was during his first year at college that Roberts began writing in earnest. Almost as soon as the term opened he wrote "An Ode to Winter" and "The Maple." The latter was one of the few poems by which his work was represented in Canadian school textbooks for many years. Another poem of the same period was "Amoris Vincula." "It was inspired more or less," said Roberts, "by a poem of Charles Pelham Mulvaney, which had appeared in *The Canadian Magazine,* and whose haunting cadences stayed with me for days." Although the poet did not include "Amoris Vincula" in his *Collected Edition,* its craftsmanship justifies attention in any study of the poet's early development.

Variants
22　stay:]　~ .　*Magazine of Poetry*

Glossary
Amoris Vincula:　the bonds of love

p. 3　THE MAPLE

The poem was first published in *Orion, and Other Poems,* 1880; lines 1-8 appeared in *The Canadian Birthday Book,* 1887; and the full poem again in *Songs of the Great Dominion,* 1889; *The Dominion Illustrated Magazine* (Nov., 1891); *Poems,* 1901/7; and *The University Monthly* (Nov., 1907). See "Amoris Vincula."

Variants
5　high]　~ ,　*Songs of the Great Dom., Univ. Monthly*
5　reach]　**brush**　*Orion, Can. Birthday Book, Songs of the Great Dom., Dom. Ill., Univ. Monthly*
6　launches,]　~ , —　*Songs of the Great Dom.*
7　love]　~ ,　*Songs of the Great Dom., Univ. Monthly*
7　above]　~ ,　*Can. Birthday Book, Songs of the Great Dom., Univ. Monthly*
8　the]　**he**　*Univ. Monthly*
11　word may be . . . locust-tree]　**word, may be, . . . locust tree**
　　　　　　　　　　　　　　　　Univ. Monthly
13　maple]　~ ,　*Songs of the Great Dom.*
14　are]　omitted in *Univ. Monthly*

14   spring-time]   **springtime**   *Univ. Monthly*

16   Winter's]   **winter's**   *Songs of the Great Dom., Dom. Ill., Univ.*
                                    Monthly

18   sifted,]   ~ ;   *Songs of the Great Dom., Univ. Monthly*

19   day–]   ~ ,   *Songs of the Great Dom.*

19   lay]   ~ ,   *Songs of the Great Dom., Univ. Monthly*

22   fresh,]   ~   *Songs of the Great Dom., Univ. Monthly*

23   stood]   ~ ,   *Songs of the Great Dom.*

24   oh!]   ~ ,   *Orion, Songs of the Great Dom., Dom. Ill., Univ.*
                                      Monthly

24   still!]   ~ .   *Univ. Monthly*

Glossary

6   *catkins*: a scaly spike of flowers

11-12 *Locust-tree . . . new-comer*: the locust-tree is not native to New
                    Brunswick but was introduced into the region by
                    plantings

p. 3 TO WINTER

The poem was first published in *Orion, and Other Poems,* 1880; lines 1-18,
40-59, and 66-79 appeared in *The Canadian Birthday Book,* 1887; and the
full poem in *Songs of the Great Dominion,* 1889. See "The Maple."

Variants

3   Twixt]   **'Twixt**   *Songs of the Great Dom.*

9   wildernesses,]   ~ .   *Songs of the Great Dom.*

18   chill]   ~ ,   *Can. Birthday Book*

30   hills,]   ~ ;   *Songs of the Great Dom.*

33   napping,]   ~ ;   *Songs of the Great Dom.*

40   And fewer]   **Fewer**   *Can. Birthday Book*

47   'Less,]   ~   *Can. Birthday Book*

51   spheres:]   ~ ;   *Songs of the Great Dom.*

53   string]   ~ ,   *Can. Birthday Book*

66   To the Autumn's . . . fulfilling;–]   **Hail the autumn's . . . fulfilling!**
                                        Can. Birthday Book

68   laughter-shaken]   **laughter shaken**   *Songs of the Great Dom.*

69   buckwheat]   ~ ,   *Can. Birthday Book*

70   fir]   ~ ,   *Can. Birthday Book*

71   juniper;]   ~ ,   *Can. Birthday Book*

72   mid]   **'mid**   *Songs of the Great Dom.*

75   Purple-cluster'd]   **Purple clustered**   *Can. Birthday Book*
76   climbing-vines]   **climbing vines**   *Can. Birthday Book*
77   Scarlet-fruited]   **Scarlet fruited**   *Can. Birthday Book*
79   came.]   ~ ,   *Can. Birthday Book*
81   land!]   ~ :   *Songs of the Great Dom.*

Glossary
77   *eglantine*:   the sweetbrier

p. 5 MEMNON

According to Pomeroy (p. 28) the poem was written in 1877. It was originally published in *Scribner's* (June, 1879); and subsequently appeared in *Orion, and Other Poems,* 1880; and *Poems,* 1901/7. *The University Monthly* (Dec., 1904) gives the following account:

> Entering the rectory study one day he showed his father some verses he had written beneath a tree on his way down from college. His father saw at once that they were good but intimated that more verses were necessary to complete the poem. His father suggested that he try to get it published and was somewhat surprised to be told that a letter to this end was already written and addressed to *Scribner's Magazine.* The poem was sent, and in a few weeks the young poet was agreeably surprised to get a letter from the editor enclosing a check in payment and a statement to the effect that it was the best poem he had received in three months, and that other productions of a like quality would be readily accepted.

Variants
3   deep,]   ~   *Scribner's*
4   cast,]   ~   *Orion*
5   wide]   **large**   *Scribner's, Orion*
6   sands; her]   **sands. Her**   *Scribner's*
7   scorched]   **scorchèd**   *Scribner's, Orion*
11   sky;]   ~ –   *Scribner's*
11   East]   **east**   *Scribner's, Orion*
14   fingers]   ~ ,   *Scribner's*
16   Day]   **day**   *Scribner's*
19   voice,]   **sound**   *Scribner's*
19   voice,]   ~   *Orion*
20   half enwound]   **half-enwound**   *Scribner's*
21   red,]   ~   *Scribner's*
24   Deep-graven . . . blast:]   **Deep graven . . . blast.**   *Scribner's*
30   hero's]   **Hero's**   *Scribner's*
31   goddess mother]   **Goddess Mother**   *Scribner's*

32 dawn-kissed] **Dawn-kissed** *Scribner's*
36 calm.] ~ : *Scribner's*
37 "Sweet mother . . . thee!] **"O Mother . . . thee.** *Scribner's*
38 massive,] ~ *Scribner's*
39 brow] ~ , *Scribner's*
43 there,] ~ *Scribner's*
44 canopy:] ~ . *Scribner's*
45 mother . . . 't is thy son prayeth thee.] **Mother . . . thy son**
            requireth thee. *Scribner's*
45 't is] **'tis** *Orion*
46 mother . . . thee!] **Mother . . . thee.** *Scribner's*
47 night] **Night** *Scribner's*
47 kind] ~ , *Scribner's, Orion*
49 come . . . my eyes,] **come,** . . . **mine eyes;** *Scribner's*
50 small] ~ , *Scribner's, Orion*
50 cries,] ~ ; *Scribner's*
52 comest–] ~ , *Scribner's*
52 surprise,] ~ ; *Scribner's* ~ – *Orion*
53 hands] ~ , *Scribner's*
54 mother . . . thy son desireth thee.] **Mother . . . 'tis thy son**
            prayeth thee. *Scribner's*
55 mother] **Mother** *Scribner's*
56 rocks] ~ , *Scribner's*
57 thee] ~ , *Scribner's*
58 wine;] ~ . *Scribner's*
61 thee] ~ , *Scribner's, Orion*
61 whilst] **whiles** *Scribner's*
62 Tithonus,] ~ ; *Scribner's*
63 willing,] ~ *Scribner's*
64 mother] **Mother** *Scribner's*
66 sea!] ~ ; *Orion*
68 night] **Night** *Scribner's*
70 bosom; music] **bosom. Music** *Scribner's*
71 sung,] ~ *Scribner's*
73 mother] **Mother** *Scribner's*
74 ravish'd . . . bed;] **ravished . . . bed?** *Scribner's*
75 thee] ~ , *Scribner's*
76 wide-opened] **wide-openèd** *Scribner's, Orion*
77 woman] ~ , *Scribner's*
79 mother . . . dead.] **Mother . . . dead?** *Scribner's*
80 Dead; . . . body slain,] **Dead!** . . . **body,–slain** *Scribner's*
81 stony-fetter'd . . . plain!] **stony-fettered . . . plain.** *Scribner's*
82 mother] **Mother** *Scribner's*
83 eyelids] **eye-lids** *Scribner's*
86 aged] **agèd** *Orion*
87 plain] ~ , *Scribner's, Orion*

88	Trojans] ~ , *Scribner's*

88 Trojans]   ~ ,   *Scribner's*
89 Phthian]   **Pthian**   *Scribner's*
91 mother, weeping,]   **Mother, weeping**   *Scribner's*
92 and, a suppliant,]   **and a suppliant**   *Scribner's*
95 oak,]   ~ ;   *Scribner's*
97 obsequies; nor]   **obsequies. Nor**   *Scribner's*
100 mother]   **Mother**   *Scribner's*
102 pyre,]   ~   *Scribner's*
103 honey,]   ~   *Scribner's*
107 And, screaming,]   **And screaming**   *Scribner's*
108 manes]   **Manes**   *Scribner's*
109 thee,]   ~   *Scribner's*
112 parch'd]   **parched**   *Scribner's*
114 Now]   ~ ,   *Scribner's*
116 snow;]   ~ :   *Scribner's*
118 night]   **Night**   *Scribner's*
119 verge.]   ~ ;   *Orion*
123 revelry,]   ~   *Orion*
124 glory]   ~ ,   *Orion*
124 dirge.]   ~ :   *Scribner's, Orion*
125 mother]   **Mother**   *Scribner's*
126 beautiful mother]   **Beautiful Mother**   *Scribner's*

Note: the stanzas are not numbered in *Scribner's*

Glossary

Memnon: the eldest son of Tithonus and Eos (Aurora). He was king of the Ethiopians and joined the Trojan army in support of Priam, his uncle and king of Troy. According to tradition, a huge statue near Thebes was erected in his memory. The statue made a musical sound when struck by the rays of the morning sun.

9   *Phoebus*: Apollo, god of the sun.

30   *Egypt's hero* is Memnon himself.

56   *Echo:* a mountain nymph.

64   *Scamander:* a river near Troy.

69   *AEmathion:* younger brother of Memnon. He seized Memnon's throne; Hercules killed him and returned the throne to Memnon.

72   *Hyperion:* father of Aurora, the Sun, and the Moon.

74   *Laconian:* Spartan. Menelaus, husband of Helen, was king of Sparta. She was taken from Menelaus by Paris, son of Priam.

76   *Ilion*: Troy

77   *Spartan woman:* Helen of Troy.

85   *Pelides:* Achilles, champion of the Greek forces.

86   *Nestor:* king of Pylos, an aged notable among the Greeks, particularly for his wisdom, justice, and eloquence.

91   *Jove:* Jupiter or Zeus. The greatest and most powerful of the Greek gods.

368

104-05   *Out of . . . birds:*   When Memnon's body was burned on a pyre,
                                the rising ashes became birds.

108   *manes:*   the spirit of a dead person.

111   *lustral drops:*   water used in the *lustrum* or rite of purification.

113   *Hesperean gate:*   the western gate in the walls of Troy.

120   *Ibis:*   a wading bird sacred in Egyptian mythology.

p. 9 ODE TO DROWSIHOOD

The poem first appeared in *Scribner's* (Nov., 1879) as "Ode to Drowsiness." It was also printed in *Orion, and Other Poems,* 1880; *The University Monthly* (April, 1883); *Poems,* 1901/7; and *Selected Poems,* 1936. According to Pomeroy (p. 28) "Ariadne" and "An Ode to Drowsihood" were written shortly after "Memnon" late in 1877.

Variants

2   Weaver]   **weaver**   *Scribner's*

3   gleams]   ~ ,   *Scribner's*

5   streams]   ~ ,   *Scribner's*

7   dusky-soft]   ~ ,   *Scribner's*

9   rest]   **Rest**   *Scribner's*

12   Nodding Spirit! Magic Comforter!]   **nodding . . . comforter**   *Scrib-*
                              ner's   **nodding spirit! magic comforter!**   *Univ. Monthly*

13   Thee, . . . speechless, I invoke,]   **Thee . . . speechless I invoke,–**
                              Scribner's

15   aged]   **agèd**   *Orion*

17   mistletoe.]   ~ :   *Scribner's*

17   This line in *Scribner's* is followed by a line of six asterisks.

18   dissolves]   **is changed**   *Scribner's*

20   interval. A]   **interval; a**   *Scribner's, Orion, Univ. Monthly*

20   billow]   ~ ,   *Scribner's*

21   oar]   ~ ,   *Scribner's*

22   pillow.]   ~ :   *Scribner's*

26   linkèd]   **linked**   *Univ. Monthly*

29   alder-boughs]   **alder boughs**   *Scribner's, Orion, Univ. Monthly*

31   endows.]   ~ ;– *Scribner's*   ~ : *Orion*

34   fetch]   **Fetch**   *Scribner's*

36   Stirs,]   ~   *Scribner's, Orion, Univ. Monthly*

37   wind,]   ~   *Scribner's*

40   ocean's]   **Ocean's**   *Scribner's*

41   throbs]   **sobs**   *Scribner's, Orion, Univ. Monthly*

43   song]   **songs**   *Scribner's*

44   downpour]   **down-pour**   *Scribner's*

49   shade]   **shades**   *Univ. Monthly*

51   reason.]   ~ :–   *Scribner's*

52   drips;]   ~ ,–   *Scribner's*

53   favors]   ~,   *Scribner's, Orion, Univ. Monthly*
53   treason.]   ~;   *Scribner's*
54   wing-tips]   ~,   *Scribner's*

Glossary
15   *Druid:*   a priest of an ancient religion in England and Europe. The
            oak and the mistletoe were sacred objects to Druids.
22   *Naiad:*   Greek goddesses of lakes, rivers, and fountains.
32   *weft:*   the cross threads in a web of cloth; a woven fabric or a web.
43   *Nereids:*   Greek goddesses of the Mediterranean Sea.
45   *Baiæ:*   a town, now submerged, on a small bay near Naples. It was
            formerly a favorite resort of the Romans.
46   *Maggiore:*   a lake in Northern Italy.
50   *Tuscan:*   pertaining to Tuscany, a region of West Central Italy.

p. 10 ARIADNE

The poem was first published in *Orion, and Other Poems,* 1880; lines 1-7
appeared in *The Canadian Birthday Book,* 1887; and the full poem again in
Poems, 1901/7. Pomeroy (p. 28) says that "'Ariadne' and 'An Ode to Drowsihood' were written shortly after 'Memnon' [1877] and also appeared in
Scribner's." A search of *Scribner's* has revealed no publication of "Ariadne"
and Roberts, in a letter to C.L. Moore (July 14, 1884), mentions only "Memnon" and "An Ode to Drowsihood" being published in *Scribner's.*

Variants
2   tranced]   **tranced**   *Orion, Can. Birthday Book*
31   the]   **th'**   *Orion*
33   moon-tracked]   **moon-track'd**   *Orion*
35   home. Ah]   **home; ah**   *Orion*
40   EVOES.]   ~ :   *Orion*
49   sea.]   ~ :   *Orion*
57   many-veined]   **many-veinèd**   *Orion*
75   past's]   **Past's**   *Orion*
77   griefs,]   ~   *Orion*
115   fills;]   ~,   *Orion*
123   hatred,]   ~   *Orion*

Glossary
Ariadne: The daughter of King Minos of Crete; she fell in love with
            Theseus, King of Athens, and helped him to kill the Minotaur
            in the Cretan Labyrinth. Theseus carried Ariadne away, but he
            abandoned her on the island of Naxos. In one legend, Ariadne
            then hanged herself. In the legend Roberts uses, she is dis-
            covered by Bacchus and marries him.

370

28	*fillets:*	bands of ribbon tied around the head or hair.
35	*chieftain:*	Theseus.
40	*EVOES:*	a Greek expression of joy or exhaltation, frequently used in the worship of Bacchus.
54	*sylvans, fauns, satyrs:*	sylvans are minor deities of the woods; fauns are rural deities; partially manlike, they were represented as having the ears, horns, tail, and hind legs of a goat. Satyrs are another rural deity, again represented as being part man and part goat.
55	*Bacchantes:*	priests or priestesses of Bacchus.
56	*Bacchus:*	also Dionysus, the Greek god of wine.
57	*thyrsus:*	a staff.
71	*subtle-tongued Ionian:*	Theseus; the Ionian Islands are off the west coast of Greece; one island, Cerigo, is off the southern coast.
81	*œnomel:*	a drink made of wine and honey.
91	*vervain:*	any plant of the genus *Verbena.*

p. 15 TO THE SPIRIT OF SONG

The poem was first published in Rose-Belford's *Canadian Monthly* (Nov., 1880); and later appeared in *Orion, and Other Poems,* 1880; *The University Monthly* (March, 1883); *The Canadian Birthday Book,* 1887; *The Magazine of Poetry* (Jan., 1889); and *Poems,* 1901/7. Pomeroy (p. 30) says that the poem was written when Roberts "was but seventeen." See also her commentary on "A Blue Blossom."

The author of the anonymous review of *Orion, and Other Poems* in *The Miramichi Advance* (Nov., 1880) discusses Roberts' classical borrowings and asks that inspiration now be found "in the scenery, the legends, the history of our own land and in the life, the thought and the labours of our own people. The field is all before him where to choose. Longfellow glanced over it and made one of its episodes a portion of the deathless heritage of song. Will our young poet take the hint? He has, we are glad to notice, faith in his own powers—an assurance that the impulse to sing is a genuine inspiration. [Lines 5-14 of the poem are quoted.] Here we have at once the confidence and the humility of genius,—the proud consciousness of power, and the reverent recognition of its source. We believe he has not been deceived and confidently look forward to a fuller demonstration of his powers in the future."

Variants

1	heaven]	~ ,	*Can. Monthly, Can. Birthday Book, Mag. of Poetry*
6	might]	~ ,	*Can. Monthly, Orion, Univ. Monthly, Can. Birthday Book, Mag. of Poetry*
8	strong;]	~ ,	*Univ. Monthly* ~ . *Can. Birthday Book*
11	bird:–]	~;–	*Univ. Monthly*

371

Glossary
    4   *ether:*   the upper region of space, the clear sky, the heavens; the medium anciently thought to fill the upper regions of the sky

p. 15 EPISTLE TO BLISS CARMAN

The poem was first published in *Orion, and Other Poems,* 1880; lines 27-32 and 53-59 are included in *The Canadian Birthday Book,* 1887; and the full poem again in *Poems,* 1901/7; and *Selected Poetry and Critical Prose,* 1974. According to Pomeroy (p. 31) "One of the most important poems in *Orion* from a philosophic as well as a personal standpoint is 'An Epistle to Bliss Carman' which was written in September, 1878, welcoming Carman to the University and paying tribute to Parkin, his master."

Variants

Title: to Bliss]   **to W. Bliss**   *Orion*
17   cool,]   ~   *Orion*
20   intervale]   **interval**   *Orion*
30   gold;]   ~ ,   *Can. Birthday Book*
58   fruit,–]   ~ ,   *Can. Birthday Book*
59   ways,]   ~   *Can. Birthday Book*
98   said.]   ~ ;   *Orion*
105   'T was]   **'Twas**   *Orion*

Glossary
18   *Fundy:*   the bay between New Brunswick and Nova Scotia
44   *wise master:*   George R. Parkin, Headmaster of Fredericton Collegiate School

p. 18 ORION

The poem originally appeared in *Orion, and Other Poems,* 1880. The Chorus (lines 239-288) was published separately in the *Canadian Illustrated News* (June, 1880). Extracts from the poem were printed in the *Canadian Birthday Book* (1887); the selections were: March 1, lines 108-115; June 7, lines 410-411, 413-423; August 21, lines 20-30; and August 28, lines 168-176. The full poem was next published in *Poems,* 1901 and 1907; but *Selected Poems,* 1936, contained only lines 1-30, 86-125, 159-190, 271-288, 393-404, and 440-466. Lines 410-439 appeared in *Selected Poems of Sir Charles G.D. Roberts,* 1955; and in *Poets of the Confederation,* 1967. The full poem was also printed in *Selected Poetry and Critical Prose,* 1974.

    Pomeroy (p. 30) says that the poem "was written at a time when Roberts was greatly under the influence of Swinburne and of the Shelley of 'Alastor' and 'Prometheus.' Although written slowly, as is the invariable custom of the poet, he was so fully possessed by it that one day while waiting for an hour at the dentist to have a tooth extracted he forgot entirely about the ordeal before him and composed six lines of the opening chorus. 'Orion' was completed well before the poet attained his nineteenth birthday."

The young Archibald Lampman in "Two Canadian Poets," (p. 410), reports that he found the publication of *Orion, and Other Poems* a clarion call to other Canadian poets. "I sat up all night reading and re-reading *Orion* in a state of the wildest excitement and when I went to bed I could not sleep. It seemed to me a wonderful thing that such work could be done by a Canadian, by a young man, one of ourselves. It was like a voice from some new paradise of art calling us to be up and doing."

An anonymous review in the *Miramichi Advance* (Nov. 4, 1880) says of the publication of *Orion, and Other Poems* that it "begins a new era in the Literary History of this Province. It has had no predecessor and it has no companion. Volumes of verse we have had, of domestic make, but no volume of poetry except the one before us. No person with poetic tastes can open it at random, and read a dozen lines, without his attention being arrested by the soul shining through the song; without feeling the force of the divine afflatus breathing through the lines; without noticing a wealth of epithet and eloquence of diction, a richness of metaphor; without being forced to acknowledge that a good thing has come out of the New Brunswick Nazareth. He is prosy indeed, even to stupidity, who can compare it to anything that has been hitherto published as the production of the Muse of New Brunswick. Others have written flowing ballads and dreamy sonnets and respectable verse of many metres, but none of them stand on the same plane with the author of *Orion*." Of "Orion" specifically, the reviewer says, ". . . the principal poem . . . is a fragment of classic story in stately blank verse. The onward flow of the story is stayed at times by rhetorical inversions and the beauty of the diction is marred by conceits after the manner of the old masters, but its current is so strong and deep, and its bosom so bedecked with flowers of song that we would not notice the faults if we were not reading to review but merely to enjoy . . . . This poem will bear reading many times, not because it is obscure and requires study, but because its beauties are so many that they cannot be taken in at once."

A review in the *Canadian Monthly* (April, 1881) says that "'Orion' . . . is epic in form: the blank verse, vigorous and musical, bears the impress of no particular school, certainly not that of the prevalent Tennysonian rhythm . . . . Surely this is poetry, thoroughly Greek, and saturated with the spirit of the glorious Greek religious art. Surely it is like what Keats wrote and Shelley; that is to say, it is true poetry, unmarked by mannerism any more than Shelley is marked by it." The same observations are repeated by W.G. MacFarlane in the *Dominion Illustrated* (Nov. 1891). "Thus far we have spoken of two sides of his genius, those that make him a Canadian poet,—his patriotic verse and his Canadian nature poems. But there is another variety of his poems to be spoken of,—those after Greek models. He was particularly fond of the literature of that language, and his 'Orion,' 'Actaeon,' and 'The Pipes of Pan' reflect somewhat the majesty and strength of Homer and the brilliance of those unsurpassed nature poems, the choruses of the Greek dramas. It may be seen, too, that he drew from the Greek wells, not only directly but also indirectly, through Keats, Shelley and other of the classical poets."

In the chapter on Roberts in *The Younger American Poets,* 1904, Jessie B. Rittenhouse wrote: "Mr. Charles G.D. Roberts presents so marked an example of evolution in the style of his work and the sources of his inspiration, that he has from volume to volume, like the nautilus, 'changed his last year's dwelling for the new,' and having entered the 'more stately mansions' has 'known the old no more.' The first chamber which he fashioned for himself in the House of Art could not long contain him, as its walls were built of myths and traditions, incapable of further expansion. This was the period of *Orion and Other Poems,* such as 'Ariadne,' 'Memnon,' and 'Launcelot and the Four Queens,' work done prior to 1880 and creditable to the initial effort of a young collegian."

In *Highways of Canadian Literature,* 1924, J.D. Logan saw *Orion* in the following perspective: "What is meant by the First Renaissance in Canadian Literature? In 1880 a young native-born Canadian, Charles G.D. Roberts, published a book of poems. The critics of England and the United States thought well of the verse. There was in it a quality that had not been in previous books of verse by native-born Canadians. The poems were marked by a certain noteworthy *artistic finish* in the craftsmanship. This was significant. Hitherto **native-born** Canadian poets had not been adroit in technique; they had been very careless about it, and some had no respect or feeling for it at all. Poetry was poetry, they thought, whether it was well dressed or not. With the publication of his *Orion,* Roberts sounded the death knell of slovenly or indifferent technique in Canadian poetry. Working with him, and largely under the influence of his ideal of technical finish in verse, were Lampman, Carman, Campbell, Pauline Johnson, Duncan Campbell Scott, Frederick George Scott, and others. They all cared supremely for fine technique in poetry."

Variants

3	ancient,]	~ *Orion*	
4	crooning]	**whispering** *Selected Poems*	
10	screens]	~ , *Orion*	
11	drawn;]	~ , *Orion*	~ ,— *Selected Poems*
20	banners]	**skirts** *Orion, Can. Birthday Book*	
22	crimson;]	~ , *Orion, Can. Birthday Book*	
26	vineyards,]	~ *Selected Poems*	
27	river-banks]	**river's banks** *Can. Birthday Book*	
28	jungles;]	~ , *Can. Birthday Book*	
29	jagg'd . . . until]	**jagged . . . till** *Can. Birthday Book*	
35	sand-level]	**sand level** *Orion*	
50	rested. Now]	**rested: now** *Orion*	
53	Apollo]	~ , *Orion*	

374

60	fanged]	**fangéd**	*Orion*
79	nigh,]	~	*Orion*
87	Lynxes]	~ ,	*Orion*
92	clouded]	**cloudy**	*Orion*
92	night,]	~	*Selected Poems*
96	shall]	**will**	*Orion*
97	wolves']	**wolf's**	*Selected Poems*
99	shall]	**will**	*Orion*
108	if, . . . pressed,]	**if . . . pressed**	*Can. Birthday Book*
109	knees perchance]	**knees, perchance,**	*Can. Birthday Book*
110	me,]	~	*Can. Birthday Book*
111	air]	~ ,	*Orion*
112	sun,–]	~ –	*Can. Birthday Book*
114	born,]	~ ,–	*Orion*
119	me;]	~ ,	*Selected Poems*
131	love's]	**Love's**	*Orion*
133	winged]	**wingéd**	*Orion*
152	turned]	~ ,	*Orion*
168	Night]	**night**	*Can. Birthday Book*
174	him;]	~ ,	*Can. Birthday Book*
176	him,]	~ .	*Can. Birthday Book*
210	white]	~ ,	*Orion*
211	death. Then]	**death; then**	*Orion*
217	fog.]	~ ;	*Orion*
219	him]	~ ,	*Orion*
234	cursed]	**curséd**	*Orion*
235	seen,]	~	*Orion*
238	lyres]	~ ,	*Orion*
239	The 1880 publication divides the next four stanzas into Strophes and Antistrophes; line 239 is designated as the beginning of Strophe A.		
239	god-begotten]	**God-begotten,**	*Can. Ill. News*
240	gods]	**Gods**	*Can. Ill. News*
241	thee]	**their**	*Can. Ill. News*
243	gods]	**Gods**	*Can. Ill. News*
247	designated as the beginning of Antistrophe A, *Orion*		
251	weaving,]	~ ;	*Can. Ill. News*
255	designated as the beginning of Strophe B, *Orion*		
256	Mother, . . . Earth]	**Mother . . . earth**	*Can. Ill. News*
262	overawed]	**over-awed**	*Can. Ill. News*
263	designated as the beginning of Antistrophe B, *Orion*		
265	pitifully,]	~	*Orion, Can. Ill. News*
271	are all]	**all are**	*Orion, Can. Ill. News*
272	Sea . . . Night]	**sea . . . night**	*Can. Ill. News*
273	Air . . . Wind]	**air . . . wind**	*Can. Ill. News*
274	Sun]	**sun**	*Can. Ill. News*
276	waters]	**Waters**	*Orion, Selected Poems*

277	Rocks] **rocks** *Can. Ill. News*	
277	rime,] ~ ; *Orion*	
278	hills] **Hills** *Orion, Selected Poems*	
278	heaven] **Heaven** *Can. Ill. News*	
278	time.] ~ ; *Orion, Can. Ill. News*	
279	Earth] **earth** *Can. Ill. News*	
281	suchlike] **such like** *Can. Ill. News*	
282	need.] ~ : *Orion*	
283	brake] **broke** *Can. Ill. News*	
284	gods . . . own.] **Gods . . . own;** *Can. Ill. News*	
285	not lacked] **lacked not** *Orion, Can. Ill. News*	
288	endure.] ~ ; *Orion*	
295	stirred,] ~ ; *Orion*	
311	Oh,] ~ *Orion*	
322	devil.] **devils,** *Orion*	
332	sky] **stars** *Orion*	
354	hills!] ~ ; *Orion*	
381	gnarled] **gnarléd** *Orion*	
392	alone,] ~ *Orion*	
407	hair,] ~ *Orion*	
419	precipices,] ~ . *Can. Birthday Book*	
421	vapours] ~ , *Can. Birthday Book*	
422	crimson] ~ , *Can. Birthday Book*	
423	day,–] ~ . *Can. Birthday Book*	
425	veiled] **veiléd** *Orion*	
426	Wherethrough] **Where-through** *Orion*	
450	bosoms, cleaving,] **bosoms cleaving** *Orion*	
451	ripples,] ~ *Orion*	
451	eachwhere] **each where** *Selected Poems*	

Glossary

Orion: In the most common classical legend, Orion was a mighty hunter, the son of Poseidon, god of the sea, and Euryale. On a visit to Chios he fell in love with Merope, daughter of King Œnopion, and cleared the island of wild beasts for her. Œnopion kept postponing the wedding and Orion, drunk, attacked Merope. As punishment, Œnopion, aided by Dionysus, the god of wine, had Orion's eyes put out while he was asleep. An oracle informed Orion to go to the East and look upon Helios, the sun god, as he rose from the sea. Orion's sight was restored. Eos, goddess of the dawn, fell in love with him and accompanied him on his intended return to Chios. Artemis, goddess of the hunt, intervened and persuaded Orion not to seek revenge, and together Artemis and Orion shared the pleasures of hunting. Apollo feared that Artemis, his sister, might fall in love with Orion and sent a giant scorpion to attack him. Orion jumped into the sea and Apollo tricked

Artemis into shooting the indistinct speck on the sea. Artemis, stricken with remorse, placed the Orion constellation in the sky in his memory.

Roberts varies the legend by omitting Orion's attack on Merope, placing the blame for his blindness solely on the treachery of Œnopion. Roberts denies Orion's desire for revenge and stops his telling of the legend with Orion in love with Eos.

29	*scaurs:*	bare rocks standing alone, or a cliff or rocky place on the side of a mountain or hill
40	*Œnopion:*	king of Chios and son of Dionysus and Ariadne
41	*Chios:*	a large Greek island in the Aegean Sea
53	*Apollo:*	the sun god
120	*Night:*	Nyx, the daughter of Chaos, the mother of Sleep, Death, and other powers
132	*Merope:*	daughter of Œnopion; she later married Cresphontes and, after he was killed, Polyphontes
142	*Colchian drug:*	Colchis is famous as the home of the sorceress Medea; it is the land where Jason went to recover the golden fleece. Colchis was associated in the popular mind with sorcery and magic.
209	*Alcmena's son:*	Hercules, fathered by Zeus
231	*the maids beloved of Doris:*	Doris was the mother of the Nereids
248	*Ocean:*	one of the Titans, predecessors to the Olympian gods
251	*Clotho:*	one of the three Fates, responsible for spinning the thread of life
282	*the twin Aloides:*	Otus and Ephialtes, sons of Poseidon and Iphimedia or Canace; they waged war on the Olympians and eventually killed each other.
283	*Hades:*	the Greek realm of the dead, less happy than the Elysian Fields but happier than Tartarus. Also, the god of the underworld
290	*Circe:*	a sorceress, famous in *The Odyssey;* she changed Ulysses' men into swine.
317	*hecatombs:*	originally the sacrifice of one hundred oxen, later the sacrifice of any large number of animals
432	*Parian stone:*	marble from the island of Paros
440	*Delos:*	a small island in the Aegean, an important centre of the worship of Apollo
448	*Nereids:*	sea goddesses, the daughters of Doris and Nereus
452	*Triton:*	a merman, son of Poseidon

p. 29 ITERUMNE

The poem was first published in Rose-Belford's *Canadian Monthly* (1880); and later appeared in *Orion, and Other Poems*, 1880; and *Poems*, 1901/7.

Pomeroy (p. 35) says that "Iterumne" was the first poem Roberts wrote at Chatham, where he moved in September, 1879. Pomeroy finds the poem "a carefully wrought sonnet with lines of considerable beauty" and she remarks that its "exceedingly serious note" was "but a mood or passing phase...." James Cappon, in *Roberts and the Influence of His Time*, 1905, pp. 18-19, writes: " . . . in *Iterumne*, he seems to breathe a mournful farewell to Arcadian legend. The breeze, he complains, is no longer blowing from Thessalian Tempe and the swift Peneus, no vision of goddess or Dryad comes to him any more: [the poem is quoted.] Very weary, surely, are the hands and eyes of one-and-twenty! But some reaction from the first ecstacy of young inspiration was natural, and the poet may already have begun to feel some shrinking and fading in that Arcadian world of his fancy. Probably also he was beginning to suspect that the temper of the age was not so favourable to that remote visionary treatment of life as it once had been. Besides, although the character of Mr. Roberts' talent is decidedly of the high traditional literary kind, he has also, as one may see from his later career, strong popular instincts, and he would soon realize that to reach any wide public in Canada he must choose themes with more of the actual life and interests of to-day in them."

Variants
Title: Iterumne]   ~ ?   *Can. Monthly, Orion*
 6   goddess]   **Goddess**   *Can. Monthly*
 7   maze;]   ~ ; –   *Can. Monthly*
12   choir]   **Choir**   *Can. Monthly*
13   grove. Nor]   **grove;–nor**   *Can. Monthly, Orion*

Glossary
Iterumne: Latin for *again?* or *once more?* The *ne* ending has the force of an interrogative.
 1   *Thessaly:*   a region of eastern Greece
 6   *Dryad:*   a nymph of the woods
12   *Apollo:*   the sun god, also the god of poetry in Greek mythology

p. 29 RONDEAU.–"HESPER **APPEARS**."

The poem was first published in the *Canadian Illustrated News* (May 10, 1879); and later appeared in *Orion, and Other Poems*, 1880; lines 1-9 are included in *The Canadian Birthday Book*, 1887; and the full poem again in *The University Monthly* (Jan., 1915). As well, the Rufus Hathaway Collection at the University of New Brunswick contains an unidentified clipping of the poem, HC.

Variants
 1   flowing]   **blowing**   *HC*
 3   low]   ~ ,   *Can. Birthday Book*

378

3   orient] **Orient** *Can. Ill. News, HC*

3   hills] ~ , *Can. Birthday Book*

4   gloaming] **gleaming** *HC*

4   distils] ~ , *Can. Ill. News, HC*

6   want] **Want** *HC*

6   assails,] ~ *Can. Ill. News*

7   Youth . . . Hope . . . Love] **youth . . . hope . . . love** *Can. Birth-day Book*

7   avails] ~ , *HC*

8   ills,] ~ *Univ. Monthly*

9   appears,] ~ . *Univ. Monthly, HC*

11   fails:] ~ . *Can. Ill. News* ~ ; *HC*

12   vexéd] **vexed** *Can. Ill. News, Univ. Monthly, HC*

12   The] **the** *Can. Ill. News*

13   yearnings] **yearning** *HC*

13   stills] ~ , *Can. Ill. News*

14   Awhile] **For now,** *Can. Ill. News*

14   wails,–] ~ – *Can. Ill. News, HC*

Glossary

Hesper: the evening star; the planet Venus

p. 30 THE SHANNON AND THE CHESAPEAKE

The poem was published only in *The Canadian Illustrated News* (Oct. 4, 1879) and in *Orion,* 1880. Pomeroy (pp. 29-30) reports that "The ballad of 'The Shannon and the Chesapeake' was an early effort which the poet himself criticized severely in later years, but which the late Rufus Hathaway always maintained was one of Roberts' finest ballads."

Variants (All variants are those which appear in the *Canadian Illustrated News.*)

1   Oh,] **O**

1   Shannon] Shannon and Chesapeake are italicized in the *Canadian Illustrated News.*

3   fought] ~ ,

6   down,] ~ –

8   o'erthrown,] ~ ;

9   Shannon] ~ ,

10   world] ~ ,

13   June,] ~ ,–

16   amaze;] ~ ; –

18   steered;] ~ –

19	bows,]	~ –
23	sullenly,]	**suddenly**
23	²one,]	~
25	blind,]	~
27	bare]	~ ,
31	fierce,]	~
38	dies.]	~ ;–
41	taffrail,]	~
46	But, oh,]	~
48	below.]	~ ,–
49	But,]	~
53	summons!]	~ !–
54	comply.]	~ :
55	men;]	~ ,
58	morn,]	~ ,–
66	apart!]	~ .
68	heart!]	~ .
69	heaven;]	~ –
70	come;]	~ –
71	now, . . . old,]	**now . . . old**

Glossary

The battle between the *Shannon* and the *Chesapeake* took place on June 1, 1813. Philip Vere Broke was captain of the *Shannon* and James Lawrence captain of the *Chesapeake.* The battle touches Canadian history as after the fight the *Chesapeake* was brought to Halifax. The mortally wounded Lawrence's plea, "Don't give up the ship!" has become proverbial.

15-16   *York, Penn, and Howe:*   The Duke of York and Admiral William Penn defeated a Dutch fleet at the battle of Lowestoft on June 3, 1665. Roberts has taken slight liberty with the date to ally it with the June 1, 1813 date of the *Shannon* and *Chesapeake* battle and with Admiral Richard Howe's defeat of the French on June 1, 1794.

51   *Watt:*   George Thomas L. Watt was First Lieutenant of the *Shannon.* He and five seamen were killed in the confusion over the flag raising. Watt lowered the American flag on board the *Chesapeake,* intending to fly the British flag above the American as a sign of the *Chesapeake's* surrender. But the lines were twisted, and when the flags were raised the American flag was above the British. The gunners on the *Shannon* immediately opened fire.

p. 32 A FAREWELL

The poem was published only in *Later Poems,* 1881, and is there dated January, 1880.

380

p. 32 BALLADE OF THE POET'S THOUGHT

The poem was first published in Rose-Belford's *Canadian Monthly* (April, 1880); and was subsequently published in *Orion, and Other Poems*, 1880; *The University Monthly* (March, 1883); *Poems*, 1901/7; and *Selected Poems*, 1936. Pomeroy (pp. 38-39) reports that Matthew Arnold mentioned several poems from *Orion* "with special commendation, particularly 'The Ballade of the Poet's Thought.'"

Variants
Title: Ballade]   **Ballad**   *Can. Monthly, Orion, Univ. Monthly*
  4   taught.]   ~ :   *Orion, Univ. Monthly*   ~ ;   *Poems* 1901/7
  5   said,–]   ~ –   *Can. Monthly*
  6   deep."]   ~ "–   *Can. Monthly*   ~ ."–   *Orion, Univ. Monthly*
  7   poet's thought]   **Poet's Thought**   *Can. Monthly;* also line 27
  9   hurry, and dust, and heat]   **hurry and dust and heat,**   *Can. Monthly*
10   free,]   ~   *Can. Monthly*
12   which he]   **which much he**   *Can. Monthly*
21   quiet]   **lonely**   *Can. Monthly*
21   spot]   ~ ,   *Orion, Univ. Monthly, Poems* 1901/7
23   said,–]   ~ –   *Can. Monthly*
ENVOI]   **L'ENVOI.**   *Can. Monthly*
25   Oh, poets]   **O Poets**   *Can. Monthly*
25   poets,]   ~   *Orion, Univ. Monthly*
25   lot,]   ~   *Can. Monthly*
28   The line is italicized in the *Canadian Monthly*.

p. 33 AT POZZUOLI

The poem was published only in *Orion, and Other Poems*, 1880. Pomeroy (pp. 28-29) reports that "Several of the short poems which were published in *Orion* were written in the classroom [at the University of New Brunswick] behind the safe seclusion of black glasses which he was obliged to wear at that time for eye trouble. The sonnet 'At Pozzuoli,' for instance, was written in the science lecture-room."

Glossary
Pozzuoli: a seaport in Southwest Italy, near Naples; the site of Roman ruins

p. 33 BALLAD OF A BRIDE

The poem was published only in *Orion, and Other Poems*, 1880.

Glossary
8   *lay:* ballad or song
11 *an':* if, an archaic form in keeping with the language of the poem
14 *Nathless:* nevertheless, another archaic form

p. 34 A BALLAD OF THREE MISTRESSES

The poem was published only in *Orion, and Other Poems,* 1880.

Glossary
10 *she:* wine
15 *Jove:* see "Memnon"
18 *Lorelie:* in Germanic mythology a siren on a rock in the Rhine river
            who by her singing lured seamen to wreck their ships

p. 35 BALLAD TO A KINGFISHER

The poem was published only in *Orion, and Other Poems,* 1880.

Glossary
11-14 *Ceyx and Alcyone* (or Halcyone): Alcyone, in Greek Mythology
                  was warned in a dream that
her husband, Ceyx, would die in a shipwreck during a storm at sea. When
she found his body washed ashore, she threw herself into the sea; she and
Ceyx were transformed into kingfishers, fabled to keep the waters calm
when they are nesting. The story is the source of the term "Halcyon days."

23   *John Milton:* Milton never specifically mentions the kingfisher, but
                  Roberts almost certainly had in mind these lines from
"On the Morning of Christ's Nativity."

> The Winds, with wonder whist,
> Smoothly the waters kiss't,
>   Whispering new joys to the mild Ocean,
> Who now hath quite forgot to rave,
> While Birds of Calm sit brooding on the charmed wave.

p. 36 A BLUE BLOSSOM

The poem was first published in *Orion, and Other Poems,* 1880; lines 1-14
appeared in *The Canadian Birthday Book,* 1887; and the full poem again in
Later Canadian Poems, 1893; and *Poems,* 1901/7. Pomeroy (p. 30) says that
"The verse of this youthful period is marked by the note of philosophic

mysticism which was to become perhaps the dominant characteristic of the poetry of Charles G.D. Roberts." She mentions "A Blue Blossom" and "To the Spirit of Song" as examples of poems in the philosophic-mystical group.

Variants
8   longing]   ~ ,   *Can. Birthday Book*
10   sight]   ~ ,   *Can. Birthday Book, Later Can. Poems*
20   scene]   **scenes**   *Orion, Later Can. Poems*
26   't is hard]   **'tis hard,**   *Orion, Later Can. Poems*

p. 36 DEDICATION OF "ORION AND OTHER POEMS"

The poem was originally published in *Orion, and Other Poems,* 1880; and later appeared in *Poems,* 1901/7; *Selected Poems,* 1936; and *Selected Poetry and Critical Prose,* 1974.

Variants
The ascription to G. Goodridge Roberts does not appear in *Orion,* and the poem is titled simply "Dedication."
3   weary]   ~ ,   *Orion, Poems* 1901/7
7   vexed]   **vext**   *Orion*
16   betray]   **bewray**   *Orion, Poems* 1901/7

Glossary
9   *Theban bees:* In classical antiquity, bees were thought to be specially inspired with wisdom from the gods. In referring specifically to Theban bees, Roberts may have had Pindar, the great lyric poet born in Thebes, in mind.

p. 37 THE FLIGHT

The poem was first published in *Orion, and Other Poems,* 1880; and later appeared in *The Magazine of Poetry* (Jan., 1889).

Variants
17   moon-lighted glades]   **moonlighted glades,**   *Mag. of Poetry*

p. 38 LAUNCELOT AND THE FOUR QUEENS

The poem was first published in *Orion, and Other Poems,* 1880; and lines 8-19, 56-66, and 275-282 appeared in *The Canadian Birthday Book,* 1887. Roberts' source for the poem is the tale of Launcelot in Book VI of Sir Thomas Malory's *Le Morte Darthur,* and he follows the essential details of Malory's story. Launcelot's song to Guinevere does not appear in the tale.

Variants

All variants are from *The Canadian Birthday Book.*
10   thrush;]   ~,
11   meads]   **weeds**
17   stirs,]   ~
57   apple-tree]   **apple tree**
58   queen,–]   ~,
60   autumn]   **Autumn**
280   blent,]   ~;

Glossary

1   *Launcelot:* knight of the **Round** Table whose love for Guinevere
                    was a part of the cause of the downfall of Arthur
11   *meads:* meadows
23   *helm:* helmet
29   *blue eggs:* the eggs of the English robin are white
38   *four queens:* Malory mentions by name only Morgan le Fay; the
                    three others he calls "the quene of North Galys Wales,
       and the quene of Estlonde, and the quene of the Oute Iles." See
       lines 96-98.
68   *eyne:* eyes, an archaic form in keeping with the language and tone
                    of the poem
84   *Certes:* certainly, another archaic form
101   *Guinevere:* wife of Arthur and in love with Launcelot
108   *aye:* always or ever, another archaism
117   *samite:* a heavy silk fabric, sometimes interwoven with gold, worn
                    in the Middle Ages
124   *wold:* an open, elevated tract of country
129   *gules:* red
129   *argent:* silver
164   *Thorough:* an archaic form of through
186   *dight:* dressed, adorned; another archaism
202   *liefer:* an archaism meaning gladly or willingly
221   *Collops:* small slices or pieces
222   *mead:* an alcoholic drink made by fermenting honey and water
226   *arras:* a tapestry or other wall hanging
230   *And:* if, another archaic form
234   *North Wales' king:* unnamed in Malory
239   *King Bagdemagus:* king of Gore, cousin-in-law to Morgan le Fay.
                    In Malory, Launcelot kept his promise to Bag-
       demagus' unnamed daughter and was victorious over the king of
       North Wales.
243   *trencher:* a flat, wooden utensil on which meat or other food was
                    formerly served or carved; another archaism
245   *Phosphor:* the morning star

p. 46 LOVE-DAYS

The poem was first published in *Orion, and Other Poems,* 1880; lines 1-5, 11-15, and 21-25 appear in *The Canadian Birthday Book,* 1887.

Variants
All variants are from *The Canadian Birthday Book.*
14   eyes,]   ~
21   way!]   ~ ,

Glossary
13   *lotus-flutes:*   In the *Odyssey,* the lotus is a plant which causes those
              who eat the fruit to become dreamy, listless, and con-
tentedly forgetful of the usual preoccupations of life. The image here,
however, is one of the persona's discontent with his own inactivity compared with the active life of all others.

p. 47 MIRIAM.–I. SAPPHICS

The poem was published only in *Orion, and Other Poems,* 1880.

Glossary
Sapphics: A sapphic is a stanzaic pattern of three verses of eleven syllables
              each (-u / -- / -uu / -u / -u) and a fourth verse of five syllables
(-uu / -u). See also "Miriam.–II. Choriambics."

p. 47 MIRIAM.–II. CHORIAMBICS

The poem appeared only in *Orion, and Other Poems,* 1880.

Glossary
Choriambics: A choriambus is a metric foot consisting of an accented
                 syllable on each side of two unaccented ones (-uu-). The
basic pattern of "Miriam" is made up of three lines, each containing a
trochee (-u), two choriambics, and an iamb (u-). The fourth line of each
stanza uses a trochee and two iambs. The usual choriambic line is a trochee,
three choriambics, and an iamb. See also "Miriam.–I. Sapphics."

p. 48 ODE TO NIGHT

The poem was published only in *Orion, and Other Poems,* 1880.

Glossary
10   *syringa:* lilac
12   *zephyr:* a mild breeze, often associated with the west
15   *lustral waters:* see "Memnon"

p. 49 ONE NIGHT

The poem appeared only in *Orion, and Other Poems,* 1880.

p. 51 RONDEAU TO A.W. STRATON

The poem appeared only in *Orion, and Other Poems,* 1880.

Glossary
A.W. Straton: Andrew William Straton (1858-1890) was a brother to the
poet Barry Straton and a cousin to both Roberts and Bliss
Carman. He published two volumes of poems: *The Building of the Bridge,*
1884; and *Idylls of the St. John,* 1887.
1   *fledge:* to enable to fly

p. 51 RONDEAU.—"WITHOUT ONE KISS."

The poem was first published in *Orion, and Other Poems,* 1880; and later
appeared in *The Magazine of Poetry* (1891). The poem, according to Pomeroy
(p. 39), was written to Mary Fenety whom Roberts was courting at the time.
"Parting one night at the gate of Linden Hall [the Fenety home] after a little
tiff, she walked haughtily into the house while the college boy went on his
way laughing repeatedly, 'Without one kiss she's gone away.'" They were
married December 29, 1880.

Variants
All variants are from *The Magazine of Poetry.*
Title: Rondeau.—"Without One Kiss."]   **Without One Kiss**
1   away,]   ~
6   so,]   ~
8   bough,]   ~
13   Love]   **love**

p. 52 SAPPHO

The poem appeared only in *Orion,* 1880.

386

Sappho: a Greek poetess of the seventh century B.C. The source of the
poem is the romantic legend that she threw herself into the sea
after being spurned by Phaon. Phaon was a boatman of Lesbos who,
legendarily, was granted beauty and youth as a reward for a favor per-
formed for Venus.

5   *curlew:* a shore bird

47   *Mitylenian:* Mitylene is another name for Lesbos, an island in the
Aegean Sea.

59   *Nereids:* sea nymphs

61   *Leucadian:* referring to Leucas, or Levkas, another Greek island.

70   *syrenal song:* the sirens sang songs which caused sailors to run their
ships onto rocks.

74   *Lesbian:* natives of Lesbos

86   *Ionian:* islands along the West coast of Greece

105   *Wine . . . leas:* lees are the sediment formed when wine is made; the
wine is drawn off and the lees thrown away.

113   *Jove:* see "Memnon"

132   *Muses:* the goddesses of poetry, music, drama, etc. Sappho was
often called the tenth Muse.

Note: *Chorus and Semi-Chorus:* In classical Greek drama the Chorus,
commentators on the action of the play, chanted and danced
their speeches. The Chorus moved in one direction during the
Strophe (here Chorus) and followed the same metrical pattern in
the Antistrophe (here Semi-Chorus) back to their original position.

p. 55 A SONG OF MORNING

The poem appeared only in *Orion, and Other Poems,* 1880.

Glossary

8   *lethe:* a river in the Hades of Greek mythology; the water caused
those who drank it to forget the past. Also, forgetfulness or
oblivion.

13   *fallow:* unseeded land

p. 55 OFF PELORUS

The poem was first published in the *Canadian Monthly* (April, 1881); and
subsequently appeared in *Later Poems,* 1881; and *In Divers Tones,* 1886. The
edition in *Later Poems* is dated February, 1881.

Variants

1   Pelorus;]   ~ ,   *Later Poems*

2   pine.]   ~ ;   *Can. Monthly, Later Poems*
4   Eachwhere]   **Each where**   *Later Poems*
7   ears,–]   ~ –   *Can. Monthly*   ~ ,   *Later Poems*
8   our eyes behold our Ithaca]   **with eyes grown drunken sail we**
                                    hence   *Can. Monthly, Later Poems*
10   ship!]   ~ ;   *Can. Monthly*   **ships:**   *Later Poems*
11   gleaming;]   ~ ,   *Can. Monthly, Later Poems*
12   lip]   **lips**   *Later Poems*
13   elysian.]   ~ !   *Can. Monthly, Later Poems*
14   mindless]   **windless**   *Later Poems*
14   pain.]   ~ !   *Can. Monthly, Later Poems*
15   behold–]   ~   *Can. Monthly, Later Poems*
15   sore-bewildering]   **sore bewildering**   *Can. Monthly*
15   vision!   ~ :–   *Can. Monthly*   ~ !–   *Later Poems*
17   us.]   ~ :–   *Can. Monthly, Later Poems*
18   Lo, . . . maids, with love-soft eyes aglow]   **Lo . . . maids with**
                                    beckoning arms divine   *Can. Monthly, Later Poems*
19   Gleaming . . . sweet]   **Throbbing . . . soft**   *Can. Monthly,*
                                    Later Poems
20   Warm lips wild with song, and softer throats than snow!]
        Throats athrob with song across the charmed brine!   *Can. Monthly*
        Throats athrob with song across the charmed brine.   *Later Poems*
21   he . . . hearkens,–]   **He . . . hearkens–**   *Later Poems*
21   song,–]   ~ –   *Can. Monthly, Later Poems*
21   forward,–]   ~ ,   *Later Poems*
22   reed.]   ~ ;   *Can. Monthly, Later Poems*
23   shoreward,–]   ~ :–   *Can. Monthly, Later Poems*
24   now;]   ~ ,   *Can. Monthly, Later Poems*
24   King . . . heed!]   **king . . . heed.**   *Later Poems*
25   luring]   **wondrous**   *Can. Monthly, Later Poems*
25   eyes']   **eyes**   *Later Poems*
26   cords!]   ~ .   *Can. Monthly, Later Poems*
27   words]   **speech**   *Can. Monthly*
28   him,]   ~   *Later Poems*
28   words.]   ~ :–   *Can. Monthly, Later Poems*
29   Wanderer, wondrous-tongued]   **wanderer, honey-tongued**   *Can.*
                                    Monthly, Later Poems
29   nigher!]   ~ ,   *Can. Monthly*   ~ ;   *Later Poems*
30   Sage of princes]   **Wisest Ruler**   *Can. Monthly, Later Poems*
30   bane]   **Bane**   *Later Poems*
30   walls!]   ~ ,   *Can. Monthly, Later Poems*
31   Whatsoe'er in all the populous earth befalls]
        Hear strange wisdom to thine uttermost desire   *Can. Monthly*
        Hear strange wisdom to thine uttermost desire,–   *Later Poems*
32   We will teach thee, to thine uttermost desire]   **Whatsoe'er in all**
        the fruitful earth befalls   *Can. Monthly, Later Poems*

388

33 So, . . . twain,] **So . . . twain** *Can. Monthly, Later Poems*
33 securer.] ~ , *Can. Monthly*
34 blade.] ~ ; *Can. Monthly, Later Poems*
36 afraid,] ~ . *Can. Monthly*
37 waste] ~ , *Can. Monthly*
37 prow,] ~ *Can. Monthly, Later Poems*
38 folding] **falling** *Can. Monthly*
38 night.] ~ :— *Can. Monthly, Later Poems*
39 yet, . . . grieving,—] **yet— . . . grieving—** *Can. Monthly,*
                                                    Later Poems

Glossary
Pelorus: the north-east point of Sicily
  5-7 *Soundless . . . ears:* The poem is based on the story of Ulysses and
                              the Sirens in *The Odyssey.* The Sirens' song
caused sailors to bring their ships close to shore where they were wrecked.
Ulysses wanted to hear the Sirens and so had himself tied to the mast of
his ship in order to insure his safety, and he ordered the crew to stop their
ears with wax. The poem is a monologue by a member of the crew, spoken
as they pass the Sirens.
  8 *Ithaca:* the homeland of Ulysses, an island off the coast of Greece.
  18 *the white-limbed maids:* the Sirens; they are also referred to as "the
                               luring death" in line 38.
  21 *the King:* Ulysses
  29-32 *"Much . . . desire.":* The stanza characterizes Ulysses. His wan-
                                derings after the Trojan War are the subject
of *The Odyssey* where he is depicted as a brilliant speaker and one of the
wiser of the Greek kings. It was his plan to build the Trojan Horse, the
device by which Troy was entered and destroyed. He is also depicted
throughout *The Odyssey* as a man interested in any new knowledge or
experience.

p. 57 A BALLADE OF PHILOMELA

The poem was published in *Later Poems,* 1882; and in *In Divers Tones,* 1886.
The edition in *Later Poems* is dated April, 1881.

Variants
All variants are from *Later Poems.*
Title: Ballade] **Ballad**
  2 utterly.] ~ ;
  3 awake.] ~ ;
  4 Flame-floods] **Flame-lances**
  5 dye,] ~
  6 dark;] ~ ,

389

6   a]   omitted
7   nigh,–]   ~ ,
11   Sat; . . . thought –"She grieves]   **Sat, . . . thought –she mourns**
12   Itylus,–]   ~ ,
13   memory."]   ~ .–
14   evening.]   ~ ,
15   Then . . . try,–]   **And . . . try,**
18   heart;]   ~ ,
19   dear]   **sore**
21   soft night . . . by.]   **noiseless . . . by:**
23   exultant, . . . descry,–]   **exultant . . . descry–**
24   sing!]   ~ .

Glossary

Philomela: daughter of Pandion, king of Athens; and sister to Procne, wife of Tereus who was king of Thrace. While escorting Philomela on a visit to her sister, Tereus raped Philomela, cut out her tongue to insure her silence, and hid her in a remote place. Philomela wove a tapestry depicting her story and sent it to Procne, who rescued her. The two sisters plotted revenge. Procne killed her son Itys, and served his flesh to Tereus. Tereus attempted to kill the two women but he was changed into a hoopoe, Philomela into a nightingale, and Procne into a swallow.

12   *Itylus:*   son of Aedon, who was the wife of Zethus, king of Thebes. In a fit of jealousy, Aedon killed her son Itylus, and she was changed into a nightingale. Roberts has evidently confused the two legends in his reference to Itylus instead of Itys.

p. 57 TO FREDERICTON IN MAY-TIME

The poem was originally published in *Later Poems,* 1881; and later appeared in *In Divers Tones,* 1886; *Poems,* 1901/7; and in *Selected Poetry and Critical Prose,* 1974. The edition in *Later Poems* is dated May 24, 1881.

Variants

All variants are from *Later Poems.*

Title: To Fredericton in May-Time]   **To Fredericton in May Time**
1   morning, . . . perfume,]   **morning . . . perfume–**
2   weather,]   ~ –
3   bees . . . birds]   **bees, . . . birds,**
7   willows,]   ~ –
8   willows,]   ~
9   dusty . . . blackbirds]   **mealy . . . black-birds**
11   Thro']   **Through**
13   sweet;]   ~ ,
14   desire!]   ~ .

p. 58 THE SLAVE WOMAN

The poem was first published in *Later Poems*, 1881; and later appeared in *The Week* (April, 1884); *The Century Magazine* (May, 1884); *In Divers Tones*, 1886; and *Poems*, 1901/7. The edition in *Later Poems* is dated June, 1881.

Variants
3   dry]   ~ ,   *Week*
6   thro']   **through**   *Later Poems, Week, Century*
6   hot,]   ~   *Later Poems*
6   apace,]   ~ ;   *Later Poems*   ~ .   *Century*
7   casts off]   **hath lost**   *Later Poems*
9   heart]   **one**   *Later Poems*
10   One]   **A**   *Later Poems*
10   moment;]   ~ ,   *Week*
11   tears.]   ~ ;   *Later Poems*

Glossary
13   *Niger:*   a river in west Africa

p. 58 LOTOS

The poem was first published in *Later Poems*, 1882; and later appeared in the *Canadian Monthly* (June, 1882); and in *In Divers Tones*, 1886. The edition in *Later Poems* is dated August, 1881.

Variants
Title: Lotos]   **Lotus**   *Can. Monthly*
6   wear.]   ~ ,   *Later Poems*
7   Sleep,]   ~   *Later Poems, Can. Monthly*
9   slumber-song]   **slumber song**   *Can. Monthly*
12   winds rustle]   **wind rustles**   *Can. Monthly*
13   Hush'dly]   **Hushedly**   *Can. Monthly*
13   brain,–]   ~ ,   *Later Poems, Can. Monthly*
14   murmur]   **murmurs**   *Later Poems*
14   bees]   ~ ,   *Later Poems, Can. Monthly*
15   whispers]   **odours**   *Later Poems*
15   ease.]   ~ ;   *Later Poems, Can. Monthly*
16   pass]   ~ ,   *Can. Monthly*
17   pain.]   ~ ;   *Later Poems, Can. Monthly*
18   wrong,]   ~   *Later Poems*
20   asleep]   **to sleep**   *Later Poems*

Glossary
Lotos: see "Love Days"

The poem first appeared in *Later Poems,* 1881; and was subsequently published in *In Divers Tones,* 1886; and in *Poems,* 1901/7. Pomeroy (p. 13)
reports that "No other work of that period [when Roberts was about twelve
years old] was published but he continued to write verse, which his father
always took seriously. He did not, however, suggest changes. If he did not
like a stanza, he would simply say, 'This needs improvement. Think it out for
yourself.' He was determined that Charles would learn self-criticism. Twelve
lines only have been preserved—the first three stanzas of 'Out of Pompeii.' At
that time the poem was called 'From Fire' and was inspired by a picture of
the destruction of Pompeii in *The London Illustrated News,* one of the innumerable pictures which papered the walls of his bedroom. It was not completed until several years after the publication of his first volume, but it
remained a faithful expression of the picture which had stirred him so deeply."
Another recollection of the poem's composition is found in a note by Roberts
in his reading copy of *Poems.* The note says, "begun when I was 13, at Westcock. Finished when I was 16, at Fredericton. First six stanzas written at
Westcock." The edition in *Later Poems,* however, is dated from Chatham,
October, 1881.

Variants
Title: Out of Pompeii]   **From Fire**   *Later Poems*
   6   sullen]   **sudden**   *Later Poems*
   9   water's]   **waters**   *Later Poems*
  11   soul,–]   ~ –   *Later Poems*
  13   fingers, groping,]   **fingers groping**   *Later Poems*
  14   mind;]   ~ ,   *Later Poems*
  18   faint, swift,]   **faint swift**   *Later Poems*
  21   then]   **but**   *Later Poems*
  27   hard,]   ~   *Later Poems*
  30   eyes.]   ~ :   *Later Poems*
  35   half curious]   **half-curious**   *Later Poems*
  37   crouched,]   ~   *Later Poems*
  40   sea-water]   **bilge-water**   *Later Poems*
  44   pure from]   **without**   *Later Poems*
  46   face,]   ~   *Later Poems*
  46   pain,–]   ~ :   *Later Poems*   ~ ;–   *IDT*
  47   sudden, . . . thronged]   **sudden . . . thronged,**   *Later Poems*
  51   dim . . . fleeing]   **dense . . . flying**   *Later Poems*
  53   fallen;]   ~ ,   *Later Poems*
  57   hearts,]   ~ ,–   *Later Poems*
  58   Mount. Clear]   **Mount; clear**   *Later Poems*
  60   here!]   ~ .   *Later Poems*
  63   safe,]   ~   *Later Poems*

Glossary
Pompeii: an ancient city in southwest Italy; it was destroyed by an erup-
tion of Mount Vesuvius in 79 A.D.

p. 61 TO THE MEMORY OF SIDNEY LANIER

The poem was first published in *Later Poems,* 1881; and later appeared in *The Current* (1883); and *In Divers Tones,* 1886. In *Later Poems* the date of composition is October, 1881.

Variants

1	rain,]	~ ; *Current*
2	leaf,]	~ ; *Current*
3	ah, . . . pain!–]	**ah!** . . . **pain!** *Later Poems*
4	slow,]	~ *Later Poems, Current*
4	grief,]	~ ! *Later Poems*
5	throbs–]	~ : *Current*
5	vain, in vain,–]	**vain! In vain!** *Later Poems, Current*
6	sheaf!]	~ . *Later Poems*
7	sheaf,]	~ *Later Poems, Current*
8	wheat,–]	~ – *Later Poems, Current*
9	Death]	**death** *Later Poems, Current*
11	prayers]	~ , *Later Poems*
13	tears. But]	**tears; but** *Later Poems*
14	me,]	~ ! *Later Poems, Current*
14	all]	**All** *Current*
15	cry!]	~ . *Later Poems, Current*
21	above.]	~ ; *Later Poems, Current*
22	Tho']	**Though** *Later Poems, Current*
23	Elder]	**elder** *Later Poems, Current*
23	Brother]	**brother** *Current*
24	space!]	~ . *Later Poems, Current*

Glossary
Sidney Lanier: American poet and critic (1842-81). He was the author
of *Florida,* 1875; *Poems,* 1876; *The Science of English Verse,* 1880; published posthumously were *The English Novel and Its Development,* 1883; and *Complete Poems,* 1884.

p. 62 A BALLADE OF CALYPSO

The poem was first published in *Later Poems,* 1881; and later appeared in *In Divers Tones,* 1886; and in *The University Monthly* (Jan. 4, 1887). The edition in *Later Poems* is dated Nov., 1881.

Variants

Title: Ballade]   **Ballad**   *Later Poems*
5   And here, of its sweet queen grown full fain,–]
                  Here of its mystical mistress fain,   *Later Poems*
5   And here]   **Here**   *Univ. Monthly*
6   poor,–]   ～ ,   *Later Poems*
9   dirges.]   ～ ;   *Later Poems*
10   gain.]   ～ ;   *Later Poems*
11   and]   **and and**   *Later Poems*
12   twain?]   ～ !   *Later Poems*
13   nor . . . retain;]   **or** . . . **retain,**   *Univ. Monthly*
14   allure;]   ～ ,–   *Later Poems*
15   toils]   **tears**   *Later Poems*
15   perils, and toils,]   **perils and toils**   *Univ. Monthly*
20   waver,]   ～   *Univ. Monthly*
21   domain.]   ～ ;   *Later Poems, Univ. Monthly*
22   immure.–]   ～ ;–   *Later Poems, Univ. Monthly*
23   ah,]   ～ !   *Later Poems, Univ. Monthly*
23   again]   ～ ,   *Later Poems*
24   secure!]   ～ .   *Univ. Monthly*
L'ENVOI]   **ENVOI**   *Later Poems*
27   mourn,]   ～   *Later Poems, Univ. Monthly*
28   secure!]   ～ .   *Later Poems*

Glossary

5   *sweet queen:*   Calypso; Ulysses stayed on Calypso's island for seven
                  years during his journey home to Ithaca from Troy.
7   *wave-worn prince:*   Ulysses
8   *Ogygian Isle:*   the mythical island of Calypso; Ogygian also means
                  of great antiquity, having to do with the reign of
                  Ogygus of Bœotia or Lycia who ruled during the first
                  Deluge

p. 62 RONDEAU (To Louis Honore Fréchette)

The poem was first published in *Later Poems,* 1881; and later appeared in
Rose-Belford's *Canadian Monthly* (Feb., 1882); and *In Divers Tones,* 1886.
The edition in *Later Poems* is dated November, 1881.

Variants

Dedication: Fréchette]   **Frechette**   *Later Poems, Can. Monthly*
1   And]   **and**   *Later Poems, Can. Monthly*
1   song]   **Song**   *Can. Monthly;* also lines 9 and 15
2   days]   ～ ,   *Can. Monthly*
3   thro']   **through**   *Later Poems*

394

4	borne,] ~ – *Can. Monthly*
5	gaze!] ~ . *Later Poems* ~ : *Can. Monthly*
7	and] **then** *Later Poems*
7	praise;–] ~ ; *Later Poems, Can. Monthly*
8	Yet] **Still** *Later Poems, Can. Monthly*
10	palaestra-plays] **palaestra plays** *Can. Monthly*
11	conqueror . . . gods] **victor . . . Gods** *Can. Monthly*
12	brows . . . born] **brows, . . . born,** *Later Poems*

Glossary

Louis Honore Fréchette: Fréchette (1839-1908) was the best known French-Canadian writer of the nineteenth century. The immediate inspiration for Roberts' poem was undoubtedly Fréchette's winning of the *Prix Montyon* of the French Academy in 1880. See *The Oxford Companion to Canadian History and Literature* (Toronto: Oxford University Press, 1967), pp. 296-297 for an account of Fréchette's life and works.

1	*Laurels . . . bays:* wreaths worn on the head to signify outstanding achievement in any endeavor.
5	*Hellas:* another name for ancient Greece.
10	*palaestra-plays:* athletic competitions.
13	*fillets:* a ribbon of cloth or other material bound around the head, here synonymous with the laurel wreath.

p. 63 A SONG OF REGRET

The poem first appeared in Rose-Belford's *Canadian Monthly* (Nov., 1881); and was included in *In Divers Tones,* 1886.

Variants
All variants are from the *Canadian Monthly.*

5	beeches] **birches**
9	beech-burrs] **birch-burrs**
10	down-patter;] **down patter,**
12	disperst] **dispersed**
13	glare] ~ ,
14	Would . . . outdare;–] **A gem's despair,**
15	'Tis] **Is**
16	flaming.] ~ ;
18	Is] **There's**
19	A . . . fire] **Acting like fire**
20	naming.] ~ ;
21	rise] ~ ,
22	a-sighing,–] ~ –
23	sighing] ~ ,
24	dies!] ~ .

The poem first appeared in *Later Poems,* 1881; and was later published in *In Divers Tones,* 1886; *Poems,* 1901/7; and *Selected Poems,* 1936. The edition in *Later Poems* is dated December 17, 1881.

Variants:

Title: Soliloquy in a Monastery] **Brother Cuthbert** *Later Poems,*
Poems, 1901/7 **Concerning Cuthbert the Monk** *IDT*

1	open! Let]	**open; let** *Later Poems*
4	it.]	~ ; *Later Poems, IDT, Poems* 1901/7
8	Monk-like . . . another!–]	**Monklike . . . another:** *Later Poems*
11	Then, . . . leave,]	**Then . . . leave** *Later Poems*
12	Eve!]	~ . *Later Poems*
16	looks –]	~ : *Later Poems* ~ . – *IDT, Poems* 1901/7
16	Hello]	**Holloa** *Later Poems*
17	keep!]	~ – *Later Poems*
18	after this line, *Later Poems* inserts:	

> Shame, man! Keep your vigil! Wake!
> Double penance else your bones
> Soon will pay with wrench and ache
> For your tempting couch of stones.
> Hard and cold your couch and cell,
> Brother, yet you slumber well!

21	are . . . cheek,]	**is . . . cheek;** *Later Poems*
22	sleeps . . . praying;–]	**sleeps, . . . praying,–** *Later Poems*
23	murmurs.]	~ : *Later Poems*
24	you.– Sleep]	**you; sleep** *Later Poems*
27	tops,]	~ *Later Poems*
28	alive,–]	~ , *Later Poems*
29	falls,]	~ *Later Poems*
30	Shivering,]	~ *Later Poems*
34	swings.]	~ ; *Later Poems*
35	bright.]	~ ,– *Later Poems*
37	speak?–]	~ ? *Later Poems*
42	whilst]	**while** *Later Poems*
47	years]	**year's** *Later Poems*
52	Iron-mouthed]	~ , *Later Poems*
54	foes!]	~ . *Later Poems*
55	he]	~ , *IDT*
58	eyes!]	~ :– *Later Poems*
59	hand]	**Hand** *Later Poems, IDT*
66	old,]	~ *Later Poems, IDT*
66	Christmastides]	**Christmas-tides** *Later Poems, IDT, Poems* 1901/7

68	him;]	~ ,	*Later Poems*

68   him;]   ~ ,   *Later Poems*
70   noise;]   ~ ;–   *Later Poems*
71   hair.–]   ~ –   *Later Poems*
74   evermore!]   ~ .   *Later Poems*
75   thee.]   ~ ;   *Later Poems*
76   Brother!]   ~ .   *Later Poems*
78   wide!]   ~ .   *Later Poems*
80   again!]   ~ .   *Later Poems*
82   pain.]   ~ ;   *Later Poems*
83   town,–]   ~ ,   *Later Poems*
85   Hungry-hearted]   ~ ,   *Later Poems, IDT*
87   poplar-tree,–]   ~ –   *Later Poems*
88   wall.]   ~ ;   *Later Poems*
91   me,]   ~ !   *Later Poems*
92   monk,]   ~   *Later Poems*
94   untold!]   ~ :   *Later Poems*
95   you're]   **your**   *Later Poems*

Glossary

1   *Cuthbert:*   The *New Catholic Encyclopedia* lists three Cuthberts, but none of the biographies match the particulars of the poem.

34   *Severn:*   a river in central Wales that flows through western England into the Bristol Channel.

p. 66 ON THE EVE OF DEPARTURE

The poem was never published and survives only in Roberts' Ernescliffe note-book at the University of New Brunswick. In ENB, just below the title, is the date January 29, 1882, and at the end of the poem is the note, "lines written in the album of Minnie Blair, one of my pupils when I was Principal of the Chatham Grammar School, at Chatham, New Brunswick, 1881-2."

p. 66 ACTÆON

The poem was initially published in *Later Poems,* 1882. A mutilated version containing lines 48-92, 95-121, 127-130, three lines which otherwise appear only in *Later Poems,* and 136-210 was published in *Our Continent* (October 17, 1883). It subsequently appeared in *In Divers Tones,* 1886; the "Appendix" to *Younger American Poets,* 1891; *Poems,* 1901/7; and in *Selected Poems,* 1936. Extracts (lines 188-210) are in *Selected Poems of Sir Charles G.D. Roberts,* 1955; and the entire poem was included in *Selected Poetry and Critical Prose,* 1974. The edition in *Later Poems* is dated March, 1882.

James Cappon, in *Roberts and the Influences of His Time* (p. 19) calls "*Actæon* . . . Roberts' most successful achievement in the region of classical idyll" and on page 21 he says that the woman of Platæa, who speaks the monologue, is "the most life-like of the few human figures, mythical or modern, that appear in Roberts' poems."

Variants

sub-heading: A Woman of Platæa Speaks] **(Duselia, a woman of Platæa, speaks.)** *Later Poems* There is no sub-heading in the *Our Continent* text.

8 people,] ~! *Later Poems*
9 you! And . . . glad,] **you;–and . . . glad** *Later Poems*
14 falls!] ~. *Later Poems*
15 hear;] ~, *Later Poems*
16 offerings,–] ~; Later Poems ~;– *IDT* **offering;** *YAP*
17 heard, and did perceive,] **heard amid their peace** *Later Poems*
18 ears,] ~ *Later Poems, YAP*
20 Tho'] **Though** *Later Poems*
27 ears. No . . . this,] **ears;–no . . . this** *Later Poems*
28 nectar cups and calm!] **nectar-cups and calm.** *Later Poems*
29 them,–] ~, *Later Poems, IDT, YAP*
30 tasks.] ~; *Later Poems*
31 long, . . . bare, . . . arm,] **long . . . bare . . . arm** *Later Poems*
32 I drew] **Drew** *Later Poems, IDT, YAP, Poems* 1901/7
33 lotus-buds,] ~ *Later Poems, IDT, YAP*
37 and smooth] **or smooth,** *Later Poems*
38 gave small] **scattered** *Later Poems*
39 god] ~, *Later Poems*
41 poppy-bells,] **poppy-blooms** *Later Poems* **poppy bells** *YAP*
42 scorn,] ~ *Later Poems*
47 fair] **sweet** *Later Poems*
48 I . . . heed] **"With how small profit,"** thought I, "men take heed *Our Con.*
49 worship] ~, *Later Poems, Our Con.*
49 heads] **head** *Our Con.*
49 heads] ~, *IDT, YAP, Poems* 1901/7
49 hands] ~, *Our Con., IDT, YAP, Poems* 1901/7
50 sacrifice] ~, *Later Poems, IDT, YAP, Poems* 1901/7
51 them] **men** *Our Con.*
52 purples] **purple** *Our Con.*
52 peace!] ~. *Later Poems* ~!" *Our Con.*
53 them,–yet–and yet] **them; yet, and yet** *Later Poems* **them once; and yet** *Our Con.* **them;–~** *IDT, YAP*
55 as] omitted in *Later Poems, Our Con., IDT, YAP, Poems* 1901/7
55 it;] ~. *Our Con.*
57 husks,] ~ – *Our Con.*
58 gods!] ~. *Later Poems*
59 questioned;] ~, *Later Poems, Our Con.*

398

61	Godlike]	**God-like** *Our Con., YAP*	
62	death,–]	~ – *Our Con., YAP*	
63	changed]	~ , *IDT, YAP*	
65	Stared . . . 'mid]	**Glared . . . mid** *Later Poems*	
65	Stared one sick]	**Gleamed white a** *Our Con.*	
70	mid]	**'mid** *YAP*	
70	hills–]	~ ,– *Later Poems*	
71	ken–]	~ ,– *Later Poems*	
74	pride.]	~ ; *Later Poems*	
75	look toward north]	**northward look** *Our Con.*	
76	long]	~ , *Later Poems*	
76	roll]	~ , *Our Con., Poems* 1901/7	
79	sunward;]	~ ;– *Later Poems* ~ – *Our Con.*	
79	wherein]	**whereon** *Our Con.*	
80	godlike . . . gods,]	**god-like . . . gods** *YAP*	
81	roamed,]	~ *Our Con.*	
83	Reverence, . . . He,]	**Reverence . . . He** *Later Poems*	
83	Cheiron!]	**Chiron.** *Our Con.*	
85	there moved none cunninger]	**none cunninger there moved** *Later Poems, Our Con.*	
90	laughing,–]	~ , *Later Poems, Our Con.*	
91	hounds.]	~ ,– *Later Poems* ~ , *Our Con.* ~ ; *IDT, YAP*	
95	out]	**forth** *Later Poems, Our Con.*	
96	Snake-root,]	~ *Our Con.*	
97	through]	**thro'** *Later Poems*	
100	gleamed,–]	~ , *Later Poems* ~ ; *Our Con.*	
101	bowshot]	**bow-shot** *Our Con.*	
102	thro' . . . low-hung]	**through . . . low hung** *Our Con.*	
104	clear,]	~ *Later Poems*	
105	further]	**farther** *Our Con.*	
106	From . . . hanging over]	**Where . . . darkened it** *Later Poems*	
106	ash-trees hanging]	**ash trees drooping** *Our Con.*	
107	But]	**Then** *YAP*	
107	shallows]	**waters** *Later Poems*	
110	beasts,]	~ *Later Poems*	
111	off,]	~ *YAP*	
116	stepping, shrinking,]	**stepping shrinking** *Later Poems, Our Con.*	
117	Here]	**There** *YAP*	
117	waterdrops]	**water drops** *Later Poems* **water-drops** *Our Con., IDT, YAP, Poems* 1901/7	
118	shoulder]	~ , *Our Con.*	
119	the washed clouds athwart]	**high light clouds that bar** *Later Poems*	
119	washed . . . blue,–]	**small . . . blue,** *Our Con.*	
120	river grasses]	**river-grasses** *Later Poems*	
122	flung.]	~ , *Later Poems* ~ : *IDT* ~ ; *YAP, Poems* 1901/7	

124   envy;]   ~ ,–   *Later Poems*
127   And]   **But**   *Our Con.*
127   She]   **she**   *Later Poems, YAP*
128   they]   **them**   *Later Poems, Our Con.*
130   beech-leaves: Ay]   **beech-leaves:–Ah**   *Later Poems*
                              beech-leaves; ay   *YAP*
130   beech-leaves . . . hair]   **beech leaves glossed with gold**   *Our Con.*
130   After this line, *Our Con.* inserts:

> Then from the cool hollowed palm the crystal stream
> Luxuriously fell lingering down her limbs,
> And flashed upon their snowiness unflushed.

133   soft,]   ~   *Later Poems, IDT, YAP*
135   After this line, *Later Poems* inserts:

> Of these grey locks I dreamed not, but for men
> Knowledge of ill is swift, and soon at hand.–
> The while from hollowed palm and cool the stream
> Luxuriously fell lingering down the limbs,
> And sparkled o'er the snowiness unflushed.

136   and]   **while**   *Later Poems, Our Con.*
137   white]   **fair**   *Later Poems, Our Con.*
138   And, . . . bunches, shed]   **And . . . bunches showered**   *Later Poems*
139   saw]   ~ –   *Our Con.*
141   laughing,–]   ~ ,   *Later Poems, Our Con., IDT, YAP*
142   hounds,]   ~ –   *Our Con.*
146   eve,]   ~   *Our Con.*
147   tall-plumed sedge]   **tall plumed reeds**   *Later Poems*
147   sedge]   **reeds**   *Our Con.*
148   spots about . . . bank,–]   **lands along . . . bank,**   *Later Poems*
                                      lands . . . bank;   *Our Con.*
151   sea;]   ~ –   *Later Poems*
151   sea;]   **tide–**   *Our Con.*
152   solitudes, . . . broad . . . plains]   **solitudes . . . broad, . . . grounds**
                                                 Our Con.
153   labours]   **labour**   *Later Poems*   **labor**   *Our Con.*
154   salt, blue, . . . mount]   **salt blue . . . Mount**   *Later Poems*
155   hills,]   ~ –   *Later Poems, Our Con.*
157   high]   ~ ,   *Our Con.*
157   days,–]   ~ –   *Our Con.*   ~ ,   *YAP*
158   dreamed . . . dreams]   **mused . . . things**   *Our Con.*
160   sorest,]   ~   *Later Poems, IDT, YAP*
160   overcome;]   ~ ,   *Later Poems, IDT, YAP, Poems* 1901/7
162   them.]   ~ ;   *Our Con.*

400

164 gods?] ~ ! *Later Poems*
165 ¹him,–] ~ – *Later Poems, Our Con.*
165 Ah] **ah,** *Our Con.*
166 ways!] ~ . *Later Poems, Our Con.*
167 ¹yet,] ~ – *Our Con.*
167 god's] **God's** *Later Poems*
168 lying] **there** *Our Con.*
173 not;] ~ , *Later Poems, Our Con.*
175 curls,] ~ *Later Poems, IDT, YAP*
176 Sun-lit,] ~ *Later Poems, IDT, YAP*
176 neck,–] ~ , *Later Poems*   ~ – *Our Con.*
177 bow] ~ , *YAP*
178 ecstacy;] ~ ,– *Later Poems*   ~ , *Our Con.*
179 close,] ~ *Our Con.*
180 red,] ~ *YAP*
181 moment. Then] **moment; then** *Later Poems, Our Con.*
183 out,–] ~ , *Later Poems*   ~ – *Our Con.*
184 dogs;] ~ – *Later Poems*
186 throat;] ~ , *Our Con.*
187 wet,] ~ *Later Poems*
188 long] ~ , *Our Con., IDT, YAP, Poems* 1901/7
189 aught] **ought** *IDT*
191 This] **Thick** *Later Poems, Our Con.*
192 not,] ~ ; *Later Poems, Our Con.*
193 hearing; but] **hearing. But** *Our Con.*
195 Unrippled,– . . . sward,] **Unrippled, . . . sward** *Later Poems*
                                  Unrippled– . . . sward *Our Con.*
196 fretful] **fitful** *YAP*
196 search,] ~ *Later Poems*
197 uneasily;] ~ ;– *Later Poems*
197 uneasily; and] **uneasily. And** *Our Con.*
199 straining] **swelling** *Later Poems*
199 throats] ~ , *Later Poems, Our Con.*
200 echoing] **sundered** *Later Poems*   **separate** *Our Con.*
202 reared,–] ~ : *Later Poems*   ~ ;– *IDT*   ~ . *YAP*
205 now] ~ , *Our Con.*
206 paling] **darkened** *Our Con.*
206 stealthy] **fitful** *Later Poems*   **rustling** *Our Con.*
           noiseless *IDT, YAP, Poems* 1901/7
207 hollow] **yellow** *Later Poems, Our Con., IDT, YAP, Poems* 1901/7
207 stirred] **moved** *Later Poems*
209 eastward] ~ , *Our Con.*

Glossary
Actæon: a hunter of Bœotia. Roberts uses only one of the several legends
           surrounding his offense and death.

Platæa: a city in Bœotia, Greece, located at the foot of Mount Cithæron, about 30 miles northwest of Athens.

6   *meed:* a reward for good service.

21   *Acheron:* one of the five rivers surrounding the Greek Hades, the river of woe. The souls of the dead had to bathe in it or cross it. Also, the name of several small rivers in Greece.

34   *himation:* a Greek garment of the classical period; it was a rectangular cloth thrown over the shoulder and wrapped around the body.

60   *thewed:* muscular

67   *Bœotia:* in ancient times a district in central Greece; Thebes was the major city.

68   *Corinthian:* Corinth was a famous city on the coast of Greece.

75   *Eleusis:* a small town about 14 miles west of Athens, sacred to Demeter—the goddess of the fertility of the earth and of man.

83   *Cheiron:* a wise and just centaur, friend and teacher to many Greek heroes, famous for his powers of prophecy and healing and his skill at hunting and music.

87   *Leto's son:* Apollo; Leto was also the mother of Artemis.

88   *Centaur:* a mythical creature, half man and half horse.

96   *snake-root:* a medicinal root.

99   *Gargaphian:* Gargaphia is the name of the valley where Actæon was killed.

102   *platan:* the plane tree, which grows wild from Italy to Persia and is used in Europe for ornament.

109   *Artemis:* one of the twelve Olympians, the virgin goddess of the hunt.

148   *Asopus:* a small river in Bœotia.

p. 71   CANOE SONG

The poem was published only in *The University Monthly* (March, 1882).

Note: The printed poem ends with line 24, "Oh, here's to the paddle, &c."

p. 72   BEFORE THE BREATH OF STORM

The poem was first published in *Later Poems,* 1882; and subsequently appeared in *In Divers Tones,* 1886; and *Poems,* 1901/7. The edition in *Later Poems* is dated September, 1882.

Variants

13   dreams;–]   ~ –   *Later Poems*
15   hills;– ... wing?]   **hills**– ... **wing?**–   *Later Poems*

p. 73 IN SEPTEMBER

The poem was first published in *Later Poems,* 1882. It subsequently appeared in *In Divers Tones,* 1886; "September" in *Through the Year with the Poets,* 1886; *Progress* (September, 1888); *The Magazine of Poetry* (January, 1889); *Songs of the Common Day and Ave,* 1893; *Poems,* 1901/7; and *Selected Poetry and Critical Prose,* 1974. Pomeroy (p. 113) says that the poem was written "in the Rectory garden at Fredericton" and the edition in *Later Poems* is dated September, 1882.

Variants

Title: In September]   **To Fredericton in September** *Progress*
1   windy, . . . afternoon]   **windy . . . afternoon,** *Through the Year*
4   grain-fields]   **grainfields** *Through the Year*
                   grain fields *Progress*
4   rune,]   ~ *Later Poems*
5   Summer]   **summer** *Through the Year*
5   soon,]   ~ *Later Poems*
7   hills,]   ~ *Progress*
13   endows:–]   ~ : *Through the Year*
14   too.]   ~ ! *Through the Year*

Glossary

4   *rune:*   a letter or character of the earliest Teutonic alphabet, frequently supposed to possess magical or mysterious powers.

p. 73 A BREATHING TIME

The poem first appeared in *The University Monthly* (November, 1882); and was later published in *The Century Magazine* (July, 1883); *In Divers Tones,* 1886; *The Magazine of Poetry* (January, 1889); and *Poems,* 1901/7. Pomeroy (pp. 47-48) incorrectly states that the poem was written during the summer or fall of 1883. She also points out (p. 48) that "A Breathing Time" was "his first experiment with the difficult classical form which he was to make so peculiarly his own—the dactylic hexameter and pentameter lines used alternately."

Variants

Title: A Breathing Time]   **A Breathing-Time** *Univ. Monthly*
1   above this line in *Univ. Monthly* is: **(Hexameters and Pentameters.)**
1   breathing time]   **breathing-time** *Univ. Monthly*
1   season.]   ~ ; *Univ. Monthly, Century*
2   life.]   ~ ; *Univ. Monthly, Century*
5   strife]   ~ , *Univ. Monthly, Century*
6   Pain,]   ~ *Univ. Monthly, Century*
6   endured;]   ~ : *Century*

7	Fighting,]	~	*Century*
8	broad . . . earth]	**broad, . . . Earth**	*Univ. Monthly*
10	Tense the unstrung]	**Calmed the o'erwrought**	*Univ. Monthly*
11	Weary]	**Feeble**	*Univ. Monthly*
12	earth's]	**Earth's**	*Univ. Monthly*
12	dreams!]	~ .	*Univ. Monthly, Century*

p. 73 IN THE AFTERNOON

The poem first appeared in *Later Poems,* 1882; and was later published in *In Divers Tones,* 1886; *Songs of the Great Dominion,* 1889; *Later Canadian Poems,* 1893; *Poems,* 1901/7; *Selected Poems,* 1936; and *Selected Poetry and Critical Prose,* 1974. Pomeroy (p. 47) incorrectly states that the poem was written in May, 1883, but the edition in *Later Poems* is dated 1882.

Variants

4	memory]	**Memory**	*Later Poems, IDT, Songs of the Great Dom., Later Can. Poems*
6	'T were]	**T' were**	*Later Poems* 'Twere *IDT, Songs of the Great Dom., Later Can. Poems*
6	forget;–]	~ ,–	*Later Poems*
8	calm.]	~ !	*Later Poems, IDT, Songs of the Great Dom., Later Can. Poems*
11	trees–]	~ ,–	*Later Poems, Songs of the Great Dom.*
17	sniff]	**snuff**	*IDT, Poems* 1901/7
21	net-reels,]	~	*Later Poems*
27	vetch and convolvulus]	**vetch, and convolvulus,**	*IDT, Songs of the Great Dom., Later Can. Poems, Poems* 1901/7
30	level,]	~	*Songs of the Great Dom.*
33	sudden, long,]	**sudden long**	*Later Poems, Songs of the Great Dom.*
40	Still-winged,]	~	*Later Poems*
42	blooms]	~ .	*Later Poems, IDT, Songs of the Great Dom., Later Can. Poems, Poems* 1901/7
47	Wind . . . afternoon,]	**–Wind . . . afternoon**	*Later Poems*
48	recalled]	**re-called**	*Later Poems*
48	June.]	~ ;	*Later Poems, IDT, Songs of the Great Dom., Later Can. Poems, Poems* 1901/7
49-60	My . . . heaven!]	omitted in *Songs of the Great Dom.*	
49	heart–]	~ ,	*Later Poems*
50	the]	**that**	*Later Poems*
56	canst . . . abate?]	**can'st . . . abate?–**	*Later Poems*
58	child-heartedness,–]	~	*Later Poems*
61	afternoon,]	~	*Later Poems*
62	tune.]	~ ;	*Later Poems*

63   voice; but . . . yet–]   **voice–but . . . yet** *Later Poems*
                                   voice; but . . . yet,– *Songs of the Great Dom.*
64   't were]   **twere**   *IDT, Songs of the Great Dom., Later Can. Poems*
64   sweetest to forget!]   **sweetest–to forget** *Later Poems*

Glossary
16-18   *Tantramar . . . Westmoreland:*   The Tantramar River is in West-
           moreland County in eastern New Brunswick.
25   *mullein:*   a weed with coarse woolly leaves and dense spikes of
           yellow flowers
27   *convolvulus:*   the morning-glory

p. 76 SONNET ON SPRING

The poem was published only in *The University Monthly* (May, 1883). It is
not signed, but it is followed, in the next column, by a poem by Roberts
which is signed. Its attribution to Roberts must remain doubtful.

p. 76 THE PIPES OF PAN

According to Pomeroy (p. 48) the poem was written in the summer of 1883,
just before the writing of "Tantramar Revisited." It was not published until
1886, in *In Divers Tones;* and it was subsequently printed in the "Appendix"
to *Younger American Poets,* 1891; *Poems,* 1901/7; *Selected Poems,* 1936;
and *Selected Poetry and Critical Prose,* 1974.

Variants
 2   withdrawn,–]   ~ ;   *IDT, YAP, Poems* 1901/7
 6   dreams,]   ~ , –   *IDT, Poems* 1901/7   ~ –   *YAP*
14   caress.]   ~ ,   *YAP*
17   nook. Two]   **nook; two** *YAP*
19   lote-leaf.]   ~ ;   *IDT, YAP*
20   roots;]   ~ ,   *IDT, YAP*
26   god's]   **gods** *YAP*
28   gloom,]   ~   *IDT, YAP, Poems* 1901/7
29   Answering. Float . . . pipes,]   **Answering; float . . . pipes** *YAP*
31   forever. Dispersed . . . Penёus]   **forever; dispersed . . . Penёus,** *YAP*
32   yon]   **there** *IDT, YAP, Poems* 1901/7
35   mortals,]   ~   *IDT, YAP, Poems* 1901/7
36   ¹at]   **in** *IDT, YAP, Poems* 1901/7
38   lips; blow, . . . away!]   **lips, blow . . . away.** *YAP*
42   the wild]   **wild life** *IDT, YAP, Poems* 1901/7

Note: in *YAP* a new stanza begins at line 31

405

Glossary

 1   *Olympus:*   the mountain home of the major Greek gods
 2   *Tempe:*   a valley between Mount Olympus and Mount Ossa
 9   *Penëus:*   a river flowing through the valley, now called the Salambria
12   *Centaur:*   see "Actæon"
13   *Artemis:*   see "Actæon"
14   *Phoebus:*   see "Memnon"
15   *dryad:*   see "Iterumne"
19   *lote-leaf:*   Roberts' poetic rendering of lotus or water lily
23   *Pan:*   god of flocks and shepherds, also the inventor of the pipe or
          flute. He is depicted as half man and half goat.

p. 78 TANTRAMAR REVISITED

The poem first appeared in *The Week* (December, 1883); and was subsequently published in *In Divers Tones*, 1886; *Songs of the Great Dominion,* 1889; *Canadian Poems and Lays*, 1893; *Poems*, 1901/7; *Oxford Book of Canadian Verse*, 1913; *Our Canadian Literature,* 1934; *Selected Poems*, 1936; *Telegraph Journal* (July, 1937); *A Book of Canadian Poetry*, 1943/8; *Selected Poems of Sir Charles G.D. Roberts*, 1955; *Canadian Anthology*, 1966; *Poets of Confederation,* 1967; and *Selected Poetry and Critical Prose*, 1974. Pomeroy (p. 48) says: "Although written when he was only twenty-three, the classical form, the originality of treatment, the vivid landscape and its intense but restrained emotion, combine to make this poem one of his masterpieces. The difficult metre, with its alternating hexameter and pentameter lines, is particularly noteworthy, for rarely has this elegiac measure, so popular with Ovid, been used in English . . . no poet, writing in English, has used it with such freedom and sustained precision as Roberts." James Cappon, in *Roberts and the Influences of His Time* (pp. 31-34) gives this evaluation: "Amongst all these varieties of the Canadian idyll, the one which leaves the strongest impression on the mind of originality in tone and treatment is *Tantramar Revisited*. . . . There is no direct picture of life in the poem, not a single human figure, but the landscape is powerfully painted in large, distant, softened traits, the true colour of elegiac reminiscence. Of direct elegiac reflection the poet has been sparing, perhaps wisely, but what there is has a sincerity which shows how deeply he felt his subject. [Almost all of the poem is here quoted.] In spite of the exotic character of the verse, which after all is a bar to the highest qualities of expression, something of the visionary eye and depth of feeling with which the poet looks on those scenes of his boyhood gets into every line. The poem is a true whole also and speaks in a subtle way to the heart. Perhaps he has lavished the resources of his style a little too freely on that description of the empty net reels. Its luxuriance is rather overpowering."

Variants
Title: Tantramar Revisited]   **Westmoreland Revisited** *Week*   **The Tan-**
         tramar Revisited *IDT, Songs of the Great Dom., Can. Poems and Lays*

406

| 2 | storm,] | ∼ | *Songs of the Great Dom., Can. Poems and Lays, Oxford Book of Can. Verse* |
| 2 | winter,] | ∼ | *Week, Songs of the Great Dom., Can. Poems and Lays, Oxford Book of Can. Verse* |

2   storm,] ∼ *Songs of the Great Dom., Can. Poems and Lays, Oxford Book of Can. Verse*

2   winter,] ∼ *Week, Songs of the Great Dom., Can. Poems and Lays, Oxford Book of Can. Verse*

4   fall'n] **fallen** *Week*

5   marred, or moulded,] **marred or moulded** *Week*

7   Earth] **earth** *Week, Oxford Book of Can. Verse, Tel. Journal*

7   shadows,–] ∼ – *Week*

8   change!] ∼ . *Oxford Book of Can. Verse*

9   Here] ∼ , *Songs of the Great Dom., Can. Poems and Lays, Oxford Book of Can. Verse*

9   woodlands,] ∼ *Week, Songs of the Great Dom., Can. Poems and Lays, Oxford Book of Can. Verse*

10   hill-tops] **hilltops** *Tel. Journal*

10   down,] ∼ *Week*

11   can] omitted in *Week*

12   orchards,] ∼ *Oxford Book of Can. Verse*

12   meadows,] **and meadows** *Songs of the Great Dom., Can. Poems and Lays, Oxford Book of Can. Verse*
    meadows *Tel. Journal*

12   wheat,] ∼ *Oxford Book of Can. Verse*

13   broad] ∼ , *Oxford Book of Can. Verse*

14   Wind-swept] **Windswept** *Oxford Book of Can. Verse, Tel. Journal*

15   sunbright] **sun-bright** *Week, Oxford Book of Can. Verse*

17   seaward] **sea-ward** *Week*

19   Yonder,] ∼ *Week*

19   toward] **towards** *Songs of the Great Dom., Can. Poems and Lays, Oxford Book of Can. Verse*

19   left,] ∼ *Week*

20   level,] ∼ *Songs of the Great Dom., Can. Poems and Lays, Oxford Book of Can. Verse*

20   grassy,] ∼ *Week*

22   for] **from** *Tel. Journal*

23   outrolled] **out-rolled** *Week*

23   river-channels] **river channels** *Week, Tel. Journal*

23   them,–] ∼ ;– *Week*

25   bay . . . Minudie.] **Bay . . . Minudie,–** *Week*

26   hills; . . . feet.] **hills, . . . feet;** *Week*

28   slim,] ∼ *Week, Songs of the Great Dom., Can. Poems and Lays, Oxford Book of Can. Verse*

28   fishing boats] **fishing-boats** *Oxford Book of Can. Verse*

29   Ah,] ∼ ! *Songs of the Great Dom., Can. Poems and Lays, Oxford Book of Can. Verse*

29   tide-mark] ∼ , *Songs of the Great Dom., Can. Poems and Lays, Oxford Book of Can. Verse, Book of Can. Poetry*

30   sun!] ∼ ; *Week*

31   net-reels] **net reels** *Week*

36	a]	**the**	*Tel. Journal*

36 a] **the** *Tel. Journal*
39 long] ~ , *Tel. Journal*
39 thro'] **through** *Oxford Book of Can. Verse*
43 marsh-owls] **marsh owls** *Week*
44 broad,] ~ *Week, Songs of the Great Dom., Can. Poems and*
                  Lays, Oxford Book of Can. Verse
45 Soon,] ~ *Week*
45 thro'] **through** *Oxford Book of Can. Verse, Tel. Journal*
45 morning,] ~ *Our Can. Lit.*
46 wind.] ~ ; *Week*
49 wave,] ~ *Week*
49 drift-net] ~ , *Oxford Book of Can. Verse, Book of Can. Poetry*
                  driftnet *Tel. Journal*
51 all. The] **all; the** *Week*
51 salt,] ~ *Week, IDT, Songs of the Great Dom., Can. Poems and*
                  Lays, Oxford Book of Can. Verse
51 margin;] ~ , *Week* **marshes** *Tel. Journal*
52 While,] ~ *Week*
54 home,–] ~ ;– *Week*
55 Yet,] ~ *Week*
55 and] **an** *Tel. Journal*
55 landscape,–] ~ – *Week*
57 haystacks,–] **hay stacks–** *Week* **haystacks,** *Oxford Book*
                  of Can. Verse
59 Ah,] **All** *Week* **Ah** *IDT*
59 rapture,–] ~ , *Week* ~ ! *Songs of the Great Dom., Can.*
                  Poems and Lays, Oxford Book of Can. Verse
59 Ah . . . rapture,–] omitted in *Tel. Journal*
60 winds . . . salt!] **wind . . . salt!–** *Week*
61 steps] ~ , *Week*
61 marshland,–] **marsh-lands,** *Week* **marsh land** *IDT*
62 off, . . . see,–] **off,– . . . see–** *Week*
63 Lest . . . sight] **Lest, . . . sight,** *Songs of the Great Dom., Can.*
                  Poems and Lays, Oxford Book of Can. Verse

Glossary

Tantramar: The Tantramar River flows near Sackville and Westcock in
        eastern New Brunswick.
22 *Cumberland Point:* now called Dorchester, a village west of
                        Westcock
25 *Minudie:* a village in Nova Scotia roughly across the Bay of Fundy
                  from Westcock

Pomeroy (pp. 52-3) reports that "The immediate result of his New York visit [1884] from a literary standpoint was two poems, 'La Belle Tromboniste' and 'The Poet is Bidden to Manhattan Island' . . . ." "La Belle Tromboniste," she says, was written "just for fun." It was first published in *Life* (May 21, 1885); and later appeared in *In Divers Tones,* 1886; and in *Cap and Bells,* 1936.

Variants

4	hair]	~ , *Life*
5	the]	**a** *Cap and Bells*
9	prodigal]	**liberal** *Life*
11	Or they]	**They** *Life*
12	quaff.]	~ ; *Life*
13	exert]	**exhaust** *Life*
17	chin]	**chair**— *Life*
18	(Not . . . !)]	**Not . . . !** *Life*
22	wet.]	~ , *Life*
28	Goodness]	**Goodness'** *Life*
30	ideal,]	~ — *Life*
31	steal—]	~ , *Life*
32	cake.]	~ ! *Life*
32	No italics appear in any line in *Cap and Bells.*	
38	call;—]	~ :— *Life*
39	petite, . . . tall—]	**petite . . . tall,** *Life*
42	pout]	**point** *Life*
43	and I know]	**and, I know,** *Life*
44	I]	(I is italicised in *Life* but not in *In Divers Tones.*)
46-47	On . . . me?—]	**Sit and toot, as thus, to me,/On her trombone tenderly?** *Life*
48	Ah,]	~ ! *Life* (entire line in italics)

See the Notes to "La Belle Tromboniste." The poem was initially published in *In Divers Tones,* 1886; and later appeared in the *King's College Record* (November, 1886); and in *Selected Poetry and Critical Prose,* 1974.

Variants
All variants are from the *King's College Record.*

1	lanes]	~ ,
3	swains]	~ ,
4	Knickerbocker]	**knickerbocker**
5	O]	**Ah,**

6	unuttered.] ~ ;
7	poet's] **Poet's**
8	buttered!] ~ .
9	Dream] **Think**
10	joy, . . . frolic.] **joy . . . frolic!**
13	poet's] **Poet's**
14	burly;–] ~
15	mind;] ~ ,–
16	early.] ~ !
17	sung, but ah, not seen–] **sung but never seen,–**
18	proper . . . Saturn–] **propor . . . Saturn**
21	poet's] **Poet's**
26	mark] **make**
27	horse–] ~ ,–
29	thousandfold] **thousand-fold**
30	But, . . . farm-yard] **But . . . farmyard**
31	drakes,] ~ ,–
32	make . . . drakes–] **make . . . drakes,**
33	Greengrocers here . . . read.] **Our green grocers . . . read;**
34	And] ~ ,
35	We lack not] **They'll find you**
38	poet's] **Poet's**
40	transformations!] ~ .
43	fields,] ~
44	new"– . . . Bowery!] **new" . . . Bowery**
46	now, . . . trust, . . . riper.] **now . . . trust . . . riper;**
48	piper.] ~ !

Glossary

3	*Phyllis:* a standard name in pastoral poetry.
4	*Knickerbocker:* originally referring to the Dutch settlers, the word is now used for any New Yorker.
18	*age of Saturn:* a period of unrestrained revelry.
20	*Arcadia:* a district in ancient Greece; it is frequently used in literature as a place of pastoral perfection.
26	*Proteus:* a sea god of Greek mythology capable of assuming various forms.
44	*"pastures new":* the last two words of the last line of John Milton's "Lycidas."
44	*Bowery:* a disreputable section of New York City.

p. 82 THE SOWER

The poem was initially published in *Manhattan Magazine* (July, 1884); and subsequently appeared in *In Divers Tones,* 1886; *American Sonnets,* 1889;

410

Later Canadian Poems, 1893; *Songs of the Common Day and Ave,* 1893; *Current Opinion* (June, 1894); *Poems,* 1901/7; *Oxford Book of Canadian Verse,* 1913; *Our Canadian Literature,* 1934; *Selected Poems,* 1936; *Selected Poems of Sir Charles G.D. Roberts,* 1955; *Poets of Confederation,* 1967; and *Selected Poetry and Critical Prose,* 1974. As well, the Rufus Hathaway Collection at the University of New Brunswick contains two unidentified clippings of the poem.

Pomeroy (p. 113) reports: "'The Sower,' which has probably been quoted most frequently in anthologies, was written for Millet's picture 'The Sower.' His friend, Richard Watson Gilder, had presented him with a fine copy which he framed and hung in his study."

Variants

| 1 | brown,] | ~ | *Manhattan Mag., IDT, Amer. Sonnets, Later Can. Poems, Current Opinion, Oxford Book of Can. Verse* |

1   brown,]   ~   *Manhattan Mag., IDT, Amer. Sonnets, Later Can.*
                                      Poems, Current Opinion, Oxford Book of Can. Verse

1   soil]   ~ ,   *Manhattan Mag., IDT, Amer. Sonnets, Later Can.*
                                        Poems, Current Opinion, Oxford Book of Can. Verse

3   sky-line,]   ~   *HC*(2)

4   aloft,]   ~   *Current Opinion, HC*(2)

7   here]   **there**   *HC*(2)

8   toil.]   ~ ;   *HC*(1)

9   glebe]   **field**   *Manhattan Mag.*

10   soil;]   ~ ,   *HC*(2)

10   though]   **tho'**   *IDT, Amer. Sonnets, Later Can. Poems, Current Opinion*

11   blind]   ~ , *HC*(1), *HC*(2)

13   in]   **from**   *HC*(1)

13   employ;–]   ~ ,–   *Manhattan Mag.*   ~ :–   *HC*(1)
                                          ~ ;   *HC*(2)

14   God-like]   **Godlike**   *IDT, Amer. Sonnets, Later Can. Poems,*
                                        Current Opinion, SOCDA, Poems 1901/7;
                                        Oxford Book of Can. Verse, Our Can. Lit.,
                                        HC(1)

Note: in *Current Opinion, Our Can. Lit.* and *HC*(2) the stanzas are not divided into octave and sestet

Glossary

9   *glebe:*   a field

p. 83 THE FOOTPATH

A holograph manuscript, evidently earlier than any printed text, is contained in the Queen's University Archives. In the manuscript the stanzas are numbered 1, 2, 3, 4, 5, 7, 6, 8, and the last stanza [9] is not numbered; MS stanzas 7 and 6 were never printed. The manuscript of "The Footpath" is followed, on the same page, by the manuscript of "Tides." Following "Tides" is Roberts' signature and the date October 3, 1884. It is unclear whether that date refers to both poems or to "Tides" only. The poem was first published in *In Divers Tones,* 1886; and was reprinted only in *Selected Poetry and Critical Prose,* 1974.

Variants

All variants are from the manuscript.

Title: The Footpath]   **The Foot-path**
  1   her . . . gone,]   **Her . . . gone**
  2   hill,]   **~ ;**
  3   hillside]   **hill-side**
  6   poplar-tree]   **poplar tree**
  7   blue]   **grey**
 10   drops and screams]   **drops & screams**
 11   Through]   **Thro'**
 12   Till . . . heaven]   **To my Paradise**
 13   Ah, . . . meet,]   **Ah . . . meet,–**
 14   I and she,–]   **I & she–**
 15   curious]   **open;**   *open* is written above *clustering* which has been crossed through
 17   Then, . . . house,]   **Ah . . . house**
 18   stars,–]   **moon,**
19-20   How . . . bars!]   **Whither, while no eye perceived,**
                                            You would lead, & leave me soon!
 20   After this stanza *MS* inserts:

7

Ah the beacon, gray with rain,
   In whose friendly shelter nigh
Strove our aching lips in vain,
   As we kissed, to say Good-bye!

6

Then how swift, alas, the night
   Ebbed, & came the unwelcome day,
And you led me from the light
   Of her loving eyes away!

 21   her]   **Her**
 24   still;]   **~ .–**
 25   she, my own,]   **She–My Own–**
 26   you, . . . allow.]   **you . . . allow;**
 28   Dare]   **Bear**

412

p. 84 IN NOTRE DAME

The poem was first published in *The Current*, 1884. Its only other appearance
was in *In Divers Tones*, 1886.

Variants
All variants are from *The Current*.
Title: In Notre Dame]   **In Notre Dame, 111 A.D.**
  1   you,]   ~ –
  6   beauty,–]   ~ –
  8   Hell or Heaven]   **hell or heaven**
 13   was. For]   **was; for**
 14   it) . . .^{2}mine!]   **it!) . . .^{2}mine**
 15   oh, my Sweet]   **O my sweet**
 16   wine!]   ~ .
 18   caresses.]   ~ : –
 21   her;]   ~ ,
 23   And]   ~ ,
 26   intense.]   ~ :
 27   queenlike,]   **queen-like;**
 28   Even . . . sense.]   **E'en . . . sense;**
 30   tears.]   ~ ;
 31   straight, and fair.]   **straight and fair;**
 34   eyes,]   ~ !
 35   love's sweetness lives]   **Love's nectar lies**
 38   emerald,–]   ~ –
 40   Heaven's . . . worse.]   **heaven's . . . worse!**
 41   bosom,–ah]   **bosom–ah,**
 42   resting-place!]   **nesting-place!–**
 45   Brittany]   ~ !

p. 85 CANADA

This poem presents one of the most interesting bibliographical entanglements
in Roberts' work. The holograph manuscript in the Rufus Hathaway Collection at the University of New Brunswick begins with a stanza which was later
deleted:

> O Thou whose young hands grasp the keys
>   To open half a continent,
> The waves of those confining seas
>   On two worlds' shores are turbulent!

In the manuscript, after this stanza had been crossed out, are numbers for
arranging the remaining stanzas. In the margin, but above the line "To front

413

the world alone" is the notation, "Insert here (3) the stanza beginning 'How long the indolence etc. CGDR.'" That stanza was the eleventh as the poem was originally written.

Two copies of a heretofore unnoticed printed text of the poem are contained in Roberts' scrapbook in the University of New Brunswick Library. This text predates all succeeding printings and has all of the indications of being a private printing, evidently prepared for personal circulation. It is printed on the two inner pages; the watermark says "Original Canadian Vellum" and contains the imprint of a beaver and a maple leaf. The outer pages are blank. At the end of the poem is Roberts' name and "Fredericton, N.B., January, 1885." The stanza "O Thou whose young hands grasp the keys" had not been deleted at the time of this printing, but the stanza "How long the indolence" has been moved from its earlier eleventh position to become the fourth stanza. All subsequent printings omit the opening manuscript-private printing stanza, and otherwise the arrangement of the stanzas remains constant.

The evidence of the manuscript and the private printing indicates a three part revision of the Hathaway manuscript. First, indication was given that the original stanza eleven should be placed in the fourth position. Then, it was decided to omit the opening stanza; but this decision was not made until after the private printing was prepared. Finally, Roberts renumbered the stanzas in the manuscript, re-ordering stanza eleven in accordance with the arrangement in the private printing, and making it stanza three after the opening stanza was crossed through.

After the private printing, the revised poem appeared in the Toronto *Globe* (January 4, 1886); *The University Monthly* (January 5, 1886); *Century* (January 31, 1886); and in *In Divers Tones,* 1886. As well, the Rufus Hathaway Collection contains another unidentified clipping of the poem identical with the text in the *Century.* Extracts of the poem, lines 1-16, were published in *The Magazine of Poetry* (January, 1889) and in *Canada* (January, 1891). The full poem was later printed in *Songs of the Great Dominion,* 1889; the "Appendix" to *Younger American Poets,* 1891; *Canadian Poems and Lays,* 1893; *Later Canadian Poems,* 1893; *A Victorian Anthology,* 1895; *Poems,* 1901/7; *Oxford Book of Can. Verse,* 1913; *Canadian Prose and Verse,* 1923; *Selected Poems,* 1936; *A Book of Canadian Poetry,* 1943/8; *Poetry of Freedom,* 1945; *Selected Poems of Sir Charles G.D. Roberts,* 1955; *Penguin Book of Canadian Verse,* 1967; and *Selected Poetry and Critical Prose,* 1974.

Pomeroy (pp. 67-8) says that Roberts' temporary devotion to the prospect of Canadian independence was brought to the fore through his work with and reaction to Goldwin Smith, an "apostle of annexation." Shortly, after the composition of "Canada," "Collect for Dominion Day" and "An Ode for the Canadian Confederacy," Roberts "became convinced that Independence would inevitably lead to Annexation, and that Canada's destiny lay within the Empire." Pomeroy also reports (p. xix) that "Canada" was "sung throughout the land as a sort of national anthem."

414

Variants

1 Child of Nations] **child of nations** *Globe, Univ. Monthly,*
                    Century, YAP, Oxford Book of Can. Verse

2 among] **amid** *MS, Globe, Univ. Monthly, Century*

2 now] ~ , *Univ. Monthly, Victorian Anth., Oxford Book of*
             Can. Verse

3 unadored] **unadorned** *Canada, Songs of the Great Dom., Can.*
             Poems and Lays, Oxford Book of Can. Verse, Can.
             Prose and Verse

4 brow,–] ~ !– *MS*   ~ ! *Globe, Univ. Monthly, Century*
             ~ : *Victorian Anth.*

6 own?] ~ ! *Globe*

10 fame,–] ~ – *Univ. Monthly, IDT, Mag. of Poetry, Canada, YAP,*
             Later Can. Poems, Oxford Book of Can. Verse
             ~ ; *Victorian Anth.*

12 name?] ~ ! *Globe*

14 manhood's] **Manhood's** *Oxford Book of Can. Verse*

15 slaves?] ~ ?– *MS*   ~ ! *Globe*

16 age.] ~ ! *MS, PP, Globe, Univ. Monthly, Century*

17 to] **in** *Globe*

18 Maple Wreath;] **maple-wreath;–** *MS*

18 Maple Wreath] **Maple-Wreath** *PP, IDT, Songs of the Great Dom.,*
             Can. Poems and Lays, Later Can. Poems,
             Victorian Anth., Oxford Book of Can. Verse
             maple-wreath *Globe, Century*
             maple wreath *Univ. Monthly*

20 beneath;] ~ ;– *MS, PP, Univ. Monthly, Century*

21 furthest] **farthest** *Globe, Univ. Monthly, Century*

23 breeze] ~ , *Globe, Univ. Monthly*

24 exhales.] ~ .– *MS*

25 Falterer,] ~ ! *MS, Globe, Univ. Monthly, Century*

26 future,–] ~ : *Victorian Anth.*

28 Champlain!] ~ . *Can. Poems and Lays*

30 Quebec,] ~ *Univ. Monthly*

30 citadel] ~ , *Globe, Univ. Monthly, Century*

33 Thou] **thou** *Globe, Univ. Monthly, Century, YAP*

34 Queenston] ~ , *IDT, Songs of the Great Dom., YAP, Can.*
             Poems and Lays, Later Can. Poems, Victorian
             Anth., Poems, 1901/7, Can. Prose and Verse

34 Lane,–] ~ – *Univ. Monthly*   ~ : *Victorian Anth.*
             ~ , *Oxford Book of Can. Verse*

36 vain!–] ~ ,– *MS, Globe, Univ. Monthly, Century*
             ~ ! *Oxford Book of Can. Verse, Can. Prose and Verse*

39 Chrysler's] **Chryslers'** *YAP*

39 Chateauguay,] ~ *Univ. Monthly*

40 ears?] ~ ! *Globe*

41   slopes,–]   ~ –   *Globe, Univ. Monthly, Century*
                   ~ ,   *Oxford Book of Can. Verse*
42   fall,–]   ~ –   *MS, PP, Globe, Univ. Monthly, Century*
                  ~ ,   *Oxford Book of Can. Verse*
43   tide–]   ~ ,–   *Victorian Anth.*   ~ ,   *Oxford Book of*
                         Can. Verse
44   call.]   ~ !   *MS, Globe, Univ. Monthly, Century*
45   wait]   **await**   *Can. Poems and Lays, Oxford Book of Can. Verse*
46   lands,–]   ~ .   *MS, Oxford Book of Can. Verse*   ~ ; –   *PP,*
                         IDT, Songs of the Great Dom., Can. Poems and Lays,
                         Later Can. Poems   ~ ;   *Globe, Univ. Monthly,*
                         Century, YAP, Victorian Anth.
48   sands.]   ~ !–   *MS*   ~ .–   *PP*
                  ~ !   *Globe, Univ. Monthly, Century*
49   O]   **Oh**   *Univ. Monthly*
49   Thy]   **thy**   *Globe, Univ. Monthly, Century*
52   streams.]   ~ ......   *MS*   ~ * * * * * *   *PP*
53   But]   –**But**   *PP*
53   country]   **Country**   *MS, PP, IDT, Songs of the Great Dom., YAP,*
                                  Can. Poems and Lays, Later Can. Poems, Victorian
                                  Anth., Oxford Book of Can. Verse
54   done,–]   ~ –   *Univ. Monthly*   ~ ;   *Oxford Book of Can. Verse*
55   breast,]   ~   *Globe, Univ. Monthly, Century*
55   o'er]   **on**   *Univ. Monthly*
55   brow,]   ~   *Globe, Univ. Monthly, Century*
56   sun]   **Sun**   *Oxford Book of Can. Verse*

Glossary
27   *Cartier:*   Jacques Cartier (1491?-c. 1557). A French navigator and
                    discoverer of the St. Lawrence River.
28   *Champlain:*   Samuel de Champlain (1567-1635). A French explorer,
                      the founder of Quebec, and the first French governor
                      of Canada.
29   *Montcalm and Wolfe:*   Louis Joseph, Marquis de Montcalm (1712-
                               1759) and James Wolfe (1727-1759). The French and
                               English Generals, respectively, of the Battle of Quebec;
                               both were killed in the battle.
34   *Queenston and Lundy's Lane:*   battle sites of the War of 1812.
39   *Chrysler's Farm and Chateauguay:*   other battle sites of the War of
                                             1812.
47-52   *And ... streams:*   A reference to the Canadian forces involved in
                               the Egyptian wars of the 1880's. Some Canadian
                               soldiers were in the army which attempted to relieve
                               General Gordon at Khartoum. See "Khartoum."

416

p. 87 MIST

The first surviving text of the poem is a manuscript (MSQ) held in the Queen's University Archives. The manuscript is an early version of the poem, and after Roberts' signature is the note: "In W.B.C.'s room, morning of Feb. 14th, 1885—(Sonnet tournament!) Subject set by Roberts. Form set by Carman." The revised poem first appeared in *In Divers Tones*, 1886. Another manuscript (MS-SOCD) now in the library of McGill University was prepared for the publication of *Songs of the Common Day* and appeared in that volume in 1893. The only other appearance of the poem was in *Poems*, 1901/7.

Variants
1   Its hand compassionate]   **It guards our sight, it**   *MSQ*
4   Strange]   **Weird**   *MSQ, IDT, MS-SOCD, SOCDA*
4   light.]   ~ .—   *MSQ*
10   And ah . . . ah]   **And Ah! . . . Ah**   *MSQ*
      And, ah! . . . ah!   *SOCDA*

p. 87 TO MY FRIEND, EDMUND COLLINS

The poem first appeared in *Rouge et Noir* (March, 1885); and was the dedicatory poem to *In Divers Tones*, 1886.

Variants
All variants are from *Rouge et Noir*.
Title: To My Friend, Edmund Collins]   **Rondel—"In Divers Tones."/**
                                              (To J.E.C.)

2   ear!]   ~ ,
5   near,]   ~ , —
6   heart . . . spring,]   **breast . . . spring,—**
8   ear!]   ~ .   Also line 14
9   thing—]   ~ ,—
12   tear.]   ~ ;

Glossary
Edmund Collins: Joseph Edmund Collins (1855-1892) was a newspaper
                    editor in Fredericton and Chatham and later a journalist
                    for the Toronto *Globe*.

p. 88 TO BLISS CARMAN

The poem was first published in *The University Monthly* (April, 1885) and later appeared in *In Divers Tones*, 1886. In the *University Monthly,* the poem

417

is the second half of "Two Quatrains." See "On Reading the Poems of Sidney Lanier." The *M* in the dedication "To M.B.C. . . ." is probably an inverted *W*.

Variants
Title: To Bliss Carman]   **II. / To M.B.C., With a Copy of Lang's**
                                "Helen of Troy" *Univ. Monthly*
1   new sung]   **new-sung** *Univ. Monthly*

Glossary
Lang: Andrew Lang (1844-1912) was an English anthropologist, Greek
           scholar, historian, journalist, poet, and novelist. His "Helen of
           Troy" was a long narrative poem in six books published in 1882.

p. 88 ON READING THE POEMS OF SIDNEY LANIER

The poem was first published in *The University Monthly* (April, 1885); and later appeared in *In Divers Tones,* 1886. A manuscript of the poem, now in The Sidney Lanier Papers, Special Collections, Tulane University, was included in a letter from Roberts to Mrs. Lanier dated February 7, 1886. In *The University Monthly,* the poem is the first half of "Two Quatrains." See "To Bliss Carman."

Variants
Title: On Reading the Poems of Sidney Lanier]   **Two Quatrains/ I./**
          To Sidney Laurier *Univ. Monthly*   **On Reading the**
          "Poems of Sidney Lanier" *MS*
1   Flute-player, that]   **Flute-Player! That** *Univ. Monthly*
                             Flute-player! That *MS*
2   sign!]   ~ :   *Univ. Monthly*   ~ ;– *MS*
3   Tho']   **Though** *Univ. Monthly, MS*
4   line.]   ~ !   *Univ. Monthly*

Glossary
Sidney Lanier: See "To the Memory of Sidney Lanier."

p. 88 TIDES

A holograph manuscript (MSP), evidently earlier than any printed text, signed by Roberts is preserved in the holdings of the Historical Society of Pennsylvania. The poem was first published in *The Century Magazine* (August, 1885); and later appeared in *In Divers Tones,* 1886; and *American Sonnets,* 1889. Another holograph manuscript (MS-SOCD) is contained in the partial manuscript book of *Songs of the Common Day* at McGill University. Later the poem was published in *Songs of the Common Day and Ave,* 1893; *Poems,* 1901/7; and *Selected Poetry and Critical Prose,* 1974.

Variants
1   still]   **quiet** *MSP*
1   out,]   ~ *Amer. Sonnets, MS-SOCD, SOCDA*
6   amid the waste]   **in the dead waste** *MSP*
8   noon-heats]   **noon heats** *MS-SOCD, SOCDA*
8   drought.]   ~ ! *MSP, Century*
12   night-watches]   **night watches** *MS-SOCD, SOCDA*
13   ere]   **are** *SOCDA*

p. 89 PROMISE

The poem first appeared in the *King's College Record* (November, 1885); and was later published in *In Divers Tones,* 1886; and *The Iceberg and Other Poems,* 1934. A note in the *King's College Record* says that it was read by Roberts before the Haliburton Club on November 21, 1885. In one of Roberts' manuscript books is a marginal note that the poem was revised in 1932.

Variants
Title: Promise]   **Foretellings** *King's Coll. Rec.*   **A Herald** *IDT*
1   spring]   **Spring** *King's Coll. Rec., IDT*
2   Over]   **O'er** *King's Coll. Rec., IDT*
5   That the winds hush to hear,—]   **That winds are hushed to hear.**
         King's Coll. Rec.   **Till winds are hushed to hear,—** *IDT*
         That winds are hushed to hear,— *MS*
8   Presence through]   **herald thro'** *King's Coll. Rec., IDT*
         Presence thro' *MS*
9   the boon]   **a boon—** *King's Coll. Rec., IDT*
11   Elusive]   **Subtle** *King's Coll. Rec., IDT*
11   though]   **tho'** *King's Coll. Rec.*
12   can I trust that word.—]   **sweetly sure the word!** *King's Coll. Rec.*
         sweetly sure that word; *IDT*
13   Even . . . soul . . . heard,]   **E'en . . . heart . . . heard** *King's Coll.
         Rec., IDT*
14   Athwart . . . wintry lea,]   **Over . . . frosty lea** *King's Coll. Rec.*
         (Over . . . frosty lea) *IDT*   **Across . . . wintry lea,** *MS*
15   Immortality.]   **immortality!** *King's Coll. Rec.*

p. 89 COLLECT FOR DOMINION DAY

According to Pomeroy (pp. 67-8) the poem was written "within a few months" of January, 1885. See "Canada" for Pomeroy's comments on Roberts' political thought at the time. The poem first appeared in *The Century Magazine* (July, 1886); and was later published in *In Divers Tones,* 1886; *Songs of the Great Dominion,* 1889; the "Appendix" to *Younger American Poets,* 1891; *The Dominion Illustrated Magazine* (November, 1891); the calendar for 1893 designed and published by the Toronto Art Students' League; *Canadian Poems and Lays,* 1893; *Poems,* 1901/7; the Toronto *Globe* (July 1, 1926); and *Selected Poems,* 1936. As well, an unidentified clipping, related to the printing in *Songs of the Great Dominion* or *Canadian Poems and Lays,* survives in the Rufus Hathaway Collection at the University of New Brunswick. Roberts evidently intended, at one time, to include the poem in *Songs of the Common Day* as a holograph manuscript is contained in the McGill University partial manuscript book prepared for that publication. The plan was changed and the poem did not appear in that volume.

Variants

Title: Collect for Dominion Day]   **Dominion Day**   *Globe*
1   nations]   **Nations**   *Songs of the Great Dom., Can. Poems and Lays, HC*
1   Help]   **help**   *Globe*
1   hand!]   ~ ,   *Songs of the Great Dom., Can. Poems and Lays, HC, 1893 Calendar*
2   to]   **To**   *MS, Globe*
2   kneel!]   ~ .   *Globe*
3   destroyer]   **Destroyer**   *1893 Calendar*
3   command]   ~ ,   *YAP*
4   tremble]   ~ ,   *1893 Calendar*
4   reel!]   ~ .   *Globe*
5   low]   **bow**   *Globe*
6   proud,]   ~ ;   *Songs of the Great Dom., Can. Poems and Lays, HC*
         ~ –   *Globe*
8   strong,]   ~   *Songs of the Great Dom., Can. Poems and Lays, HC, 1893 Calendar*
8   stern,–]   ~ ,   *Songs of the Great Dom., Can. Poems and Lays, HC, 1893 Calendar, Globe*
8   bowed!]   ~ .   *Globe*
9   unity]   **Unity**   *1893 Calendar*
9   unity,]   **Unity!**   *Globe*
9   make]   **Make**   *Globe*
10   flame,–]   ~ ,   *1893 Calendar*   ~   *Globe*
11   thine]   **Thine**   *Century, Songs of the Great Dom., Can. Poems and Lays, HC, 1893 Calendar*
11   thine]   **their**   *YAP*
11   This line is omitted in the *Globe.*
12   shame;]   ~   *Songs of the Great Dom., 1893 Calendar*
13   fever]   **feud**   *Dom. Ill.*

Glossary

11-14   *Whose . . . name.:*   A reference to the North West Rebellion of 1884-5, headed by Louis Riel (1844-85) who had earlier organized the Red River Rebellion (1869-70). Riel surrendered on May

420

15, 1885; he was tried for treason and subsequently hanged on November 16, 1885. The execution was held to be an act of injustice on the part of the Ontario government by many, particularly in Quebec, who considered Riel a champion attempting to preserve French culture.

p. 90 AN ODE FOR THE CANADIAN CONFEDERACY

According to Pomeroy (pp. 67-8) the poem was written in early 1885. It was first published in *In Divers Tones*, 1886; and later appeared in *Songs of the Great Dominion*, 1889; *Raise the Flag and Other Patriotic Canadian Songs and Poems*, 1891; *A Treasury of Canadian Verse*, 1900; *Poems*, 1901/7; *Canadian Prose and Verse*, 1923; *Selected Poems*, 1936; and *Selected Poetry and Critical Prose*, 1974. Pomeroy also reports (p. 68) that the poem was set to music by Arthur K. Putland and presented on June 12, 1938 over the national network of the Canadian Broadcasting Corporation.

Variants

1   country,]   ~ !   *Raise the Flag;* also line 13
3   range]   ~ ,   *Raise the Flag*
12   done.]   ~ !   *Raise the Flag*
15   keen]   ~ ,   *Songs of the Great Dom.*
17   Tho']   **Though**   *Raise the Flag*
17   cry]   ~ ,   *Songs of the Great Dom.*   ~ –   *Raise the Flag*
20   name,–]   ~ ;–   *IDT, Songs of the Great Dom., Treasury of Can.*
                        Verse   ~ ;   *Raise the Flag*
23   hand]   ~ ,   *Raise the Flag*
24   earth,]   ~ ,–   *Songs of the Great Dom.*   ~   *Raise the Flag*
24   land!]   ~ .   *Raise the Flag*
25   O]   ~ ,   *Raise the Flag;* also line 33
29   well]   **will**   *Treasury of Can. Verse*
30   those]   **these**   *Can. Prose and Verse*
36   Child of Nations]   **child of nations**   *Raise the Flag*

Glossary

3   *Laurentian:*   The Laurentian Mountains are in eastern Canada between the St. Lawrence River and Hudson Bay.

p. 91 THE POTATO HARVEST

A holograph manuscript, signed by Roberts and dated April 7, 1886, is preserved in the Queen's University Archives. The poem was first published in *In Divers Tones*, 1886; and subsequently appeared in *American Sonnets*, 1889; *Songs of the Common Day and Ave*, 1893; *Poems*, 1901/7; *The Oxford Book of Canadian Verse,* 1913; *Our Canadian Literature,* 1934; *Selected Poems,* 1936; *A Pocketful of Canada,* 1946; *Canadian Poems 1850-1952,* 1953; *Selected Poems of Sir Charles G.D. Roberts,* 1955; *Poets of Confederation,* 1967; and *Selected Poetry and Critical Prose,* 1974.

Variants

6 snake-fence]   ~ ,   *MS, IDT, Amer. Sonnets, SOCDA, Poems* 1901/7, *Oxford Book of Can. Verse, Our Can. Lit.*

7 pond]   ~ ,   *MS, IDT, Amer. Sonnets, SOCDA, Poems* 1901/7, *Oxford Book of Can. Verse, Our Can. Lit.*

8 supper horn.]   **supper-horn!** *MS*

10 beside]   ~ ,   *MS, IDT, Amer. Sonnets, Oxford Book of Can. Verse*

11 harvest-folk]   **harvest folk**   *IDT, Amer. Sonnets, Oxford Book of Can. Verse*

13 thunders. Down]   **thunders; down**   *MS, IDT, Amer. Sonnets, Oxford Book of Can. Verse*

13 hillside]   **hill-side**   *MS, Oxford Book of Can. Verse*

14 wain, . . . smoke.]   **wain;– . . . smoke!**   *MS*

Note: in *Our Canadian Literature* the stanzas are not divided into an octave and sestet

Glossary

14   *wain:* a cart or wagon.

p. 91 DARK

A manuscript copy of the poem (MSQ) dated September 16, 1886, and signed by Roberts is preserved in the Queen's University Archives. The poem was first published in *In Divers Tones,* 1886. Another holograph manuscript, unsigned and undated, prepared for the publication of *Songs of the Common Day* (MS-SOCD) is held by McGill University. The poem appeared in *Songs of the Common Day and Ave,* 1893; *Poems,* 1901/7; and *Selected Poems,* 1936.

Variants

3 free,–]   ~ ,   *MSQ*

5 ev'n]   **even**   *MSQ, MS-SOCD, SOCDA.* In *MS-SOCD, ev'n* has been crossed through and *even* written above it.

7 Ev'n]   **E'en** *MSQ*   **Even**   *MS-SOCD, SOCDA.* In *MS-SOCD,* the second *e* in *Even* has been written over an apostrophe.

9 thou,]   ~ , –   *MSQ*

10 The]   **This**   *MSQ*

11 desire and dream]   **desire & dream**   *MSQ*

14 gusts . . . rain!]   **drifts . . . rain.**   *MSQ*

p. 92 AFLOAT

The poem was published only in *In Divers Tones,* 1886.

Glossary
46   *nepenthe:* a drug or potion which, according to ancient writers, brought forgetfulness of sorrow or trouble.
86   *seventh . . . sphere:* in the old cosmology, there were nine spheres; the seventh was the sphere of the stars and beyond it was only the invisible Primum Mobile and the Empyrean or place of God.

p. 94 BIRCH AND PADDLE

The poem was first published in *In Divers Tones,* 1886; and subsequently appeared in *Songs of the Great Dominion,* 1889; *Canadian Poems and Lays,* 1893; *Poems,* 1901/7; *Selected Poems,* 1936; and *Selected Poetry and Critical Prose,* 1974.

Variants
6   Where]   **When**   *IDT, Songs of the Great Dom., Can. Poems and Lays*
19   left . . . unstirred]   **left, . . . unstirred,**   *Songs of the Great Dom., Can. Poems and Lays*
43   serene]   ~ ,   *Songs of the Great Dom., Can. Poems and Lays*
49   tune]   **tone**   *Poems* 1901/7
51   eyes]   ~ ,   *Songs of the Great Dom., Can. Poems and Lays*
58   face!]   ~   *Can. Poems and Lays*

Glossary
20   *phœbe-bird:* a small bird, also called the pewit or peewee

p. 96 A BIRTHDAY BALLADE

The poem appeared only in *In Divers Tones,* 1886.

p. 97 A BLUE VIOLET

The poem appeared in *In Divers Tones,* 1886; and in *The Vagrant of Time,* 1927.

Variants
All variants are from *In Divers Tones.*

Title: A]   **The**
1   ere]   **as**
4   hollows,]   ~ ,–
9   thee,]   ~ ,–
11   Ah ... *me*]   **But** ... me
12   perfume vagrants!]   **perfume-vagrants.**
16   to.]   ~ !

p. 97 A BREAK

The poem was published only in *In Divers Tones,* 1886.

p. 98 CONSOLATION

The poem originally appeared in *In Divers Tones;* 1886, and was reprinted only in *Selected Poetry and Critical Prose,* 1974.

p. 98 THE DEPARTING OF GLUSKÂP

The poem first appeared in *In Divers Tones,* 1886; and was later published in the *King's College Record* (December, 1886); *Songs of the Great Dominion,* 1889; *Canadian Poems and Lays,* 1893; *Poems,* 1901/7; and *Selected Poetry and Critical Prose,* 1974. In Roberts' 1891 *Canadian Guide-Book* (p. 158) he calls the poem "a Melicite 'Passing of Arthur.'"

Variants
Title: The Departing of Gluskâp]   **The Departing of Clote Scarp**   *IDT, King's Coll. Rec., Songs of the Great Dom., Can. Poems and Lays*
1   well-nigh]   **well nigh**   *IDT, King's Coll. Rec., Songs of the Great Dom.*
19   done]   ~ ,   *Songs of the Great Dom., Can. Poems and Lays*
26   Gluskâp]   **Clote Scarp**   *IDT, King's Coll. Rec., Songs of the Great Dom., Can. Poems and Lays*   also line 32
30   shore,]   ~   *King's Coll. Rec.*
33   little,]   ~   *IDT, King's Coll. Rec., Songs of the Great Dom., Can. Poems and Lays*
34   vanished]   **melted**   *King's Coll. Rec.*
35   beasts]   **beast**   *King's Coll. Rec.*
36   sailed,]   ~ ;   *King's Coll. Rec.*
38   where]   **when**   *King's Coll. Rec.*
41   Lo! on]   **Lo, in**   *King's Coll. Rec.*
43   again ... day]   italicized in *King's Coll. Rec.*

424

Glossary
Gluskâp: A giant and a cultural hero of the Micmac Indians; the same figure is called Clote Scarp by the Melicites.

p. 99   IMPULSE

The poem appeared only in *In Divers Tones,* 1886.

Glossary
15   *rede:* advice or plan

p. 100 THE ISLES—AN ODE

The poem was first published in *In Divers Tones,* 1886; and later appeared in the "Appendix" to *Younger American Poets,* 1891; and *A Victorian Anthology,* 1895.

Variants
6   herald,]   ~   *YAP*   **heralds**   *Victorian Anth.*
19   sight.]   ~ ;   *YAP*
20   tho']   **though**   *Victorian Anth.*
20   hid–]   ~   *YAP*   ~ ,   *Victorian Anth.*
28   tho']   **though**   *Victorian Anth.*
32   Shakspere]   **Shakespeare**   *YAP, Victorian Anth.*
34   Song of Songs]   **song of songs**   *YAP*
Note: in *A Victorian Anthology* the stanzas are not numbered

Glossary
28-34   *Here . . . them:*   Homer (ca. 1050-850 B.C.), author of *The Iliad* and *The Odyssey,* was, according to tradition, blind; Milton of course was also blind. "Omar's deep doubts" is a reference to Omar Khayyàm's (ca. 1050-1123) *Rubàiyàt,* first translated into English by Edward Fitzgerald in 1859. *The Rubàiyàt* concerns Omar's thoughts on the mysteries of existence and his Epicurean advice to eat, drink, and be merry while life lasts. *The Song of Songs* (also *The Song of Solomon*) is a poetic book of the Old Testament, the subject of which is human love and courtship.

p. 101 KHARTOUM

The poem was first published in *In Divers Tones,* 1886. It later appeared in the "Appendix" to *Younger American Poets,* 1891; and in *Poems,* 1901/7.

8   horde!]   ~ .   *YAP*

12   moods]   **mood**   *IDT, YAP*

Glossary

Khartoum: The capital of the Egyptian Sudan.

7   *Gordon:*   Charles George Gordon (1833-1885) was the English General in charge of the defense of Khartoum. He was killed when the beseiged city fell to the forces of El Mahdi in 1885.

p. 101 LIBERTY

The third stanza of the poem was quoted by Roberts, in French and in English, in his Alumni Address at the University of New Brunswick Encaenia in May, 1883. The entire speech on "The Beginnings of Canadian Literature" was printed in the St. John *Daily Telegraph* (June 29, 1883) and in *The University Monthly* (June, 1883). The full text of the poem first appeared in *In Divers Tones,* 1886; and has been reprinted only in *Selected Poetry and Critical Prose,* 1974.

Variants

All variants are from the Alumni Address. The *Daily Telegraph* and *University Monthly* texts are identical.

20   meteor]   ~ ,   The reading is considerably altered by the presence or absence of this comma. For purposes of comparison, the French text is:

> Quand j'apercois dans les fastes du monde,
> Comme un eclair, briller le doigt de Dieu.

20   dark]   In this exceptional instance I have departed from the practice of following the copy text precisely. No period appears after *dark* in *In Divers Tones,* but the syntax obviously requires one. A period does appear in the *Daily Telegraph* and *University Monthly.*

22   immortality,–]   ~ ,

Glossary

Louis Honore Frèchette: see "Rondeau."

p. 102 THE MARVELLOUS WORK

The poem was published only in *In Divers Tones,* 1886.

36   *Silurian:*   pertaining to an early Paleozoic geological period following the Ordovician period and preceding the Devonian.

37   *Devonian:*   the geological period preceding the Carboniferous or
Mississippian period.

41   *Triassic:*   The earliest division of the Mesozoic era. In all these
references Roberts is moving from the time of the Crea-
tion to the evolutionary appearance of man.

p. 104 ON THE CREEK

The poem first appeared in *In Divers Tones*, 1886; and was later published in
Songs of the Great Dominion, 1889; *Later Canadian Poems*, 1893; *Poems*,
1901/7; *Selected Poems*, 1936; and *Selected Poetry and Critical Prose*, 1974.

Variants

2   cease.]   ∼ ;   *Songs of the Great Dom.*
10   dips.]   ∼ ;   *Songs of the Great Dom.*
12   slips,]   ∼ .   *Songs of the Great Dom.*
22   plumes;]   ∼   *Songs of the Great Dom.*
24   glooms,]   ∼ .   *Songs of the Great Dom.*
27   spirits]   ∼ ,   *Songs of the Great Dom.*
33   gum,]   ∼   *Songs of the Great Dom.*
34   Breath of the]   **From clammy**   *IDT, Songs of the Great Dom.,*
Later Can. Poems
38   wings.]   ∼ ;   *Songs of the Great Dom.*
39   *chirr*]   not italicized in *IDT, Songs of the Great Dom.* or *Later*
Can. Poems
41   sere]   ∼ ,   *Songs of the Great Dom.*
46   retreat.]   ∼ ;   *IDT, Songs of the Great Dom., Later Can. Poems*
50   wing.]   ∼ ;–   *IDT, Later Can. Poems*
∼ :–   *Songs of the Great Dom.*
54   regain.]   ∼ ;   *Songs of the Great Dom.*
60   street;]   ∼ .   *Songs of the Great Dom.*

p. 106 ON THE LAGOON

The poem was first published in *In Divers Tones*, 1886; and later appeared in
The University Monthly (January, 1887) and in *The Vagrant of Time*, 1927.

Variants

Title: On the Lagoon]   **Nocturne**   *IDT, Univ. Monthly*
3   smooth,]   ∼ ,–   *IDT*   ∼ ;   *Univ. Monthly*
5   purpling]   **charmèd**   *IDT*   **mystic**   *Univ. Monthly*

6   Breathe]   **Puff**   *IDT, Univ. Monthly*
6   from]   **of**   *Univ. Monthly*
6   land,]   ~ ,–   *IDT, Univ. Monthly*
7   Till]   ~ ,   *IDT, Univ. Monthly*
7   lights]   ~ ,   *Univ. Monthly*
8-9   These are a single line in *IDT* and *Univ. Monthly*
10   The]   **A**   *IDT, Univ. Monthly*
12   snows.]   ~ ;   *Univ. Monthly*
14   The]   **A**   *IDT, Univ. Monthly*
15   half swoon]   **half-swoon**   *IDT*
16   Till . . . us]   **And thin moon-shades pace out to us**   *IDT, Univ. Monthly*
17   drift]   ~ ,   *IDT, Univ. Monthly*
17-18   These are a single line in *IDT* and *Univ. Monthly*
19   musk-rose]   **night-wide**   *IDT, Univ. Monthly*
20   the]   omitted in *IDT* and *Univ. Monthly*
21   Glide . . . of]   **Set outward voyaging**   *IDT*
                        Set seaward voyaging   *Univ. Monthly*
21   perfumes.]   ~ ,   *Univ. Monthly*
23   shadowy trees,]   **shadowed trees,–**   *IDT, Univ. Monthly*
24   night spell]   **night-spell**   *IDT, Univ. Monthly*
24   these,]   ~ ;   *Univ. Monthly*
25   Dear . . . sleep, but]   **Love . . . sleep,–we**   *IDT, Univ. Monthly*
26-27   Dissolved . . . dream.]   **To smile a little, dream, and dream.**   *IDT*
                        To smile a little, dream and dream.   *Univ. Monthly*
26-27   These are a single line in *IDT* and *Univ. Monthly*

p. 106 THE QUELLING OF THE MOOSE

The poem was first published in *In Divers Tones,* 1886; and later appeared in *Poems of Wild Life* (edited by Roberts) 1888; and *Selected Poetry and Critical Prose,* 1974.

Variants
7   Moose]   **moose**   *IDT*
11   straws]   **straw**   *IDT*
18   friend]   **Friend**   *IDT*
27   Moose]   **moose**   *IDT*
37   stood,]   ~ .   *IDT*
40   ceased. And]   **ceased; and**   *IDT*
42   hand.]   ~ !

Glossary
16   *Clote Scarp:*   See "The Departing of Gluskâp."
19   *Oolastook:*   the Indian name for the St. John river. In *Poems of Wild Life,* the spelling is Dolastook, an obvious misprint.

428

p. 108 RAIN

The poem was first published in *In Divers Tones*, 1886; and later appeared in *The Magazine of Poetry* (January, 1889); *Songs of the Common Day and Ave*, 1893; *Poems*, 1901/7; and *Selected Poetry and Critical Prose*, 1974. A manuscript of the poem survives in the McGill University partial manuscript book of *Songs of the Common Day*. In Roberts' copy of the 1901 text of *Poems*, in the Harriet Irving Library at the University of New Brunswick, line eleven "Thro' time and bitter distance" is underlined and written in the margin is, "for D C 1-16-40."

Variants

3	fro]	~ ,	*SOCDA*
4	Wave, and unweave,]	**Wave and unweave**	*MS, SOCDA*
5	plain,—]	~ —	*IDT, Mag. of Poetry*
9	if]	**If**	*MS, SOCDA*
11	Thro']	**Through**	*MS, SOCDA*
12	Her]	**her**	*SOCDA*
13	thro']	**through**	*SOCDA*
13	She]	**she**	*SOCDA*

p. 108 RECKONING

The poem was published only in *In Divers Tones*, 1886.

p. 109 SALT

The poem first appeared in *In Divers Tones*, 1886; and was later published in the *King's College Record* (February, 1887); the "Appendix" to *Younger American Poets*, 1891; and *Poems*, 1901/7.

Variants

5	strife,]	~ ;	*King's Coll. Rec.*
8	Failure,]	~	*King's Coll. Rec., YAP*
9	or]	**nor**	*King's Coll. Rec.*
10	free;]	~ ,	*YAP*
13	heart,]	~ !	*YAP*

p. 109 A SERENADE

The poem was first published in *In Divers Tones*, 1886; and later appeared in *Poems*, 1901/7; and *Selected Poetry and Critical Prose*, 1974.

p. 110 A SONG OF DEPENDENCE

The poem was published only in *In Divers Tones*, 1886.

p. 110 TO A LADY, AFTER HEARING HER READ KEATS' "NIGHTINGALE"

The poem was published only in *In Divers Tones*, 1886.

p. 111 TO S——— M———

The poem appeared only in *In Divers Tones*, 1886.

Glossary

Herrick: Robert Herrick (1591-1674), poet, the author of *Hesperides* and *Noble Numbers*. His best known poems are probably "Corinna's Going A-Maying" and "To Virgins, to Make Much of Time" with its opening line, "Gather ye rosebuds while ye may."

2 *Musæus:* a legendary Greek poet, supposedly the student of Orpheus; also a Greek poet c. 500 A.D., author of a poem on Hero and Leander, the source of Marlowe's poem on the same subject.

3 and 9 *rose, myrtle, laurel, bay:* wreathes made of any of these plants are standard headdresses associated with poets.

7 *Castaly:* Castalia; a spring on Mount Parnassus in Greece, named for the maiden Castalia who drowned in it while trying to escape the amorous pursuit of Apollo.

7 *Daphne:* another maiden fleeting the romantic advances of Apollo; she sought help from the gods and was changed into a laurel which hence became the favorite tree of Apollo.

p. 111 TOUT OU RIEN

The poem was published only in *In Divers Tones*, 1886.

p. 112 WINTER GERANIUMS

The poem appeared only in *In Divers Tones*, 1886.

430

2   *Magian:* referring to the Magi, either those who visited the infant
     Jesus or Zoroastrian priests of Ancient Media and Persia
     who were reputed to possess supernatural powers.

p. 112 MOTHER OF NATIONS

The poem was published only in the *King's College Record* (June, 1887).
Pomeroy (p. 68) says that it was written about 1886 and marks the transition
of Roberts from an advocate of independence to one who believed that
Canada's destiny lay within the Empire. She further reports that the poem
was not "considered by the author himself as worthy of inclusion in any
volume of his verse . . . . "

p. 113 A SONG OF CHEER

The poem was first published in *The Century Magazine* (January, 1888); and
subsequently appeared in *Songs of the Common Day and Ave,* 1893; and
Poems, 1901/7. A transcript of the poem in the same hand as "How the Mohawks Set Out for Medoctec" is preserved by McGill University. The transcript
was prepared for the publication of *Songs of the Common Day.*

Variants

1	up]	~ ,	*Century*		
2	tree;]	~ .	*Century*		
4	free;]	~ .	*Century*		
5	field]	~ ,	*Century*		
6	Clear . . . horn,]	**Clear, . . . horn;**	*Century*		
10	done,]	~ ;	*Century*		
12	sun;]	~ ,	*MS, SOCDA*		
15	strength,]	~ ;	*Century*		
17	goldenrod]	**golden-rod**	*Century*	**golden rod**	*MS, SOCDA*
18	hills.]	~ ;	*Century*		
19	Tho']	**Tho**	*SOCDA*		
23	That]	~ ,	*Century*		

p. 114 HOW THE MOHAWKS SET OUT FOR MEDOCTEC

The poem was first published in *The Century Magazine* (June, 1888); and
later appeared in *Progress* (June 9, 1888); *Poems of Wild Life,* 1888; *Songs of
the Great Dominion,* 1889; *Songs of the Common Day and Ave,* 1893; *Poems,*
1901/7; *Selected Poems,* 1936; and *Selected Poetry and Critical Prose,* 1974.
A scribal transcript, prepared for the publication of *Songs of the Common*

Day, is preserved at McGill University. The scribe was, perhaps, Annie Prat, Roberts' occasional secretary, and the transcript has been corrected by Roberts. The transcript was probably copied from the printing in *Poems of Wild Life* as "waves"—line 65—was omitted and later added by Roberts.

Variants
The headnote does not appear until the publication in *Poems of Wild Life.* In that text and in *Songs of the Great Dominion,* "downstream" is simply "down."

4   light.]   ~ !   *Century, Progress, Poems of Wild Life, Songs of the Great Dom., MS*   ~   *SOCDA*

8   four score,]   **four-score**   *Century, Progress*

9   Oolastook,]   ~   *Century, Progress, Poems of Wild Life, Songs of the Great Dom., MS*

23   die—]   ~ ,—   *Century, Progress*

26   devils']   **devil's**   *Century, Progress*

28   grates.]   ~ !   *Century, Progress*

31   captives]   **captives'**   *Poems of Wild Life, Songs of the Great Dom., MS*

32   well;]   ~ :   *Century, Progress, Poems of Wild Life, Songs of the Great Dom., MS, SOCDA, Poems* 1901/7

61   But]   ~ —   *Century, Progress, Poems of Wild Life, Songs of the Great Dom., MS, SOCDA*

65   waves]   omitted in *Poems of Wild Life*

68   despair,]   ~ .   *Poems of Wild Life, Songs of the Great Dom.*

69   shrills.]   ~ ..... *MS*   ~ ... *SOCDA*

71   skies]   ~ .   *Progress*

Glossary
The locations in the poem are along the St. John River, the Oolastook in the poem. The village of Madawaska is now in the state of Maine.

p. 116 BURNT LANDS

The first located publication of the poem was in *The Maple Leaf* (November 22, 1888). *The Maple Leaf* indicates that the poem had earlier appeared in *America,* but a search of that periodical has proven fruitless. After its appearance in *The Maple Leaf,* the poem was published in *Progress* (December, 1888); *Songs of the Great Dominion,* 1889; *Canadian Poems and Lays,* 1893; *Songs of the Common Day and Ave,* 1893; *A Victorian Anthology,* 1895; *Poems,* 1901/7; *Selected Poems,* 1936; and *Selected Poetry and Critical Prose,* 1974.

Variants
2   her]   **the**   *Progress*
2   blue,—]   ~ —   *Maple Leaf, Progress*

432

2   fields]   **scenes**   *Songs of the Great Dom., Can. Poems and Lays, Victorian Anth.*

3   cheer of summer]   **summer cheer of**   *Songs of the Great Dom., Can. Poems and Lays*

3   summer]   **Summer**   *Victorian Anth.*

4   scorn.]   ~ ;   *Maple Leaf*

3   bees,]   ~ .   *Maple Leaf*

5   adorn;]   ~ :   *Progress*

8   stern]   ~ ,   *Maple Leaf*

9   change.]   ~ ;   *Maple Leaf, Songs of the Great Dom., Can. Poems and Lays, Victorian Anth.*

10   spring . . . autumn]   **Spring . . . Autumn**   *Maple Leaf, SOCDA*

10   year]   **years**   *Songs of the Great Dom., Can. Poems and Lays*

11   Perchance]   **Surely**   *Songs of the Great Dom., Can. Poems and Lays*

12   Through]   **Thro'**   *Maple Leaf, Songs of the Great Dom., Can. Poems and Lays*

12   dreams,–]   ~ –   *Maple Leaf*

Note: in *A Victorian Anthology* the stanzas are not divided into an octave and sestet

p. 117 FROGS

The poem first appeared in *The Dominion Illustrated Magazine* (November, 1888); and was later published in *Songs of the Great Dominion*, 1889; *Canadian Poems and Lays*, 1893; *Songs of the Common Day and Ave*, 1893; *Poems*, 1901/7; *Selected Poems*, 1936; and *Selected Poetry and Critical Prose*, 1974.

Variants

1   Here]   ~ ,   *Songs of the Great Dom., Can. Poems and Lays*

2   weeds]   ~ ,   *Dom. Ill.*

3   heavens,]   ~   *Songs of the Great Dom., Can. Poems and Lays*

4   splendour]   **splendours**   *Dom. Ill.*

4   dyeing.]   ~ !   *Songs of the Great Dom., Can. Poems and Lays*

9   passion]   ~ ,   *Dom. Ill., Songs of the Great Dom., Can. Poems and Lays*

9   peace,]   ~ ;   *Songs of the Great Dom., Can. Poems and Lays*

10   taint.]   ~ !   *Songs of the Great Dom., Can. Poems and Lays*

11   tired ears]   **tirèd ears,**   *Songs of the Great Dom., Can. Poems and Lays*

13   tired eyelids]   **tirèd eye-lids,**   *Songs of the Great Dom., Can. Poems and Lays*

14   visions–]   ~ ,–   *Dom. Ill., Songs of the Great Dom., Can. Poems and Lays*

14   cease.]   ~ !   *Songs of the Great Dom., Can. Poems and Lays*

p. 117 THE KEEPERS OF THE PASS

The poem first appeared in the *Trinity University Review* (December, 1888); and was later published in *Songs of the Common Day and Ave*, 1893; *A Victorian Anthology*, 1895; and *Poems*, 1901/7. A holograph manuscript, part of the partial manuscript book for *Songs of the Common Day*, is held by McGill University.

Variants
The headnote does not appear in the *Trinity University Review,* and in *A Victorian Anthology* it is shortened to: "(When Adam Dulac and his comrades, sworn not to return alive, saved Montreal from the Iroquois)."

1	up.]	~ ,	*Trinity Univ. Rev.*
5	camping-ground.]	~ ,	*Trinity Univ. Rev.*
6	tamarack.]	~ ,	*Trinity Univ. Rev.*
7	near,]	~ ,–	*Trinity Univ. Rev.*
11	in]	**on**	*MS, SOCDA, Victorian Anth.*
13	we're . . . straits,]	**we've . . . straits,–**	*Trinity Univ. Rev.*
17	down.]	~ ,	*Trinity Univ. Rev.*
18	burn.]	~ ,	*Trinity Univ. Rev.*
19	brand,]	~ ,–	*Trinity Univ. Rev.*
25	break.]	~ ,	*Trinity Univ. Rev.*
33	more.]	~ ,	*Trinity Univ. Rev.*
35	sleep,–]	~ ,	*Trinity Univ. Rev.*
38	Between]	**Betwixt**	*Trinity Univ. Rev.*
43	watch,]	~ ,–	*Trinity Univ. Rev.*

p. 119 CANADIANS ARE WE

The poem was published only in the *Dominion Illustrated Magazine* (February, 1889). A holograph manuscript was included with a letter to Warner E. Colville, dated December 30, 1931. With the manuscript is a note: "If you care to print this, will you please send me three or four proof slips of it. I want to get it set to music. Is *Forum* coming regularly? Fine! I send notice. C.G.D.R."

Variants
All variants are from the manuscript.

Title:	Canadians Are We]	**A Toast for Dominion Day**	
3	is,]	~	
4	Canadians–]	~ ,	Also lines 8, 12, and 16.
10	tree,]	~ .	
13	Chateauguay–]	~	

Glossary
13 *Lundy's Lane . . . Chateauguay:* See "Canada"

434

p. 119 SEVERANCE

The poem first appeared in *Progress* (March, 1889); and was later included in the "Appendix" to *Younger American Poets,* 1891; *Songs of the Common Day and Ave,* 1893; *Poems,* 1901/7; *Selected Poems,* 1936; and *Selected Poetry and Critical Prose,* 1974. A holograph manuscript is contained in the partial manuscript book of *Songs of the Common Day* at McGill University.

In *Progress* is a notation that "'Severance,' composed by Mr. Porter, the conductor, and sung by Dr. Slayter, was a feature of the evening.–*Halifax Evening Mail.*"

Variants

3	bar]	~ ,	*Progress*		
9	Love]	**love**	*YAP*		
10	oversea,]	**over sea,–**	*Progress*	**over sea,**	*YAP*
11	land]	~ ,	*Progress*		

p. 120 THE WAKING EARTH

The poem was first published in *The Independent* (May 23, 1889); and later appeared in *Songs of the Common Day and Ave,* 1893; *Later Canadian Poems,* 1893; *Poems,* 1901/7; *Selected Poems,* 1936; and *Selected Poetry and Critical Prose,* 1974.

Variants

1   shy . . . run.]   **shy, . . . run;**   *Independent, Later Can. Poems*
2   ways.]   ~ ;   *Independent, Later Can. Poems*
3   haze,]   ~   *Independent, Later Can. Poems*
4   thin,–for Spring's begun!]   **thin–for spring's begun.**   *Independent, Later Can. Poems*
5   done.]   ~   *Independent*
6   breaks;]   ~ ,   *Later Can. Poems*
9   What]   **With**   *Poems* 1901/7   Note: In Roberts' reading copy of *Poems* in the Harriet Irving Library at the University of New Brunswick, "With" has been crossed through and "What" written above it.
11   sod.]   ~ ,   *Later Can. Poems*
12   lo,]   ~ !   *Independent, Later Can. Poems*
14   beauty, . . . god!]   **beauty . . . god.**   *Independent, Later Can. Poems*
14   god]   **God**   *SOCDA, Poems* 1901/7

p.120 THE NIGHT SKY

McGill University holds two holograph manuscripts of the poem. The first (MS) is dated August 2, 1889, and the second (MS-SOCD) is in the partial manuscript book of *Songs of the Common Day*. The poem was first published in *The Independent* (March 6, 1890); and subsequently appeared in *Songs of the Common Day and Ave*, 1893; *Later Canadian Poems*, 1893; *A Victorian Anthology*, 1895; and *Poems*, 1901/7.

Variants

1   deep]   **Deep**   *MS, Later Can. Poems, Victorian Anth.*
1   't is]   'tis   *MS, Independent, MS-SOCD, SOCDA, Later Can. Poems*
2   'T is]   'Tis   *MS, Independent, MS-SOCD, SOCDA, Later Can. Poems*
2   weigh,]   ~ ;   *Independent*
3   'T is]   'Tis   *MS, Independent, MS-SOCD, SOCDA, Later Can. Poems*
3   soundless,–]   ~ ,   *Independent, Later Can. Poems*
5   Through]   **Thro'**   *MS, Later Can. Poems*
5   realms . . . reaches]   **realms, . . . reaches,**   *MS*
7   And,]   ~   *Independent, Later Can. Poems, Victorian Anth.*
7   shoreline]   **shore-line**   *Independent*
8   the soul's]   **a man's**   *MS*
8   desire.]   ~ !   *MS*
9   deep]   **Deep**   *MS, Later Can. Poems*
9   Heaven, no]   **Heaven! No**   *MS, Independent, Later Can. Poems, Victorian Anth.*
10   may]   **shall**   *MS*
10   spheres!]   ~ .   *MS*   ~ ;   *Independent, Later Can. Poems*
12   years.]   ~ ;   *Independent, Later Can. Poems*
13   ages,]   ~ –   *Independent, Later Can. Poems*
         ~ ,–   *Victorian Anth.*
14   dream.]   ~ !   *Later Can. Poems*

Glossary
9   *Pleiad:*   a group of stars in the constellation Taurus

p.121 WHEN MILKING-TIME IS DONE

The poem first appeared in *The Youth's Companion* (July, 1889); and was later published in *Current Opinion* 1 (October, 1889); *Songs of the Common Day and Ave*, 1893; *Later Canadian Poems*, 1893; *Current Opinion* 2 (May, 1899); *Poems*, 1901/7; *Selected Poems*, 1936; *Selected Poems of Sir Charles*

436

G.D. Roberts, 1955; and *Selected Poetry and Critical Prose*, 1974. As well, an unidentified clipping—a reprint from *The Youth's Companion*—is in the Rufus Hathaway Collection at the University of New Brunswick.

Variants
Title: When Milking-Time is Done]　**The Farm at Dusk**　*Current Opinion* (1)
1　milking-time]　**milking time**　*Youth's Comp., HC, Current Opinion* (1), *Later Can. Poems, Current Opinion* (2)
2　forest home]　**forest-home**　*Youth's Comp., HC, Current Opinion* (1)
3　wide]　~ ,　*Later Can. Poems*
5　moss-cooled watering-trough]　**moss-cool watering trough**　*Later Can. Poems*
6　barnyard]　**barn-yard**　*Later Can. Poems*
8　night-hawks]　**night-jars**　*Youth's Comp., HC, Current Opinion* (1), *SOCDA, Later Can. Poems, Current Opinion* (2), *Poems* 1901/7
8　call.]　~ ;　*Later Can. Poems*
9-10　The . . . bars]　**Then, while the crickets pipe, and frogs are shrill About the slow brook's edge, the pasture bars**　*Youth's Comp., HC, Current Opinion* (1)
12　Vague . . . gleam]　**Vague, pallid shapes amid the thickets,—till**　*Youth's Comp., HC, Current Opinion* (1)
13　wilds]　**woods**　*HC, Later Can. Poems*
Note:　in *Current Opinion* (1) the poem is not divided into an octave and sestet.

p. 121　THE SUMMER POOL

McGill University holds a holograph manuscript of the poem dated September 1, 1889. The first printing of the poem was in *The Century Magazine* (October, 1891); and it subsequently appeared in *Songs of the Common Day and Ave*, 1893; *Poems*, 1901/7; and *Selected Poems*, 1936.

Variants
Title: The]　**A**　*MS, Century*
3　fir-trees]　**fir trees**　*Century*
4　iris'd]　**irised**　*Century*
9　dream,]　~ ;　*Century*
10　watch]　**wait**　*MS, Century*
10　expectancy.]　~　*SOCDA*
11　fulfils,— . . . flame,]　**fulfils, . . . flame—**　*Century*
12　jewels,]　~ —　*Century*
Note:　in *The Century Magazine* the poem is not divided into stanzas

Glossary
7   *presage:*   a presentiment or foreboding, a forecast or prediction

p. 122 THE VALLEY OF THE WINDING WATER

Two holograph manuscripts survive. The first (MS-St. John) is in the St. John's Seminary in Camarillo, California and the second (MS-SOCD) is in the partial manuscript book of *Songs of the Common Day* at McGill University. The poem was first published in *The Century Magazine* (November, 1889); and almost immediately reprinted in *Progress* (November, 1889); it was later included in *Songs of the Common Day and Ave,* 1893; *Poems,* 1901/7; and *Selected Poems,* 1936. According to Pomeroy (p. 115) the poem was written "at the same time as 'The Deserted City' and record[s] a poignant personal experience."

Variants
Title: The . . . Water]   **"The . . . Water"**   *MS-St. John.*   The title was originally enclosed in quotation marks in *MS-SOCD* but they have been crossed through.
6   emerald]   ~ ,   *MS-St. John, Century, Progress*
10   a-wing]   *SOCDA, Poems* 1901/7, and *Selected Poems* have **awing**. *MS-St. John, MS-SOCD, Century,* and *Progress* have **a-wing**, which seems to be the superior reading in the context of the stanza.
11   gladness,]   ~   *MS-St. John, Century, Progress*
13   For]   **But**   *MS-St. John, Century, Progress*
15   anguish–]   ~ ,–   *MS-St. John*   ~ ,   *Century, Progress*
16   to-day]   **today**   *MS-St. John, Progress*
16   dead.]   ~ !   *MS-St. John, Century*

p. 122 AUTOCHTHON

The poem was first published as a private printing, dated December, 1889. Its first public appearance was in the *University Quarterly Review* (February, 1890); and it was subsequently published in *Progress* (April 12, 1890); *Songs of the Common Day and Ave,* 1893; *Later Canadian Poems,* 1893; *A Victorian Anthology,* 1895; *A Treasury of Helpful Verse,* 1896; *Poems,* 1901/7; *Songs of Nature,* 1902; *Our Canadian Literature,* 1934; and *Selected Poems,* 1936.

Variants
2   grain]   ~ ,   *Univ. Quart. Rev., Progress, Later Can. Poems, Victorian Anth., Treasury of Helpful Verse, Songs of Nature*

3	suns]	**sons** *Songs of Nature*
4	rain;]	~ . *Univ. Quart. Rev., Progress*
9	wrung]	~ , *PP, Univ. Quart. Rev., Progress, SOCDA, Later Can. Poems, Victorian Anth., Treasury of Helpful Verse, Poems 1901/7, Songs of Nature, Our Can. Lit.*
13	sleep,]	~ *Univ. Quart. Rev.*
14	Wrapped]	**Wrapt** *Univ. Quart. Rev., Progress*
17	calm,]	~ ; *Treasury of Helpful Verse*
20	heed;]	~ . *Univ. Quart. Rev., Progress*
26	wave]	~ , *Progress*
29	night]	~ , *Univ. Quart. Rev., Progress*
30	dawn,]	~ ; *Univ. Quart. Rev., Progress*
32	cloud]	**clouds** *Univ. Quart. Rev., Progress*
34	of man]	**of a man** *Poems* 1901/7
38	race,]	~ ; *Univ. Quart. Rev., Progress*
39	beholds]	**behold** *Treasury of Helpful Verse*

Note: in the *University Quarterly Review, Progress, A Victorian Anthology, A Treasury of Helpful Verse,* and *Songs of Nature* the stanzas are not numbered

Glossary

Autochthon: The word originally meant one sprung from the earth itself; it also refers to the aboriginal inhabitants of a place or to indigenous animals or plants. Roberts personifies these characteristics in the poem.

p. 123 A CHRISTMAS-EVE COURTIN'

The poem first appeared in *Saturday Night* (December, 1889); and was later published in *Songs of the Common Day and Ave,* 1893; and *Harper's Weekly* (December, 1911). A transcript of the poem, in the hand of Annie Prat and corrected by Roberts, is in the partial manuscript book of *Songs of the Common Day* at McGill University.

Variants

1-8	omitted in *Harper's*	
3	drawed]	**drawd** *Sat. Night*
5	scalloped-like]	**scalloped like** *Sat. Night, MS*
8	a-layin']	**alayin'** *Sat. Night, MS*
9	a-hummin']	**ahummin'** *Sat. Night, MS*
9	a-hummin']	~ , *Harper's*
10	road;]	~ , *Harper's*
11	in]	**out** *Sat. Night;* in *MS* out has been crossed through and *in* written beside it
11	through]	**thro'** *Harper's*

11   door,]   ~   *Sat. Night, MS*   ~ –   *Harper's*

12   Crossroads]   **Cross Roads**   *Harper's*

1?   them]   **these**   *Sat. Night, Harper's;* in *MS these* has been crossed
                    through and *them* written above it

13   an']   **and**   *Sat. Night;* originally *and* in *MS*, *d* crossed through and
                    apostrophe added

14   About . . . Rome,"]   **'Bout "modern innovations!" an' "a back-**
                    woods hippodrome."   *Harper's*

14   a-driftin']   **adriftin'**   *Sat. Night, MS*

15   have Church]   **hev church**   *Harper's*

15   o']   **on**   *Sat. Night;* originally *on* in *MS*, *n* crossed through and
                    apostrophe added

16   cute red . . . pinted . . . fur]   **rose-red . . . p'inted . . . fer**   *Harper's*

17-20   omitted in *Harper's*

17   a-gittin']   **agittin'**   *Sat. Night, MS*

21   fur . . . seven;]   **fer . . . seven,**   *Harper's*

22   of Heaven]   **o' heaven**   *Harper's*

23   a-ridin']   **aridin'**   *Sat. Night, MS*

23   night . . . was]   **night, with the moon all**   *Harper's*

24   a-sparkle]   **asparkle**   *Sat. Night, MS*

25-28   omitted in *Harper's*

25   find my tongue]   **somehow say it**   *Sat. Night; somehow say it*
                    crossed through in *MS* and *find my tongue* written
                    beside it

26   But . . . it.]   **An' as fur my heart, the way it kep' jumpin' was a**
                    wonder.   *Sat. Night; An' as fur* crossed through
                    in *MS* and *But* written above it; *the way it kep'*
                    jumpin' . . . a wonder crossed through and *it sung*
                    an' sung, like canaries . . . into it written above it

30   shoulder.]   ~ !   *Harper's*

31   My heart was all afire,]   **My heart, it was all afire;**   *Harper's*

32   An' wished]   **An' I wisht**   *Harper's*

33   word;]   ~   *Harper's*

34   of]   **o'**   *Harper's*

34   sarvice]   **service**   *Sat. Night;* *e* crossed through in *MS* and *a*
                    written above it

35   sing . . . newborn]   **sing, . . . New-Born**   *Harper's*

35   King,]   ~ ;   *Sat. Night, MS*   ~ !   *Harper's*

36   of]   **o'**   *Harper's*

36   narvous]   **nervous**   *Sat. Night; a* written over *e* in *MS*

37-40   omitted in *Harper's*

42   fur]   **fer**   *Harper's*

43   overcast an' . . . fast,]   **overcast, now, an' . . . fast;**   *Harper's*

44   a-rantin']   **arantin'**   *Sat. Night, MS*

44   mountins]   **mountains**   *Sat. Night;* originally *mountains* in *MS*,
                    a crossed through

45   possessed,]   **possest;** *Harper's*
46   kind of . . . fur]   **kinder . . . fer**   *Harper's*
47   walk,]   ~ ; *Harper's*
48   her, . . . mite.]   **her,– . . . mite!** *Harper's*
49-52   omitted in *Harper's*
49   'a]   **a** *Sat. Night, MS*
53   short an' whinnied,]   **short, an' whinnied;** *Harper's*
54   cryin' too;]   **cryin', too.** *Harper's*
56   as]   omitted in *Harper's*
57   wastn't]   **wasn't** *Sat. Night, MS, Harper's*
57   skeered]   ~ , *Harper's*
58   knowed]   **knew** *Sat. Night, MS, Harper's*
58   fur her;]   **fer her.** *Harper's*
59   ²an']   ~ – *Harper's*
60   stop, . . . anyways, it . . . very]   **stop,– . . . anyways, Si, it . . . very**
                                    Harper's
61   chock full . . . say,]   **chockful . . . say;** *Harper's*
62   that]   omitted in *Harper's*
62   eyes!]   ~ . *Harper's*
63   snug,]   ~ ,– *Harper's*
65-68   omitted in *Harper's*
65   a-leadin']   **a leadin'** *Sat. Night, MS*
67   an']   **an** *Sat. Night*
67   mountin]   **mountain** *Sat. Night;* originally *mountain* in *MS, a*
                                    crossed through
68   heered]   **heerd** *Sat. Night*
71   sech]   **sich** *Harper's*
73-76   omitted in *Harper's*
75   a-growin']   **agrowin'** *Sat. Night, MS*
76   gittin']   **gettin'** *Sat. Night, MS*
77   Crossroads . . . Eve;]   **Cross Roads, . . . Eve,** *Harper's*
78   me believe . . . innovations;]   **me, we b'lieve . . . innovation.**
                                    Harper's
79   We . . . Rome]   **We like the journey home** *Harper's*
79   ain't]   **aint** *Sat. Night, MS*
79   can]   **kin** *Harper's*
79   some,]   ~ . *Sat. Night*   ~ ; *Harper's*
80   sarvice]   **service** *Sat. Night; a* written over *e* in *MS*

Glossary
10   *pung:*   a sleigh having a boxlike body on runners
40   *gossoon:*   a boy or servant
67   *"painter":*   panther

p. 126 THE FORTRESS

The poem first appeared in the *Trinity University Review* (December, 1889); and later was published in *Songs of the Common Day and Ave,* 1893; and *Current Opinion* (May, 1899). As well, an unidentified clipping is contained in the Rufus Hathaway Collection at the University of New Brunswick. The Hathaway clipping indicates that it is a reprint of the *Trinity University Review* text, to which it is identical. A holograph manuscript of the poem is in the partial manuscript book of *Songs of the Common Day* at McGill University.

Variants
All variants are from the *Trinity University Review* and the Hathaway
    clipping.
  3   heart] ~ ,
 10   siege;] ~ !
 12   tears.] ~ !

p. 126 THE FIR WOODS

As far as may be determined, the first publication of the poem was in *Songs of the Great Dominion,* 1889; but the Rufus Hathaway Collection at the University of New Brunswick contains an unidentified clipping which may precede that publication. The poem also appeared in *Canadian Poems and Lays,* 1893; *Songs of the Common Day and Ave,* 1893; *Poems,* 1901/7; *The University Monthly* (January, 1906); and *Selected Poems,* 1936.

Variants
  1   tops,] ~ *Univ. Monthly*
  3   far-off] **far off** *Univ. Monthly*
  4   Through] **Thro'** *HC, Songs of the Great Dom., Can. Poems
                  and Lays*
  5   dream-dust] **dream dust** *HC*
  6   Coral . . . rose,] **Carol . . . rose** *Univ. Monthly*
  9   profound,–] ~ – *HC*
 11   crest.] ~ : *SOCDA, Poems* 1901/7, *Univ. Monthly*
 12   lures. The] **lures; the** *Songs of the Great Dom., Can. Poems
                  and Lays*
 13   unprisoned] **imprisoned** *Songs of the Great Dom., Can. Poems
                  and Lays*
Note: in *The University Monthly* the poem is not divided into stanzas

p. 127 LIFE

The poem was published only in *The Independent* (December 10, 1891). A holograph manuscript, dated 1889, is in Roberts' Ernescliffe notebook at the University of New Brunswick. The manuscript has the text in French as well as English. The never printed French text is:

> La vie est brève.
> Un peu d'amour,
> Un peu de rêve,
> Et puis—Bon Jour!
>
> La vie est vaine.
> Un peu d'ennui,
> Un peu de peine,
> Et puis—Bonne Nuit!

p. 127 TRIUMPH

Apparently the poem was never published. It survives as an undated and unsigned holograph manuscript in the Queen's University Archives (MS) and as a signed typescript in the Mount Allison University Roberts collection (TS). The Mount Allison text contains the handwritten note "Written at King's College, Windsor, *circa* 1889."

Variants
13   Now]   originally *For*   *TS; For* crossed through and *Now*
                         written above it   **For**   *MS*
17   stranger]   **strange**   *TS*
25-30   For . . . dream!]   omitted in *MS*

p. 128 THE WINTER FIELDS

The poem originally appeared in *The Century Magazine* (January, 1890) and an unidentified clipping in the Rufus Hathaway Collection at the University of New Brunswick is a reprint of the *Century* text, evidently published soon after. The poem was also published in *Songs of the Common Day and Ave*, 1893; *Poems*, 1901/7; *Selected Poems*, 1936; *Selected Poems of Sir Charles G.D. Roberts*, 1955; *Poets of Confederation*, 1967; and *Selected Poetry and Critical Prose*, 1974. Two holograph manuscripts survive: the first is an undated manuscript, related to the *Century* text, at Queen's University (MSQ); and the second is contained in the partial manuscript book of *Songs of the Common Day* at McGill University (MS-SOCD).

Variants
1   steel.]   ~ !   *MSQ*
2   low]   ~ ,   *Century, HC*
4   Thin streaked]   **thin-streaked**   *Century, HC, MSQ*
5   dim]   ~ ,   *Century, HC*
5   fence,]   ~   *Century, HC, MSQ*
7   winter trample]   **Winter hurtle**   *MSQ*
7   by,]   ~ ;   *Century, HC*
9   Yet]   ~ ,   *Century, HC*
10   Harsh]   ~ ,   *Century, HC, MSQ*
11   glebes]   ~ ,   *Century, HC, MSQ*
12   ecstacy—]   ~ ,   *Century, HC, MSQ*   ~ ,—   *MS-SOCD*
13   summer, till]   **summer when**   *MSQ*
Note: in *MS-Q, MS-SOCD, Songs of the Common Day and Ave,* and
         Poems, 1901/7 the poem is divided into stanzas

p. 128 BLOMIDON

As far as may be determined, the poem first appeared in *The Century Maga-zine* (February, 1890); and shortly thereafter in *The Dominion Illustrated Magazine* (March, 1890). Two unidentified clippings survive, however—one in the Rufus Hathaway Collection at the University of New Brunswick and one in the partial manuscript book of *Songs of the Common Day* at McGill University. The poem was subsequently included in *Songs of the Common Day and Ave,* 1893; *Poems,* 1901/7; *Selected Poems,* 1936; and *Selected Poetry and Critical Prose,* 1974.

Variants
All variants are from the Hathaway clipping.
8   singer,]   ~
9   foam,]   ~

Glossary
Blomidon: a cape on the coast of Nova Scotia, jutting into the Bay of
            Fundy
3   *Minas:*   Minas Basin, the easternmost arm of the Bay of Fundy
7-8   *Evangeline . . . tender singer:* Henry Wadsworth Longfellow's poem
            Evangeline deals with the expulsion of the Acadians in 1755,
            as does Roberts' romance *A Sister to Evangeline,* 1898.

p. 129 THE DESERTED CITY

The poem was first published in *The Century Magazine* (March, 1890); and later appeared in *Songs of the Common Day and Ave,* 1893; *A Victorian*

444

Anthology, 1895; *Current Opinion* (May, 1899); *Poems*, 1901/7; *The Book of Poetry*, 1928; and *Selected Poems*, 1936. The Rufus Hathaway Collection at the University of New Brunswick contains an unidentified clipping of the poem, and a holograph manuscript is contained in the partial manuscript book of *Songs of the Common Day* at McGill University.

Variants

1	away.]	~ *Poems* 1901/7	~ ; *HC*
2	long.]	~ , *HC*	
3	busy,]	~ *HC*	
4	livelong]	**live-long** *MS, SOCDA, Victorian Anth., Current Opinion, Book of Poetry*	
4	day.]	~ ; *HC*	
5	hastening, gay]	**hastening gay,** *HC*	
9	'Twas]	**'T was** *Century, MS, Victorian Anth., Poems* 1901/7	
9	so,]	~ ,– *Century*	~ ; *HC*
10	therein.]	~ ; *Century*	~ , *HC*
12	din;]	~ . *Book of Poetry*	
13	been,–]	~ ;– *MS, SOCDA, Victorian Anth., Current Opinion* ~ ; *Century* ~ : *Book of Poetry* ~ . *HC*	
14	ago.]	~ ! *Century, MS*	

p. 129 THE FLIGHT OF THE GEESE

The poem was initially published in *The Independent* (April 17, 1890); and subsequently appeared in *Progress* (May 3, 1890); *Songs of the Common Day and Ave*, 1893; *A Victorian Anthology*, 1895; *Poems*, 1901/7; *Songs of Nature*, 1902; *The Bird Lover's Anthology*, 1930; *Selected Poems*, 1936; *Selected Poems of Sir Charles G.D. Roberts*, 1955; *Penguin Book of Canadian Verse*, 1967; and *Selected Poetry and Critical Prose*, 1974. A holograph manuscript is contained in the partial manuscript book for *Songs of the Common Day* at McGill University.

Variants

2	night,]	~ *Progress, MS, SOCDA*
4	sedge-flat]	**sedge flat** *Progress*
6	²The]	**the** *Independent, Progress, Bird Lover's Anth.*
8	go!]	~ . *Independent, Progress*
10	Winter's]	**winter's** *MS, SOCDA, Victorian Anth., Poems* 1901/7, *Songs of Nature, Bird Lover's Anth.*
11	solemn]	**hollow** *Independent, Progress*
12	dark]	**night** *Independent, Progress*
13	profound,]	~ : *Independent, Progress*
Note:	In *A Victorian Anthology* and *Songs of Nature* the poem is not divided into an octave and a sestet	

p. 130 THE FURROW

The poem was first published in *The Century Magazine* (April, 1890); and later appeared in *Songs of the Common Day and Ave,* 1893; *Poems,* 1901/7; and *Selected Poetry and Critical Prose,* 1974.

Variants
2   sun-rise]   **sunrise**   *Century*
7   first]   ~,   *Century*
9   team.]   ~ –   *SOCDA*
10   sea air]   **sea-air**   *Century*
12   fresh cloven steam,]   **fresh-cloven steam;**   *Century*
13   goes.]   ~ :   *SOCDA*
14   So, . . . scar, best . . . sweet.]   **So . . . scar but . . . sweet!**   *Century*
Note: in the *Century* the poem is not divided into stanzas

Glossary
5   *glebe:*   field
13   *share:*   a ploughshare

p. 130 THE NIGHT-HAWK

The poem first appeared in *The Independent* (May, 1890); and was later published in the *King's College Record* (June, 1891); *Songs of the Common Day and Ave,* 1893; *Current Opinion* (May, 1899); and *Poems,* 1901/7.

Variants
1   May,]   ~   *King's Coll. Rec.*
2   oh,]   ~   *Independent, King's Coll. Rec., SOCDA, Current Opinion*
6   rose-dusk]   **rose dusk**   *King's Coll. Rec.*
6   away,]   ~ .   *SOCDA, Current Opinion*
15   oh,]   ~   *Independent, King's Coll. Rec., SOCDA, Current Opinion*
21   hour.]   ~   *King's Coll. Rec.*

p. 131 A SONG OF GROWTH

The poem first appeared in *The Century Magazine* (August, 1890); and was later published in *Songs of the Common Day and Ave,* 1893; *Later Canadian Poems,* 1893; *A Treasury of Canadian Verse,* 1900; *Poems,* 1901/7; *The University Monthly* (March, 1907); *Oxford Book of Canadian Verse,* 1913; and *Selected Poems,* 1936. As well, the Rufus Hathaway Collection at the University of New Brunswick contains two clippings of extracts of the poem; HC(1) includes lines 1-12 and 19-24; HC(2) has only lines 7-12. In addition, the Roberts Collection at the University of New Brunswick contains yet another unidentified clipping. A holograph manuscript survives in the partial manuscript book of *Songs of the Common Day* at McGill University.

Variants

Title: A Song of Growth]   **Growth** *HC*(2)   **A Song Sung Twenty-eight Years Ago** *RC*

1   a]   omitted in *Univ. Monthly*

2   upfurled.] ~ : *Century, Later Can. Poems, Oxford Book of Can. Verse* ~ , *SOCDA, Treasury of Can. Verse, Poems* 1901/7, *Univ. Monthly, HC*(1) **unfurled** *RC*

3   span] ~ , *HC*(1)

4   It shakes . . . world,] **It will shake . . . world,–** *Later Can. Poems, Oxford Book of Can. Verse*

8   grows,] ~ ; *HC*(1)

9   Nor] **Not** *Univ. Monthly, HC*(1)

9   voice,] ~ ,– *Later Can. Poems, Oxford Book of Can. Verse, HC*(2) ~ *Univ. Monthly*

10   in] **with** *HC*(2)

10   repose,–] ~ ; *Later Can. Poems, Oxford Book of Can. Verse, HC*(2) ~ – *HC*(1), *RC*

11   rush] ~ , *Later Can. Poems, Oxford Book of Can. Verse, HC*(1), *HC*(2), *RC*

12   hush.] ~ ! *Later Can. Poems, Oxford Book of Can. Verse, HC*(2)

16   blind;] ~ , *RC*

17   But] ~ , *Century*

20   the] omitted in *Univ. Monthly*

20   rod;] ~ , *Century* ~ : *Later Can. Poems, Oxford Book of Can. Verse*

22   God,–] ~ ;– *MS, SOCDA, Treasury of Can. Verse* ~ ; *Univ. Monthly* ~ : *HC*(1) ~ – *RC*

23   Fountains] **fountains** *Later Can. Poems, Oxford Book of Can. Verse*

23   Life] **life** *Univ. Monthly*

24   cry,] ~ – *Century*

24   strife.] ~ ! *Century, Later Can. Poems, Oxford Book of Can. Verse, RC*

p. 132 THE MOWING

The poem was first published in *The Independent* (August 21, 1890); and subsequently appeared in *Songs of the Common Day and Ave*, 1893; *Poems, 1901/7; Selected Poems,* 1936; *A Book of Canadian Poetry,* 1943/8; *Canadian*

Poems 1850-1952, 1953; *Exploring Poetry,* 1955; *Selected Poems of Sir Charles G.D. Roberts,* 1955; *Poets of Confederation,* 1967; and *Selected Poetry and Critical Prose,* 1974.

Variants
All variants are from *The Independent.*
5   tireless]   **sounding**
6   triumphing]   **tireless**
8   timothy-tops and meadowsweet]   **timothy tops and meadow-sweet**
10   sun, . . . ray,]   **sun . . . ray**
14   herds]   **herd**

p. 132   A VESPER SONNET

The poem was first published in *The University Monthly* (August, 1890); and later appeared in *The Independent* (October 23, 1890); *Songs of the Common Day and Ave,* 1893; and *Poems,* 1901/7. An unidentified clipping is in the Rufus Hathaway Collection at the University of New Brunswick.

Variants
2   Celestial,]   ~   *Univ. Monthly, Independent*
4   ecstacy,]   ~   *HC*
4   dews,]   ~   *Independent, HC*
4   dream.]   ~   *Univ. Monthly*   ~ ,   *HC*
5   wine-warm]   **wine warm**   *HC*
5   dusks, . . . valley,]   **dusks . . . valley**   *Univ. Monthly, Independent*
6   casement. Cease]   **casement; cease**   *Independent*
7   the]   **that**   *Univ. Monthly*
8   supreme.]   ~ ,   *HC*
10   thin]   **their**   *HC*
10   fine,–]   ~ –   *Univ. Monthly, Independent, HC*
11   bush-fires . . . bramble-thickets]   **bushfires . . . bramble thickets**
                                     HC
11   sere,–]   ~ –   *Univ. Monthly, Independent, HC*
13   One]   **On**   *Univ. Monthly*
13   voices, . . . appear,]   **voices . . . appear**   *HC*

p. 133   LINES FOR THE TIMES

The poem was published only in *Grip* (November 29, 1890).

Glossary
One of a number of tariff "wars" between Canada and the United States was the obvious occasion for the poem.

p. 133 IN THE WIDE AWE AND WISDOM OF THE NIGHT

The poem was first published in *The Independent* (December 11, 1890); and subsequently appeared in the *King's College Record* (November, 1892); *Songs of the Common Day and Ave*, 1893; *Later Canadian Poems*, 1893; *Poems*, 1901/7; *Our Canadian Literature*, 1935; *Selected Poems*, 1936; *Selected Poems of Sir Charles G.D. Roberts*, 1955; *Poets of Confederation*, 1967; and *Selected Poetry and Critical Prose*, 1974. A holograph manuscript of the poem is contained in the partial manuscript book of *Songs of the Common Day* at McGill University.

Pomeroy (p. 92) reports that "when *Songs of the Common Day* was published, a disappointed Gilder [Richard Watson Gilder, editor of *Century Magazine* and a friend of Roberts] reproached Roberts for not having offered him 'In the Wide Awe and Wisdom of the Night,' which, he said, was the poet's finest sonnet. Roberts laughingly replied, 'But, Old Man, that's one you scornfully rejected about a year ago!' Gilder was taken aback. After a moment he said, 'That must have been when I had an attack of literary indigestion from having read too many bad poems.'"

Variants

6	orbit]	~ , *MS, SOCDA, Poems* 1901/7, *Our Can. Lit.*
10	Soul]	**soul** *Independent, King's Coll. Rec., MS, SOCDA, Later Can. Poems*
11	Till,]	~ *Poems* 1901/7, *Our Can. Lit.*
12	face,–]	~ ; *Independent, King's Coll. Rec., Later Can. Poems*
13	universe]	**Universe** *MS, SOCDA, Poems* 1901/7, *Our Can. Lit.*
14	man]	**Man** *Independent, King's Coll. Rec., MS, SOCDA, Later Can. Poems*

Note: In *Later Canadian Poems* the poem is divided into an octave and sestet.

p. 133 QUEBEC, 1757

The poem first appeared in Roberts' translation of Philippe Aubert de Gaspé's *Les Anciens Canadiens* (*The Canadians of Old*, 1890); and was later included in *The Iceberg and Other Poems*, 1934; *Selected Poems*, 1936; and *Selected Poetry and Critical Prose*, 1974.

Two typescripts are contained in the Queen's University Archives.

Glossary

Philippe Aubert de Gaspé: (1786-1871) a lawyer and sheriff of Quebec (1816-1834). He was imprisoned for debt from 1834 to 1841. *Les Anciens Canadiens* was published in 1863, and his other works are his *Mémoires* (1866) and *Divers* published posthumously in 1893.

449

7   *Angelus:*   a devotion celebrating the Annunciation; the Angelus bell
                   is sounded in the morning, at noon, and in the evening to
                   indicate the times at which the Angelus is to be recited.
8   *Beaupré and Lévis:* Beaupré is Ste. Anne de Beaupré, a city near
                   Quebec City. Lévis is a city opposite Quebec City.

p. 134 THE AUTUMN THISTLES

The poem was first published in *Canada* (January, 1891); and later appeared
in *Songs of the Common Day and Ave,* 1893; *Poems,* 1901/7; *Selected Poems,*
1936; and *Selected Poetry and Critical Prose,* 1974. A holograph manuscript
is in the partial manuscript book for *Songs of the Common Day* at McGill
University.

Variants
12   Dew-freshened . . . brave!]   **Dew freshened . . . brave** : *Canada*
13   endure . . . allow]   **endure, . . . allow,** *Canada*
14   eye.]   ~ !   *Canada*

p. 134 NEW YEAR'S EVE (After the French of Fréchette)

The poem first appeared in *The Independent* (January, 1891); and was later
published in *Songs of the Common Day and Ave,* 1893; the *Methodist Magazine and Review* (January, 1904); *The Vagrant of Time,* 1927; and *Selected
Poetry and Critical Prose,* 1974.

Variants
1   winds,]   ~   *Independent, SOCDA, Methodist Mag. and Rev.*
4   wayfarer;]   ~ ,   *Independent*
5   cries,]   ~   *Independent, SOCDA, Methodist Mag. and Rev.*
6   flood,–]   ~ ;   *Independent, SOCDA, Methodist Mag. and Rev.*
14   utters]   ~ ,   *Independent, SOCDA, Methodist Mag. and Rev.*
24   dream!]   ~ .   *Independent, SOCDA, Methodist Mag. and Rev.*
29   break–]   ~   *Independent, SOCDA, Methodist Mag. and Rev.*
31   together]   ~ ,   *Independent, SOCDA, Methodist Mag. and Rev.*
39   Him]   **him**   *Independent, Methodist Mag. and Rev.*

Glossary
Fréchette: see "Rondeau."

p. 136 MOONLIGHT

The poem was first published in *Canada* (March, 1891); and subsequently
appeared in *Songs of the Common Day and Ave,* 1893; *Poems,* 1901/7; and

450

Selected Poems, 1936. A holograph manuscript is in the partial manuscript book of *Songs of the Common Day* at McGill University.

Variants
Title: Moonlight]   **A Nocturne**   *Canada*
1   these]   **the**   *Canada*

p. 136 THE SALT FLATS

The poem was first published in *The Independent* (March 19, 1891); and sub-sequently appeared in the *King's College Record* (May, 1891); *Canada* (August, 1891); *Songs of the Common Day and Ave,* 1893; *Poems,* 1901/7; *Canadian Bookman* (August, 1933); *Our Canadian Literature,* 1934; *Selected Poems,* 1936; *Selected Poems of Sir Charles G.D. Roberts,* 1955; *Poets of Confederation,* 1967; and *Selected Poetry and Critical Prose,* 1974.

Variants
Title: The Salt Flats]   **The Salt Marshes**   *Independent, King's Coll.*
               Rec.   **The Sea-Flats**   *Can. Bookman*
1   ago]   ~ ,   *Independent, King's Coll. Rec., Our Can. Lit.*
4   flow,]   ~ ;   *Our Can. Lit.*
8   reaches]   ~ ,   *Our Can. Lit.*
13   low-lying]   **low lying**   *Independent, King's Coll. Rec.*
Note: In *Canadian Bookman* the poem is not divided into stanzas

Glossary
4   *Fundy:* see "Epistle to Bliss Carman."
5   *samphire pipes:* the samphire is an herb commonly growing in clefts of rocks near the sea; it also grows on the salt flats at the head of the Bay of Fundy, where it is **gathered** as an edible green

p. 137 FOR A BUST OF LANIER

The poem was published only in *The Independent* (April 30, 1891).

Glossary
Lanier: See "To the Memory of Sidney Lanier."

p. 137 THE CLEARING

The poem was first published in *The Independent* (August, 1891); and later appeared in *Canada* (November, 1891); *Songs of the Common Day and Ave,* 1893; *Later Canadian Poems,* 1893; *Current Opinion* (August, 1894); *Poems,*

451

1901/7; *Oxford Book of Canadian Verse*, 1913; *Selected Poems*, 1936; and *Selected Poetry and Critical Prose*, 1974. As well, the Rufus Hathaway Collection at the University of New Brunswick contains two unidentified clippings. Although the clippings are from different printings, they are textually identical abridgements containing only lines 1-4 and 9-14.

Variants

2 rain,–] ~ – *HC*
4 jarred.] ~ ... *HC*
8 marred!] ~ . *Independent, Canada, Later Can. Poems, Current Opinion, Oxford Book of Can. Verse*
10 fire-weed] **fire weed** *Independent*
10 flood] ~ , *Independent, Canada, Later Can. Poems, Current Opinion, Oxford Book of Can. Verse, HC*
11 goldenrod] **golden-rod** *Independent, Canada, SOCDA, Later Can. Poems, Current Opinion, Oxford Book of Can. Verse* **golden rod** *HC*
Note: in *Current Opinion* and *HC* the poem is not divided into stanzas

Glossary
14 *hermit:* the hermit thrush

p. 137 GREY ROCKS AND GREYER SEA

The poem was initially published in *The Century Magazine* (August, 1891); and later appeared in *Songs of the Common Day and Ave*, 1893; *Later Canadian Poems*, 1893; *Poems*, 1901/7; twice in *The University Monthly* (1–December, 1903) and (2–January, 1908); *A Little Book of Modern Verse*, 1913; *Oxford Book of Canadian Verse*, 1913; *Selected Poems*, 1936; *The Nature Lover's Knapsack*, 1947; *Selected Poems of Sir Charles G.D. Roberts*, 1955; and *Selected Poetry and Critical Prose*, 1974. As well, the Rufus Hathaway Collection at the University of New Brunswick contains two unidentified clippings; HC(1) is reprinted from the *Century*.

Pomeroy (p. 115) says that the poem was written "at the same time as 'The Deserted City' and record[s] a poignant personal experience."

Variants
Title: In *Selected Poems* the title is "Grey Rocks and the Greyer Sea." This is obviously a misprint and "the" has been crossed through in the copy of the book in the Roberts Collection at the University of New Brunswick.
1 rocks,] ~ *HC*(1), *HC*(2)
4 more.] ~ , *Univ. Monthly* (1)
10 tosses,] ~ *Century, HC*(1), *HC*(2), *Later Can. Poems, Univ. Monthly* (1), *Univ. Monthly* (2), *Oxford Book of Can. Verse*

11   the]   **a**   *Univ. Monthly* (1), *Univ. Monthly* (2)
12   dreams]   **dream**   *HC*(2)
13   rocks, . . . sea]   **rocks . . . seas**   *HC*(2)
14-15   These lines are reversed in *HC*(2).

p. 138 THE PEA-FIELDS

The poem first appeared in *The Atlantic Monthly* (August, 1891); and a holograph manuscript prepared for that publication survives in the Roberts Collection at the University of New Brunswick. The poem was later published in *Songs of the Common Day and Ave*, 1893; *Poems*, 1901/7; *Selected Poems*, 1936; *Anthology of Canadian Poetry*, 1942; *A Pocketful of Canada*, 1956; *Canadian Poems 1850-1952*, 1953; *Selected Poems of Sir Charles G.D. Roberts*, 1955; *Penguin Book of Canadian Verse*, 1967; *Poets of Confederation*, 1967; and *Selected Poetry and Critical Prose*, 1974. As well, the Rufus Hathaway Collection at the University of New Brunswick contains an unidentified clipping which was published after the poem appeared in *Songs of the Common Day and Ave*.

Variants
1   light,]   ~   *HC*
2   butterflies,]   ~   *HC*
3   whitish,]   ~   *MS, Atlantic Monthly*
4   seamaid's]   **sea-maid's**   *MS, Atlantic Monthly*
6   seas]   ~ ,   *SOCDA, HC, Poems* 1901/7
7   A-shimmer]   **Ashimmer**   *MS*   **A shimmer**   *HC*
10   fields,–]   ~ ,   *MS*   ~ –   *HC*
11   summer-time]   **summertime**   *MS*   **summer time**   *Atlantic Monthly*   **Summer time**   *HC*
12   And,]   ~   *MS, Atlantic Monthly*
13   climb]   ~ ,   *Atlantic Monthly, SOCDA, HC, Poems* 1901/7
14   grey, mossed]   **grey-mossed**   *MS*   **gray-mossed**   *Atlantic Monthly*

p. 138 THE HAWKBIT

The poem first appeared in *The Atlantic Monthly* (October, 1891); and was later published in *Songs of the Common Day and Ave*, 1893; *Poems*, 1901/7; *Songs of Nature*, 1902; and *The Home Book of Modern Verse*, 1930. As well, the Rufus Hathaway Collection at the University of New Brunswick contains an unidentified clipping of the poem. Two holograph manuscripts survive: one is preserved in the Queen's University Archives, and the other (MS-SOCD) is in the partial manuscript book of *Songs of the Common Day* at McGill University.

Variants

1   autumn]   **Autumn**   *MS-SOCD, SOCDA*
4   year!]   ~ . *HC*
5   cold]   ~ , *Atlantic Monthly, Songs of Nature, Home Book of Modern Verse*   ~ . *HC*
6   gold,]   ~ *Atlantic Monthly, Songs of Nature, Home Book of Modern Verse, HC*
10   autumn]   **Autumn**   *MS-SOCD, SOCDA*
12   spring]   **Spring**   *SOCDA*

Glossary

Hawkbit: also called the Fall Dandelion or August Flower; the flower resembles the Dandelion but the leaves are narrower and non-serrated and grow on the stem of the flower.

2   *haws:*   the fruit of the Hawthorn.

14   *Elysian:*   the Elysian Fields were the most pleasant place in the classical Greek underworld or Hades.

p. 139 MY TREES

The poem originally appeared in *The Dominion Illustrated Magazine* (1891); and was later published in *Songs of the Common Day and Ave,* 1893. A holograph manuscript is in the partial manuscript book of *Songs of the Common Day* at McGill University.

Variants

1   evening,]   ~ *Dom. Ill.*
3   firwoods]   **fir woods**   *Dom. Ill.*
4   sun]   ~ , *Dom. Ill.*
5   far … flats … seas;]   **far, … flats, … seas,**   *Dom. Ill.*
11   wings,]   ~ *MS*
12   sky.]   ~ : *Dom. Ill.*
14   through.]   ~ ; *Dom. Ill.*
15   world;–]   ~ ,– *Dom. Ill.*

p. 139 THE SILVER THAW

The poem was first published in *The Century Magazine* (March, 1892); and later appeared in *Songs of the Common Day and Ave,* 1893; *Later Canadian Poems,* 1893; *A Treasury of Canadian Verse,* 1900; *Poems,* 1901/7; *Selected Poems,* 1936; and *Selected Poetry and Critical Prose,* 1974. The Rufus Hathaway Collection at the University of New Brunswick contains an unidentified clipping of the poem which was reprinted from the *Century.*

Variants
2   snow.] ~ ; *Century, HC, SOCDA, Later Can. Poems, Treasury of Can. Verse*

7   fancy,] ~ *Century, HC, Later Can. Poems*

10   land.] ~ ; *Century, HC, SOCDA, Later Can. Poems, Treasury of Can. Verse*

11   Spring's] **spring's** *Century, HC, Later Can. Poems*

18   gleam.] ~ ; *Century, HC, SOCDA, Later Can. Poems, A Treasury of Can. Verse*

19   Spring, defeated,] **spring defeated** *Century, HC, Later Can. Poems*

22   Winter] **winter** *Century, HC, SOCDA, Later Can. Poems, A Treasury of Can. Verse, Poems* 1901/7

29   Winter's] **winter's** *Century, HC, Later Can. Poems*

30   well,] ~ *Century, HC, Later Can. Poems*

31   glory,] ~ *Century, HC, Later Can. Poems*

32   if] **through** *Century, HC*

33   silvered] **silver'd** *Treasury of Can. Verse*

33   saplings, bending,] **saplings bending** *Century, HC, Later Can. Poems*

34   gems.] ~ ; *Century, HC, SOCDA, Later Can. Poems, Treasury of Can. Verse*

35   trees, attending,] **trees attending** *Century, HC, Later Can. Poems*

40   bramble-stems] **bramble stems** *Century, HC, Later Can. Poems*

42   birth.] ~ ; *Century, HC, SOCDA, Later Can. Poems, Treasury of Can. Verse*

46   Spring] **spring** *Century, HC, Later Can. Poems, Poems* 1901/7

p. 141 THE BIRD'S SONG, THE SUN, AND THE WIND

The poem was first published in *The Century Magazine* (July, 1892); and later appeared in *Songs of the Common Day and Ave*, 1893; *A Victorian Anthology*, 1895; *Poems*, 1901/7; and *Selected Poems*, 1936. Goodridge Bliss Roberts, Charles' younger brother by ten years, died on February 4, 1892, and Pomeroy (p. 78) says that this poem "the first of several poems he was to write in Goodridge's memory" was written in the April following the death.

Variants
5   spring's] **Spring's** *SOCDA, Victorian Anth.*

5   buds] ~ , *Century*

7   spring] **Spring** *SOCDA, Victorian Anth.*   ~ , *Century*

p. 141 THE LILY OF THE VALLEY

The poem was first published in *Harper's Magazine* (May, 1892); and later appeared in *Songs of the Common Day and Ave*, 1893; *Poems*, 1901/7; *Selected Poems*, 1936; and *Selected Poetry and Critical Prose*, 1974. As well, an unidentified clipping—a reprint of the *Harper's* text—is contained in the Rufus Hathaway Collection at the University of New Brunswick.

Variants
3   forget,]   ～   *Harper's, HC*
4   In this elect,]   **This perfumed and**   *Harper's, HC*
7   sleep]   **Sleep**   *SOCDA*

p. 141 THE WILD-ROSE THICKET

The poem first appeared in *Harper's Weekly* (July 30, 1892); and was later published in *Songs of the Common Day and Ave*, 1893; *Poems*, 1901/7; *Selected Poems*, 1936; and *Selected Poetry and Critical Prose*, 1974.

Variants
9   pale]   **blue**   *Harper's*

p. 142 THE CANADA LILY

The poem was published only in *Argosy* (March, 1892).

p. 142 O SOLITARY OF THE AUSTERE SKY

A holograph manuscript, dated August 17, 1892, is reproduced in Pomeroy (opposite p. 228). The poem was first published in the *King's College Record* (May, 1893); and later appeared in *Songs of the Common Day and Ave*, 1893; *Poems*, 1901/7; *Our Canadian Literature*, 1934; *Selected Poems*, 1936; and *Selected Poetry and Critical Prose*, 1974.

Variants
Title: O Solitary of the Austere Sky]   **The Morning Star**   *King's Coll. Rec.*
1   Solitary]   **solitary**   *MS, King's Coll. Rec.*
3   station . . . by,]   **station, . . . by**   *MS, King's Coll. Rec.*
5   emerge,–]   ～ –   *MS*
7   surge,–]   ～ –   *MS*   ～ ,   *King's Coll. Rec.*
8   sleep;]   ～ ,   *King's Coll. Rec.*
9   regard!]   ～ ,   *MS*   ～ !–   *King's Coll. Rec.*

10   Invisible,–and]   **Invisible! And** *MS*   **Invisible;–and** *King's*
                Coll. Rec.
10   worth!]   ~ . *MS*
11   shard,]   ~   *MS, King's Coll. Rec.*
12   Him]   **him** *King's Coll. Rec.*
13   Eternal Soul]   **eternal soul** *King's Coll. Rec.*
14   control!]   ~ .   *King's Coll. Rec.*
Note: in the *King's College Record* the poem is divided into three qua-
            trains and a closing couplet; in *Songs of the Common Day and
            Ave* the poem is divided into an octave and sestet.

p. 142 TO G.B.R.

A holograph manuscript of the poem, dated August 19, 1892 and initialled
by Roberts, is in the Queen's University Archives. The poem first appeared in
the *King's College Record* (May, 1893); and was later included in *Songs of
the Common Day and Ave,* 1893; the last four lines served as the dedication
to *The Book of the Native,* 1896; and the entire poem appeared in *Poems,*
1901/7; and *Selected Poems,* 1936. The poem is another of the group written
for his brother, Goodridge Bliss Roberts, who died February 4, 1892. See
"The Bird's Song, the Sun, and the Wind".

Variants
Title: To G.B.R.]   **How Merry Sings the Aftermath** *MS*
                  To Goodridge Bliss Roberts *BON*
1   aftermath,]   ~   *MS, King's Coll. Rec.*
2   dew!]   ~ !– *MS*
3   hour,]   ~   *MS*
7   now–]   ~ ,–   *King's Coll. Rec.*
7   though . . . earth]   **tho'. . . Earth** *MS*
8   heart–]   ~ ,– *MS*
9   This]   **The** *BON*
10   This . . . this]   **The . . . the** *BON*
11   you]   **thee** *BON*

p. 143 THE HERMIT-THRUSH

Queen's University holds a holograph manuscript of the poem initialled by
Roberts and dated August 23, 1892. The poem was first published in *Songs
of the Common Day and Ave,* 1893; and was subsequently reprinted only in
Poems, 1901/7.

Variants
All variants are from the manuscript.

457

1   trees,]   ~
2   stream,]   ~
3   sunset]   **evening**
4   No period appears at the end of this line in *Poems;* this is un-
     doubtedly an error and a period does appear in *MS* and *SOCDA.*
5   vision;]   ~
6   calm;]   ~ .
9   Oh, . . . sphere]   **(O . . . spheres**   also lines 21 and 33
12   star!]   ~ **)**   also line 36
13   secure!]   ~ ,
22-24   These lines are represented by *etc.* in *MS.*
25   ecstatic!]   ~ ,
29   evening!]   ~ ,
31   flower]   **power**

Glossary
7   *Elysian:*   see "The Hawkbit"

p.144 THE CRICKET

A holograph manuscript of the poem, dated September 10, 1892, survives in
the Queen's University Archives. The poem was first published in *The Book
of the Native,* 1896; and later appeared in *The Living Age* (August 28, 1897);
and *Poems,* 1901/7. The *Le Gallienne Book of English and American Poetry,*
1922/35, included the first stanza only. Roberts autographed an advertisement of his 1925 Trans-Canada tour for William Arthur Deacon with the first
four lines of the poem.

Variants
Title: The Cricket]   **Song** *MS*
1   Oh,]   ~   *MS*
6   thistle-thicket]   **thistle thicket** *MS*   **thistle-thicket,**   *Living
                                                              Age*
7   pass,]   ~ ,– *MS*
8   a-wing,]   ~ ,– *MS*
13   sweet,]   ~   *MS*
14   sting!]   ~   *MS*   After this line *MS* inserts *So one has one's fling!*
16   oh,]   ~   *MS*
17   clover!]   ~ ,– *MS*
19   thistle-thicket]   **thistle thicket** *MS*
21   humming–]   ~ ,– *MS*

458

p. 144 AVE! (An Ode for the Shelley Centenary, 1892)

The poem was first published in *Ave: An Ode for the Centenary of the Birth of Percy Bysshe Shelley, August 4, 1792* in 1892. It also appeared in *Songs of the Common Day and Ave*, 1893; *Poems*, 1901/7; *Selected Poems*, 1936; *Selected Poems of Sir Charles G.D. Roberts*, 1955; and *Selected Poetry and Critical Prose*, 1974.

In a letter to Bliss Carman, dated October 29, 1892, Roberts notes that he has just completed the poem.

Variants

Title: *Ave! (An Ode for the Shelley Centenary, 1892)*]   **Ave: An Ode for the Centenary of Shelley's Birth** *Ave*   **Ave! An Ode for the Centenary of Shelley's Birth** *SOCDA, Poems* 1901/7

17	another, . . . sky,]	**another . . . sky** *Ave*
26	palm)]	**~).** *Ave* **~),** *SOCDA*
44	vetches,–]	**~ ;–** *SOCDA*
75	**awash**]	**a-wash** *Ave, SOCDA*
85	sharp,]	**~** *Ave, SOCDA*
104	Desire,]	**~** *Ave, SOCDA*
111	cradle]	**~ ,** *Ave, SOCDA, Poems* 1901/7
132	penitential,]	**~** *Ave, SOCDA*
143	loveliness]	**~ ,** *Ave*
199	o'erwearied]	**o'er-wearied** *Ave*
204	death]	**Death** *Ave*
211	Lament]	**–Lament** *Ave, SOCDA*
224	Love]	**love** *Ave, SOCDA*
259	Milton,]	**~** *Ave, SOCDA*
272	tears,–]	**~ ;–** *Ave, SOCDA*
275	lion-limbed]	**lion limbed** *Poems* 1901/7
283	forever]	**for ever** *SOCDA;* also line 293
298	seek,–]	**~ ;–** *Ave, SOCDA*

Glossary

1   *Tantramar:*   see "Tantramar Revisited"

52   *River of hubbub:* Roberts explained in *The Canadian Guide-Book* that Tantramar is a corruption of the French *Tintamarre,* meaning a hubbub

62   *Fundy:* see "Epistle to Bliss Carman"

63   *Minudie:* see "Tantramar Revisited"

64   *Chignecto:* the northern extension of the Bay of Fundy

70   *Beausejour . . . Tormentine:* Beausejour refers either to the Acadian settlement near Sackville or to the fort near the New Brunswick-Nova Scotia border. Tormentine refers either to the town or cape of the same name, on the extreme

eastern tip of New Brunswick. The distance between the two points is approximately thirty miles.

 75   *goose-tongue:* a salt marsh plant, gathered and eaten as a green
 87   *him:*   the first reference to Shelley, born August 4, 1792
108   *bays:*   see "Rondeau"
130   *Dante:*   Alighieri Dante (1265-1321) the great Italian poet, author of *The Divine Comedy* and other works
131-140 *With ... flowers:*   a reference to Shelley's expulsion from Oxford University in 1811 for the publication of a pamphlet called *The Necessity of Atheism*
142   *Alastor:*   *Alastor, or The Spirit of Solitude* was Shelley's first major poem, published in 1816
147   *Reuss and Rhine:*   both European rivers originate in Switzerland. Roberts is, of course, making Shelley's wanderings analogous to those of Alastor.
151-180 *Thyself ... blue!—:*   The references are to Shelley's poems "To a Skylark" (1820), "The Cloud" (1820), "Ode to the West Wind" (1820), and *Prometheus Unbound* (1820).
152   *Protean:*   like Proteus, the sea-god capable of assuming many forms
159   *Arnos:*   the Arno is a river in central Italy
164   *the great Titan:*   Prometheus, according to Greek mythology the creator of man. When Zeus deprived man of fire, Prometheus stole fire from Olympus and returned it to man. As punishment, Prometheus was chained to a rock where, each day, a vulture fed on his liver, and each night he was restored. He was ultimately freed by Hercules.
171   *Baths of Caracalla:*   Caracalla was a Roman emperor from A.D. 211-217
181   *Pisa:*   a city in Italy, on the Arno River
182   *ilexes:*   the ilex is a tree of the holly oak family
183   *San Giuliano:*   a town in Italy, just north of Pisa
184   *aziola:*   a small owl
185   *Serchio:*   a river in Italy, flowing north of Pisa
188   *Thy ... psalm:*   the reference is to Shelley's *Epipsychidion* (1821)
195-205 *The ... mystical:*   the reference is to Shelley's *Adonais* (1821), the elegy on the death of John Keats
211-230 *Lament ... pain:*   on July 8, 1822, Shelley was drowned in the Gulf of Spezzia while on a trip to Lerici
230   *Casa Magni:*   the villa occupied by the Shelley's, near Lerici, at the time of his death
234   *one ... graves:*   both Keats and Shelley are buried in the Protestant cemetery in Rome
251-254 *He ... Isle:*   Homer
254-256 *and ... victor:*   Aeschylus, Greek playwright, author of *Prometheus Bound;* and Shelley's own *Prometheus Unbound*

460

257-258 *and . . . divine:* King David
259 *Omar:* see "The Isles—An Ode"
259 *the Tuscan:* Dante
261-280 *Back . . . bird:* Shelley's body came ashore and was buried on
  August 16, 1822, by Byron, Trelawney, and Hunt.
278 *one . . . ghost:* Keats?

p. 153 EPITAPH FOR A SAILOR BURIED ASHORE

The poem first appeared in *Harper's Weekly* (December, 1892); and was subsequently published in *Songs of the Common Day and Ave*, 1893; *Later Canadian Poems*, 1893; *Critic* (April, 1894); *A Victorian Anthology*, 1895; *A Treasury of Helpful Verse*, 1896; *Current Opinion* (May, 1899); *A Treasury of Canadian Verse*, 1900; *Poems*, 1901/7; *Oxford Book of Canadian Verse*, 1913; *Songs of the Sea and Sailor's Chanteys*, 1924; *Selected Poems*, 1936; *The Eternal Sea*, 1946; *Selected Poems of Sir Charles G.D. Roberts*, 1955; *Poets of Confederation*, 1967; and *Selected Poetry and Critical Prose*, 1974. The Rufus Hathaway Collection at the University of New Brunswick also contains two unidentified clippings of the poem. HC(1) is evidently a reprint of the text in the *Oxford Book of Canadian Verse*.

Variants
Title: Epitaph for a Sailor Buried Ashore] **To a Sailor Buried Ashore**
  Songs of the Sea and Sailor's Chanteys
  Epitaph for a Sailor *HC*(1)
1 He who] **He, who,** *Oxford Book of Can. Verse, HC*(1)
2 clouds] ~ , *Treasury of Can. Verse*
4 change;] ~ : *Oxford Book of Can. Verse, HC*(1)
5 west . . . east] **West . . . East** *Critic, Treasury of Helpful Verse,*
  Treasury of Can. Verse, Oxford Book of Can. Verse,
  HC(1), *Songs of the Sea and Sailor's Chanteys, HC*(2)
6 of . . . and] **from . . . to** *Treasury of Helpful Verse*
6 North . . . South] **north . . . south** *Victorian Anth.*
7 Freedom's] **freedom's** *Treasury of Helpful Verse*
8 mouth;] ~ : *Oxford Book of Can. Verse, HC*(1)
9 stranger speech] **stranger-speech** *SOCDA, Critic, Current*
  Opinion, Treasury of Can. Verse, Poems 1901/7, *HC*(2)
9 speech,] ~ *Treasury of Helpful Verse*
12 lands—] ~ ,— *Critic, Treasury of Helpful Verse*

p. 154 BRINGING HOME THE COWS

The poem was initially published in *Lippincott's Magazine* (January, 1893); and later appeared in *Songs of the Common Day and Ave*, 1893; and *Poems,*

461

1901/7. As well, the Rufus Hathaway Collection at the University of New Brunswick contains an unidentified clipping which was printed, with additional variants, from *Lippincott's*.

Variants

4   cows.]   ~ !   *HC*
6   alder-boughs]   **alder boughs**   *HC*
13   bright]   **thronged**   *Lippincott's, HC*
19   Oh,]   ~   *Lippincott's, HC, SOCDA*

p. 155 THE CICADA IN THE FIRS

The poem was first published in *Harper's Weekly* (January, 1893); and was later included in *Songs of the Common Day and Ave*, 1893; *Poems*, 1901/7; and *Selected Poems*, 1936. An unidentified clipping in the Rufus Hathaway Collection at the University of New Brunswick is based on the text in *Harper's*.

Variants

1   vibrant,]   ~   *HC*
1   white]   ~ ,   *Harper's, HC*
2   firs]   **first**   *HC*
3   pale, . . . pasture-hill]   **pale . . . pasture hill**   *Harper's, HC*
3   round]   ~ ,   *SOCDA*
7   blunt-faced,]   ~   *Harper's, HC*
7   wing-notes]   **wing notes**   *HC*
9   O]   **Oh,**   *Harper's, HC*
9   came]   ~ ,   *SOCDA*
11   Summer's]   **summer's**   *Harper's, HC*
12   chord]   **note**   *Harper's, HC*

p. 155 WHITEWATERS

As far as may be determined, the poem was first published in *The Book of the Native*, 1896. There is, however, an unidentified galley sheet—evidently for periodical publication as the title is followed by Roberts' name and "King's College, Windsor, N.S." appears at the end of the poem—in the Roberts Collection at the University of New Brunswick. Certainly Roberts intended to have the poem published in a journal, as evidenced by a letter to Susan Hayes Ward of *The Independent* in 1893. No periodical publication, however, including *The Independent*, has so far come to light. The poem was again published in *Poems*, 1901/7.

Variants

1   Whitewaters]   ~ ,   *RC*

462

9	seen,] ~ *RC*
13	A-through] **All through** *RC*
38	home.] ~ ; *RC, BON*
42	last, most cherished] **latest, cherished** *RC*
52	splashed,] ~ *RC*
82	breast.] ~ .– *RC*
84	keel.] ~ ; *RC, BON*
86	moan,] ~ ; *RC*
109	he:] ~ – *RC, BON*
113	mate:] ~ :– *RC, BON*
117	irresolute] ~ ;– *RC, BON*
120	slow, . . . thirst.–] **slow . . . thirst,–** *RC, BON*
137	night . . . deep,] **night, . . . deep** *RC, BON*

Glossary

Whitewaters: The village of Whitewaters in Nova Scotia is located on the eastern side of the Blomidon Peninsula.

12   *Minas:*   see "Blomidon"

14   *Pereau:*   a small stream flowing into the Minas Basin

22   *Blomidon:*   see "Blomidon"

35   *Hally Clive:*   In a letter to Susan Hayes Ward of *The Independent* Roberts writes, "Don't you think the name *Stevie* might with advantage be changed—say to Ally or Hally? Carman is much opposed to *Stevie*."

90   *Noel's haunted wood:*   an obscure topical reference

102   *Kingsport Light:*   Kingsport is a town south of Whitewaters; apparently there was a lighthouse there at one time, but it no longer exists.

103   *Fundy:*   see "Epistle to Bliss Carman"

128   *Avon:*   a river in Nova Scotia flowing into the Minas Basin

p. 159 BUCKWHEAT

The poem first appeared in *Songs of the Common Day and Ave,* 1893; and was later included in *Poems,* 1901/7; *Selected Poems,* 1936; and *Selected Poetry and Critical Prose,* 1974.

Variant

3   comes] ~ , *SOCDA*

p. 159 CANADIAN STREAMS

The poem first appeared in *Songs of the Common Day and Ave,* 1893; and was later published in *Later Canadian Poems,* 1893; *The University Monthly* (March, 1895); *A Treasury of Canadian Verse,* 1900; *Poems,* 1901/7; the *Methodist Magazine and Review* (August, 1906); and *Selected Poems,* 1936.

Variants

1   O rivers]   **O, rivers,** *Methodist Mag. and Rev.*

2   maple-tree]   **maple tree** *Later Can. Poems, Univ. Monthly, Treasury of Can. Verse*

4   liberty!]   ~ . *Methodist Mag. and Rev.*

5   holy]   **Holy** *Univ. Monthly*

9   O]   ~ , *Methodist Mag. and Rev.;* also line 41

9   streams–]   ~ ,– *Later Can. Poems, Univ. Monthly*

12   streams!]   ~ . *Methodist Mag. and Rev.*

13   laves]   **lanes** *Univ. Monthly*

15   Richelieu]   ~ , *Methodist Mag. and Rev.*

23   thou]   ~ , *Treasury of Can. Verse*

24   Beaubassin]   **Bearubassin** *Univ. Monthly*

27   reveal,]   ~ *Later Can. Poems*

36   sweet?]   ~ ! *Later Can. Poems, Univ. Monthly*

38   trod,]   ~ *Univ. Monthly*

39   slain,–]   ~ – *Univ. Monthly, Methodist Mag. and Rev.*

40   Your]   **Their** *SOCDA, Later Can. Poems, Univ. Monthly, Treasury of Can. Verse, Poems* 1901/7, *Methodist Mag. and Rev.* Note: In Roberts' reading copy of *Poems* 1907 *Their* is crossed through and *Your*, in Roberts' hand, written in the margin.

41   waters!]   ~ , *Later Can. Poems, Univ. Monthly*

43   us . . . tone]   **us, . . . tone,** *Methodist Mag. and Rev.*

44   An extra, and perhaps non-authorial, stanza follows in *The University Monthly:*

> Sons of the North, to manhood grown,
> Be loyal, though ye stand alone;
>   Be true and strong, that men may know
> Canadian arms will guard their own!

Glossary

13 *St. Lawrence:* in Ontario and Quebec, the river flows northeast from Lake Ontario and drains the Great Lakes into the Gulf of St. Lawrence

15 *Richelieu:* in Quebec, the river flows from Lake Champlain north to the St. Lawrence

464

16	*Niagara:*	on the U.S.–Ontario border, flowing from Lake Erie into Lake Ontario
17	*Ottawa:*	roughly on the Ontario-Quebec border, the river joins the St. Lawrence at Montreal
18	*Daulac:*	see "The Keepers of the Pass"
19	*La Tour:*	either Claude de La Tour (fl. 1610-1635) or his son, Charles de Saint-Etienne de La Tour (1596-1666). Claude was an adventurer and trader; by exchanging loyalties had himself and his sons created baronets of Nova Scotia by the English. Charles refused to change loyalties and was made lieutenant-governor of a large part of Acadia by the French.
22	*Tecumseh:*	(1768-1813) chief of the Shawnee tribe and influential over all of the Indians in the Old North West. He sided with the British in the War of 1812 and was killed in the battle of Moraviantown, October 6, 1813.
24	*Twixt Beaubassin and Beauséjour:*	the Tantramar river is between Beaubassin (now Cumberland Bay) and the Acadian settlement of Beauséjour
25	*Saguenay:*	in Quebec, the river flows from Lake St. John southeast to the St. Lawrence
27	*Roberval:*	Jean François de la Rocque, Sieur de Roberval (1500?-1560?) French colonizer, viceroy, and lieutenant-general of New France. He followed the discoveries of Cartier and spent the winter of 1542-3 near Quebec City. He returned to France, with his colonists, in 1543. The exact date and circumstances of his death are unknown.
29	*Annapolis:*	in Nova Scotia, the river is near the Bay of Fundy
30	*Champlain:*	see "Canada"
32	*Pourincourt:*	Jean de Biencourt de Poutrincourt, Baron de St. Just (d. 1615), soldier and colonizer, explored Acadia in the company of Sieur de Monts. Or, his son, Charles de Biencourt de Poutrincourt (d. 1623?), who visited Acadia with the 1605 Sieur de Monts expedition. He was at one time in command of the colony at Port Royal.
32	*D'Iberville:*	Pierre le Moyne, Sieur d'Iberville (1661-1706), French explorer and naval commander whose Canadian career was largely centered around Hudson Bay. He was also governor of Louisiana from 1704-6.
35	*Saskatchewan:*	in Saskatchewan, the river flows through the central part of the province into Lake Winnipeg
36	*So . . . sweet:*	a reference to the North West Rebellions of 1870 and 1875, led by Louis Riel. See "Collect for Dominion Day"
38	*De Salaberry:*	There are three de Salaberrys of note. Ignace Michel Louis Antoine d' Irumberry de Salaberry (1752-1828).

In 1775 he participated in the defense of Quebec and was with Burgoyne at Saratoga in 1777. He was a member of the Legislative Assembly of Lower Canada from 1792-6. In 1808 he was appointed an honorary member of the Executive Council of Lower Canada and in 1817 a member of the Legislative Council.

Charles Michel d' Irumberry de Salaberry (1778-1829), the son of Ignace, he served in the British army during the Napoleonic Wars. He returned to Canada in 1810, and in 1812 was commissioned to raise among the French Canadians the Canadian Voltigeurs. In 1813 he defeated an American force at Chateaguay and was created C.B. in 1817 in recognition of his services. He became a member of the Legislative Council of Lower Canada in 1818.

Charles René Léonidas d' Irumberry de Salaberry (1820-1882), the son of Charles, he was an engineer in the North West for the Hudson Bay Company from 1855-60 and in 1869 was one of the investigators of the *Metis* problem in the Red River district. He was, for a brief period, prisoner of Louis Riel. In 1869 he was also appointed superintendent of woods and forests for the province of Quebec.

| 39 | *Wolfe:* | James Wolfe (1729-1759), the victorious British general killed at the battle of Quebec |
| 39 | *Brock:* | Sir Isaac Brock (1769-1812), British soldier sent, as lieutenant-colonel of the 49th Regiment, to Canada in 1802. Just before the beginning of the War of 1812, he was appointed president and administrator of Upper Canada. In the war, Brock captured Detroit and defeated an invading force of Americans at Queenston Heights. He was killed in the battle, October 13, 1812. |

p. 161 THE CHOPPING BEE

Queen's University holds a scribal transcript of the poem, signed by Roberts. The scribe was undoubtedly Annie Prat. The poem first appeared in *Songs of the Common Day and Ave,* 1893; and was later included in *Poems,* 1901/7; *Selected Poems,* 1936; and *Selected Poetry and Critical Prose,* 1974. As well, the Rufus Hathaway Collection at the University of New Brunswick contains an unidentified clipping of a short version of the poem which includes only lines 1-24 and 58-60.

Variants
Title: The Chopping Bee]   **The Wood Frolic** *MS, SOCDA, Poems*
          1901/7, *HC*

466

2   our]   **the**   *MS*

2   day.]   ~ ;   *HC*

3   forest, . . . high!]   **forest . . . high.**   *MS*

6   Oh, merry . . . fly!]   **Oh, the . . . high.**   *MS;* also lines 12, 24, 30, 36, 42, 48 and 54.

6   fly!]   ~ .   *HC*

8   were]   **ere**   *Poems* 1901/7; in Roberts' reading copy in the Harriet Irving Library at the University of New Brunswick *were* is written in the margin.

8   red.]   ~ ;   *HC*

9   forest, . . . high!]   **forest . . . high**   *MS*

10   lichen]   **lichens**   *MS*

11   and . . . juniper.]   **the . . . juniper;**   *HC*

13   ^{2}air]   ~ ,   *HC*

14   deep.]   ~ ;   *HC*

15   Oh, the . . . high!]   **Oh, merry . . . fly.**   *MS;* also lines 21, 27, 33, 39, 45, 51, 57.

16   blades]   ~ ,   *SOCDA, HC*

18   fly!]   ~ .   *MS*

19   hard wood . . . soft wood . . . use;]   **hard-wood . . . soft-wood . . . use,**   *MS*

20   chiefly, . . . gum,]   **chiefly . . . gum**   *HC*

22   down,]   ~ ;   *HC*

23   crown.]   ~ ;   *HC*

25   So, . . . up . . . soon;]   **Oh . . . up . . . soon,**   *MS;* in *MS up* has been crossed through

28   through the trees,]   **thro' the trees**   *MS*

31   last-returning . . . bright,]   **last returning . . . bright**   *MS*

32   frosty shadowed]   **frosty-shadowed**   *MS*

34   ceiling,]   ~   *MS*

35   onions,]   ~   *MS*

35   healing.]   ~ !   *SOCDA, Poems* 1901/7

37   dresser-shelves]   **dresser shelves**   *MS*

40   Then,]   ~   *MS*

41   pumpkinpie]   **pumpkin pie**   *MS*

43   bread-and-cheese and doughnuts . . . year!]   **bread and cheese and doughnuts . . . year,**   *MS*

47   tack;]   ~ ,   *MS*

49   funny–]   ~ ,   *MS*

52   fiddle,]   ~   *MS*

53   able,]   ~ ;   *MS*

55   go.]   ~ . . . .   *MS*

56   racing-teams . . . snow;]   **racing teams . . . snow,**   *MS*

59   stars,]   ~   *MS*

60   high!]   ~ .   *MS*

p. 163 THE COW PASTURE

McGill University holds an autographed manuscript of the poem, perhaps intended to be included in the partial manuscript book of *Songs of the Common Day*. The poem was first published in *Songs of the Common Day and Ave*, 1893; and later appeared in *Poems*, 1901/7; *Selected Poems*, 1936; *Selected Poems of Sir Charles G.D. Roberts*, 1955; and *Selected Poetry and Critical Prose*, 1974.

Variants
3   small,]   ~ *MS*
5   sparse,]   ~ *MS*
11   Through incompletion,]   **Thro' incompletion**   *MS*

p. 163 THE HERRING WEIR

The poem was first published in *Songs of the Common Day and Ave*, 1893; and later appeared in *Poems*, 1901/7; *Selected Poems*, 1936; *Selected Poems of Sir Charles G.D. Roberts*, 1955; *Penguin Book of Canadian Verse*, 1967; and *Selected Poetry and Critical Prose*, 1974.

Note: in *Songs of the Common Day and Ave* the poem is not divided into an octave and sestet

p. 164 IN AN OLD BARN

The poem first appeared in *Songs of the Common Day and Ave*, 1893; and was later included in *Poems*, 1901/7; *Selected Poems*, 1936; *A Book of Canadian Poetry*, 1943/8; *Canadian Poems 1850-1952*, 1953; *Selected Poems of Sir Charles G.D. Roberts*, 1955; *Canadian Anthology*, 1966; and *Selected Poetry and Critical Prose*, 1974. A holograph manuscript of the poem is contained in the partial manuscript book of *Songs of the Common Day* at McGill University.

Variant
13   housed,]   ~ *MS*

Glossary
2   *mows:*   the area(s) in a barn where hay, grain, etc. is stored

p. 164 INDIAN SUMMER

The poem first appeared in *Songs of the Common Day and Ave*, 1893; and was later included in *Poems*, 1901/7. A holograph manuscript is contained

468

in the partial manuscript book of *Songs of the Common Day* at McGill University.

Variants

4	number.]	An exclamation point has been crossed through in *MS*.
7	heaven]	**Heaven** *MS, SOCDA*
8	done with]	In *MS, put off* has been crossed through and *done with* written above it.
9	unlooked-for]	**unlooked for** *MS*
11	radiance,]	~ *MS*

p. 165 MARSYAS

The poem first appeared in *Songs of the Common Day and Ave*, 1893; and was later included in *A Victorian Anthology*, 1895; *Poems*, 1901/7; *Oxford Book of Canadian Verse*, 1913; *Selected Poems*, 1936; *Selected Poems of Sir Charles G.D. Roberts*, 1955; *Penguin Book of Canadian Verse*, 1967; *Poets of Confederation*, 1967; and *Selected Poetry and Critical Prose*, 1974. A holograph manuscript is contained in the partial manuscript book of *Songs of the Common Day* at McGill University.

Variants

1	little]	~ , *MS*
29	half-shut]	**half shut** *MS*
30	nor]	**Nor** *Oxford Book of Can. Verse*
31	god]	**God** *MS, SOCDA, Victorian Anth., Poems* 1901/7

Glossary

	Marsyas:	a satyr who challenged Apollo to a musical contest, the winner to treat the loser as he wanted. Apollo won the contest and flayed Marsyas alive. The poem suggests that the challenge came from Apollo.
7	*Pontic:*	the Black Sea, north of Turkey and near Greece
22	*hern:*	the heron

p. 166 MIDWINTER THAW

The poem was first published in *Songs of the Common Day and Ave*, 1893; and was later included in *Poems*, 1901/7; and *Selected Poetry and Critical Prose*, 1974. As well, the Rufus Hathaway Collection at the University of New Brunswick contains an unidentified clipping of the poem. A holograph manuscript of the poem is included in the partial manuscript book of *Songs of the Common Day* at McGill University.

3   soft]   ~ , *MS, SOCDA*

12   ghost . . . rare;] **host . . . rare,** *HC*

p. 166 THE OAT-THRESHING

The poem first appeared in *Songs of the Common Day and Ave,* 1893; and was subsequently published in *Poems,* 1901/7; *Selected Poems,* 1936; *Selected Poems of Sir Charles G.D. Roberts,* 1955; and *Selected Poetry and Critical Prose,* 1974.

Variant

2   autumn] **Autumn**   *SOCDA*

Glossary

3   *cinnabar:* bright red or vermilion

p. 167 OH, PURPLE HANG THE PODS!

The poem was probably published first in *Later Canadian Poems,* 1893; and was later included in *Songs of the Common Day and Ave,* 1893; *Poems,* 1901/7; and *Selected Poems,* 1936. Pomeroy (p. 115) says that this is another of the poems written for Goodridge Roberts.

Variants

Title: Oh, Purple Hang the Pods!] **Song** *Later Can. Poems*

2   locust-tree] **locust tree** *Later Can. Poems*

4   me!] ~ ; *Later Can. Poems*

6   autumn] **Autumn** *Later Can. Poems, SOCDA*

10   winter's] **Winter's** *Later Can. Poems, SOCDA*

11   oh,] ~ *SOCDA*

p. 167 PROLOGUE

The poem was first published in *Songs of the Common Day and Ave,* 1893; and later appeared in *Poems,* 1901/7; *Selected Poems,* 1936; and *Selected Poetry and Critical Prose,* 1974.

Variants

Note: the poem was published without title in *Songs of the Common Day and Ave* and *Poems.*

p. 167 THE PUMPKINS IN THE CORN

The poem was initially published in *Songs of the Common Day and Ave*, 1893; and later appeared in *Poems*, 1901/7; *Selected Poems*, 1936; and *Selected Poetry and Critical Prose*, 1974.

Variants
All variants are from *Songs of the Common Day and Ave*.
2   morning star]   **Morning Star**
3   autumn]   **Autumn**
6   corn,]   ~
8   autumn morns]   **Autumn morn's**

p. 168 THE SUCCOUR OF GLUSKÂP

The first identified publication of the poem is in *Songs of the Common Day and Ave*, 1893; and it was later included in *Poems*, 1901/7. However, an earlier and unidentified clipping (UC) is contained in the partial manuscript book of *Songs of the Common Day* at McGill University.

Variants
Sub-title: Melicite]   **Micmac**   *UC, SOCDA*
9   splashed]   **plashed**   *UC;* Roberts has added an *s* to correct the
                obvious error.

Glossary
Gluskâp: see "The Departing of Gluskâp"
4   *Peniawk:*   Penniac Brook; Roberts' spelling is an attempt to dupli-
                cate the Melicite word, *Pan-weè-ok.*
23   *Wahloos:*   an obscure reference
25   *sachems:*   members of the governing body of the tribe
46   *Hills of Kawlm:*   an obscure reference

p. 170 THE TIDE ON TANTRAMAR

The poem first appeared in *Songs of the Common Day and Ave*, 1893; and was reprinted only in *Poems*, 1901/7. A holograph manuscript is included in the partial manuscript book of *Songs of the Common Day* at McGill University.

Variants
6   blue]   in *MS, high* has been crossed through and *blue* written
                beside it
11   outbore]   in *MS, upbore* has been crossed through and *outbore*
                written under it

471

29	to]	**back**	*MS*
40	apart]	~ ,	*MS*
42	tall;]	~ .	*MS*
75	be?]	~ ?—	*MS, SOCDA*
80	His]	in *MS, And* has been crossed through and *His* written above it	
104	blow.]	~ ;	*MS, SOCDA*
106	gale]	in *MS,* a word has been completely blotted out and *gale* written above it	
107	white.]	~	*SOCDA*
113	Blind . . . bull]	in *MS,* a line has been completely blotted out and *Blind . . . bull* written below it	
115	The]	in *MS, That* has been crossed through and *The* written above it	
122	One]	—**One**	*MS, SOCDA*
124	Then]	—**Then**	*MS, SOCDA*
131	fisher-folk]	**fisher folk**	*MS*
138	tides.]	~ ,	*SOCDA*
139	sides.]	~ ,	*SOCDA*
149	away.]	~ !	*MS*
150	[1]Tantramar]	—**Tantramar**	*MS, SOCDA*
153	their]	**its**	*MS*

Glossary
Tantramar: see "Tantramar Revisited"

p. 174 THE STILLNESS OF THE FROST

The poem was first published in *The Century Magazine* (January, 1894); and was later included in *The Book of the Native,* 1896; *Poems,* 1901/7; *Selected Poems,* 1936; *Selected Poems of Sir Charles G.D. Roberts,* 1955; and *Selected Poetry and Critical Prose,* 1974.

Variants
10	lay'st]	**lay'dst**	*Century*
12	accord,]	~	*Century*
Note:	in *The Century Magazine* and *The Book of the Native* the poem is not divided into an octave and a sestet.		

p. 175 RESURRECTION

The poem was initially published in *Harper's Weekly* (March, 1894); and was later included in *The Book of the Native,* 1896; and *Poems,* 1901/7.

472

5   They,]   ~   *Harper's*
6   Windflower . . . may]   **Wind-flower . . . May**   *Harper's*
11 wayside]   **way-side** *Harper's*
13 hedgerows]   **hedge-rows** *Harper's, BON*
14 We, too,]   **We too** *Harper's*
15 blossom,]   ~   *Harper's*

p. 175 THE QUEST OF THE ARBUTUS

The poem first appeared in *The Century Magazine* (April, 1894); and was later included in *The Book of the Native*, 1896; and *Poems*, 1901/7. As well, the Rufus Hathaway Collection at the University of New Brunswick contains an unidentified clipping of the poem evidently related to the *Century* text. The Hathaway clipping is an abridged text having only lines 1-8 and 17-24.

Variants
4   veins!]   ~ . *HC*
5   kind,]   ~ *Century, HC*
6   behind;]   ~ : *Century, HC*
7   day,]   ~ *HC*
15 lacking,–]   ~ – *Century*
17 length]   ~ , *Century, HC*
17 nest,]   ~ *Century*
18 spring's]   **Spring's** *HC*

Glossary
Arbutus: the Trailing Arbutus, a creeping plant with fragrant white and pink blossoms

p. 176 RENEWAL

The poem was initially published in the *New Outlook* (May, 1894); and later appeared in *The Book of the Native*, 1896; and *Poems, 1901/7.*

Variants
6   dew,–]   ~ – *New Outlook*
7   dear]   ~ , *New Outlook*
8   Old,]   ~ *New Outlook*

The poem was first published in *The Century Magazine* (May, 1894); and later appeared in *Current Opinion* (July, 1894); *The Book of the Native*, 1896; *A Treasury of Canadian Verse*, 1900; *Poems*, 1901/7; *Another Book of Verses for Children*, 1907/36/71; *A Book of Lullabies*, 1925; *The Speaker* (1925); *The Poetry Book* (an abridgement containing only lines 1-12), 1926; *The Home Book of Modern Verse*, 1930; *My Poetry Book*, 1934/68; and *Poetry for Women to Speak Chorally*, 1940.

Variants

Title: Sleepy Man]   **When the Sleepy Man Comes**   *Current Opinion, The Poetry Book, Home Book of Mod. Verse, My Poetry Book*

1   Sleepy Man]   **sleepy man**   *Another Book of Verses for Children, Speaker, The Poetry Book, My Poetry Book*

1   on]   **in**   *Treasury of Can. Verse*

1   eyes]   ~ ,   *Century, Current Opinion, Book of Lullabies, The Poetry Book, Home Book of Mod. Verse, My Poetry Book*

2   Oh]   **O**   *Another Book of Verses for Children;* also lines 6, 10, 14, 18, and 22

2   weary!)]   ~),   *Another Book of Verses for Children;* also lines 14, 18, and 22

4   weary]   ~ ,   *Treasury of Can. Verse, Speaker, Poetry for Women;* also lines 8, 12, 16, 20, and 24

5   sun;]   ~   *Another Book of Verses for Children*

6   weary!)]   ~);   *Another Book of Verses for Children;* also line 10

7   one.]   ~   *Speaker*

9   castles]   **castle**   *The Poetry Book*

9   Town;]   ~   *Another Book of Verses for Children*

11   ²the]   omitted in *The Poetry Book* and *My Poetry Book*

13   dream]   **dreams**   *Treasury of Can. Verse*

13   wings]   ~ ,   *Century, Current Opinion, Speaker*
        ~ ;   *Book of Lullabies, Home Book of Mod. Verse, My Poetry Book*

17   Then]   **When**   *Treasury of Can. Verse*

17   bane]   ~ ,   *Century, Current Opinion, Treasury of Can. Verse, Speaker*   ~ ;   *Book of Lullabies, Home Book of Mod. Verse, My Poetry Book*

19   Lane,]   ~ .   *Another Book of Verses for Children, Book of Lullabies, Speaker, Home Book of Mod. Verse, My Poetry Book*

21   Wherry]   ~ ,   *Book of Lullabies, Speaker, Home Book of Mod. Verse, My Poetry Book*

23   Castle]   ~ ,   *My Poetry Book*

21   *Wherry:*   a small, light, and swift rowboat

p. 177 THE TROUT BROOK

The poem first appeared in *Harper's Weekly* (May, 1894); and was later published in *The Book of the Native*, 1896; *Current Opinion* (May, 1899); *Poems*, 1901/7; *Selected Poems*, 1936; and *Selected Poetry and Critical Prose*, 1974.

Variants
3   falling]   ~ ,   *Harper's, BON, Current Opinion*
4   golden-wings]   **goldenwings**   *Harper's*
16   tinsel]   **tinselled**   *Harper's, BON, Current Opinion*
26   reaches.]   ~ ,   *Current Opinion*
29   long, . . . done,]   **long . . . done**   *Harper's*

p. 178 THE UNSLEEPING

The poem first appeared in *The Chap-Book* (May 15, 1894) and was later published in *The Critic* (May 22, 1894); *The Book of the Native*, 1896; *Poems*, 1901/7; *Selected Poems*, 1936; *Anthology of Canadian Poetry*, 1942; *Selected Poems of Sir Charles G.D. Roberts*, 1955; and *Poets of Confederation*, 1967.

Variants
2   deep.]   ~ ;   *Chap-Book, Critic*
14   sun;]   ~ .   *Chap-Book*
24   by.]   ~ !   *Chap-Book, Critic*

p. 179 ADMITTANCE

The poem appeared only in *Lippincott's Magazine* (June, 1894).

p. 179 A HOMING SONG

The poem was first published in *The Independent* (June 28, 1894); and was reprinted only in *Sir Charles G.D. Roberts*, 1943, where Pomeroy (p. 74) reports that it was written for **Roberts'** children.

Variants
21   No comma appears after *bird* in Pomeroy, but there is no reason that the second refrain should not be identical to the first.

p. 180 THE PIPER AND THE CHIMING PEAS

The poem first appeared in *The Independent* (July 19, 1894); and was later included in *The Book of the Rose*, 1903; *Poems*, 1901/7; and *Selected Poems*, 1936.

Variants
All variants are from *The Independent*
6   ease,–]   ~ –
8   these!]   ~ ."
13   Oh, . . . Sir! That could not be!]   **Oh . . . sir, that cannot be,**
14   peas.]   ~ ;
16   bumble-bees]   **bumblebees**

Glossary
12   *Wagnerese:*   in the manner of Richard Wagner (1813-83), the German composer of vast and complex operas

p. 180 THE BALLAD OF CROSSING THE BROOK

The poem first appeared in *Scribner's* (August, 1894); and was later published in *The Book of the Native*, 1896; *Poems*, 1901/7; *Choice Readings*, 1903; *The Speaker* (1925); *Cap and Bells*, 1936; and *Selected Poems*, 1936.

Pomeroy (pp. 88-89) reports the following incident in connection with the poem.

One of his most interesting experiences in the casting of horoscopes was connected with the "dainty, dainty maid" in "The Ballad of Crossing the Brook." He and Carman were spending a few days in Washington, the guests of Richard Hovey's father and mother. At a picnic arranged in their honour, the poets met the young lady and the incident took place which suggested Roberts' ballad. She had only recently returned home from Paris after studying vocal music there for some time. Naturally she was very much pleased when the Professor of English of King's College promised to cast her horoscope.

At home in Windsor he proceeded to carry out his promise, and was amazed to find that, according to the chart, the apparently healthy young woman was suffering from a serious throat ailment. He forwarded the chart to her and said that, though in other respects the horoscope seemed applicable to her, she with her beautiful voice would be surprised to read the item about her throat. She replied that, alas, it was no surprise to her, for throat trouble had compelled her to give up singing and return home. Within a year the "throat trouble", which was tubercular, proved fatal to her.

476

Variants

Title: The] **A** *Scribner's, Speaker*
 1 a-Maying] **a-maying** *Choice Readings*
 2 degree.] ~ ; *Choice Readings*
 3 merry] ~ , *Choice Readings*
 3 forlorn,] ~ ; *Scribner's, Speaker*
 5 maid;] ~ , *Choice Readings*
 6 one.] ~ ; *Scribner's, BON, Poems* 1901/7, *Choice Readings,*
        Speaker, Cap and Bells
 7 afraid;] ~ , *Choice Readings*
 9 brook] ~ , *Choice Readings*
11 look;] ~ , *Choice Readings*
13 maid;] ~ , *Choice Readings*
15 a-near] **anear** *Choice Readings*
15 aid,–] ~ – *Scribner's, Speaker*   ~ , *Choice Readings*
18 content.] ~ ; *Choice Readings*
20 sly] **shy** *BON, Poems* 1901/7, *Choice Readings*
21 maid,] ~ *Scribner's, Speaker*
22 (O . . . done!)] **Oh, . . . done!** *Choice Readings*
23 feet] ~ , *Choice Readings*
25 Now] ~ , *Scribner's, Speaker*
25 man;] ~ , *Choice Readings*
26 over!] ~ . *Choice Readings*
27 maid–] ~ , *Scribner's, Choice Readings, Speaker*
29 So] ~ , *Scribner's, Speaker*
29 his eyes] **his honest eyes** *Choice Readings*
30 delight.] ~ , *Choice Readings*
31 maid . . . brown;] **maid, . . . brown,** *Choice Readings*
32 impish] **limpid** *Choice Readings*
33 side,] ~ ; *Scribner's, Choice Readings, Speaker*
34 word.] ~ ; *Choice Readings*
35 maid–] ~ , *Choice Readings*
35 Sir] **sir** *Scribner's, Choice Readings, Speaker*
35 said.] ~ – *Scribner's, Speaker*   ~ , *Choice Readings*
37 a-Maying] **a-maying** *Choice Readings*
38 degree.] ~ ; *Scribner's, BON, Choice Readings, Speaker*
39 She] **But she** *Scribner's, Choice Readings, Speaker*
39 forlorn] ~ , *Choice Readings*
40 sea.] ~ ! *Scribner's, Speaker*

Glossary
 8 *a-whimpling:* a whimple is a ripple or rippling in a stream

477

p. 181 KINSHIP

According to Pomeroy (pp. 92-93) the poem was offered three times to
Harper's Magazine before it was accepted. It appeared in *Harper's* (August,
1894); and was later included in *The Book of the Native*, 1896; *Poems*,
1901/7; *Our Canadian Literature*, 1935; *Selected Poems*, 1936; and *Canadian
Anthology*, 1966. An undated typescript is contained in the Roberts Collection at the University of New Brunswick.

Variants
1   vision]   ~ ,   *RC*
2   borderland]   **border-land**   *Harper's, BON, RC*
14   weaves,]   ~ –   *Harper's*
15   tree-root]   **tree root**   *Harper's*
17   hear]   omitted in *RC*
26   reveal,]   ~ ,–   *Harper's*
27   Mother,–]   ~ –   *Harper's*
40   death.]   ~ ;   *Harper's*
44   forever;]   ~ :   *BON, Poems* 1901/7, *Our Can. Lit., RC*
46   farthest]   **furthest**   *Harper's, BON, RC*

p. 183 GOLDEN-ROD

The poem was published only in *Lippincott's Magazine* (September, 1894).

p. 183 UP AND AWAY IN THE MORNING

The poem was initially published as the first of "Two Songs" in *The Century
Magazine* (September, 1894); and appeared in the same format in an unidentified clipping in the Rufus Hathaway Collection at the University of New
Brunswick. The second of "Two Songs" was "Home, Home in the Evening."
The first publication of the poem as an independent unit was in *The Book of
the Native*, 1896; and this was followed by *The Living Age* (September,
1897); *Poems*, 1901/7; and *Selected Poems*, 1936.

Variants
1   full;]   ~ :   *Living Age*
1   white.]   ~   *Century, HC, BON, Living Age, Poems* 1901/7;
                    also line 4
2   morning!)]   **morning);**   *Century, HC, BON*
                    morning).   *Living Age*
3   height;]   ~ :   *Living Age*
5   morning!)]   **morning).**   *Century, HC, BON, Living Age;* also
                    lines 7, 10, 12, 15, 17, and 20

478

6   sun.]   ~   *Century, HC, BON, Living Age, Poems* 1901/7; also
                 line 9
11   day.]   ~   *Century, HC, BON, Living Age, Poems* 1901/7; also
                 line 14
13   has ... has]   **hath ... hath**   *Century, HC*
16   long.]   ~   *Century, HC, BON, Living Age, Poems* 1901/7;
                 also line 19

p. 184 HOME, HOME IN THE EVENING

The poem was initially published as the second of "Two Songs" in *The Century Magazine* (September, 1894); and appeared in the same format in an unidentified clipping in the Rufus Hathaway Collection at the University of New Brunswick. The first of "Two Songs" was "Up and Away in the Morning." The first publication of the poem as an independent unit was in *The Book of the Native*, 1896; and this was followed by *Poems*, 1901/7; and *Selected Poems*, 1936.

Variants
2   evening!)]   ~ ,   *Century, BON;* also line 7
                 ~ .   *HC;* also lines 7 and 12
4   sea.]   ~   *Century, HC, BON, Poems* 1901/7
5   evening!)]   ~).   *Century, HC, BON;* also lines 10 and 15
9   hill.]   ~   *Century, HC, BON, Poems* 1901/7
12   evening!)]   ~),   *Century*   ~).   *BON*
13   hand,]   ~ .   *HC*
14   land.]   ~   *Century, HC, BON, Poems* 1901/7
16   door.]   ~   *Century, HC, BON*
17   evening!)]   ~);   *Century, HC*   ~).   *BON*
19   more]   ~ ,   *Century, HC, BON, Poems* 1901/7

p. 184 THE VENGEANCE OF GLUSKÂP

In November, 1894, the poem appeared in both *The Independent* and the *King's College Record*. It was later included in *The Book of the Native*, 1896; and in *Poems*, 1901/7.

Variants
Sub-title: Melicite]   **Micmac**   *Independent, King's Coll. Rec., BON*
10   again,]   ~   *Independent, King's Coll. Rec.*
21   hiding-places]   **hiding places**   *Independent, King's Coll. Rec.*
24   And ... frown]   **And, ... frown,**   *King's Coll. Rec.*
28   clay;]   ~ .   *Independent, King's Coll. Rec.*
29   sea-mews]   **seamews**   *Independent, King's Coll. Rec., BON*

Glossary
Gluskâp: see "The Departing of Gluskâp"
29   *sea-mews:*   sea gulls

p. 185 IMMANENCE

The poem was first published in the *King's College Record* (December, 1894) as one-third of a composite poem by Roberts, Carman, and Hovey. The single quatrain by Roberts also appeared in *Poems*, 1901/7; and in *Selected Poems*, 1936.

Variants
2   man's]   **Man's**   *King's Coll. Rec.*
3   wonder]   **Wonder**   *King's Coll. Rec.*
4   control]   **Control**   *King's Coll. Rec., Poems* 1901/7

p. 186 ORIGINS

The poem was first published as a manuscript facsimile in *The Chap-Book* (January, 1895); and later appeared in *The Book of the Native*, 1896; *A Treasury of Canadian Verse*, 1900; *Poems*, 1901/7; *Selected Poems*, 1936; *Selected Poems of Sir Charles G.D. Roberts*, 1955; and *Poets of Confederation*, 1967.

Variants
16   start,]   ~ !   *Treasury of Can. Verse*
21   ordain]   ~ ,   *BON*
26   birth.]   ~   *Chap-Book*
36   bequeath]   **bequeathe**   *Chap-Book, BON, Treasury of Can. Verse*
42   heard.]   ~   *Chap-Book*

p. 187 THE BROOK IN FEBRUARY

The poem was initially published in *The Outlook* (February, 1895); and later appeared in *The Book of the Native*, 1896; *Poems*, 1901/7; *The University Monthly* (February, 1905); *Selected Poems of Sir Charles G.D. Roberts*, 1955; *Canadian Anthology*, 1966; and *Selected Poetry and Critical Prose*, 1974. As well, the Rufus Hathaway Collection at the University of New Brunswick contains an unidentified clipping of the poem.

Variants
2   firs.]   ~ ;   *Univ. Monthly*   ~ ,   *HC*
7   hear–]   ~   *Outlook, BON, Univ. Monthly*

480

p. 187 EBB

The poem was first published in *The Independent* (February 28, 1895); and later appeared in *The Book of the Native*, 1896; and *Poems*, 1901/7.

p. 188 THE FROSTED PANE

The poem was first published in *The Atlantic Monthly* (February, 1895); and subsequently appeared in *The Book of the Native*, 1896; *Poems*, 1901/7; *Songs of Nature*, 1902; *University Monthly* (December, 1904); *Home Progress* (March, 1913); *Le Gallienne Book of English and American Poetry*, 1922/35; *Home Book of Modern Verse*, 1930; *Selected Poems*, 1936; *Selected Poems of Sir Charles G.D. Roberts*, 1955; and *Selected Poetry and Critical Prose*, 1974.

Variants
1   Winter]   **winter**   *Univ. Monthly*
1   noiselessly,]   ~   *Songs of Nature, Univ. Monthly, Home
           Progress, Le Gallienne, Home Book of Mod. Verse*
2   window-pane]   **window pane**   *Univ. Monthly*
5   Leaves, . . . earth,]   **Leaves . . . earth.**   *Le Gallienne*
6   grass,–]   ~ ,   *Univ. Monthly*
7   bonds . . . birth,]   **bond . . . birth**   *Univ. Monthly*

p. 188 ICE

The poem first appeared in *Lippincott's Magazine* (March, 1895); and was later included in *New York Nocturnes*, 1898; *Poems*, 1901/7; *Selected Poems*, 1936; *A Book of Canadian Poetry*, 1943/8; *Selected Poems of Sir Charles G.D. Roberts*, 1955; *Exploring Poetry*, 1955; and *Selected Poetry and Critical Prose*, 1974. As well, the Rufus Hathaway Collection at the University of New Brunswick contains an unidentified clipping of the poem.

Variants
3   still,–]   ~ ,   *Lippincott's, HC*

p. 188 AN APRIL ADORATION

As far as may be determined, the poem was first published in *The Outlook* (April, 1895). There is, however, an unidentified clipping which may be earlier (although it seems more related to the text in the *Fredericton Daily Mail*) in the Rufus Hathaway Collection at the University of New Brunswick. The poem also appeared in the *King's College Record* (May, 1895); *The Book of the Native,* 1896; *The University Monthly* (April, 1903); *Poems,* 1901/7; *The Musician* (April, 1910); *The Home Book of Modern Verse,* 1930; and the *Fredericton Daily Mail* (April, 1937).

Variants

1	morn—]	~ : HC, *Daily Mail*
3	done,]	~ *Univ. Monthly*
3	skies.]	~ *Univ. Monthly* ~ , *Home Book of Mod. Verse, Daily Mail*
5-6	Putting . . . grow.]	omitted in *HC* and *Daily Mail*
8	God]	~ , *Univ. Monthly*
9-10	And . . . praise.]	omitted in *HC* and *Daily Mail*
12	rain,]	~ . *Outlook, King's Coll. Rec.*
13	root,]	~ ; *Univ. Monthly*
16	adoration-song]	**adoration song** *Univ. Monthly, Musician*

p. 189 THE COMEDY

The poem was published only in *Lippincott's Magazine* (April, 1895).

p. 189 THE FOREST FIRE

The poem first appeared in *The Independent* (April 4, 1895); and was later published in *The Book of the Native,* 1896; *Current Opinion* (May, 1899); and *Poems,* 1901/7. As well, the Rufus Hathaway Collection at the University of New Brunswick contains an unidentified clipping reprinted, with additional variants, from the text in *The Book of the Native.*

Variants

13	roar.]	~ , *Independent, HC*
15	light,]	~ *HC*
21	zigzag]	**zig-zag** *HC*
29	saddle-bow.]	**saddlebow** *Independent* **saddle-bow,** *HC*
30	rode.]	~ ; *Independent* ~ , *HC*
31	flame]	~ , *Independent*
38	moose,]	~ *HC*
39	panther,]	~ *HC*
46	farewell.]	~ ; *Independent*
49	river.]	~ ; *Independent*
53	on.]	~ ; *Independent* ~ , *HC*
55	neck;]	~ , *HC*
59	flames,]	~ *HC*
62	renewed.]	~ ; *Independent*
63	ford,]	~ *HC*
68	come!]	~ . *HC*

48   *Old Jerry:* Pomeroy (p. 4) reports, "During these years at Westcock his father always kept a horse. Jerry, the first one, lived in the boy's memory as the most important. He was mentioned several times in *The Heart That Knows* and was a real hero in the ballad of 'The Forest Fire.'"

p. 191 TWILIGHT ON SIXTH AVENUE AT NINTH STREET

As far as may be determined, the poem first appeared in the *Maple Leaf* (April, 1895). The *Maple Leaf* printing, however, refers to an earlier appearance of the poem in *Youth's Companion*, although it has proved impossible to locate the poem in that periodical. The poem was also published in the *King's College Record* (January, 1896); *The Book of the Native,* 1896; *New York Nocturnes,* 1898; *Poems,* 1901/7; *Selected Poems,* 1936; *Selected Poems of Sir Charles G.D. Roberts,* 1955; and *Selected Poetry and Critical Prose,* 1974.

Variants

Title: Twilight on Sixth Avenue at Ninth Street] **Twilight on Sixth Avenue** *Maple Leaf, King's Coll. Rec., BON, NYN, Poems* 1901/7

3   green,] ~ *Maple Leaf*
6   of] **in** *King's Coll. Rec.*
7   clock-tower] **clock tower** *Maple Leaf*
9   houses] **windows** *King's Coll. Rec.*
10   gleam,] ~ . *Maple Leaf*
15   shadows,–] **windows–** *Maple Leaf*
19   where] **when** *King's Coll. Rec.*

p. 192 HER GLOVE BOX

The poem appeared only in *The Truth* (May 18, 1895).

p. 192 A MODERN DIALOGUE

The poem appeared only in *The Truth* (May 25, 1895).

Glossary

3   *Sarah Grand:* the penname of Frances Elizabeth Clarke (Mrs. David C. M'Fall, 1862-1943) a well known feminist of the period. She was also a novelist, her best known work being *The Heavenly Twins,* 1893. In addition, she was mayor of Bath for six terms.

p. 193 THREE GOOD THINGS

The poem first appeared in *The Bookman* (May, 1895); and was later published in the *King's College Record* (June, 1895); and *The Book of the Native*, 1896.

Variants
Motto: 1 inveni,]   ~ –   *Bookman, King's Coll. Rec.*
       2 Ludum]   **Libros**   *Bookman, King's Coll. Rec.*
       2 venerem]   **venirem**   *BON*
  1   Gods for,–]   **gods for–**   *Bookman, King's Coll. Rec.;* also
                 line 21
  2   wine!]   ~ .   *Bookman, King's Coll. Rec.*
  3   poet;–]   ~ ;   *Bookman, King's Coll. Rec.*
  5   methinks,]   ~   *Bookman, King's Coll. Rec.*
  7   libros,–]   ~ ,   *Bookman, King's Coll. Rec.*
14   way]   ~ ,   *Bookman, King's Coll. Rec.*
16   day.]   ~ ;   *Bookman, King's Coll. Rec.*
22   wine:]   ~ !   *Bookman, King's Coll. Rec.*
23   poet]   **Poet**   *Bookman, King's Coll. Rec.*
24   your]   italicized in *Bookman*

Glossary
Bona . . . vinum: literally "I have found three good things on earth, play, love, wine." Roberts' translation is certainly in keeping with the spirit of the lines. I have been unable to locate the source of the quotation.
  3   *Tiber:*   the river running through Rome
17   *Ovid, Meleager, Omar:*   Publius Ovidius Naso (43 B.C.-A.D. 18), Roman poet whose best known works are the *Ars Amatoria* (Art of Love) and the *Metamorphoses*. Meleager (c. 140-c. 70 B.C.), minor Greek poet and philosopher. Omar (see "The Isles–An Ode"). The three poets are doubtless grouped in this poem because of their similar epicurean philosophies.

p. 193 AN EPITAPH FOR A HUSBANDMAN

The poem was first published in *Cosmopolitan* (June, 1895); and later appeared in *The Book of the Native*, 1896; *The Living Age* (October, 1897); *A Treasury of Canadian Verse*, 1900; *Poems*, 1901/7; *Le Gallienne Book of English and American Poetry*, 1922/35; *Selected Poems*, 1936; *Selected Poems of Sir Charles G.D. Roberts*, 1955; and *Selected Poetry and Critical Prose*, 1974.

2   cocks,–]   ~ –   *BON, Living Age, Treasury of Can. Verse, Le Gallienne*

9   Him]   ~ ,   *Cosmopolitan*

10   again]   ~ ,   *Cosmopolitan, Treasury of Can. Verse*

13   Busy and blithe and bold] **Busy, and blithe, and bold**
               Cosmopolitan   **Busy, and blithe, and bold,** *BON,*
               Treasury of Can. Verse, Poems 1901/7, *Le Gallienne*
               Busy and blithe and bold, *Living Age*

14   morrow,–] ~ ; *Cosmopolitan*

18   dim;] ~ : *Living Age*

22   sleep,–] ~ ; *Cosmopolitan*

23   strings,] ~ – *Cosmopolitan*

p. 194 THE TRAIN AMONG THE HILLS

As far as may be determined, the poem was first published in the *King's College Record* (June, 1895). There is, however, an unidentified clipping which may be earlier in the Rufus Hathaway Collection at the University of New Brunswick. The poem also appeared in *The Book of the Native*, 1896; *Outlook* (March, 1897); *Current Opinion* 1 (July, 1897); *Current Opinion* 2 (May, 1899); *A Treasury of Canadian Verse*, 1900; and *Poems*, 1901/7.

Variants

1   silence] ~ , *HC*

5   light,] ~ . *HC*

8   thunder] **thunders** *HC, Outlook, Current Opinion* (1),
           Current Opinion (2)

9   view,] ~ *HC, Current Opinion* (1)

10   Express] ~ , *King's Coll. Rec., Treasury of Can. Verse*
           ~ . *HC*

11   happiness.] ~ .... *King's Coll. Rec., BON, Outlook, Current Opinion* (1), *Current Opinion* (2), *Treasury of Can. Verse*

13   And] –**And** *King's Coll. Rec.*

13   thronged,] ~ *HC*

p. 195 EARTH'S COMPLINES

The poem was initially published in *The Yellow Book* (July, 1895); and later appeared in *The Book of the Native*, 1896; *Poems*, 1901/7; *Selected Poems*, 1936; *Selected Poems of Sir Charles G.D. Roberts*, 1955; and *Poets of Confederation*, 1967.

7   ethereal]   **aërial**   *Yellow Book, BON, Poems* 1901/7
17   there,]   ~   *Yellow Book*
19   lilies,]   ~   *Yellow Book*

Glossary
Complines: a compline is the last of the seven canonical hours, or
the service for it, usually following vespers

p. 196 HER FAN

The poem appeared only in *The Truth* (July 13, 1895).

p. 196 THE WRESTLER

The poem initially appeared in *The Chap-Book* (July, 1895); and was later
published in *The Book of the Native*, 1896; *A Treasury of Canadian Verse,*
1900; *Poems,* 1901/7; *A Book of Poetry*, 1928; and *Selected Poems*, 1936.

Variants
1   His]   **his**   *Chap-Book*
2   show;]   ~ :   *Book of Poetry*
3   bars;]   ~ ,   *Book of Poetry*
7   Wrestler]   ~ ,   *Chap-Book, Book of Poetry*
9   crowd]   ~ ,   *Chap-Book, BON, Treasury of Can. Verse,*
Poems 1901/7, *Book of Poetry*
13   nay]   **Nay**   *Chap-Book, Book of Poetry*
14   cling.]   ~ ;   *Treasury of Can. Verse*
17   challenge–]   ~ ,   *Chap-Book, Book of Poetry*
25   him;–]   ~ ,–   *Chap-Book*   ~ –   *BON, Treasury of Can.*
Verse, Book of Poetry
26   Persepolis, and Babylon,]   **Persepolis and Babylon**   *BON,*
Treasury of Can. Verse, Book of Poetry
27   Assyria]   ~ ,   *Chap-Book*
27   dim]   ~ ,   *Chap-Book, Treasury of Can. Verse, Book of Poetry*
29   last]   **length**   *Chap-Book, BON, Treasury of Can. Verse, Book*
of Poetry
31   about]   ~ ,   *BON, Treasury of Can. Verse*
31   lights]   **stars**   *Chap-Book, BON, Treasury of Can. Verse, Book of*
Poetry

Glossary
26   *Persepolis:*   capital of the ancient Persian Empire, now in ruins in
southern Iran

486

26	*Babylon:*	capital of the ancient Babylonian and Chaldean Empires, located on the Euphrates River
27	*Assyria:*	an ancient empire in southwestern Asia, just west of the Mediterranean Sea; the capital was Nineveh
27	*Sardis:*	an ancient capital of Lydia in western Asia Minor

p. 197 AN AUGUST WOOD ROAD

The poem first appeared in *St. Nicholas* (August, 1895); and later was published in *The Book of the Native*, 1896; *The Living Age* (1897); *Poems*, 1901/7; *Selected Poems of Sir Charles G.D. Roberts*, 1955; and *Selected Poetry and Critical Prose*, 1974. As well, the Rufus Hathaway Collection at the University of New Brunswick contains an unidentified clipping, reprinted from *St. Nicholas*.

Variants
Title: Wood Road]   **Woodroad**   *St. Nicholas, HC*
2   high;]   ∼ :   *Living Age*
4   hang;]   ∼ :   *Living Age*
5   bunch-berries]   **bunch berries**   *Living Age*
6   moss;]   ∼ :   *St. Nicholas, HC, BON, Living Age*
12   pool;]   ∼ :   *Living Age*
23   good;]   ∼ :   *Living Age*

p. 198 THE WEAVER

The poem appeared only in *Lippincott's Magazine* (September, 1895).

p. 198 THE MUSE AND THE WHEEL

A manuscript of the poem, dated 8:50 p.m., October 24, 1895, is contained in the Queen's University Archives. Excerpts of the poem (lines 1-4 and 13-48) appeared in *The Truth* (May 23, 1896); the full poem was later published in the *King's College Record* (June, 1896); *The Book of the Native*, 1896; and *Selected Poems*, 1936.

Of the origin of the poem, Pomeroy (p. 80) says, "Carman bought a bicycle; whereupon Roberts, not considering it quite became his length and lankiness, gently chaffed him for it in his pseudo-classical ballad of 'The Muse and the Wheel.'"

Variants
Title: Wheel]   originally *Bicycle* in *MS*; *Bicycle* crossed through and *Wheel* written above it
1   day]   ∼ ,   *MS*

487

7   bloom]   originally *bird* in *MS; bird* crossed through and *bloom*
               written above it

11   almost]   originally *thought he* in *MS; thought he* crossed through
               and *almost* written above it

13   asleep;]   ~ , *Truth*

14   by.]   ~ ; *Truth*

15   sweep]   ~ , *MS, Truth, King's Coll. Rec.*

19   dreams,–]   ~ , *MS, King's Coll. Rec.*

20   (To . . . hollow!)]   **–To . . . hollow!–** *MS, Truth, King's*
               Coll. Rec.

21   No . . . feel]   originally *I marvel not he hardly feels* in *MS; I . . . feel*
               crossed through and *No marvel if he does not feel*
               written above it

23   gaze]   originally *eyes glance* in *MS; eyes glance* crossed through
               and *gaze* written beside it

24   queerness.]   ~ ! *MS*

25   you]   originally *this* in *MS; this* crossed through and *you* written
               above it

26   mood]   originally *life* in *MS; life* crossed through and *mood*
               written above it

29   no,]   ~ ! *King's Coll. Rec.*

29   you're . . . breed]   originally *it's . . . steed* in *MS; it's . . . steed*
               crossed through and *you're . . . breed* written above it

30   follow]   ~ , *Truth*

31   mead]   ~ , *Truth*

32   calling]   originally *whistle* in *MS; whistle* crossed through and
               calling written above it

32   Apollo!]   ~ . *Truth*

33   leap]   originally *burst* in *MS; burst* crossed through and *leap*
               written above it

34   you]   underlined in *MS; you* also underlined in *MS* lines 35, 37,
               39, and 41

38   strayed]   originally *cowered* in *MS; cowered* crossed through and
               strayed written above it

38   vale.]   ~ ; *King's Coll. Rec.*

41   poor]   ~ , *King's Coll. Rec.*

43   Pegasus]   underlined in *MS*

44   straight]   originally *safe* in *MS; straight* written above *safe* which is
               not cancelled

44   me]   underlined in *MS*

45-46   He . . . bosom]   crossed through on three lines in *MS* are *The*
               poet woke. Her / The old familiar spell / was strong /
               Interspersed with the deletions are the lines as they now
               stand.

45   olden]   ~ , *MS*

46   eager]   added with a caret in *MS*

46   bosom,]   ~ ;   *MS, Truth, King's Coll. Rec., BON*
50   trembling;]   ~ ;–   *MS*
51   woo]   originally *see* in *MS; see* crossed through and *woo* written
                above it
51   slim]   ~ ,   *King's Coll. Rec.*

Glossary
 9   *Phoebe-bird:*   see "Birch and Paddle"
14   *Muse:*   see "Sappho"
25   *Pegasus:*   a mythical winged horse, sprung from Medusa's blood
                when she was killed by Perseus, associated with the
                Muses because the stamping of his hoof caused the spring
                Hippocrene to begin flowing on Mount Helicon, an area
                sacred to the Muses
31   *Olympian mead:*   a meadow on Mount Olympus, home of the
                twelve major classical Greek deities
32   *Apollo:*   see "Iterumne"
33   *Hippocrene:*   see Pegasus
37   *Helicon:*   see Pegasus
38   *Tempe:*   see "The Pipes of Pan"

p. 200 OLIVER WENDELL HOLMES

The poem first appeared in *The Dial* (October 1, 1895); and was reprinted
only in the *King's College Record* (November, 1895).

Variants
All variants are from *The Dial.*
 1   smile–]   ~ ,–
 4   jested,]   ~
 7   mood]   ~ ,
 8   sometimes]   **often**
14   wandered]   **bowed him**

Glossary
Oliver Wendell Holmes: (1809-1894) American essayist, novelist, and
                poet; he was, as well, professor of anatomy and physi-
                ology at Harvard University from 1847-1882. His best
                known essays are in the series "Autocrat of the Breakfast-
                Table" (1857-1858), "The Professor at the Breakfast-
                Table" (1860), and "The Poet at the Breakfast-Table"
                (1872). His novels are *Elsie Venner* (1861) and *The
                Guardian Angel* (1867).

p. 200 RECESSIONAL

The poem first appeared in *The Century Magazine* (October, 1895); and was later published in *The Book of the Native*, 1896; *The Living Age*—stanzas 1-7—(October, 1897); *The University Monthly* (November, 1900); *A Treasury of Canadian Verse*, 1900; *Poems*, 1901/7; *A Little Book of Modern Verse*, 1913; *Kindergarten and First Grade*—stanzas 1-2, 4-5—(January, 1922); *Le Gallienne Book of English and American Poetry*, 1922/35; *Home Book of Modern Verse*, 1930; *Selected Poems*, 1936; *Selected Poems of Sir Charles G.D. Roberts*, 1955; and *Poets of Confederation*, 1967. As well, the Rufus Hathaway Collection at the University of New Brunswick contains an unidentified reprint of the *Century* text.

Variants

Title: Recessional]   **A Recessional** *Century, HC*   **The Recessional** *Little Book of Mod. Verse, Kindergarten, Home Book of Mod. Verse*

2   Autumn's altar-lights;]   **autumn's altar lights;** *Century, HC*
                  autumn's altar-lights: *Living Age*
                  autumn's altar-lights; *Univ. Monthly*
                  Autumn's altar lights; *Kindergarten*

7   stillness;]   ~,— *Century, HC*   ~: *Living Age*
                  ~, *Kindergarten*

10   ending,—]   ~— *Century, HC, Living Age*

17   sky]   ~, *Century, HC, Little Book of Mod. Verse, Kindergarten, Home Book of Mod. Verse*

18   by,]   ~; *Univ. Monthly*

20   Softly as]   **Softer than** *Century, HC*

21   Hark, . . . confer,]   **Hark! . . . confer—** *Century, HC*

27   joining]   ~— *Century, HC*

28   Mount, . . . star,]   **Mount . . . star** *Century, HC, Little Book of Mod. Verse, Home Book of Mod. Verse*

29   climb]   ~, *Century, HC*

30   sublime,]   ~— *Century, HC*

32   time.]   **Time:** *Century, HC*   ~; *BON, Univ. Monthly, Treasury of Can. Verse, Poems 1901/7, Le Gallienne*

Note: after line 32 in *Century, HC, BON, Univ. Monthly, Treasury of Can. Verse, Little Book of Mod. Verse, Le Gallienne,* and *Home Book of Mod. Verse* there is a concluding stanza:

> Like a plummet plunging deep
> Past the utmost reach of sleep,
>   Till remembrance has no longer
> Care to laugh or weep.

In Roberts' reading copy of *Poems* (dated 1932) at the University of New Brunswick, a period is inserted after *time* in the next to last stanza and the last stanza is crossed through.

p. 201 RECOMPENSE

A typescript, dated October 22, 1895, and initialled by Roberts, survives in the Queen's University Archives. The poem was first published in *The Atlantic Monthly* (January, 1896); and subsequently appeared in *The Book of the Native*, 1896; and *Poems*, 1901/7. As well, the Rufus Hathaway Collection at the University of New Brunswick contains an unidentified clipping which is apparently a reprint of the text in *The Atlantic Monthly*.

Variants
7	rock,]	~ *TS*
11	far]	~ , *Atlantic, HC*
13	stars;]	~ ,– *TS*
14	And . . . tell:]	**And suddenly I felt** *TS, Atlantic, HC*
15	"Beside . . . shrine]	**That at my threshold stood the shrine** *TS, Atlantic, HC*
16	dwell!"]	**dwelt.** *TS, Atlantic, HC*

p. 202 PHILLIDA'S BIRTHDAY

The poem appeared only in *The Truth* (November 16, 1895).

p. 203 THE WITCHES' FLIGHT

The poem first appeared in *The Monthly Illustrator* (December, 1895); and was later included in *The Book of the Native*, 1896; *Selected Poems of Sir Charles G.D. Roberts*, 1955; and *Poets of Confederation*, 1967.

Variants
10	air;]	~ , *Monthly Illustrator*
19	reddens;]	~ , *Monthly Illustrator*
25	^{2}mount]	~ , *Monthly Illustrator*

p. 204 A CHILD'S PRAYER AT EVENING

The poem first appeared in *A Victorian Anthology*, 1895; and was later included in *The Book of the Native*, 1896; *Poems*, 1901/7; *A Book of Lullabies*, 1925; *Selected Poems*, 1936; and *Selected Poetry and Critical Prose*, 1974.

Variants
Variants
Title: In *A Victorian Anthology*, only the Latin sub-title is given.
  6   through,]   ~   *Victorian Anth.*

Glossary
Domine, cui sunt Pleiades curae: this is the Latin equivalent of the first
            two lines of the poem

p. 204 BOHEMIA

The poem was published only in the 1896 *Calendar* of the Toronto Art Students' League.

Note: No period appears in the 1896 *Calendar* at line 16, but there
            seems no reason to omit end punctuation for this stanza and
            include it for all others.

p. 205 THE DESERTED WHARF

The poem first appeared in *Massey's Magazine* (January, 1896); and was later published in *The Book of the Native*, 1896; *The Nation* (March, 1897); *The Living Age* (April, 1897); *Poems*, 1901/7; *Selected Poems*, 1936; and *Selected Poetry and Critical Prose*, 1974.
    Pomeroy (pp. 93-94) reports that the poem was written during a storm when Roberts and Carman were crossing from Yarmouth to Boston by ferry. Carman, very seasick, wrote an immediate and ribald parody.

Variants
Title: The Deserted Wharf]   **The Lone Wharf**   *BON, Nation, Living*
                Age, Poems 1901/7
  3   tides]   **tiles**   *Living Age*
  3   Tantramar.]   ~   *Massey's*
 13   sea!]   ~   *Massey's;* also line 26
 23   gloom,]   ~   *Massey's*

p. 206 THE ELEPHANT AND THE PANSY-BLOSSOM

The poem appeared only in *The Truth* (January 4, 1896).

Glossary
  8   *Aubrey Beardsley:*   Aubrey Vincent Beardsley (1872-1898), the
                leading English illustrator of the 1890's, particularly in *The
                Yellow Book* and *The Savoy* periodicals. Next to Oscar Wilde,

492

Beardsley was the outstanding figure in the Aesthetic movement of the period, a movement characterized by affectation of speech and manner and eccentricity in clothing.

p. 207 NATIVITY

The poem was first published in *Lippincott's Magazine* (January, 1896); and was reprinted only in *McBride's Magazine* (December, 1914).

p. 207 A SPRING COLLOQUY

The poem was published only in *The Century Magazine* (February, 1896). A much later typescript—Sir Charles G.D. Roberts is typed at the bottom of the poem—is in the Lloyd Roberts Collection at the University of New Brunswick. The typescript contains the notation *"The Century,* April, 1896."

p. 208 THE STIRRUP CUP

The poem first appeared in *Lippincott's Magazine* (February, 1896); and was later included in *New York Nocturnes*, 1898; and *Selected Poems*, 1936.

Variants
All variants are from *Lippincott's Magazine.*
1   Life ... stirrup]   **Life, ... stirrup,**
2   me,–]   ~ ,
3   sea,–]   ~ ,
4   that land ... lies.]   **the land, ... lies!**
6   know!]   ~ .

Glossary
Stirrup cup: a drink traditionally offered to a departing guest on horseback or at the beginning of a hunt

p. 208 THE LAUGHING SALLY

The poem was first published in *The Century Magazine* (March, 1896); and later appeared in *The Book of the Native*, 1896; *Steps to Oratory*, 1900; *Poems*, 1901/7; and *Selected Poems*, 1936.

Variants
Title: The Laughing Sally]   **The Ballad of the "Laughing Sally"**
         Century, Steps to Oratory

1	Pernambuco.] ~ *Century, Steps to Oratory*	
2	Yeo] ~ , *Century, Steps to Oratory*	
3	away!)] ~ !)– *Century, Steps to Oratory*	
10	Pernambuco;] ~ , *Century, Steps to Oratory*	
12	King's] **king's** *Century, Steps to Oratory*	
12	ship] ~ , *Century, BON, Steps to Oratory, Poems* 1901/7	
14	day,] ~ ; *BON, Poems* 1901/7	
16	quarry,] ~ *Century*	
19	shore,] ~ *Century, Steps to Oratory*	
20	river-mouth] **river mouth** *Century, Steps to Oratory*	
22	channel] ~ , *Century, Steps to Oratory*	
23	keel,–] ~ ; *Century, Steps to Oratory*	
24	book,] ~ – *Century, Steps to Oratory*	
26	ghost,] ~ *Century, Steps to Oratory*	
31	King's . . . war.] **king's . . . war;** *Century, Steps to Oratory*	
32	red cross] **Red Cross** *Century, Steps to Oratory*	
46	A boat] **Her boats** *Century, Steps to Oratory*	
47	she brought–] **they brought:** *Century, Steps to Oratory*	
48	King's . . . France] **king's . . . France,** *Century, Steps to Oratory*	
49	King's] **king's** *Century, Steps to Oratory*	
51	then–] ~ : *Century, Steps to Oratory*	
53	English men] **Englishmen** *Century, Steps to Oratory*	
55	river.] ~ ; *Century, Steps to Oratory*	
59	red cross] **Red Cross** *Century, Steps to Oratory*	
61	had not] **hadn't** *BON, Poems* 1901/7	
65	a-row] **arow** *Century, Steps to Oratory*	
67	dawn-rays] **dawn rays** *Century, Steps to Oratory*	
69	guns] ~ , *Steps to Oratory*	
74	turned, and stared;–] **turned and stared** *Century, Steps to Oratory*	
77	red-cross . . . serene!] **Red Cross . . . serene.** *Century, Steps to Oratory*	
78	Pernambuco,–] ~ *Century, Steps to Oratory*	
79	Yeo] ~ , *Century, Steps to Oratory*	
82	day.] ~ ! *Century, Steps to Oratory*	

Glossary

1	*Pernambuco:*	a seaport in eastern Brazil, also called Recife
28	*liana:*	a climbing plant or vine

p. 210 THE LITTLE FIELD OF PEACE

The poem was initially published in *Scribner's* (March, 1896); and subsequently appeared in *The Book of the Native,* 1896; *The Living Age* (March, 1897); *Poems,* 1901/7; and *Selected Poems,* 1936.

4   this] **the** *Scribner's*
5   little] ~ , *Scribner's*
6   find] **learn** *Scribner's*
6   sweet;] ~ : *Living Age*
7   play,] ~ *Living Age*
15   heed,–] ~ – *Scribner's*
17   stalk,–] ~ – *Scribner's*
20   day.] ~ ; *Scribner's*
25   Ah!] ~ , *Scribner's*
30   content;] ~ , *Scribner's*   ~ : *Living Age*

Glossary
16   *tansy:* a common strong-scented herb

p. 211 THE FLOCKS OF SPRING

The poem was initially published in *Munsey's Magazine* (April, 1896); and was later included in *Poems, 1901/7*; and *Selected Poetry and Critical Prose,* 1974.

Variants
6   Spring] **spring** *Munsey's Magazine*
9   wind,–] ~ – *Munsey's Magazine*
12   free,] ~ ; *Munsey's Magazine*
14   hours;] ~ , *Munsey's Magazine*

p. 212 THE JONQUIL

The poem first appeared in *The Independent* (April 16, 1896); and was subsequently published in *The Book of the Native,* 1896; and *Poems, 1901/7*. As well, the Lloyd Roberts Collection at the University of New Brunswick contains an unidentified clipping of the poem.

Variants
1   bulb] ~ , *LRC*
4   spring] **Spring** *BON*
5   heat,] ~ *Independent*
8   enchanter's] **Enchanter's,** *BON*
10   noon] ~ , *Independent, LRC*
12   cocoon.] ~ ; *Independent*
14   tears,–] ~ ; *Independent*   ~ , *LRC*

p. 212 AN OBLATION

An undated but autographed typescript in the Queen's University Archives is apparently earlier than any printed text of the poem. The poem was first published in *The Chap-Book* (April, 1896); and was later included in *The Book of the Native*, 1896; and *Poems*, 1901/7.

Variants
Title: An Oblation]   originally *An Oblation* in *TS; April* added between the words with a caret.
1-4   Behind . . . dreams.]   in *TS:*

> When all that is not seems,
> Behind the speaking streams,
> Sat the Artificer
> Of things and deeds and dreams.

11   spring]   **Spring**   *TS, BON*
18   afar,]   ~   *Chap-Book*
26   brook,–]   ~ ,   *Chap-Book*
27   leaves,–]   ~ ,   *Chap-Book*
28   took.]   ~ ;   *TS*
30   oblation]   originally *oblations* in *TS; s* crossed through
31   arbutus,]   ~ ,–   *Chap-Book*
33   shadowy]   **speaking**   *TS, Chap-Book, BON*
34   Birth and Death]   **Death and Birth**   *TS, Chap-Book, BON*
35   palm,]   ~   *Chap-Book*
36   wide;]   ~ ;–   *TS, Chap-Book, BON*

Glossary
21   *mead:*   a meadow
31   *arbutus:*   see "The Quest of the Arbutus"

p. 213 WITH ALL HER FAULTS

The poem appeared only in *The Truth* (April 18, 1896).

Glossary
27   *Lippi:*   Fra Lippo Lippi (c. 1406-69) an Italian painter and the subject of a poem by Robert Browning

p. 214 INSPIRATION

The poem was published only in *The Bookman* (May, 1896).

496

p. 215 THE JAR

The poem was published only in *Lippincott's Magazine* (June, 1896).

p. 215 TWO SPHERES

The poem first appeared in *Munsey's Magazine* (July, 1896); and was later included in *The Book of the Native*, 1896; and *Poems,* 1901/7.

Variants
2   his]   **His**   *Munsey's Magazine*; so also in lines 3 and 4
5   he]   **He**   *Munsey's Magazine*

Glossary
15   *Arcturus:*   a first magnitude star in the constellation Boötes

p. 216 O CLEAREST POOL

The poem was first published in *Canadian Magazine* (August, 1896); and appeared again only in *Poems,* 1901/7.

Variants
All variants are from *Canadian Magazine.*
8   life and love]   **love and life**
9   old]   ~ ,
10   hold,–]   ~ –
17   crystal]   **clearest**
22   divine!–]   ~ !
23   Knowing . . . more,]   **–Knowing . . . more**
26   smile!]   ~ .

p. 217 YE POET AND HIS IDEAL

The poem appeared only in *The Truth* (August 8, 1896).

Glossary
1   *A . . . slim:*   an obvious reference to Bliss Carman
16   *Izrafel . . . beeves:*   in the Islamic religion, the archangel who will sound the trumpet to announce the Day of Resurrection; traditionally angels do not eat, thus he would not dream of "beeves"
25-28   *Or . . . pay:*   referring to Helen and the Trojan War. The Simois is a river near Troy

29   *Lilith:*   in Rabbinical literature she was Adam's first wife and was
              displaced by Eve
37   *Muse:*   see "Sappho"

p. 218 THE STACK BEHIND THE BARN

The poem was first published in *The Truth* (September 5, 1896); and was reprinted only in *Poems*, 1901/7. See "The Farmer's Winter Morning" for Pomeroy's comment on the poem.

Variants
All variants are from *The Truth.*
 1   here,]   ~
 2   weeds.]   ~ ;
 6   home-farm,–]   ~ :
 9   barn-yard]   **barnyard**
11   ³dear . . . garden-smell]   **dear, . . . garden smell**
17   play-house]   **playhouse**
18   goldenrod,]   **golden-rod**
24   drop]   **jump**
26   O]   ~ ,
28   you,]   ~ .
29   Life]   **life**

p. 219 IN THE ORCHARD

As far as may be determined, the poem first appeared in *Massey's Magazine* (October, 1896). There is, however, an unidentified clipping which may be earlier in the Rufus Hathaway Collection at the University of New Brunswick. The *Methodist Magazine and Review* (May, 1904) contains a reprint of the *Massey* text and illustration. The poem was also published in *Poems*, 1901/7; and *Selected Poems*, 1936.

Variants
 3   stir,]   ~   *Massey's, Methodist Mag. and Rev., HC*
 4   by.]   ~ ;   *Massey's, Methodist Mag. and Rev., HC*
 7   expectancy.]   ~ ,   *Massey's, Methodist Mag. and Rev., HC*
11   arcade!]   ~ ,   *Massey's, Methodist Mag. and Rev., HC*
13   afraid?]   ~ ;   *Massey's, Methodist Mag. and Rev., HC*
14   air]   ~ ,   *HC*
15   prayer.]   ~ ,   *Massey's, Methodist Mag. and Rev., HC*
              ~ ;   *Poems 1901/7*
16   way.]   ~ ;   *Massey's, Methodist Mag. and Rev., HC*

p. 220 DEW

The poem was first published in *Lippincott's Magazine* (November, 1896); and that text, with variants, was reprinted in the *New Outlook* (November, 1896).

Variants
1   done,]   ~   *New Outlook*
2   Earth]   **earth**   *New Outlook*

p. 220 THE FARMER'S WINTER MORNING

The poem first appeared in *The Truth* (December 19, 1896); and was later included in *Poems,* 1901/7; *Selected Poems,* 1936; and *Selected Poetry and Critical Prose,* 1974.

Pomeroy (p. 2) gives the following account:

Like other little boys he found the barn at Westcock an excellent place in which to play both summer and winter. Particularly did he enjoy the barn-yard and the stack of hay adjoining the barn. His memory of these, in later years, gave birth to three poems: "In the Barn-Yard's Southerly Corner," "The Farmer's Winter Morning," and "The Stack Behind the Barn."

Variants
All variants are from *The Truth.*
1   wide,]   ~
2   barn-yard.]   ~ !   also lines 6, 14, 18, 26, and 30
7   brand.]   ~ ;
8   latch.]   ~ !   also lines 12, 20, 24, and 32
17 eyes]   No period appears in *Selected Poems,* but one is present in *Truth* and *Poems,* 1901/7. There is no intrinsic reason why the period should not appear and I have taken the earlier readings to be correct.
19 stalls,]   ~
21 falls.]   ~ ;
25 tins]   ~ ,
27 begins.]   ~ ;
34 straw,–]   ~ ,
36 (And . . . latch.)]   **And . . . latch.**

The first two datable publications of the poem, in *Scribner's* (May, 1894); and *A Victorian Anthology*, 1895; were short versions containing only lines 1-8, 21-24, and 29-44. The first publication of the full poem was in *The Book of the Native*, 1896; and this was followed by *Poems*, 1901/7; *The Home Book of Modern Verse* (as in *Scribner's*), 1930; *Our Canadian Literature*, 1934; *Selected Poems*, 1936; *The Nature Lover's Knapsack* (as in *Scribner's*), 1947; and *Selected Poems of Sir Charles G.D. Roberts* (lines 1-8, 13-16, 21-32, and 41-44), 1955. As well, the Rufus Hathaway Collection at the University of New Brunswick contains an unidentified clipping which includes lines 1-20.

Variants

Title: Afoot] **Comes the Lure of Green Things** *HC*
2 flowing,–] ~ – *Scribner's, Victorian Anth., Home Book of Mod. Verse, HC*
3 Desire] **desire** *Scribner's, Victorian Anth., BON, Home Book of Mod. Verse, HC;* also line 23 in all texts except *HC*
15 flapping,] ~ *HC*
18 resume,–] ~ – *HC*
22 Where . . . wending,–] **When . . . wending–** *Scribner's, Victorian Anth., Home Book of Mod. Verse*
24 Dream] **dream** *Scribner's, Victorian Anth., BON, Home Book of Mod. Verse, Our Can. Lit.*
28 Vision.] ~ *Poems 1901/7, SP*
34 Death] **death** *Scribner's, Victorian Anth., Home Book of Mod. Verse*
36 days;] ~ :– *BON* ~ : *Poems 1901/7, Our Can. Lit.*
38 are,] ~ ,– *BON*
39 zenith,] ~ ,– *BON*
40 star,] ~ ,– *BON*
41 Till, . . . tears,] **Till . . . tears** *Scribner's, Victorian Anth., Home Book of Mod. Verse*

Glossary

32 *Bedouins:* nomadic Arabs or any wanderer

A holograph manuscript of the poem survives in the Queen's University Archives. The poem was first published in *The Book of the Native*, 1896; and later appeared in *Poems*, 1901/7; and *Selected Poems*, 1936.

Variants
All variants are from the manuscript.

3	apples,]	~
11	cider-presses]	**cider presses**
20	apples;]	~ . also line 32
27-8	maples . . . haze]	In *MS*, Roberts had originally written *pumpkins in the field	Are revealed.* This has been crossed through and *maples are ablaze	In the haze* has been written above it.
30	fruiting song]	**fruiting-song**
37	O]	~,
38	apples;]	~ ,
42	song!]	~ .

p. 223 BESIDE THE WINTER SEA

The poem first appeared in *The Book of the Native,* 1896; and was later published in *The Living Age* 1 (April 13, 1897); *The Living Age* 2 (November 13, 1897); *Poems,* 1901/7; *Selected Poems,* 1936; *Selected Poems of Sir Charles G.D. Roberts,* 1955; *Poets of Confederation,* 1967; and *Selected Poetry and Critical Prose,* 1974.

Variants

2	ago,]	~ . *Living Age* (1)	
8	walking,]	~ *Living Age* (1)	
9	on;]	~ : *Living Age* (2)	
11	feet;]	~ : *Living Age* (2)	
15	sea's;–]	~ ; *Living Age* (1)	~ :– *Living Age* (2)
21	rose]	~ , *BON, Living Age* (1) and (2), *Poems* 1901/7	
21	mine!]	~ . *Living Age* (1)	

p. 224 BUTTERFLIES

The poem was first published in *The Book of the Native,* 1896; and was later included in *Poems,* 1901/7; *Selected Poems,* 1936; and *Selected Poetry and Critical Prose,* 1974.

p. 224 THE HEAL-ALL

As far as may be determined, the poem first appeared in *The Book of the Native,* 1896. There is, however, an unidentified clipping which may be earlier in the Rufus Hathaway Collection at the University of New Brunswick. Further, the Hathaway clipping is supposedly reprinted from *Harper's Bazaar,* although it has proved impossible to locate the poem in that periodical. The poem also appeared in *Poems,* 1901/7; and *Selected Poems,* 1936.

4   fame!] ~ . *HC*
18   me and thee] **thee and me** *HC*
19   brave,–] ~ , *HC.* In *Poems* 1901/7 the dash after the comma
                  has been omitted, but in Roberts' reading copy he has
                  replaced the dash
21   gain,–] ~ – *HC*
22   Life] **life** *HC*

Glossary
Heal-All: a flower reputed in folk-medicine to possess a variety of
            curative powers

p. 225 JULY

The poem was first published in *The Book of the Native,* 1896; and later appeared in *Poems,* 1901/7; and *The University Monthly* (May-June, 1912).

Variants
Title: July] **Playgrounds of Old Sol** *Univ. Monthly*
3   Where . . . bee] **When . . . bees** *Univ. Monthly*
6   blue,–] ~ , *Univ. Monthly*
8   renew;] ~ . *Univ. Monthly*
10   oxeye] **ox-eye** *BON, Univ. Monthly*
12   alive;] ~ . *Univ. Monthly*
16   confer;] ~ . *Univ. Monthly*
20   dream;] ~ . *Univ. Monthly*
21   adventure] ~ , *Univ. Monthly*
22   dun.] ~ , *Univ. Monthly*

p. 226 LOVE'S TRANSLATOR

The poem first appeared in *The Book of the Native,* 1896; and was later published in *Munsey's Magazine* (May, 1903); and *Poems,* 1901/7.

Variants
All variants are from *Munsey's Magazine.*
1   mist,] ~
5   tall] ~ ,
17 poppy-bud] **poppy bud**
19 blood] ~ ,
21 that] **the**

p. 226 MOTHERS

As far as may be determined, the poem first appeared in *The Book of the Native*, 1896. There is, however, an unidentified clipping which may be earlier in the Rufus Hathaway Collection at the University of New Brunswick. The poem was reprinted only in *Poems, 1901/7.*

Variants
All variants are from the Hathaway clipping.
Title: Mothers]   **Guests from Paradise**
4   Him]   **him**
7   Child]   **child**

p. 227 TRYSTING SONG

As far as may be determined, the poem first appeared in *The Book of the Native,* 1896; but the Rufus Hathaway Collection at the University of New Brunswick contains an unidentified, and perhaps earlier, clipping of the poem. The only other publication was in *Poems, 1901/7.*

Variants
All variants are from the Hathaway clipping.
Title: Trysting Song]   **The "Trysting Song":–**
2   near.]   **~ ,**
14   heart . . . wild.]   **heart, . . . wild,**
23   a]   omitted

p. 228 A WAKE-UP SONG

The poem was first published in *The Book of the Native,* 1896; and was subsequently included in *Poems, 1901/7;* and *Selected Poems,* 1936. As well, an unidentified clipping is contained in the Rufus Hathaway Collection at the University of New Brunswick. Pomeroy (pp. 73-74) reports that the poem was written for Roberts' children, and she identifies "Golden Head" as the baby of the family and "Brownie" as the daughter next to the baby in age.

p. 228 WHERE THE CATTLE COME TO DRINK

The poem was first published in *The Book of the Native,* 1896; and was later included in *Poems, 1901/7; Selected Poems,* 1936; *Selected Poems of Sir Charles G.D. Roberts,* 1955; and *Selected Poetry and Critical Prose,* 1974.

p. 228 AYLESFORD LAKE

The poem was first published in *Massey's Magazine* (January, 1897); and was later reprinted only in *Poems,* 1901/7. The poem was inspired, according to Pomeroy (p. 139), by a camping trip [1895?] which included Roberts and members of the Prat and Clark families to Aylesford Lake, located in central Nova Scotia.

Variants
10   beaches,–]   ~ ,   *Massey's Mag.*
12   sky,–]   ~ ,   *Massey's Mag.*

p. 229 THE SOLITARY WOODSMAN

The poem was first published in *The Century Magazine* (January, 1897); and was subsequently included in *New York Nocturnes,* 1898; *Poems,* 1901/7; *Our Canadian Literature,* 1934; *Selected Poems,* 1936; *A Book of Canadian Poetry,* 1943/8; *A Pocketful of Canada,* 1946; *Selected Poems of Sir Charles G.D. Roberts,* 1955; *Canadian Anthology,* 1966; *Poets of Confederation,* 1967; and *Selected Poetry and Critical Prose,* 1974. As well, an unidentified clipping, reprinted with additional variants from the *Century Magazine,* survives in the Rufus Hathaway Collection at the University of New Brunswick.

Variants
1   lake-water]   **lake water**   *HC*
2   alder-bushes]   **alder bushes**   *NYN*
4   hushes,–]   ~ –   *HC*
8   lamp,–]   ~ –   *HC*
9-10   These lines are reversed in *Century* and *HC*
10   cornel]   **coral**   *HC*
12   fellow,–]   ~ –   *HC*
16   swamp,–]   ~ –   *HC*
17-18   These lines are reversed in *Century* and *HC*
19   summer-sleekened]   **summer sleekened**   *HC*
20   bed,–]   ~ –   *HC*
23   wood-road]   ~ ,   *HC*
27   rising]   ~ ,   *HC*
32   forest-side]   **forest side**   *Century, HC*
38   bluejay]   **blue-jay**   *Century, HC, NYN*
42   afternoon;]   ~ ,–   *NYN, Poems* 1901/7, *Our Can. Lit.*
44   noon.]   ~ ;   *Century, HC*
46   humming,–]   ~ –   *HC*

504

p. 231 LIFE AND ART

The poem first appeared in *The Century Magazine* (February, 1897); and was later included in *New York Nocturnes*, 1898; *Poems*, 1901/7; *Canadian Singers and Their Songs*, 1925; and *Selected Poems*, 1936. The text in *Canadian Singers and Their Songs* is a photographed reproduction of the poem in manuscript. An unidentified clipping is in the Rufus Hathaway Collection at the University of New Brunswick and was reprinted from *Century*.

Variants
Title: Life and Art]   **Life**   *Century, HC*
1   Art–]   ~ ,   *Century, HC*
3   form,]   ~   *Century, Can. Singers*
4   fidelity,]   ~ ;   *Century*   ~ .   *HC*
5   craving]   **longing**   *Can. Singers*

p. 231 TO A MIRROR

The poem was published only in *Lippincott's Magazine* (February, 1897).

p. 231 PHILLIDA'S LENT

The poem appeared only in *The Truth* (April 22, 1897).

p. 232 THE TOWER BEYOND THE TOPS OF TIME

The poem first appeared in the *King's College Record* (June, 1897); and was later published in *New York Nocturnes*, 1898; *The Living Age* (August, 1898); *Poems*, 1901/7; *Selected Poems*, 1936; *Selected Poems of Sir Charles G.D. Roberts*, 1955; and *Selected Poetry and Critical Prose*, 1974.

Variants
Title: The Tower Beyond the Tops of Time]   **Beyond the Tops of Time**   *King's Coll. Rec., NYN, Living Age, Poems* 1901/7. In Roberts' reading copy of *Poems* in the Harriet Irving Library at the University of New Brunswick is Roberts' marginal note: "By far the greater part of this poem was written in a dream. The title, in my dream, was 'The Tower Beyond the Tops of Time.'"
2   watched,]   ~   *King's Coll. Rec., Living Age*
2   feared.]   ~ ;   *King's Coll. Rec.*
7   flame;–]   ~ –   *Living Age*
20   dead.]   ~ ,   *King's Coll. Rec.*

21	awe,]	~ *King's Coll. Rec.*
23	cried–]	~ : *King's Coll. Rec.*
28	thing,–]	~ – *Living Age*
32	Hosannas]	**hosannas** *King's Coll. Rec., Living Age*
32	cease;]	~ : *Living Age*
33	frays,]	~ ; *King's Coll. Rec.*
34	lotus-pools]	**lotus pools** *Living Age*
35	gaped and cried–]	**gaped, and cried;** *King's Coll. Rec.*
38	vain.]	~ : *King's Coll. Rec.*
40	pain]	~ , *King's Coll. Rec., NYN, Living Age*
45	I,]	~ : *King's Coll. Rec.*
50	heart-beat?–Thrice]	**heartbeat?–thrice** *King's Coll. Rec.*
52	spheres,–]	~ – *Living Age*
54	sky.]	~ , *King's Coll. Rec.*
58	I,]	~ : *King's Coll. Rec.* ~ – *NYN, Living Age*
59	cried–]	~ : *King's Coll. Rec.*
61	sleep,–]	~ : *King's Coll. Rec.* ~ – *Living Age*
65	I,]	~ : *King's Coll. Rec.* ~ – *NYN, Living Age*
67	answered,]	~ : *King's Coll. Rec.* ~ – *NYN, Living Age*
67	wise]	~ , *Living Age*
68	seem.]	~ ; *King's Coll. Rec.*

Glossary

31   *sard and chrysoprase:*   brownish-red and apple-green quartz

33   *Valhalla:*   In Scandinavian mythology, the hall of immortality for the souls of heroes killed in battle

p. 234 WHEN THE CLOVER BLOOMS AGAIN

The poem was first published in *The Century Magazine* (June, 1897); and was subsequently included in *New York Nocturnes,* 1898; *Poems,* 1901/7; and *Selected Poems,* 1936. According to Pomeroy (p. 151) Richard Watson Gilder, editor of *The Century Magazine,* said of the poem that it was "one of those perfect lyrics which will find a place in the best anthologies." As Pomeroy notes, however, "no anthologist has ever noticed it."

Variants

4	completer,]	~ *NYN*
6	over sea]	**oversea** *Century*
8	sleeping,]	~ : *Century*
12	place,]	~ *Century*
13	long,]	~ *Century*

p. 235 THE HERMIT

The poem was first published in *Munsey's Magazine* (August, 1897); and was later included in *New York Nocturnes,* 1898; *Poems,* 1901/7; and *Selected Poems,* 1936.

Variants
5   sleep]   ~ , *Munsey's*
7   endless]   ~ , *Munsey's*
10   unperturbéd]   **unperturbed** *NYN*
13   Life]   **life** *Munsey's*
18   name,–]   ~ – *Munsey's*
19   Fate]   **fate** *Munsey's*
22   crown,–]   ~ – *Munsey's*

p. 236 **MARJORY**

The poem first appeared in *The Truth* (August, 1897); and was later included in *New York Nocturnes,* 1898; *Poems,* 1901/7; and *Selected Poems,* 1936.

Variants
Sub-title: ***The Truth*** and *New York Nocturnes* include the sub-title *A Backwoods Ballad.*
6   grey]   **gray**, *Truth*
7   wind,]   ~ *Truth*
7   sun]   ~ , *NYN*
13   rattle]   ~ , *Truth*
14   hour of the]   **hour, the** *Truth*
18   lane.]   ~ ; *Truth*
19   milking,–]   ~ – *Truth*
22   o'er!]   ~ . *Truth*
28   a]   **the** *Truth*
31   familiar,–]   ~ – *Truth*
33   garden;–]   ~ ; *Truth*
35   fox-glove . . . pansy,]   **foxglove** . . . **pansy**– *Truth*

Glossary
34   *mignonette:*   a fragrant yellowish green flower; also called reseda
35   *fox-glove bell:*   a bell shaped flower of the figwort family; also called fairy gloves

The poem was first published in *The Independent* (September, 1897); and was later included in *New York Nocturnes*, 1898; *A Treasury of Canadian Verse*, 1900; *Poems*, 1901/7; *Selected Poems*, 1936; and *Selected Poetry and Critical Prose*, 1974.

Variants
All variants are from *A Treasury of Canadian Verse*.
4   wrought,–]   ~ ;
5   heed]   **hand**
10   throat,]   ~

Glossary
7   *speedwell:*   one of the various low herbs of the figwort family, bearing blue or white flowers, also called *bird's eye* or *veronica*
12   *Arcturus:*   see "Two Spheres"

p. 238 TEARS

The poem was published only in *Lippincott's Magazine* (October, 1897).

p. 238 NIGHT IN A DOWN-TOWN STREET

The poem was first published in *The Century Magazine* (December, 1897); and later appeared in the *King's College Record* (October, 1898); *New York Nocturnes*, 1898; *Canadian Verse*, 1900; *Poems*, 1901/7; *Selected Poems*, 1936; and *Selected Poems of Sir Charles G.D. Roberts*, 1955.

Variants
Title: in]   **on**   *Century*
1   gloom,]   ~   *Century*
2   repose]   ~ ,   *Century*
9   woods]   ~ ,   *Century*
12   unveiled . . . here.]   **unveiled, . . . here!**   *Century*
13   street is a grim]   **street, a hollow**   *Century*
15   That knows no more]   **Remembers not**   *Century*
18   dry.]   ~ ,   *Can. Verse*
21   moon]   ~ ,   *Century*

The poem was first published in *The Independent* (December 2, 1897); and later appeared in *New York Nocturnes*, 1898; *A Treasury of Canadian Verse*, 1900; *Poems*, 1901/7; *Selected Poems*, 1936; and *Selected Poetry and Critical Prose*, 1974.

Pomeroy (p. 152) makes the following observation:

> The love poems in *New York Nocturnes* introduce a new note in the poetry of Roberts. There were several love poems in the poetry of the Windsor period, but they generally lacked the emotional intensity, and the spirit of worship and adoration which characterize the Nocturnes. "A Nocturne of Consecration" is the most significant and impassioned. Upon its publication in *The New York Independent*, Richard Henry Stoddard, the well-known poet and editor of *The New York Evening Mail*, went to the office of the editor of *The Independent*, Dr. William Hayes Ward, and said, "This is the greatest love poem in the language since Spenser's 'Epithalamium.'"

Variants

1	Dear]	**dear** *Independent*
3	you,]	~ *Independent*
4	through]	**thro',** *Independent*
6	tears,]	~ *Independent*
11	said— . . . through]	**said: . . . thro'** *Independent*
13	Through . . . long,]	**Thro' . . . long** *Independent*
15	made.]	~ ; *Independent*
16	her]	**Her** *Independent, NYN, Treasury of Can. Verse*
17	air—]	~ : *Independent*
22	eclipse.]	~ ; *Independent*
25	Kind, . . . companionable,]	**Kind . . . companionable** *Independent*
29	said—]	~ : *Independent*
31	love, . . . lees;]	**love . . . lees,** *Independent*
36	stir;]	~ , *Independent*
39	her.]	~ , *Independent*
39	her]	**Her** *NYN, Treasury of Can. Verse;* so also in lines 45, 51, and 64
40	earth—]	~ : *Independent*
41	child.]	~ ; *Independent*
43	birth]	~ , *Independent, Treasury of Can. Verse*
45	given?]	~ — *Independent*
48	heaven]	**Heaven** *Independent*
50	thereof.]	~ ? *Independent*
54	new!]	~ . *Independent*
58	said—]	~ : *Independent*

60	mine,]	~	*Independent*
60	she]	**She**	*NYN, Treasury of Can. Verse*
63	this,–]	~ ,	*Independent*
64	know.]	~ ;	*Independent*
65	unaware,]	~ .	*Independent*
67	me. Make]	**me; make**	*Independent*
67	hers]	**Hers**	*NYN, Treasury of Can. Verse*
68	ministers,–]	~ :	*Independent*
80	surprise,]	~	*Independent*

81   I have added the closing quotation marks, doubtless omitted when the decision was made to delete the three lines which follow in all texts except *Selected Poems*.

81   After this line *Independent, NYN, Treasury of Can. Verse* and *Poems* 1901/7 inserts:

> In other worlds expect another joy
> Of her*, which blundering fate shall not annoy,
> Nor time or change destroy.

> * Her in *NYN* and *Treasury of Can. Verse*

82   Dear . . . long, . . . through]   **dear . . . long . . . thro'**   *Independent*

p. 241 MY GARDEN

The poem initially appeared in *Munsey's Magazine* (January, 1898); and was later included in *New York Nocturnes*, 1898; and *Poems*, 1901/7.

Variants

1	grime]	~ ,	*Munsey's*
2	summer-time]	**summer time**	*Munsey's, NYN*
4	Paradise,]	~	*Munsey's*
17	hair,–]	~ ,	*Munsey's*
22	heart-beat]	**heart beat**	*Munsey's*
26	touch,–]	~ ,	*Munsey's*

p. 242 A STREET VIGIL

The poem was first published in *The Chap-Book* (January 15, 1898); and was later included in *New York Nocturnes*, 1898; and *Poems*, 1901/7.

Variants

3	little,]	~	*Chap-Book*
10	my life's]	**all my**	*Chap-Book, NYN*
12	fame]	~ ,	*NYN*
14	little, . . . cease]	**little . . . cease,**	*Chap-Book*

510

p. 242 AT THE RAILWAY STATION

The poem was initially published in *Harper's Weekly* (February 5, 1898); and later appeared in *New York Nocturnes*, 1898; *Poems*, 1901/7; *The Living Age* (August, 1902); and *The University Monthly* (November, 1902).

Variants
<table>
<tr><td>1</td><td>light,]</td><td>~ ;</td><td>*Harper's*</td></tr>
<tr><td>2</td><td>go,]</td><td>~ ;</td><td>*Harper's*</td><td>~ .</td><td>*Living Age, Univ. Monthly*</td></tr>
<tr><td>5</td><td>change,]</td><td>~ ;</td><td>*Harper's*</td></tr>
<tr><td>14</td><td>throng.]</td><td>~ ;</td><td>*Harper's*</td></tr>
<tr><td>18</td><td>blank,]</td><td>~</td><td>*Harper's*</td></tr>
<tr><td>23</td><td>mine,–]</td><td>~ –</td><td>*Living Age, Univ. Monthly*</td></tr>
</table>

p. 243 IN A CITY ROOM

The poem was first published in *Munsey's Magazine* (February, 1898); and was later included in *New York Nocturnes*, 1898; *Poems*, 1901/7; and *Selected Poetry and Critical Prose*, 1974.

Variants
1   O]   **Oh,**   *Munsey's*

p. 243 IN THE SOLITUDE OF THE CITY

The poem first appeared in *The Independent* (February 10, 1898); and was later included in *New York Nocturnes*, 1898; and *Poems*, 1901/7.

Variants
4   thou . . . thou]   **Thou . . . Thou**   *Independent*

p. 244 A NOCTURNE OF EXILE

The poem was first published in *The Bookman* (February, 1898); and later appeared in *The Living Age* (February, 1898); *New York Nocturnes*, 1898; and *Poems*, 1901/7.

Variants
<table>
<tr><td>5</td><td>^{3}years]</td><td>~ ,</td><td>*Bookman, Living Age*</td></tr>
<tr><td>8</td><td>thee.]</td><td>~ !</td><td>*Bookman, Living Age*</td></tr>
<tr><td>11</td><td>joy,–]</td><td>~ –</td><td>*Bookman, Living Age*</td></tr>
<tr><td>17</td><td>shut; thy]</td><td>**shut. Thy**</td><td>*Bookman, Living Age*</td></tr>
<tr><td>18</td><td>eyes.]</td><td>~ .–</td><td>*NYN*</td></tr>
<tr><td>19</td><td>throng!]</td><td>~ ;</td><td>*Bookman, Living Age*</td></tr>
</table>

p. 245 A NOCTURNE OF TRYSTING

The poem was first published in *The Bookman* (February, 1898); and later was included in *New York Nocturnes*, 1898; *Poems*, 1901/7; and *Selected Poems*, 1936.

Variants
5   with] **for** *Bookman*
10-11   prevision / Of the flower that] **prevision of the flower / That**
             Bookman

p. 245 PRESENCE

The poem was initially published in *Munsey's Magazine* (February, 1898); and was later included in *New York Nocturnes*, 1898; *Poems*, 1901/7; *Selected Poems*, 1936; and *Selected Poetry and Critical Prose*, 1974.

Variants
Title: Presence] **Her Presence** *Munsey's*
5   livelier] **lovelier** *Munsey's*
7   notes.] **~ ;** *Munsey's*
10   after this line, *Munsey's* adds:

> The world has changed since you have come my way.
> Love, is this life I only learn today?

p. 245 LIFE AND THE ARTIST

The poem appeared only in *Harper's Weekly* (March 5, 1898).

p. 246 THAW

The poem was published only in *Lippincott's Magazine* (March, 1898).

p. 246 A NOCTURNE OF SPIRITUAL LOVE

The poem was first published in *The Independent* (May 26, 1898); and later appeared in *A Treasury of Canadian Verse*, 1900; *Poems*, 1901/7; and *Selected Poems*, 1936.

512

Variants

2   Sleep . . . free.]   **Sleep, . . . free!** *Independent, Treasury of Can. Verse*

3   child,]   ~ ,– *Independent, Treasury of Can. Verse*

8   Passion,] ~ *Independent, Treasury of Can. Verse*

9   heart! and now,–] **heart! And now–** *Independent, Treasury of Can. Verse*

14   unseen,–] ~ , *Independent, Treasury of Can. Verse*

15   ah, . . . thy] **ah . . . Thy** *Independent, Treasury of Can. Verse*

21   wonderful.] ~ ! *Independent, Treasury of Can. Verse*

22   divine.] ~ ! *Independent, Treasury of Can. Verse*

23   dream] **dreams** *Independent, Treasury of Can. Verse*

p. 247 IN THE CROWD

The poem was first published in *Lippincott's Magazine* (September, 1898); and was subsequently included in *New York Nocturnes*, 1898; *Poems*, 1901/7; and *Selected Poems*, 1936. As well, an unidentified clipping, reprinted from *Lippincott's Magazine*, survives in the Rufus Hathaway Collection at the University of New Brunswick.

Variants

Title: In the Crowd] **In a Crowded Street** *Lippincott's, HC*

p. 247 ON THE ELEVATED RAILWAY AT 110TH STREET

As far as may be determined, the poem first appeared in *Scribner's* (October, 1898). There is, however, an unidentified clipping, which may be earlier, in the Rufus Hathaway Collection at the University of New Brunswick. The poem was also published in *Poems*, 1901/7; *The Poetic New World*, 1910; *Selected Poems*, 1936; and *Selected Poetry and Critical Prose*, 1974.

Variants

Title: On the Elevated Railway at 110th Street] **A New York Nocturne** [sub-title] **On the Elevated at 110th Street** *Scribner's* **On the Elevated** *HC* **On the Elevated Railroad at 110th Street** *Poems* 1901/7, *Poetic New World*

5   stars.] ~ , *Scribner's, HC, Poetic New World*

6   below] ~ , *HC*

9   shadow towers] **shadow-towers** *Scribner's*

10   grim] ~ , *HC*

14   mount, and plain,] **mount and plain** *HC*

p. 247 AT THY VOICE MY HEART

The poem first appeared in *The Century Magazine* (November, 1898); and was later included in *Poems, 1901/7*; and *Selected Poems, 1936*. On March 18, 1933, the Elson Club sponsored a national tribute to Roberts; and Pomeroy (p. 313) reports that this poem was sung at the meeting, the music written by Dr. Healey Willan.

Variants
Title: At Thy Voice My Heart]   **A Song**   *Century*
  3   night]   ~ ,   *Century*

p. 248 A BALLAD OF MANILA BAY

The poem was first published in *Harper's Magazine* (December, 1898); and later appeared in *Current Opinion* (February, 1899); *Our Country in Poem and Prose*, 1899; *Ballads of American Bravery*, 1900; *Poems, 1901/7*; *Poems of American History*, 1922; and *Great Americans, As Seen by the Poets*, 1933. In addition, there is an unidentified clipping—a reprint from *Harper's*—in the Rufus Hathaway Collection at the University of New Brunswick.

Variants
  3   gate,–]   ~ –   *HC*   ~ .   *Great Americans*
  6   sea-room.]   ~ ,   *Current Opinion, Our Country, Ballads of Amer.*
              Bravery   ~   *Poems of Amer. Hist., Great Americans*
 12   thunders]   **thunder**   *Current Opinion*
 15   roared–]   ~   *Our Country*
 18   waves;]   ~ :   *HC*
 20   rave,]   ~ .   *Our Country, Ballads of Amer. Bravery, Poems of*
              Amer. Hist., Great Americans
 22   elate,]   ~ .   *Great Americans*
 24   a]   **the**   *Current Opinion*
 29   oppose,–]   ~ –   *HC*
 34   shattering]   **shattered**   *Ballads of Amer. Bravery, Poems of Amer.*
              Hist., Great Americans
 38   Bay;–]   ~ –   *HC*   ~ :–   *Ballads of Amer. Bravery, Poems of*
              Amer. Hist., Great Americans
 42   doom,–]   ~ –   *HC*
 45   brave]   ~ ,   *Our Country*
 46   and]   **not**   *Our Country*
 49   ¹Bay!]   ~ ;   *Our Country*
 51   strong]   ~ ,   *Ballads of Amer. Bravery, Poems of Amer. Hist.,*
              Great Americans
 53   Drake]   ~ ,   *Our Country*
 57   the]   omitted in *Our Country*
 62   blow,–]   ~ –   *HC*

514

Manila Bay: A large bay in the Philippine Islands, scene of the first battle of the Spanish-American War (May 1, 1898) between the American and Spanish Asiatic Fleets. The city of Manila, capital of the Philippines, is on the eastern shore.

1   *Corregidor:*   The largest of the three small islands guarding the entrance to Manila Bay. For inexplicable reasons, the batteries on Corregidor did not fire on the American ships as they passed.

4   *Captain:*   Commodore (afterward Admiral) George Dewey (1837-1917) commander of the American fleet

5-16   The American fleet, in the predawn morning of May 1, was able to slip past the fortifications at the entrance of Manila Bay practically unnoticed. The feared mines were faulty and none exploded. A single battery on El Fraile, smallest of the islands in the entrance, fired a few shots as the ships passed but did no damage.

27   *Kalibuyo and Salinas:*   towered outpost on the southeast shore of Manila Bay

29   *Cavité:*   the island fortress and arsenal of the Spanish fleet, in Bakor Bay

38   *Bakor Bay:*   a small cove on the southeast side of Manila Bay

47   *the dauntless boat:*   The *Reina Christina,* flagship of the Spanish fleet, attempted to engage the American flagship, the *Olympia,* but was driven off and sank.

53   *Drake:*   Sir Francis Drake (c. 1540-1596) British Admiral, buccaneer, and circumnavigator of the globe

55   *Farragut:*   David Glasgow Farragut (1801-1870) American Admiral, victor in the Civil War battles of New Orleans and Mobile Bay

56   *Blake:*   Robert Blake (1599-1657) British Admiral

63   *Nelson:*   Viscount Horatio Nelson (1758-1805) British Admiral, famed for victories over Napoleon, especially the Battle of Trafalgar (1805)

p. 250 THE ATLANTIC CABLE

The poem was first published in *New York Nocturnes,* 1898; and was reprinted only in *Poems,* 1901/7.

The Atlantic Cable: The first Atlantic Cable was completed on July 27, 1886 from Heart's Content, Newfoundland to Valentia, Ireland.

p. 250 AT TIDE WATER

As far as may be determined, the poem first appeared in *New York Nocturnes,*
1898. There is, however, an unidentified clipping, which may be earlier, in
the Rufus Hathaway Collection at the University of New Brunswick. The
poem also appeared in *Poems,* 1901/7; *Selected Poems,* 1936; *An Anthology
of Canadian Poetry,* 1942; *The Penguin Book of Canadian Verse,* 1967; and
Selected Poetry and Critical Prose, 1974.

Variants
1   Autumn]   **autumn**   *HC*
2   flats,]   ~   *HC*
3   marshes,–]   ~ –   *HC*
4   Land . . . abide,]   **land . . . abide.**   *HC*
5   tranquil,]   ~   *HC*
11   heaven's]   **Heaven's**   *NYN, Poems* 1901/7
14   breath,–]   ~ –   *HC*
15   desire,]   ~   *HC*
16   laughter,]   ~   *HC*
18   surprise.]   ~ ;   *HC*
19   contemplation,]   ~   *HC*

p. 251 DREAM-FELLOWS

The poem first appeared in *New York Nocturnes,* 1898; and was reprinted
only in *Poems,* 1901/7.

Variants
44   white,]   ~   *NYN*

p. 253 AN EVENING COMMUNION

The poem was first published in *New York Nocturnes,* 1898; and was later
included in *Poems,* 1901/7; *Selected Poems,* 1936; and *Selected Poetry and
Critical Prose,* 1974.

Variants
10   hour]   ~ ,   *NYN, Poems* 1901/7

p. 254 THE FALLING LEAVES

As far as may be determined, the poem first appeared in *New York Nocturnes,*
1898. There is, however, an unidentified clipping which may be earlier in the

516

Rufus Hathaway Collection at the University of New Brunswick. The poem later appeared in *A Treasury of Canadian Verse*, 1900; *Poems*, 1901/7; *Methodist Magazine and Review* (November, 1904); *Selected Poems*, 1936; *Selected Poems of Sir Charles G.D. Roberts*, 1955; and *Selected Poetry and Critical Prose*, 1974.

Variants
5 He] **he** *Treasury of Can. Verse*
7 recalling] ~ , *NYN, Treasury of Can. Verse, Poems* 1901/7,
          Methodist Mag. and Rev.
8 Eternity] **eternity** *HC*

p. 254 A FOREWORD TO *NORTHLAND LYRICS*

The poem first appeared in *The Canadian Magazine* (December, 1898); and was subsequently published as the foreword to *Northland Lyrics*, 1899. The poem is also included in Pomeroy's biography, p. 161.

Variants
All variants are from *The Canadian Magazine.*
Title: Northland] **Norland**
1 Sisters and brothers] **Sisters, and Brothers**
3 close-knit] **close knit**
4 sweet,] **dear**
8 others . . . word,] **other . . . word**
9 Northland] **northland**

Glossary
Sub-title: *E.R. MacD., W.C.R., T.G.R.:* Elizabeth Roberts MacDonald,
          William Carman Roberts, and Theodore Goodridge Roberts

p. 254 THE IDEAL

The poem was first published in *New York Nocturnes*, 1898; and was reprinted only in *Poems*, 1901/7.

p. 255 IN DARKNESS

The poem was first published in *New York Nocturnes*, 1898; and was reprinted only in *Poems*, 1901/7.

p. 255 NOCTURNES OF THE HONEYSUCKLE

The poem first appeared in *New York Nocturnes,* 1898; and was reprinted only in *Poems,* 1901/7.

p. 256 O THOU WHO BIDD'ST

The poem was first published in *New York Nocturnes,* 1898; and was later included in *Poems,* 1901/7; and *Selected Poems,* 1936.

p. 256 **THE STREET LAMPS**

The poem first appeared in *New York Nocturnes,* 1898; and was later published in *Poems,* 1901/7; and *Selected Poems,* 1936.

p. 257 AT THE DRINKING FOUNTAIN

The poem was first published in *Lippincott's Magazine* (January, 1899); and later appeared in *Current Opinion* (April, 1899); *Poems,* 1901/7; and *Selected Poetry and Critical Prose,* 1974.

Variants
Title: Drinking Fountain]   **Drinking-Fountain**   *Lippincott's, Current Opinion*
3   thro']   **through**   *Lippincott's, Current Opinion*
4   drifts.]   ~ ,   *Current Opinion*

p. 257 JONATHAN AND JOHN

The poem was first published in *The Century Magazine* (January, 1899); and was later included in *Poems,* 1901/7; and *Selected Poems,* 1936.

Variants
2   bout.]   ~ ;   *Century*
7   Will]   In the margin of Roberts' reading copy of *Poems* at the University of New Brunswick, he has crossed through *Will* and written *Would.* The change was not incorporated in *Selected Poems.*
14   fret]   ~ ,   *Century, Poems* 1901/7
16   good;]   ~ ,   *Century*

Glossary
Jonathan and John: traditional names for the United States and England. The names are used in this sense in the last paragraph of Henry David Thoreau's *Walden.*
13-16   *When ... good:*   the American Revolution

p. 258 KINSMEN STRONG

The poem was initially published in *Pall Mall Magazine* (March, 1899); and was reprinted only in *Poems*, 1901/7.

Variants
All variants are from *Pall Mall Magazine.*
1-4   Italicized
 2   strong]   ~ ,
17   note ... ye,]   **note, ... ye**
27   barren,]   ~
34   part]   ~ ,
40   hand.]   ~ ;

Glossary
20   *thews:*   muscles or sinews

p. 259 A REMORSE

The poem was first published in *Lippincott's Magazine* (March, 1899); and later appeared in *The Book of the Rose*, 1903; and *Poems*, 1907. As well, an unidentified clipping—a reprint from *Lippincott's*—is in the Rufus Hathaway Collection at the University of New Brunswick.

Variants
Title: A Remorse]   **In the Night**   *Lippincott's, HC*
 1   love]   **Love**   *Lippincott's*
 1   dead.]   ~ :   *Lippincott's*   ~ ;   *HC*
 2   this!—]   ~ ,—   *Lippincott's*   ~ —   *HC*
 8   remained]   **was left**   *Lippincott's, HC*
 8   unsaid;—]   ~ ;   *HC*
11   "O God!" ... aloud—"She]   **"Oh, God," ... aloud, "she**
       Lippincott's   "O God," ... aloud, "she   *HC*
Note: in *Lippincott's Magazine* and the Hathaway clipping the poem is divided into three quatrains

p. 259 A SONG FOR APRIL

The poem originally appeared in *The Century Magazine* (May, 1899); and was later included in *Poems, 1901/7*; and *Selected Poems*, 1936. As well, an unidentified clipping is preserved in the Rufus Hathaway Collection at the University of New Brunswick.

Variants
Title: A Song for April]   **A Song for Spring**   *Century*
1   ^{2}list . . . confer.]   **List . . . confer:**   *Century*
8   ^{2}up . . . world's]   **Up . . . mold's**   *Century*
12   sleep]   ~ ,   *Century*
14   ^{2}see]   **See**   *Century*
15   wind,]   ~   *HC*
20   silvery shrill]   **silvery-shrill**   *Century*
20   This line is omitted in *HC*.

p. 260 BROOKLYN BRIDGE

The poem was first published in *The Atlantic Monthly* (June, 1899); and later appeared in *Poems, 1901/7*; *The Poetic New World*, 1910; *Poems of American History*, 1922; *Canadian Poems 1850-1952*, 1953; *Canadian Anthology*, 1966; and *Selected Poetry and Critical Prose*, 1974.

Variants
8   As]   **For**   *Atlantic, Poetic New World, Poems of Amer. Hist.*
10   sun,]   ~ ;   *Atlantic, Poetic New World, Poems of Amer. Hist.*
15   arch.]   ~ ,   *Atlantic, Poetic New World, Poems of Amer. Hist.*

Glossary
Brooklyn Bridge: a suspension bridge, 5989 feet long, connecting the boroughs of Manhattan and Brooklyn; it was begun in 1867 and completed in 1884.

p. 260 A STREET SONG AT NIGHT

The poem first appeared in *Cosmopolitan* (1899); and was reprinted only in *Poems, 1901/7*.

Variants
All variants are from *Cosmopolitan.*
Title: A Street Song at Night]   **A Night Song in the Street**
1   Here mid]   **Here, 'mid**
5   together,]   ~ —

520

9   know.]   ~ ;
18   throng.]   ~ ,
19   lips]   ~ ,

Glossary
3   *car lights:*   i.e., street-car lights

p. 261 THE WHITE FROST

The poem was published only in *Lippincott's Magazine* (January, 1900).

p. 261 CHILD OF THE INFINITE

The poem was first published in *Pall Mall Magazine* (February, 1900); and was later included in *The Book of the Rose,* 1903; *Poems,* 1907; *Selected Poems,* 1936; *Selected Poems of Sir Charles G.D. Roberts,* 1955; and *Selected Poetry and Critical Prose,* 1974.

Variants
1   Wind, and Flame]   **Flame, and Wind**   *Pall Mall*
2   Day]   ~ ,   *Pall Mall, Poems* 1907
2   Night,–]   ~ !   *Pall Mall*
3   endure. Shall]   **endure,–shall**   *Pall Mall*
5   return. Shall]   **return,–shall**   *Pall Mall*
7   mighty. But]   **mighty, but**   *Pall Mall*
9   Sun]   The italicized stanza designations appear only in *Selected*
                  Poems.
11   I,]   ~   *Pall Mall*
16   waste]   ~ ,   *Pall Mall, BOR, Poems* 1907
21-26, 27-32   These stanzas are reversed in *Pall Mall.*
22   world,]   ~ ;   *Pall Mall*
24   ocean]   **Ocean**   *Pall Mall*
30   reinitiant]   **re-initiant**   *Pall Mall*

p. 263 THE AIM

As far as may be determined, the poem was first published in the *Criterion* (April, 1900). There is, however, an unidentified clipping which may be earlier in the Rufus Hathaway Collection at the University of New Brunswick. The poem also appeared in *Current Literature* (August, 1900); *The Book of the Rose,* 1903; *The Book Buyer* (February, 1904); *Poems,* 1907; as an advertisement for Roberts' Trans-Canada Tour in 1925; in *Selected Poems,* 1936, *Masterpieces of Religious Verse,* 1948; *Selected Poems of Sir Charles G.D.*

Roberts, 1955; the *Penguin Book of Canadian Verse*, 1967; and *Selected Poetry and Critical Prose*, 1974.

Variants

4   soul,]   ~ .   *HC*
5   worth,–]   ~ –   *Current Lit.*
6   act,]   ~ ,–   *Criterion*   ~ –   *Current Lit.*
9   desire.]   ~ ,   *Criterion, Current Lit.*
10   Thy]   **thy**   *BOR, Book Buyer*
10   sight:–]   ~ –   *Criterion, Current Lit.*
15   my . . . strive.]   **the . . . strive;**   *Criterion, Current Lit.*
16   Thy]   **thy**   *HC*

Glossary

6   *scamped:*   to perform work carelessly or dishonestly

p. 263 ATTAR

The poem first appeared in *The Smart Set* (May, 1900); and was later included in *The Book of the Rose*, 1903; *Poems*, 1907; and *Selected Poems*, 1936. As well, the Rufus Hathaway Collection at the University of New Brunswick contains an unidentified clipping, reprinted from *The Smart Set*.

Variants

2   summer . . . south]   **Summer . . . South**   *Smart Set, HC*
8   love]   **Love**   *Smart Set, HC*
14   me,–]   ~ !–   *Smart Set, HC*
16   me!]   ~ .   *Smart Set, HC*
20   after this line, *Smart Set, HC, BOR,* and *Poems* 1907 add:

> The white flower of your feet,
> How sacred and how sweet to me!–
> From some close-hung and censered shrine
> Borne to make life divine to me.

22   me!–]   ~ !   *BOR, Poems* 1907
23   censered]   **censured**   *HC*   **cloistered**   *BOR, Poems* 1907

Glossary

Attar: a perfume or oil obtained from flowers; here used in the sense of essence

522

The poem was first published in the *Saturday Evening Post* (May, 1900); and was later included in *The Book of the Rose*, 1903; *Poems*, 1907; *Selected Poems*, 1936; *Selected Poems of Sir Charles G.D. Roberts*, 1955; and *Poets of Confederation*, 1967.

Pomeroy (p. 5) gives the following account of the genesis of the poem:

> When Charles was nine years old a great storm, known later as the Saxeby Gale, broke down the dykes and flooded all the marshes of the Tantramar. The phenomenal tide carried far inland, almost half a mile above the ordinary tide-level, an old ship which was never restored to her element. The young lad liked to play around the wrecked ship. To him "it ached to be in the sea again." Years passed. The little boy of the Tantramar had become the busy writer in scenes far distant. One day he recaptured a boyhood dream and wrote the ballad entitled "The Stranded Ship."

Variants

1	her.]	~	*Sat. Evening Post*
3	more. The]	**more; the**	*Sat. Evening Post*
5	her. No]	**her; no**	*Sat. Evening Post*
5	^{2}more]	In *Selected Poems* the line ends with a period. In this instance I have taken the earlier readings to be correct.	
7	journey. For]	**journey; for**	*Sat. Evening Post*
15	Vast]	**vast**	*Sat. Evening Post*
18	track.]	~, *BOR* **trackt,** *Poems*, 1907; Roberts has crossed through the erroneous *t* in his reading copy of *Poems*.	
19	calm]	~,	*Sat. Evening Post*
26	more, . . . slips,]	**more . . . slips**	*Sat. Evening Post*
28	time.]	~,	*Sat. Evening Post*
29	Ceylon,–]	~ –	*Sat. Evening Post*
30	St. John.]	~ ;	*Sat. Evening Post*
31	coffee-bags,–]	**coffee-bales–** *Sat. Evening Post* **cotton-bales,–** *BOR, Poems* 1907	
37	sun]	~,	*Sat. Evening Post*
38	sailors . . . done!]	**shipmen . . . done.**	*Sat. Evening Post*
43	long]	~,	*Sat. Evening Post*
50	inland]	~,	*Sat. Evening Post*

The poem first appeared in *The Century Magazine* (June, 1900); and was later included in *The Book of the Rose*, 1903; *Poems*, 1907; and *Selected Poems*, 1936.

2   curled,]   ~! *Century*
3   for] **to** *Century*
6   the wild] **your hushed** *Century*   **the hushed** *BOR,*
                        Poems 1907
6   heart,] ~! *Century*
7   bee . . . wings,] **bee, . . . wings** *Century*
10   fire,] ~! *Century*
14   madness] **wonder** *Century*
16   Even] **E'en** *Century*
17   rose,] ~! *Century*
18   done] ~, *Century*

p. 266 THE ROSE OF MY DESIRE

The poem was first published in *The Smart Set* (June, 1900); and was later included in *The Book of the Rose,* 1903; *Poems,* 1907; and *Selected Poems,* 1936. As well, an unidentified clipping (RC) is pasted in the front of Roberts' reading copy of *Poems,* 1901, in the Roberts Collection at the University of New Brunswick.

Variants

1   O] **Oh,** *RC*
3   eastern] **Eastern** *Smart Set, RC*
6   camphor-trees] **camphor trees** *Smart Set, RC*
14   ^{2}star] ~, *Smart Set, RC, BOR, Poems* 1907
17   homeless] ~, *Smart Set, RC, BOR, Poems* 1907
22   flame] ~, *Smart Set, RC, BOR, Poems* 1907
23   ^{1}it] ~, *Smart Set, RC, BOR, Poems* 1907
24   burned] **turned** *Smart Set, RC*
27   O wild,] **Oh, wild** *RC*

p. 267 AWAY, SAD VOICES

The poem first appeared in *The Saturday Evening Post* (August, 1900); and was later included in *The Book of the Rose,* 1903; and *Poems,* 1907.

Note: in *The Saturday Evening Post* and *The Book of the Rose* the
         poem is divided into two quatrains

p. 267 THE FEAR OF LOVE

The poem first appeared in *The Smart Set* (August, 1900); and was later in-cluded in *The Book of the Rose*, 1903; *Poems*, 1907; *Selected Poems*, 1936; and *Selected Poetry and Critical Prose*, 1974. As well, an unidentified clipping—a reprint from *The Smart Set*—is in the Rufus Hathaway Collection at the University of New Brunswick. Pomeroy (p. 203) notes that this poem is Roberts' "first experiment in *vers libre*."

Variants
6   joy]   ~ ,   *Smart Set, HC, BOR, Poems* 1907
12   eyes]   ~ ,   *Smart Set, HC, BOR, Poems* 1907

p. 268 THE COVERT

The poem first appeared in *The Smart Set* (September, 1900); and was later included in *The Book of the Rose*, 1903; and *Poems*, 1907.

Variants
1   Sharp]   **Oh, sharp**   *Smart Set*
7   sorrow of life]   **Sorrow of Life**   *Smart Set*
8   hair!]   ~ .   *Smart Set*

p. 268 HOW LITTLE I KNEW

The poem first appeared in *The Saturday Evening Post* (October, 1900); and was later included in *The Book of the Rose*, 1903; and *Poems*, 1907. As well, an unidentified clipping—a reprint from *The Saturday Evening Post*—is in the Rufus Hathaway Collection at the University of New Brunswick.

Variants
1   knew,]   ~   *HC*
2   eyes]   ~ ,   *HC*
3   this,–]   ~ –   *Sat. Eve. Post, HC*
9   known; for]   **known! For**   *Sat. Eve. Post, HC*
11   Months . . . memory]   **Years . . . pulses**   *Sat. Eve. Post, HC*
12   pulses]   **memory**   *Sat. Eve. Post, HC*
16   world]   **worlds**   *Sat. Eve. Post, HC*

Glossary
6   *harebell:*   an herb with blue, bell shaped flowers

p. 269 NEW DEAD

The poem was first published in *The Outlook* (November, 1900); and was later included in *The Book of the Rose,* 1903; *Poems,* 1907; and *Selected Poems,* 1936. An unidentified clipping in the Rufus Hathaway Collection at the University of New Brunswick is a reprint of the text in *Outlook.*

Pomeroy (p. 204) says that the poem was written after the death of Roberts' friend, Richard Hovey. Hovey, an American, was co-author with Bliss Carman of *Songs of Vagabondia.* He died in 1900 at the age of thirty-six.

Variants

9	world]	**World**	*Outlook, HC*
10	smile,–]	~?–	*Outlook, HC*
14	night,–]	~ –	*Outlook, HC*
16	sight,–]	~ –	*Outlook, HC*
19	stopt]	**stopped**	*HC*
25	slips,–ah]	**slips . . . Ah**	*Outlook, HC*
26	outworn!]	~ –	*Outlook, HC*
27	strong]	~ ,	*Outlook, HC*
28	new born!]	**new-born.**	*Outlook, HC*

p. 270 IN APIA BAY

The poem evidently first appeared in *The Youth's Companion,* but it has proved impossible to locate the issue in which the poem appeared. The text in *Ballads of American Bravery,* 1900, is a reprint from *The Youth's Companion,* and the poem was also included in *Poems of American History,* 1922.

Variants

23	dragged,]	~ .	*Ballads of American Bravery*

Glossary

Apia Bay: In *Poems of American History* is the note:

> On March 15, 1889, a hurricane visited the Samoan Islands. There were in the harbor of Apia, at the time one English, three German, and three American war-ships, sent there to safeguard the interests of their respective countries. The English ship, the *Calliope,* succeeded in steaming out of the harbor, the crew of the American flagship *Trenton* cheering her as she passed. The *Trenton* was wrecked a few minutes later, as were the five other ships in the harbor.

Morituri vos salutamus: the salutation of the Roman gladiators, "We who are about to die salute you."

526

p. 272 THE ROSE'S AVATAR

The poem was first published in *The Smart Set* (February, 1901); and later appeared in *The Book of the Rose,* 1903; and *Poems,* 1907. As well, an un-identified clipping–a reprint from *The Smart Set*–is in the Rufus Hathaway Collection at the University of New Brunswick.

Variants
2   sang.]   ~ ,   *Smart Set, HC*
6   fire.]   ~ ;   *Smart Set, HC*
13   East,]   **east**–   *HC*
14   South,–]   **South**–   *Smart Set*   **south**–   *HC*
15   love and tears]   **tears and love**   *Smart Set, HC*
16   thy]   **your**   *Smart Set, HC*
Note: in *The Smart Set* and the Hathaway clipping the poem appears as four quatrains

Glossary
Avatar: in the Hindu religion the descent of a deity to the earth in an incarnate form; the incarnation of a spirit
2   *Saadi:*   a Persian poet (c. 1200) whose principal works were two collections of verse, the *Gulistan* or *Rose-Garden* and the *Bustan* or *Tree-Garden*
9   *seraglio:*   a harem
11   *Mænad:*   a female attendant of Bacchus, the Greek god of wine

p. 272 THE PIPERS OF THE POOLS

The poem was first published in *Lippincott's Magazine* (April, 1901); and was later included in *The Book of the Rose,* 1903; *Poems,* 1907; and *Selected Poems,* 1936. As well, the Rufus Hathaway Collection at the University of New Brunswick contains an unidentified clipping of the poem, an abridged reprint–with additional variants–of the text in *Lippincott's.*

Variants
1   pools]   ~ ,   *Lippincott's, HC*
2   in.]   ~ ;   *Lippincott's, HC*
6   air]   ~ ,   *Lippincott's, HC*
9   cold]   **old**   *HC*
11   the]   So in all texts except *Selected Poems* which has *and;* I have assumed the earlier readings to be correct in this instance.
13-16   omitted in *HC*
13   earth]   ~ ,   *Lippincott's*
18   time:]   ~ ;   *HC*
19   sapwood]   **sap-wood,**   *Lippincott's*   **sapwood,**   *HC*

20   ¹climb,]   ~   *Lippincott's, HC*
23   off]   **of**   *Poems* 1907
26   bee,]   ~ ,–   *Lippincott's*   ~ –   *HC*
27   children,]   ~   *BOR, Poems* 1907
28   Flower and wing]   **Wing by flower**   *Lippincott's, HC*
29-32   omitted in *HC*
30   arise;]   ~ ,   *Lippincott's, BOR, Poems* 1907
33   in to]   **into**   *Poems* 1907   Note: Roberts corrected this printing
         error in his reading copy of *Poems.*
34   ³soon]   ~ ,   *Lippincott's, HC*
36   moon!]   ~ .   *Lippincott's, HC*

p. 273 THE ROSE OF LIFE

The poem first appeared in *The Century Magazine* (April, 1901); and was later published in *The Book of the Rose,* 1903; *Poems,* 1907; and *Selected Poems,* 1936. As well, an unidentified clipping—a reprint with many additional variants of the *Century* text—is contained in the Rufus Hathaway Collection at the University of New Brunswick.

Variants
1   Rose . . . garden:]   **rose . . . garden;**   *HC*
4   glad;]   ~ :   *HC*
6   gold;]   ~ :   *HC*
9   wisdom,]   ~ .   *HC*
10   know,]   ~ .   *HC*
15   Answered:]   ~ ;   *HC*
18   noon;]   ~ :   *HC*
24   vain,]   ~ .   *HC*
27   witness, each,]   **whiteness, each**   *HC*
28   Ancient]   ~ ,   *Century, HC, BOR, Poems* 1907
33   beauty:]   ~ ;   *HC*
34   thronged]   ~ ,   *HC*
36   wronged;]   ~ ,   *Century, HC, BOR, Poems* 1907
38   omitted in *HC*
39   bite]   **bits**   *HC*

p. 274 THE NATIVE

The poem was first published in *The Saturday Evening Post* (May, 1901); and was later included in *The Book of the Rose,* 1903; *Poems,* 1907; *Selected Poems,* 1936; and *Selected Poetry and Critical Prose,* 1974.

Variants
11   veins]   ~ ,   *Sat. Eve. Post, BOR*
26   fate.]   ~ :   *Sat. Eve. Post*

p. 275 INVOCATION

The poem was first published in *The Smart Set* (October, 1901); and was later included in *The Book of the Rose*, 1903; and *Poems*, 1907.

p. 276 THE WISDOM OF LOVE

The poem initially appeared in *Munsey's Magazine* (November, 1901); and was later included in *The Book of the Rose*, 1903; and *Poems*, 1907.

Variants
3   inscrutable,]   no comma appears in *Poems*, 1907; I have assumed
          the earlier readings to be correct in this instance

p. 277 IN THE BARN-YARD'S SOUTHERLY CORNER

The poem first appeared in *Poems*, 1901/7; and was later included in *Selected Poems*, 1936; *The Book of Canadian Poetry*, 1943/48; *Twentieth Century Canadian Poetry*, 1953; and *Selected Poetry and Critical Prose*, 1974. For Pomeroy's comment see "The Farmer's Winter Morning."

p. 278 THE LOGS

The poem first appeared in *Poems*, 1901/7; and was later included in *Selected Poems*, 1936; and *Selected Poetry and Critical Prose*, 1974.

p. 279 NEW LIFE

The poem was published only in *Poems*, 1901/7.

p. 279 THE SKATER

As far as may be determined, the poem first appeared in *Poems*, 1901/7. There are, however, two unidentified clippings which may be earlier in the Rufus Hathaway Collection at the University of New Brunswick. The poem was also published in *Canadian Prose and Verse*, 1923; *Selected Poems*, 1936; *Canadian Anthology*, 1966; and *Selected Poetry and Critical Prose*, 1974.

Variants

1   feet . . . steel]   **feet, . . . steel,**   *HC*(2)
2   wingéd]   **winged**   *Poems* 1901/7, *HC*(1), *HC*(2), *Can. Prose and Verse*
6   glimmering,]   ~   *HC*(1)
10   Winter's]   **winter's**   *HC*(1), *HC*(2)
10   rests]   **lies**   *HC*(1)
12   hollows]   **echoes**   *HC*(1)
15   behind]   ~ ,   *HC*(2)
16   ²faster]   ~ ,   *HC*(2)
19   speed]   ~ ,   *HC*(1), *HC*(2)
20   seed,–]   ~ –   *HC*(1)   ~ ,   *HC*(2)
24   sleep.]   ~ ,   *Can. Prose and Verse*
25   near.]   ~ ,   *HC*(1)
26   fear.]   ~ ;   *Poems* 1901/7, *HC*(1), *HC*(2), *Can. Prose and Verse*

p. 280 THE GREAT AND THE LITTLE WEAVERS

The poem was first published in *Munsey's Magazine* (April 27, 1902); and later appeared in *The Book of the Rose*, 1903; *Poems*, 1907; *Selected Poems*, 1936; and *Selected Poems of Sir Charles G.D. Roberts*, 1955.

Variants

2   sleep.]   ~ ;   *Munsey's*
6   white-thorn . . . gust,]   **whitethorn . . . gust;**   *Munsey's*
7   cloud-rose]   **cloud rose**   *Munsey's*
8   earth-rose]   **earth rose**   *Munsey's*
14   tires,]   ~ ;   *Munsey's*
15   bird-song]   **bird song**   *Munsey's*
16   fires,]   ~ ;   *Munsey's*
18   flute-cry]   **flute cry**   *Munsey's*
22   death,]   ~ ;   *Munsey's*
23   dew]   ~ ,   *Munsey's*
24   breath,]   ~ ;   *Munsey's*
25   ere the]   **ere yet the**   *BOR*
26   new-old]   **new old**   *Munsey's*
32   years;]   ~ .   *Munsey's*
36   hearse.]   ~ ;   *Munsey's*
39   kindreds]   **Kindreds**   *Munsey's*
41   Love]   **love**   *Munsey's*
42   latch,]   ~ –   *Munsey's*
43   (In]   **In**   *Munsey's*
44   catch),]   **catch–**   *Munsey's*
46   vain,–]   ~ ;   *Munsey's*

Glossary
14   *Titan:*   In ancient Greek mythology, the children of Uranus (heaven) and Gaea (earth); they overthrew their parents and for a time ruled the world until they, in turn, were overthrown by Zeus, a son of the leading Titan, Cronus. The word is commonly used to describe anyone or anything of enormous size.

34   *beldame:*   an old woman, especially one who is ugly; a hag

p. 282   HEAT IN THE CITY

The poem initially appeared in *The Outlook* (July, 1902); and was subsequently published in *Current Opinion* (September, 1902); *The Book of the Rose,* 1903; *Poems,* 1907; *Selected Poems,* 1936; and *Selected Poems of Sir Charles G.D. Roberts,* 1955.

Variants
2   slow.]   ~ ;   *Current Opinion*
6   sleep.]   ~ ,   *Outlook*   ~ ;   *Current Opinion*
15   stoops]   **stoop**   *Current Opinion*
16   fear]   **dread**   *Outlook, Current Opinion*

p. 282   AT THE WAYSIDE SHRINE

The poem first appeared in *Munsey's Magazine* (October, 1902); and was later included in *The Book of the Rose,* 1903; and *Poems,* 1907.

Variants
All variants are from *Munsey's Magazine.*
Title: At the Wayside Shrine]   **At Sainte Anne de Beaupré**
2   saint!–]   ~ !
11   grace,–]   ~ ,
12   ignorance,]   ~
22   delight,–]   ~ –

Glossary
Ste. Anne de Beaupré: a shrine to Sainte Anne, the traditional name for the mother of Mary, is located at Ste. Anne de Beaupré, near Quebec City.

p. 283   SHEPHERDESS FAIR

The poem first appeared in *The Smart Set* (December, 1902); and was later included in *The Book of the Rose,* 1903; and *Poems,* 1907.

11   now . . . noon]   **now, . . . noon,**   *Smart Set*

p. 284 THE UNKNOWN CITY

The poem was first published in *Scribner's* (September, 1903); and later appeared in the *Windsor Magazine* (June, 1908); *The Living Age* (July, 1908); *New Poems,* 1919; *The Sweet o' the Year and Other Poems,* 1925; *Canadian Poets,* 1926; *The Vagrant of Time,* 1927; *The Golden Treasury of Canadian Verse,* 1928/9; *Songs of the Maritimes,* 1931; *Our Canadian Literature,* 1934; *Selected Poems,* 1936; *Poets of Confederation,* 1967; and *Selected Poetry and Critical Prose,* 1974.

A holograph manuscript, dated March 14, 1903, is contained in Roberts' notebook at the University of New Brunswick. A single typescript, probably prepared for the publication of *The Sweet o' the Year* or *The Vagrant of Time,* is in the Queen's University Archives.

Variants

1-16   There . . . foam.]   In *NB* the lines appear in the order 1-2, 11-16, and 3-10 on the first page of the poem. This page is crossed through; but the poem is continued, beginning with the revised lines 11-16, on the following page. The second page is not cancelled.

1   lies]   **is**   *NB*

1   inaccessible,]   ~   *NB, Scribner's, Windsor, Living Age*

6   snows,]   ~ ;   *Windsor, Living Age*

7   imminent]   originally *sunsweet* in *NB; sunsweet* crossed through and *imminent,* preceded by an obliterated word, written above it

9   war.]   ~ ,   *NB, Windsor, Living Age, NP, TS, Sweet o' the Year, Can. Poets, VOT, Golden Treasury of Can. Verse, Songs of the Maritimes*

11-16   White . . . foam.]   the cancelled stanza in *NB* is:

> White-walled and jettied on the peacock tide,
> Rose roofed and purple skied,
> It greets the happy dreamers coming home
> Soft with slow oars over the foam

In the second line, *purple* is written above *violet* which has been cancelled, and *with slow oars* is written above the uncancelled phrase *oared across.*

11   White-walled]   **White walled**   *Windsor, Living Age*

12   enskied,]   ~ ;   *Golden Treasury of Can. Verse*

14   ever-living]   **everlasting**   *Windsor, Living Age*
14   green,]   ~ ;   *Golden Treasury of Can. Verse*
15   turning]   originally *coming* in *NB; coming* crossed through and
                  turning written beside it
17   musical]   ~ ,   *Windsor, Living Age*
18   fountains' shadowy]   **shadowy fountains'**   *NB*
19   With . . . rose]   **With daffodil & lavender rose**   *NB*
19   rose]   ~ ,   *Scribner's, Windsor, Living Age, NP, TS, Sweet o' the*
                  Year, Can. Poets, VOT, Golden Treasury of Can. Verse,
                  Songs of the Maritimes, Our Can. Lit.
21   dye,]   ~   *Windsor, Living Age*
23   chambers,]   originally *courts are* in *NB; courts are* crossed through
                  and *chambers* written above it
24   faëry]   originally *mystic* in *NB; mystic* crossed through and *fairy*
                  written above it
24   circumstance,–]   ~ –   *Scribner's, Windsor, Living Age*
25   lean some time]   **lean, some time,**   *NB, Scribner's*
                  lean, sometime,   *Windsor, Living Age*
28   pure,]   ~   *Songs of the Maritimes*
29   This . . . emprise.]   cancelled above this line in *NB* is:

                    This is that city

31   do,]   ~   *NB, Scribner's, Windsor, Living Age*
33-42   Here . . . tongue.]   In *Scribner's* the lines are:

          Here is fulfilled each hope that soared and sought
          Beyond the bournes of thought;–
          The chorded cadence art could ne'er attain
          Crowns the imperfect strain;
          The obdurate marble yields; the canvas glows;
          Perfect the column grows;
          And the song that seemed to die unsung
          Triumphs upon the tongue.
          Here the high failure, not the level fame,
          Attests the spirit's aim,–
          And hero hearts, by too frail flesh forsworn,
          At last forget to mourn.

     In *Windsor Magazine* and *The Living Age* the lines are:

          Here is fulfilled each hope that soared and sought
          Beyond the bournes of thought.
          The obdurate marble yields; the canvas glows;
          Perfect the column grows;
          The chorded cadence art could ne'er attain

Crowns the imperfect strain;
And the great song that seemed to die unsung
Triumphs upon the tongue.
Here the high failure, not the level fame,
Attests the spirit's aim;
And here the hearts by too frail flesh forsworn,
At last forget to mourn.

35   Here . . . sought]   cancelled above this line in *NB* is:

Here every childlike hope that soared & sought
Beyond the bournes of thought

37-42   The . . . tongue.]   in *NB* the lines are:

Here the great song that seemed to die unsung
Triumphs upon the tongue,
The obdurate marble yields, the canvas glows,
Perfect the column grows,
The chorded cadence art could ne'er attain
Crowns the imperfect strain.
And hero hearts, by too frail flesh forsworn,
At last forgets to mourn.
Here the high failure, not the sordid fame,
Attests the spirit's aim.

In the seventh line, *And* is written above *The,* and in the ninth
line *Here* is written above *And; The* and *And* have been cancelled.

p. 285 WHEN IN THE ROWAN TREE

The poem first appeared in the *Canadian Magazine* (October, 1905); and was
later published in the *Windsor Magazine* (November, 1908); *New Poems,*
1919; and *The Vagrant of Time,* 1927. In Roberts' notebook in the Roberts
Collection at the University of New Brunswick is a manuscript copy of the
poem dated March 15, 1903. The entire poem is crossed out in the notebook
by two large crosses.

Variants
Title: When in the Rowan Tree]   **You** *Can. Mag., Windsor*
1   rowan tree]   **rowan-tree** *Windsor*
3   quiet dusk]   *quiet evening dusk* in *NB; evening* crossed through
4   All lilied]   originally *Light odored* in *NB. Light odored* crossed
                     through and *All lilied* written above it
4   lilied]   **livid** *Can. Mag.*

534

4   you,]   ~   *Windsor*

6   me,]   ~ ;   *NB*

7   tender]   originally *kindly* in *NB; kindly* crossed through and
                       loving tender written above it

7   dark]   **night**   *Can. Mag.*

8   you.]   **You!** *NB*   **YOU!**   *Windsor;* also line 16

9   across]   *far on* in *NB* and *over* written above *far on*

12   you,]   ~ ;   *Windsor*

14   ²red]   ~ ,   *Can. Mag.*

15   to me means love,]   **means love to me;** *NB*

p. 286 WHEN THE CLOUD COMES DOWN THE MOUNTAIN

The poem first appeared in *New Poems*, 1919; and was later included in
Canadian Poets, 1926; *The Vagrant of Time*, 1927; and *Selected Poems*, 1936.
    A holograph manuscript, dated March 15, 1903, "S.J.R.R." is contained
in Roberts' notebook at the University of New Brunswick.

Variants
All variants are from Roberts' notebook.

1   mountain,]   ~

4   eaves,–]   ~ ,

7   life with the drenched brown]   *life* crossed through in *NB; drink-*
                       ing grass crossed through and *live brown* written above
                       it. Obviously there was a still later revision of this line.

p. 286 COAL

The poem was first published in *The Book of the Rose*, 1903; and was reprinted only in *Poems*, 1907.

p. 286 THE CONSPIRATORS

As far as may be determined, the poem was first published in *The Book of the
Rose*, 1903. However, an unidentified clipping which may be earlier is con-
tained in the Rufus Hathaway Collection at the University of New Brunswick.
The poem also appeared in *Poems*, 1907.

Variants
All variants are from the Hathaway clipping.

2   three]   ~ ,

4   life]   **Life**   also line 19

8   treasons]   ~ ,

12	bitterer . . . plaint,]	**bitterest . . . plaint.**
14	thee,]	~ ;
16	taint,]	~ ;
22	breath!]	~ .

p. 287 THE FIRST PLOUGHING

As far as may be determined, the poem was first published in *The Book of the Rose,* 1903. There is, however, an unidentified clipping which may be earlier in the Rufus Hathaway Collection at the University of New Brunswick. The poem also appeared in *Poems,* 1907; *Selected Poems,* 1936; and *Selected Poems of Sir Charles G.D. Roberts,* 1955.

Variants
All variants are from the Hathaway clipping.

4	hill.]	~ ,
6	till.]	~ !
9	flycatcher–]	~ ,
17	high-hole]	**highhole** also line 29
17	grove]	~,
18	clear:]	~ ;
19	way]	~ ,
22	woodgrubs]	**wood-grubs**
23	ploughing, . . . ploughing,]	**ploughing–** . . . **ploughing–**
26	steam.]	~
29	tumbles,]	~ ;
30	gleam;]	~ ,
31	sod]	**soil**
32	winter's]	**winter**

Glossary

| 17 | *high-hole:* the flicker |

p. 288 LINES FOR AN OMAR PUNCH-BOWL

The poem first appeared in *The Book of the Rose,* 1903; and was later included in *Poems,* 1907; and *Selected Poetry and Critical Prose,* 1974.

Variants

| 33 | No comma appears after *be* in *Poems,* but one is so placed in *The Book of the Rose.* In this instance I have chosen the earlier reading. |

Glossary
Omar: see "The Isles–An Ode"

536

C.B.:   Cleo Huneker Bracken, a noted sculptress of the time; sister-in-law to Roland Perry, also a sculptor and painter, whose studio (Pomeroy, p. 169) was a "popular rendezvous for the circle to which Roberts and Carman belonged. . . ."

p. 289 MY HEART IS A HOUSE

As far as may be determined, the poem first appeared in *The Book of the Rose,* 1903. However, the Rufus Hathaway Collection at the University of New Brunswick contains an unidentified clipping which may be earlier. The poem also appeared in *Poems,* 1907; and *Selected Poems,* 1936.

Variants
5   beat,–]   ~ –   *HC*
6   feet.]   ~ ;   *HC*
7   For]   All texts except *Selected Poems* begin with *My* at lines 7, 13, 19, and 25; but in Roberts' reading copy of *Poems,* he has written *For* at line 7 and *But* at lines 13, 19, and 25. In *Selected Poems,* however, *For* appears at the beginning of line 25.
23   wold]   **world**   *HC, Poems* 1907
23   dread,–]   ~ –   *HC*

Glossary
23   *wold:*   an open and elevated tract of country

p. 290 ON THE UPPER DECK

The poem was first published in *The Book of the Rose,* 1903; and was later included in *Poems,* 1907; and *Selected Poems,* 1936.

Variants
18   air?]   ~ ?–   *BOR, Poems* 1907

p. 293 WHEN MARY THE MOTHER KISSED THE CHILD

The poem was first published in *The Book of the Rose,* 1903; and later appeared in *Methodist Magazine and Review* (December, 1905); *Poems,* 1907; *Selected Poems,* 1936; *Selected Poems of Sir Charles G.D. Roberts,* 1955; and *Poets of Confederation,* 1967.

Variants
Title: the Mother]   omitted in *Methodist Mag. and Rev.*

| 1 | Child] | ~ , | *Methodist Mag. and Rev.* |

1   Child]   ~ ,   *Methodist Mag. and Rev.*
1   Child]   **child**   *Poems* 1907
9   broke]   ~ ,   *Methodist Mag. and Rev.*
14 guest,–]   ~ –   *Methodist Mag. and Rev.*
15 side,–]   ~ –   *Methodist Mag. and Rev.*
16 Heaven ... Earth denied,–]   **heaven ... earth denied–**
      Methodist Mag. and Rev.
22 wings,]   ~ .   *Methodist Mag. and Rev.*

p. 294 ALL NIGHT THE LONE CICADA

The poem first appeared in *The Century Magazine* (March, 1907); and was later included in *New Poems,* 1919; *Poetry Cure,* 1925; *Canadian Poets,* 1926; *The Vagrant of Time,* 1927; *Selected Poems,* 1936; and *Selected Poetry and Critical Prose,* 1974. As well, the Rufus Hathaway Collection at the University of New Brunswick contains two unidentified clippings of the poem. HC(1) is a reprint of the *Century* text, but HC(2) does not identify any source.

A holograph manuscript, with a concluding date of December 11, 1904, is in the earliest of the Roberts notebooks at the University of New Brunswick.

Variants
Note: In *NB,* dated March 20, 1903, is the following cancelled stanza:

> All night the lone cicada
>   Was shrilling in the rain
> And the cloud adown the mountain
>   Kept spilling into the plain.
> And the long clouds of the mountain
>   Darkened the lights in the plain.

    In the first line, *lone* is written above *grim* which has been cancelled. Apparently the third and fourth lines were cancelled before the fifth and sixth lines were written. In the last line, *Darkened* is written below *Dark* and *Hid* which have been crossed through; also cancelled is *of* before *in.*

2   rain,]   ~ –   *Century, HC*(1)*, HC*(2)*, Can. Poets*
5   tossing]   originally *high, blown* in *NB; high* crossed through and *wind* written above it
5   tossing]   **wind-blown**   *Century, HC*(1)*, HC*(2)*, Can. Poets*
6   high]   originally *brave* in *NB; brave* crossed through and *high* written above it
9   To looming vasts]   originally *The unseen sleep* in *NB; The ... sleep* crossed through and *To ... vasts* written above it
9   mountain,]   ~   *Century, HC*(1)*, HC*(2)*, Can. Poets*

10   To shadowy deeps]   originally *The sunlit blur* in *NB; The . . .*
                 blur crossed through and *And lonely vasts* written above
                 it; *And lonely vasts* cancelled; *To* added at the beginning
                 of the line and *shadowy deeps* written beside *And lonely*
                 vasts.
10   To . . . plain]   **And . . . plain,**   *Century, HC*(1), *HC*(2), *Can. Poets*
12   vain,–]   ~ ;   *NB*   ~ ,   *Century*   ~ .   *HC*(1), *HC*(2),
                 Can. Poets
13   my]   omitted in *NB; the* added with a caret
13   my . . . spirit,]   **the . . . spirit**   *Century, HC*(1), *HC*(2), *Can. Poets*
14   my]   omitted in *NB; the* added with a caret
14   my]   **the**   *Century, HC*(1), *HC*(2), *Can. Poets*
15   failure]   ~ ,   *Century, HC*(1), *HC*(2), *Can. Poets*

p. 295 BEPPO'S SONG (From "The Sprightly Pilgrim")

The poem was published only in *The Vagrant of Time,* 1927.

Pomeroy (p. 80) reports: "Carman visited at Windsor when he was writing
Songs of the Sea Children [1904] and, after he had read some of the most
impassioned lyrics (and they were impassioned!), Roberts announced that he
was going to write *Songs of the He Children.* The first and only one of this
proposed series was 'Beppo's Song'."

Glossary
"The Sprightly Pilgrim":   apparently a projected work which was never
                 completed. See "Philander's Song."

p. 295 PHILANDER'S SONG (From "The Sprightly Pilgrim")

The poem first appeared in *The Vagrant of Time,* 1927; and was later in-
cluded in *Songs of the Maritimes,* 1931; *Selected Poems,* 1936; *The Book of
Canadian Poetry,* 1943/48; *Selected Poems of Sir Charles G.D. Roberts,* 1955;
Poets of Confederation, 1967; and *Selected Poetry and Critical Prose,* 1974.

A holograph manuscript, evidently earlier than any printed text, is preserved in the Queen's University Archives.

Variants
Sub-title: From "The Sprightly Pilgrim"]   **From the Fantasy of *The***
                 Sprightly Pilgrim *MS*
6 look]   originally *glance* in *MS; glance* crossed through and *look*
                 written above it.

Glossary
   1   *Anacreon:* a Greek poet of the sixth century B.C. whose poems
                 celebrated love and wine

539

p. 295 MONITION

The poem was first published in *The Century Magazine* (January, 1907); and was later included in *Canadian Poets,* 1916/26; *New Poems,* 1919; *The Vagrant of Time,* 1927; *Selected Poems of Sir Charles G.D. Roberts,* 1955; and *Selected Poetry and Critical Prose,* 1974. As well, an unidentified clipping, reprinted from *Century,* is contained in the Rufus Hathaway Collection at the University of New Brunswick.

The first two lines of the poem, dated October 13, 1904; and on a later page the full poem, dated December 5, 1905 is contained in Roberts' notebook at the University of New Brunswick.

Variants
1-2   In *NB*(1) the first two lines are:

> The fall wind blowing from the world's end
> Estranged the city square.

> *Estranged* is written above *Made strange* which has been crossed through, and *square* is written after *street* which is also crossed through.

1   A faint]   originally *The Fall* in *NB*(2); *The Fall* crossed through and *A faint* written above it
2   street.]   ~ ,   *HC, Can. Poets*
3   strange]   partially crossed through in *NB*(2); evidently there was a later decision to retain it
9   eyes]   ~ ,   *Century, HC, Can. Poets*
12   How brief]   *How very brief* in *NB*(2); *very* crossed through
12   day.]   ~ !   *NB*(2)

p. 296 FROM THE HIGH WINDOW OF YOUR ROOM

The poem was first published in *New Poems,* 1919; and later appeared in *The Vagrant of Time,* 1927; and *Selected Poetry and Critical Prose,* 1974.

A holograph manuscript, dated December 23, 1905 at the top and December 24, 1905 at the bottom, is contained in Roberts' notebook at the University of New Brunswick.

Variants
All variants are from Roberts' notebook.
6   day:]   ~ .
7   ethereal]   originally *aerial; ethereal* written above *aerial*
8   away.]   ~ !
12   mystic]   *heavenly* written above *mystic*
13   It]   originally *The glow; The glow* crossed through and *It* written above

540

14   veiled . . . paradise]   **strange . . . Paradise**

15   face,—]   ~ —

Note: Two unrhymed variant couplets are written sideways in the
margin of *NB*:

> The light that over Earth's descending rim
> Upwakes, pure & mystical as prayer.

> Then, then I turn, & find them in
> The wonder of your waking eyes.

p. 296 THE HOUR OF MOST DESIRE

The poem first appeared in *New Poems,* 1919; and was later included in *The
Sweet o' the Year and Other Poems,* 1925; *The Vagrant of Time,* 1927;
Selected Poems, 1936; and *Selected Poetry and Critical Prose,* 1974.

A holograph manuscript—dated January 4, 1906 at the top and January 9,
1906 at the bottom—is contained in Roberts' notebook at the University of
New Brunswick.

Variants

Note: Eight lines, crossed through, appear in *NB* before the present
first line:

> It is not in the dark
> That I desire you most,
> When I toss restlessly
> And grope to touch your face.

> Nor is it in the day
> When ceaselessly I turn
> Longing to meet your eyes
> For solace or for joy.

       In the fourth line, *touch* is written above *feel* which has been
cancelled.

8   in dream]   **asleep**   *NB*

9   work]   originally *toil* in *NB; toil* crossed through and *work* written
beside it

9   work—]   ~ ,—   *NB, NP*

10   When, . . . success,]   **When . . . success**   *NB*

11   Or]   Originally *And* in *NB; And* crossed through and *Or* written
above it

11   pain,]   ~   *NB*

13   rest,—]   ~ ,   *NB, NP, Sweet o' the Year, VOT*

18   most—]   ~ ,—   *NB, NP*

The poem first appeared in *Craftsman Magazine* (December, 1906); and was later published in *Windsor Magazine* (June, 1907); *Canadian Poets,* 1916/26; *New Poems,* 1919; *The Sweet o' the Year,* 1925; *The Vagrant of Time,* 1927; *The Golden Treasury of Canadian Verse,* 1928/29; and *Selected Poems,* 1936. As well, an unidentified clipping, reprinted from *Craftsman Magazine,* is contained in the Rufus Hathaway Collection at the University of New Brunswick.

A holograph manuscript of the poem, dated January 4, 1906 "on train—Boston to N.Y." at the top and January 11, 1906 at the bottom is contained in Roberts' notebook at the University of New Brunswick.

Variants

2   earth.]   **Earth.** *Craftsman, HC*   **earth!** *Windsor*

3   divine,]   ~ *Windsor*

5   Though]   **If** *NB*   **Tho'** *Craftsman, HC*

6   Through]   **This** *NB*

6   long-endured]   *endured* added with a caret in *NB*

7   Of nights]   originally *Of grinding nights* in *NB; grinding* crossed through

9   life]   **Life** *NB, Craftsman, HC, Can. Poets*

12   thick-perfumed]   added with a caret in *NB*

13-16   written in the margin of *NB* with an arrow to indicate its position

13   earth]   ~ , *NB, Windsor, Can. Poets*   **Earth,** *Craftsman, HC*

17   Before this line in *NB* a line has been obliterated.

17   And]   added with a caret in *NB*

17   earth,–]   ~ , *NB*   **Earth–** *Craftsman, HC*
          earth;– *Windsor*

18   earth]   **Earth** *Craftsman, HC*

19   thou]   **Thou** *Craftsman*

19   with]   originally *of* in *NB; of* crossed through and *with* written beside it

19   seed of suns]   originally *breath of fire* in *NB;* **breath of fire** crossed through and *seed of suns* written above it

20   fire]   a word has been obliterated in *NB* and *fire* written above it

20   blood!]   ~ . *NB, Craftsman, HC, Can. Poets, Golden Treasury of Can. Verse*

21   though]   **tho'** *Craftsman, HC*

24   powers.]   ~ ! *Windsor*

25-28   Thine . . . dew.]   This stanza has been added at the end of the poem with an arrow to indicate its position.

26   unpreëmpted]   **unpre-empted** *Golden Treasury of Can. Verse*

28   dew.]   ~ , *Golden Treasury of Can. Verse*

30   tree]   This word is crossed through in *NB;* evidently there was a later decision to retain it.

31 run] ~, *Craftsman*
33 sea.] ~! *Craftsman, HC, Can. Poets*
Note: In all texts except *The Vagrant of Time* and *Selected Poems* lines
21-33 are a single stanza.

p. 298 THE GOOD EARTH

As far as may be determined, the poem was first published in *The Outlook* (March, 1906). There are, however, two unidentified clippings which may be earlier in the Rufus Hathaway Collection at the University of New Brunswick. The poem also appeared in *Canadian Poets*, 1916/26; *New Poems*, 1919; *The Vagrant of Time*, 1927; and *Songs of the Maritimes*, 1931.

A holograph manuscript of the poem, dated April 9, 1905 "(on train)" at the top and April 14, 1905 beside stanza six—which is written sideways in the margin—is contained in Roberts' notebook at the University of New Brunswick. In the notebook the stanzas were originally arranged so that the present stanza five was the third stanza with all the other stanzas following in order, but Roberts has numbered the stanzas in the margin (1, 2, 5, 3, 4, 6) to arrive at the arrangement of the printed texts.

Variants
Title: The Good Earth]   **A Spring Prayer** *NB*
 2   air;]   ~, *NB*
 3   piping of the]   *poignant trill* in *NB* and *call* written under *trill*
                          poignant call of   *Outlook, HC(1), HC(2)*
 4   bare;]   ~, *NB*   ~ *HC(1)*
 5   wood,]   ~ *Outlook, HC(1), HC(2)*
 6   stir;]   ~,– *NB*   ~, *Outlook, HC(2)*   ~ *HC(1)*
 7   ardent]   originally *pulsing* in *NB; pulsing* crossed through and
                  ardent written above it
 9   spring]   **Spring** *NB, Outlook, HC(1)*
11   Pour]   originally *Breathe* in *NB; Breathe* crossed through and *Pour*
             written above it
12   pure,]   ~ *HC(1)*
12   fire.]   ~! *Outlook, HC(1), HC(2), Can. Poets*
13   waters,]   ~ *HC(1)*
13   free]   ~, *NB*
15   me,]   ~ *HC(1)*
15   dream]   **dreams** *NB*
16   clean]   **close** *HC(1)*
16   strong.]   ~! *Outlook, HC(1), HC(2), Can. Poets*
17   Earth]   **earth** *Outlook, HC(1), HC(2)*
17   warm]   originally *strong* in *NB; strong* crossed through and *warm*
             written above it

18   renew.]   ~ ;   *NB, Outlook, HC*(2)   ~ ,   *Songs of the*
                  Maritimes   **renews**   *HC*(1)
20   Simple]   ~ ,   *HC*(2)
20   glad,]   ~   *HC*(1), *Songs of the Maritimes*
20   you.]   ~ !   *Outlook, HC*(1), *HC*(2), *Can. Poets*
22   waiting]   **winging**   *HC*(1), *HC*(2)
24   resume.]   ~ !   *NB, Outlook, HC*(1), *HC*(2), *Can. Poets*

p. 299 O EARTH, SUFFICING ALL OUR NEEDS

The poem first appeared in *Craftsman Magazine* (March, 1907); and was later published in *Current Opinion* (May, 1907); *Windsor Magazine* (August, 1907); *Canadian Poets*, 1916/26; *New Poems*, 1919; *The Sweet o' the Year*, 1925; *The Vagrant of Time*, 1927; *Songs of the Maritimes*, 1931; *Our Canadian Literature*, 1935; *Selected Poems*, 1936; and *Selected Poetry and Critical Prose*, 1974. As well, an unidentified clipping, reprinted from *Craftsman Magazine*, is contained in the Rufus Hathaway Collection at the University of New Brunswick.

A holograph manuscript, variously dated—the first two lines April 16, 1905; the third and fourth lines December 26, 1905; stanzas three and four January 28, 1906; and stanzas two and five June 21, 1906—is contained in Roberts' notebook at the University of New Brunswick. The stanzas are numbered to arrive at the arrangement in all printed texts, though obviously they were not composed in that order.

Variants
Title: O Earth, Sufficing All Our Needs]   **Sufficing Earth**   *Windsor*
1   earth]   **Earth**   *NB, HC*
1   needs,]   ~ ;   *NB*
2   spirit]   ~ ,   *HC, Can. Poets*
3   patient while]   originally *vainly do* in *NB; vainly do* crossed
              through and *patient while* written above it
4   blue!]   ~ .   *Craftsman, HC, Current Opinion*
5   unseen,]   ~   *Songs of the Maritimes*
7   calls,]   ~   *NB*
8   Veiled]   The line begins with *And* in *NB; And* has been crossed
              through and *Veiled* (with a capital *V*) written beside it.
8   reassurance,]   ~   *NB, Current Opinion*   **re-assurance**   *NP,*
              Sweet o' the Year, VOT, Songs of the Maritimes, Our Can. Lit.
8   mean.]   ~ !   *Craftsman, HC, Current Opinion, Can. Poets*
9   gone]   ~ ,   *HC, Current Opinion, Can. Poets*
10   through your]   originally *thro' the* in *NB; the* crossed through
              and *your* written above it
10   through]   **thro'**   *Craftsman, HC, Current Opinion, Can. Poets*

544

10 withdrawn;] ~ . *Craftsman, Current Opinion* ~ *HC*
        ~ , *Windsor* ~ : *Can. Poets*

11 they remain] originally *do they rest* in *NB; do they rest* crossed
        through and *they remain* written beside it

12 pass] originally *roam* in *NB; pass* written above *roam*

12 sequence] originally *tallies* in *NB; sequence* written above *tallies*

13 far . . . Heaven] originally *doubtful & remote* in *NB; doubtful &*
        remote crossed through and *far and strange the heaven*
        written above it

13 Heaven] **heavens** *Craftsman, HC, Current Opinion, Can. Poets*
        heaven *Windsor*

13 but very] originally *but dear & near* in *NB; but dear & near*
        crossed through and *but very* written above it

14 Your] originally *His* in *NB; His* crossed through and *Your* written
        above it

15 At times] **Sometimes** *Windsor*

15 we almost] **almost we** *NB*

15 door swung wide] **gate swung wide** *NB*

15 wide.] ~ ,– *NB* ~ – *Craftsman, HC, Current Opinion,*
        Can. Poets ~ , *Windsor*

16 An] **Some** *NB*

16 hear.] ~ ! *Craftsman, HC, Current Opinion*

17 Heaven–] ~ , *NB* **heaven** *Craftsman, HC, Current*
        Opinion, Windsor, Can. Poets

17 just.] ~ ! *Windsor*

18 know–] ~ , *NB, Craftsman, HC, Current Opinion, Windsor,*
        Can. Poets

19 I have sought] **Though I seek** *Craftsman, Windsor*
        Tho' I seek *HC, Current Opinion, Can. Poets*

19 His] **the** *NB, Craftsman, HC, Current Opinion, Windsor, Can.*
        Poets **his** *NP*

19 farthest] **furthest** *NB, Craftsman, Current Opinion, Windsor*

19 star–] ~ , *Craftsman, HC, Windsor, Can. Poets*
        ~ . *Current Opinion*

20 But here I find Him] **Here I shall find him** *NB*
        ***Here* shall I find Him** *Craftsman, Current Opinion*
        Here shall I find Him *HC, Windsor, Can. Poets*

20 Him,] ~ *Songs of the Maritimes*

20 quickening] **deathless** *NB, Craftsman, HC, Current Opinion,*
        Windsor, Can. Poets

p. 299 UNDER THE PILLARS OF THE SKY

The poem was first published in *Windsor Magazine* (September, 1907); and later
appeared in *Craftsman Magazine* (October, 1907); *Canadian Poets*, 1916/26;

New Poems, 1919; *The Sweet o' the Year,* 1925; *The Vagrant of Time,* 1927;
Selected Poems, 1936; and *Selected Poems of Sir Charles G.D. Roberts,* 1955.

A holograph manuscript—the first three stanzas dated March 17, 1907
"S.S. Carmania. Atlantic" and the fourth stanza dated March 20, 1907—is
contained in Roberts' notebook at the University of New Brunswick.

Variants
1   Under]   originally *Among* in *NB; Among* crossed through and
                   Under written above it
2   at life]   originally *with clouds* in *NB; with clouds* crossed
                   through and *at life* written above it
2   life,]   **Life—** *Windsor*   **Life,** *Craftsman*
3   grave]   originally *great* in *NB; grave* written above *great* which
                   has not been crossed through
3   day]   **Day** *Windsor*
4   Was . . . play.]   originally *I made but matter of my play!* in *NB;*
                   Was matter of my trivial written under the original line
5   stars . . . night,]   **Stars . . . Night** *Windsor*
6   delight,]   ~ ;— *NB*   ~ . *Windsor, Craftsman*
7   eyes,]   ~ *Windsor, Craftsman*
7-8   In *NB* the last two lines originally were:

> And now, alas, too late, I see
> The purpose of Eternity.

In this stanza *purports* is written below *purpose.*
Another attempt at the last two lines is written sideways in the
margin of the notebook:

> And now, when all is done, I see
> The doorway to Eternity

These two versions are crossed through and under a heavy line
is written:

> Till now, with startled eyes, I see
> The portents of Eternity.

Over *startled* Roberts wrote *wakening,* but evidently decided to
retain the original word.

p. 300 EASTWARD BOUND

The poem was first published in *The Century Magazine* (April, 1910); and was
later included in *New Poems,* 1919; *The Vagrant of Time,* 1927; *Off to*

Arcady, 1933; *Selected Poems,* 1936; and *Selected Poems of Sir Charles G.D. Roberts,* 1955.

A holograph manuscript dated "Nov. 2, 1907, SS Kaiser Aug. Vict." is contained in Roberts' notebook at the University of New Brunswick.

Variants

1	arc]	originally *stage* in *NB; stage* crossed through and *arc* written beside it
2	sun;]	~ , *NB* ~ : *Off to Arcady*
6	Draws]	originally *Goes* in *NB; Goes* crossed through and *Draws* written above it
6	dawn,]	~ ; *Century* ~ . *NP*
10	rise, and sweep, and fall,–]	**rise and sweep and fall,** *Century*
10	sweep]	**roll** *NB*
11	sea,–]	~ , *Century*

p. 300 THE BANQUET

As far as may be determined, the poem first appeared in *Poems,* 1907. There is, however, an unidentified clipping which may be earlier in the Rufus Hathaway Collection at the University of New Brunswick. Further, the Hathaway clipping claims to be reprinted from *Harper's Magazine,* although it has proved impossible to locate the poem in that periodical. The poem was also included in *Selected Poems,* 1936.

Variants

2	spread,–]	~ :– *HC*
3	Laughter . . . love]	**Laughter, . . . love,** *HC*
4	Sleep]	~ , *HC*
4	toil the gritty]	**work, the bitter** *HC*
		work the bitter *Poems* 1907

p. 300 HILL TOP SONGS: I

As far as may be determined, the poem first appeared in *New Poems,* 1919. There is, however, an unidentified clipping, which may be earlier, in the Rufus Hathaway Collection at the University of New Brunswick. The poem was also published in *Canadian Poets,* 1916/26; *Contemporary Poetry,* 1923; *The Sweet o' the Year,* 1925; *The Vagrant of Time,* 1927; and *Selected Poems,* 1936.

A holograph manuscript, the first thirteen lines dated Pont Levoy, April 26, 1909 and the last two lines—written sideways in the margin—dated April 27, 1909 is contained in Roberts' notebook at the University of New Brunswick. In the notebook the title is Hill Top Songs and there are two poems, of which this is the second. However, when the poems have been printed together, this one has always been the first. See also "Hill Top Songs: II."

Variants

Title: Hill Top Song] **Hill Top Songs I** *NP, Can. Poets, Contemp.*
                              Poetry, Sweet o' the Year, VOT

  2   the] **my** *NB*

  2   clear,] ~ . *NP, HC, Can. Poets, Contemp. Poetry, Sweet o'*
                   the Year

3-4   In *NB* originally

> The high Unseen appear;
> Wisdom draws near

These two lines are crossed through and are followed by

> Desire being still,
> The High Unseen appear.

Roberts has written over a small *h* in *High* to make it a capital.

  3   still,] ~ *NP, HC, Can. Poets, Contemp. Poetry, Sweet o' the*
                   Year

  8   sheep's pasturing] originally *sheep's high pasturing* in *NB; high*
                          crossed through

10   sweet;] ~ . *NB*

13   fate;] ~ . *NB*   ~ : *HC*

p. 301 HILL TOP SONGS: II

The poem was first published in *McLure's Magazine* (March, 1910); and was later included in *Canadian Poets,* 1916/26; *New Poems,* 1919; *Contemporary Poetry,* 1923; *The Sweet o' the Year,* 1925; *The Vagrant of Time,* 1927; and *Selected Poems of Sir Charles G.D. Roberts,* 1955. As well, an unidentified clipping, reprinted from *McLure's Magazine,* is contained in the Rufus Hathaway Collection at the University of New Brunswick.

A holograph manuscript, dated Pont Levoy, April 21, 1909, is contained in Roberts' notebook at the University of New Brunswick. See "Hill Top Song."

Variants

Title: Hill Top Songs: II] **Hill Top Song** *McLure's*
                             Hilltop Song *HC*

  4   shadows] **colours** *NB*   colors *McLure's, HC*

10   goes] originally *sweeps* in *NB; sweeps* crossed through and *goes*
                  written above it

11	smells, . . . sounds,]	**smells . . . sounds** *NB, McLure's, HC*
12	Mount]	originally *Go up* in *NB; Mount* written above *Go up*
12	sky;]	~ : *McLure's, HC*
13	the door of]	added with a caret in *NB*
16	the . . . close]	originally *the dear earth close* in *NB;* the corrected phrase, adding only *how,* is written above the original
16	heaven]	**Heaven** *NB*

p. 301 THE PLACE OF HIS REST

The poem was first published in *New Poems*, 1919; and was later included in *Canadian Prose and Verse*, 1923; *Canadian Poets*, 1926; *The Vagrant of Time*, 1927; *Our Canadian Literature*, 1934; *Selected Poems*, 1936; *Selected Poems of Sir Charles G.D. Roberts* (omitting lines 25-28 and 45-48), 1955; and *Poets of Confederation* (also omitting lines 25-28 and 45-48), 1967.

A holograph manuscript dated May 24, 1909 at the top and May 25, 1909 at the bottom at Pont Levoy is contained in Roberts' notebook at the University of New Brunswick. A note at the top of the poem says, "*in dream. Dreamed L. read it to me from a book of my own verse.*" The dream is described by Pomeroy (p. 223) and she identifies "L." as Mrs. Morris, an American friend of Roberts.

Variants

Title:	The Place of His Rest]	**Meadow Rest** *NB*
5	washed]	originally *wide* in *NB; wide* crossed through and *washed* written above it
6	stream;]	~ ,– *NB*
9-16	The . . . dragon-fly.]	These stanzas are reversed in *NB* with marginal numbers to indicate the correct order.
11	brown;]	~ , *NB*
12	reed;]	~ . *NB*
15	ringed;]	~ *NB*
16	dragon-fly]	**dragon fly** *NB, NP, Can. Prose and Verse, Can. Verse, VOT*
17	rushes]	~ , *NP, Can. Prose and Verse, Can. Verse*
18	breast]	originally *rest* in *NB; rest* crossed through and *breast* written beside it
20	rest.]	~ ; *NB*
21	far-flown]	**far-flying** *NB*
26	Where now]	originally *Upon where* in *NB; Upon where* crossed through and *Where now* written over and above it
27	the]	originally *his* in *NB; the* written over *his*
28	Of . . . eyes,]	originally *All praise in his kind eyes;* in *NB; All . . . kind* crossed through and *Of his weary* written over and above it

549

28   eyes,]   ~ :   *NP, Can. Prose and Verse, Can. Verse, VOT, Our Can. Lit.*

33-35   Well . . . number] in *NB* originally:

> How well to his slumber
> Attends the year then!
> Soft rains without number

These lines have been crossed through and the stanza approximately as it now stands is written below them.

33   Well]   originally *How well* in *NB; How* crossed through and *And* written over it

34   year:]   ~ !– *NB*

35   number]   ~ , *NB, Can. Prose and Verse*

36   noons,]   ~ *NB*

37-38   With . . . hours] above these lines in *NB* is:

> With the balm of night
> And the calm of dawn

These lines have been crossed through.

37   With]   written over an undecipherable word in *NB*

38   dark,]   ~ *Can. Prose and Verse*

39   Brooding]   originally *Drooping* in *NB; Drooping* crossed through and *Brooding* written beside it

41   speeds]   originally *leads* in *NB; leads* crossed through and *speeds* written above it

43   softly]   originally *tenderly* in *NB; tenderly* crossed through and *softly* written above it

44   tomb!–]   ~ ,– *NB*

45   white-thorn]   **white thorn** *NP, Can. Prose and Verse, Can. Verse*

45   nears]   omitted in *Can. Prose and Verse*

46   cowslip goes]   written above two obliterated and undecipherable words in *NB*

47   appears;]   ~ , *NB*

Glossary

1   *marsh-mallows:* a member of the Mallow family of herbs; the marsh-mallow, as the name implies, grows in marshy areas and has a pink flower

p. 303 IN THE VALLEY OF LUCHON

The poem first appeared in *Windsor Magazine* (November, 1909); and was later included in *New Poems*, 1919; and *The Vagrant of Time*, 1927.

5   villages;]   ~ ,   *Windsor Mag.*
8   loud]   ~ .   *Windsor Mag.*
18   comes,]   ~   *Windsor Mag.*

Glossary
Luchon: a village in the south of France. Pomeroy (pp. 185-88)
            describes Roberts' tour in the summer of 1904.

p. 303 ON THE ROAD

The poem was first published in *Pall Mall Magazine* (May, 1913); and subsequently appeared in *The Living Age* (May 31, 1913); *Literary Digest* (June 14, 1913); *Canadian Poets,* 1916/26; *New Poems,* 1919; *The Brunswickan* (November, 1925); *The Vagrant of Time,* 1927; *A Golden Treasury of Canadian Verse,* 1928; and *Selected Poems,* 1936.

A holograph manuscript of the poem, dated "Torquay, Devon, Jan. 19, 1913," is contained in Roberts' notebook at the University of New Brunswick. The Lloyd Roberts Collection, also at the University of New Brunswick, contains a typescript of the poem autographed by Roberts and dated "Torquay, Jan. 1913."

Variants
1   brown]   added with a caret in *NB*
3   ask]   **asked**   *NB; ed* squeezed in, suggesting an addition
3   meet.]   ~ ,   *Brunswickan*
4   answers]   **answered**   *NB*
4   looks]   originally *looked* in *NB; ed* crossed through and *s* written
               above it
5   "Only more hills and more hills]   originally *"Only more hills* in
               NB; a lot added with a caret between *more* and *hills;* following *a lot, & more hills* is written above the line. Nothing is
               cancelled in *NB.*
6   last.]   ~ !   *LRC, Pall Mall, Living Age, Lit. Digest*
               ~ ;   *Brunswickan*
7   am]   originally *was* in *NB; am* written above *was*
7   see]   originally *saw* in *NB; see* written above *saw*
7   is]   **originally** *was* in *NB; is* written above *was*
8   hate]   originally *loathed* in *NB; ed* crossed through and *s* written
               above it
8   I've]   originally *I had* in *NB; had* crossed through and *'ve*
               written over it
9   I've tramped it too long]   originally *I had fared too far* in *NB;*
               have written above *had* and *journey'd* written above *fared*
               which has been crossed through

551

9   tramped it]   **wandered**   *LRC*

9   is]   originally *was* in *NB; is* written above *was*

10   hill.]   ~ ;   *NB*

12   a-tiptoe]   **a-tip-toe**   *LRC*   **a tip-toe**   *Can. Poets, NP, Brunswickan*

13   far]   ~ ,   *Pall Mall, Living Age, Lit. Digest, Can. Poets, NP, Brunswickan, VOT, Golden Treasury of Can. Verse*

13   strife.]   ~ ,   *Brunswickan*   ~ ;   *Golden Treasury of Can. Verse*

14   wide]   **long**   *NB*

15   but]   ~ ,   *Lit. Digest*

15   oh,]   omitted in *NB*   ~ !   *Pall Mall, Lit. Digest*   ~ ;   *Living Age*

15   core;]   ~ ,–   *NB, LRC*   ~ ,   *Pall Mall, Living Age, Lit. Digest*

14-15   I . . . core;]   under a heavy line in the margin of *NB* are the variant lines:

> For I have lived long, & bit deep in the
>   apple of life, &
> Sweet enough at the rind, but so sweeter
>   by far at the core!

16   be gained]   **the prize**   *NB*

16   gained]   ~ ,   *LRC, Pall Mall, Living Age, Lit. Digest, Can. Poets, NP, Brunswickan, VOT, Golden Treasury of Can. Verse*

17   climb]   written over an undecipherable word in *NB*

17   climb.]   ~ –   *Golden Treasury of Can. Verse*   ~ ,   *Brunswickan*

18   The demand]   **And the claim**   *NB; And* written over an undecipherable word

18   time.]   **Time.**   *Pall Mall, Living Age, Lit. Digest*   **time;**   *Golden Treasury of Can. Verse*

20   ventured and visioned]   **visioned & ventured**   *NB*

21   So . . . dark,]   originally *And when, at the last, my feet stumble in ultimate dark* in *NB; at the last* crossed through and *failing, shall* added with a caret. The line *And when, at the last, my feet stumble in ultimate dark* is repeated after the date at the end of the poem.

22   faint]   added with a caret in *NB*

22   high lift]   originally *adventurous* in *NB; adventurous* crossed through and *high lift* written above it

22   pathway shall]   **path may**   *NB*

23   There]   omitted in *NB*

23   I'll]   **I shall**   *NB*

23   down]   omitted in *NB*

24   What . . . glow.]   originally *New hills shall < . . . . > when I walk in the morning glow* in *NB. What* is added before *New; hills* is crossed through and *summit*

written below it. Under this line is written the line as it now stands; the only variant is *will* for *shall.*

p. 304 GOING OVER [*The Somme, 1917*]

The poem was first published in *New Poems*, 1919; and was later included in *The Vagrant of Time*, 1927; *Songs of the Maritimes*, 1931; *Selected Poems*, 1936; *Canada Speaks of Britain*, 1941; *Twentieth Century Canadian Poetry*, 1953; and *Selected Poetry and Critical Prose*, 1974.

Two typescripts—TS(1) and TS(2)—are contained in the Queen's University Archives. TS(2) was apparently prepared for the publication of *Canada Speaks of Britain*. Also, an untitled holograph manuscript, dated London, October 20, 1918, is contained in Roberts' notebook at the University of New Brunswick.

Variants
Sub-title: The Somme, 1917]   omitted in *NP, VOT, Songs of the Maritimes, SP*
1   heart]   ~ .   *NB, NP, VOT, Songs of the Maritimes, SP, TS*(1)
5   Where my]   originally *Where were the* in *NB; the* crossed through and *my* written beside it
6   dark]   **night**   *NB*
7   slipping.]   ~ ,   *Songs of the Maritimes, TS*(1)   ~ ;   *SP*
8   out-flare]   **up-flare**   *NB*
8   Verge,]   ~ .   *TS*(1)
9   a-flower]   **aflower**   *NB, SP*
10   saying?– ... along.–]   **saying? ... along.**   *NB*
11   I]   no italics in *Songs of the Maritimes*
11   along?]   ~ ?–   *NB*
11   breathing]   **drinking**   *NB*
13   Over]   originally *Up and over* in *NB; Up and* crossed through, capital *O* written over *o*

Glossary
8   *Verys:*   flares fired from pistols
Note: Roberts served in the British and Canadian Armies from 1914-1918.

p. 305 CAMBRAI AND MARNE (1914-1918)

As far as may be determined, the poem first appeared in *The Bookman* (December, 1918). There is, however, an unidentified clipping which may be earlier in the Rufus Hathaway Collection at the University of New Brunswick. The poem appeared as well in *New Poems*, 1919; *Canadian Poets*, 1926; *The*

Vagrant of Time, 1927; and *Canada Speaks of Britain,* 1941. Two typescripts, evidently prepared for the publication of *Canada Speaks of Britain,* are in the Queen's University Archives.

Variants

Note: The dates (1914-1918) appear as a part of the title only in the two Queen's University typescripts and in *Canada Speaks of Britain.*

1	trenches]	**columns** *Bookman*
2	away.]	~ , *Bookman*
5	hordes]	~ , *HC, Bookman, Can. Poets*
6	swords,]	~ ; *Bookman*
7	still,]	~ *Bookman*
8	up]	~ , *Bookman*
10	Their]	**The** *HC, Can. Poets*
10	down.]	~ ; *HC, Bookman, Can. Poets*
12	beetfields]	*Canada Speaks of Britain* has *beetfield* but all other texts, except *Bookman,* show *beetfields.* In this instance I have taken the earlier readings to be correct.
14	fell.]	~ ; *HC, Bookman, Can. Poets*
15	ere]	**e're** *VOT*
18	fall–]	~ ,– *Bookman*
19	obeyed,]	~ *Bookman*
21	retreat,]	~ . *Bookman* ~ ; *Can. Poets*
22	defeat.]	~ ; *HC, Can. Poets*
26	went;]	~ , *HC, Bookman, Can. Poets*
27	turned]	~ , *HC, Can. Poets*
29	stood–]	~ ,– *Bookman*
30	blood.]	~ ; *Can. Poets*
33	fire.]	~ , *HC, Can. Poets*
34	mire.]	~ ; *HC, Can. Poets*
35	retreat,]	~ *HC, Bookman, Can. Poets*
37	flung]	**drove** *HC, Can. Poets*
38	track.]	~ ; *HC, Bookman, Can. Poets*
40	ways]	**way** *Bookman*
41	ford,]	~ *HC, Bookman, Can. Poets*
44	Cambrai!]	~ . *HC*

Glossary

Cambrai and Marne: Cambrai is a city in northern France, the scene of World War I battles in 1917 and 1918. The Marne is a river in north-east France which flows west to the Seine near Paris; it was the scene of World War I battles in 1914 and 1918.

p. 306 TO SHAKESPEARE, IN 1916

The poem first appeared in *Poems of the Great War,* 1918; and was later included in *New Poems,* 1919; *The Vagrant of Time,* 1927; and *Canada Speaks of Britain,* 1941.

Two typescripts are contained in the Queen's University Archives.

Variants
All variants are from *Poems of the Great War.*
Title: To Shakespeare, In 1916]   **To Shakespeare, 1916**
  4   thrust!]   ~ .
5-8   How . . . Malines!]   omitted
  9   consoled]   ~ ,—
 10   (Who knew'st . . . well)]   **Who knewest . . . well,—**
 11   sloth,]   ~
 13   assured.]   ~ !
 15   earth,—]   ~ —
 16   ²tramp, . . . feet.]   **tramp . . . feet!**

Glossary
  6   *the acclaim:*   In *Canada Speaks of Britain* is the note, "The Germans were enthusiastic admirers of Shakespeare."
  7   *Lusitania:*   a British steamship sunk on May 7, 1915 by a German submarine. The sinking was one of the events which led to the entry of the United States into World War I.
  8   *Malines:*   the French name for Mechlin, Belgium. The city was heavily damaged in both World Wars.

p. 306 THE STREAM

As far as may be determined, the poem was first published in *New Poems,* 1919. There is, however, an unidentified clipping which may be earlier in the Rufus Hathaway Collection at the University of New Brunswick. The poem later appeared in *The Sweet o' the Year,* 1925; *The Vagrant of Time,* 1927; *Songs of the Maritimes,* 1931; and *Selected Poetry and Critical Prose,* 1974.

A holograph manuscript, with the first four lines dated "London, Dec. 26, 1918," lines five through eighteen dated December 29, 1918, and the last stanza dated January 1, 1919, is contained in Roberts' notebook at the University of New Brunswick.

Variants
  2   flows.]   ~ ; *NB*   ~ , *HC*   ~ *Songs of the Maritimes*
  3   a-gleam]   **agleam** *NB*
  6   through]   **thro'** *NB*

555

7-18 Its . . . shade.]   In *NB* these stanzas are reversed and partially combined; marginal numbers indicate the correct order. However, the present stanza two is combined with the present stanza three:

> There summer sleeps
> Unstirred by any storm;   (2)
> The shy mouse creeps
> Thro' grasses hushed and warm

Before *shy* a *w* has been crossed through and added with a caret above *grasses* is *tall weeds.*

> Its waters glide
> In shimmering sun & air,
> A fairy tide
> Of memories dear & fair;   (1)
> And the shy snipe,
> Alighting unafraid,
> With sudden pipe
> Startles the dreaming shade

In shimmering is written above an undecipherable word or words followed by *with* which has been crossed through.

11   sleeps]   ∼ ,   *HC*
13   creeps]   ∼ ,   *HC*
19-24   So . . . tears!]   in *NB* originally:

> Ah, long ago—
> And through how many tears,
> Its roses glow!
> Still my memory hears
> Across the sundering years
> Its silver flow.

This stanza has been crossed through and below it is written:

> So long ago!
> Still, still my memory hears
> Across the sundering years
> Its silver flow.
> Its roses glow,
> Ah, thro' how many tears!

20   ²still]   ∼ ,   *HC*
22   years–]   ∼ ,–   *NP*

p. 307 THE SUMMONS

The poem was first published in *New Poems*, 1919; and later appeared in *The Sweet o' the Year*, 1925; *Canadian Poets*, 1926; *The Vagrant of Time*, 1927, *Songs of the Maritimes*, 1931; *Selected Poems*, 1936; and *Selected Poems of Sir Charles G.D. Roberts*, 1955.

A holograph manuscript, dated London, January 13, 1919, is contained in Roberts' notebook at the University of New Brunswick.

Variants

1   west]   **West**   *NB*
2   Flaming and]   **Flaming,**   *NB*
3-4 Two lines are here obliterated in *NB*, and two other lines are written under them.
3   Upsprings my soul from his]   **My heart upsprings from its**   *NB*
10   torn]   ~ ,   *Songs of the Maritimes*
14   trumpets blown and blown!]   **wild trumpets blown.**   *NB*

p. 308 EPITAPH FOR A CERTAIN ARCHITECT

The poem was first published in *Canadian Bookman* (August, 1925); and later appeared in *The Vagrant of Time*, 1927; *Selected Poems*, 1936; *The Modern Muse*, 1936; and *Selected Poetry and Critical Prose*, 1974.

A holograph manuscript—dated November 3, "SS. K.A.V." at the top; January 10, 1919 at line five; and January 16, 1919 "London" at the end—is contained in Roberts' notebook at the University of New Brunswick.

Variants

Title: Epitaph for a Certain Architect]   **For a Builder's Tomb**   *NB*
         Epitaph   *Can. Bookman, VOT, Mod. Muse*
Note: In the margin of *NB* is an alternate arrangement of three of the lines in the first stanza:

         Remains the stones he hewed and piled.
         His name the jeer of fool & child.
         His fame the mock of shallow wits.

1   mock]   originally *sport* in *NB; sport* crossed through and *scorn* written above it; *scorn* then crossed through and *mock* written above it
1   wits]   originally *brows* in *NB; brows* crossed through and *wits* written above it
3   fixed in form]   **bade endure**   *NB*
5   scorn]   originally *scorns* in *NB;* final *s* crossed through
5   way]   **hand**   *NB*

557

6	well]	**half** *NB*
10	enscroll]	**scroll** *NB*
12	This]	originally *This* in *NB; is* crossed through and *e* written above
12	fame.]	~ *Mod. Muse*
14	Impregnable]	**Imperishable** *NB*
15	Through]	**Thro'** *NB*
16	His]	**This** *NB*
16	outwear]	originally *challenge* in *NB;* written below *challenge* is *confront* and *outwear.* None of the words have been cancelled.

Note: At the end of the poem in *NB* is a rough alternate last line:

His dream shall stand tower last confronting time.

stand and *tower* have been crossed through

p. 308 THE SWEET O' THE YEAR

The poem was first published in *To-Day* (March-August, 1920); and subsequently appeared in the *Literary Digest* (June, 1920); *The Sweet o' the Year and Other Poems,* 1925; *The Vagrant of Time,* 1927; *The Golden Treasury of Canadian Verse,* 1928-9; *Songs of the Maritimes,* 1931; *What I Like in Poetry,* 1934; and *New Harvesting,* 1938.

A holograph manuscript—the first ten lines dated "on train, Folkestone to London, March 25, 1908" and the remainder January 26 and February 5, 1919—is contained in Roberts' notebook at the University of New Brunswick. In addition, an undated typescript in the Queen's University Archives and another typescript was included in a letter to A.M. Stephen, dated March 26, 1942.

Variants

1-2	The . . . again;]	These lines are reversed in *NB,* but there are numbers at the end of the lines rearranging them.
1	hills]	**fields** *NB*
3-4	All . . . aisles]	These are a single line in *NB:*

All down the humming orchard aisles

Written sideways in the margin is:

Down shadowy miles
Of orchard aisles
The pink-lip snows are seen again.

6-7 To . . . plot]   a single line in *NB*
8-9 Come . . . bergamot]   a single line in *NB*
10   ardent]   **tender**   *NB;* above *tender,* but crossed through, is
                     yearning
11   The . . . again]   originally *Grackle & thrush are here again* in *NB;*
                     the entire line is crossed through
11   swallow is]   originally *swallows are* in *NB;* final *s* in *swallows*
                     and *are* crossed through. Originally *swallow's* in
                     TS(1); *'s* crossed through and *is* written in the
                     margin.
12-13 To . . . thrush,]   a single line in *NB*
12   thorn-bush]   **thorn bush**   *To-Day*
14   painted-wings]   **Painted-Wings**   *To-Day, Lit. Digest*
14   again.]   ~ ;   *Golden Treasury of Can. Verse, What I Like in*
                     Poetry, TS(2)
15   young]   originally *warm* in *NB; warm* crossed through and
                     young written in parentheses in the margin
19   Warm . . . again,]   repeated, without change, in the margin of *NB*
19   again,]   ~   *TS*(1)
20   again.]   ~ ;   *To-Day, Lit. Digest*
21   aflush]   **a-flush**   *To-Day*
22   rush,]   ~   *Songs of the Maritimes*
23   To . . . again]   *The heart's desire attains again* written sideways
                     in the margin of *NB*
23   Heart's Desire]   **heart's desire**   *NB*
26   defeat,]   ~   *To-Day, Lit. Digest*
27   Lord]   **lord**   *To-Day, Lit. Digest*

Glossary
  9   *bergamot:*   a small tree of the citrus family

p. 309 THE FLOWER

The poem was first published in *New Poems,* 1919; and was reprinted only in
The Vagrant of Time, 1927.

Glossary
  4   *lotus-airs of Ind.:*   in *The Odyssey,* the eating of the lotus flower
                         resulted in indolence and laziness; *Ind.* is, of
                         course, a poetic abbreviation for India

As far as may be determined, the poem first appeared in *New Poems*, 1919. There is, however, an unidentified clipping which may be earlier in the Rufus Hathaway Collection at the University of New Brunswick. Further, the Hathaway clipping notes that it is a reprint from *The Smart Set*, but it has proved impossible to locate the poem in that periodical. The poem was later included in *The Vagrant of Time*, 1927.

Variants

Title: With April Here]   **At the Gates of Spring**   *HC*
11   Spring,–]   **spring–**   *HC*

p. 310 SISTER TO THE WILD ROSE

The poem was published only in *The Vagrant of Time*, 1927.

Three holograph manuscripts, all dated August 27, 1926, survive. The first is in Roberts' notebook (NB); the second is in his Ernescliffe notebook (ENB); and the last is in the Lloyd Roberts Collection (LRC). All three copies are in the library at the University of New Brunswick. Also, two autographed typescripts are in the Queen's University Archives. At least one of the typescripts was prepared for the publication of *The Vagrant of Time* and Roberts has designated it as the final revised copy.

Pomeroy (p. 274) says that the poem was written for Roberts' granddaughter—Lloyd Roberts' daughter—Patricia Bliss Roberts who was eighteen when the poem was composed.

Variants

Title: Sister to the Wild Rose]   originally *I Know a Maid* in *NB; I . . .*
                    Maid crossed through and *Sister . . . Rose* written above
                    it   **I Know a Maiden Like a Flower**   *ENB*
                    untitled   *LRC*
1   maiden . . . flower,]   **maid who's . . . flower–**   *NB*
2   Flower-sweet, dainty]   **Flower-sweet! Dainty**   *NB;* also lines 6
                    and 10
3   Sister . . . wild]   **Sister she to the shy wild**   *NB;* the start of a
                    word has been obliterated before *she* and *shy* has been
                    crossed through
4   marguerite.]   **~ !**   *LRC*
5   her,]   **Her–**   *NB*
7   And . . . blue]   **And in her eyes the fairy blue**   *NB*
8   meet.]   **~ !**   *NB, LRC*
9   Light]   originally *Cool* in *NB; Cool* crossed through and *Light*
                    are written above it

9   Light . . . blossom]   originally *Her hands are like the foam of the meadows* in *ENB; Light* is written in the margin before *Her; are like the foam of the meadows* has been crossed through and *light as the cherry flower* written above it; in the superimposed line *light* and *flower* have been crossed through and above *flower* is *bloom* which has also been crossed through; finally *blossom* is written below *flower*

9   Light her hands]   **Her hands are light**   *LRC*

9   as the cherry blossom,]   originally *as the foam of the apple bloom—* in *NB; apple* crossed through and *grass* written above it. See also 9(2).

9   blossom]   **bloom**   *LRC;*   also in the final revised typescript *bloom* has been crossed through and *blossom* written above it

12   As . . . feet.]   **As her little dancing feet!**   *NB*

p. 310 ASTEROPE

The poem was first published in *The Century Magazine* (August, 1904); and was reprinted only in *The Vagrant of Time,* 1927.

Two holograph manuscripts survive. The first, dated February 16, 1903, is in Roberts' notebook (NB) and the second is in another notebook kept by Roberts during his stay at the Ernescliffe (ENB). In ENB is the note, "Written at New York, Feb. 16, 1903, never published. Revised, Toronto, 1926." As well, a typescript (TS) is in the Queen's University Archives. TS notes, "These verses were originally perpetrated on Staten Island, N.Y., in 1903; but as I could not then get them quite right I laid them aside. Have just now revived and revised them. C.G.D.R. September 1926."

Variants

Title: Asterope]   **Down the Ways of Dream**   *Century*

2   starry-eyed,]   ~ —   *Century*

3   Tears and]   **Wayward**   *Century*

3   lips]   ~ ,   *NB*

4   by]   **at**   *Century*

6   shining]   originally *yellow* in *NB; yellow* crossed through and *golden* written above it

6   shining]   **golden**   *Century*

6   lands,—]   ~ ,   *Century, ENB, TS*

9-16   Wind . . . feet.]   These stanzas are reversed in *NB* with numbers written above them to indicate the correct order.

9   of]   originally *of* in *NB; of* crossed through and *o'* written beside it

9   of]   **o'**   *Century*

9   hath]   originally *hath* in *NB; hath* crossed through and *has*
                written above it
9   hath]   **has**   *Century*
10   sighing tree,–]   **tossing tree,**   *NB, Century*
14   sweet.]   ~ ;   *Century*
16   fell]   **fall**   *TS*
17   that]   originally *that* in *NB; that* crossed through and *the* written
                above it
18   Where waits]   originally *And* in *NB; And* crossed through and
                  Where waits written above it
20   A-crowding]   **Crowding**   *NB*
Note: In *NB* an alternate fifth stanza follows and is crossed through:

> Somewhere down the ways of dream
> Waits my starry-eyed,–
> All the happy things of earth
> Crowding at her side.

Glossary
Asterope: In Greek mythology one of the seven daughters of Atlas who
             were set by Zeus among the stars, thus forming the Pleiades in
             the constellation Taurus.

p. 311 TO-DAY

The poem was first published in *The Brunswickan* (November, 1926); and was
later included in *The Vagrant of Time,* 1927; *Selected Poems,* 1936; and
Selected Poems of Sir Charles G.D. Roberts, 1955.

    Two holograph manuscripts are contained in the two Roberts notebooks
at the University of New Brunswick. In NB the poem is dated "on train, Aug.
28, 1926" at the top and "Toronto, Sept. 1, 1926" at the bottom. The text
in ENB is dated from Toronto, September 1, 1926. In addition, an autographed typescript of unknown date is contained in the Queen's University
Archives.

Variants
Title: To-Day]   In *ENB* the alternate titles *The Splendour of Today*
                      and *The Wondrous Age* have been crossed through
                      and the title as it now stands written in large script
                      above them. In *TS Today* is typed but above it *The*
                      Splendour of is written in script but then crossed
                      through.
2   goatboy]   **goat-boy**   *NB*
3   go,]   ~   *ENB*
5   I, . . . stream,]   **I . . . stream**   *NB*

6	heroes]	originally *hear* in *ENB; hear* crossed through and *heroes* written above it
10	eyes, unsealed,]	**eyes unsealed** *NB*
14	splendour]	**wonder** *NB*
14	To-Day]	**Today** *NB, TS, Brunswickan*
16	reach]	originally *reach* in *NB; reach* crossed through and *power* written above it. Originally *power* in *ENB; power* lightly crossed through and *reach* written above it.

Glossary

1	*Hybna:*	So in all texts. Either an obscure reference or a mistaken spelling of Hybla, a town in Sicily celebrated for the honey produced there and having, hence, the poetic meaning of sweet or mellifluous.
2	*the goatboy:*	probably Pan, but the reference is either obscure or Roberts is freely borrowing a familiar pastoral image.
5	*Nashwaak:*	a river which joins the St. John River just above Fredericton

p. 311 HATH HOPE KEPT VIGIL

The poem was first published in the *Dalhousie Review* (1926); and was later included in *The Vagrant of Time*, 1927; *The Modern Muse*, 1936; *Selected Poems*, 1936; *Selected Poems of Sir Charles G.D. Roberts*, 1955; and *Selected Poetry and Critical Prose*, 1974.

In Roberts' notebook, the first three lines and the first word of the fourth line are written in ink and dated from London, January 16, 1919. The full poem follows in NB and is dated from Toronto, September 3, 1926. Another holograph manuscript is included in Roberts' Ernescliffe notebook and is also dated September 3, 1926.

Variants

3	hath]	originally *that* in *ENB; that* crossed through and *hath* written above it
4	number,]	~ . *Dal. Rev.*
6	being?]	originally followed by a comma in *NB;* then a question mark and a dash added
8	blooms within its]	*splendours in* in parentheses written below *within its* in *NB*
11	Will]	originally *Shall* in *NB; Shall* crossed through and *Will* written above it. Originally *With* in *ENB; With* crossed through and *Will* written beside it
12	strong]	originally *glad* in *NB; glad* crossed through and *strong* written below it

2   *cerements:*   waxed cloth, used especially for wrapping the dead, or any other graveclothes

p. 312 SPRING BREAKS IN FOAM

As far as may be determined, the poem was first published in *The Vagrant of Time,* 1927; it later was included in *Selected Poems,* 1936; *Selected Poems of Sir Charles G.D. Roberts,* 1955; and *Selected Poetry and Critical Prose,* 1974.

Two holograph manuscripts are contained in the two Roberts notebooks at the University of New Brunswick. NB is obviously a rough draft of the poem. The entire poem in NB is dated "Ventor, I.W., Ap. 12, 1922" but Pomeroy (p. 329) points out that "in the late summer of 1926 he was looking over a note book when his eyes fell on two lines [the first two lines of the poem] which he had written at Ventor several years before. Soon the entire poem was completed. . . ." ENB is dated "Ventor, Ap. 1922 & Toronto, Sept. 4, 1926." There is a note *"Canadian Bookman"* in ENB but it has proved impossible to locate the poem in that periodical. In addition, a single autographed typescript is contained in the Queen's University Archives.

Variants

2   bough.]   ~ ; *NB*   ~ , *TS*

3   Whitethroat]   originally *Cl* < . . > *ffinch* in *NB; Cl* < . . > *ffinch* crossed through and *Whitethroat* written above it

5   copse]   ~ , *NB*

6   And]   originally *With* in *NB; With* crossed through and *And* written above it

7   is one ecstacy]   originally *wakes to rapture* in *NB; wakes to rapture* crossed through and *is one ecstacy* written above it

8   Of]   originally *Again* in *NB; Again* crossed through and *Of* written above it

9-12 And . . . eyes.]   crossed through in *NB* is:

> And at your eyes
> My dream & my desire
> Awake to rapture
> In life's renewing fire.

In the second line *My* is written beside *The* which has been crossed through. The third line is written above *Crave to rapture* which has been cancelled. In the last line *In life's* is written above *The spring's* which has been crossed through.

11   ²long] added with a caret in *ENB*

12   At]   originally *Melts at* in *ENB; Melts* crossed through and *a*
             capitalized
12   dear]   added with a caret in *ENB*

p. 312 THE VAGRANT OF TIME

The poem was first published in *Saturday Night* (December 4, 1926); and was
later included in *The Vagrant of Time*, 1927; *Our Canadian Literature*, 1934;
Selected Poems, 1936; *Selected Poems of Sir Charles G.D. Roberts*, 1955;
and *Selected Poetry and Critical Prose*, 1974.

Holograph manuscripts are contained in the two Roberts notebooks (NB
and ENB) at the University of New Brunswick. The first stanza of the poem,
crossed through in NB, is dated "Hyeres-Toulon, Ap. 1908." The full text in
NB is dated from Toronto—September 5, 1926 at the beginning of the poem;
September 6, 1926 at the cancelled final two stanzas; and September 7, 1926
at the end of the two revised final stanzas. The text in ENB is dated September 7, 1926.

Three typescripts are held in the Queen's University Archives. TS(1) was
evidently written before the publication in *Saturday Night*. TS(2) displays
editorial marks for printing and TS(3) is designated as the "Final revised
copy"–apparently for the publication of *The Vagrant of Time*–and is initialled
by Roberts.

Pomeroy (p. 223) says that the poem was begun at Pont Levoy, not at
Hyeres-Toulon. On page 330 she remarks that Roberts spoke "often of the
poem as his spiritual autobiography" and she remarks that it "is this revelation of the poet's character through his spiritual experiences that makes the
poem one of special significance."

Variants
Title: The Vagrant of Time]   originally *The Eternal Vagabond* in
             NB; The Eternal Vagabond crossed through and *Vagrant of
             Time* written beside it. Originally *The Vagabond of Time* in
             ENB; The Vagabond crossed through and *Vagrant* written
             above it. *The* omitted in *TS*(1), *Sat. Night, TS*(2) and *TS*(3).
1-4   I . . . hands.]   The first text of this stanza, crossed through in
             NB reads:

> I travel north, I voyage south,
> I taste of life in many lands,
> With ready wonder in my eyes
> And strong adventure in my hands,

> In the first line *travel* and *voyage* have been crossed through
> and *voyage* and *wander* have been, respectively, written above
> them. All other *NB* variants are from the later, full, text.

1   journey]   **wander**   *NB*
4   strong]   originally *stout* in *NB;* *stout* crossed through and *strong* written above it
5-12   I . . . door.]   These stanzas are reversed in *NB* with numbers written above them to indicate the correct order.
6   West;]   **west;**   *NB*   **west,**   *ENB*   west;   *TS*(1), *Sat. Night, TS*(2), *TS*(3)
7   their]   **the**   *NB*
7   catch]   originally *catch* in *NB; catch* crossed through and *hear* written beside it. Originally *hear* in *ENB, TS*(2), and *TS*(3); *hear* crossed through and *catch* written beside it in all three cases.   **hear**   *TS*(1), *Sat. Night*
8   my]   originally *their* in *ENB; their* crossed through and *my* written above it
9   East]   **east**   *ENB, TS*(1), *Sat. Night, TS*(2), *TS*(3)
12   guess]   originally *call* in *NB; call* crossed through and *sense* written above it
12   through]   **thro'**   *NB*
12   close-shut]   **unopened**   *NB.* Originally *unopened* in *ENB; close-shut* written above *unopened* which has not been crossed through
13-24   In . . . gleam.]   These stanzas were composed in the order 6, 4, 5 and numbers have been written above them in *NB* to indicate the correct order
13-20   In . . . urge.]   Numbers above these stanzas in *ENB* indicate an original order of 4, 5; Roberts changed his mind and renumbered them 5, 4. Still later, he renumbered them again 5, 4. The stanzas appear in the 5, 4 order in *TS*(1) and *Sat. Night.* In *TS*(2) they are written 5, 4 but there is an arrow to rearrange them. In *TS*(3) the stanzas are still reversed but there is a marginal note to transpose them.
14   season . . . content,]   **little . . . content;**   *NB*
15   Till]   **then**   *NB*
15   fare]   originally *go* in *NB; go* crossed through and *fare* written above it
17   down]   originally *by* in *ENB; by* crossed through and *down* written above it
21-24   In . . . gleam.]   originally stanza 9 in *ENB* but with a number 6 written above it to indicate the correct order
22   dream.]   ~ ;   *NB, ENB*   ~ ,—   *TS*(1)   In *TS*(2) and *TS*(3) a comma was originally written after *dream* but in both cases the comma has been crossed through and a period added.

25-28   Great . . . cot.]   designated as stanza 12 in *NB;* originally stanza
                                 12 in *ENB* but with a number 7 written above
                                 it to indicate its correct position
25   Great]   **Good**   *NB*
26   not,–]   ~ ,   *NB*
27   Grip]   originally *Clasp* in *NB; Clasp* crossed through and *Grip*
                    written above it
27   hall or camp]   originally *camp or* in *NB; camp or* crossed through
                           and *court or camp* written beside it. In *ENB,*
                           court is crossed through and *hall* written above it.
28   Greet]   originally *Meet* in *NB; Meet* crossed through and *Greet*
                    written above it
28   court or cot]   originally *town* in *NB; town* crossed through and
                          hall or cot written beside it. In *ENB* the phrase was
                          originally *hall or cot; hall* has been crossed through
                          and *court* written above it.
29-36   Down . . . stars.]   These stanzas were originally designated as
                               stanzas 7 and 8 in *NB;* 7 and 8 crossed
                               through and 8 and 7 written above them. The
                               movement of the original stanza 12 (see above
                               25-28) has, of course, now made these stanzas
                               8 and 9.
31   bright . . . bees]   **the bees and droning flies**   *NB*
34   When . . . unbars]   originally *I lie and watch the unfathomed stars*
                               in *NB;* the entire line is crossed through and
                               below it is written *When upon the vaulted night
                               my sense unbars.* In the new line *upon the* is
                               crossed through; *night* is crossed through and
                               space written below it; *sense* is crossed through
                               and *sense* is rewritten below it.
35   I . . . night]   originally *I swing through space* in *NB;* the entire
                          line is crossed through and written below it is *I
                          pitch my tent and bed the night.* In the new line *bed*
                          is crossed through and *camp* written below it.
35   tent,]   ~   *Sat. Night*
42   chill]   originally *those* in *NB; those* crossed through and *cold*
                    written beside it
43   shins . . . feet]   **shins, . . . feet,**   *NB, ENB*
44   fists]   ~ ,   *NB, ENB*
46   pause to]   **halt, and**   *NB*
47   gipsying]   **journeying**   *NB.* Originally *journeying* in *ENB;*
                      journeying crossed through and *gipsying* written above it
48   a-many]   originally *so many* in *ENB; so* crossed through and *a-*
                    written above it
48   true.]   ~ !   *NB*

49-56 So . . . skies.]   Crossed through in *NB* is the first attempt at
these two stanzas:

> And when at last I hang my cloak
>   Behind the Last Inn's noiseless door,
> And occupy the cold guest room cold
>   Where no one has ever lodged before,
>
> Content I'll sleep & unafraid,
>   That when they knock I may arise
> Strong for the new adventure
>   Under new suns and vaster skies.

In the first line *at last I hang* is crossed through and *someday
hanging* written above it. In the third line *And occupy* is
crossed through and *I'm shown into* written above it; also
[1]*cold* is crossed through. In the fourth line *no one* is crossed
through and *none* written beside it. Written below these
crossed out stanzas is the text approximately as it now stands.

49   So]   **And**   *NB*
49   drop]   **loose**   *NB.* Originally *loose* in *ENB; loose* crossed through
and *drop* written above it
51   lone]   **strait**   *NB.* Originally *strait* in *ENB; strait* crossed through
and *lone* written above it
52   no guest]   **no one has**   *NB.* Originally *none has* in *ENB; none
has* crossed through and *no guest* written above it
53   lie,–]   ~   *NB*   ~ , *ENB*
55   quest new ventures]   originally *front new ventures* in *NB; front*
and *ventures* crossed through and *quest* and
wonders, respectively, written above them
56   Essay]   **Venture**   *NB.* Originally *Voyage* in *ENB; Voyage*
crossed through and *Essay* written above it
56   suns]   originally *seas* in *ENB; seas* crossed through and *suns*
written above it

p. 314 IN THE NIGHT WATCHES

The poem was first published in *Willison's Monthly* (January, 1927); and was
later included in *The Vagrant of Time,* 1927; *Songs of the Maritimes,* 1931;
Selected Poems, 1936; *New Harvestings,* 1938; *Selected Poems of Sir Charles
G.D. Roberts,* 1955; *Penguin Book of Canadian Verse,* 1967; and *Selected
Poetry and Critical Prose,* 1974.
Two holograph manuscripts are contained in the two Roberts notebooks
at the University of New Brunswick. The poem occupies three pages in NB
and is written in pencil except for a few corrections. The first page is dated

September 10, 1926; the second page is undated; and the third is dated September 22, 1926. ENB is dated September 22, 1926. Three typescripts are in the Queen's University Archives. TS(1) is undated and unsigned. TS(2) is autographed but undated. TS(3) notes that it is the final revised copy and was, thus, prepared for some publication of the poem. No edition, however, precisely matches TS(3), a strange circumstance.

Variants

1   spent]   **night**   *TS*(1)

1   are]   originally *were* in *NB; were* crossed through and *are* written above it

1   tamarack]   originally *mulberry* in *NB; mulberry* crossed through and *poplar* written above it; *poplar* then crossed through and *tamarack* written below *mulberry*

3   wan]   originally *pale* in *NB; pale* crossed through and *wan* written above it

3   misshapen]   **mis-shapen**   *Willison's*

4   out]   **far**   *NB*

6   solitude]   originally *lone lands* in *NB; lone lands* crossed through and *solitude* written above

6   sleeps,–]   ~ –   *Willison's*

8   longing,]   ~ ,–   *ENB, TS*(3)

9   in my shack]   added with a caret in *ENB*

9   the marshes]   originally *the forest-girt marshes* in *ENB; forest-girt* crossed through

10   oh so far]   **oh, so far,**   *Willison's*

14   slender]   originally *young* in *NB; young* crossed through and *slender* written above it

14   saplings]   added with a caret in *NB*

14   its]   **my**   *ENB*

14   With . . . surely;]   below and to the right of this line in *NB* is the cancelled line:

To baffle the wind & the rain storm.

15-16   In . . . shy,]   these lines are reversed in *NB;* but there are marginal numbers, in ink, to place them in the order of the printed texts

15   play,]   ~   *ENB*

16   shy,]   ~   *ENB*

17   In . . . night.]   following this line, but cancelled, in *NB* is:

(And my long thoughts stab me with longing,)

See line 8. And, there is an uncancelled line:

O so dear, O so far, O so unforgotten in dreams,

See line 37.

18 Awake . . . square,]   written as two lines in *ENB:*

Awake,
Wide-eyed I watch my window-square

18 wide-eyed,]   ~   *Willison's, TS*(1), *TS*(2), *VOT, Songs of the
                              Maritimes, New Harvestings*
18 my]   originally *the* in *NB; the* crossed through and *my* written
              above it
18 window-square,]   ~   *TS*(3)
20 not! . . . not!]   **not, . . . not,**   *NB*   **not! . . . not,**   *ENB*
21 ache]   **Ache**   *Willison's*
21 memory,]   ~   *ENB, Willison's, TS*(3)
21 me by]   added with a caret in *NB*
21 by,]   ~   *ENB, TS*(3)
21 spare,]   ~ !   *Willison's, TS*(1), *TS*(2)
23 Once and again]   **Once and again,**   *ENB*
                               Once, and again,   *TS*(3)
25 firs,]   ~   *TS*(2)
27 brushes at]   **lifts**   *NB*
28 feet]   **steps**   *NB*
29 leaves]   ~ ,   *ENB*
30 On . . . floor?]   before this line, but cancelled, in *NB* is:

No more! No more!

31-32   From . . . fly.]   these lines are reversed in *NB*
31 From the still]   **Out on the**   *NB*
33 The . . . clear!]   the line is crossed through in *ENB* and in another
                              ink the same words are written above it
33 The . . . clear!]   following this line in *NB* and *ENB* is:

(No more! No more!)

The phrase is in ink in *NB*, and in *ENB* it is cancelled and
below the cancelled line is:

Almost I see the wide, slow ripple circling to the shore.

wide, slow is added with a caret

33   The ... clear!]   below this line, but cancelled in *NB* is:

O so dear, O so far, O so unforgotten in dream.

See line 37.

33   splash,]   ~ *Willison's, TS*(2)

34   Almost ... shore.]   omitted in *NB*

34   wide,]   ~ *Willison's, TS*(2)

35   rest. But]   **rest; but**   *NB, Willison's, TS*(2)

35   faint]   originally *fainting* in *NB; ing* crossed through

36   Long, long]   added with a caret in *NB*

36   peace . . .]   ~ !******* *NB*   ~ .*******_ *ENB*
                ~ . *Willison's, TS*(2)

37   Dear ... Far]   **dear ... far** *NB*

37   Unforgotten-in-dream,]   **unforgotten in dream!** *NB*
                             Unforgotten in dream *ENB, TS*(1), *TS*(3)
                             unforgotten in dream *TS*(2), *Songs of the Maritimes*

38   reach of my questing]   originally *mountain & stream* in *NB;*
                       mountain & stream crossed through and *reach of my*
                       questing written above it in ink

38   questing.]   ~ , *Willison's, TS*(3), *Songs of the Maritimes*

40   heart]   originally *heart's call* in *NB; heart's call* crossed
                       through and *heart* written above it

40   sleep,]   ~ *Willison's*

43   my]   originally *a quiet* in *NB; a quiet* crossed through and *my*
                       written above

44   heart,]   ~ *ENB, Willison's*

45   night)]   ~ ,) *TS*(2)

Glossary

  9   *Margaree:*   a river and a lake in Cape Breton, Nova Scotia

p. 315 THESE THREE SCORE YEARS

The poem was first published in the *Montreal Star* (June 30, 1927) with the note: "Written by Charles G.D. Roberts / Famous Canadian Poet / for The New Brunswick Celebration of Canada's Diamond Jubilee / and for The T. Eaton Co. Limited." The only other publication of the poem was in *Selected Poems*, 1936.

The first four lines of the poem appear in the earliest of the Roberts notebooks at the University of New Brunswick and are dated "Pont Levoy, France, June 3, 1909." The entire poem appears in Roberts' Ernescliffe notebook and is dated June 26, 1927. Two typescripts survive. The first is in the Lloyd Roberts Collection (LRC) at the University of New Brunswick; it is autographed and was apparently made after the publication in the *Montreal Star*.

The other typescript is in the Queen's University Archives; there are some printing notations in Roberts' hand and the typescript was apparently prepared for the publication of *Selected Poems*.

Variants
Title: *NB* is untitled.
Sub-title: Ode] **Song** *ENB, Montreal Star, LRC*
1   Oh] **It's Oh** *NB*
2   my own] originally *one's own* in *NB; one's own* crossed through
          and *my old* written above it
2   home;] ~ , *ENB, Montreal Star, LRC*
3   ¹the] added with a caret in *NB*
3   chase the] originally *follow* in *NB; follow* crossed through and
          chase the written above it
3   across] originally *along* in *NB; along* crossed through and *across*
          written above it
3   meadows] ~ , *ENB, Montreal Star, LRC*
4   deep] originally *green* in *NB; green* crossed through and *deep*
          written above it
5   exile . . . days] **Exile . . . day** *ENB*
7   ways] originally *days* in *ENB; days* crossed through and *ways*
          written beside it
7   ways,] ~ *Montreal Star, LRC*
13   this] added with a caret in *ENB*
15   blind] ~ , *ENB*
15   Ignorance] originally *Indolence* in *ENB; Indolence* crossed
          through and *Ignorance* written above it.
          Indolence *Montreal Star*
22   eyes,] ~ *Montreal Star*
24   wrought,] ~ *Montreal Star, LRC*
35   icepeaks] **ice-peaks** *ENB, LRC*
35   will.] ~ *TS*
41   These] **The** *ENB*
42   true,] originally followed by a question mark in *ENB;* question
          mark crossed through and a comma followed by a dash
          added.   ~ ,– *LRC*
47   cheer,] ~ *ENB, LRC*
48   clear,] ~ *ENB, LRC*
50   side,] ~ *ENB, Montreal Star, LRC*
51   laughed] ~ , *ENB*   ~ ; *LRC*
65   heart this] added with a caret between these words in *ENB*
          is *for aye*

Glossary
38-39 *And . . . signed.:* A reference to Thomas D'Arcy McGee (1822-
          1905), of Irish birth, an American immigrant in 1842, he

572

moved to Montreal in 1857. He was elected to the House of Assembly in 1858 and in 1864 was a member of the Great Coalition Ministry for the Confederation of the British North American Colonies. He was a delegate to the Charlottetown and Quebec Conferences and was elected to Parliament in 1867. An opponent of the attempt by the Fenians to foster disloyalty among Irish immigrants, he was assassinated April 7, 1868. As well as being a statesman, McGee was a journalist, a poet, and the writer of numerous prose works. See the entry in the *Oxford Companion to Canadian History and Literature.*

44-51   *Make . . . died.:*   all references are to scenes of battles in World War I

50   *Lion:*   the traditional symbol of England

p. 317 BE QUIET, WIND

The poem was originally published as a privately printed Christmas card for 1928; it later appeared in *The Iceberg and Other Poems,* 1934; *Selected Poems,* 1936; *Anthology of Canadian Poetry,* 1942; and *Selected Poems of Sir Charles G.D. Roberts,* 1955.

Two holograph manuscripts survive in the two Roberts notebooks at the University of New Brunswick. In NB the poem is dated Seattle, August 6 at the top, "on train" August 22 beside the fourth stanza, and Winnipeg, August 23, 1928 at the bottom. The Ernescliffe notebook (ENB) manuscript is also dated Winnipeg, August 23, 1928. ENB has the note, "sold to Harper's Bazaar, June 1929" but it has proved impossible to locate the poem in that periodical.

Four typescripts survive. The two in the library at the University of New Brunswick, TS(1) and TS(2), are apparently related and are earlier than any printed text. Both are signed by Roberts. The two typescripts in the Queen's University Archives are also apparently related, and at least one of them was evidently prepared for the publication of *The Iceberg and Other Poems.*

Variants

Title: Be Quiet, Wind]   no title   *NB.* Originally *My Heart and I* in *ENB; My . . . I* crossed through and *Be Quiet, Wind* written above it.

1   wind]   **Wind**   *NB, ENB, Xmas card*

3   rivulet,]   ~   *NB, ENB, TS*(1), *TS*(2), *Xmas card, TS*(3), *TS*(4), *Iceberg*

4   stealthily]   **soft as sleep**   *NB.* Originally *soundlessly* in *ENB; stealthily* written under *soundlessly* which has not been crossed through. In *TS*(3) and *TS*(4) *soft as sleep* reappears, but in the galley proofs of *The Iceberg and Other Poems* in the Queen's University Archives Roberts has crossed through *soft as sleep* and written *stealthily* in the margin.

573

5   whisperings]   **whispering**   *NB, ENB, TS*(3), *TS*(4)   Note: In the
              galley proofs of *The Iceberg and Other Poems* Roberts
              has added an *s*.
6   whip-poor-will]   **whippoorwill**   *NB*
7   slow . . . the]   **dew-drip from the overburden**   *NB*
7   rose–]   ~ ,–   *NB, ENB, TS*(1), *TS*(2), *TS*(4)   ~ ,   *Xmas card*
8   You, even]   **You. Even**   *NB*
9   must have]   originally *want the* in *NB; want the* crossed through
              and *must have* written above it
9   now,]   ~   *NB, ENB, TS*(1), *TS*(2)
11   all]   **what**   *NB*
11   me–]   ~ ,   *TS*(1), *TS*(2)   ~   *Xmas card*
12   Now,]   ~   *NB, Xmas card*
14   spell,–]   ~ ,   *TS*(1), *TS*(2), *Xmas card*
15   While we commune]   originally *And we are lost* in *NB; And we
              are lost* crossed through and *While we con-
              fer* written above it
15   commune]   originally *confer* in *ENB; confer* crossed through and
              commune written above it
16   deep]   **dear**   *NB*

p. 318 PAN AND THE ROSE

The poem was first published in *The Iceberg and Other Poems,* 1934; and was
reprinted only in *Selected Poems, 1936.*

Two holograph manuscripts are contained in the two Roberts notebooks
at the University of New Brunswick. In NB the poem is dated from Burnaby
Lake, July 31, 1928 for lines 1-23; the notation "Vancouver, Aug. 2" appears
beside line 24; and "Winnipeg, Aug. 24" appears at the end of the poem.
ENB is dated from Burnaby Lake, July 21 [31?] and from Winnipeg, August
24, 1928.

Three typescripts survive, all apparently earlier than any printed text.
TS(1) is signed by Roberts and is in the Lloyd Roberts Collection at the
University of New Brunswick. TS(2) and TS(3) are in the Queen's University
Archives and either one or both were apparently prepared for the publication
of *The Iceberg and Other Poems.*

Variants
3   The]   **With the**   *NB.*   Originally *With the* in *ENB; With* crossed
              through
4   Adrip]   **A-gleam**   *NB, TS*(1).   Originally *A-gleam* in *ENB; gleam*
              crossed through and *drip* written above it.
              A-drip   *TS*(2), *TS*(3)
5   thrust]   **pushed**   *NB.*   Originally *pushed* in *ENB* and *TS*(1);
              pushed crossed through and *thrust* inserted

574

5   through]   **thro'** *NB*

6   Stamped]   originally *And spurned* in *NB; And spurned* crossed
              through and *Stamped* written above it

7   scanned]   originally *sniffed at* in *NB; sniffed at* crossed through
              and *scanned* written above.   **scared** *TS*(2), *TS*(3)

10   blossom,]   ~ ,– *TS*(1)

11   rose]   **Rose** *ENB*

11   but half open]   originally *half opening just unfolding* in *NB;*
              half . . . unfolding crossed through and *half open*
              rewritten at the end of the line

12   insistent]   **ardent** *NB*

12   sun,–]   ~ , *NB, TS*(1)

14   ecstacy,]   comma crossed through in *NB*   ~ *TS*(1)

15   The]   **And the** *TS*(1)

15   perilous perfume]   originally *perfume & wonder* in *NB; perfume &*
              wonder crossed through and *perilous perfume* written
              at the end of the line

17   hot]   originally *wild* in *NB; wild* crossed through and *hot* written
              above it

19-20   The . . . dew.]   originally *Pan set his mouth / To the trembling*
              blooms in *NB;* these two lines are crossed through and
              the new lines written beside them

19   tender]   originally *frail* in the revised line in *NB; frail* crossed
              through and *tender* written above it

22   wonder,]   ~ *ENB, TS*(1)

23   distillage]   originally *draught* in *NB; draught* crossed through and
              nectar written beside it. Originally *nectar* in *ENB* and
              TS(1); *nectar* crossed through and *distillage* inserted

24   that]   **their** *NB, TS*(1). Originally *that* in *ENB; that* crossed
              through and *their* written above it; *their* then crossed
              through and rewritten below the line

25   thereafter]   **after** *NB*

27   lone]   added with a caret in *NB*

28   stream,–]   ~ , *NB.* Originally followed by a semi-colon in *ENB;*
              then a dash drawn through the period of the semi-colon

30   nymphs]   **maids** *NB.* Originally *nymphs* in *ENB; nymphs*
              crossed through and *maids* written above it; *maids* then
              crossed through and *nymphs* rewritten in the margin.
              Originally *maids* in *TS*(2); *maids* crossed through and
              nymphs written in the margin

30   copses,–]   **thickets,** *NB.* Originally *thickets* in *ENB* and *TS*(1);
              thickets crossed through and *copses* inserted

31   heart tormented]   **wild heart thirsting** *NB*

31   tormented,]   ~ *TS*(1)

33   that assuages them]   originally *he drains* in *NB; he drains* crossed
              through and *that assuages them* written in the margin

Pan: see "The Pipes of Pan"

   7   *Dianthe:*   also Diana, among other powers she was—as the allusion
                       here implies—goddess of the moon

p. 319 UNSAID

The poem was first published, privately, as a Christmas card for 1929; it was
later included in *The Iceberg and Other Poems,* 1934; and *Selected Poems,*
1936.

Two holograph manuscripts are contained in the two Roberts notebooks
at the University of New Brunswick. NB is dated December 29 and 30, 1928.
ENB is dated December 31, 1928 and January 11, 1929. ENB contains a note
that the poem was sold to *Harper's Bazaar,* June 1929, but it has proved
impossible to locate the poem in that periodical. Another holograph manuscript—MS(1)—is undated and is in the Roberts Collection at the University
of New Brunswick. The Queen's University Archives contain yet another
holograph manuscript—MS(2)—which is dated 1931-32. In addition, the
Queen's University Archives also contain a typescript probably prepared for
the publication of *The Iceberg and Other Poems.*

Variants

   1   a]   originally *an* in *NB; an* crossed through and *a* written beside it
   2   web]   originally *pair* in *ENB; pair* crossed through and *web*
                 written above it
   2   moonbeam]   originally *moonlight* in *NB; light* crossed through
                 and *beam* written beside it
   3   head]   originally *dream* in *NB; dream* crossed through and *head*
                 written beside it
   5   lovely]   before this word in *NB* a word has been obliterated
   5   scarce-thought]   originally *half-thought* in *ENB; half* crossed
                 through and *scarce* written above it
   6   even my]   originally < > *lips* in *NB;* the first word is obliterated,
                 lips is crossed through and *even my* is written above
                 the cancelled words
   6   had]   originally *tears* in *NB; tears* crossed through and *had*
                 written above it
   6   unsaid.]   ~ !   *MS*(2); also line 12
   6   After this line, *NB* has only a sketch of the remainder of the poem:

> And then my eyes looking into your dream,
> Uncovered there all the wonderful things,
> The half-thought things I had left unsaid.
> Found there hidden,
> Cherished & hidden
> The darlingest things I had left unsaid.

In the second line, *Uncovered* is written above *Found* and *the wonderful things* is written below *I had left unsaid.* The original word and phrase has been crossed through.

In *ENB,* crossed through, are the following lines:

> And then my eyes, surprising your dream,
> Found there hidden,
> Cherished forbidden,
> All the wonderful things they had left unsaid.
> The scarce-thought things I had left unsaid.

In the first line, *surprising* is written above *looking into* and in the third line *forbidden* is written above *and hidden;* the original phrases have been crossed through. In the fourth line, *All* is written in the left hand margin and *they had left unsaid* is written above the cancelled phrase *the disastrous things.* In *ENB* the second stanza, approximately as it now stands, follows.

7	slumbering]	originally *sleeping* in *ENB; sleeping* crossed through and *slumbering* written above it
8	surprise.]	~ , *ENB* ~ ; *Xmas card*
9	dream;]	~ , *ENB, Xmas card* ~ ,– *MS*(2)
9	hidden,–]	~ – *ENB, Xmas card* ~ , *MS*(2)
10	Sleeping]	–**Sleeping** *MS*(2)
10	cherished]	~ , *MS*(1), *MS*(2), *TS, Iceberg*
10	though]	originally *and* in *ENB; and* crossed through and *though* written above it
10	forbidden,–]	~ – *ENB, Xmas card* ~ , *MS*(2)
11	All]	–**All** *MS*(2)

p. 319 BAT, BAT, COME UNDER MY HAT (A Modernity)

The poem was first published in *The Iceberg and Other Poems,* 1934; and was reprinted only in *Selected Poems,* 1936.

A holograph manuscript with the notation "On train. June 12, 1929" is contained in Roberts' Ernescliffe notebook at the University of New Brunswick. The Queen's University Archives holds two typescripts with marginal corrections in Roberts' hand.

Variants

1	friends]	originally *man friends came* in *ENB; man friends came* crossed through and *men* written above it
5	known,]	~ *ENB, TS*(1), *TS*(2)
6	Then had they]	originally *They had* in *TS*(1); *Then* written in the margin and an editorial line drawn to reorder *They had.* Originally *They had then* in *TS*(2); *They had then* crossed through and *Then had they* written in the margin

7	things,]	~ *ENB*
9	Where . . . Why]	no italics in *ENB* here or in line 10
15	sinning;]	~ . *ENB*
22	Life]	**life** *ENB*
22	poorer,]	comma crossed through in *ENB*
23	unsurer,]	~ *ENB*
24	securer,]	~ *ENB* ~ ,– *TS*(1)
25	brief]	**strange** *ENB, TS*(1), *TS*(2), *Iceberg*

Glossary
17 *Vega . . . Arcturus:* Vega is a first **magnitude** star in the constellation Lyra, and Arcturus is a star of the same
magnitude in the constellation Boötes.

p. 320 SPIRIT OF BEAUTY

The poem was first published, privately, as a Christmas card for 1930; it later
appeared in *Harper's Bazaar* (January, 1931); *The Iceberg and Other Poems,*
1934; *Selected Poems,* 1936; and *Selected Poetry and Critical Prose,* 1974.

Three holograph manuscripts survive in the two Roberts notebooks at the
University of New Brunswick. In NB the poem is dated June 11 at the beginning and June 12, 1930 at the end. The first copy in ENB is dated June 12,
1930; this copy is crossed through and there is a note to see the revised form
on the following page. The revised, second, copy in ENB is dated June 13,
1930 and is the first text of the poem to divide the stanzas into quatrains
rather than couplets. An undated holograph manuscript (MS) and a typescript
are in the Queen's University Archives.

Variants
Note: in *NB* and *ENB*(1) the stanzas are couplets throughout, as:

> Spirit of Beauty, never shall you escape me.
> Through glad or bitter days hearten and shape me.

4	Hearten]	**strengthen** *NB*
5	see]	~ , *NB, ENB*(1), *Xmas card*
7	knew]	**could** *NB, ENB*(1). Originally *could* in *ENB*(2); *could* crossed through and *knew* written above it
7	dream]	~ , *ENB*(1)
9	were]	added with a caret in *NB*
10	whitethroat's]	**white-throat's** *NB, MS*
10	plaining,]	~ *ENB*(1), *ENB*(2), *MS, Xmas card, Harper's*
12	low]	**wet** *NB*. Originally *wet* in *ENB*(1); *wet* crossed through and *low* written above it
12	raining,]	~ *ENB*(1), *MS, Xmas card, Harper's*

578

15   an empty]   originally *the lonely* in *NB; the* crossed through and *a*
                   written above it
16   And a far bell]   originally *& in far bells* in *NB;* then *a* added with
                          a caret between *in* and *far*
16   And]   originally *in* in *ENB*(1); *in* crossed through and *and* written
                above it
17   clasp]   originally *clasp* in *ENB*(1); *clasp* crossed through and *hold*
                  written above it. Originally *hold* in *ENB*(2); *hold* crossed
                  through and *clasp* written above it
17   warm, dear]   **dear, warm**   *NB, ENB*(1)
17   hand]   ~ ,   *Xmas card*
19   lean to]   **touch**   *NB, ENB*(1). Originally *touch* in *ENB*(2); *touch*
                    crossed through and *lean to* written above it
19   lips of]   originally *lips that of* in *ENB*(2); *that* crossed through
19   love]   ~ ,   *Xmas card*
21   Night]   **night**   *Harper's*
21   comes]   ~ ,   *ENB*(1)
22   the]   **my**   *NB*
23   cold,]   ~   *NB*
24   shall]   **will**   *NB, ENB*(1), *Harper's*

p. 321 THE ICEBERG

The poem was first published in *The University of Toronto Quarterly* (October, 1931); and later appeared in *The Iceberg and Other Poems*, 1934; *Selected Poems*, 1936; *Selected Poems of Sir Charles G.D. Roberts*, 1955; and *Selected Poetry and Critical Prose*, 1974.

Two holograph manuscripts are contained in the two Roberts notebooks at the University of New Brunswick. NB has three cancelled lines dated September-October, 1928; the full NB text is dated February 17, 1931 at the beginning of the poem and March 9, 1931 at the end. ENB has the notation, "Finished March 9th. Revised March 13th, 1931." Three typescripts survive. TS(1) is autographed and is in the Lloyd Roberts Collection at the University of New Brunswick. TS(2) is in the Queen's University Archives. Both TS(1) and TS(2) are apparently earlier than *The University of Toronto Quarterly* text. TS(3) is also in the Queen's University Archives. It has some editorial notations and was probably prepared for the publication of *The Iceberg and Other Poems*.

Pomeroy (pp. 332-333) says of the poem:

In February, 1931, as he was recovering from his illness, [hypertension of the nerves; its effect on Roberts is described on pp. 311-312] he started *The Iceberg,* and even after the first two stanzas were completed he said, "I don't know whether I'll be able to finish it or not;" and his listeners, although silent, also questioned the final outcome. He had written the first three lines several years before, so the idea of the poem, according to his custom, had been simmering for a long time. The poem, however, grew steadily and, in less than two months, was completed. Hitherto *Ave*, the first great ode in Canadian literature, which Roberts wrote for the Shelley Centenary in 1892, was considered the poet's finest achievement. To some readers *Ave*, classical both in thought and form, will remain the greater; to others *The Iceberg*, classical in its lucidity and melodiousness of expression but modernistic in its irregularities of form and pure objectivity, will take precedence even of *Ave*.

As in the past Roberts had instinctively adapted himself to the period in which he was writing. *Orion* (1880) and *Ave* (1892) belonged to their periods, and just as faithfully does *The Iceberg* belong to the twentieth century. It is forceful and direct, strong without violence, profound yet never obscure.

Meanwhile, the poet's writer-friends in Toronto had been strongly impressed by the poet's method of writing. They already knew *about* it. But during those weeks they often saw him at work, saw him prowling up and down his studio, while he carefully considered the new lines before committing them to paper—there was never any suggestion of haste. The visitors knew that the few, and to them already faultless, lines which constituted the day's work would be again subjected to the most rigid criticism the next morning, before the new day's work began. To them genius *did* appear as "the infinite capacity for taking pains." The writer well remembers hearing the poet read, one evening, the lines describing the shipwreck. Still in the mood of the poem, he began his accustomed prowling, and this time *thinking aloud* of what was to follow. Suddenly he interrupted the flow of thought saying, "Why, there are two more lines." The prowling continued for a few silent minutes. Then he wrote them down.

> The long, insidious fingers of the sun
> Their stealthy depredations wrought upon me.

At the next reading, "long" had been changed to "sweet."

Variants

1-3 The following lines, dated September-October, 1928—Toronto, appear on a different page from the rest of the poem in *NB*. They were evidently a first start (see Pomeroy above) and the revised lines do appear with the full text. The early entry reads:

> I was spawned from the glacier,
> North beyond Cape Chidley
> By a thousand miles.

All further *NB* variants are from the full text.

4   and the spawning]   written above an undecipherable word in
           line three of *NB*

5   vast]   originally *huge* in *NB; huge* crossed through and *vast*
           written above it

6   aloft]   originally *aloft with smoking sides* in *NB; with . . . sides*
           crossed through. Written across the margin is:

          Shaking down cataracts from its smoking sides.

8-9   With . . . sea.]   These lines, crossed through, originally appear as
           lines 4 and 5 in *NB;* they are repeated in their proper position.

9   Outraged]   originally *Startled* in *NB;* when the line was revised
           Startled was replaced by *Outraged.*

12   Crawling]   originally *Crawling over* in *NB; over* crossed through

12   ³crawling]   added in *NB* above the beginning of *irresistibly* which
           has been crossed through and then the full word
           written beside it

13   ice,]   ~ ;   *TS*(2)

16   immeasurable]   originally *the desolation* in *NB;* added with a caret
           above the line is *infinite wastes of immeasurable;*
           infinite wastes of is crossed through

21   low]   **slow**   *NB*

21   winnowing]   ~ ,   *TS*(2)

22   fleet-winged]   **timid**   *NB*

22   death,–]   ~ .   *TS*(1), *TS*(3)

23   backward-glancing fox]   originally *drifting fox* in *NB; drifting fox*
           crossed through and *backward-glancing fox* written
           beside it

24   Half]   **A moment**   *NB*

24   and vanishing]   **then fading**   *NB; ing* written over *es*

26   Stalking]   **Seeking**   *NB*

26   Stalking his prey]   following this line in *NB, ENB, TS*(1), *TS*(2) is:

          Where no prey was nor would be.

          The line is cancelled in *ENB.*

27   white sky]   originally *sky* in *NB; sky* crossed through and *white*
           sky written beside it

28   Only]   originally *Watching* in *NB; Watching* crossed through and
           Only written above it

28   wind screaming]   **winds that screamed**   *NB*

29   night–]   ~ ,   *NB*

30   night, naked, . . . over]   **night naked . . . above**   *NB*

32   cry]   originally *voices* in *NB; voices* crossed through and *cry*
           written beside it

33   where]   **as**   *NB*

37   close ranked] **close-ranked** *NB, UTQ*

38   scarlet] ~ , *NB*

39   sphere] ~ , *NB*

39   Hunted . . . sphere] following this line, but cancelled, in *NB* is:

From the horizon

40-41   And . . . died.] a single line in *NB*

43   indifferent, serene] **serene, indifferent** *NB*

44   Over] **Above** *NB*

45   But] **And** *NB*

45   afloat] originally *afloat, I drifted* in *NB; I drifted* crossed through

46   In . . . tide] **Seized in the stealthy grip of the huge tide** *NB;*
            the squeezed between *in* and *stealthy*

47-48   Began . . . doom] Earlier attempts at these lines are crossed
        through in *NB:*

South Began my drift to a remote
And unimaginable doom

Evidently *South* was the first beginning of the line; it was
crossed through and *Began* written beside it. In the second
line, *unimagined doom* was cancelled and *unimaginable doom*
written beside it; then the entire line was cancelled and
relocated.

47   south] ~ , *NB*

48   doom.] ~ , *TS*(2)

51   Shearing] originally *Ploughing* in *NB; Ploughing* crossed through
            and *Shearing* written above it

52   Ploughing] originally *Clearing* in *NB; Clearing* crossed through
            and *Ploughing* written above it

52   wide-flung ice-fields in] **mighty ice-fields** *NB;* in addition, a
            word has been obliterated between *fields* and *in*

52   ice-fields] **icefields** *TS*(2)

53   my] **their** *ENB*

53   ponderous flanks] *ponderous* written below two undecipherable
            words and *s* in *flanks* crossed through in *NB*

56   radiance;] ~ , *NB*

59   Life] ~ , *NB, ENB, TS*(1), *TS*(2), *UTQ, TS*(3), *Iceberg*

59   aswarm] **a-swarm** *TS*(1), *TS*(2), *UTQ, TS*(3)

61   tiny] **shoaling** *NB*

61   small pale] originally *tiny* in *NB; tiny* crossed through and *small
            pale* written above it

61   pale squid] originally *pale countless squid* in *ENB; countless*
            crossed through

61   squid,–] ~ *NB*

62   struck]   **shows**   *NB*
63   screamed]   originally *screamed* in *ENB; screamed* crossed
                    through and then rewritten beside it
64   themselves, and rose,]   **themselves and rose**   *NB*
65   A . . . hid]   originally *A clamourous cloud of wings that hid* in
                    NB; A . . . hid crossed through and *A clamour of*
                    weaving wings, that hid written in the margin
66   Momently my face]   *My face a moment* written above an unde-
                    cipherable line in *NB*
67   The]   omitted in *NB*
68   agape,]   ~   *ENB, TS*(2)
69   spoil, and slept,]   **spoil and slept**   *NB*
70   humped forms]   **black shapes**   *NB*
70   awash]   **a-wash**   *ENB, TS*(1), *TS*(2), *UTQ, TS*(3)
70   softly,–]   ~ ,   *NB, UTQ*   ~ ;   *ENB, TS*(2)
71   Or . . . nosed]   **Or plunged to the deep and nosed along**   *NB*
72   Along . . . roots]   **My ribbed and sunken sides**   *NB*
73   And . . . cod]   There is a two line equivalent in *NB:*

            Scraped clean their infested hides
            And scattered the pasturing cod.

74   voyaged on,]   **journeyed on**   *NB*
76   calving]   originally *calving* in *NB; calving* crossed through and
                    whelping written above it; *whelping* then crossed
                    through
77   Mild-featured,]   omitted in *NB*
77   innocent-eyed,]   ~   *TS*(1), *UTQ, TS*(3)
77   and]   **all**   *NB*
80   Of Hudson Strait]   originally part of line 79 in *NB;* crossed through
                    and then rewritten on a single line
81   Chidley]   **Chidleigh**   *NB*
82   seethe]   originally *roar* in *NB; roar* crossed through and *strive*
                    written below it
83   along]   **past**   *NB*
84   many-watered]   **many watered**   *TS*(3)
86   Dark . . . dark]   **Cape . . . Cape**   *NB*
87-90   And . . . hung]   in *NB:*

            And came at last off lone Belle Isle, the bane
            The bane of ships and snare of bergs
            And snare of bergs.
            Here, by the deep, conflicting currents drawn,
            A space I hung swing
            This way & that, I hung and swing
            I hung

In the first line, *at last* is crossed through and *off* written over an undecipherable word. In the second line, *The bane* is crossed through and *of* capitalized; *and snare of bergs* is cancelled. In the fourth line, *the* is an addition to the original line. The fifth and sixth lines are cancelled.

89   drawn,]   ~ *ENB*

90   hung,]   ~ *ENB, TS*(2)

91   swung,]   ~ *TS*(2)

92   Gulfward]   **gulfward** *TS*(2)

93   alien]   added with a caret in *TS*(2)

95-96   But . . . fate,]   a single line in *NB*

95   But]   originally *And* in *TS*(2); *And* crossed through and *But* written above it

95   then]   **now** *NB*

95   off-shore]   **off shore** *UTQ, TS*(3)

97   pressed]   originally *fought* in *NB; fought* crossed through and *thrust* written above it

100   South-east . . . Bauld]   two cancelled lines follow in *NB:*

> And slanted out Atlantic ward until
> Faded from view the loom of Newfoundland,

See below lines 103 and 105

103   out]   added with a caret in *TS*(1)

103   Atlanticwards]   *s* crossed through in *TS*(1)

104   treacherous swaths of fog]   **treacherous coils of mist** *NB; treacherous* written beside *writhing* which has been cancelled

108-111   A . . . gone]   originally in *NB:*

> A towering miracle of white
> The cynosure of passing ships
> That wondered & were gone

These lines, beginning with *of white* are cancelled. The revised lines then follow.

110   I was]   added in the margin of *NB*

112   wreathed]   **dark** *NB*

112   them beyond the verge]   This is written above and below several obliterated words in *NB*

114   stars and calm,]   **stars,–** *NB*

114   calm,]   ~ ,– *ENB, TS*(1), *TS*(2), *UTQ, TS*(3)

115   up]   added with a caret in *TS*(1)

116   throb]   originally *throb* in *NB; throb* crossed through and *pulse* written above it

116   long-drawn]   **long drawn** *TS*(1), *TS*(2)

117-118   Luminous . . . rows]   a single line in *NB*

117   behind]   originally *behind* in *NB; behind* crossed through and
           astern written beside it
118   sharp, small]   *small sharp* written above the line as an addition
           in *NB*
119   lay]   originally *was* in *NB; was* crossed through and *lay* written
           above it
120   off to leeward,]   omitted in *NB*
121   Blurring . . . line.]   This line is a part of line 120 in *NB*. Following
           is a line which does not appear in any other text:

           Lying in wait for the predestined hour.

122   day,]   ~ ;   *NB*
124-125   By . . . night]   a single line in *NB:*

           At noon White-blind, and in the night

       At noon written in the margin.
124   noon,]   ~   *ENB, TS*(1), *TS*(2), *UTQ, TS*(3)
124   blind-white,]   **blind-white**   *ENB*   **blind white**   *TS*(2)
126   and smothering]   originally *imperishable, baffling* in *NB;*
           imperishable, baffling crossed through and *and*
           smothering written above
126   sight.]   ~ ,   *TS*(2)
127   Folded . . . unconcerned]   in *NB:*

           I floated waiting, waiting & guessed not what
           And heeding not,
           My heart unconcerned.

       In the second line a word has been obliterated before *not,* and
       in the third line *incurious* is written above
129   not,]   ~   *TS*(1)
131   small]   **slow**   *NB*
131   lapping along]   In *NB, working and fretting* have been cancelled
           and *lapping around* has been written below the line
132   Lipping . . . breath]   **Lipping & lisping, whispering under breath**
           NB; under crossed through and *with bated* written above it
133   A]   originally *With* in *NB; With* crossed through and *The* written
           in the margin
134   heard remote]   **heard, remote,**   *NB*
135   carrying]   **echoing**   *NB*
137   love]   **great**   *NB*
138   Louder . . . rose]   **Louder grew**   *NB*
139   deepening]   **widening**   *NB*

139   then passed on]   **athwart the dark**   *NB; athwart* written beside
        throu which has been crossed through
140   Diminishing, and dying,–]   **Diminished, and diminished, and
                                    passed on.**   *NB*
140   dying,–]   ~ ;   *ENB, TS*(2)   ~ ,   *TS*(1), *UTQ*
141   And ... around]   **And a great silence fell**   *NB*
142   in]   added with a caret in *ENB* and *TS*(1)
143-144   Those ... death]   In *NB:*

> That casual undertone,
> That whispering of expectancy;
> And time stood still.

        In the first line, *casual undertone* is written beside *whispering
        of expectancy* which has been cancelled. In the second line,
        of death follows the semi-colon, but it has been cancelled.
145   And]   crossed through in *NB*
145-146   And ... approaching.]   a single line in *NB*
146   thud]   **throb**   *NB*
147-148   Near ... loud,]   a single line in *NB*
149   thick]   **blind**   *NB*
150   and hiss of waters]   originally *of trampled waters* in *NB; of ...
        waters* crossed through and *& hiss of waters* written above it
151   unseen, unseeing]   originally *unswerving and* in *NB; unswerving
                           and* crossed through and *unseen, unseeing*
                           written beside it
152   stood across]   originally *hove toward across* in *NB; hove ...
                       across* cancelled and *lay athwart* written above it
153-158   And doom.]   in *NB:*

> And then, a startled blare of hooting thunder,
> A glare of sudden, stabbing search lights
> That pierced not, but dispersed, the gloom, and there
> I towered, a dim immensity of doom.–

        In the first line, *And* is an addition written in the margin and
        startled is written beside *sudden* which has been crossed
        through. In the fourth line, *towered* is written beside *stood*
        which has been crossed through.
156   gloom;]   ~ ,   *ENB, TS*(2)
156-157   That ... there]   originally a single line in *ENB; and there*
                            crossed through in line 156 and rewritten as a new line
160   tortured waters]   originally *tortured waters* in *NB; tortured
                          waters* crossed through and *surges* written above it
160   screws]   added with a caret in *NB*
161   Reversed]   This is the last word of line 160 in *NB.*

161   thundered]   omitted in *NB*
162-163   Yet . . . helm,]   a single line in *NB:*

>   Yet on she came; but answering desperate helm,

162   drew]   originally *crept* in *ENB; crept* crossed through and *drew*
           written beside it
164-165   She . . . me;]   a single line in *NB:*

>   Swerved, & came broadside, almost scaping free,

166   a]   **one**   *NB*
166   faces, blanched]   **faces, white, blanched**   *ENB; white* crossed
           through. It cannot be determined if *white* was first can-
           celled and *blanched* written beside it or if the original
           phrase was *white, blanched*
166   blanched]   **which**   *NB*
167   turned . . . eyes]   **and eyes**   *NB*
168   Astare;]   **Staring,**   *NB*
168   one . . . cry]   **long wavering yell**   *NB*
168   long,]   ~   *ENB, TS*(2)
169   gored . . . through,]   **projecting, ripped her through**   *NB*
170-172   Ripping . . . steep]   in *NB:*

>   From stem to stern, and she drifted solemnly
>   Till her tall funnels leaned against my side

In the first line, *solemnly* is written beside *slowly* which has
been cancelled.
173   sprang . . . boats]   **sprang for the life boats**   *NB*
173   stumbling, for]   originally *stumbling and struggling, for* in *ENB;*
           and struggling crossed through
173   the boats]   *life* added with a caret between *the* and *boats* in
           ENB; life then cancelled
174   my . . . foundations]   originally *the warmer seas* in *NB; the . . .*
           seas crossed through and *my deep foundations* written
           beside it
175   those . . . hour]   **the . . . time**   *NB*
176-177   When . . . her]   a single line in *NB*
179-187   And . . . Wallowing,]   in *NB:*

>   And ice rained crashing down upon her
>   As my enormous mass hung over her decks,
>   And one long moan of horror rose, and was still
>   As I turned over, wallowing sluggishly,

In the first line, *ice* is written beside *blocks* which has been crossed through; between *rained* and *crashing* a word has been obliterated. In the third line, *one* and *moan* are written above *a* and *groan* which have been cancelled.

181 obliterating,–]   ~ .–   *ENB*   ~ .   *UTQ*
183 Babel]   **babel**   *TS*(1)
183 prayers]   ~ ,   *ENB, TS*(1), *TS*(2), *UTQ*
184 escaping]   ~ ,   *ENB, TS*(1), *TS*(2), *UTQ*
189 heaved up]   **streaming**   *NB*
190 And . . . emerging]   above this line, but cancelled, in *NB* is:

> And now from fogs emerging,–
> With contours altered, and my skyey crest
> Degraded to the deeps

191 traversed]   **sailed in**   *NB*
194 origin, my]   **origin and**   *NB*
195 and]   added with a caret in *ENB* and *TS*(1)
196 overwhelming ruin]   **wheming death**   *NB; death* is written beside an obliterated word and *dreadful* which has been cancelled. A number one is written above *death* and a number two over *wheming*. The word *wheming* is an obvious error; in *NB* it was originally *overwheming* but *over* has been crossed through.
197 pale, alien bulk]   **pale shape**   *NB; pale* written above *weak* which has been cancelled
197 pale,]   ~   *TS*(2)
198 ambient sheen]   originally *circumambience of sheen* in *NB; circum* and *of* crossed through and a *t* written over *ce* in *ambience*
199 outspread,]   ~ ,–   *TS*(2)
200 gulf]   **sea**   *NB;* originally *sea* in *ENB; sea* crossed through and *gulf* written above it
201-202   I . . . knew]   a single line in *NB*
201 in]   **with**   *NB*
202-203   Nor . . . girth]   originally a single line in *ENB* with a diagonal line to separate them
203 swiftly]   in *NB* an undecipherable word has been crossed through above *swiftly*
204 caresses]   **persuasion**   *NB*
204 breath]   originally *breath of* in *ENB; of* crossed through in line 204 and becomes the first word of line 205
205 soft]   **warm**   *NB*
205 sucked . . . strength]   **diminished me**   *NB*
205 how]   originally *what* in *NB; what* crossed through and *how* written above it
206 sweet,]   ~   *NB*

207 Their]   cancelled in *NB*

207 upon]   originally *on* in *NB; on* crossed through and *upon* written
                above it. Originally *on* in *ENB; up* squeezed in. In *TS*(1),
                up is added with a caret.   **on**   *TS*(2)

211 With]   **In** *NB*

213 sunlit]   **sun lit**   *NB, TS*(1), *TS*(3)

214 Back . . . elude]   an additional line appears above this in *NB:*

And plunge again

216 Day after day]   originally *Days on days* in *NB;* the *s* of *Days* and
                on days are crossed through, and *after* is written
                above *on days.* Beside the crossed through words
                is *radiant day.*

219 lithe]   originally *little* in *TS*(1); *little* crossed through and *lithe*
                written in the margin

219 sides]   **flanks** *NB*

220 speed]   **speed of flight**   *NB*

221 That]   **The** *NB*

222 followed hungering]   **following hungry**   *TS*(2)

224 rolling]   **that went** *NB*

226 rhythmically]   **in slow rhythm**   *NB*

227 Their . . . way]   two lines in *NB; Their . . . / Heading. . . .*

227 blunt black bodies]   originally *black bodies* in *NB; bodies* crossed
                through and *blunt bodies* written beside it

227 way]   ~ ,   *TS*(2)

228-229   Until . . . light.]   a single line in *NB:*

Until they vanished in the dazzling light

234 In . . . caught;–]   **Lapped in luxurious peace**   *NB; in* written
                beside *round* which has been crossed through

234 caught;–]   ~ ,–   *ENB, TS*(1), *TS*(2), *UTQ*

235 noon]   **day** *NB*

235 a wave]   added with a caret in *NB*

236 sobbing]   **whispering** *NB.* Originally *whispering* in *ENB;*
                whispering crossed through and *sobbing* written above it

238 gone;]   ~ – *NB*   ~ , *ENB*

240 Nor . . . content]   **And well content I was**   *NB, ENB, TS*(1),
                TS(2), *UTQ, TS*(3), *Iceberg*

242 sight,]   ~ *NB*

243 warm, wild]   **wild warm**   *NB*

246 amber]   **rose** *NB.* Originally *rose* in *ENB; rose* crossed through
                and *amber* written above it

248 Glowing . . . heat]   **And glowed & shimmered in the scalding
                heat** *NB*

589

248 with]   added with a caret in *TS*(1)
251 disdain,]   ~ ;   *ENB, TS*(2)
252 fallen]   **shrunken**   *NB*
253 foraging]   **great white**   *NB*
254 Stooped . . . feet]   **stooped to me, hovering, touched me with pink feet**   *NB*
255 And . . . away]   **And, startled, whirled & skreeled away**   *NB;* *whirled & skreeled* written above *skreeled & whirled* which have been cancelled
257 Last]   originally *Then* in *NB; Then* crossed through and *Last* written above it
258 glancing]   **gleaming**   *NB.*   Originally *gleaming* in *ENB; gleaming* crossed through and *glancing* written beside it
259 on the slow-pulsed swell]   originally *on the slow-pulsed blue* in *NB; slow . . . blue* crossed through and written above it is *on the slanting swell* which is also cancelled. Below the two cancelled phrases is *on the slow-pulsed swell*
260 And . . . frame]   written above this line, but cancelled, in *NB* is:

> Until at last I melted softly
> Dissolved at last in the enfolding sea
> Ready to disappear
> And merge forever in the solvent tide

261-262   Dissolved . . . light]   a single line in *NB; many coloured* written after *coloured* which has been crossed through
264 in]   originally *in* in *ENB; in* crossed through and *with* written above it; *with* then crossed through and four periods marked under the original word.   **with**   *TS*(1), *TS*(2)
264 all-solvent]   **solvent**   *NB*

Glossary
3   *Cape Chidley:*   the northernmost tip of Labrador; a thousand miles due north would be near the Elizabeth Islands.
36   *flaming Polar cohorts:*   the Northern Lights
80   *Hudson Strait:*   the body of water connecting Hudson Bay and the Atlantic Ocean. The Strait is just south of Baffin Island.
86   *Mokkowic . . . Napiskawa:*   Cape Mokkowik (Makkovic) is approximately half way down the coast of Labrador. I have not been able to locate Cape Napiskawa, but from the context of the poem I assume it to be between Mokkowic and Belle Isle.
87   *Belle Isle:*   an island at the northern entrance to the Gulf of St. Lawrence, between Newfoundland and Labrador.

590

100 *Bauld:* the northern tip of Newfoundland, approximately twenty-five miles south of Belle Isle.

183 *Babel:* the town, and specifically the tower, mentioned in the Bible. In order to stop the erection of the tower, God caused each person to speak in a different language. By analogy, any greatly confused shouting or disorder.

p. 327 TO A CERTAIN MYSTIC

The poem was first published in the *Queen's Quarterly* (July, 1931); and later appeared in the *Literary Digest* (December, 1931); as a privately printed Christmas card for 1931; in *The Iceberg and Other Poems*, 1934; *Selected Poems*, 1936; and *Selected Poetry and Critical Prose*, 1974.

According to Roberts' notebook, the fourth stanza was composed first, at Pont Levoy, September 18, 1909. The remainder of the poem, including the unrevised last stanza, is dated from Toronto March 20, 1931; the revised last stanza is dated March 22. In Roberts' Ernescliffe notebook the poem, including the unrevised last stanza, is dated March 22, and the revised last stanza March 23. Two typescripts and a manuscript—evidently written in the order TS(1), MS, TS(2)—are contained in the Queen's University Archives.

Variants

Title: To a Certain Mystic]   **To a Psychomant**   *NB. ENB* has two titles: **Lines to a Certain Mystic** and **A Mystic.**   **A Mystic**   *TS*(1)

1   see.]   ~ ,   *Lit. Digest*

2   no one else could]   **others could not**   *NB, Xmas card*

2   hear:–]   **hear–**   *NB*   ~ :   *ENB, Queen's Quart., Lit. Digest, Xmas card*   ~ ;   *TS*(1)

5   voyaging the]   originally *voyaging on the* in *NB; on* crossed through

5   vision]   originally followed by a comma in *ENB;* comma crossed through

7   fragrance,]   ~   *NB*

7   wafted]   originally *breathed* in *ENB; breathed* crossed through and *wafted* written above it   **breathed**   *Queen's Quart., Lit. Digest*

9   And . . . continents]   preceding this line, crossed through, in *NB* are three earlier attempts:

And in the pearl of dawn did you divine
And did
And did you mark at dawn

591

In the first line *divine* is crossed through and *descry* written beside it before the entire line was crossed through.

9   from strange continents] originally *from a strange continent* in *NB;* *a* crossed through, *continent* crossed through and *countries* written above it

9   continent]   originally followed by a comma in *ENB;* comma crossed through   *~ , TS*(1)*, Queen's Quart., Lit. Digest*

10   knows,–]   *~ – Lit. Digest*

11   leafage]   originally *leafage* in *NB;* *leafage* crossed through and *branches* written above it. Originally *branches* in *ENB;* *branches* crossed through and *leafage* written above it. Originally *branches* in *TS*(1)*;* *branches* crossed through and *leafage* written in the left margin.

11   Eternal]   originally *of Life* in *NB;* *of Life* crossed through and *Eternal* written beside it. Originally *Eternal* in *ENB;* *Eternal* crossed through and *of Life* written above it, then *of Life* crossed through and *Eternal* rewritten in the margin.

11   Eternal,]   *~ Xmas card*

12   Imperishable]   **imperishable** *Queen's Quart., Lit. Digest*

13   And]   **But** *Queen's Quart., Lit. Digest, Xmas card*

13   spirit]   **Spirit** *NB*

14   that]   originally *the* in *TS*(1)*;* *the* altered to *that*

14   unknown sea,]   **Unknown Sea?** *NB*

15   rumour]   **Rumour** *NB, ENB*

16   lands]   **worlds** *NB, ENB, TS*(1)*, Queen's Quart., Lit. Digest, Xmas card*

17   Ah]   originally *Oh* in *NB;* *O* altered to *A*   **Oh** *TS*(1)

18   sign,]   originally followed by a question mark in *NB;* question mark crossed through and a comma added

19   small]   **pearl-white** *NB*

19   seed,]   *~ NB, ENB*

21-24   But . . . must.]   There are two versions of this stanza in *NB* and *ENB;* in each of these notebooks the first attempt is crossed through and the revised text, approximately as it now stands, written below it. In *TS*(1) the variant stanza is not cancelled, nor is the revised one added. The three early texts are slightly different from each other.

NB: But you came empty-handed, and with tongue
        Babbling confusion; and men mocked at you!
    And some, we half believed you, wistfully,
        Having illusions too,–that might prove true.

ENB:	But you came empty-handed, and your tongue
	Babbling confusion. And men mocked at you.
	Yet some—we half believed you, wistfully,
	Having illusions too—which might prove true!

TS(1)	But you came empty-handed, and your tongue
	Babbled confusion; and men mocked at you.
	Yet some—we half believed you, wistfully,
	Having illusions too, that might prove true!

There are a few variants in the revised texts.

21   empty handed,]   ~ *NB, ENB, TS*(2); in *TS*(2) there is a double space in the line, suggesting that the comma did not strike hard enough to print

22   none]   **now**   *TS*(2); an obvious typographical error

Glossary

6   *shallop:*   a small, light boat
7   *Elysian:*   see "The Hawkbit"

p. 328 TAORMINA

The poem was first published in the *Dalhousie Review* (October, 1932); and was later included in *The Iceberg and Other Poems,* 1934; *Selected Poems,* 1936; *Selected Poems of Sir Charles G.D. Roberts,* 1955; and *Selected Poetry and Critical Prose,* 1974.

Two holograph manuscripts are contained in the two Roberts notebooks at the University of New Brunswick. NB is dated May 3, 1932 at the top, May 5 at line 30, and May 6 at the end of the poem. ENB is dated May 6, 1932.

Two typescripts survive. The first is in the Rufus Hathaway Collection at the University of New Brunswick; it is autographed and evidently earlier than any printed text. The second typescript is in the Queen's University Archives and is apparently later than the *Dalhousie Review* text; it was perhaps prepared for the publication of *The Iceberg and Other Poems.*

Pomeroy (pp. 333-4) gives the genesis of the poem:

The following spring, May, 1932, "Taormina" was written. Over twenty-one years had elapsed since he had *lived* the poem in "the little tumbled city on the height" (the ancient Hellenic city of Taormina in Sicily) when there fell from a book, which he had picked up casually from his shelves, a withered almond flower. At once was released a flood of memories. Although it was already an early hour of the morning, sleep did not come until many of the singing lines had been committed to paper.

Variants

Title: Taormina] **Ricorditi di me [My Memories]** *NB*
1   above this line in *NB* is:

> Taormina. Taormina.
> And the month of the almond blossom!

2   Basking] **Dreaming** *NB*
2   sea] originally *blue* in *NB; blue* crossed through and *sea* written
      above it
2   sea!] ~ .– *ENB*
3   pale,] ~ *NB, ENB, TS*(1)
3   ghosts] **ghost** *NB*
3   come] added with a caret in *ENB*. Originally *comes* in *TS*(1); *s*
      crossed through
4   call] **calls** *NB*. Originally *calls* in *TS*(1); *s* crossed through
4   the] added with a caret in *NB*
4   me] originally *you* in *NB; you* crossed through and *me* written
      above it
4   me!] ~ . *TS*(1)
5   Taormina, Taormina,] **Taormina. Taormina.** *TS*(1); also lines
      11, 17, 23, 34, and 41
6   month] **scent** *TS*(1)
7-10 In . . . desire!] crossed through in *NB* is:

> 1   How far have danced your feet since that bright hour
> 2   That brought us to the land of our delight!
>   And I remember many things tonight.
> 3   In an old book I find a withered flower

> *bright hour* is written above *fair day* which has been crossed
> through, and *find* is written above *found* which has also been
> cancelled

7   flower,] ~ ,– *TS*(1)   ~ *Dal. Rev., TS*(2)
12   Oh] **And** *NB*
12   Oh,] originally followed by a comma in *ENB;* comma crossed
      through in line 12 and omitted in lines 24 and 42
13   monastery] *monastery* and, above it, *convent* have both been
      crossed through in *NB*
14   flung   added with a caret in *NB*
14   upclamber] ~ , *NB*   **up clamber** *TS*(1)
15   In] normally spaced in *NB* but preceded by an illegible word in
      the margin
15   cling] ~ , *ENB, TS*(1), *Dal. Rev.*
15   fall,–] ~ – *TS*(1)

594

16   Brave]   originally *Those* in *ENB; Those* crossed through; *The* and
           Bold written above *Those* and then cancelled. *Brave*
           written below the original word. Originally *Bold* in *TS*(1);
           Bold crossed through and *Brave* written in the margin.
16   purple]   originally *crimson* in *ENB; crimson* crossed through and
           purple written above it
19   above this line, but cancelled, in *NB* is:

           We dreamed upon the wall, and, hand in hand,
           We caught our breath

19   breath,]   ~ *NB, ENB, TS*(1)
21   Soaring above]   originally *Above* in *NB; Soaring* added with a
           caret in the margin
22   Enmeshed]   **Meshed**   *NB*. Originally *Meshed* in *ENB* and *TS*(1);
           En added and *M* altered to *m*
25   Corydon,–]   ~ , *NB*
26   Of]   originally *How* in *NB; How* crossed through and *Of* written
           above it
26   dark locks]   *dark* written over an undecipherable word in *NB* and
           locks written above *hair* which has been crossed
           through
26   locks,–]   ~ *NB*
27   grieving]   originally *leaning* in *NB; leaning* crossed through and
           grieving written above it
28   rocks]   ~ , *NB*
29   the]   omitted in *NB;* added with a caret in *ENB*
29   blossom,–]   ~ . *NB*   ~ ;– *ENB*
30-39   Of . . . flame!]   These stanzas are reversed in *NB*.
30   Of]   originally *Of* in *ENB* and *TS*(1); *Of* crossed through and *And*
           written above it; *And* then crossed through and *Of* rewritten
           in the margin of each text
31   veiled the slim]   **sheltered the white**   *NB*
32   pines]   ~ , *NB*
33   caught her close,]   **clasped her close**   *NB*
36   above this line, but cancelled, in *NB* is:

           We laughed to see the goat-herd rend apart
           The vines that sheltered Cloe and her dreams.

36   then–]   ~ *NB*   ~ , *ENB, TS*(1)
36   me!]   ~ . *NB, ENB*
38   sea–]   ~ ,– *NB, TS*(1)   ~ ; *ENB*
39   flame!]   ~ . *NB, TS*(1)   ~ .– *ENB*
40-42   The . . . blossom.]   omitted in *NB*
40   dies. The]   **dies,–the** *NB*   **dies–the** *TS*(1)
40   me.]   ~ ! *ENB*

Glossary

16   *bougainvilleas:*   an ornamental shrub with small flowers
20   *Aetna:*   an active volcano in eastern Sicily
25   *Battos . . . Corydon:*   Battos was a shepherd of the mythical land
          of Arcadia and Corydon is a shepherd who appears in the
          "Idylls" of Theocritus and the "Eclogues" of Virgil; the
          names are conventional in pastoral poetry
26   *Amaryllis:*   a shepherdess in the works of Theocritus, Virgil, and
          Ovid; another conventional name in pastoral poetry
27-33   *Of . . . wrath:*   either obscure legends or imagined ones appro-
          priate to the pastoral mood of the poem

p. 329 PRESENCES

The poem was first published in the *Queen's Quarterly* (1932); and later appeared in the *Literary Digest* (January, 1933); *The Iceberg and Other Poems,* 1934; *Selected Poems,* 1936; and *Selected Poetry and Critical Prose,* 1974.

There are two entries in Roberts' notebook; the first stanza is dated "March 17, 1907, S.S. Carmania"; the full poem appears on another page and is dated May 12, 1932 at the top and May 13 at the bottom. Another holograph manuscript, dated May 13, 1932, is contained in Roberts' Ernescliffe notebook. Three typescripts are contained in the Queen's University Archives.

Variants

2   cabin]   **lonely**   *NB*(1). Originally *lonely* in *NB*(2); *lonely* crossed
          through and *cabin* written above it
4   walks]   **walked**   *NB*(1). Originally *walked* in *NB*(2); *ed* crossed
          through and *s* written above it
4   tops]   ~ ,   *ENB*
5   Across . . . sill]   originally *It danced* in *NB*(1); *It danced* crossed
          through and *Across . . . sill* written beside it
6   trembled]   ~ ,   *ENB*
9   Was]   originally *Was* in *ENB; Was* crossed through and *Is* written
          above it
9   light can]   **light could**   *NB*(2). Originally *air could* in *ENB; air*
          crossed through and *light can* written above it
10   whirl up,]   ~   *TS*(1), *TS*(2), *TS*(3), *Queen's Quart., Lit. Digest*
11   fall–]   ~ ,–   *ENB*
12   they had]   **if they'd**   *NB*(2)
13   harebells]   **hare-bells**   *NB*(2), *ENB, TS*(1), *TS*(2), *TS*(3), *Queen's
          Quart., Lit. Digest*
15   aswing,]   originally followed by a question mark in *ENB;* question
          mark crossed through and a comma added

596

16	Tho' . . . glade]	originally *Tho' not another blade or leaf* in *NB; not . . . leaf* crossed through and *all about the forest glade* written above it; then *all about* crossed through and *up & down* written below the line
23	hair,–]	~ – *NB*(2), *Lit. Digest*
24	there!]	~ . *NB*(2)
27	come]	originally *are* in *NB*(2); *are* crossed through and *come* written above it

p. 330 RE-BIRTH

As far as may be determined, the poem first appeared in *The Iceberg and Other Poems,* 1934. However, an unidentified clipping which may be earlier is included in a letter from Roberts to A.M. Stephen, dated December 25, 1934. The poem was also included in *Selected Poems,* 1936.

Two holograph manuscripts are included in the two Roberts notebooks at the University of New Brunswick. Both manuscripts are dated from the Ernescliffe, September 22, 1932.

Two typescripts survive. TS(1) is in the Rufus Hathaway Collection at the University of New Brunswick. It is signed by Roberts and also dated September 22, 1932. A few corrections are made in Roberts' hand. TS(2) is in the Queen's University Archives and was probably prepared for the publication of *The Iceberg and Other Poems.*

Variants
Title: Re-Birth] untitled *NB.* both *Rebirth* and *Renascence* in
        ENB **Rebirth** *TS*(1)
Note: Cancelled in *NB,* before the poem proper begins, are the following lines:

> Before the mists of temporal
> forgetting closed about me
> Back, back, back, but ever striving up
> Till I came < . . . > darkness of the tomb
>
> (I was snared once again in the kindly flesh of man)
>
> For an age I had lain in the darkness of the tomb,
> I had slept in the stillness of the tomb.
> It seemed I had dreamed in the deeps of this oblivion
> I had dreamed far back, back, back, but ever striving up
> Till I came into this darkness of the tomb.

1   stumbled]   **struggled**   *NB*

1   slime]   originally *slime* in *NB; slime* crossed through and another
                     word, also crossed through, written above it. The space was
                     left blank with four periods under the original word.

1   heights]   **height**   *NB*

3   age]   **Age**   *TS*(2)

3   pulseless, senseless dark]   originally *darkness of the tomb* in *NB;*
                     darkness . . . tomb crossed through and *pulseless . . .*
                     dark written above it, then *senseless* crossed through

3   dark,]   ~ :   *TS*(1)   ~ ;   *TS*(2), *Xmas clipping*

4   darkness]   **blackness**   *ENB*

7   the long-forgotten]   written above an **undecipherable** phrase in *NB*

7   immemorial]   written above an undecipherable phrase <   > *of
                     the* in *NB*

8   I . . . sleep.]   Two cancelled lines precede this in *NB:*

                     I shed my <   > & breathed into the light.
                     I emerged, I breathed up into the light.

8   fled up]   **sped upward**   *NB*

9   soul,]   ~   *NB*

10   floated]   **swam**   *NB*

14   shadows to a blissful gloom]   originally *golden shadows into
                     space* in *NB; golden . . . space* crossed through and
                     to . . . gloom written above it

15   sweetly assuaged]   **assuaged in full content**   *NB*

17   In . . . seemed,]   **From afar, yet in my heart,**   *NB*. Originally
                     From far off, yet in my heart in *ENB; From . . . heart*
                     crossed through; also crossed through above the phrase
                     is *From afar* and *Far off;* written to the side, above the
                     cancelled phrase, is *In my heart, as it seemed*

17   heart,]   comma crossed through in *TS*(1)

17   faint]   originally *feeble* in *ENB; feeble* crossed through and *faint*
                     written above it

19   groping . . . satisfied;]   **thirst was sweetly assuaged**   *NB*

19   groping]   added with a caret in *ENB*

19   was satisfied]   originally *was richly satisfied* in *ENB; richly*
                     crossed through

20   slumbered]   originally *slept* in *NB; slept* crossed through and
                     slumbered written beside it

20   wrapt]   added with a caret in *NB*

21   Once . . . man.]   **I was snared once again into the kindly flesh of
                     Man,**   *NB*

21   man.]   ~ ;   *TS*(1), *TS*(2), *Xmas clipping*

22   closed . . . sight]   originally *sealed and lulled my sight* in *NB; and
                     lulled my* crossed through and *away the spirit's* written above it

22   closed]   originally *sealed* in *ENB* and *TS*(1); *sealed* crossed through
                    in both texts and *closed* written above
23   shut]   **closed**   *NB*. Originally *closed* in *ENB* and *TS*(1); *closed*
                    crossed through in both texts and *shut* written above
24   I had seen, far off,]   **I saw once more**   *NB*. Originally *I saw far*
                    off in *ENB; I . . . off* crossed through and *I had seen*
                    from afar written above it; then *from afar* crossed
                    through and *far off* written beside it. The phrase *I had*
                    seen, far off, is repeated at the bottom of the poem.
24   I had seen]   **I saw**   *TS*(1)
24   far off]   originally *afar* in *TS*(1); *afar* crossed through and *far off*
                    written below it

p. 331 THE SQUATTER

The poem first appeared in the *Queen's Quarterly* (May, 1933); and was later
included in *The Iceberg and Other Poems,* 1934; *Selected Poems,* 1936;
Selected Poems of Sir Charles G.D. Roberts, 1955; and *Selected Poetry and*
Critical Prose, 1974.

Two manuscripts of the poem are contained in the two Roberts notebooks
at the University of New Brunswick. In *NB* the poem is dated from the
Ernescliffe, September 23 at the beginning and October 2, 1932 at the end.
At the bottom of *ENB* is October 2, 1932 and a notation of its sale to (or if
the note is late, its appearance in) the *Queen's Quarterly.*

Three typescripts survive. TS(1) and TS(3) are in the Queen's University
Archives. TS(1) is evidently earlier than any printed text, and there are several
corrections in Roberts' hand. TS(3) was apparently prepared for the publication of *The Iceberg and Other Poems.* TS(2) is in the Roberts Collection at
the University of New Brunswick; it is signed by Roberts and, although dated
from the Ernescliffe October 2, 1932, is a relatively clean copy and probably
was prepared at some time between TS(1) and TS(3).

Variants
Note: in *NB* the stanzas are written in the order 1, 4, 2, 3, 7, 5, 6, 8, 9,
         10, 11, 12, 13, 16, 17, 14, 15, 18, 19, 20, 21, 22, 23, and there
         are marginal numbers to place the stanzas in the proper order
Title: The Squatter]   originally *The Lone Clearing* in *NB; The Lone*
                    Clearing crossed through and *The Squatter's*
                    Clearing written above it
1   Round]   **Around**   *NB*
2   Clearly]   **Sweetly**   *NB*
2   whitethroats call]   **whitethroat calls**   *ENB*
3   Across]   originally *Athwart* in *NB; Athwart* crossed through and
                    Across written above it; *Across* then cancelled and
                    Over written in the margin. The entire poem is written

599

in pencil in *NB* except the line through *A cross* and the
word *Over,* suggesting a later revision

3   dusk]   ~ , *ENB*

4   empty]   originally *paling* in *NB; paling* crossed through and
empty written beside it

5   Amber and apple-green]   originally *Amber & inert* in *NB; Amber*
crossed through and then rewritten above the original
word

6   A]   originally *One* in *NB; One* crossed through and *A* written
over it

6   and twangs her]   originally *with a twang of her* in *NB; with* crossed
through and *and* written above it; *a* crossed through and
the written above it but then cancelled; *s* added to
twang and *of* cancelled

7   astir]   originally *stirs* in *NB; a* added and *s* cancelled

9   smoke of a]   originally *scent of the* in *NB; scent* and *the* crossed
through and *smoke* and *a* written above the respec-
tive cancelled words

10   The . . . spruces]   originally *The dark firs crowding* in *NB; firs
crowding* crossed through and *spired spruces* written
above; a *2* is written above *dark* and a *1* above *spired*

11   snake fence, breathless]   originally *ragged fence* in *NB; ragged*
crossed through and *snake* written above it; *breathless*
does not appear in *NB*

11   breathless,]   ~ . *TS*(2)

13   wet]   written above an undecipherable word in *TS*(1)

14   brook flows murmuring]   **spring flows softly** *NB*

15   The]   originally *The* in *NB; The* crossed through and *A* written
above it

15   The . . . cow-bell]   **A cow drinks. The bell** *NB*

15   drinks,–the]   originally *drinks,–and the* in *TS*(1); *and* crossed
through

15   tonk-tonk]   **tonk-a-tonk** *NB.* Originally *tonk-a-tonk* in *TS*(1);
a crossed through

17   lounges]   **idles** *NB.* Originally *idles* in *TS*(1); *idles* crossed
through and *lounges* written above it

18   damp air,]   **cool air** *NB*

18   Sniffs . . . rain.]   Following this line, but cancelled, in *NB* is:

He seats himself,
Stiffly upon the door-sill,
And slowly fills his pipe, and smokes, and

See lines 23-24

19   has made]   originally *makes* in *NB; makes* crossed through and
has made written above it

19	meal,–] ~ – *ENB*	
20	Fat] added in the margin of *NB*	
20	bacon, . . . cakes,] **bacon . . . cakes** *NB*	
20	cakes,] ~ *TS*(3)	
21	ruddy-brown] **ruddy brown** *NB, ENB*	
23	door-sill] **door sill** *ENB*	
26	birch logs] **wood-pile** *NB* **birch-logs** *ENB*	
27	fresh white chips] **white birch-chips** *NB*	
27	fresh] ~ , *TS*(1), *TS*(2)	
33	through] **thro'** *ENB*	
33	twilight] originally *dusk* in *TS*(1); *dusk* crossed through and *twilight* written beside it	
34	fragrance] **perfume** *NB*	
36	brush-fire] **brushfire** *TS*(3), *Iceberg*	
36	ascending] originally *ascending* in *NB*; *ascending* crossed through and *upspiralling* written above it	
37-39	Deepens . . . moth.] omitted in *ENB*	
38	The . . . night-hawk] **Hushed are the white throats The night- hawk** *NB*	
39	Drops . . . night-moths] originally *Drops from the sky* in *NB*; *Drops from the sky* crossed through and written under it is:	

Descending, silently zigzags over the alder-tops

40	is dreaming] **dreams** *NB*	
41	he . . . winter] **he dreams & plans** *NB*	
42	He'll . . . brook] **To clear another field, beyond the brook** *NB*	
42	out] originally *down* in *TS*(1); *down* crossed through and *out* written below it	
42	brook.] ~ ; *TS*(1), *TS*(2), *TS*(3)	
43-45	He'll . . . stack] in *NB:*	

Vaguely he plans
To build a bigger barn
Next year, & get himself another horse.

46	He . . . stretches] originally *The squatter rises* in *NB; The . . . rises* crossed through and *He rises, stretches,* written above	
47	Goes . . . closes] **He goes in and shuts** *NB;* there is some evi- dence of an attempt to cancel *He* and to capitalize the g in *goes*	
48	beside] **by** *NB*	
50	lights . . . strewn] **picks out the scattered** *NB*	
50	chips.] ~ , *TS*(3)	
51	For . . . rabbit] **the dog darts across it, chasing a startled rabbit** *NB*	

51   dog]   ~ , *ENB*

52   lean]   omitted in *NB*

53   squatter]   ~ , *NB*

54   Knitting]   originally *Knitting* in *NB; Knitting* crossed through and *Wrinkling* written below it

54   Knitting . . . paper]   **Wrinkling his brows over a month old paper** *NB*

56   Humped]   written above a crossed through and undecipherable word in *NB*

56   remote]   written beside an undecipherable word in *TS*(1)

59   rounder . . . white]   **round and glassy white** *NB*

59   rounder]   **round** *TS*(3)

60   up]   **in** *NB*

60   sky]   ~ , *ENB, Queen's Quart.*

60   over]   originally *on* in *TS*(1); *on* crossed through and *over* typed above it

62   Illusively]   **Glassily** *NB*

63   lop-sided]   **lopsided** *ENB*

63   stack by the barn]   **fodder-stack** *NB*

64   floods]   originally *looks* in *NB; looks* crossed through and *floods* written above it

64   window,–]   ~ . *NB*

65   in his bunk]   originally *in his bunk in the bright* in *NB;* the phrase is crossed through and several periods written under it to indicate that the line is not complete

65   Below this line, but cancelled, in *NB* is:

In his bunk, on the mattress stuffed

66   green]   omitted in *NB*

66   fir]   originally *spruce* in *NB; spruce* crossed through and *fir* written above it

66   tips,]   ~ *NB*

67   From]   **In** *NB*

68-69   The . . . clearing]   in *NB:*

The great horned owl hoots thrice.
Then the silver silence closes down on the clearing.

69   the silence]   perhaps inadvertently omitted in *TS*(1) and then **written** in the margin

69   once more]   originally *again* in *TS*(1); *again* crossed through and *once more* written below it

The poem was first published in *The Iceberg and Other Poems,* 1934; and was later included in *Selected Poems,* 1936; *Selected Poems of Sir Charles G.D. Roberts,* 1955; and *Selected Poetry and Critical Prose,* 1974.

Two holograph manuscripts survive in the two Roberts notebooks at the University of New Brunswick. A fragment in NB is dated from Bond Lake, July 14, 1929; and the full poem is dated November 27, 1932 at the top, October 13, 1934 at the second stanza, and October 14, 1934 at the bottom. The text in ENB is dated October 14, 1934 and has a note *"New Outlook"* and "End of *'The Iceberg and Other Poems.'*" It has proved impossible to locate the poem in *New Outlook.*

Four typescripts survive. TS(1), TS(2), and TS(3) are in the Queen's University Archives. TS(1) is autographed by Roberts and then a line has been drawn through the signature; there are corrections in Roberts' hand. TS(2) is signed by Roberts and is dated as having been "Written Oct. 14, 1934." Above the title, written in Roberts' hand, is "In memory of G. Goodridge Roberts" and at the bottom of the poem is "For L.P. from C.G.D.R." TS(3) is unsigned and undated and there are corrections in Roberts' hand. TS(4) is in the Roberts Collection at the University of New Brunswick; it is a clear copy and is signed by Roberts.

Variants

1-2	As . . . tears.]	These two lines, on a different page in *NB* from the full text, are dated "Bond Lake, July 14/29."
3	Under . . . heard]	written above this line and crossed through in *NB* is:

> In the bright stir of summer pomp
> I heard the spending years
> I heard

3	Under]	**Beneath** *NB; Beneath* written beside *I heard* which has been crossed through. See above.
3	Under the summer's]	**Beneath the Summer's** *TS(2)*
5	No italics in the refrain in *TS*(4)	
5	Oh,]	~ *ENB;* also lines 11, 17, 23, 29, and 35
5	sweet . . . swift]	above these words in *NB* are the numbers 2 and 1 respectively. Also line 11.
5	sweet]	originally *swift* in *ENB* and *TS*(1); *swift* crossed through and *sweet* inserted. Also lines 11, 17, 23, 29, and 35.
5	swift]	originally *sweet* in *ENB* and *TS*(1); *ee* altered to *if.* Also lines 11, 29, and 35 in *ENB;* lines 11 and 35 in *TS*(1).
5	years! The . . . years!]	**years, the . . . years,** *NB;* also lines 11 and 35.

7   slopes]   originally *hill* in *NB; hill* crossed through and *slope* written above it

8   marshlands]   originally *meadows* in *NB; meadows* crossed through and *marshlands* written above it

9   And,] ~ *NB, ENB, TS*(1), *TS*(2); comma added in the left hand margin in *TS*(3)

9   hurrying pale] **gliding slow** *NB.* Originally *gliding slow* in *ENB; gliding slow* crossed through and *hurrying pale* and an obliterated word written above it.

9   dikes,] ~ *ENB, TS*(1), *TS*(2)

10   My] **The** *NB.* Originally *The* in *ENB; The* crossed through and *My* written above it.

12   away!] ~ . *NB;* also lines 18, 24, and 36

13-18   The . . . away] originally the sixth stanza in *NB* with a marginal number to indicate its correct position

13   tang] originally *scent* in *NB; scent* crossed through and *tang* written above it

13   buckwheat] originally *clover* and an undecipherable word in *NB; buckwheat* written above the cancelled words

14   Were . . . air] originally *Filled all the streaming air* in *NB; Filled all* crossed through and *Breathed on* written above it. *Breathed* and *streaming* then crossed through; *Were* written in the margin before *Breathed* and *breathing* written under *streaming*.

16   one] originally *one* in *NB; one* crossed through and *him* written above it

17   swift] originally *beloved* in *NB; be* crossed through. So also line 23 in *NB.* Originally *loved* in *ENB* and *TS*(1); *loved* crossed through and *swift* written above. So also line 23 in *ENB* and lines 23 and 29 in *TS*(1).

19-24   I . . . away!] originally the third stanza in *NB* with a marginal number to indicate its correct position

20   old grey] **little** *NB*

20   grey] added with a caret in *ENB* and *TS*(3); omitted in *TS*(1) and *TS*(2)

21   Kneeling,] ~ *ENB*

22   that] **the** *TS*(2)

24   that] **have** *NB;* also line 30

25-30   I . . . away!] originally the fourth stanza in *NB* with a marginal number to indicate its correct position

25   form.] ~ , *NB*

26   hymning] before this word in *NB* is a cancelled word or the beginning of a word which is undecipherable

26   choir.] ~ .— *NB*   ~ .***** *ENB*

27   Shadows!—and] **Shadows! And** *NB*   **Shadows.— and** *ENB* **Shadows! and** *TS*(2)

27 dreams!]   ~ .   *ENB*
31-36   He . . . away!]   originally the fifth stanza in *NB* with a mar-
                               ginal number to indicate its correct position
31   sleeps;–how]   **sleeps, how**   *NB*   **sleeps:–How**   *ENB*
                      sleeps:–how   *TS*(1), *TS*(3)   **sleeps!–how**
                      TS(2)
32   withdrawn]   ~ ,   *NB*
33   woods,]   ~   *NB*
33   ²these]   **and**   *NB, TS*(1), *TS*(2). Originally *and* in *ENB* and
                      TS(3); *and* crossed through and *these* written above
34   These]   **And**   *NB, TS*(1), *TS*(2). Originally *And* in *ENB* and
                      TS(3); *And* crossed through and *These* written above
34   dawn.]   ~ !   *ENB, TS*(2)
35   ²years!]   ~ !*****   *ENB, TS*(1), *TS*(2)
                      ~ !–   *TS*(4), *Iceberg*
36   have]   **that**   *NB*

Glossary
Westcock: a village in eastern New Brunswick, Roberts' boyhood home
10   *Tantramar:*   see "Tantramar Revisited"

p. 334   TWILIGHT OVER SHAUGAMAUK

The poem was first published in the *Queen's Quarterly* (Spring, 1937); and
later appeared in *Twilight Over Shaugamauk and Three Other Poems,* 1937;
and *Canada Speaks of Britain,* 1941. In addition, an unidentified clipping,
evidently later than the *Queen's Quarterly* text, is in the scrapbook of A.M.
Stephen at the University of British Columbia.

Two holograph manuscripts are contained in the two Roberts notebooks
at the University of New Brunswick. NB has the first two lines dated August
5, 1905. A very rough draft of a first stanza is dated October 15, 1928.
The full text in NB is dated February 18 by the first line, February 25 at
the end of the first stanza, October 18 at the beginning of the third stanza,
and October 20, 1936. ENB is dated October 20, 1936. Still another holograph manuscript is in the Queen's University Archives. It is dated January
23, 1937 and notes that it was transcribed for Lorne Pierce. Three typescripts survive. TS(1) is inscribed for Dora Pomeroy and is pasted into the
copy of *The Iceberg* in the Roberts Collection at the University of New
Brunswick. Both the Pierce manuscript and TS(1) were evidently prepared
before the publication in the *Queen's Quarterly.* TS(2) and TS(3) were prepared for publications of the poem, perhaps for *Twilight Over Shaugamauk
and Three Other Poems* and *Canada Speaks of Britain,* respectively. TS(2)
and TS(3) are in the Queen's University Archives.

Variants

1 The first appearance of this line in *NB*, written *Back to old Sanga-*
mauk / My heart is turning, is dated August 5, 1905. Another beginning is dated October 15, 1928 and reads:

> Back to old Shagamauk
> My heart is turning.
> With old dear memories
> My heart is burning.
> Goodie & Andie & Jim,
> Mumsie, & he, the beloved
> Leader of the Clan, the Boy

All further *NB* references are to the full text of the poem.

1 you]   originally *old* in *NB; old* crossed through and *wild* written
above it
1 Shaugamauk,]   ~   *NB*
1 turning!]   ~ .   *NB, ENB, Pierce MS*
2 Your . . . dusk.]   written above this line, but cancelled, in *NB* is:

> I hear again your shallow rapids call. brawl. spill.
> Call to me, rapidly

2 Your]   **The** *NB*
3 I . . . burning.]   written above this line, but cancelled, in *NB* is:

> I breathe the dew-drenched tamaracks' faint musk,
> And the acrid sweet of the brush fires burning.

3 sniff]   **breathe** *NB, Pierce MS.* Originally *breathe* in *ENB* and
TS(1); *breathe* crossed through and *sniff* added.
3 burning.]   ~ ;   *NB*   ~ ,   *Stephen clipping*
4 breathe]   originally *breathe* in *NB; breathe* crossed through and
sniff written in the margin. Originally *sniff* in *ENB* and
TS(1); *sniff* crossed through and *breathe* added.
sniff *Pierce MS*
4 your]   **the** *NB*
4 poignant]   originally *faint* in *NB; faint* crossed through; below it,
also crossed through, is *cool* and *elusive*. Above *faint*
is *subtle*. Originally *subtle* in *ENB* and *TS*(1). In *ENB*,
subtle is crossed through and written above and below
the word are *poignant, chilly, cool,* and *poignant*
again. At the bottom of the page in *ENB* is: "I
breathe your tamarack's evanescent musk." In *TS*(1),
subtle is crossed through and *poignant* written below it.
subtle *Pierce MS, Queen's Quart.*

5   I . . . appearing]   written above this line, but cancelled, in *NB* is:

> In the pale sky a thin young moon appearing
> Tangled among the spruce tops,
> From the lone cabin in the hillside clearing
> A light shines suddenly to call me home.

Written in the margin beside these lines is:

> A dog's bark echoes softly through my heart.

5   once more]   originally *again* in *ENB; again* crossed through and
                         once more written above it
5   your . . . appearing]   **a . . . appearing,** *NB*
6   Through . . . apart]   **(A sliver of silver), pale, remote, apart**. *NB;*
                         In the margin is: (*Through the black branches*).
6   Through]   **Thro'** *ENB*
7   on]   **in** *NB*
8   faintly]   **softly** *NB*. Originally *softly* in *ENB; softly* lightly
                         crossed through and *faintly* (*?*) written lightly above it
8   through]   **thro'** *ENB*
9   I . . . keeping]   written above this line, but cancelled, in *NB* is:

> I must forget,—but you are unforgetting

10   Some part]   **Something** *NB*
11   My words, my songs, my]   **words my dreams my** *NB*. Originally
                         My thoughts, my words in *ENB; thoughts* crossed through
                         and *songs* written above it. A number 2 and 1 appear above
                         songs and *words,* respectively.
12   Will . . . flow]   following this line in *NB* is an obliterated word
                         followed by *so singing on forever I*
13-14   Waters . . . calling.]   omitted in *NB*
14   hearing]   originally *to hear* in *ENB; to hear* crossed through and
                         hearing written above
14   shallows]   **shadows** *TS*(3), *CSOB*. In Roberts' copy of *Canada*
                         Speaks of Britain at the University of New Brunswick,
                         d has been crossed through and *ll* written over it.

Glossary
Shaugamauk: a stream north of Fredericton, flowing into the St. John
                River.

The poem was first published in the *Dalhousie Review* (1937-38); and later appeared in *Twilight Over Shaugamauk and Three Other Poems,* 1937; and *Canada Speaks of Britain,* 1941.

Two holograph manuscripts are contained in the two Roberts notebooks at the University of New Brunswick. In NB, lines 1-8 are dated Febraury 14, lines 9-12 are dated February 16, and lines 13-28 are dated February 17, 1937. Also in NB is the note "last stanza fundamentally changed Feb. 24/37." ENB is dated February 24, 1937.

Seven typescripts survive. TS(1) through TS(5) are all apparently earlier than any printed text. TS(6) and TS(7) were apparently made after the publication of *Twilight Over Shaugamauk* but before the publication of *Canada Speaks of Britain.* TS(2) is autographed and is in the Roberts Collection at the University of New Brunswick. In the same collection is TS(5), autographed and with the note "For Dora Pomeroy. C.G.D.R." TS(5) is added as an insert in *The Iceberg and Other Poems.* TS(3) is autographed and is located in the Lloyd Roberts Collection at the University of New Brunswick. TS(1), TS(4), TS(6), and TS(7) are in the Queen's University Archives; all except TS(7) are autographed.

Variants

Note: *TS(6)* and *TS(7)* have the never printed sub-title *Spain, 1937.*

1   borders]   **marge**   *NB;* in parenthesis at the end of the line is:

Along the borders of evening

2   cool.]   ~ ;   *NB, Dal. Rev.*
4   pool.]   ~ ;   *NB, TS(2), Dal. Rev.*
5   the]   **their**   *ENB, TS(1)*
5   through]   **thro'**   *ENB, TS(1), TOS*
6   The]   originally *Thro' the* in *ENB; Thro'* cancelled
6   one;]   ~ ,   *NB*
7   lusty]   originally *slow stepping* in *NB; slow stepping* crossed through and *lusty* written above it
7   lad]   originally *boy* in *NB; boy* crossed through and *hand* written above it; *hand* then crossed through and *boy* rewritten below the original word
7   free]   omitted in *NB*
8   For soon]   originally *Because* in *NB; Because* crossed through and *For soon* written above it
9   war-torn]   originally *troubled* in *NB;* in the margin, dated February 27, is *In war-torn lands afar.* Originally *troubled* in *ENB; troubled* crossed through and *war-torn* written above and below it.   **troubled**   *TS(1), TS(2), TS(3), TS(4), TS(5), Dal. Rev., TOS*

Originally *troubled* in *TS*(6); *troubled* crossed through and *war-torn* written above it.

10 Red ... fade] crossed through above this line in *NB* is:

Some other where, not here

10 fade.] ~ ; *TS*(2), *Dal. Rev.*
11 Temples ... down] crossed through above this line in *NB* is:

And towers & temples

11 down] ~ , *NB*
12 dismayed.] **afraid**; *NB*
13 loud] **hoarse** *NB*
13 shouting,] ~ ; *ENB, TS*(1), *TOS*
14 bleed and] **mad with** *NB*
15 The ... sod,–] **Then the blood soaks into the sand.** *NB; Then* cancelled and rewritten; *soaks* written above *sinks* which has been crossed through
16 Then ... quiet] **And at last falls quiet** *NB;* originally *And falls, at last, quiet; at last* crossed through in first version, added with a caret in second; *comes* written under *falls,* but *falls* is not cancelled.
16 Then] originally *Then* in *ENB; Then* crossed through and *And* written above it
17-28 On ... done] a note in *NB* says "last stanza fundamentally changed Feb 24/37." The original, cancelled, stanza is:

The cows stray out in the pasture
 Under the sicker moon
The farm hand whistles light hearted
 For soon his toil is done
Tomorrow he'll sweat at the plow again
 And rest at the fall of dew;
And still the frogs will go on piping
 As when old Earth was new.

In the third line, *hand* is written above *boy* and in the sixth line *at* is written above *till; boy* and *till* have been cancelled.

18 face.] ~ ; *TS*(2), *Dal. Rev.*
19 sly] ~ , *ENB, TS*(1), *TS*(2), *TS*(3), *TS*(4), *TS*(5), *Dal. Rev., TOS, TS*(6)

27   from fields]   *the* added with a caret in *ENB* and *TS*(6); *the* then
                        crossed through.   **from the fields**   *TS*(3),
                        TS(4), *Dal. Rev.*   Originally *from the fields* in
                        TS(5); *the* crossed through
27   fields–]   ~ ,   *ENB, TS*(1), *TOS*

p. 335 AS DOWN THE WOODLAND WAYS

The poem was first published in the *Queen's Quarterly* (1937); and later
appeared in *Twilight Over Shaugamauk and Three Other Poems*, 1937; *Canada
Speaks of Britain*, 1941; *Twentieth Century Canadian Poetry*, 1953; and
Canadian Anthology, 1966.

Two holograph manuscripts survive in the two Roberts notebooks at the
University of New Brunswick. NB is a fragment containing stanzas one and
two, six lines not used in the final text, and a draft of the final couplet. NB
is dated February 5, 1936 over the first two lines; March 11 appears beside
the third line. ENB is dated March 31, 1937, and "Queen's Quarterly" is
written at the bottom of the poem.

Five typescripts survive. TS(1) is autographed by Roberts and is in the
Roberts Collection at the University of New Brunswick. TS(2) is inserted in
the copy of *The Iceberg and Other Poems* at the University of New Brunswick; it is autographed and also inscribed "For Dora Pomeroy. C.G.D.R."
TS(3) and TS(4) are in the Queen's University Archives; both were probably
prepared for a publication of the poem. TS(3) is autographed. TS(5) was included in a letter, dated January 4, 1941, to Ralph Gustafson. TS(5) is
autographed.

Variants
1   As . . . went]   **As I went down the woodland way**   *NB; woodland*
                        way written above *forest path* which has been
                        crossed through
2   asleep]   ~ ,   *TS*(1)
3   felt]   originally *heard* in *NB; heard* crossed through and *felt*
                written above it
3   surge]   originally *stir* in *NB; stir* crossed through and *surge*
                written above it
3   endless]   added with a caret in *NB*
3   life]   following this word in *NB* and crossed through are *invisible,*
                unseen, and another word which has been obliterated
5   urge]   **stir**   *NB*
5   quickening mould]   **mould & dew**   *NB*
5   quickening]   **living**   *TS*(1), *TS*(2)
6   had been once]   **once had been**   *NB*
                        had been, once   *Queen's Quart.*
7   Mount . . . again]   **Slow   mounting to the bloom again**   *NB*

610

7	to bloom again]	**again to bloom** *ENB*
8	At]	**In** *TS*(1)
8	its]	**their** *NB*
9-18	I . . . same:—]	omitted in *NB*
10	decay,]	~ *ENB, TS*(1), *TS*(2)
11	pillared]	**spires of** *TS*(1), *TS*(2)
12	On]	originally *In* in *ENB* and *TS*(1); *In* crossed through and *On* written in the margin
14	crawling, perished]	*perished, crawling* in *ENB* with a line and a note to transpose the order. **perished, crawling** *TS*(1)
17	through]	**thro'** *TS*(1), *TS*(2)
18	same:—]	~ : *ENB*
19	pang]	**pangs** *NB.* Originally *pangs* in *TS*(1); *s* crossed through
19	life]	**chance** *NB*
20	Destruction]	originally *Distraction* in *TS*(2); *i* and *ra* crossed through, *e* and *ru* written in the margin to correct the obvious typographical error
20	a name]	**rebirth** *NB; rebirth* written above two obliterated words, but not *a name*
20	name.]	~ ! *ENB, TS*(1)
Note:	Written across the margin of *NB* is:	

> Life, not death, it is that lays its finger on
> all that hath being
> Death but the mask of life,
> The change from life to life.
>
> When life was launched it contained
> at its heart the divine seed of discontent.

p. 336 TWO RIVERS

The poem was initially published in the *Dalhousie Review* (1937-38); and was later included in *Twilight Over Shaugamauk and Three Other Poems*, 1937; *Canada Speaks of Britain*, 1941; and *Selected Poetry and Critical Prose*, 1974.

Two holograph manuscripts are contained in the two Roberts notebooks at the University of New Brunswick. NB is variously dated—March 20, 1937 at the beginning of the poem, April 3 beside line 7, April 20 beside line 46, May 2 beside line 49, May 12 beside line 59, May 16 and 17 beside line 73, and May 18 at the end of the poem. ENB is dated May 18, 1937. As well, two typescripts survive. TS(1) is in the Lloyd Roberts Collection at the University of New Brunswick. TS(1) is autographed by Roberts and is apparently earlier than any printed text. TS(2) is in the Queen's University Archives and was prepared for the publication of *Canada Speaks of Britain* as evidenced by its proof marks and "Recent Miscellaneous Poems" written above the title.

Variants

Sub-title: St.] **Saint** *Dal. Rev., TOS.* Originally *Saint* in *TS*(2); *Saint* crossed through and *St.* written above it. *NB* has no sub-title.

1   heart]   ~ , *NB*

2   And . . . leave]   originally *Wherever I may be* in *NB; Wherever . . . be* crossed through and *And neither can I leave* written beside it

3   When . . . long]   originally *And whose memory lingers long with one* in *NB; And* cancelled; *lingers* cancelled and *stays too* written above it. In the margin is *loiters with one too long*

4   tugs my sleeve]   originally *calls to me* in *NB; calls to me* cancelled and *tugs my sleeve* written in the margin. Under *tugs* is written *plucks.*

4   tugs]   originally *tugs* in *ENB; plucks* is crossed through above *tugs* which has not been cancelled

4   The . . . sleeve.]   three cancelled lines follow in *NB:*

> Wherever I may roam.
> One urges me to wandering
> The other calls me home.

5   my blood and bone]   originally *my blood & bone* in *NB; very* added with a caret between *my* and *blood; & bone* crossed through

6   will]   **shall** *NB.* Originally *shall* in *ENB; shall* crossed through and *will* written above it

7   Along]   originally *In my* in *NB; In my* crossed through and *Within* written above; *Within* then cancelled and *Along* written beside it

8   incessantly]   originally *unceasingly* in *NB; incessantly* written, in parenthesis, beside *unceasingly*

10   And]   originally *Urges* in *NB; And* written over *Urges*

10   fickle]   originally *fickle* in *NB; fickle* crossed through and an undecipherable word written below it

11   strange desires]   originally *hot unrest* in *NB; unrest* crossed through and *desires* written above it

13   The . . . flood]   written across the margin, with a line drawn to below *The . . . flood* is:

> Would win me back from wandering
> My boyhood's fickle counsellor

13   a . . . flood]   originally *tranquil, proud, true* in *NB; tranquil . . .*
                            true crossed through and *a strong & tranquil* written
                            beside it

13   flood]   originally followed by a comma in *ENB;* comma crossed
                            through

14   breast,]   ~ *Dal. Rev., TOS.* Comma added in the margin of
                      TS(2)

16   desire with rest]   originally *my feet with peace* in *NB; my feet*
                                  crossed through and *desire* written above;
                                  peace crossed through and *rest,* in parenthesis,
                                  written beside it

17-20   To . . . change,–]   There are three roughly comparable versions
       of this stanza in *NB.* In its proper sequence is:

> Tantramar, Tantramar
>   Because I played beside
> Your flutter and ebb & flow
>   And chased your wandering tide,

Above the first line, *my moonstruck* is written, but the entire
stanza is crossed through. Written across the margin is:

> Tantramar. Tantramar.
> The moon on Tantramar
>   I see once more
> across the estranging, changing years
> Past Sackville to the sea
> Past Westcock to the sea
> You & the new moon, hand in hand,
> Twin arbiters of change

In the second line, *moon on* was originally *moonlight over;*
light and *over* have been cancelled and *on* written above *over.*
In the fifth line, *to the sea* is cancelled and two or three undecipherable words followed by *round* are written above. All
of the lines are then cancelled. Out of sequence, but with a
marginal number to indicate its correct position is:

> To you, my moonled Tantramar
>   I turn, who taught my feet to range,–
> You & the vagrant moon conspiring,
>   Twin arbiters of change

In the first line, *moonled* was originally *moonstruck; struck*
was cancelled and *led* written above it. In the third line, *vagrant
moon conspiring* is written above *moon ever whirling* which has
not been cancelled.

21   To . . . Tantramar]   originally *Tantramar, my Tantramar* in *NB;*
              Tantramar, my crossed through and *My wild*
              momentous written above
23   wastes . . . green]   originally *long, green, winding dykes* in *NB;*
              long . . . dykes crossed through and *wind-swept wastes*
              of green written above
25   floods . . . tumbling]   originally *waters flooding* in *NB; waters*
              flooding crossed through and *floods come tumbling*
              written above
26   fill]   **brim**   *NB.* Originally *brim* in *ENB; brim* crossed through
              and *fill* written above it
28   afloat.]   originally followed by a semi-colon in *ENB;* semi-colon
              altered to period
29   venturing]   originally *faltering* in *NB; faltering* crossed through
              and *venturing* written above it
31   with . . . sea]   originally *back rolling to the sea* in *NB; back rolling*
              crossed through and *with laughter back* written
              above; *the* cancelled
33-40   Far . . . run]   These stanzas are reversed in *NB* with marginal
              numbers to indicate their correct position.
33   Far . . . farms]   **Through Midgic's far green farms**   *NB*
34   And . . . fill]   **And for a moment are still**   *NB*
35   back]   originally *back* in *NB; back* crossed through and *down*
              written above it
37   Draining . . . red]   originally *Heave empty* in *NB; And Heaving*
              written in the margin; *Heave empty* crossed
              through and *your vast red* written above
39   You tremble down the]   **Aghast within your**   *NB*
39   gleaming]   originally *gaping* in *ENB; gaping* crossed through and
              gleaming written above it
40   whimper]   originally *whisper* in *ENB; s* altered to *m*
40   run;]   ~ .   *NB*
41   But, . . . repenting]   **But . . . repenting,**   *NB*
42   roar]   originally *shout* in *ENB; shout* crossed through and *roar*
              written above it
42   again]   originally *to brim* in *NB; to brim* crossed through and
              again written above
43   brim]   originally *fill* in *ENB; fill* crossed through and *brim* written
              above it
43   dykes]   **channels**   *NB*
45   estranging, . . . years,]   **estranging . . . years**   *NB*
46-48   Blind . . . Tantramar]   in *NB:*

              You draw & drive me, Tantramar,
              Content alone in discontent,
              Blind puppet of my restless star.

614

Part III St.]   **Saint**   *Dal. Rev., TOS.* Originally *Saint* in *TS*(2); *Saint*
                  crossed through and *St.* written above it

49-54   To . . . stream]   above the revised lines, and dated May 2, 1937,
                  in *NB* is:

> [1]   To you I turn, to you I turn again,
> [2]   Always with deep joy I turn St. John
> [3]   To you great river, constant tide,
>
> [4]   To you I turn, to you I turn again,
> [5]   With deepest joy I turn
> [6]   To you, St. John, great river, constant tide
> [7]   Breast full of memories & dreams beside
> [8]   Whose green banks I was born.
>
> [9]   A babe I left you, & a youth returned
> [10]   To where my kinfolk dwell

In the first line, *est* has been cancelled at the end of *deep*. In
the third line, *great river, constant tide* is written below *my
strong & constant tide* which has been cancelled. The fifth
line originally began with *Always* but it has been crossed
through. In the sixth line, *St. John* is added with a caret
between *you* and *great* and cancelled at the end of the line;
tide is written above *stream* which has been crossed through.
In the eighth line, *green banks* is written, in parenthesis,
below *waters* which has been cancelled. The revised stanza,
approximately as it now stands, follows in *NB*.

49   again, St. John]   originally *St. John again* in *NB*; *St. John* crossed
                  through before *again* and rewritten after

50   tide,–]   ~ , *NB*

50   tide]   originally *tide* in *ENB*; *floods* is crossed through above
                  tide which is not cancelled

51   With . . . you]   originally *To you with deepest joy* in *NB*; a line
                  then drawn to move *To you* after *joy*

51   a full heart]   originally *deepest joy* in *ENB*; *deepest joy* crossed
                  through and *joy & trust* written above; *joy & trust*
                  then cancelled and *a full heart* written below the
                  original phrase

53   A . . . youth]   written in the margin of *NB* is:

> A babe I left you & a youth returned,

54   you,]   added with a caret in *ENB*

56   dream.]   ~ ; *NB*

57-68   Your . . . moon.]   These stanzas were composed in the order
4, 5, 3 in *NB;* a marginal number properly
locates the third stanza

57   Your broad]   originally *My little city* in *NB; My . . . city* crossed
through and *Your blue* written beside it

57   tide sweeps]   **tides sweep**   *TS*(1)

59-60   where . . . dead]   at the top of the page in *NB* containing the
St. John section of the poem is:

Where sleeps the dust, where sleeps
The dust of my beloved dead.

And, written across the margin is:

Forever unforgotten sleeps the dust
Of my beloved dead.

61   withdrawn]   originally *you draw* in *NB; you draw* crossed through
and *withdrawn* written above

62   from the wash]   originally *amber clear* in *NB; amber clear* crossed
through and *from the wash* written beside it

64   Swamps]   originally *Dark swamps* in *NB; Dark* cancelled and
initial *s* of *swamps* capitalized

65   From]   originally *And* in *NB; And* crossed through and *From*
written above it

65   far and]   **little**   *NB*

68   alien]   **waning**   *NB.* In *Dal. Rev., TOS, TS*(2), and *CSOB,*
Roberts has included the note, "The sources of the St.
John are in Maine."

68   Under . . . moon.]   Four partially legible lines and one obliterated
line follow in *NB.* Also, an arrow is drawn to
locate the lines above line 61, but all five
lines are cancelled.

From many a < > tide you take
And many a tribute stream flows in
    To swell your long tide flood lapping to the far off sea
    Tribute ? on your long course to sea
    < . . . . >

70   fortunate]   **tranquil**   *NB.*   Originally *tranquil* in *ENB; tranquil*
crossed through and *fortunate* written above it

71   the barrier heights]   originally *your bulwark hills* in *NB; your*
cancelled and *the* written above it

71   barrier]   originally *bulwark* in *ENB; bulwark* crossed through
and *barrier* written above it

616

71   heights]   originally *heights* in *ENB; hills* is crossed through above
                  heights which is not cancelled

73   guard]   ~ , *ENB*

74   While]   **Where** *NB*

74   Fundy's]   *'s* added in the margin of *TS*(2)

74   floods]   **tides** *NB*. Originally *tides* in *ENB; tides* crossed through
                    and *floods* written above it

77   that]   **the** *NB*

78   first the Ships of Freedom]   **erst the ships of freedom** *NB*.
                  Originally *erst the ships of freedom* in *ENB; erst* altered
                  to *first; s* and *f* capitalized

79   begirt]   originally *begirt* in *ENB; begirt* crossed through and *engirt*
                  written beside it; *engirt* then cancelled and *begirt*
                  rewritten beside it. Originally *engirt* in *TS*(1); *en* crossed
                  through and *be* written above it

80   bears]   originally *bears* in *NB;* altered to *wears*. Originally *wears*
                  in *ENB; wears* crossed through and *bears* written above it

81   rock-bound]   **rock-based** *NB*

82   birthright]   **origin** *NB*

82   still,]   ~ ! *NB*

83   fronts]   originally *confronts* in *NB; con* crossed through

83   o'er mastering]   in *NB conspiring* is written above *o'er mastering*
                  which has not been cancelled

85   River]   **river** *NB*

86   endless]   *endless* is written above *unending* in *ENB;* but *unending*
                  has not been cancelled

87   will come back]   **shall return** *NB*. Originally *shall return* in
                  ENB; will is cancelled above *shall* which is not crossed
                  through; *return* is cancelled, and crossed through above
                  and below it are *I'll turn on back; again* is written above
                  on and *turn back; come back* is then written at the
                  end of the line

Glossary

33   *Midgic's farms:*   Midgic is a village north of Sackville

35   *Sackville's studious halls:*   Mount Allison University is located in
                  Sackville

58   *Where . . . bred:*   Roberts is alluding either to the Loyalists' settle-
                  ment of Fredericton or to his personal experiences
                  in the city

63   *Temiscouata:*   Lake Temiscouata is in Quebec, just north of the
                  Maine border

64   *Allegash:*   the St. John River begins in the Allegash Lake in
                  northern Maine and the Allegash River joins the St.
                  John while it is still in Maine

78-80   *Where . . . fame:*   the first Loyalists landed at the city of St.
John, and the city still bears the appellation
The Loyalist City

p. 339 PEACE WITH DISHONOUR

The poem first appeared in *Saturday Night* (October 1, 1938); and was later published in the *Canadian Poetry Magazine* (December 3, 1938); *Canada Speaks of Britain,* 1941; and *Selected Poetry and Critical Prose,* 1974.

Two holograph manuscripts are contained in the two Roberts notebooks at the University of New Brunswick. NB is dated September 18 at the top and September 20, 1938 at the bottom. ENB is dated September 20, 1938.

Five typescripts survive. TS(1) is in the Lloyd Roberts Collection at the University of New Brunswick. It is autographed by Roberts and is addressed "For Leila. Love from C.G.D.R." TS(2) is in the Roberts Collection at the University of New Brunswick and is autographed. TS(1) and TS(2) are apparently earlier than any printed text. TS(3), also in the Roberts Collection, is apparently later than the text in *Saturday Night.* It is addressed "For Roderick Kennedy,—Greetings & regards! Yours ever Charles G.D. Roberts." TS(4), in the Queen's University Archives, is evidently later than the *Canadian Poetry Magazine* text, and TS(5), also in the Queen's University Archives, was prepared for the publication of *Canada Speaks of Britain.*

Variants

Title: Peace With Dishonour]   **In Time of Despondency**   *NB, TS*(1),
TS(2), *Sat. Night.* Originally *In Time of Despondency*
in *ENB; In . . . Despondency* crossed through and
Peace—With Dishonour written above it

1   The . . . woman,]   above this line in *NB* is a cancelled first stanza:

Outside the wind sobs in the dead spruce
Tapping my window pane.
Its branches tap my window pane.
One dead branch taps my window pane.
The slow rain Drips endlessly the slow reluctant rain
The tale of Earth's misuse
Bewailing

In the first line *dead* is written above *old* which has been crossed through. In the third line *Its* is written in the margin before *Whose* which has been cancelled. In the fifth line an undecipherable word is written under *endlessly* and *slow* is written under *dull. The slow rain* and *The tale of* are crossed through in the fifth and sixth lines respectively. In *ENB* is:

Outside the wind sobs in the dead spruce.
A dead branch taps my window pane.
Drips sullenly the dull, reluctant rain,
Bewailing Earth's misuse.

Above *Bewailing,* which has not been cancelled, is *Lamenting.*
There is a marginal note to omit this stanza in *ENB*. See "In
Time of Earth's Misuse".

1   woman]   **women**   *TS*(1), *TS*(2), *Sat. Night, TS*(3), *Can. Poetry
          Mag.* Originally *women* in *TS*(4) and *TS*(5); *e* altered
          to *a* in both cases

2   bomb]   originally *bombs* in *NB; s* crossed through

3   stricken,]   ~   *TS*(2), *Sat. Night, TS*(3)

3   death–]   ~ ,–   *TS*(1), *TS*(2), *TS*(3), *Can. Poetry Mag.*
          ~ .   *Sat. Night*

4   These . . . human!]   **These are but human.**   *NB*

4   These, alas]   **These, these, alas**   *Sat. Night*

4   human!]   ~ .   *TS*(1), *TS*(2), *Sat. Night, TS*(3), *Can. Poetry Mag.*

5   sinks–]   ~ ,   *NB*   ~ ,–   *ENB, TS*(1), *TS*(2), *Sat. Night,
          TS*(3), *Can. Poetry Mag.*

6   pass]   ~ ,   *NB*

6   sick]   originally *sickening* in *ENB* and *TS*(3); *ening* crossed
          through   **sickening**   *TS*(1), *TS*(2), *Sat. Night*

7   Time's]   **the years'**   *NB*

7   stream.]   ~ .–   *ENB, TS*(1), *TS*(2), *TS*(3), *Can. Poetry Mag.*

8   Oh]   originally *Ah* in *ENB; Ah* crossed through and *Oh* written
          above it

9   oh]   added with a caret in *NB*

9   oh]   originally *ah* in *ENB; a* altered to *o*   **ah**   *TS*(1), *TS*(2)
          Ah   *Sat. Night*

9   soul.]   ~ !   *NB, ENB, TS*(1), *TS*(2), *Sat. Night, TS*(3), *Can.
          Poetry Mag.*

10 dishonour brief, cowed]   **dishonour brief cowed**   *NB*
          dishonour, a brief, cowed   *TS*(1), *TS*(2), *Sat. Night*
          Originally *dishonour, a brief, cowed* in *TS*(3); *a*
          crossed through   **dishonour, brief, cowed**   *Can.*
          Poetry Mag.

10 peace.]   ~ ,   *NB*

11 Freedom]   **freedom**   *ENB, TS*(1), *TS*(2), *Sat. Night, TS*(3),
          Can. Poetry Mag.

11 pack.]   ~ ;–   *NB*   ~ .–   *TS*(1), *TS*(3), *Can. Poetry Mag.*
          ~ ,–   *TS*(2)

12 This endures.]   added in the margin of *NB*

12 This]   **–This**   *ENB, Sat. Night*

12 For]   originally *for* in *NB; for* crossed through

12 this cringes] **this must cringes** *ENB; must* crossed through and
         s presumably added to *cringe*
         this must cringe *TS*(1), *TS*(2), *TS*(3)

p. 339 IN TIME OF EARTH'S MISUSE

The poem was first published in *Maclean's Magazine* (March, 1940); and was reprinted only in *Canada Speaks of Britain,* 1941.

 Two holograph manuscripts are contained in the two Roberts notebooks at the University of New Brunswick. In NB, two related lines are dated March 16, 1936, and the full poem is dated February 8, 1940. ENB is dated February 9, 1940. Three typescripts survive. The first is in the Lloyd Roberts Collection (**LRC**) at the University of New Brunswick; it is unsigned and undated but was evidently prepared after the publication in *Maclean's.* TS(1) and TS(2) are in the Queen's University Archives, and both were prepared for the publication of *Canada Speaks of Britain.* TS(1) has only the first two stanzas as the page ends at that point.

Variants

Title: Misuse] originally *Distress* in *NB* and *ENB; Distress* crossed
       through and *Misuse* added

Note: In *NB,* dated March 16, 1936, are the lines:

Outside the wind sobs in the old spruce
The voice of Earth's unrest.

     All further *NB* references are to the full text, dated February 8, 1940.

1 spruce.] ~ , *LRC*
3 Drips] originally *Drips sullenly* in *NB; sullenly* cancelled
3-4 Drips . . . grieves,] a single line in *NB*
5 misuse–] ~ ; *NB* ~ ,– *ENB* ~ , *LRC*
6 Lamenting] originally *Lamenting* in *NB; Lamenting* crossed
       through and *Bewailing* written above it
6 blood-lust] **blood lust** *LRC*
7 spew] originally *drool* in *NB; drool* crossed through and *spew*
     written above it
7 spew] **spread** *LRC*
7 the] omitted in *LRC, TS*(1), *TS*(2)
8 stretch . . . hands,] **lift maimed hands to heaven** *NB*
8 stretch] originally *lift* in *ENB; lift* crossed through and *stretch*
     written above it
8 heaven] **Heaven** *LRC*
8 hands,] ~ *ENB, LRC*
9 shriek] **cry** *NB.* Originally *cry* in *ENB; shriek* written above *cry*

10   oh]   **Oh**   *Maclean's, TS*(2)
10   alas–]   **alas,** *NB*   **alas!–** *ENB*   **Alas** *LRC*
                 Alas– *Maclean's, TS*(2)
11   What if too late?–]   **–Now, perhaps,–** *NB.* Originally *Never*
                 perhaps! in *ENB; Never perhaps!* crossed through and
                 What . . . late?– written above it.
                 Never perhaps– *Maclean's*
11   Thrust]   **thrust** *LRC*
12   rust!]   ∼. *NB*
Note: In *TS*(1), *TS*(2), and *Canada Speaks of Britain* Roberts has
         appended the note: "When this poem was written it was aimed
         in bitter protest at the neutrals. Since then the scene has changed.
         There are no more neutrals. The United States is an undeclared
         ally. The protest has no longer any point. I include the verses
         merely as a matter of record."

p. 340 FORGET NOT, THOU

The poem was first published in *Saturday Night* (July, 1940); and was reprinted only in *Canada Speaks of Britain*, 1941.

Two holograph manuscripts are contained in the two Roberts notebooks
at the University of New Brunswick. NB is dated May 12 at the beginning
and May 26 and 27, 1940, at the end of the poem. ENB is dated May 27,
1940. Three typescripts are contained in the Queen's University Archives.
TS(1) is signed by Roberts and is apparently earlier than the text in *Saturday
Night*. TS(2) and TS(3) were prepared for the publication of *Canada Speaks
of Britain*.

Variants
Title: Forget Not, Thou]   *NB* is untitled. *ENB* has the titles *Prayer
          in Time of Dejection* and *Too Long We Wait*. In *TS*(1)
          Prayer in Time of Dejection is written above *Too Long
          We Wait*. The title in *Saturday Night* is *Too Long We
          Wait*. The original title in *TS*(2) is *Too Long We Wait;
          Too . . . Wait* is crossed through and *Forget Not, Thou*
          is written above it.
1   not, Thou]   **not Thou,** *NB*
1-2   Forget . . . Mine.]   a single line in *NB*
2   Mine]   **mine**   *TS*(1)
2-3   I . . . Thou,]   a single line in *NB*
3   not Thou,]   **not, Thou** *NB*
4   Compassion!]   ∼. *NB*
5-6   The . . . overflowing!]   a single line in *NB*
7   (Thou . . . now!)]   **Thou . . . now!** *NB*
7   Thou God]   **Thou, God,** *ENB*

621

9   they]   **Thy children**   *NB*
10   Thy children,]   omitted in *NB*
11   obscene . . . reviles]   **Mad . . . mocks**   *NB*
11   name]   **Name**   *TS*(1), *Sat. Night*
12-18   And . . . long!]   in *NB* the last lines are:

> And boasts his shame
> And treads down mother & babe
> In the bloody spew of his hate?
> O God who seest all, too long we wait!
> Forget not Thou.

13   down, mother]   **down, down, mother**   *ENB, TS*(1), *Sat. Night,*
TS(2). Originally *down, down, mother* in *TS*(3);
second *down* crossed through

16   all,]   ~   *ENB, TS*(1), *Sat. Night, TS*(2), *TS*(3)

p. 340 CANADA TO FRANCE

The poem was first published in *Saturday Night* (July, 1940); and later appeared in the *Canadian Poetry Magazine* (September, 1940); and *Canada Speaks of Britain*, 1941.

Two holograph manuscripts are contained in the two Roberts notebooks at the University of New Brunswick. NB is dated June 26 at the beginning and June 30, 1940 at the end of the poem. ENB is dated June 30, 1940. Three typescripts survive. TS(1) and TS(2) are in the Queen's University Archives. TS(1) is dated June 30, 1940, but it was evidently prepared after the publication of the poem in *Saturday Night* and the *Canadian Poetry Magazine*. TS(2) was prepared for the publication of *Canada Speaks of Britain*. TS(3) was included in a letter to Ralph Gustafson, dated January 4, 1941, but it is based on an earlier text of the poem.

Variants

Title: Canada to France]   **To France, June 1940**   *NB, Sat. Night,*
Can. Poetry Mag., TS(3). Originally *To
France, June 1940* in *ENB; Canada* added
with a caret before *to.*

1   upon]   **unto**   *NB*
2   our France]   added with a caret in *NB*
2   bright]   above this word, but cancelled, in *ENB* is *great*
5   From dotards]   originally *From cowards and dotards* in *NB;
cowards* crossed through and *slothful* written
above; *slothful* then cancelled
5   butchering]   originally *obscene* in *NB; obscene* crossed through;
crossed through as well are *assassin's* and *beast's;*

622

Black Butcher's is written above *obscene*. Originally
Mad Beast's in *ENB*; *Mad Beast's* crossed through;
obscene written above and then cancelled; *butchering*
written above

6   "Honour"]   **Honour**   *NB*

6   slit]   originally *cut* in *NB; cut* crossed through and *slit* written
above it

6   throat!–]   ~ .   *NB*   ~ !   *Sat. Night*

7   Never for]   originally *Not* in *NB; Not* crossed through and *Never
for* written above it

7   cowed traitors]   originally *foresworn and craven* in *NB; foresworn
and craven* crossed through and *cowed traitors*
written above it

8   The right]   **Title**   *NB*

9   Upon]   **Over**   *NB*

9   brought]   originally *bowed* in *ENB; bowed* crossed through and
brought written above it

9   low]   originally *down* in *NB; down* crossed through and *low*
written above it

10   homes]   originally *houses* in *ENB; houses* crossed through and
homes written above it

10   soul enchained]   originally *children weeping* in *NB; weeping*
crossed through and *slain* written beside it.
Originally *children starve* in *ENB; children
starve* crossed through and *soul enchained*
written above.   **children slain**   *TS*(3)

11   But . . . know]   cancelled above this line in *NB* is:

But courage!

11   darkest]   **blackest**   *NB*. Originally *blackest* in *ENB; blackest*
crossed through and *darkest* written above it

12   that . . . stained]   **shall redeem from stain**   *NB, TS*(3).
Originally *shall redeem from stained* in *ENB;
that* added with a caret; *redeem from* crossed
through and *purge thy* written above; *ed*
crossed through in *stained*

13   Banner, and above]   originally *Thy Flag, their honour,* in *NB;
their honour,* crossed through and *banner
& above* written above

13   Banner]   **Thy banner**   *ENB, TS*(3)

14   See]   **Watch**   *NB, Sat. Night, TS*(3). Originally *Watch* in *ENB;
Watch* crossed through and *See* written above it

p. 341 THE RAVAGED LANDS

The poem was first published in *Saturday Night* (August, 1940); and later appeared in the *Canadian Poetry Magazine* (September, 1940); and *Canada Speaks of Britain,* 1941.

Two holograph manuscripts are contained in the two Roberts notebooks at the University of New Brunswick. NB has a cancelled first stanza dated May 12, 1940. The revised first stanza and stanzas two and three are dated May 16; stanzas four and five are dated July 21; and stanza six is dated July 28, 1940. In ENB, stanzas one through five are dated July 22; a cancelled stanza six is dated July 28; and the revised stanza six is dated July 29, 1940. Three typescripts survive. TS(1), autographed, is included in a letter to Ralph Gustafson, dated January 4, 1941. TS(2) and TS(3) are in the Queen's University Archives. TS(2) is signed by Roberts and contains the revised title in his hand. TS(3) was prepared for the publication of *Canada Speaks of Britain.*

Variants

Title: The Ravaged Lands]   **Poland, May, 1940**   *NB. ENB* has three
           titles: *The Ravaged Lands, Not Here Comes Spring,*
           and *The Trail of the Hun.*   **Not Here Comes Spring**
           Sat. Night, Can. Poetry Mag.   *TS*(1) has the *Not*
           Here Comes Spring and the sub-title *For Poland, 1941.*
           The original title in *TS*(2) is *Not Here Comes Spring;*
           Not . . . Spring is crossed through and *The Ravaged*
           Lands (Poland, 1939-40) is written above it.

Note: In *NB*, a cancelled stanza, dated May 12, reads:

           Oh, not this year comes Spring
              To the ravaged lands
           Gutted with fire, laid waste
              By ravaging hands.

           All further *NB* references are to the full text, dated June 16,
           July 28 and 29, 1940.

1   Oh,]   ~   *ENB*
1   spring]   **Spring**   *NB, ENB, Sat. Night, Can. Poetry Mag., TS*(1),
                           TS(2), *TS*(3)
2   darkened]   originally *scourged* in *NB; scourged* crossed through
                   and *darkened* written above it
5   Not]   originally *Oh not* in *NB; Oh* cancelled and *n* altered to *N*
7   blooms and wings]   originally *blooms and wings* in *NB;* altered
                           to *wings and blooms.*   **wings and blooms**
                           Can. Poetry Mag.
10   summer's]   **Summer's**   *NB, ENB, Sat. Night, TS*(1)
10   breath:–]   ~ :   *NB*

12	Deep]	originally *And* in *NB; And* crossed through and *Deep* written above it
12	death!]	~ . *NB, ENB, Can. Poetry Mag.*
13	fields–]	~ , *NB*
14	women's]	**woman's** *Sat. Night, Can. Poetry Mag., TS*(1)
14	weeping]	~ , *ENB*
15	children's starving]	**starved children's** *NB*
15	cries]	~ , *ENB*
17	Oh,]	omitted in *NB*
17	bitter]	originally *grim* in *ENB; grim* crossed through and *bitter* written above it
18	(Far off]	**Afar** *NB*
18	off,]	~ *Can. Poetry Mag.*
18	fated,)]	~) *NB* ~ , *Can. Poetry Mag.*
19	will not be assuaged]	**shall not die** *NB*
19	will]	originally *shall* in *NB; shall* crossed through and *will* written above it
20	sated,–]	~ . *NB, Sat. Night*
21-24	Till . . . paid.]	a cancelled stanza in *ENB* reads:

Till at last has come the hour
So long delayed
When the bitter score shall be,
To the utter most, paid.

A revised stanza follows in *ENB*

21	comes at length]	**as last has come** *NB*
22	(Too]	**So** *NB, ENB*
22	delayed)]	~ , *NB* ~ *ENB*
23	grim]	**bitter** *NB.* Originally *bitter* in *ENB; bitter* crossed through and *grim* written above it
24	last tear]	originally *uttermost* in *NB; To the last tear* written below the line.

p. 342 CANADA SPEAKS OF BRITAIN

The poem was first published in *Maclean's Magazine* (October 1, 1940); and later appeared in *Voices of Victory,* 1941; *Canada Speaks of Britain,* 1941; *Flying Colours,* 1942; and *An Anthology of Canadian Poetry,* 1942.

Two holograph manuscripts are contained in the two Roberts notebooks at the University of New Brunswick, and a third manuscript is in the Lloyd Roberts Collection. NB is dated July 28, 1940 at the top and August 18, 1940 at the bottom. ENB is dated August 19, 1940.

Three typescripts survive. TS(1) is dated August 19, 1940 and is in the Queen's University Archives; it is apparently earlier than any printed text.

TS(2) and TS(3) are evidently later than the *Maclean's* text. TS(2), although dated August 19, 1940, was included in a letter of January 4, 1941 to Ralph Gustafson. TS(3) is in the Queen's University Archives and was obviously prepared for the publication of *Canada Speaks of Britain*.

Variants

Title: Canada Speaks of Britain] **Britain—The Empire to** *NB*
Originally *The Empire Speaks of Britain* in *ENB, LRC, TS*(2), and *TS*(3); *The Empire* crossed through and *Canada* written above it in all cases. **The Empire Speaks of Britain** *TS*(1), *Maclean's*

1-4 This . . . again.] There are two early versions of this stanza in *NB:*

> This is that bastioned rock about whose base
> < · >
> Forever the storm of alien fury thunders in vain
> Surge after surge against its iron face
> Floods up to reel in ruins back again.

In the first line *about* is written above *against* which has been crossed through. The second line is obliterated. In the third line *fury thunders* is written above *wrath* which has been cancelled. The second of the early versions is:

> This bastioned rock that holds the seven seas
> In f< . . > perpetual, against whose base
> Thunders in vain the fury of our foes,

The second word in the second line is not clear; but it is probably *fee*. All further *NB* variants are from the full text of the poem.

3 Storm up] originally < > *rage* in *NB;* the first word is obliterated, both are crossed through, and *Storm up* is written above them. *Storm* is written above *Surge* which has been crossed through.

4 flaming] **ruinous** *NB*

5 This, this is] originally *This is that* in *NB; that* crossed through

5 This,] ~ — *ENB*

5 bulwark] originally *Mother* in *NB; Mother* crossed through and *bulwark* written above it

5 breed] originally *race* in *NB; race* crossed through and *breed* written beside it

6 Our . . . hate.] crossed through above this line in *NB* is:

> And hope <   > of our faith

626

6   hordes]   originally *assaults* in *NB; assaults* crossed through and
              hordes written above it
6   hate.]   ~ , *TS*(3)
7   Smite . . . smitten;]   **Strike . . . stricken–** *NB*
8   Yet . . . fate.]   **But steadfast she against all strokes of Fate.** *NB*
8   Yet]   **But** *ENB, LRC, TS*(1), *Maclean's.* Originally *But* in *TS*(2)
              and *TS*(3); *But* crossed through and *Yet* written in the
              margin.
8   fate]   **Fate** *Maclean's*
9   shall;–but]   **shall. But** *NB*   **shall; but** *ENB, Maclean's*
10   ships and planes]   **ships, and planes,** *Maclean's*
11   break,–]   ~ ;– *ENB*   ~ – *Maclean's*
12   temper]   originally *steel* in *NB; steel* crossed through and *temper*
              written beside it
12   temper,–]   ~ , *NB*   ~– *Maclean's*
13   we]   added with a caret in *NB*
13   answer]   ~ , *ENB*
13   breath,–]   ~ ; *NB*   ~ , *ENB, Maclean's*
              ~ .– *Voices of Victory*
Note: in *Maclean's Magazine* the poem is not divided into stanzas

p. 342 EPITAPH FOR A YOUNG AIRMAN

The poem was first published in *Saturday Night* (October, 1940); and later
appeared in *The Brunswickan* (November, 1940); and *Canada Speaks of Britain*,
1941.

Two holograph manuscripts are contained in the two Roberts notebooks
at the University of New Brunswick. NB is dated September 28 at the top and
beside a cancelled first stanza; the revised first stanza is dated October 13
and October 17, 1940 at the end of the poem, followed by two alternate
last stanzas. ENB is dated October 18 but there is a note that it was revised
December 4, 1940–that is, after the publications in *Saturday Night* and *The
Brunswickan.* A third holograph manuscript is in the Lloyd Roberts Collection (LRC) at the University of New Brunswick and was apparently made
before the revisions in ENB. LRC is autographed and dated October 18,
1940. Three typescripts, all dated October 16, 1940, survive. TS(1) and TS(3)
are in the Queen's University Archives. TS(2), despite its date, was included
in a letter to Ralph Gustafson, dated January 4, 1941.

Variants
Title: Epitaph for a Young Airman]   *NB* has the alternate titles
          Epitaph, St. Paul's, The Fleet, The Great Reunion, and *Blood
          and Tears* above the cancelled first stanza. The correct title
          appears before the revised first stanza.

Note: a cancelled first stanza in *NB* reads:

> He who but yesterday
> The lad with morning in his eyes
> Would soar on sundering wing
> To clear the skies

All further *NB* references are to the full text of the poem.

1   eager]   originally *soaring* in *NB; soaring* crossed through and *eager* written above it.   **tireless** *Sat. Night, Brunswickan*

2   eyes] ~ , *NB*

3   and hurl]   originally *to fling* in *NB; to fling* crossed through and *and hurl* written above it

4   through] **to** *NB*

4   skies,–] ~ – *Brunswickan* ~ ;– *LRC, ENB*

5   Would . . . thin]   the line is illegible in places in *NB;* the legible words are:

> He would soar <   > the <   > air of heights

He and *soar* have been cancelled as have the two illegible words.

6   For . . . labouring] **When strives the faltering** *NB; strives* and *faltering* are written above *halts* and *fainting* which have been cancelled.

7   fling]   originally *shout* in *NB; shout* crossed through and *fling* written beside it

8   death,–] ~ ; *LRC, ENB*

9   plunge] **drive** *NB*

9   scathing . . . fire] **hail of chattering guns** *NB*

9   scathing] **withering** *Sat. Night, Brunswickan*

10   screaming] **shrieking** *NB*

11   ravening horde] **slaughterers** *NB*

11   ravening] **slaughtering** *Sat. Night, Brunswickan, LRC.* Originally *slaughtering* in *ENB; slaughtering* crossed through and *ravaging* written above it; *ravaging* then cancelled and *ravening* written beside it. Originally *slaughtering* in *TS*(1); *slaughtering* crossed through and *ravening* written in the margin. **ravaging** *TS*(2), *TS*(3)

12   hell,–] ~ ;– *LRC, ENB*

13   He . . . sleep] in *NB,* in parenthesis to the side and below the line is:

> Lapped in his deep-sea grave

13   today]   originally *tonight* in *NB; tonight* crossed through and
                today written above it. Originally *today* in *ENB; today*
                crossed through and *tonight* written above it.
13   today,]   ~ —   *Sat. Night, Brunswickan*   ~   *TS*(1)
                tonight—   *TS*(2), *TS*(3)
13   how]   originally *so* in *LRC; so* crossed through and *how* written
                above it
13   how . . . sleep]   originally *how deep a sleep* in *ENB; how . . . sleep*
                crossed through and *so deep a sleep* written above
                it; *so* then cancelled and *how* rewritten above it
13   sleep,]   ~ —   *Sat. Night, TS*(2), *TS*(3)   ~   *Brunswickan,*
                TS(1)
14   wave,]   ~   *NB*
14   wave]   **tide**   *Sat. Night, Brunswickan, TS*(1). Originally *tide* in
                LRC and *ENB; tide* crossed through and *wave* written
                above it
15   heeds]   originally *dreams* in *NB; heeds* is written above *dreams*
                but *dreams* is not cancelled.   **dreams**   *Sat. Night,*
                Brunswickan, LRC, ENB. Originally *dreams* in *TS*(1),
                TS(2) and *TS*(3); *dreams* crossed through and *heeds*
                written in the margin in all three cases.
15   task]   **work**   *NB*
16   those . . . save]   **whom to save he died**   *Sat. Night, Brunswickan,*
                TS(1). Originally *whom to save he died* in *LRC*
                and *ENB.* In *LRC, whom to save* is crossed
                through and *them* is written above; *to save* is
                added at the end of the line. In *ENB, whom . . .*
                died is crossed through and *those he died to*
                save written above it.
16   those]   **them**   *TS*(2), *TS*(3)
Note: in *NB* there are two alternate versions of the last stanza:

He sleeps today how deep a sleep,
    Lapped in his deep-sea grave,
Nor heeds (dreams) how well his task was done
    For those he died to save.

He sleeps today how deep a sleep,
    Beneath the Channel tide,
Nor heeds (dreams) how well his task was done
    For whom to save he died.

The poem was published only in *Saturday Night* (May, 1942).

Two holograph manuscripts are contained in the two Roberts notebooks at the University of New Brunswick. In NB the title only is dated May 27, 1941. A few rough lines are dated July 18 and 19, 1941. The date of March 16, 1942 appears at the end of the full poem. ENB is dated March 16, 1942. Four typescripts survive. TS(1) is autographed and was included in a letter to Ralph Gustafson dated January 4, 1942. TS(2) is similarly autographed and was included in a letter to A.M. Stephen dated March 26, 1942. TS(3) is also autographed and is in the J.D. Logan Collection at Acadia University. TS(4) was included in a letter to B.K. Sandwell, editor of *Saturday Night,* and is dated April 21, 1942. The letter to Sandwell says:

> Do you want to publish this poem? If you care for it,
> I would want it *featured.* It is being set to music. Healy
> Willan & Dan Haman (of Romanelli's) are working on it,
> with a view to putting it "on the air."
>
> It may strike you as journalism rather than poetry,–but
> I think I can claim it has guts!

The poem appeared on page one of *Saturday Night.*

Variants

Title: Song for Victory Delayed]   originally *The Empire's Song
          for Victory* in *NB; The . . . Victory* crossed through
          and *A . . . Delayed* written above it

Sub-title: Une heure viendra qui tout paiera]   omitted in *NB, ENB,
          TS*(2), *TS*(3). "A time will come when all will be
          repaid."

Note: Before the poem proper in *NB* are the following lines:

[1]   No easy task is ours.
[2]   For us the tears, the smart,
[3]   The crash of bombs by day,
[4]   By night the deadlier threat.

[5]   Teeth clenched to endure
        With set teeth to endure is written in the margin
[6]   And strength that shall not tire,
[7]   Through deadly days, through flaming nights
[8]   The test of blood & fire.

[9]   Not yet is victory ours,
[10]   The battle not yet won

In the first line, *is* is written above *be* which has been cancelled. In the second line, *tears* is written above the cancelled word *blood*. Before *day* in the third line, *night* has been cancelled. In the sixth line, *And* is written above *With* which has been crossed through. And, in the seventh line, *blood* (before *deadly*) and *through flaming* have been cancelled. All other *NB* variants are from the full text of the poem.

2   Far . . . yet]   originally *The victory is not yet* in *NB;* in parenthesis beside this line is:

(Far off is victory yet.)

2   is]   originally *is* in *ENB; is* crossed through and *the* written above it.   **the**   *TS*(2)

4   sweat.]   ~ ,   *NB*

5   us]   ~ ,   *ENB*

5   with will]   originally *with steadfast* in *NB; steadfast* crossed through and *will* written beside it

7   teeth]   ~ ,   *ENB*

8   test]   originally *trial* in *ENB; trial* crossed through and *test* written above it

9   blindness, folly]   **folly, blindness**   *NB*

9   sloth,]   ~   *ENB*

10   Still . . . price]   **Must still be paid the price**   *NB*

10   price,–]   ~ ,   *Sat. Night*

11-12   The . . . sacrifice]   in *NB:*

still to pay the price,–
A People's heart uptorn
In blinding sacrifice

9-12   For . . . sacrifice.]   The stanza as it now stands follows the above first attempt in *NB*.

13   On . . . die]   **We die on every shore**   *TS*(1)

13-16   On . . . down.]   The entire stanza is written in the margin of *NB:*

On every shore we die,
On every sea we drown,–
But dying we shall prove
The worth of our renown.

A cancelled stanza in *ENB* reads:

On every shore we die,
On every sea go down,

And dying we declare
The worth of our renown.

There are also two revised versions of the stanza in *ENB:*

We die on every shore.
In every sea we drown.
Adventuring every sky
To death our sons go down.

On every shore we die.
In every sea we drown.
Adventuring every sky
To death our sons go down.

16   Our . . . down]   **To death our sons go down**   *TS*(2)

17-20   Yet . . . undismayed,]   Two versions of this stanza, with many cancellations in each, appear in *NB:*

For purged by fire we front
The fury undismayed,
Knowing our hour will come
And the dread score be paid.

purged by flame we front
The fury undismayed,
With faith that flinches not
And hope unafraid.

17   Yet]   originally *But* in *ENB; But* crossed through and *Yet* written above it

19   flinches not]   originally *flinches not* in *ENB;* altered to *will not flinch.*   **does not flinch**   *TS*(2)

20   And high hearts]   originally *With courage* in *ENB; With courage* crossed through and *And high hearts* written above it

20   undismayed.]   ~ ,—   *ENB*

21   strikes]   originally *comes* in *NB; comes* crossed through and *strikes* written above it

22   Big . . . fate]   originally *When we with hearts elate* in *NB; When . . . elate* crossed through and *Big with the world's fate* written above it

23   scourge . . . doom]   originally *crush and smite to doom* in *NB; crush . . . doom* crossed through and *scourge to their just doom* written above it

632

23   scourge]   originally *hurl* in *ENB; hurl* crossed through and *scourge*
                 written above it
23   just]   originally *just* in *ENB; just* crossed through and *belated*
                 written above it; *belated* then cancelled and *just* rewritten
                 below the original word
24   shattered]   originally *reeling* in *ENB; reeling* crossed through
                 and *shattered* written above it

p. 344 RESURGANT

The poem was first published in *Saturday Night* (July, 1942); and was reprinted only in *Flying Colours,* 1942.

Two holograph manuscripts are contained in the two Roberts notebooks
at the University of New Brunswick. NB is described below. ENB is dated
April 8 and 9, 1942. A typescript, dated 1942 and signed by Roberts, is in
the Queen's University Archives.

Variants
In *NB,* dated August 12, 1934, is the single line:

         Clear & high summons the trumpet

Dated January 6, 1941, is:

                 Resurgant
     They all shall rise again. They all shall rise.
       Up from the slough of undeserved defeat,

The full poem, variously dated and many times revised, is often illegible.
As nearly as I can determine, the text is as follows. I have numbered the
legible lines.

                 Resurgant
   1   They all shall rise,
   2   They all shall rise again,
   3   The new dawn in their eyes.

   4   Oh clear & high summons the trumpets
   5   Before the gates of Dawn.
      [Lines 1-5 are cancelled.]
   6   What though their ramparts be falling   March 29/42
      [followed by four cancelled lines beside which
       line 7 is written]
   7   What tho' their streets run red;

8	Over cradle and altar
9	The brute battalions tread; Ap. 4

10	What tho' their ramparts be fallen;
11	Their streets with blood run red

[*with blood* appears in parenthesis at the end of the
line with an arrow to indicate its correct position]

12	And over cradle and altar
13	The brute battalions tread:

14	Tho' flame has harrowed their village

[line 14 and four largely illegible lines following are
cancelled as is the refrain "Yet . . . Dawn."]

15	Tho' flame has ravaged their villages
16	And gutted are byre and stead
17	Yet ever for vengeance cry the bones
18	Of their unburied dead
19	And clear & High etc.

[written across the margin is:]
Their fields laid waste with fire
    Their swords have not burned down
[Then an obliterated line]
And ever for vengeance cry the bones
    Of their unburied dead,

[four cancelled lines follow]

20	In the black slough of defeat
21	Their heads are still unbowed
22	In death they are still defiant
23	& even in their chains, proud;
24	And they shall rise again
25	They all shall rise
26	To a world made clean & free
27	And a New Dawn in their eyes

28	They all shall rise again,
29	They all shall rise
30	To a world made clean & free
31	And the new Dawn in their eyes
32	To a world made clean
33	As it never yet has been
34	A world at last made safe & free

[a cancelled line ending with *liberty* follows] Ap.7&8/42

35   In the black slough of defeat
36   Are still their heads unbowed.
37   They front death still defiant,   Ap. 9/42
38   Even in chains still proud,
39   But they shall rise again
40   From the long day all shall rise
41   With the daybreak on their foreheads
42   And the New Dawn in their eyes,–
43   To a new Earth purged with tears (blood?)
          [an obliterated line follows]
44   As it never before has been,
45   A world for justice, faith, good will
46   Made free at last & clean.

47   Oh clear & high summons the trumpets
48   Before the gates of Dawn.

5   And]   **Tho'** *ENB*
7   flame]   originally *fire* in *ENB; fire* crossed through and *flame* written above it
8   Tho']   **And** *ENB*
10   dead:–]   ~ ;– *TS, Sat. Night*
11   Yet]   originally *But* in *TS; But* crossed through and *Yet* written above it
12   Dawn.]   ~ ! *ENB*
14   unbowed;]   ~ : *TS*
15   Defiant they]   originally *They* in *ENB; Defiant* added at the beginning of the line and cancelled at the end
16   In]   originally *Even in* in *TS; Even* crossed through and *i* altered to *I*
16   proud;]   ~ :– *TS*   ~ . *Sat. Night*
17   again:–]   ~. *ENB, TS*
17   following this line, but cancelled, in *ENB* is:

          They all shall rise,
        With the daybreak on their brows
        And the new Dawn in their eyes,
          To a day born clean and free,–
          To a world made clean
          As it never before has been,
          A world at last made glad and free
          For Man and Liberty

The lines, approximately as they now stand, follow.
18   shall they]   **they shall** *ENB*
20   eyes,]   ~ *ENB*
21   new world]   **New Earth** *ENB*

p. 344 PHILLIDA'S BLUE RIBBON

As yet, no publication of the poem, except in Pomeroy's *Sir Charles G.D. Roberts,* has come to light.

Of the poem Pomeroy (pp. 94-5) writes:

> It is not surprising to learn that the poet, who was always an enthusiastic dancer, sometimes found an inspiration at the dance. At a fancy dress ball his partner lost a length of blue ribbon which had been serving her as a criss-crossed garter. The poet gallantly pocketed it. He was granted permission to keep the ribbon if he would promise solemnly to write a poem about it. That was sufficient inspiration. He wrote "Phillida's Blue Ribbon." . . . This was but one of many poems concerning Phillida—an imaginary character, so the poet assures us!—which were never included in any volume, although published at the time in *The Smart Set* or in *Truth* when Peter McArthur was editor. About ten or twelve years later the poet was taken to a semi-private entertainment in New York and, unknown to the performers, was seated unobtrusively at the back of the room. One of the artists, a complete stranger to Roberts, was a reciter who, after rendering a couple of selections, announced that her next number would be a poem by the well-known poet, Charles G.D. Roberts, which he had written specially for her. She read "Phillida's Blue Ribbon!" She little guessed that a much-amused Roberts was in the audience!

Although I have been unable to locate the poem in *The Smart Set* or in *Truth*—or any other periodical—the poem was probably written in the mid-1890's if Pomeroy's story of it may be taken at face value.

p. 345 MAY-NIGHT

Apparently the poem was never published, and it survives only as a manuscript in Roberts' scrapbook at the University of New Brunswick. The handwriting is not that of Roberts, and his authorship of the poem must remain conjectural. The manuscript is dated 25 May, 1919.

p. 346 COLOUR TOASTS

The poem was never published, and the two surviving typescripts have the notation "For private circulation only." TS(1) is in the Queen's University Archives and contains stanzas 1-10; it is autographed by Roberts and there is the additional note "Other colours to be added in due time!" TS(2) is in the private possession of Nelson Ball who bought it at an auction in Toronto; this text is initialled by Roberts and contains stanzas 1-8. In addition, a holograph manuscript of stanza 11 is in the Queen's University Archives.

636

INDEX OF FIRST LINES

A brown, sad-coloured hillside, where the soil : p. 82

A child, I set the thirsting of my mouth : p. 101

A faint wind, blowing from World's End : p. 295

A girl's voice in the night troubled my heart : p. 304

A high bare field, brown from the plough, and borne : p. 91

A hollow on the verge of May : p. 99

A little brown old homestead, bowered in trees : p. 166

A little grey hill-glade, close-turfed, withdrawn : p. 165

A little tumbled city on the height : p. 328

A poet was vexed with the fume of the street : p. 32

A small blue flower with yellow eye : 36

A snowy path for squirrel and fox : p. 187

A wind blew up from Pernambuco : p. 208

A wistful poet long and slim : p. 217

Above the blindness of content : p. 235

Above the hollow deep where lies : p. 247

Across the fog the moon lies fair : p. 167

Afloat : p. 92

Ah, Love, what would I give just for a little light : p. 47

Ah me! No wind from golden Thessaly : p. 29

All deserted to wind and to sun : p. 96

All night long the light is lying : p. 228

All night the lone cicada : p. 294

Although you might surmise : p. 202

Amber and blue, the smoke behind the hill : p. 167

An azure splendour floats upon the world : p. 15

An eagle city on her heights austere : p. 133

An elegant Elephant walked one day : p. 206

As down the woodland ways I went : p. 335

As I came over Westcock Hill : p. 333

As once by Hybna's emerald flow : p. 311

As one who sleeps, and hears across his dream : p. 223

As the will of last year's wind : p. 290

At evening, when the noise of life is done : p. 220

At evening, when the winds are still : p. 139

At evening, where the cattle come to drink : p. 228

At Pozzuoli on the Italian coast : p. 33

At thy voice my heart : p. 247

Awake, my country, the hour is great with change : p. 90

Away, sad voices, telling : p. 267

Back to the bewildering vision : p. 181

Back to the green deeps of the outer bay : p. 163

Back to you, Shaugamauk, my heart is turning : p. 334

Be quiet, wind, a little while : p. 317

Before the breath of storm : p. 72

Before the feet of the dew : p. 195

Before our trenches at Cambrai : p. 305

Behind the fateful gleams : p. 212

Behind the veil that men call sleep : p. 251

Beside the wharf at Whitewaters : p. 155

Blossom that spread'st, ere spring brings in : p. 97

Breather of honeyed breath upon my face : p. 9

Bring orange-blossoms fairly twined : p. 33

Broods the hid glory in its sheath of gloom : p. 245

By the long wash of his ancestral sea : p. 210

Calls the crow from the pine-tree top : p. 287

Came Pan to the garden : p. 318

Charm of the vibrant, white September sun : p. 155

Clearest pool, my wondering joy : p. 216

Come, Death, sit down with me : p. 286

Come, Red Mouse : p. 203

Comes the lure of green things growing : p. 221

Comrade of the whirling planets : p. 176

Crimson swims the sunset over far Pelorus : p. 55

Cuthbert, open! Let me in : p. 64

Daffodil, lily, and crocus : p. 175

Dawn like a lily lies upon the land : p. 245

Day long, and night long : p. 303

Dear blossom of the wayside kin : p. 224

Dear ! Dear : p. 227

Dear Heart ! between us can be no farewell : p. 98

Dear Heart, the noisy strife : p. 104

Dear Poet, quit your shady lanes : p. 81

Dear, you have come into my loving heart : p. 345

Deep in the hush of those unfathomed glooms : p. 286

Deeps of the wind-torn west : p. 307

Did Winter, letting fall in vain regret : p. 141

Ere the spring comes near : p. 89

Ever just over the top of the next brown rise : 303

Eyes of the city : p. 256

Faithful reports of them have reached me oft : p. 100

Far up the lonely strand the storm had lifted her : p. 264

Father of nations! Help of the feeble hand : p. 89

Father, who keepest : p. 204

Fill high to its quivering brim : p. 34

For a little while : p. 127

For days the drench of noiseless rains : p. 175

Forever shed your sweetness on the night : 255

Forget not, Thou who saidst : p. 340

Frail lilies that beneath the dust so long : p. 311

Friend, those delights of ours : p. 94

From gab of jay and chatter of crake : p. 57

From the high window of your room : p. 296

Gluskâp, the friend and father of his race : p. 184

Grey rocks, and greyer sea : p. 137

Grows the great deed, though none : p. 114

Haughty glass, be not so vain : p. 231

He builds not anxiously by rule and line : p. 214

He stops beside the crowded curb, and lifts : p. 257

He that so often bade us smile : p. 200

He who but yesterday would roam : p. 153

He who would mount on eager wing : p. 342

He who would start and rise : p. 193

Her hair it floated fair and free : p. 52

Here clove the keels of centuries ago : p. 136

Here in the red heart of the sunset lying : p. 117

Here is a breathing time, and rest for a little season : p. 73

Here is the street : p. 242

Here mid the hasting and eddying faces : p. 260

Here on the hill : p. 300

Here the night is fierce with light : p. 242

Here's to the girl who dresses in *white* : p. 346

Here's to the glory of the land that we name : p. 119

Hesper appears when flowing gales : p. 29

His fame the mock of shallow wits : p. 308

How grave she sits and toots : p. 80

How little I knew, when I first saw you : 268

How long it was I did not know : p. 232

How merry sings the aftermath : p. 142

How shrink the snows upon this upland field : p. 166

How sombre slope these acres to the sea : p. 130

How sweetly on the autumn scene : p. 138

Hung like a rich pomegranate o'er the sea : p. 10

I am for the open meadows : p. 225

I am the man who found a flower : p. 309

I am the spirit astir : p. 122

I dreamed last night my love was dead : p. 259

I had stumbled up thro' Time from the slime to the heights : p. 330

I have a garden in the city's grime : p. 241

I have faced life with courage,—but not now : p. 255

I have lived long, and watched out many days : p. 66

I hear the low wind wash the softening snow : p. 129

I know a maiden like a flower : p. 310

I know a stream : p. 306

I might not, coming to the realms of bliss : p. 179

I sat and read Anacreon : p. 295

I see the harsh, wind-ridden, eastward hill : p. 163

I soothe to unimagined sleep : p. 178

I talked about you, Dear, the other night : p. 239

I thieved a skein of gossamer thread : p. 319

I voyage north, I journey south : p. 312
642

I walk the city square with thee : p. 247

I was spawned from the glacier : p. 321

If I should take my pen in hand : p. 192

In an enchanted gloom : p. 198

In divers tones I sing : p. 87

In smart attire my Phillida : p. 231

In the heart of a man : p. 131

In the southward sky : p. 63

In the wide awe and wisdom of the night : p. 133

In thronged procession gliding slow : p. 278

It is not in the day : p. 296

It is so long ago: and men well-nigh : p. 98

Its breath, which cools her breast to snow : p. 196

Its hand compassionate guards our restless sight : p. 87

Kingfisher, whence cometh it : p. 35

Laurels for song! And nobler bays : p. 62

Life at my stirrup lifted wistful eyes : p. 208

Life said to the Artist: Tell my dream : p. 245

Lightly He blows, and at His breath they fall : p. 254

List! List! The buds confer : p. 259

Love hath given the day for longing : p. 109

Love, if you love me, love with heart and soul : p. 111

Love, what were fame : p. 110

Mary, when the childing pain : p. 226

Miriam, loved one, were thy goings weary : p. 47

My feet are set for other ways : p. 32

My glad feet shod with the glittering steel : p. 279

My heart is a house, deep-walled and warm : p. 289

My life she takes between her hands : p. 276

Never poet : p. 111

Night; and the sound of voices in the street : p. 243

No easy task is ours : p. 343

No lifeless thing of iron and stone : p. 260

Not in the eyed, expectant gloom : p. 238

Not only far away and long ago : p. 207

Not only in the cataract and the thunder : p. 185

Not upon thee the shame, not upon thee : p. 340

Not yet, for all their quest of it, have men : p. 102

Now along the solemn heights : p. 200

Now, for the night is hushed and blind with rain : p. 91

Now heap the branchy barriers up : p. 117

Now that Canadian barley can't go in : p. 133

O apple leaves, so cool and green : p. 219

O breath of wind and sea : p. 109

O Child of Nations, giant-limbed : p. 85

O city night of noises and alarms : p. 243

O deep of Heaven, 't is thou alone art boundless : p. 120

O earth, sufficing all our needs, O you : p. 299

O Life, how slight : p. 127

O little rose, O dark rose : p. 265

O rivers rolling to the sea : p. 159

O shepherdess fair, the flocks you keep : p. 283

O Solitary of the austere sky : p. 142

O the sun has kissed the apples : p. 222

O Thou who bidd'st a million germs decay : p. 256

O Thou who hast beneath Thy hand : p. 237

O Thou who lovest not alone : p. 263

O tranquil meadows, grassy Tantramar : p. 144

O Voice : p. 275

O what avails the storm : p. 112

O wild, dark flower of woman : p. 266

Oh, clear and high summons the trumpet : p. 344

Oh, fierce is the heat : p. 179

Oh, it was a dainty maid that went a-Maying in the morn : p. 180

Oh, not this year comes spring : p. 341

Oh, purple hang the pods : p. 167

Oh, shout for the good ship Shannon : p. 30

Oh some are for the cities of men : p. 295

Oh, take me into the still places of your heart : p. 267

Oh, tenderly deepen the woodland glooms : p. 3

Oh the coast of green Bohemia : p. 204

Oh, the scent of the hyacinth blossom : p. 97

Oh, to be a cricket : p. 144

Oh to be back where the oatfields are blowing : p. 315

Omar, dying, left his dust : p. 288

On other fields and other scenes the morn : p. 116

On the pale borders of evening : p. 335

Once in a garden, when the thrush's song : p. 224

One night came Winter noiselessly, and leaned : p. 188

Out of the dreams that heap : p. 186

Out of the frost-white wood comes winnowing through : p. 174

Out of this night of lonely noise : p. 244

Outside the wind sobs in the old spruce : p. 339

Over the scorching roofs of iron : p. 282

Over the tops of the houses : p. 191

Over the tops of the trees : p. 143

Path by which her feet have gone : p. 83

Penning his comedy called "Man," the Master : p. 189

Pipers of the chilly pools : p. 272

Poet and Flute-player, that flute of thine : p. 88

Ringed with the flocking of hills, within shepherding watch of Olympus : p. 76

Ripe grew the year. Then suddenly there came : p. 183

Rocks, I am one with you : p. 274

Round the lone clearing : p. 331

Ruin and death held sway : p. 270

Ruling with an iron hand : p. 3

Said Life to Art—"I love thee best : p. 231

Sang the sunrise on an amber morn : p. 188

Save what the night-wind woke of sweet : p. 59

September is here, with the ripened seeds : p. 218

Set in the fierce red desert for a sword : p. 101

Sharp drives the rain for me : p. 268

Sharp drives the rain, sharp drives the endless rain : p. 108

She rose in the night and fled : p. 37

Shedding cool drops upon the sun-baked clay : p. 58

Should Jonathan and John fall out : p. 257

Since I have felt upon my face thy tears : p. 279

Sing, Boys, sing : p. 71

Sisters and brothers, not by blood alone : p. 254

Sleep, sleep, imperious heart! Sleep, fair and undefiled : p. 246

So little and so kind a shrine : p. 282

Sometimes you saw what others could not see : p. 327

Soothe, soothe : p. 106

Spirit of Beauty : p. 320

Spring breaks in foam : p. 312

Spring, summer, autumn, winter : p. 236

Stumps, and harsh rocks, and prostrate trunks all charred : p. 137

Subtler than all sorceries : p. 2

Sullenly falls the rain : p. 61

Summers and summers have come, and gone with the flight of the swallow : p.78

Sun, and Moon, and Wind, and Flame : p. 261

Sun's up; wind's up! Wake up, dearies : p. 228

Tantramar! Tantramar : p. 170

The airs that blew from the brink of day : p. 177

The bird's song, the sun, and the wind : p. 141

The dark rose of your mouth : p. 263

The earth lay black and weeping, till from God : p. 261

The fifers of these amethystine fields : p. 136

The great and the little weavers : p. 280

The green marsh-mallows : p. 301

The happy valley laughed with sun : p. 168

The large first stars come out : p. 253

The long tides sweep : p. 205

The loud black flight of the storm diverges : p. 62

The morning sky is white with mist, the earth : p. 134

The morning star was bitter bright, the morning sky was grey : p. 161

The night was grim and still with dread : p. 189

The noon has dried thy dewdrops from my wings : p. 48

The northern summer, bright like flame : p. 142

The poet took his wheel one day : p. 198

The red and yellow of the Autumn salt-grass : p. 250

The red flame of war, the anguish of woman : p. 339

The Rose spoke in the garden : p. 273

The shadow of the poplar : p. 329

The smell of burning weeds : p. 298

The snow'd laid deep that winter from the middle of November : p. 123

The sweet-mouthed shore hath wed the singing sea : p. 46

The tide falls, and the night falls : p. 119

The tide goes out, the tide goes out; once more : p. 187

The upland hills are green again : p. 308

The valley of the winding water : p. 122

The wash of endless waves is in their tops : p. 126

The wide, white world is bitter still : p. 220

The winds are up with wakening day : p. 113

The winds are whispering low their dirges drear : p. 1

The wood is cold, and dank, and green : p. 49

There came a day of showers : p. 139

There grew a rose more wonderful : p. 272

There lies a city inaccessible : p. 284

There lies a little city leagues away : p. 129

There was a little piper man : p. 180

These are the fields of light, and laughing air : p. 138

These first-fruits, gathered by distant ways : p. 36

This antique song, new sung in fashion new : p. 88

This band of true patrician hue : p. 344

This giant nerve, at whose command : p. 250

This is a wonder-cup in Summer's hand : p. 121

This is that bastioned rock where dwell the Free : p. 342

This is that black rock bastion, based in surge : p. 128

This is the song : p. 258

This is the voice of high midsummer's heat : p. 132

This morning, full of breezes and perfume : p. 57

This smell of home and honey on the breeze : p. 159

This supreme song of him who dreamed : p. 110

This violet eve is like a waveless stream : p. 132

This windy, bright September afternoon : p. 73

Though o'er the board the constellations shine : p. 300

Three good things I've thanked the Gods for : p. 193

Through cold and dreary winter Nature sleeps : p. 76

Through its brown and withered bulb : p. 212

Through the still dusk how sighs the ebb-tide out : p. 88

Tide's at full; the waves break white : p. 183

Time in the long, chill Norland silence slept : p. 246

Time is a deep-mouthed jar, pictured and dim : p. 215

To Beauty and to Truth I heaped : p. 201

To fledge the hours with mirth and ease : p. 51

To Her, when life was little worth : p. 254

To Her whose fame, these fifty years : p. 112

To him the vision and the peace belong : p. 137

To you, dear girl, and other friends like you : p. 66

Tons upon tons the brown-green fragrant hay : p. 164

Twelve good friends : p. 319

650

Two mighty arms of thunder-cloven rock : p. 18

Two rivers are there hold my heart : p. 336

Under the pillars of the sky : p. 299

Up, heart of mine : p. 297

Vast, unrevealed, in silence and the night : p. 194

Violet, Violet, where did you capture : p. 207

We mount the arc of ocean's round : p. 300

Weary, forsaken by fair, fickle sleep : p. 5

Weird Night has withdrawn : p. 55

What bold : p. 192

What matter that the sad gray city cleeps : p. 108

What touch hath set the breathing hills afire : p. 164

When chars the heart to ashes in its pain : p. 238

When first did I perceive you, when take heed : p. 84

When frogs make merry the pools of May : p. 130

When God sends out His company to travel through the stars : p. 196

When I was but a lad : p. 213

When in the rowan tree : p. 285

When Mary the Mother kissed the Child : p. 293

When milking-time is done, and over all : p. 121

When potatoes were in blossom : p. 154

When snows the dead earth cumber : p. 1

When tent was pitched, and supper done : p. 106

When the cloud comes down the mountain : p. 286

When the clover blooms again : p. 234

When the crows fly in from sea : p. 184

When the frost is white on the fodder-stack : p. 277

When the grey lake-water rushes : p. 229

When the lights come out in the cottages : p. 301

When the little spent winds are at rest in the tamarack tree : p. 314

When the partridge coveys fly : p. 197

When the Sleepy Man comes with the dust on his eyes : p. 176

When the white moon divides the mist : p. 226

When winter is done, and April's dawning : p. 211

When Winter scourged the meadow and the hill : p. 188

Where a little-trodden byway : p. 38

Where are the kind eyes gone : p. 269

Where humming flies frequent, and where : p. 141

Wherefore awake so long : p. 58

While eager angels watched in awe : p. 215

While raves the midnight storm : p. 126

White as fleeces blown across the hollow heaven : p. 15

Whither down the ways of dream : p. 310

Wind of the summer afternoon : p. 73

Winds here, and sleet, and frost that bites like steel : p. 128

With April here : p. 309

With shy bright clamour the live brooks sparkle and run : p. 120

With what white wrath must turn thy bones : p. 306

Without one kiss she's gone away : p. 51

Ye night winds, shaking the weighted boughs : p. 134

Your threats how vain, Corregidor : p. 248

INDEX OF TITLES

Actæon : p. 66, n. 397
Admittance : p. 179, n. 475
Afloat : p. 92, n. 423
Afoot : p. 221, n. 500
Aim, The : p. 263, n. 521
All Night the Lone Cicada : p. 294, n. 538
Amoris Vincula : p. 2, n. 364
Apple Song : p. 222, n. 500
April Adoration, An : p. 188, n. 481
Ariadne : p. 10, n. 370
As Down the Woodland Ways : p. 335, n. 610
Ascription : p. 237, n. 508
Asterope : p. 310, n. 561
At Pozzuoli : p. 33, n. 381
At the Drinking Fountain : p. 257, n. 518
At the Railway Station : p. 242, n. 511
At the Wayside Shrine : p. 282, n. 531
At Thy Voice My Heart : p. 247, n. 514
At Tide Water : p. 250, n. 516
Atlantic Cable, The : p. 250, n. 515
Attar : p. 263, n. 522
August Wood Road, An : p. 197, n. 487
Autochthon : p. 122, n. 438
Autumn Thistles, The : p. 134, n. 450
Ave! (An Ode for the Shelley Centenary, 1892) : p. 144, n. 459
Away, Sad Voices : p. 267, n. 524
Aylesford Lake : p. 228, n. 504
Ballad of a Bride : p. 33, n. 381
Ballad of Crossing the Brook, The : p. 180, n. 476
Ballad of Manila Bay, A : p. 248, n. 514
Ballad of Three Mistresses, A : p. 34, n. 382
Ballad to a Kingfisher : p. 35, n. 382
Ballade of Calypso, A : p. 62, n. 393
Ballade of Philomela, A : p. 57, n. 389
Ballade of the Poet's Thought : p. 32, n. 381
Banquet, The : p. 300, n. 547
Bat, Bat, Come Under My Hat : p. 319, n. 577
Be Quiet, Wind : p. 317, n. 573
Before the Breath of Storm : p. 72, n. 402
Beppo's Song : p. 295, n. 539

Beside the Winter Sea : p. 223, n. 501
Birch and Paddle : p. 94, n. 423
Bird's Song, the Sun, and the Wind, The : p. 141, n. 455
Birthday Ballade, A : p. 96, n. 423
Blomidon : p. 128, n. 444
Blue Blossom, A : p. 36, n. 382
Blue Violet, A : p. 97, n. 423
Bohemia : p. 204, n. 492
Break, A : p. 97, n. 424
Breathing Time, A : p. 73, n. 403
Bringing Home the Cows : p. 154, n. 461
Brook in February, The : p. 187, n. 480
Brooklyn Bridge : p. 260, n. 520
Buckwheat : p. 159, n. 463
Burnt Lands : p. 116, n. 432
Butterflies : p. 224, n. 501
Cambrai and Marne : p. 305, n. 553
Canada : p. 85, n. 413
Canada Lily, The : p. 142, n. 456
Canada Speaks of Britain : p. 342, n. 625
Canada to France : p. 340, n. 622
Canadian Streams : p. 159, n. 464
Canadians Are We : p. 119, n. 434
Canoe Song : p. 71, n. 402
Child of the Infinite : p. 261, n. 521
Child's Prayer at Evening, A : p. 204, n. 491
Chopping Bee, The : p. 161, n. 466
Christmas-Eve Courtin', A : p. 123, n. 439
Cicada in the Firs, The : p. 155, n. 462
Clearing, The : p. 137, n. 451
Coal : p. 286, n. 535
Collect for Dominion Day : p. 89, n. 419
Colour Toasts : p. 346, n. 636
Comedy, The : p. 189, n. 482
Consolation : p. 98, n. 424
Conspirators, The : p. 286, n. 535
Covert, The : p. 268, n. 525
Cow Pasture, The : p. 163, n. 468
Cricket, The : p. 144, n. 458
Dark : p. 91, n. 422
Dedication of "Orion and Other Poems" : p. 36, n. 383
Departing of Gluskâp, The : p. 98, n. 424
Deserted City, The : p. 129, n. 444
Deserted Wharf, The : p. 205, n. 492
Dew : p. 220, n. 499
Dream-Fellows : p. 251, n. 516

Earth's Complines : p. 195, n. 485
Eastward Bound : p. 300, n. 546
Ebb : p. 187, n. 481
Elephant and the Pansy-Blossom, The : p. 206, n. 492
Epistle to Bliss Carman : p. 15, n. 372
Epitaph for a Certain Architect : p. 308, n. 557
Epitaph for a Husbandman, An : p. 193, n. 484
Epitaph for a Sailor Buried Ashore : p. 153, n. 461
Epitaph for a Young Airman : p. 342, n. 627
Evening Communion, An : p. 253, n. 516
Falling Leaves, The : p. 254, n. 516
Farewell, A : p. 32, n. 380
Farmer's Winter Morning, The : p. 220, n. 499
Fear of Love, The : p. 267, n. 525
Fir Woods, The : p. 126, n. 442
First Ploughing, The : p. 287, n. 536
Flight, The : p. 37, n. 383
Flight of the Geese, The : p. 129, n. 445
Flocks of Spring, The : p. 211, n. 495
Flower, The : p. 309, n. 559
Footpath, The : p. 83, n. 411
For a Bust of Lanier : p. 137, n. 451
Forest Fire, The : p. 189, n. 482
Foreword to *Northland Lyrics,* A : p. 254, n. 517
Forget Not, Thou : p. 340, n. 621
Fortress, The : p. 126, n. 442
Frogs : p. 117, n. 433
From the High Window of Your Room : p. 296, n. 540
Frosted Pane, The : p. 188, n. 481
Furrow, The : p. 130, n. 446
Going Over : p. 304, n. 553
Golden-Rod : p. 183, n. 478
Good Earth, The : p. 298, n. 543
Great and the Little Weavers, The : p. 280, n. 530
Grey Rocks and Greyer Sea : p. 137, n. 452
Hath Hope Kept Vigil : p. 311, n. 563
Hawkbit, The : p. 138, n. 453
Heal-All, The : p. 224, n. 501
Heat in the City : p. 282, n. 531
Her Fan : p. 196, n. 486
Her Glove Box : p. 192, n. 483
Hermit, The : p. 235, n. 507
Hermit-Thrush, The : p. 143, n. 457
Herring Weir, The : p. 163, n. 468
Hill Top Songs: I : p. 300, n. 547
Hill Top Songs: II : p. 301, n. 548

Home, Home in the Evening : p. 184, n. 479
Homing Song, A : p. 179, n. 475
Hour of Most Desire, The : p. 296, n. 541
How Little I Knew : p. 268, n. 525
How the Mohawks Set Out for Medoctec : p. 114, n. 431
Ice : p. 188, n. 481
Iceberg, The : p. 321, n. 579
Ideal, The : p. 254, n. 517
Immanence : p. 185, n. 480
Impulse : p. 99, n. 425
In a City Room : p. 243, n. 511
In an Old Barn : p. 164, n. 468
In Apia Bay : p. 270, n. 526
In Darkness : p. 255, n. 517
In Notre Dame : p. 84, n. 413
In September : p. 73, n. 403
In the Afternoon : p. 73, n. 404
In the Barn-Yard's Southerly Corner : p. 277, n. 529
In the Crowd : p. 247, n. 513
In the Night Watches : p. 314, n. 568
In the Orchard : p. 219, n. 498
In the Solitude of the City : p. 243, n. 511
In the Valley of Luchon : p. 303, n. 550
In the Wide Awe and Wisdom of the Night : p. 133, n. 449
In Time of Earth's Misuse : p. 339, n. 620
Indian Summer : p. 164, n. 468
Inspiration : p. 214, n. 496
Invocation : p. 275, n. 529
Isles—An Ode, The : p. 100, n. 425
Iterumne : p. 29, n. 377
Jar, The : p. 215, n. 497
Jonathan and John : p. 257, n. 518
Jonquil, The : p. 212, n. 495
July : p. 225, n. 502
Keepers of the Pass, The : p. 117, n. 434
Khartoum : p. 101, n. 425
Kinship : p. 181, n. 478
Kinsmen Strong : p. 258, n. 519
La Belle Tromboniste : p. 80, n. 409
Laughing Sally, The : p. 208, n. 493
Launcelot and the Four Queens : p. 38, n. 383
Liberty : p. 101, n. 426
Life : p. 127, n. 443
Life and Art : p. 231, n. 505
Life and the Artist : p. 245, n. 512
Lily of the Valley, The : p. 141, n. 456

Lines for an Omar Punch-Bowl : p. 288, n. 536
Lines for the Times : p. 133, n. 448
Little Field of Peace, The : p. 210, n. 494
Logs, The : p. 278, n. 529
Lotos : p. 58, n. 391
Love-Days : p. 46, n. 385
Love's Translator : p. 226, n. 502
Maple, The : p. 3, n. 364
Marjory : p. 236, n. 507
Marsyas : p. 165, n. 469
Marvellous Work, The : p. 102, n. 426
May-Night : p. 345, n. 636
Memnon : p. 5, n. 366
Midwinter Thaw : p. 166, n. 469
Miriam.–I./Sapphics : p. 47, n. 385
Miriam.–II./Choriambics : p. 47, n. 385
Mist : p. 87, n. 417
Modern Dialogue, A : p. 192, n. 483
Monition : p. 295, n. 540
Moonlight : p. 136, n. 450
Mother of Nations : p. 112, n. 431
Mothers : p. 226, n. 503
Mowing, The : p. 132, n. 447
Muse and the Wheel, The : p. 198, n. 487
My Garden : p. 241, n. 510
My Heart is a House : p. 289, n. 537
My Trees : p. 139, n. 454
Native, The : p. 274, n. 528
Nativity : p. 207, n. 493
New Dead : p. 269, n. 526
New Life : p. 279, n. 529
New Year's Eve : p. 134, n. 450
Night in a Down-Town Street : p. 238, n. 508
Night-Hawk, The : p. 130, n. 446
Night Sky, The : p. 120, n. 436
Nocturne of Consecration, A : p. 239, n. 509
Nocturne of Exile, A : p. 244, n. 511
Nocturne of Spiritual Love, A : p. 246, n. 512
Nocturne of Trysting, A : p. 245, n. 512
Nocturnes of the Honeysuckle : p. 255, n. 518
O Clearest Pool : p. 216, n. 497
O Earth, Sufficing All Our Needs : p. 299, n. 544
O Little Rose, O Dark Rose : p. 265, n. 523
O Solitary of the Austere Sky : p. 142, n. 456
O Thou Who Bidd'st : p. 256, n. 518
Oat-Threshing, The : p. 166, n. 470

Oblation, An : p. 212, n. 496
Ode for the Canadian Confederacy, An : p. 90, n. 421
Ode to Drowsihood : p. 9, n. 369
Ode to Night : p. 48, n. 385
Off Pelorus : p. 55, n. 387
Oh, Purple Hang the Pods : p. 167, n. 470
Oliver Wendell Holmes : p. 200, n. 489
On Reading the Poems of Sidney Lanier : p. 88, n. 418
On the Creek : p. 106, n. 427
On the Eve of Departure : p. 66, n. 397
On the Elevated Railway at 110th Street, p. 247, n. 513
On the Lagoon : p. 106, n. 427
On the Road : p. 303, n. 551
On the Upper Deck : p. 290, n. 537
One Night : p. 49, n. 386
Origins : p. 186, n. 480
Orion : p. 18, n. 372
Out of Pompeii : p. 59, n. 392
Pan and the Rose : p. 318, n. 574
Pea-Fields, The : p. 138, n. 453
Peace With Dishonour : p. 339, n. 618
Philander's Song : p. 295, n. 539
Phillida's Birthday : p. 202, n. 491
Phillida's Blue Ribbon : p. 344, n. 636
Phillida's Lent : p. 231, n. 505
Piper and the Chiming Peas, The : p. 180, n. 476
Pipers of the Pools, The : p. 272, n. 527
Pipes of Pan, The : p. 76, n. 405
Place of His Rest, The : p. 301, n. 549
Poet is Bidden to Manhattan Island, The : p. 81, n. 409
Potato Harvest, The : p. 91, n. 421
Presence : p. 245, n. 512
Presences : p. 329, n. 596
Prologue : p. 167, n. 470
Promise : p. 89, n. 419
Pumpkins in the Corn, The : p. 167, n. 471
Quebec, 1757 : p. 133, n. 449
Quelling of the Moose, The : p. 106, n. 428
Quest of the Arbutus, The : p. 175, n. 473
Rain : p. 108, n. 429
Ravaged Lands, The : p. 341, n. 624
Re-Birth : p. 330, n. 597
Recessional : p. 200, n. 490
Reckoning : p. 108, n. 429
Recompense : p. 201, n. 491
Remorse, A : p. 259, n. 519

Renewal : p. 176, n. 473
Resurgant : p. 344, n. 633
Resurrection : p. 175, n. 472
Rondeau.—"Hesper Appears" : p. 29, n. 378
Rondeau.—"Without One Kiss" : p. 51, n. 386
Rondeau to A.W. Straton : p. 51, n. 386
Rondeau / To Louis Honore Fréchette : p. 62, n. 394
Rose of Life, The : p. 273, n. 528
Rose of My Desire, The : p. 266, n. 524
Rose's Avatar, The : p. 272, n. 527
Salt : p. 109, n. 429
Salt Flats, The : p. 136, n. 451
Sappho : p. 52, n. 386
Serenade, A : p. 109, n. 429
Severance : p. 119, n. 435
Shannon and the Chesapeake, The : p. 30, n. 379
Shepherdess Fair : p. 283, n. 531
Silver Thaw, The : p. 139, n. 454
Sister to the Wild Rose : p. 310, n. 560
Skater, The : p. 279, n. 529
Slave Woman, The : p. 58, n. 391
Sleepy Man : p. 176, n. 474
Soliloquy in a Monastery : p. 64, n. 396
Solitary Woodsman, The : p. 229, n. 504
Song for April, A : p. 259, n. 520
Song for Victory Delayed : p. 343, n. 630
Song of Cheer, A : p. 113, n. 431
Song of Dependence, A : p. 110, n. 430
Song of Growth, A : p. 131, n. 446
Song of Morning, A : p. 55, n. 387
Song of Regret, A : p. 63, n. 395
Sonnet on Spring : p. 76, n. 405
Sonnet / On the Dying Year : p. 1, n. 363
Sower, The : p. 82, n. 410
Spirit of Beauty : p. 320, n. 578
Spring : p. 1, n. 363
Spring Breaks in Foam : p. 312, n. 564
Spring Colloquy, A : p. 207, n. 493
Squatter, The : p. 331, n. 599
Stack Behind the Barn, The : p. 218, n. 498
Stillness of the Frost, The : p. 174, n. 472
Stirrup Cup, The : p. 208, n. 493
Stranded Ship, The : p. 264, n. 523
Stream, The : p. 306, n. 555
Street Lamps, The : p. 256, n. 518
Street Song at Night, A : p. 260, n. 520

Street Vigil, A : p. 242, n. 510
Succour of Gluskâp, The : p. 168, n. 471
Summer Pool, The : p. 121, n. 437
Summons, The : p. 307, n. 557
Sweet o' the Year, The : p. 308, n. 558
Taormina : p. 328, n. 593
Tantramar Revisited : p. 78, n. 406
Tears : p. 238, n. 508
Thaw : p. 246, n. 512
These Three Score Years : p. 315, n. 571
Those Perish, These Endure : p. 335, n. 608
Three Good Things : p. 193, n. 484
Tide on Tantramar, The : p. 170, n. 471
Tides : p. 88, n. 418
To a Certain Mystic : p. 327, n. 591
To a Lady, / After Hearing Her Read Keats' "Nightingale" : p. 110, n. 430
To a Mirror : p. 231, n. 505
To Bliss Carman / With a Copy of Lang's "Helen of Troy" : p. 88, n. 417
To Fredericton in May-Time : p. 57, n. 390
To G.B.R. : p. 142, n. 457
To My Friend, / Edmund Collins : p. 87, n. 417
To S—— M—— : p. 111, n. 430
To Shakespeare, In 1916 : p. 306, n. 555
To the Memory of Sidney Lanier : p. 61, n. 393
To the Spirit of Song : p. 15, n. 371
To Winter : p. 3, n. 365
To-Day : p. 311, n. 562
Tout ou Rien : p. 111, n. 430
Tower Beyond the Tops of Time, The : p. 232, n. 505
Train Among the Hills, The : p. 194, n. 485
Triumph : p. 127, n. 443
Trout Brook, The : p. 177, n. 475
Trysting Song : p. 227, n. 503
Twilight on Sixth Avenue at Ninth Street : p. 191, n. 483
Twilight Over Shaugamauk : p. 334, n. 605
Two Rivers : p. 336, n. 611
Two Spheres : p. 215, n. 497
Under the Pillars of the Sky : p. 299, n. 545
Unknown City, The : p. 284, n. 532
Unsaid : p. 319, n. 576
Unsleeping, The : p. 178, n. 475
Up and Away in the Morning : p. 183, n. 478
Vagrant of Time, The : p. 312, n. 565
Valley of the Winding Water, The : p. 122, n. 438
Vengeance of Gluskâp, The : p. 184, n. 479
Vesper Sonnet, A : p. 132, n. 448

Wake-Up Song, A : p. 228, n. 503
Waking Earth, The : p. 120, n. 435
Wayfarer of Earth : p. 297, n. 542
Weaver, The : p. 198, n. 487
Westcock Hill : p. 333, n. 603
When in the Rowan Tree : p. 285, n. 534
When Mary the Mother Kissed the Child : p. 293, n. 537
When Milking Time is Done : p. 121, n. 436
When the Cloud Comes Down the Mountain : p. 286, n. 535
When the Clover Blooms Again : p. 234, n. 506
Where the Cattle Come to Drink : p. 228, n. 503
White Frost, The : p. 261, n. 521
Whitewaters : p. 155, n. 462
Wild-Rose Thicket, The : p. 141, n. 456
Winter Fields, The : p. 128, n. 443
Winter Geraniums : p. 112, n. 430
Wisdom of Love, The : p. 276, n. 529
Witches' Flight, The : p. 203, n. 491
With All Her Faults : p. 213, n. 496
With April Here : p. 309, n. 560
Wrestler, The : p. 196, n. 486
Ye Poet and His Ideal : p. 217, n. 497

SOURCES OF THE POEMS

A. Publications of Roberts' Poems

Orion, and Other Poems. Philadelphia: Lippincott, 1880.
Later Poems. Fredericton: private printing, 1881.
Later Poems. Fredericton: private printing, 1882.
Canada. Fredericton: private printing, 1885.
In Divers Tones. Boston: D. Lothrop, 1886 and Montreal: Dawson Bros., 1887.
Autochthon. Windsor, N.S.: private printing, 1889.
Canadians of Old, The. a translation of Phillippe Aubert de Gaspé's *Les Anciens Canadiens*. New York: Appleton, 1890 and Toronto: Hart, 1891.
Ave: An Ode for the Centenary of the Birth of Percy Bysshe Shelley, August 4, 1792. Toronto: Williamson Book Co., 1892.
Songs of the Common Day, and Ave: An Ode for the Shelley Centenary. London: Longman's, Green, 1893 and Toronto: William Briggs, 1893. [Ryerson Press.]
Book of the Native, The. Boston, New York, and London: Lamson and Wolfe, 1896 and Toronto: Copp, Clark, 1896.
New York Nocturnes. Boston, New York, and London: Lamson and Wolfe, 1898.
Poems. New York, Boston, Chicago: Silver, Burdett, 1901.
Book of the Rose, The. Boston: L.C. Page, 1903.
Poems. Boston: L.C. Page, 1907.
New Poems. London: Constable, 1919.
Sweet o' the Year and Other Poems, The. Toronto: Ryerson Press, 1925.
Vagrant of Time, The. Toronto: Ryerson Press, 1927.
Iceberg and Other Poems, The. Toronto: Ryerson Press, 1934.
Selected Poems. Toronto: Ryerson Press, 1936.
Twilight Over Shaugamauk, and Three Other Poems. Toronto: Ryerson Press, 1937. [private printing.]
Canada Speaks of Britain. Toronto: Ryerson Press, 1941.
Selected Poems of Sir Charles G.D. Roberts, The. Ed. and with an introduction by Desmond Pacey. Toronto: Ryerson Press, 1955.
Selected Poetry and Critical Prose: Charles G.D. Roberts, Literature of Canada: Poetry and Prose in Reprint, No. 9. Ed. and with an introduction by W.J. Keith. Toronto and Buffalo: University of Toronto Press, 1974.

B.   Anthologies

American Sonnets. Selected and edited, with an introduction by W.
    Sharp. London: Walter Scott and New York: W.J. Gage, 1889.
Another Book of Verses for Children. Ed. E.V. Lucas. London: Wells,
    Gardner, Darton, 1907.
Anthology of Canadian Poetry (English). Comp. by Ralph Gustafson.
    Harmondsworth, Middlesex, England: Penguin, 1942
Ballads of American Bravery. Ed. Clinton Scollard. New York: Silver
    Burdett, 1900.
Bird Lover's Anthology, The. Comp. by Clinton Scollard and Jessie B.
    Rittenhouse. Boston and New York: Houghton Mifflin, 1930.
Book of Canadian Poetry: A Critical and Historical Anthology, The.
    Ed. with an introduction and notes by A.J.M. Smith. Rev ed.
    Chicago: University of Chicago Press, 1948.
Book of Canadian Prose and Verse, A. Comp. and ed. by Edmund K.
    Broadus and Eleanor H. Broadus. Toronto: Macmillan, 1923.
Book of Lullabies, A. Ed. Elva S. Smith. Boston: Lothrop, Lee, and
    Shepard, 1925.
Book of Poetry, The. Ed. E. Markam. Vol. II. New York: W.H. Wise,
    1928.
Canadian Anthology. Ed. Carl F. Klinck and R.E. Watters. Rev. ed.
    Toronto: Gage, 1966.
Canadian Birthday Book, The. Comp. by Seranus [pseud.], S. Frances
    Harrison (Riley). Toronto: Blackett Robinson, 1887.
Canadian Poems, 1850-1952. Ed. Louis Dudek and Irving Layton.
    2nd. ed. Toronto: Contact Press, 1953.
*Canadian Poems and Lays: Selections of Native Verse, Reflecting the
    Seasons, Legends and Life of the Dominion.* Arranged and edited
    by William D. Lighthall. London: Walter Scott, 1893.
Canadian Poets. Ed. John W. Garvin. Rev. ed. Toronto: McClelland
    and Stewart, 1926.
*Canadian Singers and Their Songs: A Collection of Portraits and Auto-
    graphed Poems.* Ed. Edward S. Caswell. Rev. ed. Toronto:
    McClelland and Stewart, 1925.
Cap and Bells: An Anthology of Light Verse by Canadian Poets.
    Chosen by John W. Garvin. Toronto: Ryerson Press, 1936.
*Choice Readings for Public and Private Entertainments, and for the Use
    of Schools, Colleges, and Public Readers, with Elocutionary
    Advice.* Ed. R.M. Cumnock. Rev. ed. Chicago: A.C. McClurg,
    1903.
Contemporary Poetry. Ed. M. Wilkinson. New York: Macmillan, 1923.
Eternal Sea, The. Ed. W.M. Williamson. New York: Coward McCann,
    1946.
Exploring Poetry. Ed. M.L. Rosenthal. New York: Macmillan, 1955.
Flying Colours: An Anthology. Ed. Sir Charles G.D. Roberts. Toronto:
    Ryerson Press, 1942.

Golden Treasury of Canadian Verse, The. Chosen by Alexander M. Stephen. Toronto: Dent, 1928/9.

Great Americans, As Seen by the Poets. Ed. Burton Stevenson. Philadelphia: J.B. Lippincott, 1933.

Home Book of Modern Verse, The. Ed. Burton Stevenson. Sixth ed. New York: Holt, Rinehart, and Winston, 1930.

Later Canadian Poems. Ed. James E. Wetherell. Toronto: Copp Clark, 1893.

Le Gallienne Book of English and American Poetry, The. Ed. Richard Le Gallienne. Rev. ed. New York: Garden City, 1935.

Little Book of Modern Verse, A. Ed. Jessie B. Rittenhouse. Boston and New York: Houghton Mifflin, 1913.

Masterpieces of Religious Verse. Ed. J.D. Morrison. New York: Harper and Row, 1948.

Modern Muse, The. Ed. The English Association. Oxford: Oxford University Press, 1936.

My Poetry Book. Ed. G.T. Huffard et al. New York: Holt, Rinehart, and Winston, 1968.

Nature Lover's Knapsack, The. Ed. E.O. Grover. New York: Crowell, 1947.

New Harvesting: Contemporary Canadian Poetry, 1918-1938. Chosen by Ethel Hume Bennett. Toronto: Macmillan, 1938.

Northland Lyrics. By William Carman Roberts, Theodore Roberts, and Elizabeth Roberts MacDonald. Selected and arranged by Charles G.D. Roberts. Boston: Small Maynard, 1899.

Off to Arcady. Ed. M.J. Herzberg. New York: American Book Co., 1933.

Our Canadian Literature: Representative Verse, English and French. Chosen by Bliss Carman and Lorne Pierce. Rev. ed. Toronto: Ryerson Press, 1934.

Our Country in Poem and Prose. Ed. Eleanor A. Persons. New York and Cincinnati: American Book Co., 1899.

Oxford Book of Canadian Verse, The. Chosen by Wilfred Campbell. Toronto: Oxford University Press, 1913.

Penguin Book of Canadian Verse, The. Ed. with an introduction and notes by Ralph Gustafson. Rev. ed. Harmondsworth, Middlesex: Penguin Books, 1967.

Pocketful of Canada, A. Ed. John Daniel Robins. Toronto: Collins, 1946.

Poems of American History. Ed. Burton Stevenson. Freeport, N.Y.: Books for Libraries Press, 1922.

Poems of the Great War. Ed. John William Cunliffe. New York: Macmillan, 1918.

Poems of Wild Life: An Anthology. Ed. Charles G.D. Roberts. London: Walter Scott and Toronto: Gage, 1888.

Poetic New World, The. Ed. L.H. Humphrey. New York: Holt, 1910.

Poetry Book, The. Ed. Miriam Blanton et al. Vol. II. New York: Rand McNally, 1926.

Poetry Cure, The. Ed. Robert H. Schauffler. New York: Dodd, Mead, 1925.

Poetry for Women to Speak Chorally. Ed. Marion P. Robinson and Rozetta L. Thurston. Boston: Expression Co., 1940.

Poetry of Freedom. Ed. William Rose Benét and Norman Cousins. Toronto: Random House, 1945.

Poets of the Confederation. Ed. with an introduction by Malcolm Ross. Toronto: McClelland and Stewart, 1960.

Raise the Flag and Other Patriotic Canadian Songs and Poems. Toronto: Rose, 1891.

Songs of the Great Dominion: Voices from the Forest and Waters, the Settlements and Cities of Canada. Selected and edited by W.D. Lighthall. London: Walter Scott, 1889.

Songs of the Maritimes: An Anthology of the Poetry of the Maritimes Provinces of Canada. Ed. Elizabeth Ritchie. Toronto: McClelland and Stewart, 1931.

Songs of Nature. Ed. John Burroughs. New York: McLure Phillips, 1902.

Songs of the Sea and Sailor's Chantey's. Ed. Robert Frothingham. Cambridge, Mass.: Houghton Mifflin, 1924.

Steps to Oratory. Ed. F.T. Southwick. New York: American Book Co., 1900.

Through the Year With the Poets. Ed. Oscar Fay Adams. Boston: Lothrop, 1886.

Treasury of Canadian Verse, A. Ed. T.H. Rand. Toronto: Briggs, 1900.

Treasury of Helpful Verse, A. Selected by John W. Chadwick and Annie Hathaway Chadwick. Boston: L.C. Page, 1896.

Twentieth Century Canadian Poetry. Ed. Earle Birney. Toronto: Ryerson Press, 1953.

Victorian Anthology, A. Ed. Edmund Clarence Stedman. Boston and New York, 1895.

Voices of Victory: Representative Poetry of Canada in Wartime. Compiled by Amabel King. Toronto: Macmillan, 1941.

What I Like in Poetry. Compiled by W.L. Phelps. New York and London: Scribner's, 1934.

Younger American Poets. Ed. Douglas B.W. Sladen. New York: Cassell, 1891.

C.   Periodicals and Newspapers

Atlantic Monthly, The. Boston.
Book Buyer, The. New York.
Bookman, The. New York.

Brunswickan, The. (*University Monthly*). Fredericton.
Calendar, 1893. Toronto Art Students' League. Toronto.
Calendar, 1896. Toronto Art Students' League. Toronto.
Canada. Benton, N.B.
Canadian Bookman. Toronto.
Canadian Illustrated News, The. Montreal.
Canadian Magazine. Toronto.
Canadian Monthly (*Rose Belford's*). Toronto.
Canadian Poetry Magazine. Toronto.
Century Magazine, The. New York.
Chap-Book, The. London.
Cosmopolitan. New York.
Craftsman Magazine. Eastwood, N.Y.
Criterion. London.
Critic. New York.
Current, The. Chicago.
Current Literature (*Opinion*). New York.
Current Opinion. New York.
Daily Telegraph, The. St. John, N.B.
Dalhousie Review. Halifax, N.S.
Dial, The. New York.
Dominion Illustrated Magazine, The. Montreal.
Fredericton Daily Mail, The. Fredericton.
Globe, The. Toronto.
Grip. Toronto.
Harper's Bazaar. New York.
Harper's Magazine. New York.
Harper's Weekly. New York.
Independent, The. New York.
Kindergarten and First Grade. Springfield, Mass.
King's College Record. Windsor, N.S.
Life. New York and Chicago.
Lippincott's Magazine (*McBride's*). Philadelphia.
Literary Digest. New York.
Living Age, The. Boston.
Maclean's Magazine. Toronto.
Magazine of Poetry, The. New York.
Manhattan Magazine. New York.
Maple Leaf, The. Albert, N.B.
Massey's Magazine. Toronto.
McBride's Magazine (*Lippincott's*). Philadelphia.
McLure's Magazine. New York.
Methodist Magazine and Review, The. Toronto.
Monthly Illustrator, The. New York.
Montreal Star, The. Montreal.
Munsey's Magazine. New York.

667

Musician, The. Philadelphia, Boston, and New York.
Nation, The. New York.
New Outlook (*Outlook*). New York
Our Continent. Philadelphia.
Outlook, The (*New Outlook*). New York.
Pall Mall Magazine. London.
Progress. Chicago.
Queen's Quarterly. Kingston, Ontario.
Rouge et Noir. Paris.
Saturday Evening Post, The. Philadelphia.
Saturday Night. Toronto.
Scribner's. New York.
Smart Set, The. New York.
Speaker, The. Philadelphia.
Saint Nicholas. New York.
Telegraph Journal, The. St. John, N.B.
To-Day. London.
Trinity University Review. Toronto.
Truth, The. New York.
University Monthly, The. (*Brunswickan*). Fredericton.
University of Toronto Quarterly. Toronto.
University Quarterly Review. Toronto.
Week, The. Toronto.
Willison's Monthly. Toronto.
Windsor Magazine. London.
Yellow Book, The. New York.
Youth's Companion, The. Boston.

D.   Biography

Sir Charles G.D. Roberts: A Biography. Elsie M. Pomeroy. Toronto:
Ryerson Press, 1943.

BIBLIOGRAPHY

Anon.   "Charles G.D. Roberts." *Acta Victoriana,* 55 (March-April, 1931), 15.

_____.   "Diamond Jubilee." *Canadian Bookman,* 15 (March, 1933), 38.

_____.   Obituary. *Canadian Poetry,* 7 (Dec., 1943), 5-6.

_____.   Obituary. *Current Biography 1944.* New York: Wilson, 1945, p. 599.

_____.   Obituary. *Time,* 42 (Dec. 6, 1943), 76.

_____.   Obituary. *Wilson Library Bulletin,* 18 (Jan., 1944), 367.

_____.   "Seventy-Fifth Birthday." *Canadian Bookman,* 17 (Sept., 1935), 109.

Archer, William. "Charles G.D. Roberts." *Poets of the Younger Generation.* London: Lane, 1902, pp. 362-372.

Bailey, A.G. "Creative Moments in the Culture of the Maritime Provinces." *Culture and Nationality.* Toronto: McClelland and Stewart, 1972, pp. 54-55.

Benet, W.R. "The Phoenix Nest." *Saturday Review of Literature,* 27 (March 4, 1944), 24.

Benson, Nathaniel A. "Dean of Canadian Letters." *Saturday Night,* 47 (April 25, 1931), 5.

_____.   "Sir Charles G.D. Roberts." *Leading Canadian Poets.* Ed. W.P. Percival. Toronto: Ryerson Press, 1948, pp. 184-192.

Brown, E.K. *On Canadian Poetry.* 1944; rpt. Ottawa: Tecumseh, 1973, pp. 46-53.

Cappon, James. *Charles G.D. Roberts.* Toronto: Ryerson Press, 1925.

_____.   *Roberts and the Influence of His Time.* 1905; rpt. Ottawa: Tecumseh, 1975.

Carman, Bliss. "Contemporaries: V, Charles G.D. Roberts." *Chapbook,* 2 (Jan. 1, 1895), 163-171.

Cogswell, Fred. *Charles G.D. Roberts and His Works* (Canadian Writers and Their Works Series: Poetry, Vol. II). Downsview, Ontario: ECW Press, 1983.

_____.   *Proceedings of the Sir Charles G.D. Roberts Symposium.* Ed. Carrie MacMillan. Halifax: Nimbus Press, 1984.

_____.   *The Sir Charles G.D. Roberts Symposium.* Ed. and Introduced by Glenn Clever. Ottawa: University of Ottawa Press, 1984.

Daniells, Roy. "Lampman and Roberts." *Literary History of Canada.* Ed. Carl Klinck. Toronto: University of Toronto Press, 1965, pp. 389-405.

Deacon, William Arthur. "Sir Charles G.D. Roberts: An Appreciation." *Canadian Author and Bookman,* 19 (Dec., 1934), 4.

669

DeMille, A.B. "Canadian Celebrities: XVI, The Roberts Family." *Canadian Magazine,* 15 (Sept., 1900), 426-430.

Djwa, Sandra A. "Metaphor, World View and the Continuity of Canadian Poetry: A Study of the Major English Canadian Poets with a Computer Concordance to Metaphor." Ph.D. dissertation, University of British Columbia, 1968.

Edwards, Mary Jane, Paul Denham and George Parker. "Introduction to 'Charles George Douglas Roberts'." *The Evolution of Canadian Literature in English: 1867-1914.* Evolution in Canadian Literature in English, series II. Toronto and Montreal: Holt, Rinehart and Winston, 1973, pp. 141-145.

Edgar, Pelham. "Charles G.D. Roberts." *Acta Victoriana,* 52 (Jan., 1928), 33-34.

————. "Sir Charles G.D. Roberts and His Times." *University of Toronto Quarterly,* 13 (Oct., 1943), 117-126. Also in *Across My Path.* Ed. Northrop Frye. Toronto: Ryerson Press, 1952, pp. 99-108.

————. "Sir Charles G.D. Roberts, 1860-1943." *Royal Society of Canada Proceedings and Transactions,* Third series, 38, (1944), 111-114.

Forbes, E.A. "The Development of Style and Thought in the Poetry of Charles G.D. Roberts, 1877-1897." M.A. thesis, University of New Brunswick, 1953.

Gammon, Donald B. "The Concept of Nature in Nineteenth Century Canadian Poetry, with Special Reference to Goldsmith, Sangster and Roberts." M.A. thesis, University of New Brunswick, 1948.

Harkins, Edward F. "The Literary Career of Roberts." *Little Pilgrimages Among the Men Who Have Written Famous Books.* Boston: Page, 1902, pp. 299-315.

Henry, Lorne J. "Sir Charles G.D. Roberts (1860-1943)." *Canadians: a Book of Biographies.* Toronto: Longman's, 1950, pp. 69-75.

Herriman, Dorothy C. "Sir Charles G.D. Roberts: 80 Years Young (1860-1940)," *Canadian Author,* 16 (Jan., 1940), 5.

Keith, W.J. *Charles G.D. Roberts.* Studies in Canadian Literature Series. Toronto: Copp Clark, 1969.

————. "Introduction." *Selected Poetry and Critical Prose: Charles G.D. Roberts.* Literature of Canada: Poetry and Prose in Reprint series. Toronto: University of Toronto Press, 1974.

Kirkconnell, Watson. "Sir Charles G.D. Roberts: A Tribute." *Canadian Author and Bookman,* 19 (Dec., 1943), 3.

Lampman, Archibald. "Two Canadian Poets" with a prefatory note by E.K. Brown. *University of Toronto Quarterly,* 13 (July, 1944), 406-423.

Lesperance, John. "The Poets of Canada." *Royal Society of Canada Proceedings and Transactions,* First series, 2 (1844), 42ff.

Livesay, Dorothy. "Open Letter to Sir Charles G.D. Roberts." *Canadian Bookman,* 21 (April, 1939), 34-35.

670

Lock, D.R. "Charles G.D. Roberts." *World Wide,* 31 (July 25, 1931), 1187.

Marquis, T.G. "Prominent Canadians XXI: Professor Charles G.D. Roberts, M.A." *The Week,* 5 (July 26, 1888), 558-559.

_____. "Roberts." *Canadian Magazine,* 1 (Sept., 1893), 572-575.

_____. "Songs of the Common Day." *The Week,* 10 (Sept. 22, 1893), 1023.

Massey, Vincent. "Roberts, Carman, Sherman: Canadian Poets." *Canadian Author and Bookman,* 23 (Fall, 1947), 29-32.

Matthews, Robin. "Charles G.D. Roberts and the Destruction of the Canadian Imagination." *Journal of Canadian Fiction,* I, 1, 47-56.

Middleton, J.E. "Dean of Canadian Letters." *Saturday Night,* 58 (June 19, 1943), 20-21.

O'Hagan, Thomas. "Two Canadian Poets." *Dominion Illustrated,* 1 (Oct. 27, 1888), 263.

Pacey, Desmond. *Creative Writing in Canada.* Rev. ed. Toronto: Ryerson Press, 1961.

_____. "Introduction." *Selected Poems of Sir Charles G.D. Roberts.* Toronto: McGraw-Hill Ryerson, 1955.

_____. "Sir Charles G.D. Roberts." *Our Living Tradition,* Fourth series. Ed. Robert L. McDougal. Toronto: University of Toronto Press, 1962. Also in Pacey's *Essays in Canadian Criticism.* Toronto: Ryerson Press, 1969, pp. 180-187

_____. "Sir Charles G.D. Roberts." *Ten Canadian Poets.* Toronto. Ryerson Press, 1958, pp. 34-58.

Pierce, Lorne Albert. "Charles G.D. Roberts." *Three Fredericton Poets: Writers of the University of New Brunswick and the New Dominion.* Toronto: Ryerson Press, 1933, pp. 11-17.

Pollock, F.L. "Canadian Writers in New York." *Acta Victoriana,* 22 (April, 1899), 434-439.

Pomeroy, Elsie. "A Canadian Author's Welcome in Italy, and a Few Memories of the Poet." *Atlantic Advocate,* 52 (March, 1962), 57-59.

_____. *Sir Charles G.D. Roberts: A Biography.* Toronto: Ryerson Press, 1943.

_____. *Tributes Through the Years: The Centenary of the Birth of Sir Charles G.D. Roberts, January 10, 1960.* Toronto: Pomeroy, 1959.

Reid, R.L. "Charles G.D. Roberts, Poet and Novelist." *British Columbia Monthly,* 24 (March, 1925), 7.

Rhodenizer, V.B. "Who's Who in Canadian Literature: Charles G.D. Roberts." *Canadian Bookman,* 8 (Sept., 1926), 267-269.

Rittenhouse, Jessie B. "Charles G.D. Roberts." *The Younger American Poets.* Boston: Little Brown, 1904, pp. 132-150.

Roberts, Lloyd. *The Book of Roberts.* Toronto: Ryerson Press, 1923.

Rogers, A. Robert. "American Recognition of Bliss Carman and Sir Charles G.D. Roberts." *Humanities Association Bulletin,* 22, ii, 19-25.

Ross, Malcolm. "Introduction." *Poets of The Confederation.* Toronto: McClelland and Stewart, 1960.

———. "A Strange Aesthetic Ferment." *Canadian Literature,* 68-69 (Spring-Summer, 1976), 13-25.

Ross, P.D. "A Very Great Canadian." *Canadian Author and Bookman,* 19 (Sept., 1943), 12.

Roy, George Ross. "Charles G.D. Roberts." *Le sentiment de la nature dans la poesie canadienne anglaise, 1867-1918.* Paris: Nizet, 1961.

Smythe, A.A.E. "Charles G.D. Roberts." *Canadian Bookman,* 7 (Feb., 1925), 25.

Stephen, A.M. "The Poetry of C.G.D. Roberts." *Queen's Quarterly,* 36 (Jan., 1929), 48-64.

Stevenson, Lionel. *Appraisals of Canadian Literature.* Toronto: Macmillan, 1926.

Stevenson, O.J. "New Visions and Brave Ventures." *A People's Best.* Toronto: Musson, 1927, pp. 85-94.

Stringer, Arthur. "Eminent Canadians in New York: II, The Father of Canadian Poetry." *National Monthly,* 4 (Feb., 1904), 61-64.

———. "Wild Poets I've Known: Charles G.D. Roberts." *Saturday Night,* 57 (April 11, 1942), 25.

Sykes, W.J. "Charles G.D. Roberts." *Acta Victoriana,* 17 (Jan., 1894), 112-115.

Whiteside, Ernestine R. "Canadian Poetry and Poets." *McMaster University Monthly,* 8 (Oct., 1898), 21-28.